Sources of Information in the Social Sciences

Thompson M. Little
Leatrice Kemp

JAMES P. SHENTON
BERT F. HOSELITZ
HANS L. ZETTERBERG
FELIX M. KEESING
ROBERT I. WATSON
WILLIAM W. BRICKMAN
HEINZ EULAU

Sources of Information in the Social Sciences

A GUIDE TO THE LITERATURE

Carl M. White and Associates

 THE BEDMINSTER PRESS

Copyright © 1964, The Bedminster Press,
Vreeland Avenue, Totowa, New Jersey
Manufactured in the United States of America
by H. Wolff Book Manufacturing Co., Inc., New York
Library of Congress Catalog Card Number: 63–13892

Contents

Preface

This study was made possible by the interest and encouragement of the Faculty of Letters of the University of Ankara, the American Library Association and the Ford Foundation. Brief information follows about those whose work has brought it into being. Reference is made in each case to the chapter or chapters to which they have contributed.

Brickman, William W. Professor of educational history and comparative education, Graduate School of Education, University of Pennsylvania. *Guide to research in educational history* (New York University Bookstore, 1949); co-author, with G.Z.F. Bereday and G.H. Read, *The changing Soviet school; the Comparative Education Society field study in the USSR* (Houghton, 1960); *Religion, government and education* (Society for the Advancement of Education, 1961). EDUCATION.

Eulau, Heinz. Professor of political science, Stanford University. *Class and party in the Eisenhower years* (Free Press, 1962); co-author, *The legislative system: explorations in legislative behavior* (Wiley, 1962); editor, with others, *Political behavior* (Free Press, 1956); joint editor with J.C. Wahlke, *Legislative behavior* (Free Press, 1959); general editor, *International yearbook of political behavior research*; associate editor, *International encyclopedia of the social sciences*. Formerly fellow, Center for Advanced Study in the Behavioral Sciences. POLITICAL SCIENCE.

Hoselitz, Bert F. Professor of economics and the social sciences, University of Chicago. Editor, *A reader's guide to the social sciences* (Free Press, 1959); *Sociological aspects of economic growth* (Free Press,

1960); editor, *Journal of economic development and cultural change*, 1954-1961. One year residence at the Center for Advanced Study in the Behavioral Sciences. Has served (one year) as specialist on economic aspects of metropolitan planning on a Ford Foundation project in India; has served as industrial economist for the UN Technical Assistance Administration and several times as consultant to UNESCO. ECONOMICS AND BUSINESS ADMINISTRATION.

Keesing, Felix M. Late professor of anthropology, Stanford University. *The Menomini Indians of Wisconsin* (The American Philosophical Society, 1939); *The South seas in the modern world* (Day, 1941); *Culture change; an analysis and bibliography of anthropological sources* (Stanford Univ. Press, 1953); with Marie M. Keesing, *Elite communication in Samoa, a study of leadership* (Stanford Univ. Press, 1956); *Cultural anthropology; the science of custom* (Rinehart, 1958). ANTHROPOLOGY.

Kemp, Leatrice. Former Reference Librarian, New York Life Insurance Company. ECONOMICS AND BUSINESS ADMINISTRATION, EDUCATION.

Little, Thompson M. Librarian, School of Library Service Library, Columbia University. Formerly, Principal librarian, Humanities and Social Sciences Division, Stanford University Library. LITERATURE OF SOCIAL SCIENCE, HISTORY, SOCIOLOGY, ANTHROPOLOGY, PSYCHOLOGY, POLITICAL SCIENCE.

Shenton, James P. Associate professor of history, Columbia University. *Robert John Walker; a politician from Jackson to Lincoln* (Columbia Univ. Press, 1962); two-volume history text in preparation for publication by Doubleday in 1962-63. Executive committee, American Catholic Historical Assoc. HISTORY.

Watson, Robert I. Professor of psychology and Director, graduate training program in clinical psychology, Northwestern University. *Psychology of the child* (Wiley, 1959); *The clinical method in psychology* (Harper, 1951); *The great psychologists; from Aristotle to Freud* (Lippincott, 1963). PSYCHOLOGY.

White, Carl M. Program specialist in library development, The Ford Foundation; Library adviser to the Federal Government of Nigeria. Editor, *Modern kütüphaneciligin esaslari* (Ankara, Guven Matbaasi, 1961; English edition in press, Pergamon Press); *Origins of the American library school* (Scarecrow Press, 1961). EDITOR AND COMPILER.

Zetterberg, Hans L. Associate professor of sociology, Columbia University. *On theory and verification in sociology* (Stockholm, Almquist and Wiksell; New York, Tressler Press, 1954); *Sociology in the United States of America; a trend report* (UNESCO, 1956); joint editor, with Iago Galdston, *Panic and morale* (International Universities Press, 1958); *Social theory and social practice* (Bedminster, 1962); joint editor, with Murray Gendell, *A sociological almanac for the United States* (Bedminster, 1961). SOCIOLOGY.

Mr. Little and Mrs. Kemp have rendered invaluable aid in bringing a basic list of reference works up-to-date and revising annotations. Mr. Little and his wife, Mrs. Barbara M. Little, have further assisted the Editor in checking for accuracy, preparing final copy and seeing the volume through the press. In an even larger sense this is a cooperative venture;

for librarians, social scientists, and even students have contributed advice and suggestions which have made it a work of many hands. I shall not try to list them all but wish heartily to thank them all. The scene of much of our work has been the libraries of Columbia, Harvard (especially the Baker Library) and Stanford. Librarians at these institutions have gone out of their way to give the project a boost; it is fitting, therefore, to conclude this paragraph with a grateful salute to them and to those others, unknown to us, who helped shape the collections which have served us so well.

Documentation in the social sciences is varied in form and content, written for people in many walks of life, and fills several miles of shelving in libraries that try to keep up with it. Graduate students who qualify for positions as professional librarians have to learn about this vast preserve, and it is their need of guidance that explains the origin of this book.

How is this guidance to be given? Nobody is fully satisfied with answers found so far, but everybody is getting interested in the search, as publications continue to multiply and acreage for their housing and use expands. The plan followed in this book is mainly the result of experience with students in a course on social science literature offered by the graduate School of Library Service, Columbia University. If the procedure has merit, it arises from the simple act of seeing, within all these tiered rows of books, a highly organized system of communicating information. Some elements of the system are sources which exist to report research; others exist to take such reports and piece them together into competent summaries of present knowledge; still others, to list or review new publications, explain the nomenclature, or perform some other helpful function. Each type of source, in short, has its job to do. The task of this book is to place in the reader's hands a sort of chart and compass to use in finding his way around and learning how the system works.

A preliminary edition of the book was used to inaugurate instruction in subject bibliography in the Faculty of Letters, University of Ankara, where the writer served as Director of the Institute of Librarianship (1959-61) and as Chair Professor of Library Science (1960-61). Turkish scholars and librarians were interested in using this method of study as a guide to the stage of development of the literature in a given field. It was observed, however, that scholarly libraries in Turkey are not at present able to obtain all the output in the social sciences. Appraisals of the literature of the several fields would be helpful in making necessary decisions on works for first purchase. The suggestion has led to effort on a scale which probably might not have been exerted otherwise, but the treatment is more rounded as a result. No aspect of the literature is slighted; and within each grouping or category, an attempt is made to identify the more crucial works.

For each subject, the treatment falls into two parts. First a specialist,

sought out for his grasp of the literature, presents a bibliographical review of basic monographic works for a collection of substantive material.
This review is followed by a list of reference works. Informative annotations are provided for all works except those adequately explained by
the title. Specialized works are included, especially when they exemplify
types of sources important for reference purposes. First priority goes to
works which may be looked upon as basic for a program of service to a
general clientele made up of scholars, students and the public at large. If
some stress falls on bibliographies, it is because they serve as controls for
opening doorways to even vaster information and to sources that are
more obscure.

Certain fields are included which do not fall wholly within the social
sciences, but it is simpler to include them than to cull out that part of
the literature that does. This tendency toward inclusiveness has another
aspect. History includes reference works on biography and geography;
sociology, works on demography, social service, race relations, public
opinion, gerontology; anthropology, works on ethnology, ethnography,
folklore, linguistics, pre-history and non-classical archeolgy; political
science, works on public administration, international relations and government publications.

All contributions are signed, with names of contributors appearing
at the end of the contribution to improve the format. All works designated as of first importance are coded to facilitate cross reference, and
these are indexed. Works mentioned more casually are not indexed, although many of these are important also. Sources where material is indexed are included as a reference aid. Space is saved by the use of abbreviations in the attached list.

Carl M. White

August 5, 1962

List of Abbreviations Used in This Volume

Each chapter contains, under the heading *Sources of scholarly contributions—journals*, a representative listing of scholarly periodicals. For each is given: Title, dates, place of publication, publisher, frequency and an indication of whether the title is indexed or abstracted. The listing of indexing or abstracting services for a journal is as complete as possible, whether the contents are indexed fully or selectively. Care has been taken to gather this information in one place so as to enlarge the usefulness of the work.

Agr Ind	Agricultural index.
App Sci Tech	Applied science and technology index
Art	Art index
Aust PAIS	Australian public affairs information service
Bibl Deut Zeit	Bibliographie der deutschen Zeitschriftenliteratur (Abt. A, Internationale Bibliographie der Zeitschriftenliteratur)
Bibl Fremd Zeit	Bibliographie der fremdsprachigen Zeitschriftenliteratur (Abt. B, Internationale Bibliographie der Zeitschriftenliteratur)
Biol Abst	Biological abstracts
Br Ed Ind	British education index
Br Subj Ind*	British subject index
Bull Anal	Bulletin analytique de documentation politique, économique et sociale contemporaine

* In January 1962 the *British subject index* was expanded to become the *British humanities index* and the *British technology index*.

Bull Sig	Bulletin signaletique. Pt. 19 Sciences humaines, philosophie
Bus Per	Business periodicals index
Cath Ind	Catholic periodical index
Chem Abst	Chemical abstracts
Doc Econ	Documentation économique
Econ Abst	Economic abstracts
Ed Ind	Education index
Empl Rel Abst	Employment relations abstracts
Engr Ind	Engineering index
Fin Ind	Financial index
Funk & Scott	Funk & Scott index of corporations and industries
Hist Abst	Historical abstracts
Ind Art	Industrial arts index
Ind Lab Art	Index to labor articles
Ind Lab Un Per	Index to labor union periodicals
Ind Leg Per	Index to legal periodicals
Ind Sel Per	Index to selected periodicals
Int Ind	International index
Int Pol Sci Abst	International political science abstracts
Lab Pers Ind	Labor personnel index
Lib Lit	Library literature
Lib Sci Abst	Library science abstracts
Math R	Mathematical reviews
Med Lit *	Current list of medical literature
19 RG	Nineteenth century readers guide
Nutr Abst	Nutrition abstracts
NZ Ind	Index to New Zealand periodicals
PAIS	Public affairs information service
Poole	Poole's index to periodical literature
Psych Abst	Psychological abstracts
QC Ind Med	Quarterly cumulative index medicus (to 1956)
RG	Readers guide
Sci Abst	Science abstracts
Soc Abst	Sociological abstracts

* Beginning with vol. I, 1960, *Index medicus,* new series supersedes *Current list of medical literature* (v. 1-36, 1941-1959) and cumulates annually into *Cumulated index medicus.*

Trop Abst	Tropical abstracts
UN Lib	United Nations. Library, Geneva. Monthly list of selected articles.
WSJ	Wall Street journal index
assoc.	association
Aufl.	Auflage
augm.	augmented
Ausg.	Ausgabe
bear.	bearbeitet
comp.	compiled, compiler
corr.	corrected
dept.	department
ed., éd.	editor, edited, edition, édition, edicion, edicão, edizióne, editóre.
eds.	editors
enl.	enlarged
gänz.	gänzlich
Govt. Print. Off.	U.S. Government Printing Office
hrsg.	herausgeben
Hrsg.	Herausgeber
in prep.	in preparation
Jahrg.	Jahrgang
Lfg.	Lieferung
n.F.	neue Folge
n.s.	new series
nouv.	nouvelle
pref.	preface
prelim.	preliminary
ptg.	printing
pts.	parts
rev.	revised
tr.	translated, translator
umgearb.	umgearbeitet
univ.	university
verb.	verbessert
verm.	vermehrt

Sources of Information in the Social Sciences

1

The Literature of Social Science

This work is intended as a guide to the literature of the social sciences.

Scope and purpose. Definitions of social science vary. The focus shifts as findings are systematized and then revised in the light of further research. For purposes of selecting the fields to be treated here, social scientists may be described as those who employ objective methods in the study of the behavior of man in any and all of its complex forms. Qualifying contributions on this broad subject originate in various disciplines, but there are five which mainly account for the rapid increase in reliable knowledge of it: sociology, psychology, anthropology, economics and political science. History and education are added to round out the list to be treated. Education is more an art than a science, but is included, first, because it draws liberally on studies of human behavior by supporting disciplines and, second, because of scientific research that is being done within the field itself. History has close ties with the humanities which, while they too are concerned with man, his ways and works, rely on different methods of work—on the use of critical analysis, the creative imagination, and the arts of expression and persuasion. For a century and more, however, historians have been busy perfecting and applying methods of objective inquiry, and the results have brought them recognition as social scientists. No field, as a matter of fact, surpasses history in successfully combining methods that have arisen from the two great scholarly traditions: the humanistic and the empirical.

The purpose of this book is to introduce the literature of these seven fields, and in addition to introduce works of more general scope which are to be treated briefly in this chapter. In the arrangement of subjects, history is placed first, because of the role it has played in intellectual orientation ever since attempts at rational explanation of things began. Political science is concerned with the most ambitious—or, should one say, the most massive?—of all human undertakings, in the course of which man draws on all he knows, or thinks he knows, about himself and others. It is, accordingly, put at the end. Nothing is said for the arrangement of other subjects except that it has proved useful in teaching.

Certain other decisions on scope and purpose should be noted. The book discusses methods of investigation that have been used in developing knowledge of the subject, fundamental insights around which the existing fabric of thought about it has been woven, the work of those who have done the most to further the progress of the subject, the emergence of branches of the subject and their relations to one another: all these are treated rather from the standpoint of mapping than of mining the veins of ore to be found in the literature. This latter responsibility, the task of introducing the subjects themselves, is left to systematic treatises and encyclopedias. The task of this guide is bibliographical: it is to map the way through the total documentation of social science as it stands on the shelves of well-rounded library collections.

Since the object is to introduce the literature as a whole, monographic works and reference works are both treated. The term "monograph" is used in contrast both with "serial publication" and with "secondary source," but it is proposed to use here a more general meaning which contrasts it with a work of reference. This is a convenient way to separate substantive literature, organized to be read through, from works which are designed rather to be referred to.[1] Scholarly journals are treated here among works used for reference.

The development of guides limited to reference works has come a long way since publication, in 1902, of Alice B. Kroeger's 104-page *Guide to the study and use of reference books*. Guides which include monographic works also are not so well developed, although the number is growing. Recent examples include: Lester Asheim, *Humanities and the library* (Chicago, American Library Association, 1957); Bert F. Hoselitz, ed. *A reader's guide to the social sciences* (Glencoe, Ill., Free Press, 1960); Peter R. Lewis, *The literature of the social sciences* (London, Library Association, 1960); Louise N. Malclès, *Les sources du travail bibliographique* (Genève, E. Droz, 1950-52); and Jesse H. Shera, *Historians, books and libraries* (Cleveland, Press of Western Reserve University, 1953). The origin of these and kindred surveys having a scope broader

[1] The distinction has its merits in spite of exceptional cases—as of the Dean of a well-known graduate school who confided, in 1940, that he had just read through the *Encyclopedia of the social sciences*.

than reference books is explained by circumstances which can be indicated in a general way as follows.

The evolving social control over the accumulated work of the mind. First to be mentioned is the growth of subject literature to the point where guidance is increasingly sought by those who use it. Chauncey M. Louttit observed in the preface of his *Handbook of psychological literature* (Bloomington, Ind., Principia Press, 1932) that "The literature of psychology is so voluminous and so scattered that professional men, as well as students, are often at a loss when searching for material on subjects with which they are not familiar." In the period leading up to World War II, consciousness of this drawback was deepening, and was not limited to psychology. One of the working papers used in planning Unesco described how bibliographical problems had, by 1945, grown to such a degree that it would take cooperation on an international scale to cope with them.[2] They had arisen too slowly to attract much attention, but as the stream of book production grew bigger, between the fifteenth and twentieth centuries, the ability of the individual to keep track of intellectual advances was gradually overtaxed. Adjustments to this first breakdown of arrangements lessened dependence on private libraries and stimulated development of great institutional libraries supported at public expense. Later came the breakdown of the idea of a library of record which, so far as it met expectations, enabled the individual to keep up with intellectual progress by accumulating all the literature on different subjects in a single place. As single-location access gave way, the stream of books once more swirled "beyond the control of man, wherever he found himself unaided by bibliographical facilities." The name commonly applied to this third method of keeping track of the intellectual output, viz., the aiding of access to material by listing it, is "bibliographical control."

Much progress has been made since 1945 toward reasserting social control over an ever-enlarging stream of documentation through better bibliographical control. The improvements are the work, not only of Unesco, but of national libraries including the Library of Congress and a host of cooperating professional associations. One of the more influential studies of the period was devoted to bibliographical services in the social sciences.[3] Based on an examination of the working needs of scholars and of the condition of social science literature, the study recommended various improvements in services, ranging all the way from better listing of new publications to searching analyses of progress based

[2] An article based on this report to the Department of State and the Conference of Allied Ministers of Education appeared in the *Library journal*, v. 71, April 1, 1946: 435-38, under the title, "The position of the book and the library in the program of the United Nations Educational, Scientific and Cultural Organization."
[3] Chicago. University. Graduate Library School and Social Science Division. Bibliographical services in the social sciences. *Library quarterly*, v. 20, April 1950: 79-99.

on reviews of the literature. Later pages of this work note several improvements that have originated since—sometimes in consequence of—these recommendations. Better listing of new publications is being done in several countries, and this benefits workers in all fields. As for the social sciences, the most conspicuous improvement has been along the line of better abstracting for subjects where bibliographical services have been weak. As for those "tools of orientation" (Louttit's phrase) whose function is to "open the ramifying paths" of the literature, some good guides for single disciplines, for government publications, etc., have been produced; but general guides to the monographic and reference literature are fewer and more experimental in nature.

Subject specialists comprise only a portion of the population interested in social science literature. Society's ways of making this voluminous material serviceable places the librarian at the crossroads of lanes of communication, where most of the clamor for bibliographical guidance is heard. It is, of course, clear that librarianship is a social institution—a method of putting to use and maintaining control over the accumulated work of the mind. It is also clear that, as a form of social control, the library relies on all three types of administrative control alluded to above: control over information through the use of librarians who have knowledge of the literature; control through provision of direct physical access to books; and control through the preparation and use of bibliographical aids. To provide good library service to all the people, in a century which has brought an explosion of specialized information, many librarians have divided up the total intellectual record into subject collections of broad scope, with a literature specialist in charge of each division. It is a trend that is related to older ways of decentralizing library collections for use and takes more than one form. The thing to note for present purposes is the premium it places on good working knowledge of subject literature, and this has augmented the demand for bibliographical guides which systematically map the territory.

As the demand for literature specialists in libraries has risen, critical attention has turned to methods of producing them. British librarians rely on a system of guided reading and examinations; German librarians, on prolonged subject training. The historic position of the American library school is close to the German practice in treating subject-literature training as a responsibility of subject departments; but the results have not been very satisfactory. Scholars in subject departments who profess competence to handle bibliographical instruction in all branches of their subject are rare, while courses covering all branches of the subject, though not unknown, are rarer still. Moreover, bibliographical instruction is usually organized in terms of needs of those who are qualifying as subject specialists. Students whose professional interests lie outside teaching and research in that field usually have to adjust to a pattern of organization ill-adapted to their needs. Now and then a course is found which is organized for broader cultural purposes. A good example is a course on "The literature of American history," taught for years at Columbia University by Allan Nevins. A survey and critical appraisal of American history and historians built around works which stand out as landmarks, this course served many students from other departments. A more typical procedure is to distribute bibliographical instruction among content courses of a department, with an occasional course on methods of research dealing at length with bibliographical problems. It is a procedure which obviously might take several years for a student who sets out to acquaint himself with the literature of three or four or more disciplines. No library school has had the temerity to make such a regimen prerequisite to admission or, after admission, prerequisite to graduation.

The recruiting of ready-made literature specialists has not worked out well either. Recruits who hold the Master's degree in a subject often measure up well, but no prediction can easily be made about two Bachelors from separate departments of economics (to take an example), except that their knowledge of economics literature will vary, and that both are likely to be unfamiliar with a wealth of material that is much used in the best libraries of economics and business. German dependence on "doctor" librarians seeks to resolve the problem through prolonged formal training, but the price paid is a status system which, as German librarians have pointed out, acts as a barrier to professional unity and good morale. A point to be borne in mind is that the librarian who learns, by whatever procedure, the literature of one subject does not by that act gain a working knowledge of others. The problem to be faced is that the new type of subject divisions that have been found useful in asserting social control over large segments of the intellectual record tends to be broader in scope than the lines of departmental organization that are used for purposes of administering instruction and research.

There is, as a result, a fair amount of agreement among faculties of library schools on two propositions. First, all prospective librarians require basic bibliographic instruction for which subject-matter courses are no substitute. Second, university instruction is on the whole poorly organized to provide training in subject bibliography of the scope required by literature specialists, especially by those who have charge of collections comprising the literature of two or more disciplines. The search for ways of altering and supplementing the traditional handling of subject bibliography makes it apparent that success depends on teaching aids. All of the guides named above have some relation to this search on the part of librarians for aid in gaining a firmer, more comprehensive grasp of subject literature. The attempt is made in this work to deal authoritatively with the literature, on a plane commensurate with the breadth of interest of library literature specialists in the social sciences. If it succeeds in its mission, it should serve others whose interest in the literature is of comparable range.

Subject collections as sources of information. The original preface of Melvin G. Mellon's *Chemical publications, their nature and use* (New York, McGraw, 1928) justifies the study of subject bibliography on the ground that a library collection remains a closed store of information until one learns how to open it up. "The chemical literature" to be found in a well-equipped library, he says, "is the storehouse of the available information of chemical science and chemical industry. Such a storehouse—the permanent memory of the chemist—can be opened only by those who have become acquainted with its contents. The successful searcher must have acquired the necessary technique—the knowledge of how and where to find desired information in the library."

Social science materials are found wherever we turn, and they are heavily used. They make up complete libraries, are very prominent in all libraries of a general nature, and, in collections devoted to the physical, mathematical and life sciences, or to medicine, engineering, the fine arts, etc., they are normally in greater demand than materials from any other field outside the specialty of the collection itself. This record of usefulness is explained primarily by the harvest of information pertinent to human needs which social scientists have brought to the common store; but it is explained no less by that whole complex of factors which has given information of all sorts its prominence in modern life. It would divert the discussion to do more than allude to this phenomenon. In the aggregate, of course, the fund of tested knowledge, data and expert opinion which we label "information" is extraordinary both in range and bulk. Methods of supplying the information thus amassed have steadily improved, and, as access has broadened, attitudes toward utilizing it have undergone change. The results are the most dramatic in communities and nations which formerly depended on ways handed down, but are now readier to think and act in terms of the best information available from any quarter. Indeed, it has become fashionable for all nations nowadays to strive to some degree to close the gap between tested knowledge, on the one hand, and those social practices, on the other, whose validity rests solely, or mainly, on their serviceability in times past. Those nations which most consistently use reliable information employ a variety of techniques that affect both the production and the use of social science materials. They encourage: the advancement of knowledge as a matter of public policy; systematic reporting of programs and activities of private organizations and government agencies; large-scale gathering of statistical data, etc. They organize a variety of services to aid in making all this information available, and they train managers in business, labor, government and education to put it to effective use.

While practices of coping with man's information problems need further study, librarians have already learned enough about readers and about the way to build collections to develop what the literature calls a functional philosophy of librarianship. This is a shorthand description of the practice of studying the problems, interests and needs of a community (school, university, suburban, industrial or other) and building library collections and activities around the aspirations and working habits of the people to be served. The start is thus made from *within* the informing process: as soon as an image is formed of the information requirements, the librarian starts marshaling the information sources that will best serve them.

One thing that emerges from library experience in these matters is that requests for information tend to group themselves around broad functional categories which, in library parlance, are referred to as types of request. For example, one library may have requests for names and addresses of lawyers or business organizations. Another may supply none of these but will supply information of exactly the same type about psychologists or educators. So different in substance are the two sets of requests in such a case that entirely different stocks of sources will be required to handle them; but the function of supplying *directory* information is one that both have to perform.

The procedure to be followed in this volume builds upon the everyday experience of libraries in the grouping of requests into major types. It seeks to organize the treatment in terms of the way that subject literature functions as a collection of information sources. It is an approach which offers: a useful method of opening up the rich and ever-expanding store of information to be found in social science literature; a method of taking stock of the capability of the literature, as presently developed in individual fields, for meeting society's information requirements; and an opportunity to identify the more crucial sources now at hand in each major category. It is an approach which opens an even wider vista of problems, which cannot be fully treated here, such as: how the form of bibliographic organization used here for grouping types of sources can be further perfected; to what extent types of sources which are highly developed in one subject correspond to types found in others; and what criteria can be evolved from a study of "best" examples of sources of a given type for use in improving documentation and book selection.

TYPES OF SOURCES

While the shaping of individual collections depends upon demands of the clientele, book selection for subject fields, if based on knowledge of popular demand alone, misses the elemental point that the subject itself demands certain types of material for readers who would know it. What is the backbone of social science literature, the essential working equipment for getting at the knowledge, data and expert opinion for scholars, students and the public at large? It is impossible to give a pat answer to this question, but it is worth stating, for it has been in mind enough to throw light on the selection, grouping and exposition of sources that are to be met in the coming pages.

Each of the social sciences has its peculiarities, and since organization is the handmaiden of exposition and not its master, the treatment in these eight chapters tries to adapt itself to the strucure of the literature as determined by the way it has developed. The following outline, however, encompasses basic types of information commonly demanded of subject collections, and has been used as a pattern of treatment as far as it is found applicable. In an area where terminology is a problem interpretations are inserted after the headings to clarify the meanings of terms.

Introductions and systematic sources. Like the god, Janus, the scientific process faces in two directions at once. It begins by breaking down the field of study into problems which are attacked one at a time, and the resultant findings are the raw materials of scientific knowledge. Then, as the results of inquiry accumulate, the findings are systematized. This obverse side of the process means taking inventory and fitting the fragments into a coherent pattern where, as in a mosaic, each fragment gains meaning from being seen in relation to others. One of the recurring demands on social science collections is for information of this sort: the mind reaches for synthesis, in this sphere as elsewhere, as the ivy reaches for light.

The feature that sets this type of source apart is the work of systematizing the information, but this is, of course, done in various ways and at various levels. The theme treated may be broad or narrow; the author may be a specialist or a layman; and the treatment may be popular or learned, depending on the audience for which it is written. An elementary textbook on psychology is a work of synthesis, the same as a handbook summing up the status of knowledge for psychologists. Both require skills different from conducting research, and one is not *ipso facto* easier than the other because it is done for novices.

The *Standard catalog for public libraries* can be used to make more concrete the point that this type of source takes in a very wide variety of material. This well-known aid to book selection double-stars current works which are recommended for first purchase. The following were recently among the double-starred choices in the social sciences: George F. Kennan, *Russia and the West under Lenin and Stalin* (Boston, Little, 1961); John F. Kennedy, *The strategy of peace,* ed. by Allan Nevins (New York, Harcourt, 1960); Martin Mayer, *The schools* (New York, Harper, 1961); Ruth Strang, *Helping your gifted child* (New York, Dutton, 1960); and Vance O. Packard, *The waste makers* (New York, McKay 1960). These are but random examples from the steady stream of presentations on some aspect or other of political science, education, psychology, economics, etc. They are all written for non-specialists and contribute toward informed citizenship, toward informed parenthood, general enlightenment and the deepening of the reading habit in general.

The point having been made, it is not necessary to dwell on the riches and uses of assorted veins of material which are systematic sources of one kind or another. For the purpose of developing a useful general guide to social science literature, it seems fitting to concentrate under the heading "Introductions and systematic sources" on short syntheses written by professionals. And in this first chapter, only those works will be listed which bring together findings from more than one discipline.

A word should be added about an important class of professionally-written summaries that are not confined to scientific content. John B. McMaster, A *school history of the United States* (New York, American Book Co., 1897) and Jacques Barzun and Henry P. Graff's *The modern researcher* (New York, Harcourt, 1957) are both introductory works. One treats historical content: the other, the task and technique of the competent report-writer—whether historian or some other. It is an important distinction, and provides insight into the condition of the literature if it is found, for example, that the true summary of knowledge, the type confined to content, is not yet well developed. On this subject more will be said later on.

Histories. These contain connected accounts of how the subject has advanced and of those whose work accounts for the progress.

Sources on the status of the specialty. These are systematic assessments of study, teaching, public recognition.

Works on method. These selections define and explain procedures that scholars have evolved for use in developing objective conclusions about the subject.

Contributions to different branches of the subject. The literature takes shape around major break-throughs in one direction or sector after another. The major sources under this heading are the milestones along each trail that has been blazed back and forth across the area.

Guides to the literature. Used carelessly, this term refers to any work which is intended to aid someone in the use of books. For example, Jack A. Clarke, *Research materials in the social sciences* (Madison, Univ. of Wisconsin Press, 1959)—a good annotated list of general works—is referred to as a "guide," because it was prepared to aid graduate students who are starting to do research. Intent is important, for it governs the selection and organization of material and affects usefulness in other subtle ways; but as used here, the term "guide" is reserved for the type of bibliographical source which systematizes and introduces the literature. Its function is analogous to that of a good systematic introduction to the content of the subject. Normally the treatment is illuminated by connected discussion: it differs from the bibliography, to be mentioned as a separate type farther on, in that it does more than simply list, or list and annotate.

Reviews of the literature. One of the most frequent requests is for information to aid in evaluating books. The organization of these sources is undergoing change. The traditional and still the most important source is the book review section of scholarly journals, literary magazines and newspapers. Psychologists led in developing a more systematic type of review using the literature as a basis of evaluating the status of research in different areas. Two other ways of accomplishing this end are likewise illustrated by psychology. One is to abandon the scattering of responsibility among several journals and centralize responsibility in a special book-reviewing organ—in this case *Contemporary psychology.* The other way, regular inventories of research progress based on the literature, is accomplished by an *Annual review of psychology.* It goes a step beyond the work of the *Psychological bulletin,* its precursor, by reviewing progress more thoroughly and more regularly.

It is important to relate the various sources of critical information about the literature to one another, and this heading is the means used to do so.

Abstracts and digests. These contain no critical evaluation such as that found in Reviews of the literature (above). Abstracting has developed into a recognized technique whose purpose is to describe the essential features of the contribution considered as a whole. Digests are enough alike to justify treatment under the same heading. They are usually current but sometimes retrospective.

Bibliographies and indexes. Exhibiting extremes in scope, purpose and make-up, bibliographies and indexes share responsibility for listing books, articles, etc., according to some pattern—whether by author, title, subject, form, date of publication, or some other. An especially valuable sub-class is the bibliography of bibliographies. These are both current and retrospective. The service of the bibliography may be limited to selection, organization and listing; but often further information is supplied by discussing the literature item by item. This type of discussion, annotation, may be expository, critical or promotional.

Dictionaries. These are sources whose primary purpose is to define the meaning of words and phrases.

Encyclopedias and encyclopedic sets. These comprehensive syntheses of knowledge are produced by cooperative effort. They are further distinguished from handbooks (as that term is used here) by scholarly treatment which normally places the subject in historical perspective, identifies those who have furthered its advancement and facilitates reference to the most pertinent literature. Encyclopedias customarily break down the treatment into topics which are then arranged alphabetically, but this is a matter of form of presentation. The same intellectual function can be, and is, performed by the encyclopedic set, which arranges the presentation in systematic form. Accordingly, the two forms of treatment are placed under a common heading.

Directories and biographical information. Here we locate factual information about people, organizations, places and things.

Atlases, pictorial works. These are sources which map, picture, or present information in some other graphic manner.

Handbooks, manuals, compendia. The *vade mecum* derived its name from being needed at hand for constant use. It was the forerunner of the modern handbook—defined here as a source of much-used information in handy form. The parliamentarian's manual of procedure will be less used by the historian than a compendium of dates or other factual information, but both sources illustrate the modern tendency among intellectual workers of all classes to use information of one kind or another in their specialties so constantly that it enhances their efficiency to have it close at hand in very practical form.

Yearbooks. Their distinguishing feature is annual reporting, which in form varies from systematic accounts of recent developments to periodic revision of basic data in tabular form. Up-to-date information is so important in modern affairs that certain yearbooks perform a function indistinguishable from that of handbooks as above defined. The line drawn between these two types of sources depends less on whether "handbook," "yearbook," etc. appears in the title than on whether annual up-dating is a primary determinant of the tool's usefulness.

Statistical sources. The most useful ones commonly share characteristics of handbooks and yearbooks. This class is treated separately, because it is another type of source whose singularity lies in communicating information in quantitative form.

Original sources. These are other sources besides statistics which are likewise of fundamental importance in documentation and research.

Sources of scholarly contributions. Here we have the journals which play the major role in reporting research; monograph series which extend the reporting process by publishing studies too long for journals to handle; organizations which exist to promote research or which in other ways significantly influence the development of the literature.

Sources of current information. This category covers professional journals, bulletins or other channels through which professionals obtain news reports or minutes of official meetings, exchange professional opinion and keep up to date with all other important professional news—new activities, promotions, deaths, etc.

Sources of unpublished information. Most common here are the unpublished dissertations, but we also have other unpublished studies, reports of research in progress, etc.

Mellon's *Chemical publications* uses another pattern of bibliographic organization which is well known among subject bibliographers.[4] There the literature of the subject is divided into three main categories: (1) primary sources (periodicals, institutional publications, literature on patents, dissertations, manufacturers' technical bulletins); (2) secondary sources (periodicals and serials devoted to indexing, abstracting and reviews; bibliographies; reference works, monographs and textbooks); and (3) tertiary sources (publications about chemical literature; language dictionaries; trade catalogs, directories, and biographical dictionaries). A fourth section is devoted to the technique of making searches in chemical literature. "Tertiary sources" were included the first time in the third edition (1958). It is useful for anyone who is to do research, or work with researchers, to get acquainted with the literature as a set of sources which bear directly or indirectly on promoting the advancement of knowledge; the hierarchical scheme has proved its usefulness for this purpose. When, however, the object is to interpret the information capabilities of the literature for readers of all sorts, who turn to subject collections with all sorts of requests, the hierarchy breaks down and becomes a source of confusion. What is to be gained by insisting that a trade catalog is a "tertiary" source, when for certain purposes it is a primary source? The information-requirements of modern man have a leveling tendency. A source gains status, not by being born to high or low station, but by speaking on some important subject clearly and with authority. The

---

[4] For an illustration of the influence of Mellon on bibliographic organization in the social sciences, see: Louttit, Chauncey M. *Handbook of psychological literature.* Bloomington, Ind., Principia Press, 1932. p. 7-8.

latest news release from the Weather Bureau is, for its purposes, the peer of basic statistical material from the Census Bureau. The best history of New York City is no substitute for the City telephone directory, and the reports of the Securities Exchange Commission do a job that research reports in journals or dissertations cannot do.

MONOGRAPHS

Introductions and systematic accounts. The results of scientific inquiry are brought together to some extent in many works, but good general summaries are scarce. Three of superior merit are listed below. Two are textbooks; the third a "factbook," taking in the work of the behavioral sciences and is the best summary of tested knowledge available. The term "behavioral science" is used in the literature in two ways. It commonly refers to sociology, psychology, and anthropology, but is coming to refer quite as much to consistent application of objective methods to the study of human behavior in the broadest sense of that term.

A1. Berelson, Bernard and Gary Steiner. Human behavior; an inventory of scientific findings. New York, Harcourt, 1964. (In preparation)
A2. Hunt, Elgin F. Social science; an introduction to the study of society. 2d ed. New York, Macmillan, 1961. 887 p.
A3. Ross, Ralph G. and Ernest van den Haag. The fabric of society; an introduction to the social sciences, under the general editorship of Carl Latham and Robert K. Merton. New York, Harcourt, 1957. 777 p.

All three of these accounts are written for non-specialists. The literature is weak in general systematic accounts of a more specialized nature. There is no adequate handbook, in the German sense of a summing up of existing knowledge for the ready use of the scholar; and the only comprehensive encyclopedias are out of date or in preparation. Any list of contributions toward bettering the situation would include work of Talcott Parsons and Pitirim A. Sorokin mentioned later in sociology—work which, in trying to find a basic consensus, has as one effect shown that current thought is not ready for it.

There are conflicting explanations of why sources of this more specialized variety are limited in comparison with other fields. One is that the profession cultivates imaginative use of theoretical construction in forming hypotheses necessary for fact-finding, but neglects it for broad-gauged integration of results or for planning research to aid this process. The other explanation is that empirical inquiry, for all its progress, has not yet produced enough results to make possible generalization of the more comprehensive variety. Too many pieces of the mosaic, it is felt, are still missing. There is evidence to support both sides.

Both parties agree, however, that the difficulty is related to how the work of social scientists is organized. While quantity of research by itself is not enough, effective interdisciplinary synthesis stands to benefit from more cross-disciplinary efforts at the fact-finding level. To date, most or the content of social science has been developed by scholars who are, for example, political scientists or historians first and social scientists second. Accordingly, monographic literature is largely treated in subsequent chapters on separate disciplines, since this chapter is generally the place for noting significant works which cut across several or all of these disciplines.

The Social Science Research Council was established in 1923. It originated with, and has in turn led, a movement out of which has come much of the progress along interdisciplinary lines. Harry E. Barnes, ed., *The history and progress of the social sciences* (New York, Knopf, 1925), an early interdisciplinary contribution, brought together specialists in history, human geography, biology, social psychology, economics, political science, jurisprudence and ethics who produced competent summaries on the progress and aspirations of their several specialties. But as a reviewer was quick to point out, "The interrelation of the various fields is . . . left to the intelligence of the reader." William F. Ogburn and Alexander A. Goldenweiser, eds., *Social sciences and their interrelations* (Boston, Houghton, 1927) were more successful. Thirty-nine specialists were set to analyzing the interests and tools held in common by some fourteen specialties dealing with "Man in society" and what type of cross-fertilization and cooperation the future interests of responsible scholarship required. The book was to gain recognition as a milestone, but the pull of inertia was still heavy at the time. It is not surprising to find one reviewer remarking that "the disappointment of the volume lies in the fact that first-rate minds were set to the performance of a second-rate task." The *Encyclopedia of the social sciences* further demonstrated the mutual interests and interdependence of several disciplines within which the tradition of independence had been strong. The effect was to accelerate interdisciplinary cooperation and to pave the way for some measure of reorganizing inquiry to keep pace with momentous change of the twentieth century. The works below are selected to interpret the interrelationship of the social sciences, to describe how bridges of cooperative effort are being built between them and how, in the process, the working habits and orientation of social scientists are being altered.

A4. Seligman, Edwin R.A. What are the social sciences? *Encyclopedia of the social sciences.* New York, Macmillan, 1937. v. 1. p. 3-7.

A5. Komarovsky, Mirra, *ed.* Common frontiers of the social sciences. Glencoe, Ill., Free Press, 1957. 439 p.

A6. White, Leonard D., *ed.* The state of the social sciences; papers presented at the 25th anniversary of the Social Science Research Building, University of Chicago, Nov. 10-12, 1955. Chicago, Univ. of Chicago Press, 1956. 504 p.

A7. Gillin, John P., *ed.* For a science of social man; convergences in anthropology, psychology and sociology. New York, Macmillan, 1954. 296 p.

A8. Berelson, Bernard, *ed*. The behavioral sciences today. New York, Basic Books, 1963. 278 p.

This is the place to remark upon a peculiarity in the literature of synthesis in social science. Scientific inquiry is a human enterprise as well as a knowledge-producing tool. Those in charge must be decisive in their purposes and methods. In the last four decades or so, social scientists have bent to the pursuit of knowledge in a climate of confusion about the enterprise in their custody. While advancing knowledge, they have simultaneously been re-examining the tools and organization of inquiry that are used in their field. The literature reflects this dual purpose; indeed, some of the finest work of synthesis is devoted quite as much to the meaning, scope, organization and responsibilities of the enterprise as to the content of knowledge derived therefrom. Three summaries which stress content were named at the outset. They are supplemented by the following, in which proportionately greater stress falls upon the nature, role and significance of social science.

A9. Bruner, Jerome S., *ed*. Toward a common ground: international social science. New York, Society for the Psychological Study of Social Issues, 1947. 66 p. (*Journal of social issues*, v. 3, no. 1, Winter, 1949)

A10. Chase, Stuart. The proper study of mankind; an inquiry into the science of human relations. Rev. ed. New York, Harper, 1956. 327 p.

A11. Dahl, Robert, *et al*. Social science research on business; product and potential. New York, Columbia Univ. Press, 1959. 185 p.

A12. Lerner, Daniel, *ed*. The human meaning of the social sciences. New York, Meridan, 1959. 317 p.

A13. Lerner, Daniel and Harold D. Lasswell. The policy sciences; recent developments in scope and method. Stanford, Calif., Stanford Univ. Press, 1951. 344 p.

A14. Lundberg, George A. Can science save us? 2d ed. New York, Longmans, 1961. 150 p.

A15. Lynd, Robert S. Knowledge for what? The place of social science in American culture. Princeton, N.J., Princeton Univ. Press, 1939. 248 p.

A16. University of Chicago Round Table. Prospects for the scientific study of human relations; a radio discussion by James B. Conant, Robert Redfield and George D. Stoddard, including a supplement on Social science and education for a democracy. Chicago, 1947. (No. 510, Dec. 28, 1947)

There is a great abundance of even more specialized sources on the role of the social sciences and their significance for human needs. To illustrate this policy-making may be chosen as one special area. A series of brochures prepared by the Russell Sage Foundation for the *American sociological review* describes the role which sociology is able to play in supplying invaluable information in such widely separated practical arts as military affairs, mental health, correction and education. The importance of the social sciences as contributors toward intelligent determination of public policy, including intelligent handling of technical aid administered by governments, is brought out by the following:

A17. Hoselitz, Bert F., *ed*. The progress of underdeveloped areas. Chicago, Univ. of Chicago Press, 1952. 296 p.

A18. Kraus, Hertha, *ed*. International cooperation for social welfare, a new reality. Philadelphia, American Academy of Political and Social Science, 1960. 222 p. (*Annals*, v. 329, May 1960)

A19. Myrdal, Gunnar. The theoretical assumption of social planning. *Transactions of the 4th world congress of sociology*. London, International Sociological Assoc., 1959. v. 2. p. 155-167.

A20. Russell Sage Foundation. Effective use of social science research in the federal services. New York, 1950. 47 p.

A21. Spicer, Edward H., *ed*. Human problems in technological change; a casebook. New York, Russell Sage Foundation, 1952. 301 p.

Histories. There is no adequate history of the social sciences. The one that comes closest to the mark is Howard Becker and Harry E. Barnes, *Social thought from lore to science.* Florjan Znaniecki, *Cultural sciences, their origin and development* (Urbana, Univ. of Illinois Press, 1952) is less a disciplined application of historical analysis than a presentation of a point of view making selected use of historical materials for support. Sources of biographical information are better represented, although coverage is piecemeal. Bert F. Hoselitz, ed. *A reader's guide to the social sciences* is a contribution whose usefulness is weakened by splitting attention between introducing seven subjects and introducing their literature; an introductory chapter contains an unexcelled short history of the social sciences.

A22. Becker, Howard and Harry E. Barnes. Social thought from lore to science. 3d ed., expanded and rev. New York, Dover, 1961. 3 v.

A23. Hoselitz, Bert F., *ed*. A reader's guide to the social sciences. Glencoe, Ill., Free Press, 1959. 256 p.

A24. Kardiner, Abraham and Edward Preble. They studied man. Cleveland, World, 1961. 287 p.

A25. Odum, Howard W., *ed*. American masters of social science; an approach to the study of the social sciences through a neglected field of biography. New York, Holt, 1927. 411 p.

A26. Schumpeter, Joseph A. Ten great economists from Marx to Keynes. New York, Oxford Univ. Press, 1951. 305 p.

Study, teaching and the public's opinion of the social sciences. Democratic societies have a deep commitment to training for good citizenship. How to meet this responsibility is another thing: it has taken and continues to take much thought and experimentation. One apparently permanent innovation is a curriculum of social studies for youth. The concept, no less than the educational reorganization required to introduce it, is largely the work of social scientists. Of the voluminous literature on the subject three sources are cited as high lights of the creative effort and organization that went into the innovation.

A27. American Historical Association. *Commission on the Social Studies in the Schools*. Report. New York, Scribner, 1932-41. 16 pts.
A28. National Society for the Study of Education. *Committee on Social Studies in the Elementary School*. Social studies in the elementary school, ed. by Nelson B. Henry. Chicago, 1957. 320 p.
A29. Wesley, Edgar B. and Stanley P. Wronski. Teaching social studies in high schools. 4th ed. Boston, Heath, 1958. 628 p.

In general, the best sources on academic status are to be found in the literature on individual disciplines. For example, the Unesco series, *Documentation in the social sciences*, contains studies of the present status of three disciplines: economics, sociology, and political science. But the reports are published separately, and each belongs with its own subject. There are surveys, of unequal merit, on the handling of social sciences in different institutions and countries, including the USSR, of which the following are better examples:

A30. Harvard University. The behavioral sciences at Harvard; report by a faculty committee, June 1954. Cambridge, 1954. 518 p.
A31. UNESCO. The teaching of the social sciences in the United Kingdom. Paris, 1953. 140 p. (Its Teaching in the social sciences)
A32. UNESCO. The teaching of the social sciences in the United States, ed. by H.W. Ehrmann. Paris, 1954. 150 p. (Its Teaching in the social sciences)

Considerable information on careers in the social sciences is available in reference books, magazines and some monographs. Perhaps the most revealing documentation on public attitudes deals with the debate on the proper position of the social sciences in American life that occurred while the National Science Foundation was being established. The best summary for the defense is to be found in Lundberg's *Can science save us?*, already listed. The best summaries of the debate itself, including the literature, are to be found in: Harry Alpert, The social science research program of the National Science Foundation, *American sociological review*, v. 22, Oct. 1957:582-85; and George A. Lundberg, The Senate ponders social science, *The scientific monthly*, v. 64, May 1947:397-411.

Method. Science is a rigorous way of thinking, which supplies objectivity greater than can be expected from common sense. In consequence, the rise of any specialty in which scholars succeed in developing a respected fund of verified knowledge has invariably been accompanied by the perfection of tools of analysis for the purpose. The first among the social sciences to develop distinctive, fruitful methods applicable to the phenomena they sought to illuminate were history, psychology and anthropology. Economics is one of the oldest of the social disciplines, and it has some claim to inclusion among these; but its present effectiveness as a science does not date back very far. Political science was at first strongly influenced by methods of law and jurisprudence, while educators who were not trained in the methods of some other discipline tended, until recently, to be interested more in practical problems than in special tools of scholarship. Sociology presents a mixed picture of an early commitment to objective study held back by the complexity of its subject no less than by the grip of philosophic analysis and the urgencies of social reform. Stuart A. Rice edited for a committee of the Social Science Research Council a significant early contribution, *Methods in social science, a case book* (Chicago, Univ. of Chicago Press, 1931). In it he observed that some social scientists believe the advancement of knowledge to be the result of piercing insight of great minds; that lesser minds, lacking the genius for telling discovery, lay greater store by method; and hence, that the appearance of special concern with method is a sign of decadence. However, in the next generation virtually all sociologists rallied behind the move to refine and perfect the tools of research. The following list stresses sources broader in range than one discipline. In so doing, it indicates the origin of methods which have interdisciplinary application. Together the five contributions document the important bearing of scientific method on controlled investigation.

A33. Barzun, Jacques and Henry P. Graff. The modern researcher. New York, Harcourt, 1957. 386 p.
A34. Festinger, Leon and Daniel Katz, *eds*. Research methods in the behavioral sciences. New York, Dryden, 1953. 660 p.
A35. Goode, William J. and Paul K. Hatt. Methods of social research. New York, McGraw, 1952. 386 p.
A36. Research methods in social relations, by Claire Selltiz and others. Published for the Society for the Psychological Study of Social Issues. Rev. New York, Holt, 1959. 622 p.
A37. Young, Pauline V. Scientific social surveys and research; an introduction to the background, content, methods, principles and analysis of social studies with chapters on statistics, scaling techniques, graphic presentation and human ecology, by Calvin Schmid. 3d ed. Englewood Cliffs, N.J., Prentice Hall, 1956. 540 p.

Contributions to social science of an interdisciplinary character. The interdisciplinary movement has been accompanied by an erosion of barriers between disciplines. This raises the question of whether social sciences in the plural are in process of being replaced by a single science of social man. The shape of the future is not visible, but social science emerges from most systematic treatises on content and method in one of two lights. In one, "social science" is less a discipline where scientific effort prevails than the product of effort i.e., the sum of authentic knowledge of human behavior considered without reference to disciplines which may have contributed it. In another light, "social science" is associated with objective inquiry, and in this sense methodology is its differentiating characteristic: it stands for rigorous thought, for utilizing fruitful methods pioneered by any and all disciplines.

As for "barriers" between disciplines, this figure of speech is linked with a premise which is falling into disrepute. The generation of *The*

history and prospects of the social sciences assumed that social scientists
are all brothers by virtue of belonging to a family of diciplines bound together by a common subject (human behavior or "man in society," to
employ Ogburn and Goldenweiser's phrase). The subject, however, is
divided into as many "fields" as there are academic departments where
work is done on it; these are in turn divided by "barriers." The arrangement of the specialties remains much the same today because of the way
study and professional training are organized. But it is closer to the spirit
of the profession to describe human behavior as an open field of scientific
inquiry within which specialists operate wherever they are equipped to
do so. The tie that binds is changing: for example, mutual interests and
training may bring an empirically-minded political scientist into closer
working relations with a psychologist than with a political philosopher;
the latter's contribution to political science is not deprecated on that
account. The point to stress is that human behavior is a unity or con-
tinuum. The several methods for learning about it differ in perspective
for purposes of analysis.

Later chapters cite prominent studies in the development of the various disciplines within the scope of this book. Here studies are cited to
show the meaning and progress of interdisciplinary research. Some of the
works chosen emphasize the fruitfulness of applying to a common problem, such as the wartime experiences of the soldier, methods of investigation which have originated in more than one discipline. Others take a
problem which has been well studied in one field—for instance, administration in political science—and provide some germinal restatement
which brings it within the scope of fresh methods of analysis from outside. It is the leaven of such experiences that is subtly altering the concept as well as the literature of the social sciences.

A38. Almond, Gabriel A. and James S. Coleman, *eds.* The politics of de-
        veloping areas. Princeton, N.J., Princeton Univ. Press, 1961. 591 p.
A39. Lasswell, Harold D. Power and personality. New York, Norton, 1948.
        262 p.
A40. McClelland, David C. The achieving society. New York, Van Nos-
        trand, 1961. 512 p.
A40a. Myrdal, Gunnar. An American dilemma; the Negro problem and
        modern democracy, with the assistance of Richard Steiner and
        Arnold Rose. New York, Harper, 1944. 2 v.
A40b. Simon, Herbert A. Administrative behavior; a study of decision-
        making processes in administrative organization. 2d ed. with new
        introduction, with a foreword by Chester I. Barnard. New York,
        Macmillan, 1957. 259 p.
A40c. Studies in social psychology in World War II, prepared and ed. under
        the auspices of a special committee of the Social Science Research
        Council. Princeton, N.J., Princeton Univ. Press, 1949-50. 4 v.
        v.1 Stouffer, S.A., *et al.* The American soldier: adjustment dur-
            ing army life. 1949. 599 p.
        v.2 Stouffer, S.A., *et al.* The American soldier: combat and its
            aftermath. 1949. 675 p.

v.3 Hovland, C.I., *et al.* Experiments on mass communication. 1949. 340 p.
v.4 Stouffer, S.A., *et al.* Measurement and prediction. 1950. 756 p.

A40d. Warner, William L., *ed.* Yankee city series. New Haven, Conn., Yale Univ. Press, 1941-59. 5 v.
v.1 Warner, W.L. and P.S. Lunt. The social life of a modern community. 1941. 460 p.
v.2 Warner, W.L. and P.S. Lunt. The status system of a modern community. 1942. 246 p.
v.3 Warner, W.L. and Leo Strole. The social systems of American ethnic groups. 1945. 318 p.
v.4 Warner, W.L. and J.O. Low. The social system of the modern factory; the strike, a social analysis. 1947. 245 p.
v.5 Warner, W.L. The living and the dead; a study of the symbolic life of Americans. 1959. 528p.

An extended appraisal of the first two, and most significant, *Studies in social psychology in World War II* is to be found in Robert K. Merton and Paul F. Lazarsfeld, eds. *Continuities in social research; studies in the scope and method of the "American soldier"* (Glencoe, Ill., Free Press, 1950). A sixth volume, *Data book for the Yankee city,* has been announced for the *Yankee city series.*

Carl M. White

GUIDES TO THE LITERATURE

A41. Carr, Edwin R. Guide to reading for social studies teachers. Washington, National Council for the Social Studies, 1951. 154 p. (National Council for the Social Studies. Bulletin, no. 26)
An annotated bibliography of some 500 English language books and 50 periodicals published mainly in the 1940's and selected for their significance in the study and teaching of social studies. An excellent selection, with informative and descriptive, rather than critical, annotations. Includes very few reference works or biographies. Arrangement is alphabetical by author under: economics, sociology and anthropology, political science, geography, American history, world history, social studies, education and the social sciences. Author index.

A42. Lewis, Peter R. Literature of the social sciences; an introductory survey and guide. London, Library Association, 1960. 222 p.
Originally intended as a brief guide for students preparing for the final examination given by the Association, the work was expanded into a broad general survey in an attempt to compensate for the lack of general guides to social science literature. International in scope, with emphasis upon the practical side of the social sciences and upon those titles which are particularly useful to British readers. Ten major areas are covered in individual chapters (with subdivisions): social sciences in general; economics; eco-

nomic history and conditions; economic history, Great Britain; statistics; commerce and industry; political science and public administration; law; international affairs; and sociology. Contents of each chapter vary, but a selection of bibliographic sources, guides and reference works is given, followed by a survey of the developments within the subject area including representative and/or significant monographs and periodicals. This is followed by a discussion of library resources and problems (e.g., cataloging, acquisition, etc.). The whole work is in the format of a bibliographical essay which allows only brief comments upon any title but permits the inclusion of a large number of works. General index. An excellent survey within self-imposed limits.

A43. Malclès, Louise-Noëlle. Les sources du travail bibliographique. Geneva, Droz; Lille, Giard, 1950-1958. 3 v. in 4.
Designed to serve as a guide to all types of reference and source materials —bibliographies, encyclopedias, dictionaries, atlases, texts, important periodicals, collections. Many of the references cited are to be found in Winchell (A46) and Walford (A45), but for materials of Europe and the Middle East this work substantially supplements the American and English manuals. While basic works of earlier dates are included, emphasis has been on the publications of the last 25 years and particularly 1940-1950. Entries are classified under broad categories with many subdivisions. Chapter headings and many subheadings are followed by analytical comment, and, though few references are separately annotated, most are gouped with a descriptive note. Vol. 1 is devoted to general bibliographies, vol. 2 (in 2 parts) to specialized sources in the humanities and social sciences and vol. 3 to specialized sources in the natural and applied sciences. Topics covered in vol. 2 of special interest are: prehistory, anthropology, ethnology, sociology, linguistics, history, geography, political, economic and social sciences, language, literature and history of Slavic and Balkan countries, the Near East, Middle East and Far East. Author subject and title index for each volume.

A44. Totok, Wilhelm and Rolf Weitzel. Handbuch der bibliographischen Nachschlagewerke. Frankfurt am Main, Klostermann, 1954. 258 p.
The German counterpart to Malclès (A43), Winchell (A46) and Walford (A45). Although primary emphasis is upon bibliographical reference works, some attention is given to encyclopedias, biographical dictionaries, etc. as well as leading periodicals. The 1,800 entries are grouped in two main sections. The first, "general bibliography," is subdivided by types, bibliographies of bibliographies, national bibliographies, library catalogs, etc. The second part, "specialized bibliographies," is arranged by subject, with short sections on history, folklore, political science, economics, geography, anthropology and sociology. Most items are annotated. Emphasis is upon Western European and American material. Coverage is less extensive than in other general guides to reference works.

A45. Walford, Arthur J., ed. Guide to reference material. London, Library Association, 1959. 543 p. Supplement, 1963.
A recent annotated guide to reference sources and bibliographies, with emphasis upon current works and material published in Great Britain. More than 3,000 items are arranged according to the 1957 abridgment of the UDC. Much material in librarianship and general bibliography is omitted, as are some older items now out of print or not readily accessible. Significant bibliographies and literature surveys appearing in periodicals

have been included. Annotations are full, informative, and often cite additional sources. Author, title and subject index. Suppl. adds ca. 2,000 items published 1957-1961. Second edition planned for 1965.

A46. Winchell, Constance M. Guide to reference books, 7th ed. Chicago, American Library Assoc., 1951. 645 p. Supplement, 1950-1952 by C.M. Winchell and O.A. Johnson, 1954; Second supplement, 1953-1955 by C.M. Winchell, 1956; Third supplement, 1956-1958, by C.M. Winchell, 1960; Fourth supplement, 1959-1962, by C.M. Winchell, 1963.
The authoritative work on reference books. Arrangement is systematic by discipline in general accord with the Dewey classification. Annotations are good, but are not uniformly provided. International in scope, with less emphasis upon Scandinavia. Full index. Kept up to date by the semi-annual supplements appearing in the January and July issues of *College and research libraries*. 8th ed. in preparation.

REVIEWS OF THE LITERATURE

A47. American Academy of Political and Social Science. Annals. v. 1+ 1890+ Philadelphia. bi-monthly.
The *Annals* are symposia, with each issue devoted to a specific topic. Included also is an extensive "Book Department," which surveys 400-450 new titles a year in all fields of political and social sciences. The signed critical reviews (325-1,000 words) are classified by broad subjects which vary from time to time but include: political theory, sociology, anthropology, economics, American government and history, Asia and Africa, psychology, European history and government, international relations, etc. Although emphasis is upon American writing and American affairs the works reviewed are international in scope and include a few important titles in foreign languages.

A48. Inter-American review of bibliography. v. 1+ 1951+ Washington, Pan American Union, Dept. of Cultural Affairs. quarterly.
The Pan American Union (and its Columbus Memorial Library) acts as a bibliographical center for the Organization of American States and through this publication coordinates reports and activities in the member states. Each issue contains: articles of special interest; critical review articles (6-10 a year); 25-30 signed book reviews (200-1,500 words); and "Recent books," a listing of 1,000-1,500 items a year relating to Latin America, classified under 23 major headings including anthropology, economics, education, geography, history, labor and social affairs, psychology, political science and sociology. There is also a useful section on the publications of the OAS and its specialized agencies. Annual index of authors and contributors.

A49. International review of social history. v. 1+ 1956+ Assen, Netherlands, Van Gorcum. 3 a year.
Issued from 1937-1940 and 1950-1955 as the *Bulletin* of the International Institute of Social History. Includes an annotated bibliography of 800-1,000 books a year, representing a broad selection in European languages. Each title is abstracted or commented upon in 200 words or less. Arrangement is under broad subject and country headings, with an index of names and an index of countries and subjects. Emphasis on social and labor problems.

A50. International social science journal. v. 1+ 1941+ Paris, UNESCO. quarterly.

"Reviews of documents and books" is a major section of this journal devoted to the social sciences and their relationships to international organizations. 600-700 publications of the U.N. and the specialized agencies are listed each year with short descriptive annotations. 25-50 books a year are given short (ca. 400 words) critical reviews. "Books received" lists 200-300 titles a year with brief explanatory annotations.

ABSTRACTS AND DIGESTS

A51. Bulletin signalétique. Sect. 19; Sciences humaines, philosophie. Paris, Centre National de la Recherche Scientifique, 1961+ quarterly.

Title varies: v. 1-9 (1947-1955) *Bulletin analytique: Philosophie*; v. 10-14 (1956-1960) *Bulletin signalétique*; Pt. 3 *Philosophie, sciences humaines.* One section of an abstracting service, with a wide subject range and world coverage. Includes extensive sections on psychology (ca. 4,000 items a year); sociology (ca. 2,500 items a year); education (ca. 1,200 items a year) and shorter sections on geography, linguistics, philosophy of history and political philosophy. Brief, indicative abstracts of articles and book reviews from a large number of periodicals from many countries. Annual indexes of authors and concepts.

A52. International journal of abstracts; statistical theory and method. v. 1+ 1959+ Edinburgh, published for the International Statistical Institute by Oliver and Boyd. quarterly.

Aim of this new journal is to give as complete a coverage as possible to articles in the field of statistical theory and new contributions to statistical method. 700-1,000 items are abstracted annually from 250 journals, research reports, conference papers, symposia and seminars. Classified arrangement. The annual index supplement includes an author index, list of abstractors, list of journals and an index to book reviews in 30 major journals.

A53. Social science abstracts; a comprehensive abstracting and indexing journal of the world's periodical literature in the social sciences. New York, Social Science Abstracts, Inc., 1929-1933. 5 v.

Published monthly, with annual author and subject indexes under the auspices of the Social Sciences Research Council. During its short-lived existence it presented 70,464 abstracts of articles appearing in over 4,000 journals. Covered human geography, cultural anthropology, history, economics, political science, sociology and statistics. Classified arrangement. V. 5 is an author and subject index, with an extensive list of periodicals in the social sciences. Discontinued for lack of funds.

A54. Soviet periodical abstracts; Asia, Africa and Latin America. v. 1+ May 1961+ New York, Slavic Languages Research Institute. quarterly.

A55. ————; Soviet society. v. 1+ May, 1961+ New York, Slavic Languages Research Institute. quarterly.

The first title abstracts articles published in current Soviet journals which are selected to give an idea of the Russian view on Asian, African and Latin American affairs; the second, articles relating to education, sociology, philosophy, public administration and non-governmental institutions. Articles from the daily press are excluded. Indication is given of those titles which are translated in the *Current digest of the Soviet press.* (A59) The annotations (100-200 words) present the views of the original author. Also useful is *L'U.R.S.S. et les pays de l'est; revue des revues* v. 1+ 1960+ (Paris, S.E.D.E.S. quarterly) the abstract journal of the Centre de Recherches sur l'U.R.S.S. et les Pays de l'Est, University of Strasbourg which presents selected abstracts in French from Russian, Polish and Yugoslav periodicals.

A56. Tropical abstracts. v. 1+ 1946+ Amsterdam, Royal Tropical Institute. monthly.

Largely agricultural in orientation, but includes material on economic and social affairs, economic geography and international organizations. 2,000-3,000 items for over 300 journals are abstracted annually. International in scope. Classified arrangement, with an annual subject index.

A57. World agricultural economics and rural sociology abstracts. v. 1+ 1959+ Amsterdam, North Holland Publ. Co. quarterly.

An international abstract journal, covering the literature of agricultural economics and rural sociology in the broadest sense, including agricultural policy, land reform, farm labor, marketing, agrarian reform, etc., as well as agricultural education, legislation, geography and history. The entries (books and articles) are arranged under 52 subject headings with annual author, subject and geographic indexes. Restricted to publications of a scholarly nature. Works of purely local interest are excluded.

News Digests

A58. Asian recorder; a weekly digest of Asian events with index. Jan. 1955+ Delhi, Sankaran. weekly.

A loose-leaf news service in the style of *Keesing's contemporary archives* (A61). The news items are summarized from Asian and foreign newspapers, periodicals, official publications and reports. Sources are identified, (no pages or dates) and references to previous articles are included. Geographical coverage includes all of Asia and the Middle East, as well as some African areas, with emphasis on India. (Beginning in Jan., 1962 a separate *African recorder* has been published fortnightly.) Quarterly index with annual cumulation.

A59. Current digest of the Soviet press. v. 1+ Feb. 1, 1949+ New York, Joint Committee on Slavic Studies. weekly.

Sponsored by the American Council of Learned Societies and the Social Science Research Council. Each issue gives a complete weekly index of the contents of the two leading Soviet dailies, *Pravda* and *Izvestia*, and a digest of the news, translated in full or condensed, from other newspapers and periodicals. Arrangement is by subject matter—special features, foreign affairs (by region) and domestic affairs. Each item is fully documented. Time lag for *Pravda* and *Izvestia* is about one month, longer for others. Quarterly indexes include not only the contents of the *Current digest* but also other translations of Soviet materials (e.g., the items translated in *Soviet studies*) and the contents of Soviet publications printed in English.

A60. Facts on file; world news digest with index. v. 1+ 1940+ New York, Facts on File. weekly.

A loose leaf news service which records without comment or bias all vital news of the week under such headings as world affairs, national affairs, foreign affairs, Latin America, economy, arts and sciences, education and religion, sports, and obituaries. The news section is continuously paged, and the items include references to previous articles on the same topic. Indexes are issued bi-weekly and monthly which cumulate quarterly with the fourth quarterly index being the annual index. Items are brief and factual. Sources are not indicated. Three five-year indexes (1946-1950; 1951-1955; 1956-1961) have been issued.

A61. Keesing's contemporary archives; weekly diary of important world events with index kept continually up-to-date. v. 1+ July 1, 1931+ London, Keesing's. weekly.

"Reports, statistics and data selected, condensed, translated, summarized and indexed from newspapers, periodicals and official publications of the United Kingdom, the Commonwealth and foreign countries, as well as from information supplied by the recognized international news agencies." Items included are more strictly political and economic in nature and are more fully reported than in the comparable *Facts on file*. Reproduces speeches and the texts of documents (often in full), as well as statistical tables and maps. The sources of each report are identified but specific details (date, pages, etc.) are not given. V. 1-9 (1931-1952/54) covered three years each; thereafter two years. Subject index appears biweekly and quarterly, the latter being cumulated from the beginning of the volume until a final consolidated index is issued for the completed volume. A cumulative name index is published quarterly.

BIBLIOGRAPHIES—CURRENT

A62. American Bibliographical Service. Quarterly check-list series. Darien, Conn., 1958+

A series of select lists of current books, monographs, brochures and separates published in western languages. Series of interest include: Classical studies, v. 1+ 1958+; Psychology, v. 1+ 1961+; Linguistics, v. 1+ 1958+; Economics and political science, v. 1+ 1958+; Ethnology and sociology, v. 1+ 1958+; Medievalia, v. 1+ 1959+; Oriental studies, v. 1+ 1959+; and Renaissance studies, v. 1+ 1959+. In each series the 300-700 items a year are listed alphabetically by author, with an annual author, editor and translator index. No annotations, but full bibliographical details including publisher's address and price. See also B324.

A63. American bibliography of Slavic and East European studies, 1956+ Bloomington, Ind., 1957+ annual. (Indiana University. Publications. Slavic and East European series, v. 1, 10, 18, 21+)

The first issue (1956) included only the humanities. Social science material was added in the volume for 1957. 1,300-1,800 items per year include books and articles written by Americans anywhere or published in America (including all the Americas), classified under 11 major headings, including for the social sciences: geography, anthropology and archeology, history, political science, law, economics, education and folklore. No annotations. Author index. For the period 1945-1957 see Robert F. Byrnes' *Bibliography of American publications on East Central Europe, 1945-1957*. (Bloomington, Ind., Indiana Univ. Press, 1958. 213 p. [Indiana University. Publications. Slavic and East European series, v. 12]), a classified listing of 2,810 items. East Germany, Greece and the USSR excluded. See also Dagmar

Horna's *Current research on Central and Eastern Europe* (New York, Mid-European Studies Center, 1956. 251 p.) the first part of which lists 1,214 American research topics. The second section is a roster of the 700+ scholars whose research is listed. Gives academic training, present address and employment.

A64. Androit, John L. Guide to U.S. government statistics. 3d ed. rev. and enl. Arlington, Va., Documents Index, 1961. 402 p.

An annotated guide to the statistical contents of the voluminous output of Federal publications. The 1,777 entries are arranged by government agency, listing for each the various publications containing statistical data. Includes "one-time" works as well as serial material. The works listed range from one-table news releases to large compilations of statistical data covering many subjects. Subject and agency indexes. Future volumes planned biennially (in odd years). A supplemental volume which will contain the background and interrelationship of various series, etc. is in preparation. To be revised biennially.

A65. Arctic Institute of North America. Arctic bibliography; prepared for and in cooperation with the Department of Defense. Washington, Govt. Print. Off., 1953+ v. 1+ (In progress)

An extensive annotated bibliography, designed to provide a key to scientific publication in all languages, relating to the Arctic and sub-Arctic areas. Included is material on administration and government, Eskimos, archeology, economic and social conditions, expeditions, mapping, population, communication, psychology, education, colonization transportation and ethnographic material for the peoples native to the North. V. 1-3 constitute the basic set (authors, A to Z and an index). V. 4+ are in a sense annual volumes. Two parts: (1) an alphabetical author listing, with full bibliographical details, including transliteration and translation of foreign and Cyrillic titles. Concise abstracts with location given for the copy used; (2) an extensive subject-geographic index. Especially valuable for Russian and Scandinavian sources. V. 1-9, 56,278 items.

A66. Australian public affairs information service. A subject index to current literature. no. 1+ July 1945+ Canberra, Commonwealth National Library. monthly, cumulated annually since 1955.

A subject index to current books, pamphlets, articles and government publications concerning Australian politics, economics and social affairs received by the Library from any English language country. Indexes ca. 450 Australian periodicals. No author index.

A67. Bibliografia brasileira de ciências sociais. v. 1+ 1954+ Rio de Janeiro, Instituto Brasileiro de Bibliografia e Documentaçâo. annual.

An annual classified listing of works on social science subjects written by Brazilian authors, by foreigners living in Brazil and works dealing with Brazil. Its 1,600-2,200 entries a year include books, articles (from ca. 100 Brazilian periodicals), pamphlets, reports, etc. arranged by the Universal Decimal Classification with alphabetical author and subject indexes. Covers sociology, statistics, political science, economics, law, public administration, social welfare, commerce and trade, and folklore.

A68. "Bibliografia italiana delle scienze sociali." *Rivista internazionale de scienze sociali*. Ser. 3 v. 28+ 1958+ Milan.

This annual classified bibliography of Italian works (500-1,000 books and articles a year) is primarily devoted to economics and political science.

1957 is covered in v. 28. This journal, published bimonthly since 1893, also reviews 100-150 books per year (500-1,500 words).

A69. Bibliographic index; a cumulative bibliography of bibliographies, 1937+ New York, Wilson, 1938+ semi-annual with cumulations.
An alphabetical subject listing of bibliographies published in books, pamphlets and periodicals since 1937. Ca. 1,500 periodicals (including some foreign titles) are examined regularly. Valuable listing, especially for minor topics.

A70. Bibliographie der Sozialwissenschaften. 42. Jahrg. n.F. Jahrg. 1+ 1950+ Göttingen, Vandenhoeck and Ruprecht. 3 a year.
An extensive classified bibliography surveying German and foreign language publications, books and articles, in all branches of the social sciences. The old series, *Bibliographie der Staats-und Wirtschaftswissenschaften* v. 1-39 (1905-1943), was restricted more to economics and politics. The new series is wider in scope, and its 5,000+ items a year include works in sociology, anthropology and social psychology. Annual author index and catchword subject index. Issued with *Jahrbuch für Sozialwissenschaft*, but the bibliography is separately paged. V. 42 covers 1948 to 1950. V. 40 (1943-1945) and v. 41 (1945-1947) are planned for future publication. This gap is, meanwhile, partially filled for German works by *Das deutsche sozialwissenschaftliche Schrifttum der Jahre 1939-1945* (Kiel Universtät, Institut für Weltwirtschaft, Bibliothek, Kiel, 1949. 51 p.), a highly selective listing of 630 significant works of a scientific nature in the social sciences.

A71. Bibliography of Asian studies, 1956+ *Journal of Asian studies* Sept. 1957+ annual.
Began as *Bulletin of Far Eastern bibliography* 1936-1940; from 1941-1956 issued in the *Far Eastern quarterly*. An extensive current bibliography (3,000-5,000 items, books, pamphlets, articles, etc.) of writings on Asia in general, China, Japan, Korea, Mongolia, Tibet, Siberia, Burma, Thailand, Vietnam-Cambodia-Laos, Malaya, Indonesia, Philippine Islands, South Asia and India. Entries are arranged geographically and subdivided by subject. Covers all topics, including history, geography, politics, economics and other social science areas. With few exceptions references are in western languages. Author index.

A72. Book review digest. v. 1+ 1905+ New York, Wilson. monthly, with semi-annual and annual cumulations.
Indexes and quotes from selected book reviews in ca. 75 English and American periodicals, principally general in character but including 15 major social science journals. Arranged by author with title and subject indexes.

A73. Brussels. *Université Libre. Institut de Sociologie Solvay.* Revue de l'Institut de Sociologie. v. 1+ 1920+ Brussels. quarterly.
Scholarly sociological journal which included, from 1920-1956, a long classified bibliography of international literature in the social sciences. 4,000 items a year. Two parts, books and articles, subdivided into sections on sociology, political science, economic science, social economy, ethnology, history, law and statistical methodology with further subject subdivisions. Publication suspended 1940-1947. The first issue in 1948 covered material published up to 1946. With v. 30 (1957) the bibliography was abandoned. Included also are critical book reviews and review articles.

A74. Fondation Nationale des Sciences Politiques. Bulletin analytique de documentation politique, économique et sociale contemporaine. v. 1+ 1946+ Paris, Presses Universitaires de France. monthly.

A classified list of periodical articles (3,000-4,000 a year) selected from ca. 1,000 leading journals in all European languages, with brief annotations or abstracts. Two main sections: (1) "Problemes Nationaux," arranged by country with subject subdivisions, i.e., education, political parties, industry, etc.; and (2) "Relations internationales," subdivided by political studies, social studies, economic studies and regional studies. Includes some government documents. Material abstracted is usually current within 3 or 4 months. Annual subject index with a list of periodicals examined. Replaces the *Bulletin bibliographie de documentation internationale contemporaine* issued from 1926 to 1940.

A75. Handbook of Latin American studies. v. 1+ 1936+ Gainesville, Fla., Univ. of Florida Press. annual.

An extensive annotated bibliography of important books, articles, pamphlets, maps and documents relating to Latin America. Specific fields vary from year to year, but regularly span most of the social sciences and humanities. Originally a listing of one year's publications, a single volume now (since 1957) includes all important publications seen by the contributing editors for the first time, regardless of imprint date. The 3,000-6,000 entries a year are classified according to disciplines, including sections on anthropology, economics, education, geography, history and sociology. Author index and, since v. 18, a subject index. Annotations, mostly in English, are critical as well as descriptive. Vols. 1-8, 11 and 22 contain special articles on some phase of life and culture, bibliographical problems, or inter-American relations. See also *Current Caribbean bibliography* v. 1+ 1951+ (San Juan, Puerto Rico, Caribbean Commission. annual) and *Bibliográfia de Centroamérica y del Caribe,* 1956+ (Madrid, Agrupación Bibliográfica Cubana Jose Toribió Medina, 1958+ irreg.) Cumulative index v. 1-25 is in preparation.

A76. Humaniora Norvegica; the year's work in Norwegian humanities, ed. by Harald L. Tveterås. v. 1+ 1950+ Oslo, Univ. of Oslo Press, 1954+ annual.

Presents in English an annual survey, bibliographical and critical, of current Norwegian research in the Humanities. Consists of signed reviews or review articles of all books and important journal articles published in Norway or written by Norwegians. The classified arrangement includes psychology, education, economics, sociology and politics, law, folklore, ethnology and ethnography, archeology, history, local history, social history and geneaology. Reviews of individual books are quite detailed and often include references to other reviews. Index of authors and reviewers. From v. 2+ each volume covers two years.

A77. An index to book reviews in the humanities. v. 1+ March, 1960+ Detroit, Phillip Thomson. quarterly.

Lists reviews from 480 British and American journals ranging from the popular and general to the scholarly. The term "humanities" is broadly interpreted to include all adult books except scientific and technical works. 114 periodicals in the social sciences are surveyed, and reviews of books in education, law, archeology, history, psychology, sociology, geography, economics and folklore are included. Foreign language journals are not indexed, but foreign books reviewed in English language journals are included. Arrangement is alphabetical by author, with the citation including the name of the reviewer. No indication given of the length of the review.

A78. Index translationum. Repertoire international des traductions. International bibliography of translations. Paris, International Institute of Intellectual Cooperation, 1932-40. nos. 1-31; n.s. v. 1+ 1948+ Paris, UNESCO, 1949+
The first series appeared quarterly; the new series is annual. The translations are arranged first by the country in which they were published and then by subject under the 10 general headings of the UDC. Complete bibliographical information is given, including the original language, title, publisher, and date when available. Both series include indexes of authors, publishers and translators. Vols. 1-13 in the new series have listed 271,871 items from 63 countries including over 55,000 items of specific social science interest.

A79. "International bibliography of statistics." *Revue de l'Institute International de Statistique.* v. 1+ 1933+ La Haye, Stockum. irregular.
2,500-3,500 items are listed annually in a detailed classification scheme. Includes books, government publications, articles in official and unofficial periodicals covering the current statistical literature of many countires. No indexes. See also *Metron; Rivista internazionale di statistica* (v. 1+ 1920+ Rome, Instituto di Statistica, irregular.) which devotes ⅓ of each issue to a classified bibliography of publications bearing upon the use of statistics in all disciplines. The Royal Statistical Society. *Journal* (v. 1+ 1839+ London. quarterly) and the American Statistical Society. *Journal* (v. 1+ 1888+ Washington. quarterly) include critical book reviews, and lists of periodical articles and books.

A80. Internationale Bibliographie der Zeitschriftenliteratur. Osnabrück, Dietrich, 1897+.
The most extensive of periodical indexes; published semi-annually, in 12-15 Lieferung, with no cumulations. Abteilung A: *Bibliographie der deutschen Zeitschriftenliteratur, mit Einschluss von Sammelwerken.* 1897+. Alphabetical subject listing with author index. Indexes some 3,600 German-language periodicals and 45 newspapers. Abteilung B: *Bibliographie der Fremdsprachigen Zeitschriftenliteratur; Répertoire bibliographique international des revues; International index to periodicals,* 1911-19, 1925+. An alphabetical subject index to some 3,200 periodicals and general works in the principal non-German languages. Index of authors since 1925. Vols. for 1920-24 and 1943-49 in preparation. Abteilung C: *Bibliographie der Rezensionen und Referate,* v. 1-77, 1900-1943. A comprehensive listing of book reviews. From 1901-1911 only German reviews indexed; from 1912-1943 two series were published, one indexing reviews in 3,000 German periodicals and the other indexing reviews in 2,000 non-German periodicals.

A81. Pan American Union. *Columbus Memorial Library.* List of books accessioned and periodical articles indexed. v. 1+ 1950 Washington, D.C. monthly.
An up-to-date and extensive guide to current Latin American materials. It is useful within the limitations of an uncumulated classified list without author indexing. Two parts: (1) Books and (2) Periodical articles. The list of articles (ca. 3,600 a year) has been since 1951 the most comprehensive guide to the contents of Latin American periodicals containing social sciences material of reference value. Added quarterly features include "New periodical titles" and "Documents of the OAS and publications of the Pan

American Union." *Index to Latin American periodical literature 1930 to 1960* (Boston, G.K. Hall, 1961. 6 v.) will in essence be the cumulation for the *Accessions list.* The 250,000 entries represent cards originally in the general catalog of the Columbus Memorial Library which have now been withdrawn and published for the first time. A further retrospective index is Sturgis E. Leavitt's *Revistas hispanoamericanas; índice bibliográfico, 1843-1935.* (Santiago de Chile, Fondo Histórico y Bibliográfico Jose Toribio Medina, 1960. 589 p.), a classified listing of 30,107 articles from 56 journals with a separate section for translations and an index of names. *Index to Latin American periodicals; humanities and social sciences* v. 1+ 1961+ (Boston, G.K. Hall, quarterly) is a new index to 331 periodicals published in Latin America prepared by the Columbus Memorial Library and the N.Y. Public Library. *Fichero bibliográfico hispanoamericano* v. 1+ 1961+ (New York, Bowker, quarterly) is a classified bibliography of new books in the Spanish language offered for sale in Latin America. Index of authors and titles.

A82. Public Affairs Information Service. Bulletin. v. 1+ 1915+ New York. weekly, cumulated annually.

PAIS is a selective but comprehensive subject index to current literature on economics, social conditions, politics, government, international relations, and public administration. Restricted to the English language but including publications in English from all countries, it lists current books, pamphlets, government documents, many periodical articles, and some analytical entries for collected works, symposia, yearbooks, etc., with emphasis in selection on factual and statistical information. Bibliographical detail is sufficient for identification, and many items have brief explanatory items. Cumulated 5 times per year, the 5th being the permanent annual volume which includes a "Key to Periodical References," a "Directory of Publishers and Organizations," and a list of "Publications Analyzed."

A83. UNESCO. *Research Centre on the Social Implications of Industrialization in Southern Asia.* Southern Asia social science bibliography, 1952+ Calcutta, 1954+ annual.

Volume 8 (1959), published in 1960, merges two former separate publications, the *South Asia social science abstracts* and the *South Asia social science bibliography.* Geographical coverage was extended to include Burma, Indonesia, Malaya and Singapore, the Philippines, Thailand and Vietnam in addition to India, Pakistan and Ceylon. It is a classified bibliography of 1,500-2,000 English and French language items a year, including books, pamphlets and articles (from over 125 journals) published in Southern Asia. Vague or ambiguous titles are briefly annotated, and important articles on social and economic development are fully abstracted. Covers sociology, social anthropology, political science and economics. Author and subject indexes.

A84. United Nations. *Library, Geneva.* List mensuelle d'articles sélectionnés. Monthly list of selected articles. V. 1+ 1929+ monthly.

Begun by the League of Nations and continued by the U.N., this current bibliography provides a survey of articles selected from 2,000 periodicals on political, legal, economic, financial and social problems. The 7,000-odd entries a year are classified broadly by subject, with subdivisions. No annotations. Wide international coverage. No cumulations or annual indexes. A comparable list, issued by the United Nations Library in New York, *List of selected articles.* (v. 1+ 1949+ monthly) refers solely to articles on the U.N., the specialized agencies, and topics currently before the General Assembly.

A85. United Nations. *Library, Geneva.* Liste mensuelle d'ouvrages cata-logués à la Bibliothèque des Nations Unis. Monthly list of books catalogued in the Library of the United Nations. V. 1+ 1928+ Geneva, League of Nations, 1928-45; United Nations, 1946+
"A selected list of works relating to questions of every kind studied by the organs of the United Nations." (Explanatory note.) 3,000-4,000 items are listed annually. Systematic arrangement in 7 groups including a section devoted to reference works and library science. Full bibliographic details and U.D.C. classification numbers are given. No annotation. Excludes U.N. publications. Annual index of authors and main entries.

A86. U.S. *Bureau of the Census.* Bibliography of social science peri-odicals and monograph series. Washington, Govt. Print. Off., 1961+ (For-eign social science bibliographies series P92 no. 1+) (In progress)
A new series of bibliographies of social science periodicals and mono-graph series published in Communist Bloc and other countries using so-called "difficult" languages. The series in general will cover the period 1950-1960 and is restricted to the holdings of the Library of Congress. When completed it will include a separate volume for each of the follow-ing areas: Albania, Bulgaria, Mainland China, Taiwan, Czechoslovakia, Denmark, Finland, East Germany, Greece, Hong Kong, Hungary, Iceland, Japan, North and South Korea, Norway, Poland, Rumania, Sweden, Turkey, USSR and Yugoslavia. It will cover in total ca. 1,000 periodicals and sepa-rate titles in 400-500 monograph series. The entries are classified under 15 major headings. Information given for periodicals includes: issuing agency (transliterated and translated); title (in original language, transliterated and translated); publication information; indication of book reviews, news notes, summaries, etc.; a brief statement of coverage; 5 representative arti-cles from recent issues; and Library of Congress holdings. For monograph series: issuing agency; series title; details of each title in the series. Indexes of subjects, titles, authors and issuing agencies.

Newspaper Indexes

A87. New York Times index. v. 1+ 1913+ New York, New York Times. semi-monthly with annual cumulation.
An extensive and detailed index to the Last Edition with exact citation to date, page and column with many cross references. The brief synopsis under each entry often make reference to the paper itself unnecessary. Can be utilized as a guide to current reporting in other newspapers. An earlier index covering 1851-58; 1860-1905 is available on microfilm.

A88. Times, London. Official index, 1906+ London, The Times. quar-terly.
Detailed alphabetical index referring to date, page and column. See also *Palmer's index to the Times newspaper, 1790-1941* (London, Palmer, 1868-1943) a much briefer and less accurate index but valuable because of the period covered.

A89. Wall Street Journal: Index. v. 1+ 1958+ New York, Dow, Jones & Co. monthly with annual cumulation.

See also: A59

General

A90. Albert, Ethel M., *et al.* A selected bibliography on values, ethics and esthetics in the behavioral sciences and philosophy, 1920-1958. Glencoe, Ill., Free Press, 1959. 342 p.

An annotated bibliography of 1,991 items (books and articles) selected from over 6,000 titles collected during a research project. Significant works are listed for the following areas: anthropology (303 items); psychology (330 items); sociology (387 items); political science, public administration, and government (143 items); economics (166 items); philosophy (600 items); related areas outside the behavioral sciences (162 items). Material from public opinion, attitudes, prejudice, communication, decision-making, law and religion has only selective representation. Entries are arranged by author under 7 large subject areas with a classified index and author index. Annotations are brief.

A91. American Universities Field Staff. A select bibliography; Asia, Africa, Eastern Europe, Latin America. New York, 1960. 534 p.

Lists the most useful books and journals in western languages (mostly English) for the college student and general reader. Of the more than 7,000 items covering the religion, philosophy, history, economics, and culture of the non-Western peoples, the more important ones are indicated by the letters A and B and are annotated. Index of authors and titles. Arrangement is geographical with subject subdivisions. *Supplement* 1961 adds 500 items published between June 1959 and June 1961.

A92. Association index; a source-list of directories and other publications listing associations. Los Angeles, Metropolitan Research Co., 1958. 122 p.

An annotated bibliography of 1,083 directories, annuals, yearbooks, and periodicals which list current non-governmental associations and societies in the U.S. and Canada. Arrangement is alphabetical by title or organization. "Finding list" includes subjects, titles, authors, sponsoring agencies, and abbreviations. Annotations are concise and descriptive.

A93. Besterman, Theodore. A world bibliography of bibliographies and bibliographical catalogues, calendars, abstracts, digests, indexes and the like. 3d and final ed., Rev. and greatly enl. throughout. Genève, Societas Bibliographica, 1955-56. 4 v.

The major work in its field. An alphabetical subject arrangement of 84,403 separately published bibliographies with an author index (v. 4). No annotations except for an estimate of the number of items included in each bibliography cited. 4th ed. in preparation.

A94. Bowker, R.R., *comp.* Publications of societies; a provisional list of the publications of American scientific, literary and other societies, from their organization. New York, Publishers' Weekly, 1899. 181 p.

Lists publications of over 1,000 national, state or general American learned societies to the year 1898, arranged alphabetically by society name. No index. Primarily of historical significance.

A95. Culver, Dorothy C. Methodology of social science research; a bibliography. Berkeley, Univ. of California Press, 1936. 159 p.

A bibliography of materials published in English from 1920-1936 on the types of methods and techniques which have been used in social sciences research. Although much of the material has now been superseded, the basic ideas and procedures are still valid. Excludes psychology and education. Includes listings on: methodology of special fields; sources of material and information; use of libraries; collection and analysis of data; and the preparation of the manuscript. Some of the 1,509 items have brief annotations. Author and subject indexes. A current survey is "Selected articles and documents on methodology and research in the social sciences" a regular feature since 1950 in the *American political science review.*

A96. Farber, Evan I. Classified list of periodicals for the college library. 4th ed. rev. and enl. to July, 1957. Boston, Faxon, 1957. 146 p. (Useful reference series no. 86)

An annotated, classified listing of 601 English language periodicals (includes 14 in French and German) with an alphabetical title index. 209 titles in social sciences fields: classics and archeology (12); economics and business administration (45); education (42); geography (10); history (16); political science (36); psychology (27); and sociology and anthropology (21); plus 46 general periodicals. Full bibliographical details are given. Extremely useful for its descriptive annotations as to the nature of the individual titles and special departments or features (especially bibliographical sections).

A97. Fondation Nationale des Sciences Politiques. Bibliographies françaises de sciences sociales. v. 1+ Paris, 1960+ (In progress)

A new series of bibliographical studies of significant recent French publications in various social science subjects. V. 1, "Science politique en France," is a classified listing of 603 items with short descriptive annotations and an author index. V. 2, L'administration française; administrations centrales," lists 951 items published from 1944-1958. Classified with author index. Future volumes will cover local administration, French rural society, political parties and movements, publications of the Ministry of Foreign Affairs, etc. Some of these titles and others of social science significance appear in English as volumes of the *French bibliographical digest* Series II, published by the Cultural Center of the French Embassy in New York (see D 247).

A98. Grandin, A. Bibliographie générale des sciences juridiques, politiques, économiques et sociales de 1800 à 1925. Paris, Recueil Sirey, 1926. 3 v.

———. Supplément 1-19; 1926-1950. Paris, Recueil Sirey, 1928-1951.

An extensive bibliography of monographic works in the French language in the fields of law, politics, economics and sociology. Systematic arrangement with 16 subject groups. Legal literature constitutes at least half of the average volume. The balance contains area sections, very full for Belgium, Switzerland and France overseas; less so for other countries, and sections on finance, political economy and sociology. Theses and government publications are included. Full bibliographical details are given, but no annotations. Subject and author indexes. Continued to some extent by *Bibliographie; histoire, sciences politiques, économiques et sociales.* (Paris, Librairie du XXᵉ Siècle, 1958-1961. 2 v.) V. 1 lists 7,000 works published in France from 1953 to 1958. V. 2 adds material appearing Sept., 1958 to June, 1961. Classified arrangement. Author, title, date, and price only. No index. See also Gabriel Lepointe *Éléments de bibliographie sur l'histoire des institutions et faits sociaux 987-1875.* (Paris, Éditions Montchrestien, 1958. 232 p.) 3,324 items appearing from 1926 to 1956.

A99. Index bibliographicus: directory of current periodical abstracts and bibliographies . . . 3d ed. completely rev. Paris, UNESCO, 1951-52. 2 v.

A directory of serials devoted to abstracts or bibliographies, or journals carrying regular sections of abstracts, book reviews or bibliography. V. 1 is devoted to science and technology. V. 2 covers social sciences, education and humanistic studies. The entries are classified according to the U.D.C. and coded symbols indicate for each title its frequency, language, coverage, and average number of items. International in scope. Subject and title indexes. Coding system is inconvenient and the distinction between titles entirely and partially bibliographical is not well brought out. Ed. 4 with a separate volume devoted to the social sciences is in preparation and will provide more details for each title.

A100. Inter American Statistical Institute. Bibliography of selected statistical sources of the American nations. Bibliografía de fuentes estadísticas escogidas de las naciones Americanas. 1st ed. Washington, 1947. 689 p.

A comprehensive bibliographical guide to the principal statistical materials of the 22 American nations, including data, analyses, methodology, laws, and organization of statistical agencies. 2,500 titles are classified first by country and then by subject with detailed alphabetical and classified indexes. The annotations are factual on content and are given in two languages (English and one other). Gives detailed information on the statistical publications of each country and also has a section on general statistical works. Kept up to date by the quarterly bibliography appearing in *Estadística: journal of the Inter American Statistical Institute.* v. 1+ 1943+ (Washington. quarterly).

A101. A London bibliography of the social sciences. London, London School of Economics and Political Science, 1931-32. 4 v.; Supplements (v. 5-11). 1934-1960.

The subject catalog of several libraries: The British Library of Political and Economic Science, Edward Fry Library of International Law, Goldsmith's Library of Economic Literature, National Institute of Industrial Psychology, Royal Anthropological Institute, Royal Institute of International Affairs, the Royal Statistical Society. V. 1-5 record all works held in 1931; V. 6 (1937) carries this record to 1936 for the first 3 libraries only. V. 7-11 show additions to the British Library of Political and Economic Science and the Edward Fry Library through 1955. The largest subject bibliography of its kind (over 840,000 items). Arrangement is chronological under subjects or their subdivisions. Entries carry abbreviated bibliographical detail without annotation, but the presence of a bibliography is indicated. Slavonic languages included in suppl. 4 (V. 10-11) which also lists Russian materials for 1936-1950. Author indexes given in V. 4 (for V. 1-3), 5 and 6, but not in later volumes. There are tables of subject headings and subject subdivisions. The British Library of Political and Economic Science issues also a current mimeographed *Monthly list of additions to the Library.*

A102. Maunier, René. Manuel bibliographique des sciences sociales et économiques. Paris, Sirey, 1920. 228 p.

An older but still useful guide to bibliographies and reference books in the social science fields published during the 18th and 19th centuries.

A103. Ulrich's periodical directory: a classified guide to a selected list of current periodicals, foreign and domestic. 10th ed. New York, Bowker, 1963. 667 p.

A select listing of ca. 20,000 current titles, classified by broad subject, with a title and subject index. Gives full bibliographical information, indication of special features (e.g., bibliographies, indexes, book reviews, etc.), and shows where a title is indexed or abstracted.

A104. Union of International Associations. Directory of periodicals published by international organizations. 2d ed. Brussels, 1959. 241 p. (It's Publication no. 162)

Gives founding date, frequency, publisher, size and descriptive comments for 1,340 titles arranged by subject under 2 broad subdivisions: (1) supranational and intergovernmental organizations and (2) international non-governmental organizations. Only current items are included. "Periodical" is broadly interpreted. Agency and title index.

A105. UNESCO. General catalogue of UNESCO publications and UNESCO sponsored publications, 1946-1959. Paris, UNESCO, 1962. 217 p.

An important classified catalog of 2,681 items either published by Unesco itself, by some other body under Unesco contract or under Unesco auspices. Unesco documents, usually printed in limited quantities, are not included. Multi-lingual publications are listed under each language with cross references to other languages. Separate listing of official publications. Full bibliographical details. No annotations. List of film strips and art slides. List of publishers. General index of authors, titles and series titles.

A106. UNESCO. List mondiale des périodiques spécialisés dans les sciences sociales. World list of social science periodicals. 2d ed. rev. and enl. Paris, 1957. 210 p. (It's Documentation in the social sciences)

A bibliography of 941 periodicals current in 1955 published in 62 countries. Includes only those periodicals which specialize in the social sciences as a whole or one of these sciences. Excludes general psychology, law, history, geography, and philosophy. Includes only periodicals of a scientific nature—no fact providing publications, newspapers or purely bibliographical periodicals. Arrangement is alphabetically by country with indexes by title, by scientific institution, by subject and by discipline, i.e., anthropology, economics, etc. Title given in translation for lesser known languages. Three categories of information given: (1) editorial information (2) practical information (frequency, publisher, tables, indexes, date of first issue) and (3) description of average issue (pages, number and length of articles, subjects included, etc.).

A107. UNESCO. A selected inventory of periodical publications. Paris, 1951. 129 p. (Bibliographies in the social sciences)

Part 1 deals with the problem of documentation services in the social sciences. Part 2 provides a listing of 59 major bibliographical services. Details of publication, subject coverage, special features, time lag, etc., are systematically stated in each case. Indexes of titles, countries of publication, languages of publication, kinds of services (e.g., abstracts, bibliographies), disciplines, and geographical areas. A supplement (1953) covers an additional 15 services and includes corrections.

A108. U.S. *Library of Congress. Census Library Project.* Statistical bulletins; an annotated bibliography of the general statistical bulletins of major political subdivisions of the world. Prepared by Phyllis G. Carter. Washington, 1954. 93 p.

An annotated listing by country of official general statistical bulletins issued more frequently than annually and which cover statistics in several subject fields. Each entry is fully annotated giving bibliographical data, history and content information. Companion volume to *Statistical yearbooks* (A109).

A109. U.S. *Library of Congress. Census Library Project*. Statistical yearbooks; an annotated bibliography of the general statistical yearbooks of major political subdivisions of the world. Prepared by Phyllis G. Carter. Washington, 1953. 123 p.

A comprehensive survey, retrospective and current, of statistical annuals published by the governments of ca. 200 countries or areas in the world. Arrangement is by continent subdivided by country. Each entry is annotated, information being given on historical background, data covered, and the contents of the most recent issue. Included in the absence of a regular statistical yearbook is any reasonable equivalent which may serve the same purpose. Companion volume to *Statistical bulletins* (A108).

A110. Viet, Jean. International cooperation and programs of economic and social development; an annotated bibliography. Paris, UNESCO, 1962. 107 p. (International Committee for Social Sciences Documentation. Reports and papers in the social sciences, 15)

A select, classified bibliography of 1,141 books and articles concerned with one aspect of underdevelopment—the definition, formulation and execution of programs of international cooperation. 4 major sections: (1) general; (2) bi-lateral; (3) multi-lateral; and (4) regional assistance programs. Author index. Supplements the author's earlier work *Assistance to underdeveloped countries; an annotated bibliography*. (Paris, UNESCO, 1957. 83 p. [Reports and papers in the social sciences, 8].)

A111. Zischka, Gert A. Index lexicorum; Bibliographie der lexikalischen Nachschlagewerke. Wien, Brüder Hollinek, 1959. 290 p.

A bibliography of encyclopedia-type reference works (specialized encyclopedias and dictionaries, handbooks, glossaries, yearbooks, gazetteers, etc.). International in scope, but particularly strong for German works. The 7,000 titles are grouped in 21 sections, the first devoted to general works; the remainder to subject areas (including history, psychology, education, economics, folklore, geography, politics and biography). Some brief annotations. Index of personal names and subject headings.

Africa

The sources of information on the African continent are quite diverse. The current bibliographies listed in the preceding section contain material on Africa and consulting A *bibliography of African bibliographies* (A114 below) reveals the numerous scholarly works available. Other important sources are the national and trade bibliographies of the major colonial powers and the printed catalogs of special library collections, *e.g.* Royal Empire Society, London. *Subject catalogue of the library of the Royal Empire Society*. (London, 1930-37. 4 v.). The items listed below are a selection of recent bibliographical tools important as a general introduction to Africa or as guides to further research. See also: A91, E123, E127.

A112. Blaudin de Thé, Bernard M.S., *ed*. Essai de bibliographie du Sahara français et des régions avoisinantes. 2. éd. Paris, Arts et Métiers Graphiques, 1960. 258 p.

A classified bibliography of 9,301 items (books and articles) related to French Africa. Author index.

A113. International African Institute. Select annotated bibliography of tropical Africa. New York, Twentieth Century Fund, 1956. 481 p.
5,099 books and articles covering geography, ethnography, government, economics, education, missions and health. No indexes.

A114. South African Public Library, Cape Town. A bibliography of African bibliographies south of the Sahara. 4th ed. Cape Town, 1961. 79 p. (Grey bibliographies, no. 7)
A classified bibliography of over 1,300 bibliographical sources dealing with all aspects of African culture arranged according to the abridged U.D.C. with author and general subject index. Over one-third of the items listed deal with social science subjects. Includes bibliographies in periodicals and monographs, as well as separately published items. Some contents notes. To be kept up to date by supplements appearing in the *Quarterly bulletin of the South African Library*.

A115. U.S. *Library of Congress. Africana Section.* Serials for African studies. Compiled by Helen F. Conover. Washington, 1961. 163 p.
An alphabetical listing of ca. 2,000 serials concerned with all phases of African life. Includes all significant continuing sources of information (e.g., monograph series, yearbooks, institutional reports, etc.) and periodicals which carry articles about Africa on a fairly regular basis. Some descriptive annotations. General index and index of organizations.

A116. U.S. *Library of Congress. European Affairs Division.* Introduction to Africa; a selective guide to background reading. Prepared by Helen F. Conover. Washington, 1952. 237 p.
A bibliographical study designed for general orientation to Africa. Arrangement is by region and country with some subject subdivisions. The 1,000+ references are chiefly to recent literature, in English. Lengthy and informative annotations. Brought up to date by the more comprehensive publications: U.S. Library of Congress. General Reference and Bibliography Division. *Africa south of the Sahara; a selected, annotated list of writings, 1951-1956* (Washington, 1957. 269 p.); and *North and Northeast Africa; a selected, annotated list of writings, 1951-1957*. (Washington, 1957. 182 p.).

Asia and the Pacific

Many Asian areas have been the subject of major bibliographical studies which are basic to research and which cover the literature in European languages from the 15th century to 1937: Henri Cordier's "Bibliographie des pays d'Extreme-Orient" in three parts, *Bibliotheca sinica* (2 éd. Paris, Guilmoto, 1904-08. 4 v.; Supplement, 1922-24), *Bibliotheca japonica* (Paris, Leroux, 1912. 762 col.) *Bibliotheca indosinica* (Paris, Leroux, 1912-1932. 4 v.); Friedrich von Wenckstern's A *bibliography of the Japanese empire* (Leiden, Brill, 1895; Tokyo, Maruya, 1907. 2 v.) and its continuation by Oskar Nachod *Bibliographie von Japan.* (Leipzig, Hiersemann, 1928-40. 6 v.); *Orientalische bibliographie,* 1887-1911 (Berlin, Reuther, 1888-1922. 26 v. annual). Listed below are a selection of recent bibliographical studies of works in Western languages dealing with Asian areas. See also: A91, B345, B346, B365, E160, E161, E164, E167.

A117. Bangkok. Chulalongkorn University. *Central Library*. Bibliography of material on Thailand in Western languages. Bangkok, 1960. 325 p.

A118. Borton, Hugh, *et al*. A selected list of books and articles on Japan in English, French and German. Rev. and enl. ed. Cambridge, Harvard Univ. Press for the Harvard-Yenching Institute, 1954. 272 p.

A selective and critical bibliography of 1,781 works relating to the humanities and the social sciences published up to 1952. Analytical index of authors, titles and subjects. Some brief evaluative annotations.

A119. Chicago. *University. Philippine Studies Program*. Selected bibliography of the Philippines topically arranged and annotated. New Haven, Conn., Human Relations Area files, 1956. 138 p. (Behavior science bibliographies)

A120. Leeson, Ida. A bibliography of bibliographies of the South Pacific. Published under the auspices of the South Pacific Commission. London, Oxford Univ. Press, 1954. 61 p.

A selective listing of 376 bibliographic monographs or publications which include important bibliographies arranged by area and subject. Brief descriptive annotations. Author index.

A121. New York University. *Burma Research Project*. Annotated bibliography of Burma. New Haven, Conn., Human Relations Area Files, 1956. 230 p. (Behavior science bibliographies)

An annotated bibliography of 1,018 items (books, articles, documents and pamphlets) on all aspects of Burmese life. *Burma; an annotated bibliographical guide 1900-1960* is being prepared by the Orientalia Division of the Library of Congress.

A122. U.S. *Library of Congress. Orientalia Division*. Southeast Asia; an annotated bibliography of selected reference sources. Compiled by Cecil Hobbs. Washington, 1952. 163 p.

A bibliographical study of some 350 items designed as a guide to further research rather than a comprehensive listing. Full descriptive annotations. Index of authors and subjects. A revised edition is in preparation.

A123. U.S. *Library of Congress. Reference Department*. Introduction to Asia: a selective guide to background reading. Prepared by L.K. Quan. Washington, 1955. 214 p.

An annotated bibliography of 811 authoritative works, mostly in English, on all the countries of the Asian continent (including the Near and Middle East; excluding Asiatic Russia) intended for the general reader.

A124. Yüan, T'ung-li. China in western literature: a continuation of Cordier's Bibliotheca Sinica. New Haven, Conn., Far Eastern Publications, Yale Univ., 1958. 802 p.

Classified listing of 10,000 books and monographs published from 1921 to 1957 in English, French, German and Portuguese. Index of names. Intends to be a comprehensive listing and no attempt has been made to select or reject any items.

Latin America

See also: A91, B301.

A125. Bayitch, Stojan A. Latin America; a bibliographical guide to economy, history, law, politics and society. Coral Gables, Fla., Univ. of Miami Press, 1961. 335 p. (Interamerican legal studies, no. 6)

A selected listing of ca. 10,000 English language works (books and articles) intended as a research guide for the general reader. Classified arrangement with brief subject index. Emphasizes legal material. Treatment uneven in the other subjects covered. No annotations.

A126. Behrendt, Richard F.W. Modern Latin America in social science literature; a selected, annotated bibliography of books, pamphlets, and periodicals in English in the fields of economics, politics and sociology of Latin America. (Hamilton, N.Y., 1949. 152 p.)
An older, but still important work listing ca. 1,000 works many with brief, but critical annotations. Classified and geographical arrangement with an author index. A supplement published in 1950 covers the writings of 1949 and 1950.

A127. Jones, Cecil K. A bibliography of Latin American bibliographies. 2d ed. Rev. and enl. Washington, Govt. Print. Off., 1942. 311 p. (U.S. Library of Congress. Latin American series, no. 2)
A basic, selective listing of bibliographies, some collective biography, histories of literature and reference works useful to bibliographic research. 3,016 entries (books and articles), arranged geographically, often with descriptive but little critical comment. Author, title, subject index. Supplemented by the "Bibliographies, lists and indexes" subsections in the *Handbook of Latin American Studies* (A75).

A128. Zimmerman, Irene. A guide to current Latin American periodicals; humanities and social sciences. Gainesville, Fla., Kallman Pub. Co., 1961. 357 p.
An annotated, evaluative bibliography of 668 active periodicals from 26 Latin American countries and the U.S. (by Latin Americans, inter-American agencies, or published in the U.S. for Latin American circulation.) The basic presentation is by country, followed by a classified section and a chronological listing. Each country, subject section and chronological period is prefaced by an explanatory introduction. The very full and evaluative annotations give information on editors, history, coverage, policies, volumes published, etc. Index of titles. Another useful source is Pan American Union. *Repertorio de publicaciones periódicas actuales latin americanas. Directory of current Latin American periodicals.* (Paris, UNESCO, 1958. 266 p. [UNESCO bibliographic handbooks, no. 8]) which contains 3,376 entries of which over half (1612) are in the social sciences. Arranged by U.D.C. classification with a geographical and subject index. Bibliographic details only, no annotations. Lack of alphabetical title index limits its usefulness.

Middle East
See also: E161.

A129. Ettinghausen, Richard, *ed.* A selected and annotated bibliography of books and periodicals in western languages dealing with the Near and Middle East with special emphasis on medieval and modern times; completed Summer 1951, with supplement, December, 1953. Washington, Middle East Institute, 1954. 137 p.
A classified bibliography of the most significant recent books, periodicals (no articles) and maps intended for general use. 2,059 annotated items are classified by area and subject with an author index. Includes: geography, history, law, archeology, economics, anthropology, political science and edu-

cation. Periodical literature is covered in the "Bibliography of periodical literature" *Middle East journal,* v. 1+ 1947+ (Washington. quarterly), a selective and annotated bibliography covering history and politics, economic and social conditions, geography, bibliography and book reviews. Some 13,000 items listed to date. Israel is excluded in both these works because of the extensive coverage in *Palestine and Zionism* v. 1+ 1946+ (New York, Zionist Archives and Library. bimonthly with annual cumulations), an index to current books, pamphlets, and periodical literature on Israel, Palestine and Zionism and to some extent, the Arab world in general.

A130. International Committee for Social Sciences Documentation. Retrospective bibliography of social science works published in the Middle East; U.A.R., Iraq, Jordan, Lebanon, 1945-1955. Cairo, UNESCO Middle East Science Cooperation Office, 1959. 299 p.
A classified bibliography of books, articles, pamphlets and near print reports published in the Middle East. Arrangement is first by country then by subject with three major headings: (1) sociology, social psychology, anthropology; (2) political science and (3) economics. Titles in Arabic are transliterated and translated. The 3222 items include English and French language titles. Author index. No annotations. A second volume, *Social sciences bibliography: Arab countries of the Middle East 1955-1960* published in 1961 adds 1270 items.

A131. Pearson, James D. Index Islamicus, 1906-1955; a catalogue of articles on Islamic subjects in periodicals and other collective publications. Cambridge, Eng., Heffer, 1958. 897 p.
Lists ca. 26,000 articles in western languages from 510 periodicals. Includes law, geography, history, anthropology, demography, folklore and education. North Africa, the Middle East and East and Central Asia are covered in detail, while countries on the fringes of Islamic territories are treated selectively. Five year supplements are planned. The first covering 1956-1960 was published in 1962. Currently supplemented by "Abstracta Islamica" an annual bibliography of books and articles appearing in the *Revue des études Islamique* (v. 1+ 1927+ Paris).

DICTIONARIES

A132. Gale Research Company. Acronyms dictionary; a guide to alphabetic designations, contractions and initialisms: Association, aerospace, business, electronic, government, international, labor, military, public affairs, scientific, societies, technical, transportation, and United Nations. 1st ed. Detroit, 1960. 211 p.
Includes some 12,000 entries. Acronyms are American except where specifically designated UN, international, German or some other nationality.

A133. Inter American Statistical Institute. Statistical vocabulary. 2d ed. Washington, Pan American Union, 1960. 83 p.
Designed to promote uniform inter-American terminology this work consists of (1) a main list of over 1,300 English language terms with equivalents in Spanish, Portuguese and French and (2) separate Spanish, Portuguese and French alphabetical indexes, each keyed to the English equivalents.

A134. International Statistical Institute. Multilingual list of terms frequently used in official statistics. (In preparation)
When complete will contain ca. 3,000 terms equated in many languages. A preliminary French-English and English-French list will be published in 1963.

A135. Kendall, Maurice G. and William R. Buckland. A dictionary of statistical terms. 2d ed. Edinburgh, published for the International Statistical Institute by Oliver and Boyd, 1960. 575 p.
Two main parts: (1) a dictionary of ca. 1,000 terms and definitions in English, and (2) four glossaries of equivalent terms (without definitions) for German, French, Italian and Spanish. Each of the glossaries has page references to the basic English text. The only change in the 2d ed. (first ed. 1957) is the addition of a combined glossary of equivalent terms. In addition to terms that are wholly statistical, the dictionary includes some terms of a semi-mathematical nature, and those of a statistical character used in other sciences, as well as terms originating in other sciences of special interest to statisticians.

A136. Kolb, William L. and S.J. Gould, *eds.* UNESCO dictionary of the social sciences. (In preparation)
The cooperative effort of 250 scholars this interdisciplinary dictionary will contain definitional essays (1-10 pages) for ca. 1,000 selected terms in anthropology, sociology, economics, political science and social psychology. For each term an effort will be made to indicate its etymology; the variation of scientific usage in different disciplines, traditions and English speaking countries; and finally the "common core" of meaning, if any, that can be found. Will exclude exclusively historical terms, proper names of people and places, and theoretical essays. Publication scheduled for 1963.

A137. Zadrozny, John T. Dictionary of social science. Washington, Public Affairs Press, 1959. 367 p.
Briefly defines ca. 4,000 terms and phrases primarily drawn from sociology, political science and economics with some representation from population, psychology, physical anthropology, prehistory and jurisprudence. No attempt is made to "standardize" the vocabulary of the social sciences or to appraise all the variations of each term. Attempts to bridge the gaps between the occupational vocabularies of the various fields. The definitions are clear and concise—though at times too brief. Does not assign a particular definition to a specific field.

ENCYCLOPEDIAS AND ENCYCLOPEDIC SETS

A138. Enciclopedia di scienze politiche, economiche e sociali. Bologna, C. Zuff, 1956+ v. 1+ (In progress)
The first encyclopedia of the social sciences in Italian. It is to be international in scope covering all major areas in the social sciences with some emphasis on Southern Europe. The articles vary in length, are signed by specialists and carry brief bibliographies. Includes short biographies. Only one volume, A-Ben published to date.

A139. Encyclopedia of the social sciences. New York, Macmillan, 1930-35. 15 v.

An excellent synthesis and comprehensive survey of knowledge in the social science fields to 1930, projected and prepared under the auspices of 10 learned societies with the assistance of hundreds of scholars from all over the world. The first part of its 349 page introduction includes a discussion of the meaning of the social sciences and a history of their chronological development, followed by a country by country survey of the social sciences as disciplines. The main portion of the work aims to cover all important concepts and ideas in political science, economics, law, anthropology, sociology, penology, and social work, and, in addition the social aspects of many other subject areas. Brief biographical articles make up 20% of the contents. The lengthy articles are prepared by specialists and carry brief, but adequate bibliographies. Entries are alphabetically arranged with cross-references and a subject index. A new encyclopedia of the social sciences, covering the advances during the past 25 years, is being prepared under the direction of Prof. W. Allen Wallis and Dr. David L. Sills. To be published jointly by Free Press, Macmillan and Colliers Encyclopedia in 1965.

A140. Hamburg. Welt-Wirtschafts-Archiv. Länderlexikon. Hamburg, Verlag Weltarchiv GMBH, 1955-1960. 3 v.
An encyclopedia of the social and economic structure of the major nations, dependencies and geographical areas of the world. The 252 entries (from 1-70 pages long) are classified by major region. Topics covered include: governmental structure, politics, social organization, geography, economics, finance, agriculture, trade, industry and education. Some historical orientation, but emphasis is upon current conditions. Bibliographies, illustrations, maps, etc. New edition of v. 1 in preparation.

A141. Handwörterbuch der Sozialwissenschaften. Stuttgart, G. Fischer, 1952+ Lfg. 1+ (In progress)
To be completed in 12 volumes and index volume, this comprehensive encyclopedia is the successor to the *Handwörterbuch der Staatswissenschaften* (H318) and intends to cover all branches of the social sciences whereas its predecessor was primarily concerned with political science. The signed articles are long and appended with excellent bibliographies. International in scope with articles on countries and geographical areas, international organizations, people (20% of the articles are biographical) and subjects.

DIRECTORIES AND BIOGRAPHICAL INFORMATION

A142. American men of science; a biographical directory, ed. by Jaques Cattell. v. 5 The social and behavioral sciences. 10th ed. Tempe, Ariz., Jaques Cattell Press, 1962. 1,220 p.
Provides biographical data on ca. 24,000 Americans and Canadians in the fields of anthropology, economics, geography, political science, psychology, sociology and statistics. History and the humanities are included in *Directory of American scholars*, ed. by Jaques Cattell. 3d ed. (New York, Bowker, 1957. 836 p. see G275). Information given: full name, position, address, field of specialization, birthplace, degrees, positions held, memberships, and research specialties.

A143. Annuaire des organisations internationales. Yearbook of international organizations. Brussels, Union des Associations Internationales, 1948+ annual.

A reliable and up-to-date source of information on nearly 150 inter-governmental and over 1,200 independent non-governmental international organizations. Information for each entry includes: name (in French, English, Spanish and German), address, very brief history, membership, officers, finances, intergovernmental and nongovernmental relations, current activities, and publications (brief). General index in French and English. Index of abbreviations or initials. Supplemented by *International associations* v. 1+ 1949+ (Brussels, Union of International Associations. monthly) which carries current news and amendments to the *Yearbook*. For a chronological listing see *The 1978 international organizations founded since the Congress of Vienna* (H335); for additional details on publications see *Directory of periodicals published by international organizations* (A104).

A144. Asia Society. American institutions and organizations interested in Asia; a reference directory, ed. by Ward Morehouse and Edith Ehrman. 2d ed. New York, Taplinger, 1961. 581 p.

Contains descriptive listings of over 1,000 programs relating to Asia conducted by American organizations. For each entry: name, address, name and title of principal officers, data on organization, publications, and activities relating to Asia. The last includes geographical coverage, staff and a description of the program. Appendices include a listing of Asian and U.S. diplomatic and consular offices and information centers. Alphabetically indexed for institutions, departments, programs, committees, and all non-listed institutions cited in the *Directory*.

A145. Current biography. v. 1+ 1940+ New York, Wilson. monthly with annual cumulations.

Impartial, informal, well-written sketches of contemporary personalities in some 40 professional areas. Contains individual photographs, pronunciation of difficult names and references to additional material. Each issue contains a cumulated index of the previous issues. The annual volume for 1950 contains a cumulative index for 1940-1950; the 1960 volume for the years 1951-1960.

A146. Directory of special libraries and information centers, ed. by Anthony T. Kruzas. Detroit, Gale Research Co., 1963. 767 p.

The directory, to be published triennially, will supply data on all types of information units in business and industrial organizations, governmental agencies, educational institutions, research institutes, and trade and professional associations in the U.S. and Canada. Its main objective will be to provide current and continuing listings of specialized knowledge in all subject fields. Arranged alphabetically by name with subject index.

A147. Directory of university research bureaus and institutes. 1st ed. Detroit, Gale Research Co., 1961. 199 p.

Lists ca. 1,300 university and college sponsored bureaus, institutes, centers, experimental stations and laboratories in the U.S. and Canada which have been set up on a permanent basis and carry on a continuing program of research. The entries are arranged by broad subject fields with indexes of sponsoring agencies, city and state. Information includes: name of bureau or institute; director; founding date; budget; and staff. A short description of activities follows and, for some, principal serial publications and special conferences are listed.

A148. Encyclopedia of associations. 3d ed. Detroit, Gale Research Co., 1961. 2 v.

V. 1 lists 12,000 U.S. national organizations, associations, societies, federations, chambers of commerce, unions and other non-profit membership groups. The entries are grouped by field (agriculture, business, education, government, etc.) and then indexed by name, keyword and subject. For each is given: name, address, acronym, membership, activities and purpose, research and educational programs, staff, special committees, publications and meetings. V. 2 is a geographic-executive index.

A149. International Committee for Social Sciences Documentation. International repertory of social sciences documentation centres. Paris, UNESCO, 1952. 42 p.

A selective register of leading research institutions arranged by country. Data given on the directorship, organization, subjects covered, publications and services, the latter including statistics on library holdings, and special services. Centers are reported for 12 European countries, Australia, Canada, India and the U.S. plus 6 international organizations.

A150. International Institute of Political and Social Sciences Concerning Countries of Differing Civilizations. Répertoire international des centres d'étude des civilisations et de leurs publications. International guide to study centers on civilizations and their publications. Brussels, 1955. 156 p.

A directory of world research centers concerned with anthropological, historical and socio-economic studies of civilizations of the world. The 275 centers are classified into 23 civilization groups or areas with an alphabetical index of institutions and a geographic index of headquarters. For each center is given; address, date of founding, directorship, objectives, current periodical publications and titles of monographs (since 1945). Exclusively educational institutions are omitted.

A151. International who's who, 1935+ London, Europa Publications, 1935+ annual.

Slightly irregular in frequency, this directory of prominent personages of the world contains 8,000 to 13,000 entries per year. Prior to 1935 it formed a part of the loose-leaf service *Europa* (A169). Short but authoritative biographies give name, title, dates, nationality, education profession, career, works (scientific, literary, artistic, etc.) and address.

A152. International yearbook and statesmen's who's who, 1953+ London, Burke's Peerage. annual.

A reference work which combines data about political and economic conditions of the world with an international biographical directory which gives brief sketches of some 10,000 individuals of international standing—statesmen, diplomats, military leaders, clergy, industrialists, etc. The information on various countries, arranged alphabetically, is much the same as in *Statesman's Yearbook* (A170) but with more detailed statistical information.

A153. Keeling, Guy A. Trusts and foundations; a select guide to organizations and grant-making bodies operating in Great Britain and the Commonwealth. Cambridge, Eng., Bowes & Bowes, 1953. 194 p.

The first guide of its kind to British charitable trusts and foundations. The 1,000 entries are arranged alphabetically by name with a classified subject index and an alphabetical subject index. Information given includes: name, address, history, purposes, financial data and publications. Future editions are planned.

A154. National Research Council. Scientific and technical societies of the United States and Canada. 7th ed. Washington, 1961. 494 p. (National Research Council. Publ., 900)

A directory of professional and selected amateur societies in scientific and technical fields (including anthropology, archaeology, geography and psychology). Both national and local membership societies are included. Lists 1,836 societies (1,597 American, 239 Canadian) giving for each: address, officers, history, purpose, membership, library, research funds, publications and professional activities. Arranged alphabetically with two indexes (American and Canadian) which include subjects, periodical titles, names of medals, prizes, etc. and changes in the names of societies since 1955.

A155. New York. Foundation Library Center. The foundation directory. New York, Russell Sage Foundation, 1960. 817 p.

Successor to *American foundations and their fields*, VII (1955), this directory provides data on 5,502 nongovernmental, non-profit foundations in the United States based upon the records of the Russell Sage Foundation and the American Foundation Information Center, publishers of the earlier work. Arrangement is alphabetical under state with a special section for New York City. Information given (as of 1958) includes: name, address, date of founding, donor, purposes and activities, financial data, and officers. Indexes are by fields of interest, personal names and foundation names. News and developments are reported in *Foundation news* the bimonthly bulletin of the Center.

A156. Pan American Union. *Social Sciences Section*. Guía de instituciones y sociedades en el campo de las ciencias sociales. 2d ed. corr. y aumentado. Washington, 1952-54. 2 v.

A listing of professional societies (national and regional), research institutions and other organizations with social science activities. V. I, 240 entries for the United States. V. II, 455 entries from 20 Latin American countries. Gives name, address, officials, purpose and publications. Personal name and subject indexes.

A157. Scientific and learned societies of Great Britain; a handbook compiled from official sources. 60th ed. London, Allen and Unwin, 1962. 219 p.

Two sections: Part I lists organizations conducting officially sponsored (government) research. Part II is a classified listing of over 600 individual societies. Sections of major importance in the social sciences are (1) general science, (8) geography, geology and mineralogy, (9) archeology and history, (10) anthropology and sociology, and (12) economics, statistics and political science. Information given: address, phone, objectives, membership and fees, meetings, publications and library facilities. Alphabetical index.

A158. Social Science Research Council. Fellows of the Social Science Research Council, 1925-1951. New York, 1951. 473 p.

Contains biographical sketches of the 1,028 persons who have held fellowships of the SSRC for the period covered. Information given, emphasizing the individual's career as a social scientist, includes: name, type of fellowship and dates, vital statistics, family, education and degrees, full-time positions held, military service, present position, academic prizes, fellowships awarded, honorary degrees, memberships, publications (limited to 10), description of the work done under the fellowship program and current research. Arranged alphabetically with a classified list by category of fellowship and fields of interest.

A159. UNESCO. *Social Science Clearing House.* Foundations with social science activities; an international catalog. Paris, 1957. 89 p. (International Committee for Social Sciences Documentation. Reports and papers in the social sciences, no. 7)

A listing of 158 foundations in 22 countries, giving for each a detailed and specific description of current or recently completed social science research, with statements on training programs, lists of recent publications, grants and subsidies made during recent years, financial data, and a listing of donors and staff. Arranged by country. Criteria for selection is outlined in the preface.

A160. UNESCO. *Social Science Clearing House.* International organizations in the social sciences. Rev. ed. Paris, 1961. 145 p. (International Committee for Social Sciences Documentation. Reports and papers in the social sciences, no. 13)

A summary description of 18 international non-governmental organizations which devote their activities to the social sciences and have been approved for consultative relationship with Unesco (e.g., International Economic Association, International Union of Scientific Psychology). Each entry includes information on: (1) organization and aims; (2) activities including publications and meetings and (3) annexes which include past officers, committees, affiliates, constitutions. More detailed information than is included in most directories.

A161. UNESCO. *Social Science Clearing House.* Research councils in the social sciences. Paris, 1955. 54 p.; Addenda, 1956. 23 p. (International Committee for social sciences documentation. Reports and papers in the social sciences no. 3, 6)

Lists and describes 22 national research councils in 14 countries partly or wholly active in the social sciences. Information given includes organization, aims and activities, publications, and officials.

HANDBOOKS, MANUALS, COMPENDIA

A162. Actividades estadisticas de las naciones Americanas . . . 2. ed. Washington, Instituto Interamericano de Estadistica, 1954+ (In progress)

A compendium of information on the statistical services and activities in each of the 22 nations of the Western Hemisphere. This series of handbooks (one for each country) is a revision and expansion of the information given in *Statistical activities of the American nations.* (Washington, Inter American Statistical Institute, 1941. 842 p.) The format of each handbook is identical and includes (in Spanish): a general introduction; fundamental legislation and organization of the national statistical system; censuses; statistical information currently compiled; participation in international activities; major statistical organizations; statistical education; an English language summary; and a bibliography of periodical publications that contain statistical data. No indexes.

A163. Collision, Robert L. Bibliographical services throughout the world, 1950-1959. Paris, UNESCO, 1961. 240 p. (UNESCO bibliographical handbooks, no. 9)

The culmination of a series of reports inaugurated in 1955. The first part, arranged by country, describes bibliographical achievements in over 100 countries or territories. It indicates progress in national bibliography, library cooperation, current special bibliography and retrospective bibliography. The second part summarizes the bibliographical work of more than 80 international organizations. No index. Kept up-to-date by Unesco's *Bibliography, documentation, terminology* v. 1+ 1962+ (Paris, UNESCO. bi-monthly).

A164. Merrill, John C. A handbook of the foreign press. Baton Rouge, Louisiana State Univ. Press, 1959. 394 p.

Short, general introductions to the press systems of over 44 countries and geographical areas. Contains informed opinion on the contents of both metropolitan dailies and provincial papers, including founding date, circulation, editorial policies, etc. Well documented. Arranged by area with alphabetcal indexes of persons, organizations and publications. An older but still useful work for comment on editorial policy is U.S. Library of Congress. European Affairs Division. *European press today* (Washington, 1949. 152 p.), a critical annotated guide to ca. 1,000 newspapers and periodicals. A recent and more detailed analysis for Latin America is *Political newspapers and journals of Latin America* (n.p., Seminar on Acquisition of Latin American Library Materials, Carbondale, Ill., 1961. Working paper no. 3. 133 l.

A165. U.S. *Bureau of the Budget. Office of Statistical Standards.* Statistical services of the United States government. Rev. ed. Washington, Govt. Print. Off., 1963. 136 p.

A basic guide. Part I describes the statistical system of the Federal government. Part II describes briefly the principal economic and social statistical series collected by the government and, under each of ca. 50 subject headings (population, labor force, retail prices, education, etc.), includes what agencies are concerned and what kinds of data are collected. References are made to the bibliography in Appendix II. Appendix I describes the area of statistical responsibility for each agency and Appendix II gives an annotated bibliography of principal periodical statistical publications, arranged by agency. No index.

A166. U.S. *Library of Congress. General Reference and Bibliography Division.* World list of future scientific meetings. Part II. Social, cultural, commercial, humanistic. no. 1+ June, 1959+ Washington, Govt. Print. Off. monthly

A comprehensive listing of meetings which have been internationally organized, financed or sponsored; or which have international (three or more countries) participation. Arranged chronologically with subject, sponsoring body and geographical indexes. From Sept., 1946 to Oct., 1961 the State Department issued quarterly a *List of international conferences and meetings* which listed international meetings of an intergovernmental nature with annotations giving the background, agenda and expected participation. The Union of International Associations publishes the *International congress calendar* (Brussels, 1961+ annual), a chronological listing of international congresses, conferences, meetings and symposia scheduled to take place in the current year and subsequent years. The Union also publishes *Bibliographie courante des documents, comptes rendus et actes des réunions internationales* v. 1+ Jan., 1961+ (Brussels. monthly)

A167. Worldmark encyclopedia of nations. New York, Worldmark Press, 1960. 1456 p.

A compendium of information on 103 countries and 16 international organizations. Part I is arranged alphabetically by country with the information for each under 50 subject headings (*e.g.*, population, ethnic groups, history, government, international cooperation, economic policy, education, press, religion, etc.) plus a bibliography of further sources. Part II describes in some detail the history, development and programs of 16 organizations of the U.N. system (ILO, FAO, WHO, GATT, ICAO, etc.). Especially useful in smaller libraries, but does not equal the standard sources available in larger collections. Edition 2 in preparation.

YEARBOOKS

A168. Annual register of world events; a review of the year . . . v. 1+ 1758+ London, 1761+ annual.

The venerable yearbook of world events first edited by Edmund Burke. The events of the past year are presented in essay style, each topic being prepared by a specialist and including summaries of many important speeches. Although international in scope, British affairs receive the fullest treatment. Organization of contents has varied but in general the following topics are covered: history of the United Kingdom, the Commonwealth, international organizations, foreign history (by country or regional group); religion; science; law; arts and literature; economics; texts of important public documents; obituaries, and a chronicle of world events. Index of names and subjects. A general index for the years 1758-1819 was published in 1826.

A169. The Europa yearbook, 1959+ London, Europa Publications. 2 v. a year.

Supersedes *Europa: the encyclopaedia of Europe* (1926-1958) and *Orbis: the encyclopaedia of extra-European countries* (1938-1958) which were published in looseleaf format. A reliable and valuable international reference book. Contains more directory information than the *Statesman's yearbook* (A170). Vol. I covers European organizations (OEEC, NATO, Council of Europe, etc.) and European countries. Vol. II covers Africa, the Americas, Asia and Australasia as well as the U.N. and regional organizations (SEATO, Arab League, Caribbean Commission, etc.). For each country it gives a statistical summary followed by information on the constitution, government, politics, legal system, religion; directories of the press, publishers, banks, industrial organizations, unions, learned societies, research institutes, libraries, museums and universities. Because of its wider geographical scope Vol. II is more compressed than Vol. I. Sections on international organizations include the texts of important documents, e.g., the Warsaw Pact of 1955. Europa Publications also issues *The Middle East* (1948+ irregular) and *World of learning* (1947+ annual) and *British Commonwealth* (1956+ irregular) in the same general format.

A170. Statesman's yearbook; statistical and historical annual of the states of the world . . . v. 1+ 1864+ London, New York, Macmillan. annual.

A comprehensive, up-to-date and reliable compendium of information on all countries of the world. Part I deals with international organizations. Part II covers the British Commonwealth in detail. Part III surveys the

U.S. with subheadings for the individual states and possessions. Part IV covers "Other countries" with; breakdowns for the dependencies of Belgium, Netherlands, Portugal, and Spain; full treatment of the French Community; and subsections for the German Länder, the Persian gulf states and the Republics of the USSR. Each entry includes systematic statements and statistics on political history, heads of state, constitution and government, area and population, religion, education, justice, finance, defense, production, commerce, money and banking, and weights and measures. Diplomatic representatives (including embassy staff) to and from Great Britain and (since the 1960-61 vol.) the U.S. are listed for each country. Entries for Commonwealth nations also carry a listing of major diplomatic representatives. Each unit or subsection is followed by a short list of references. The extensive index is made up almost wholly of place names.

A171. World almanac and book of facts, 1868+ New York, New York World-Telegram, 1868+ annual.

The most comprehensive and useful of the American almanacs. Provides statistical data and concise information on all aspects of current affairs (religious, political, social, economic, etc.). Sources are cited for most statistics. Detailed index. British counterpart is Joseph Whitaker's *An Almanack* . . . (London, Whitaker, 1868+ annual).

See also: A151, A152.

STATISTICAL SOURCES

A172. Basic facts and figures; international statistics relating to education, culture and mass communication. v. 1+ 1952+ Paris, UNESCO. annual.

This useful compendium summarizes the data submitted to Unesco in accordance with Article VII of its constitution. It consists of 34 tables providing information for 215 separate territorial units. Data for education include extent of illiteracy, educational attainment, estimated school population, number of schools and teachers, and expenditure on education. The second section provides information on libraries and their collections and on museums. Part 3 deals with book production and translations. The last section covering information media gives data on newspapers and periodicals, consumption of paper, films, radio broadcasting and television. Introductory text for each section and explanatory notes for each table. See also (A177).

A173. California. University. *University at Los Angeles. Center of Latin American Studies.* Statistical abstract for Latin America, 1955+ Los Angeles. annual.

Presents current statistical data on all Latin American countries and dependencies. Information on area, population, social organization, economic characteristics, finances and foreign trade. Occasional special topics are included. Notes and source information accompany tables. Bibliography.

A174. Council of Europe. *Secretariat.* Données statistiques. Statistical data. v. 1+ 1954+ Strasbourg. annual.

A compilation of statistical data for the member countries of the Council of Europe and associated overseas areas; covering population, industry, agriculture, transport, foreign trade, national prosperity (national product, standard of living, prices, etc.) and finance. Each year one of the many aspects of European statistics receives special attention—hence, many tables do not appear regularly. Each volume carries a cumulative list of tables and a key word index which refers to tables published in the current or previous volumes. Sources are cited.

A175. International Statistical Institute. Statistique internationale des grandes villes. La Haye, 1954+ irreg.

A series of volumes of statistical data relative to European towns of more than 100,000 inhabitants. Five series will cover the following topics: (1) population and vital statistics; (2) housing; (3) economic data; (4) public utilities; and (5) culture. One volume of statistical data covering a period of 4-7 years will be published each year. An earlier series covering 1928-1934 was published in 1938-1940. See also (A176).

A176. International statistical yearbook of large towns. v. 1+ 1962+ The Hague, International Statistical Institute. biennial.

Contains tables on population, vital statistics, data on unemployed, motor vehicles, telephone, radio, tourism, water supply, theaters, museums, art galleries, cinemas, and libraries for major European and selective non-European cites. Will complement and bring together information appearing in separate volumes of *Statistique internationale des grandes villes* (A175) which will continue to be published.

A177. U.N. *Statistical Office.* Compendium of social statistics. New York. (In progress)

Work has begun on this extensive statistical survey to be published in 1963 and once every 4 years thereafter. It will serve as a companion to the *World social survey* and aims to give indications of levels of living in the various countries. Its major sections will include: (1) population and vital statistics; (2) health conditions; (3) food consumption and nutrition; (4) housing; (5) education and cultural activities; (6) labor force and conditions of employment; (7) social security and (8) income and expenditure.

A178. United Nations. *Statistical Office.* Statistical yearbook. no. 1+ 1948+ New York. annual.

Continues the *Statistical yearbook of the League of Nations, 1926-1942/44* (Geneva, 1927-45). Tables cover population, manpower, agriculture, production, mining construction, consumption, transportation, external trade, wages and prices, national income, finance, social statistics, education and culture. Normally a 10-20 year span is given for each series. Subject and country indexes. Sources are cited. Textual material (including indexes) are in French and English. Current data for many tables are published regularly in the U.N. Statistical Office's *Monthly bulletin of statistics* (No. 1+ 1947+ New York. monthly).

A179. U.S. *Bureau of the Census.* County and city data book, 1956+ Washington, Govt. Print. Off., 1957+ irregular.

Earlier editions for 1949 (1952); 1952 (1953). A supplement to the *Statistical abstract of the United States* (A182) combining two separate earlier publications *Cities supplement* (1944) and *County data book* (1947). Gives 133 items for each county in the U.S. and 130 items for each of the 484 cities having 25,000+ inhabitants. Includes population, dwelling units, retail trade, wholesale trade, selected service trades, manufactures, vital statistics and agriculture for county units. Adds city government, finances, school systems, hospitals and climate for city units. Comparable information given for geographic regions and divisions, states, and standard metropolitan areas. Also includes descriptive text and source notes.

A180. U.S. *Bureau of the Census.* Congressional districts data book (Districts of the 87th Congress). Washington, Govt. Print. Off., 1961. 150 p.

The latest supplement to the *Statistical abstract of the United States* (A182). Brings together a variety of statistical information not available elsewhere or available only in diverse sources. Table I presents 135 items on population, area, elections and housing for all 437 Congressional districts. Table II presents 125 items (vital statistics, bank deposits, retail trade, local governments, etc.) for the 297 districts which consist of one or more entire county units. Table III presents 72 items pertaining to the nonwhite population in selected districts.

A181. U.S. *Bureau of the Census.* Historical statistics of the United States, Colonial times to 1957. Washington, Govt. Print. Off., 1960. 789 p.

Compiled by the Bureau of the Census with the cooperation of the Social Science Research Council, this supplement to the *Statistical abstract of the United States* presents in concise format more than 8,000 statistical time series (mostly on an annual basis) which cover the period from 1610-1957. Includes data on every major aspect of the nation's social and economic development. The statistics are accompanied by text notes which specify the sources of the data, include references to other sources, discuss the historical development of the data and evaluate their reliability. Separate chapter on Colonial statistics and a 15-page subject index. Similar compilations for other countries include: Italy. Istituto Centrale di Statistica. *Sommario di statistiche storiche italiane, 1861-1955.* (Rome, 1958. 233 p.); Sweden. Statistiska Centralbyrån. *Historisk statistik för Sverige.* (Stockholm, 1955-1960. 3 v.); B.R. Mitchell and P. Deane. *Abstract of British historical statistics.* (Cambridge, Eng., University Press, 1962. 513 p.).

A182. U.S. *Bureau of the Census.* Statistical abstract of the United States. v. 1+ 1878+ Washington, Govt. Print. Off., 1879+ annual.

The standard summary of statistics on the social, political and economic organization of the U.S. It serves also as a guide to other statistical publications and sources by means of the introductory text to each section, the source notes for each table, and the "Bibliography of sources." Emphasis is given primarily to national data. To meet the need for more detailed information for small areas (cities, counties, metropolitan areas, etc.) a series of supplements to the *Abstract* has been issued. (See A179, A180, A181.) Most nations have a comparable publication, e.g., Gt. Brit. Central Statistical Office. *Annual abstract of statistics* (v. 1+ 1840+); France. Direction de la Statistique Générale. *Annuaire statistique de la France.* (v. 1+ 1877+); Italy. Istituto Centrale di Statistica. *Annuario statistico italiano.* (v. 1+ 1878+).

See also: A152, A169, A170, A171.

SOURCES OF SCHOLARLY CONTRIBUTIONS

A183. *Journals.*

American Academy of Political and Social Science. Annals. v. 1+ 1890+
Philadelphia. bi-monthly.
Bibl Fremd Zeit; Bull Anal; Bull Sig; Doc Econ; Econ Abst; Hist Abst;
Int Pol Sci Abst; PAIS; Psych Abst; RG; Soc Abst; UN Lib.

American behavioral scientist. v. 1+ 1957+ Princeton, N.J. monthly
except July and August. (Title v. 1-3; PROD.)
PAIS

American journal of economics and sociology. v. 1+ 1941+ New York.
quarterly.
Bibl Fremd Zeit; Bull Anal; Bull Sig; Econ Abst; Int Ind; PAIS; Soc Abst;
UN Lib.

American Philosophical Society. Proceedings. v. 1+ 1838+ Philadel-
phia. bi-monthly.
Bibl Fremd Zeit; Biol Abst; Bull Sig; Chem Abst; Nutr Abst; PAIS;
Soc Abst.

American Statistical Association. Journal. v. 1+ 1888+ Washington,
D.C. quarterly.
Bibl Fremd Zeit; Biol Abst; Bull Anal; Bull Sig; Bus Per Ind; Doc Econ;
PAIS; Psych Abst; Soc Abst; UN Lib.

Américas. v. 1+ 1949+ Washington, D.C. Pan American Union.
monthly. (Supersedes in part the *Bulletin of the Pan American Union,*
1893-1948.)
Bibl Fremd Zeit; Bull Anal; PAIS; RG.

Annales; économies, sociétés, civilisations. v. 1+ 1946+ Paris, Colin.
bi-monthly.
Bibl Fremd Zeit; Bull Anal; Bull Sig; Doc Econ; Int Pol Sci Abst;
UN Lib.

Behavioral science. v. 1+ 1956+ Ann Arbor, Mental Health Research
Institute, Univ. of Michigan. quarterly.
Bull Anal; Bull Sig; Psych Abst; Soc Abst.

Daedalus; journal of the American Academy of Arts & Letters. v. 1+
1846+ Cambridge, Mass. quarterly.
Biol Abst; Bull Sig; Chem Abst; Eng Ind; Math R; PAIS; Sci Abst.

Diogenes; an international review of philosophy and humanistic studies.
v. 1+ 1953+ New York, International Council for Philosophy and Humanistic Studies. quarterly.
Bull Anal; Bull Sig; Int Pol Sci Abst; PAIS; Soc Abst.

Estadística. v. 1+ 1943+ Washington, Inter American Statistical Institute. quarterly.
Bibl Fremd Zeit; PAIS; UN Lib.

Jahrbuch für Sozialwissenschaft. v. 1+ 1950+ Göttingen, Germany,
Van den hoeck und Ruprecht. irregular. (Contains the separately paged
Bibliographie der Sozialwissenschaften.)

Bibl Deut Zeit; Bull Anal; Bull Sig; Doc Econ; Int Pol Sci Abst; Econ Abst.

Journal of conflict resolution. v. 1+ 1957+ Chicago, Univ. of Chicago Press. quarterly.
PAIS; UN Lib.

Journal of human relations. v. 1+ 1952+ Wilberforce, Ohio, Central State College. quarterly.
Ind Sel Per; PAIS; Psych Abst; Soc Abst.

Journal of inter-American studies. v. 1+ 1959+ Gainesville, Fla. School of Inter-American Studies, Univ. of Florida. quarterly.
PAIS.

Kyklos; internationale Zeitschrift für Sozialwissenschaften. v. 1+ 1947+ Basel, Kyklos-Verlag. quarterly.
Bibl Deut Zeit; Bull Sig; Doc Econ; Econ Abst; PAIS; Soc Abst; UN Lib.

Revista interamericana de ciencias sociales. v. 1-7 1950-1956; 2d series v. 1+ 1961+ Washington, D.C., Pan American Union. (Formerly *Ciencias sociales; notas e informaciones*, 1950-1956.) quarterly.

Revue de psychologie des peuples. v. 1+ 1946+ Le Havre, Institut Havrais de Sociologie Économique et de Psychologie des Peuples. quarterly.
Bull Anal; Bull Sig; Psych Abst; UN Lib.

Rivista internazionale di scienze sociali. v. 1+ 1892+ Milano. quarterly.
Bull Anal; Doc Econ; Econ Abst; Int Pol Sci Abst; Soc Abst; UN Lib.

Royal Statistical Society. Journal. v. 1+ 1838+ London. (Series A: General; quarterly. Series B: Methodological; semi-annual.)
Bibl Fremd Zeit; BR Subj Ind; Bull Anal; Bull Sig; Doc Econ; Econ Abst; PAIS; Soc Abst; UN Lib.

Slavic review. v. 1+ 1941+ Seattle, Wash., American Association for the Advancement of Slavic Studies. quarterly. (From V. 1-20; 1941-1961 called American Slavic and East European Review.)
Bibl Fremd Zeit; Bull Anal; Bull Sig; Hist Abst; Int Ind; PAIS.

Social forces; a scientific medium of social study and interpretation. v. 1+ 1922+ Baltimore, Md., Williams and Wilkins. quarterly.
Bibl Fremd Zeit; Bull Anal; Bull Sig; Int Ind; Int Pol Sci Abst; PAIS; Psych Abst; Soc Abst.

Social problems. v. 1+ 1953+ Brooklyn, N.Y., Society for the Study of Social Problems. quarterly.
PAIS; Psych Abst; Soc Abst.

Social research; an international quarterly of political and social science. v. 1+ 1934+ New York, New School for Social Research. quarterly.
Bibl Fremd Zeit; Bull Anal; Bull Sig; Doc Econ; Econ Abst; Int Ind; PAIS; Soc Abst; UN Lib.

Social science. v. 1+ 1925+ Winfield, Kansas, National Social Science Honor Society, Phi Gamma Mu. quarterly.
Bibl Fremd Zeit; Bull Anal; Bull Sig; PAIS.

Southwestern social science quarterly. v. 1+ 1920+ Baton Rouge, La., Southwestern Social Science Association. quarterly.
Doc Econ; Int Ind; PAIS.

A184. *Organizations*

American Academy of Political and Social Science. Philadelphia. Founded 1889.

American Association for the Advancement of Science. Washington, D.C. Founded 1848. (Section E, Geology and geography; H, Anthropology; I, Psychology; K, Social and economic science; L History and philosophy; Q, Education).

American Philosophical Society. Philadelphia. Founded 1743.

Centre National de la Recherche Scientifique. Paris. Founded 1939.

Centro Latinoamericano de Investigaciones en Ciencias Sociales. Rio de Janeiro. Founded 1957.

Columbia University. Bureau of Applied Social Research. New York. Founded 1937.

Foundation for Research on Human Behavior. Ann Arbor, Mich. Founded 1952.

Institute for Social Research, Oslo. Founded in 1948.

Inter-American Economic and Social Council. Washington, D.C. Founded 1945.

International Committee for Social Sciences Documentation. Paris. Founded 1950.

International Institute of Differing Civilizations. Brussels. Founded 1894.

International Social Science Council. Paris. Founded 1952.

International Statistical Institute. The Hague. Founded 1885.

National Institute of Economic and Social Research. London. Founded 1938.

National Institute of Social Sciences. New York. Founded 1899.

National Institute of Social and Behavioral Science. Washington, D.C. Founded 1959.

New York University. Research Center for Human Relations. New York. Founded 1949.

P.E.P. (Political and Economic Planning) Trust. London. Founded 1931.

Russell Sage Foundation. New York. Founded 1907.

Social Science Research Council. New York. Founded 1923.

Society for the Study of Social Problems. Chambersburg, Pa. Founded 1951.

Tavistock Institute of Human Relations. London. Founded 1946.

Union of International Associations. Brussels. Founded 1907.

University of Michigan. Institute for Social Research. (Survey Research
            Center, and the Research Center for Group Dynamics) Ann
            Arbor. Founded 1946.

University of North Carolina. Institute for Research in Social Science.
            Chapel Hill, N.C. Founded 1924.

A185. *Monograph Series*

American Philosophical Society. Memoirs. v. 1+ 1935+ Philadelphia.

Columbia University. Studies in the social sciences. v. 1+ 1891+ New
York. (Former title: Studies in history, economics and public law.)

Human Relations Area Files. Survey of world cultures. [v. 1+] 1958+
New Haven.

Ibero-Americana. v. 1+ 1932+ Berkeley, Univ. of California Press.

Indiana University. Social science series. v. 1+ 1939+ Bloomington, Ind.

Johns Hopkins University. Studies in historical and political science.
v. 1+ 1883+ Baltimore.

London. University. School of Economic and Political Science. Studies in
economic and political history. v. 1-110, 1896-1936; new series unnumbered
1947+ London.

National Institute of Economic and Social Research. Economic and
social studies. v. 1+ 1942+ London, Cambridge Univ. Press.

Pan American Union. Social Science Section. Social science monographs.
no. 1+ 1955+ Washington, D.C.

Social Science Research Council. Bulletin. no. 1+ 1930+ New York.

Social Science Research Council. Monographs. v. 1+ 1948+ New York.

Stanford University. Stanford series in history, economics and political
science. v. 1+ 1922+ Stanford, Calif.

University of California. Publications in culture and society. v. 1+
1945+ Berkeley.

University of Illinois. Studies in the social sciences. v. 1+ 1912+
Urbana.

University of Michigan. Publications in history and political science.
v 1+ 1911+ Ann Arbor.

University of Michigan. Institute for Social Research. Research Center
for Group Dynamics. Publications. no. 1+ 1951+ Ann Arbor.

SOURCES OF CURRENT INFORMATION

A186. ACLS newsletter. v. 1+ 1949+ New York, American Council of
Learned Societies. monthly except July and August.

Includes information on the administration of ACLS, its own activities and those of its 30 constituent societies. The March issue is a "directory issue" with detailed information on each of the 30 societies.

A187. Bollettino delle ricerche sociali. v. 1+ 1961+ Bologna, Il Mulino. bi-monthly.
Includes: reports of current research in the various social science fields; information on research centers and the teaching of the social sciences; news and information on conferences, meetings, etc.; and bibliographies.

A188. International social science journal. v. 1+ 1949+ Paris, UNESCO. quarterly.
Serves as the official organ for the International Committee of Comparative Law, International Committee for Social Sciences Documentation, International Economic Association, International Political Science Association, International Sociological Association, International Social Science Council and the World Association for Public Opinion Research for which it publishes official proceedings and other communications. Part I of each issue is devoted to articles on a given social science problem. Part II, "World of the social sciences," gives current information on the activities of social science organizations, research institutions and study centers throughout the world. News of conferences, meetings, symposia, etc. is listed. Also includes reviews of books and documents. See (A50). *Indexed in:* Bibl Fremd Zeit; PAIS; Psych Abst; Soc Abst; UN Lib.

A189. Social Science Research Council. Items. v. 1+ 1947+ New York. quarterly.
The news and information medium for the Council. Includes articles on current developments, committee reports, personal news, publications, grants, etc.

A190. UNESCO bulletin for libraries. v. 1+ 1947+ Paris, UNESCO. bi-monthly.
Articles on libraries and developments in library science throughout the world, with special emphasis on the work of Unesco and other international agencies in the fields of bibliography, publications, exchange, etc. *Indexed in:* Bibl Fremd Zeit; Lib Lit; Lib Sci Abst; PAIS.

A191. *Selected daily newspapers*
Il Corriere della Sera. Milan, 1876+; Daily telegraph. London, 1855+; Excelsior. Mexico City, 1917+; Le Figaro. Paris, 1854+; Frankfurter Allgemeine. Frankfurt am Main, 1949+; Globe and mail. Toronto, 1844+; La Prensa. Buenos Aires, 1869+; Manchester guardian. Manchester, Eng., 1821+; Le Monde. Paris, 1861+ (Pre-war title: Le Temps); Neue Zürcher Zeitung. Zurich. Switz., 1779+; Pravda. Moscow, 1912+; The Times. London, 1785+.
Atlanta constitution. Atlanta, Ga., 1868+; Chicago tribune. Chicago, 1847+; Christian science monitor. Boston, 1908+; Los Angeles times. Los Angeles, 1881+; New York times. New York, 1851+; St. Louis post dispatch. St. Louis, Mo., 1878+; Wall Street journal. New York, 1889+; Washington post. Washington, D.C., 1877+.

SOURCES OF UNPUBLISHED INFORMATION

A192. Dissertation abstracts. v. 1+ 1938+ Ann Arbor, Mich., University Microfilms, 1938+ monthly.
Published as *Microfilm abstracts* 1938-1949. A compilation of abstracts (ca. 600 words) of doctoral dissertations submitted by 141 cooperating institutions. Arranged under 31 major subject headings with author and subject (since v. 22 July, 1961) indexes which are cumulated annually. Limitations: some institutions do not send all of their dissertations; various institutions began participating at different times while other major universities do not participate at all, e.g., Harvard, and University of Chicago. In 1956 "Index to American doctoral dissertations," began appearing as no. 13 of *Dissertation abstracts* and continues *Doctural dissertations accepted by American universities* 1933/44-1954/55. (New York, Wilson, 1934-1955. 22 v.) It consolidates into one list titles of dissertations for which doctoral degrees were granted in the U.S. during the academic year covered. Broad subject arrangement with author index. Preceded by U.S. Library of Congress. Catalog Division. *List of American doctoral dissertations printed in 1912-1938*. (Washington, Govt. Print. Off., 1913-1940. 26 v.)

A193. Dossick, Jesse J. Doctoral research on Russia and the Soviet Union. New York, New York Univ. Press, 1960. 248 p.
A classified listing of 960 dissertations accepted by American, Canadian and British universities through 1959. Twenty-three major sections including: archeology and anthropology; communications; education; geography; psychology; history; sociology; economics; history; political science; and international law and relations. Each section is preceded by a brief introductory essay and followed by a bibliographical listing "Aids to further research." British dissertations are listed separately. No index.

A194. France. Ministère de l'Éducation Nationale. Direction des Bibliothèques de France. Catalogue des thèses de doctorat soutenues devant les universités françaises. Nouvelle séries. Année 1959+ Paris, 1960+ annual.
Title 1884-85-1958, *Catalogue des thèses et écrits Academiques.* . . . The official French listing. Arranged since 1914 by facultés. Author and subject indexes have not been issued since 1929. Beginning in 1930 theses were also listed in *Bibliographie de la France* as Supplement D.

A195. Index to theses accepted for higher degrees in the universities of Great Britain and Ireland. v. 1, 1950-51+ London, Aslib, 1954+ annual.
Classified arrangement with indexes of authors and subject headings. Gives name of author, university and degree, and title of the thesis. No annotations. 2 to 3 year time lag. There is no prior national listing.

A196. Jahresverzeichnis der deutschen Hochschulscriften. Bd. 1, 1885+ Berlin, Börsenverein der deutschen Buchhändler, 1887+
Publisher and title vary. The official German listing including all universities since 1885, all Technische Hochschulen since 1913 and Hochschulen der Länder since 1924. Arrangement has varied. Since Bd. 52 (1936) arrangement is by place with author and subject indexes.

A197. National Institute of Economic and Social Research. Register of research in the social sciences in progress and in plan and directory of research institutions. no. 1-13. London, Cambridge Univ. Press, 1943-1956.
A basic guide to current social research carried on in the British Isles for

the period covered. The projects reported by participating institutions are arranged first by broad subject and then by institution. Ph.D theses are listed separately in each section. Indexes of institutions, subjects, research-ers' names. Each entry is fully described. Ph.D. theses are listed until finished; other entries are dropped after two years if no new information is received. The directory of research institutions was begun in no. 6 (1948-49) giving information on the functions and policy, organization, research arrangements and publications for 50-60 research institutions. Supplemented by Gt. Brit. Dept. of Scientific and Industrial Research. *Register of research in the human sciences, 1960-61.* (London, Stationery Office, 1962), a classified listing of 308 projects in the major social science areas with institution and subject indexes. Future editions planned.

A198. "Osteuropa-Dissertationen." *Jahrbücher für Geschichte Osteuropa* n.s. v. 1+ 1951+ Munich, Isar Verlag. quarterly.
Instituted on a biennial basis starting with the 1953 volume which covered the period 1945-1950. Classified list of dissertations on all subjects relating to Eastern Europe done in European countries and the U.S. 2,546 titles listed to date. Author and subject index.

A199. Ottawa. Canadian Bibliographic Centre. Canadian graduate theses in the humanities and the social sciences, 1921-1946. Ottawa, Printer to the King, 1951. 194 p.
Of the 3,043 theses listed 1,557 are concerned with social science subjects. Classified arrangement subdivided by university. Gives author, title, degree, date and professor in charge. Some entries have descriptive content notes. Author index.

A200. Social Science Research Council of Australia. Bibliography of research in the social sciences in Australia, 1954-1960. Canberra, 1958-1961. 2 v.
A register of current research designed to supplement *Australian social science abstracts* (Melbourne, Social Science Research Council, 1945-1954. semi-annual). The first vol. covers 1954-1957; the second, 1957-1960. The 1,866 items are classified by broad subject with an author index. Information includes researcher's name, title or description of the research, institution, starting and completion dates, and publication information. Includes work done at non-university institutions.

A201. Stucki, Curtis W. American doctoral dissertations on Asia, 1933-1958. Ithaca, N.Y., Cornell Univ. Press, 1959. 131 p. (Cornell University. South East Asia Program. Data paper no. 37)
Lists 1,762 dissertations dealing with all aspects of Asian culture. Heaviest emphasis is in economics, education, history and political science. Covers the Far East, Central Asia, S.E. Asia, South Asia and the Pacific Islands. Arrangement is geographical with subject subdivision and an author index. The appendix lists 164 MA theses on Asia written at Cornell during the period covered.

A202. Theses on Pan American topics prepared by the candidates for degrees in the universities and colleges in the United States. 3d ed. rev. and enl. Washington, Pan American Union, 1941. 170 p. (Pan American Union. Columbus Memorial Library. Bibliographic series, no. 5)
An alphabetical author listing of 1671 doctor's and master's theses prepared between 1869 and 1940 as reported by 86 American institutions. Subject index. Supplemented by: A *bibliography of unpublished doctoral*

dissertations and master's theses dealing with the governments, politics and international relations of Latin America, prepared by Harry Kantor (Gainesville, Fla., Inter-American Bibliographical and Library Association, 1953. 85 p.), a classified listing of 973 items prepared between 1908 and 1952; and Edward Marasciulo's *Survey of research and investigations in progress and contemplated in the field of Latin American subjects . . .* (Gainesville, Fla., School of Inter American Studies, 1953. 24 p.), 519 items; and three editions of *Survey of investigations in progress in the field of Latin American Studies* (Washington, Pan American Union, 1956, 58 p.; 1959, 76 p.; 1963, 80 p.).

A203. United Nations. *Economic and Social Council.* Catalogue of economic and social projects of the United Nations and the specialized agencies. no. 1-5, March 1949-1955. New York. irreg.

A descriptive catalog of studies and research, technical services and operational activities. Arranged under the various departments and divisions of the U.N., the numbered entries explain the current projects fully. Includes bibliographical data for continuing publications and monographs as well as details of the work of committees, training centers, regional meetings, etc. Excellent general index. No. 5 covering 1954 was published in 1955. No more issued.

A204. UNESCO. International register of current team research in the social sciences (1950-1952); a tentative survey. Paris, 1955. 312 p. (It's Documentation in the social sciences)

Developed as a pilot project in the area of social science documentation, this work lists research projects undertaken or in progress by research institutes in 41 countries and 14 dependent areas. The United Kingdom is excluded as current research for the period was covered in *Register of research in the social sciences* (A197). No entries for the U.S. Instead a bibliographical survey of 117 lists or directories of research conducted in the U.S. is given. The *Register* lists 1,018 projects; arranged by country and subdivided by subject. Index of research institutions and a subject index.

A205. UNESCO. *Research Centre on the Implications of Industrialization in Southern Asia.* Research information bulletin; social science projects in southern Asia. v. 1+ 1956+ Calcutta. annual.

A current listing and description of research completed or in progress in the countries of southern Asia (India, Ceylon, Indonesia, Pakistan, Philippines, etc.) concerned with social sciences subjects. Arranged under 7 major headings with subject, name and geographic indexes.

A206. UNESCO. Thèses de sciences sociales; catalogue analytique international des thèses inédites de doctorat, 1940-1950. Paris, 1952. 236 p.

A Unesco project which coordinated information furnished by 22 member countries and Germany regarding theses for the doctorate completed and accepted by universities but unpublished during the 10 years of World War II and the reconstruction period. The 3,215 entries are listed under 10 major divisions (with subdivisions) and subdivided by language. Titles are given in French except for works in English or Afrikaans (trans. into English) with an indication of the language of the original. Information includes: author, university and department, degree, country and date. Author, subject and geographical indexes.

A207. U.S. *Dept. of State. Office of Intelligence Research.* External research list no. 1+ Washington, 1952+ irreg.

A series of individual research lists based on the catalog of social science research on foreign areas compiled by the External Research Division from information from scholars throughout the U.S. At the present they are revised twice a year; in April, lists of research in progress; in October, completed projects. The present series covers: (1) USSR and Eastern Europe; (2) East Asia; (3) Southeast Asia; (4) South Asia; (5) Western Europe; (6) Middle East; (7) Africa; (8) American Republics; (9) British Commonwealth; and (10) International affairs. No cumulation. Occasional brief author annotations. No index.

Thompson M. Little
Carl M. White

2

History

History is the intellectual discipline which studies the past in order to provide it with a rational explanation. Though it is an ancient discipline, it reveals an ever-changing aspect, as the historian seeks to achieve a more precise reconstruction of past events. No part of the human experience is closed to him as a source of evidence. When he has completed his research, the historian has two forms in which he may present the results. He may give a narrative account in which he seeks to tell the story, or he may emphasize interpretation in order to explain why historical events took a particular course. It is not unlikely that the two approaches will often be combined.

As the historian goes about his work, he may seek to recreate the past as it really was, trying to establish the hard core of historical fact which embodies "objective" truth. He may instead eschew this task for the larger job of discovering the universal laws which govern the historical past. In this effort the historian either interprets "the record of the past in the light of its own ideas" or accepts the proposition "that knowledge of the past has come down through one or more human minds, has been processed by them, and therefore cannot consist of elemental and impersonal atoms which nothing can alter." If he has chosen the former path, he has accepted the possibility that the past can be recaptured in its essentials; but if he has followed the second route, he has tacitly admitted that history is a never-ending search for an ever-elusive truth. In the first instance, the historian has assumed the existence of an objective truth; in the second instance, he treats the writing of history as a subjective matter.

The task of composing history confronts the historian with problems of causation and evidence. Within the realm of causation he must deal with the question of origins, inevitability, the relationship between men and events, and the boundary between past and present. The scope of evidence is no less challenging. The modern historian is confronted with an abundance of evidence that for sheer bulk threatens to engulf him. The reverse dilemma faces the historian of ancient or medieval times, both of whom must deal with a paucity of evidence. Since much of our evidence is transmitted through the fallible memory of man, the historian must endlessly scrutinize his evidence. He must choose between conflicting sources and must be prepared to defend his decision. And he must be able to construct from the multiplicity of his evidence an explanation which flows logically from it. Ultimately the historian's task is to render a judgment from the material he has examined, with the knowledge that acceptance of his decision depends on the care with which he formulates his judgment.

Works which seek to explain the nature of history are:

B1. Barraclough, Geoffrey. History in a changing world. Oxford, Blackwell, 1955. 246 p.
B2. Berlin, Isaiah. Historical inevitability. London, Oxford Univ. Press, 1954. 78 p.
B3. Bloch, Marc L.B. The historian's craft. New York, Knopf, 1953. 197 p.
B4. Carr, Edward H. What is history? New York, Knopf, 1962. 209 p.
B5. Collingwood, Robin G. The idea of history. New York, Oxford Univ. Press, 1956. 339 p.
B6. Geyl, Pieter. Use and abuse of history. New Haven, Conn., Yale Univ. Press, 1955. 97 p.
B7. Stern, Fritz R., *ed.* The varieties of history from Voltaire to the present. New York, Meridan Books, 1956. 427 p.

THE ANCIENT HISTORIANS

Man, from his most distant origins, has wished to understand his past. He has always sensed that his present was rooted in bygone time. In the beginning, man and nature were one; man believed that magic controlled his environment; he embedded in his myths rituals which had to be followed if he were to obtain effective results over nature. As he achieved greater control over his surroundings, he translated his totems, taboos, and myths into a personalized religion. His gods were peculiarly his own, and the events that had revealed the divine were known only to his worshippers. Divine events transcended history; as long as man failed to develop a sense of time, his past remained hidden in mythology—a set of revealed and accepted myths.

The ancient Greeks were the first people to transcend myth and write history. Beginning with Herodotus, the assumption was made that questions about the past could be both posed and answered. Past events were assumed to have had a specific location in time and to have involved humans whose behavior determined the events. Herodotus described his researches as "history," the Greek word for investigation or inquiry, the results of which would be available to posterity. Although the histories of Herodotus still contain a substantial appeal to myth, the bulk of his research is directed toward ascertaining the truth.

A major deficiency of Herodotus, his failure to indicate the sources of his evidence, is not present in Thucydides. Eyewitness accounts, critically evaluated, were the major source for both Thucydides and Herodotus; but only the former historian described the critical tests he made to insure the veracity of his accounts. Such sources possessed the inherent limitation of a short perspective. In addition, whereas Herodotus is content to attempt a description of what happened, Thucydides seeks to expose through historical analysis the laws of human behavior. His reports of various figures are founded on the unhistorical presumption that their speeches could be deduced from the logic of a given situation. At best, these speeches become the addresses Thucydides would have given under the circumstances.

Not until the second century B.C., some two hundred years after the death of Thucydides, did the Greeks produce another great historian in Polybius. He took for himself the titanic theme of Rome's conquest of the world. Though prejudiced against Carthage, Polybius carefully explored his sources, often travelling great distances to verify his conclusions. He was profoundly concerned with the causes of events and the underlying principles of history. Believing that the governors of the future could learn from the past how to bear the inevitable tragedies of their lives, Polybius was also concerned with conveying the lessons of history. Man cannot avoid his fate, only meet it with sensitive awareness. Implicit in Polybius is the idea that fate masters man.

In Livy, the Romans obtained an historian whose concern was to convey to the Roman common man the glories of Roman history. He failed to check his sources carefully, emphasizing that his concern with history was as a source of moral examples for the present. The greatest of Roman historians was Tacitus, who viewed the transition from Roman Republic to Empire as an unmitigated disaster. His bias toward the Roman senate led him to neglect the administrative achievements of the early Caesars. In addition, he is prone to view the whole of history as a struggle between the forces of good and the forces of evil. The result is a systematic distortion of human nature that transfers a Tiberius from the realm of humanity to that of caricature. The great defect of all ancient history remained its failure to develop a detachment in its treatment of events. Emphasizing as it did the role of personality in the course of history, it concluded that events were the consequence of human decision, and that responsibility rested with man.

The following works are basic to an understanding of ancient history.

B8. Bury, John B. The ancient Greek historians. New York, Dover, 1958. 281 p.
B9. Childe, Vere G. What happened in history. Rev. ed. Harmondsworth, Middlesex, Penguin Books, 1954. 288 p.
B10. Herodotus. Herodotus; the histories, tr. by A. de Sélincourt. Baltimore, Penguin Books, 1954. 599 p.
B11. Laistner, Max L. W. The greater Roman historians. Berkeley, Univ. of California Press, 1947. 196 p.
B12. Livy, Titus. History of Rome, tr. by D. Spillan and C.R.Edmonds. New York, Harper, 1892. 2 v.
B13. Polybius. The histories of Polybius, tr. by E.S. Shuckburgh. London, Macmillan, 1889. 2 v.
B14. Thucydides. Thucydides; history of the Peloponnesian war, tr. by R. Warner. Baltimore, Penguin Books, 1954. 533 p.

THE CHRISTIAN AND MEDIEVAL HISTORIANS

The major preoccupation of the Christian historian was to establish that human history was the visible manifestation of divine will. The nature of the divinity was beyond the ken of man. The ancient insistence upon the pre-eminence of human will was replaced by the thought that human action merely reflected God's purposes. Although man still remained the agent of historical action, he no longer determined events, but gained his importance as the vehicle of God's intentions. Earthly institutions have temporal existence but cease to have eternal significance. The essence of history is change, in which established institutions survive only to meet the immediate purposes of a historical process. Since the Christian message is universal, the theme of Christian history is universal; it transcends time and place. The events of the present are viewed from the perspective of the future advance of the Christian ideal. Tomorrow is a fulfillment and carries with it the implication that the events of history were mere incidents in a single chronology. So far as the Christian historian was concerned, the apocalyptic event was the birth of Christ. Thus all history was dated either before or after this event.

The medieval historian continued along the path set out by his Christian predecessors. Since he did not possess a critical faculty, he was prone to uncritical reports of what he had heard. The Christian presumption that all of history is revelation led naturally to the conclusion that future developments in history could be deduced from the past. This single-minded obsession with God's purpose limited the scope of historical investigation. It did not concern itself with extensive research and saw no value in seeking perspective. Instead, it contemplated the gift given to mankind by God the Father through Christ his Son.

Some compelling insights into the thinking of Christian and medieval historians are obtained by reading:

B15. Augustinus, Aurelius, Saint, Bishop of Hippo. The City of God, tr. and ed. by M. Dods. New York, Hafner, 1948. 2 v.
B16. Geoffrey of Monmouth. History of the kings of Britain. The Sebastian Evans translation rev. by W. Dunn. New York, Dutton, 1958. 281 p.
B17. Orosius, Paulus. Seven books of history against the pagans, tr. by I.W. Raymond. New York, Columbia Univ. Press, 1936. 436 p.
B18. Otto, Bishop of Freising. The two cities, tr. by C.C. Mierow, ed. by A.P. Evans and C. Knapp. New York, Columbia Univ. Press, 1928. 523 p.

THE RENAISSANCE HISTORIANS

Although modern historians are vigorously divided over the existence or non-existence of the Renaissance, it is evident that a shift away from the universal emphasis of Christian-medieval historiography to that of the humanistic emphasis of antiquity occurred in the 15th and 16th centuries. Unlike the ancients, however, the Renaissance historian viewed the human as a creature of emotion and impulse whose history exposed his passionate bias. A healthy skepticism replaced the simple-minded credulity of too many medieval historians. Instead of seeking the divine purpose, the historian was redirected to interest himself in the past for the sake of the past. To establish the facts is a sufficient justification, and there followed from this intention the conclusion that history is neither a guide for the present nor a prophecy of the future. The basis for an independent discipline of history had been established.

Useful examples of Renaissance history are:

B19. Foxe, John M. The acts and monuments of J. Foxe. 4th ed. London, Religious Tract Society, 1877. 8 v.
B20. Machiavelli, Niccolò. The history of Florence and of the affairs of Italy from the earliest times to the death of Lorenzo the Magnificent. New York, Harper, 1960. 417 p.
B21. Vasari, Giorgo. The lives of the most eminent painters, sculptors, and architects. London, Macmillan, 1912-1915. 10 v.

THE ENLIGHTENMENT HISTORIANS

Voltaire and Hume inaugurated the modern conception of history. Possessed of an intense anti-religious bias, they tended to write history as a polemic for their time. Their antipathies and prejudices often overrode the historian's obligation to attempt to understand the function of an institution or a belief. Both men, however, accepted the task of the historian as one which required the disentangling of fact from the web of distortion. Historical evidence required careful scrutiny, scrutiny which aimed to establish the facts of an event as exactly as possible. Voltaire added the further modification of making the subject of history the total experience of a people. He viewed with distaste the medieval age; he consigned to it the role of a dark age. The main goal of the enlightenment historian was to subject human experience to reason, in the expectation that by so doing the historian could discern the laws which govern human life. Inherent, therefore, in the enlightenment view of history was the idea that history had an existence of its own, independent of the existence of either man or God.

An awareness of the meaning of enlightenment history is best obtained by consulting:

B22. Hume, David. History of England from the invasion of Julius Caesar to the abdication of James the Second, 1688. New York, Harper, 1850. 6 v.

B23. Hume, David. "Of the populousness of ancient nations." In *Essays and treatises on several subjects.* London, J. Jones, 1822. 2 v.

B24. Voltaire, François M.A. The age of Louis XIV, tr. by M.P. Pollack. London, Dent, 1951. 475 p.

B25. Voltaire, François M.A. Essai sur les moeurs et l'esprit des nations. Paris, Werdet, 1829. 4 v.

B26. Gibbon, Edward. The history of the decline and fall of the Roman Empire. New York, Heritage Press, 1946. 3 v.

B27. Kant, Immanuel. Idea of a universal history on a cosmo-political plan, tr. by T. de Quincey. Hannover, Sociological Press, 1927. 14 p.

B28. Montesquieu, Charles L. Montesquieu's considerations on the causes of the grandeur and decadence of the Romans, tr. by J. Baker. New York, Appleton, 1894. 526 p.

THE MODERN HISTORIAN

George Friedrich Hegel completed the task of giving to history a distinct role as an independent discipline. His *Philosophy of history* seeks to demonstrate, through a comprehensive analysis of world history, the inherent logic and purpose of historical development. The external purpose of history as set forth by the Christian historian is here translated into an internal, continuing purpose of cosmic dimensions. History assumes its own identity, in which man achieves freedom. Since, in Hegel's view, freedom and moral reason are one, history is the continuing process within which man progresses toward a fuller recognition of himself as a thinking being within his social environment. The whole of history is the history of thought, and the task of the historian is to penetrate into the thought processes which govern human behavior. Every act within history contains an inherent logic that emerges from the thought processes of the actors who made the events.

Hegel's emphasis was upon the emergence of the state as an institution in which occurred an ever fuller participation of humanity. His political emphasis, however, distorts the human experience, for it neglects the multiple facets of that experience. It did inaugurate a form of history that systematically analyzed one aspect of the human experience. Thus Karl Marx emphasized the economic side of human experience with particular emphasis upon the history of capitalism; Leopold von Ranke analyzed the development of Protestantism; Benedetto Croce explored the history of liberty; and Friedrich Meinecke concerned himself with the doctrine of *raison d'état*. Intensive but comprehensive analysis was the hallmark of these historians. Their weakness was to view the human experience with a lopsided perspective that emphasized a single theme or dimension within history.

The following works should be consulted:

B29. Croce, Benedetto. History as the story of liberty, tr. by S. Spriggen. New York, Meridan Books, 1955. 333 p.
B30. Gooch, George P. History and historians in the nineteenth century. Boston, Beacon, 1959. 547 p.
B31. Hegel, Georg W. The philosophy of history. New York, Dover, 1956. 457 p.
B32. Marx, Karl. Capital; a critique of political economy. New York, Modern Library, 1936. 869 p.
B33. Marx, Karl. The class struggle in France (1848-1850). New York, International Publishers, 1934. 159 p.
B34. Marx, Karl. The civil war in France. New York, International Publishers, 1940. 96 p.
B35. Marx, Karl. The Eighteenth Brumair of Louis Bonaparte. New York, International Publishers, 1935. 128 p.
B36. Meinecke, Friedrich. Machiavellism; the doctrine of Raison d'état and its place in modern history, tr. by D. Scott. New Haven, Conn., Yale Univ. Press, 1957. 438 p.
B37. Ranke, Leopold von. History of the Reformation in Germany, tr. by S. Austin. London, Longman, Brown, Green and Longmans, 1845-1847. 3 v.

THE GERMAN SCHOOL

The concern with comprehensive historical themes was paralleled, in the 19th century, by a concern for the peculiar development of a particular people. Even in Hegel, the preoccupation with the theme of freedom was complemented with his concern for the unique role of the German in achieving the consummate freedom. The emergence of a defined conception of nationalism, a term which entered language only after the Congress of Vienna in 1815, turned the historian to the search for those historical experiences which differentiated a particular people. From what had been essentially a cosmopolitan concern the historian turned inward to parochial themes. In the aftermath of Prussia's overwhelming defeat by Napoleon, Prussian intellectuals, following the injunction of their king, committed themselves to "make up by intellectual strength what we have lost in material power." In a surge of redirected patriotism, German historians turned their energy to an intensive analysis of evidence. Systematic compilations of Latin inscriptions, medieval manorial rolls, and manuscripts, were supplemented by new editions of histories and other sources. Attention was increasingly given to the development of institutions from their earliest origins. Sources were closely analyzed to establish their creditability. From this effort there emerged a school of history known as positivism. Its concern was to ascertain facts and to set forth fixed laws of historical development. The emphasis upon fact encouraged the writing of monographs rather than comprehensive history. As the historian narrowed his range of research, he extended the scope of his tools: he now accepted philology, archaeology, and subsequently such disciplines as sociology and psychology as legitimate sources for techniques with which to analyze historical problems. From this proliferation of new techniques came a concern for the precise formulation and exact presentation of materials. The finest expression of the new spirit was stated by Ranke, when he called for the writing of history "as it actually happened."

Gems of 19th century German history are:

B38. Mommsen, Theodor. The history of Rome. Glencoe, Ill., Free Press, 1957. 5 v.
B39. Niebuhr, Barthold G. The history of Rome, tr. by J.C. Hare and C. Thirlwall. London, Walton, 1855-60. 3 v.
B40. Ranke, Leopold von. History of the Latin and the Teutonic nations, 1494 to 1514, tr. by G.R. Denis. London, G. Bell, 1909. 448 p.
B41. Treitschke, Heinrich G. von. History of Germany in the nineteenth century. New York, McBride, Nast, 1915-1919. 7 v.

THE FRENCH REVOLUTION

Germany was not alone in its development of a particularistic approach to history. In France, where the Revolution had released a truly titanic energy, events that shook the nation and the world to its foundations soon captivated the historical imagination. The origins of the revolution, the events which brought upheaval to a nation and a continent for over a quarter of a century, and the complex personality of Napoleon occupied the center of French historical thought. But analysis of the event alone was not enough. It was necessary for the French historian to establish it as the climactic event in history. "History is the drama of liberty," Herder, a German historian, argued, "the protest of the human race against the world which enchains it, the freedom of the spirit, the reign of the soul." France and its revolution were treated as the inaugural of democracy both at home and abroad. The civilizing mission of France was traced to its origins. Equally fascinating was the French historian's concern with Napoleon. The extraordinary career of the Corsican who skyrocketed from obscurity to immortality posed a dilemma: did the man determine the events or did the events make the man? The 19th-century version of liberalism, which emphasized individual responsibility, manifested itself in the tendency of the 19th-century historian to focus his attentions on the actions of the man. An even more significant trend was the sophistication of the historian's concept of the historical period. The French Revolution achieved the status of a historical climax; the events preceding it were treated as preparatory to the Revolution, and those that followed it were regarded as a fulfillment of its progressive implications. Inherent in this treatment was the assumption that what was destroyed by revolutionary action was inferior to what followed.

The literature of the French Revolution and its antecedents is vast. The following works have achieved the status of classics:

B42. Aulard, François V.A. The French Revolution; a political history 1789-1804, tr. by B. Miall. 3d ed. London, Unwin, 1910. 4 v.
B43. Geyl, Pieter. Napoleon, for and against, tr. by O. Renier. New Haven, Conn., Yale Univ. Press, 1949. 477 p.
B44. Lefebvre, Georges. The coming of the French Revolution, tr. by R.R. Palmer. New York, Vintage Books, 1957. 191 p.
B45. Lefebvre, Georges. The French Revolution from its origins to 1793, tr. by E.M. Evanson. New York, Columbia Univ. Press, 1962. 365 p.
B46. Mathiez, Albert. The French Revolution, tr. by C.A. Phillips. New York, Knopf, 1928. 509 p.
B47. Michelet, Jules. Historical view of the French Revolution from its earliest indications to the flight of the king in 1791, tr. by C. Cocks. New ed. London, H.G. Bohn, 1860. 602 p.
B48. Tocqueville, Alexis de. The old regime and the French Revolution, tr. by S. Gilbert. Garden City, N.Y., Doubleday, 1955. 300 p.

NINETEENTH-CENTURY BRITISH HISTORIANS

The inward-looking views of European historians in the 19th century was invariably conditioned by the peculiar history of their native countries. As the German historians worked to provide Germany with an identity in the absence of German unity and the French viewed the transcendent implications of their Revolution, the British historians contemplated the remarkable durability of their island kingdom. In their effort to explain the distinctive character of their national institutions, British historians systematically analyzed medieval institutions. The tendency of European historians, especially of the French, to view it as a "dark age" was rejected. For the British it was the time in which their present institutions were rooted.

Change in history took on an evolutionary character, with the emphasis on gradual alteration rather than on revolutionary upheaval. The interrelationship between past and present was omnipresent in British life. The durability of British institutions was accepted as proof of their obvious superiority A preoccupation with origins, a sense of rapport with the past rather than a repudiation of it, a belief in the distinctiveness of British experience—these were the hallmarks of British history during the 19th century.

The following works reveal the foregoing tendencies:

B49. Acton, John E. Essays in freedom and power. New York, Noonday Press, 1955. 350 p.
B50. Froude, James A. History of England from the fall of Wolsey to the death of Elizabeth. New York, Scribner, Armstrong, 1872. 12 v.
B51. Green, John R. A short history of the English people. New York, Harper, 1876. 823 p.
B52. Hallam, Henry. The constitutional history of England from the accession of Henry VII to the death of George II. New York, Harper, 1870. 737 p.
B53. Kemble, John M. The Saxons in England, rev. by W.D. Birch. London, Quaritch, 1876. 2 v.
B54. Lecky, William E.H. A history of England in the eighteenth century. New York, Appleton, 1892-93. 7 v.
B55. Macaulay, Thomas B. History of England from the accession of James II. New York, Dutton, 1953. 4 v.
B56. Maitland, Frederic W. The constitutional history of England, ed. by H.A.L. Fisher. Cambridge, Eng., University Press, 1961. 548 p.
B57. Maitland, Frederic W. Domesday Book and beyond. London, Fontana Library, 1960. 605 p.

Herbert Butterfield in his *The Whig interpretation of history* (New York, Scribner, 1951) B58, has written a sharp criticism of the British historian's tendency to view the process of history as one of progress.

NINETEENTH-CENTURY AMERICAN HISTORIANS

No less emphatic in their assertion of uniqueness were the American historians. The democratic impulse that permeated 19th century American life attracted the attention of the great French historian, Tocqueville. His assumption that a great experiment in equality was being conducted in America was accepted as an a priori truth by Americans. They took their lead from George Bancroft, who stated that "The United States have the precedence in the practice and defence of the equal rights of man." In addition, Bancroft venerated democratic man. His heroes were those men who had demanded individual liberty and expressed confidence in the good sense of the people. The idealization of the past which flowed from such treatment provoked a counter-response, beginning with Richard Hildreth, who took a dimmer view of human nature and expressed sharp reservations about both the American past and the consequences of mass democracy. Equally attractive to the American historian was the struggle waged between man and nature in the New World. This was redefined by Francis W. Parkman as a struggle between the French and English to implant their civilization in the New World wilderness. William Prescott turned his attention to the Spanish conquest and revealed a tolerance of Spanish institutions that provoked a sharp counter-response from John L. Motley, who insisted on treating Protestantism as obviously superior to Catholicism. Complementing these broadly based and controversial interpretations were the responsible, thorough studies of the pre-Civil War and the Jeffersonian period by John B. MacMaster and Henry Adams respectively. The overall achievement of American historians during the 19th century is best summed up as one of excellent literature but mediocre scholarship.

The following works are the most durable American works of the 19th century:

B59. Adams, Henry. History of the United States of America. New York, Scribner, 1891-98. 9 v.
B60. Bancroft, George. History of the United States of America from the discovery of the continent. New York, Appleton, 1891-92. 6 v.
B61. Hildreth, Richard. History of the United States of America. Rev. ed. New York, Harper, 1880. 6 v.
B62. MacMaster, John B. A history of the people of the United States from the Revolution to the Civil War. New York, Appleton-Century, 1931-38. 8 v.
B63. Motley, John L. The rise of the Dutch Republic. New York, Harper, 1900. 5 v.
B64. Parkman, Francis. Pioneers of France in the New World. Boston, Little, Brown, 1907. 491 p.
B65. Prescott, William H. A history of the conquest of Mexico. New York, Heritage Press, 1949. 558 p.

THE TWENTIETH-CENTURY HISTORIAN

In the 20th century, the task of recreating the past has been complicated by the addition of new sources and new techniques. The historian has lost much of the optimism of the nineteenth century. Two world wars that have shattered whole societies, subverted institutions, and revealed dimensions of human behavior that destroyed the simple view of man as an essentially rational and good creature. Historians have been compelled to re-examine their past assumptions. In an uncertain world they have accepted tentative, rather than absolute, conclusions; eager to obtain a fuller comprehension of their own discipline, they have made use of the approaches of other disciplines. The whole of human experience occupies their attention. The proclivity of the 19th-century historian to render moral judgments has been modified as the historian seeks instead to understand, rather than judge, the past. The interrelationship of past, present, and future is accepted as a fixed point. Minute and meticulous analysis of evidence is accepted as the necessary condition for reaching an awareness of the morphology of human affairs. "The subject matter of history is human affairs, men in action, things which have happened and how they happened; concrete events fixed in time and space, and their grounding in the thoughts and feelings of men—not things universal and generalized; events as complex and diversified as the men who wrought them, those rational beings whose knowledge is seldom sufficient, whose ideas are but distantly related to reality, and who are never moved by reason alone." In the foregoing words Sir Lewis B. Namier has summed up the temper of the 20th-century historian.

A fuller awareness of the 20th-century historian's intentions is found in the following works:

B66. Geyl, Pieter. Debates with historians. New York, Meridan Books, 1961. 405 p.
B67. Geyl, Pieter. Encounters in history. Cleveland, Meridan Books, 1958. 287 p.
B68. Huizinga, Johan. Men and ideas. New York, Meridan Books, 1959. 378 p.
B69. Namier, Lewis B. Avenues of history. London, Hamish Hamilton, 1952. 202 p.

BASIC WORKS IN HISTORY

The number of historical publications is so voluminous that it is unlikely that any bibliography could contain more than a small fraction of the total. The purpose of this section is to provide a listing of basic works in the major fields of history. It is designed to provide an interested reader with a beginning upon which he can subsequently build a more intensive reading.

ANCIENT HISTORY: Two solid texts of the Grecian and Roman period are John B. Bury, A *history of Greece to the death of Alexander the Great,* revised by Russell Meiggs (3d ed. London, Macmillan, 1951) B70 and Max Cary, A *history of Rome down to the reign of Constantine* (2d ed. London, Macmillan, 1954) B71. Social and economic conditions in Rome and Greece are perceptively analyzed by the great historian Mikhail Rostovfsev, *The social and economic history of the Hellenistic world* (Oxford, Clarendon Press, 1941) B73, and *The social and economic history of the Roman Empire,* revised by P. M. Fraser (2d ed. Oxford, Clarendon Press, 1957) B74. William W. Tarn, *Hellenistic civi-*

lization, revised by G. T. Griffith (3d ed. London, E. Arnold, 1952) B75, and Harold Mattingly, *Roman imperial civilization* (Garden City, N.Y., Doubleday, 1959) B76 are two excellent surveys. A classic of French historical literature is Numa D. Fustel de Coulanges, *The ancient city; a study on the religion, law and institutions of Greece and Rome* (Garden City, N.Y., Doubleday, 1956) B77. For a brilliant analysis of the declining days of Rome consult Sir Samuel Dill, *Roman society in the last century of the western empire* (2d rev. ed. New York, Meridan Books, 1958) B78, and the provocative Richard M. Haywood, *The myth of Rome's fall* (New York, Crowell, 1958) B79.

BYZANTINE HISTORY: Byzantine civilization has been under a pall in the West ever since the 18th century philosophies dismissed it as a decadent, superstition ridden society. Only within the last three decades of the 20th century has interest revived. The third volume of Gibbon's *The history of the decline and fall of the Roman Empire* (New York, Heritage Press, 1946) B80 provides an excellent insight into the limitations of pre-20th century treatments of Byzantine history. Steven Runciman, *Byzantine civilization* (New York, Meridan Books, 1956) B81 presents a lucid, cogent account of the subject. Two excellent detailed studies are Georg Ostrogorsky, *History of the Byzantine state,* tr. by Joan Hussey (New Brunswick, N.J., Rutgers Univ. Press, 1957) B82, and Alexander A. Vasiliev, *History of the Byzantine empire, 324-1453* (2d English ed. Madison, Univ. of Wisconsin Press, 1928) B83. Both of the foregoing contain excellent introductory bibliographical essays for those wishing more particular studies.

MEDIEVAL HISTORY: For the sake of clarity I have defined the medieval period as extending from the 6th to the 15th century A.D. A good beginning is Henri Pirenne, *A history of Europe,* tr. by B. Miall (Garden City, N.Y., Doubleday, 1958) B84, and his more specialized *Economic and social history of medieval Europe,* tr. by I. E. Clegg (New York, Harcourt, Brace, 1937) B85. The latter book contains the thesis that the Arab conquest of the Mediterranean littoral in the 8th and 9th centuries consigned Western Europe to an economic and cultural deadend. The foregoing is fully set forth in two Pirenne classics, *Mohammed and Charlemagne,* tr. by B. Miall (New York, Meridan Books, 1957) B86, and *Medieval cities,* tr. by F. D. Halsey (Garden City, N.Y., Doubleday, 1956) B87. A comprehensive critique of the Pirenne thesis is found in Alfred F. Havighurst, *The Pirenne thesis; analysis, criticism, and revision* (Boston, Heath, 1958) B88. An acute analysis of the social stresses that accompanied the transititon from antiquity to medievalism is found in C. Delisle Burns, *The first Europe; a study of the establishment of medieval Christendom, A.D. 400-800* (London, Allen and Unwin, 1947) B89. Two excellent texts are Christopher H. Dawson, *The making of Europe; an introduction to the history of European unity* (London, Sheed and

Ward, 1932) Bgo, and George G. Coulton, *Life in the middle ages* (New
York, Macmillan, 1930) Bg1. Valuable specialized studies are George G.
Coulton, *Medieval village, manor and monastery* (New York, Harper,
1960) Bg2; Eileen E. Power, *Medieval people* (Garden City, N.Y.,
Doubleday, 1954) Bg3; Helen Waddell, *The wandering scholars*
(Garden City, N.Y., Doubleday, 1955) Bg4; and Otto F. von Gierke,
Political theories of the Middle Age, tr. by Frederic W. Maitland (Boston, Beacon Press, 1958) Bg5. The dominant institution of the medieval
period—the Church—has been extensively treated. Consult Jakob
Burckhardt, *The age of Constantine the Great*, tr. by M. Hadas (Garden City, N.Y., Doubleday, 1956) Bg6 which deals with the shattering
impact of Christianity on the pagan Roman Empire. An excellent summary of Christian doctrine is found in Adolf von Harnack, *Outlines of
the history of dogma*, tr. by E. K. Mitchell (Boston, Beacon Press, 1957)
Bg7 which is a distillation of Harnack's classic seven volume study of the
subject. A major study of the interrelationship of church and state during the period is Steven Runciman, *A history of the crusades* (Cambridge, Eng., University Press, 1951-54) Bg8. A provocative series of
essays that deals perceptively with the role of Augustinian thought is Martin C. D'Arcy, et. al., *St. Augustine* (New York, Meridan Books, 1957)
Bg9. Among selected studies of unusual value are: Helen Waddell, *The
desert fathers* (Ann Arbor, Univ. of Michigan Press, 1957) B100;
George G. Coulton, *Inquistion and liberty* (Boston, Beacon Press,
1959) B101; Steven Runciman, *The medieval Manichee; a study in
Christian dual heresy* (New York, Viking, 1961) B102; and Henry C.
Lea, *The history of sacredotal celibacy in the Christian Church* (New
York, Russell and Russell, 1957) b103. The classic study of the Holy
Roman Empire remains James Bryce, *The Holy Roman Empire* (Lon-
don, Macmillan, 1919) B104.

THE RENAISSANCE: Few debates among historians are more
energetic than that over whether there was or was not a Renaissance. The
conception of the masterful Swiss historian Jacob Burckhardt that the
Renaissance constituted a distinct break with the past has been challenged
by historians who see the distinctive characteristics of the Renaissance as
a gradual development within medieval life. For opponents of Burckhardt
the Renaissance constituted not a beginning but the end of a process.
For a thorough history of the changing interpretations of the Renaissance consult Wallace K. Ferguson, *The Renaissance in historical
thought: five centuries of interpretation* (Boston, Houghton Mifflin,
1948) B105. Jacob Burckhardt, *The civilization of the Renaissance in
Italy* (New York, Modern Library, 1954) B106, is one of the great historical classics which has retained much of its pertinence and intellectual
vitality. The most important challenger of Burckhardt's thesis is
the Dutch historian Johan Huizinga, whose *The waning of the middle*

ages (Garden City, N.Y., Doubleday, 1954) B107, is a *tour de force*. A good introductory account to the history of the Renaissance is Wallace K. Ferguson, *The Renaissance* (New York, Holt, 1940) B108. Two accounts by a single author Ferdinand Schevill, *The Medici* (New York, Harper, 1960) B109, and *History of Florence from the founding of the city through the Renaissance* (New York, Harcourt, Brace, 1936) B110, have the virtue of succinct presentation. An incisive treatment of Italian painting is that of Bernard Berenson, *The Italian painters of the Renaissance* (New York, Meridan Books, 1957) B111. An excellent description of the interaction of Renaissance and Reformation is found in Johan Huizinga, *Erasmus and the age of Reformation*, tr. by F. Hopman (New York, Harper, 1957) B112.

THE REFORMATION: The religious upheaval that swept Europe during the 16th and 17th centuries has been productive of an extensive and still growing literature. It has attracted the attention of some of the greatest modern historians. A masterpiece is Ernst D. Troeltsch, *The social teaching of the Christian churches*, tr. by O. Wyon (New York, Harper, 1960) B113. A solid Protestant account is Henry P. Smith, *The age of the Reformation* (New York, Holt, 1920) B114. A brief survey of the English Reformation is given in Frederick M. Powicke, *The Reformation in England* (London, Oxford Univ. Press, 1941) B115. Two accounts of the interdependence of Protestantism and Capitalism that have achieved the stature of classics are Max Weber, *The Protestant ethic and the spirit of capitalism*, tr. by T. Parsons (New York, Scribner, 1948) B116, and Richard H. Tawney, *Religion and the rise of capitalism, a historical study* (New York, Penguin Books, 1947) B117.

MODERN EUROPE: The singular impact of western Europe on the world since the 16th century is neatly suggested in Arnold J. Toynbee's brief *The world and the West* (New York, Oxford Univ. Press, 1953) B118. An excellent one volume general history of Europe in the modern era which views Europe as central to the events of the era is Robert R. Palmer, *A history of the modern world* (New York, Knopf, 1950) B119.

EUROPE IN THE 16TH AND 17TH CENTURIES: The following works have the virtue of lucidity and thoroughness: R. Trevor Davies, *The golden century of Spain, 1501-1621* (London, Macmillan, 1937) B120; Conyers Read, *The Tudors; personalities and practical politics in sixteenth century England* (New York, Holt, 1936) B121, which should be supplemented by Sir John E. Neale, *Queen Elizabeth I; a biography* (New York, Doubleday, 1957) B122, and *Elizabeth I and her parliaments* (New York, St. Martin's Press, 1953-58) B123. A brilliant treatment of 16th-century English-Spanish rivalry is Garrett Mattingly, *The Armada* (Boston, Houghton Mifflin, 1959) B124. Events of the lowlands are dealt with in Pieter Geyl, *The revolt of the Netherlands, 1555-1609* (2d ed. New York, Barnes and Noble, 1958) B125, and *The Netherlands divided*, tr. by S. T. Bindoff (London, Williams and Norgate, 1936) B126. French affairs are covered in Franklin C. Palm, *Calvinism and the religious wars* (New York, Holt, 1932) B127, and Warren H. Lewis' spirited *The splendid century; life in the France of Louis XIV* (New York, Doubleday, 1957) B128. An important account of the economic factors that underlay the Puritan Revolution in Great Britain is Richard H. Tawney, *The agrarian problem in the sixteenth century* (London, Longmans, Green, 1912) B129. A thorough treatment of the religious wars of the 17th century is Cicely V. Wedgwood, *The Thirty years war* (Garden City, N.Y., Doubleday, 1961) B130. A good account of 17th century events is found in George N. Clark, *The seventeenth century* (2d ed. Oxford, Clarendon Press, 1947) B131. A provocative supplement to the foregoing is Basil Willey, *The seventeenth century background; studies in the thought of the age in relation to poetry and religion* (London, Chatto and Windus, 1934) B132. The Puritan and the Glorius Revolutions of Great Britain are well covered in George M. Trevelyan, *England under the Stuarts* (London, Methuen, 1947) B133, and the latter revolution is treated brilliantly in Trevelyan's *The English revolution, 1688-1689* (London, Butterworth, 1938) B134.

EUROPE IN THE 18TH CENTURY: A good beginning is Walter L. Dorn, *Competition for empire, 1740-1763* (New York, Harper, 1940) B135. A lucid summary of British Empire history before the American Revolution is Lawrence H. Gipson, *The coming of the Revolution, 1763-1775* (New York, Harper, 1954) B136. A major study of extraordinary detail that has had profound consequences on the study of history is Sir Lewis B. Namier, *The structure of politics at the accession of George III* (2d ed. London, Macmillan, 1957) B137. A work that sees the latter half of the 18th century as the seedbed of democracy is Robert R. Palmer, *The age of the democratic revolution* (Princeton, N.J., Princeton Univ. Press, 1959) B138. Though subjected to much criticism Carl L. Becker's essay, *The heavenly city of the eighteenth-century philosophers* (New Haven, Conn., Yale Univ. Press, 1959) B139, has the virtue of originality. A delightful treatment of some aspects of Italian history during the 17th and 18th centuries is found in Harold M. Acton, *The last Medici* (Rev. ed. New York, St. Martin's Press, 1958) B140. A good account of the waning years of the 18th century is Leo Gershoy, *From despotism to revolution, 1763-1789* (New York, Harper, 1944) B141.

THE FRENCH REVOLUTION AND THE ERA OF NA-POLEON: In addition to the works mentioned earlier the reader would find Crane Brinton, *A decade of revolution, 1789-99* (New York, Harper, 1934) B142, and James M. Thompson, *The French Revolution* (Oxford, Blackwell, 1943) B143, useful. Robert R. Palmer, *Twelve who ruled* (Princeton, N.J., Princeton Univ. Press, 1941) B144 recreates the time of the terror excitingly. A good study of the effects of the revolution on Germany is George P. Gooch, *Germany and the French Revolution* (London, Longmans, Green, 1920) B145. A short but perceptive analysis of the great conservative critic of the French Revolution, Edmund Burke, is Charles Parkin, *The moral basis of Burke's political thought* (Cambridge, Eng., University Press, 1956) B146. Geoffrey Bruun, *Europe and the French imperium, 1799-1814* (New York, Harper, 1938) B147, is reliable. A readable though excessively patriotic account of Britain during the Napoleonic Wars is Arthur Bryant, *The years of endurance, 1793-1802* (London, Collins, 1942) B148; *The years of victory, 1802-1812* (London, Collins, 1944) B149; and *The age of elegance, 1812-1822* (London, Collins, 1950) B150. Friedrich von Gentz, *The French and American Revolutions compared,* tr. by John Q. Adams (Chicago, Gateway Editions, 1955) B151 is a classic of unusual interest.

EUROPE IN THE 19TH CENTURY: An unusually fine text is David Thomson, *Europe since Napoleon* (New York, Knopf, 1957) B152. The years immediately after the Napoleonic wars are ably covered in Frederick B. Artz, *Reaction and revolution, 1814-1832* (New York, Harper, 1934) B153. For a detailed treatment of the Congress of Vienna consult Sir Harold Nicolson, *The Congress of Vienna, a study in allied unity: 1812-1822* (New York, Harcourt, Brace, 1946) B154, and Henry A. Kissinger, *A world restored* (London, Weidenfeld and Nicolson, 1957) B155. Of unusual merit are the several volumes of Elie Halévy's *A history of the English people in the nineteenth century,* tr. by E. I. Watkin and D. A. Barker (London, E. Benn, 1949-52. 6 v.) B156. The first volume, *England in 1815,* is a stunning performance. *The liberal awakening, 1815-1830; The triumph of reform, 1830-1841;* and *The rule of democracy, 1905-1914,* are fine but do not quite match the first performance. Still good but lacking the polish of the preceding works are his *Victorian years, 1841-1895,* and *Imperialism and the rise of labour, 1895-1905.* A remarkable achievement is Elie Halévy, *The growth of philosophic radicalism,* tr. by M. Morris (Boston, Beacon Press, 1955) B157, which deals with the growth of utilitarianism in England. For a sound and brief history of industrialization see Thomas S. Ashton, *The industrial revolution, 1760-1830* (London, Oxford Univ. Press, 1948) B158, which should be read as a corrective to John L. and Barbara Hammond, *The village labourer* (London, Longmans, Green, 1948) B159, and *The town labourer, 1760-1832* (London, Longmans, 1917) B160. The Hammonds have summarized their views in *The bleak age* (West Drayton, Middlesex, Penguin Books, 1947) B161. The continuing impact of revolutionary ideas on France is found in John P. Plamenatz, *The revolutionary movement in France,1815-1871* (London, Longmans, Green, 1952) B162. The British historian A. J. P. Taylor has done exten-

sive work in the history of Central Europe during the 19th century and
the first decade of the 20th century. His work is provocative and invari-
ably lively. See *The struggle for mastery in Europe, 1848-1918* (Oxford,
Clarendon Press, 1954) B163, which is an excellent diplomatic history;
The Hapsburg monarchy, 1809-1918 (London, Hamilton, 1948) B164,
which should be supplemented by Z. A. B. Zeman, *The break-up of the
Habsburg empire, 1914-1918* (London, Oxford Univ. Press, 1961)
B165. Taylor is at his epigramatic best in *Bismarck, the man and states-
man* (New York, Knopf, 1955) B166, and *The course of German history*
(New York, Coward-McCann, 1946) B167. Two works that reveal the
catholic scope of Sir Lewis Namier's interest are *Vanished supremacies*
(New York, Macmillan, 1958) B168, and *1848; the revolution of the intellectuals* (London, Oxford Univ. Press, 1957) B169. Two ideological
developments of the 19th century are well treated in Guido de Ruggiero,
The history of European liberalism, tr. by R. G. Collingwood (Boston,
Beacon Press, 1959) B170, and Edmund Wilson, *To the Finland station* (Garden City, N.Y., Doubleday, 1953) B171, which deals with the
revolutionary tradition in Europe and the rise of socialism. An impressive history of modern France is John P. T. Bury, *France, 1814-1940*
(Philadelphia, Univ. of Pennsylvania Press, 1949) B172. Anyone interested in the development of nationalism should consult Carlton J. H.
Hayes, *The historical evolution of modern nationalism* (New York,
Macmillan, 1948) B173, and Hans Kohn, *Prophets and peoples; strug-
gles in nineteenth century nationalism* (New York, Macmillan, 1946)
B174.

THE HISTORY OF RUSSIA: A brief but thorough account is
Richard D. Charques, *A short history of Russia* (New York, Dutton,
1958) B175. A longer account is found in Michael T. Florinsky, *Russia:
a history and interpretation* (New York, Macmillan, 1953) B176. An unusually thoughtful account is Sir John Maynard, *Russia in flux before
October* (London, V. Gollancz, 1941) B177. Two good accounts of the
decline and fall of the Russian monarchy are Hugh Seton-Watson, *The
decline of imperial Russia, 1855-1914* (New York, Praeger, 1952) B178,
and Sir Bernard Pares, *The fall of the Russian monarchy* (New York, Vintage Books, 1961) B179. Several specialized studies of imperial Russia are
useful. Among these are Nicolas Berdyaev, *The origin of Russian Communism*, tr. by R. M. French (London, Centenary Press, 1937) B180;
Geroid T. Robinson, *Rural Russia under the old regime* (New York,
Longmans, Green, 1932) B181; and Edward H. Carr, *Michael Bakunin*
(New York, Vintage Books, 1961) B182. Franco Venturi, *Roots of
revolution; a history of the Populist and Socialist movements in nineteenth century Russia* (New York, Knopf, 1960) B183, is a major contribution to an understanding of the domestic origin of the Russian
Revolution.

THE RUSSIAN REVOLUTION: Leon Trotsky, *The history of the Russian Revolution*, tr. by Max Eastman (Ann Arbor, Univ. of Michigan Press, 1957) B184, is both a history and a historical document composed by one of the makers of the Revolution. William H. Chamberlin, *The Russian Revolution, 1917-1921* (New York, Macmillan, 1935) B185, is a responsible though limited study. John W. Wheeler-Bennett, *The forgotten peace, Brest-Litovsk, March, 1918.* (New York, Morrow, 1939) B186, contains much interesting material of early Communist foreign policy and of the kind of peace a triumphant imperial Germany inflicted upon the defeated Russia. Bertram D. Wolfe, *Three who made a revolution, a biographical history* (New York, Dial Press, 1948) B187, is important; it should be supplemented by Isaac Deutscher, *Stalin, a political biography* (New York, Oxford Univ. Press, 1949) B188. For events since the revolution consult Edward H. Carr, *The Bolshevik Revolution, 1917-1923* (London, Macmillan, 1950-53) B189.

EUROPE IN THE 20TH CENTURY: A good textual account is that of H. Stuart Hughes, *Contemporary Europe: a history* (Englewood Cliffs, N.J., Prentice-Hall, 1961) B190. The immediacy of the events of the 20th century makes it difficult to obtain the detached accounts that are a key ingredient in the making of good history. Two treatments of imperialism are particularly useful: John A. Hobson, *Imperialism; a study* (3d ed. London, Allen and Unwin, 1938) B191, and William L. Langer, *The diplomacy of imperialism, 1890-1902* (2d ed. New York, Knopf, 1956) B192. A durable account of the events before and after World War I is Raymond J. Sontag, *European diplomatic history, 1871-1932* (New York, Century, 1933) B193. Sidney B. Fay, *The origins of the World War* (New York, Macmillan, 1930) B194, is a good account. A well written account of the events immediately prior and during the first months of the war is Barbara W. Tuchman, *The guns of August* (New York, Macmillan, 1962) B195. A brief but adequate account of the war is found in Cyril Falls, *The Great War* (New York, Putnam, 1959) B196. A shrewd insight into the period between the two world wars is found in Edward H. Carr, *The twenty years' crisis, 1919-1939* (London, Macmillan, 1940) B197. A controversial treatment of the origins of World War II which has provoked angry protests is A. J. P. Taylor, *The origins of the Second World War* (London, Hamilton, 1961) B198. Franz L. Neumann, *Behemoth: the structure and practice of National Socialism* (New York, Oxford Univ. Press, 1959) B199, remains the best analysis of the Nazi movement. A popular account is William L. Shirer, *The rise and fall of the Third Reich* (New York, Simon and Schuster, 1960) B200. A first rate account of the Spanish civil war is found in Hugh Thomas, *The Spanish civil war* (New York, Eyre, 1961) B201.

AMERICAN HISTORY: Two reliable texts in American history are Richard Hofstadter, William Miller, and Daniel Aaron, *The United*

States; the history of a republic (Englewood Cliffs, N.J., Prentice-Hall, 1957) B202, and Harry J. Carman, Harold Syrett, and Bernard Wishy, *A history of the American people* (2d ed. rev. New York, Knopf, 1960) B203.

Colonial period: An excellent one-volume text is Curtis P. Nettels, *The roots of American civilization* (New York, Crofts, 1938) B204, which should be supplemented by Oscar T. Barck, Jr., and Hugh T. Lefler, *Colonial America* (New York, Macmillan, 1958) B205. Charles M. Andrews, *The colonial period of American history* New Haven, Conn., Yale Univ. Press, 1934-38) B206, remains the definitive account. The background of English migration is set forth with distinction in Wallace Notestein, *The English people on the eve of colonization, 1603-1630* (New York, Harper, 1954) B207. Two studies of unusual value are Bernard Bailyn, *The New England merchants in the seventeenth century* (Cambridge, Harvard Univ. Press, 1955) B208, and Perry Miller, *The New England mind* (Boston, Beacon Press, 1961) B209. On colonial southern life see Carl Bridenbaugh, *Myths and realities; societies of the colonial South* (Baton Rouge, Louisiana State Univ. Press, 1952) B210. A major revision of the extent of franchise and other democratic devices is set forth in Robert E. Brown, *Middle-class democracy and the revolution in Massachusetts, 1691-1780* (Ithaca, N.Y., Cornell Univ. Press, 1955) B211.

The American Revolution: A brief but succinct account of the revolutionary period is found in Edmund S. Morgan, *The birth of the republic, 1763-89* (Chicago, Univ. of Chicago Press, 1956) B212. This should be read in conjunction with John C. Wahlke, *The causes of the American Revolution* (Rev. ed. Boston, Heath, 1962) B213, which brings together a number of conflicting interpretations. The best recent work on the subject is John C. Miller, *Origins of the American Revolution* (Rev. ed. Stanford, Calif., Stanford Univ. Press, 1959) B214. Carl Becker, *The Declaration of Independence* (New York, P. Smith, 1933) B215, remains a classic evaluation of the ideas that inspired the document. Still valuable is Randolph G. Adams, *Political ideas of the American Revolution* (Durham, Trinity College Press, 1922) B216. An excellent summary of the historical treatment of George III is given by Herbert Butterfield, *George III and the historians* (Rev. ed. New York, Macmillan, 1959) B217. The best account of the Confederation period is Merrill Jensen, *The new nation* (New York, Knopf, 1950) B218. For an inspired treatment of the social implications of the Revolution see J. Franklin Jameson, *The American Revolution considered as a social movement* (New York, P. Smith, 1926) B219. Charles A. Beard, *An economic interpretation of the Constitution of the United States* (New York, Macmillan, 1913) B220, remains the most influential account although it should be read in light of the severe strictures placed on it by Robert E. Brown, *Charles Beard and the Constitution; a critical analy-*

sis of "An economic interpretation of the Constitution" (Princeton, N.J., Princeton Univ. Press, 1956) B221.

The early Republic: The best survey of the Federalist period is John C. Miller, *The Federalist era, 1789-1801* (New York, Harper, 1960) B222. No less useful is Leonard D. White, *The Federalists; a study in administrative history* (New York, Macmillan, 1948) B223. White's *The Jeffersonians; a study in administrative history, 1808-1829* (New York, Macmillan, 1951) B224, is an excellent study of Jeffersonian administrative practices. Two dependable political studies are Noble E. Cunningham, *The Jeffersonian Republicans* (Chapel Hill, Univ. of North Carolina Press, 1957) B225, and Manning J. Dauer, The *Adams Federalists* (Baltimore, Johns Hopkins Press, 1953) B226. The following biographies are useful: Gilbert Chinard, *Honest John Adams* (Boston, Little, Brown, 1933) B227; John C. Miller, *Alexander Hamilton; portrait in paradox* (New York, Harper, 1959) B228; Marcus Cunliffe, *George Washington, man and monument* (Boston, Little, Brown, 1958) B229; and Albert Nock, *Jefferson* (New York, Harcourt, Brace, 1926) B230. Charles A. Beard, *Economic origins of Jeffersonian democracy* (New York, Macmillan, 1915) B231, still remains of value. On the later Jeffersonians see George Dangerfield, *The era of good feeling* (New York, Harcourt, Brace, 1952) B232, an impressive achievement. A great two volume biography is Samuel F. Bemis, *John Quincy Adams and the foundations of American foreign policy* (New York, Knopf, 1949) B233, and *John Quincy Adams and the union.* (New York, Knopf, 1956) B234.

Jacksonian democracy: A good introductory study is Glyndon G. Van Deusen, *The Jacksonian era, 1828-1848* (New York, Harper, 1959) B235. It should be read with Leonard D. White, *The Jacksonians; a study in administrative history, 1829-1861* (New York, Macmillan, 1954) B236. Frederick J. Turner, *The United States, 1830-1850* (New York, Holt, 1935) B237, remains a durable monument to one of America's great historians. A brilliant but controversial interpretation is Arthur M. Schlesinger, Jr., *The age of Jackson* (Boston, Little, Brown, 1945) B238. A provocative study is found in Marvin Meyers, *The Jacksonian persuasion; politics and belief* (Stanford, Calif., Stanford Univ. Press, 1957) B239. A major challenge to accepted treatments of Jacksonian democracy is Lee Benson, *The concept of Jacksonian democracy* (Princeton, N.J., Princeton Univ. Press, 1961) B240. A major revision of accepted concepts is found in Bray Hammond, *Banks and politics in America; from the Revolution to the Civil War* (Princeton, N.J., Princeton Univ. Press, 1957) B241. For ante-bellum reform see Alice F. Tyler, *Freedom's ferment* (Minneapolis, Univ. of Minnesota Press, 1944) B242, which has the virtue of a spirited presentation. A great study of Jacksonian democracy is found in Alexis de Tocqueville, *Democracy in America* (New York, Knopf, 1945) B243. Frederick J. Turner, *The frontier in American history* (New York, Holt, 1948) B244, is still important. Economic developments in the period are best treated in George R. Taylor, *The transportation revolution, 1815-1860* (New York, Rinehart, 1951) B245. On expansionist tendencies in the 19th century see Albert K. Weinberg, *Manifest destiny; a study of nationalist expansionism in American history* (Baltimore, Johns Hopkins Press, 1935) B246. Alfred H. Bill, *Rehearsal for conflict* (New York, Knopf, 1947) B247, is a lively treatment of the Mexican War.

The disruption of the Union: Basic to a treatment of the antebellum period is Allan Nevins, *Ordeal of the Union* (New York, Scribner, 1947) B248, and *The emergence of Lincoln* (New York, Scribner, 1950) B249. R. F. Nichols, *The disruption of American democracy* (New York, Macmillan, 1948) B250, and Avery O. Craven, *The coming of the Civil War* (2d ed. Chicago, Univ. of Chicago Press, 1957) B251, are important. Two works on slavery which illuminate the subject are Kenneth Stampp, *The peculiar institution: slavery in the ante-bellum South* (New York, Knopf, 1956) B252, and Stanley Elkins, *Slavery; a problem in American institutional and intellectual life* (Chicago, Univ. of Chicago Press, 1959) B253.

Civil War and Reconstruction: The basic text on the subject remains James G. Randall, *The Civil War and Reconstruction* (2d. ed. New York, Heath, 1961) B254. This should be supplemented with Allan Nevins, *The war for the Union* (New York, Scribner, 1959-60) B255. Benjamin P. Thomas, *Abraham Lincoln* (New York, Knopf, 1952) B256, is the best single volume account of the Civil War president's life. Clement Eaton, *A history of the Southern Confederacy* (New York, Macmillan, 1961) B257, is reliable. A brief but responsible treatment of Reconstruction is John H. Franklin, *Reconstruction: after the Civil War* (Chicago, Univ. of Chicago Press, 1961) B258. Two works by the same author deal perceptively with southern history after Reconstruction: C. Vann Woodward, *Origins of the New South, 1877-1913* (Baton Rouge, Louisiana State Univ. Press, 1951) B259, and *The strange career of Jim Crow* (New York, Oxford Univ. Press, 1955) B260.

Late 19th century: Several specialized studies of interest are Samuel P. Hays, *The response of industrialism, 1885-1914* (Chicago, Univ. of Chicago Press, 1957) B261; Thomas C. Cochran and William Miller, *The age of enterprise; a social history of industrial America* (Rev. ed. New York, Harper, 1961) B262; Robert G. McCloskey, *The American Supreme Court* (Chicago, Univ. of Chicago Press, 1960) B263; and Oscar Handlin's incisive essay on immigration, *The uprooted* (Boston, Little, Brown, 1951) B264. Matthew Josephson, *The politicos, 1865-1896* (New York, Harcourt, Brace, 1938) B265, is an irreverent account of fin de siècle politics.

Progressivism: Three publications of the New American Nations series that are excellent surveys of the period are: Harold U. Faulkner,

Politics, reform and expansion, 1890-1900 (New York, Harper, 1959) B266; George E. Mowry, *The era of Theodore Roosevelt, 1900-1912* (New York, Harper, 1958) B267; and Arthur S. Link, *Woodrow Wilson and the progressive era, 1910-1917* (New York, Harper, 1954) B268. Three perceptive treatments of American reform temperament are Richard Hofstadter, *The age of reform* (New York, Knopf, 1955) B269; Henry F. May, *The end of American innocence* (New York, Knopf, 1959) B270; and Eric F. Goldman, *Rendevous with destiny* (New York, Knopf, 1952) B271.

The twenties and normalcy: A solid but dull account of the roaring twenties is found in John D. Hicks, *Republican ascendancy, 1921-1933* (New York, Harper, 1960) B272. A charmingly written study of the period which has the virtue of provocative thinking is William E. Leuchtenburg, *The perils of prosperity, 1914-1932* (Chicago, Univ. of Chicago Press, 1958) B273. Frederick L. Allen, *Only yesterday* (New York, Harper, 1931) B274, has achieved the stature of a classic. Isabel Leighton, ed., *The aspirin age, 1919-1941* (New York, Simon and Schuster, 1949) B275, treats of the foibles of the twenties and thirties.

The New Deal and after: In history there occurs the moment when the facts of history become blurred by the direct involvement in the events of the authors of history. The present and past are too intertwined to permit a detached analysis. The safest approach to the period is a text treatment. For the 20th century Oscar T. Barck, Jr., and Nelson M. Blake, *Since 1900* (3d ed. New York, Macmillan, 1959) B276, is very good. On the depression see Broadus Mitchell, *The depression decade; from new era through New Deal, 1929-1941* (New York, Rinehart, 1947) B277. James M. Burns, *Roosevelt; the lion and the fox* (New York, Harcourt, Brace, 1956) B278, is the best one volume account of the four term president. Basil Rauch, *The history of the New Deal, 1933-1938* (New York, Creative Age Press, 1944) B279, is thorough. On foreign affairs see Allan Nevins, *The New Deal and world affairs* (New Haven, Conn., Yale Univ. Press, 1950) B280. For American entrance into World War II consult William L. Langer and S. Everett Gleason, *The challenge of isolation, 1937-1940* (New York, Harper, 1952) B281, and *The undeclared war, 1940-1941* (New York, Harper, 1953) B282. A good but controversial history of World War II is Chester Wilmot, *The struggle for Europe* (New York, Harper, 1952) B283. An excellent summary of the events between 1945-1955 is found in Eric F. Goldman, *The crucial decade: America, 1945-1955* (New York, Knopf, 1956) B284. A responsible text in foreign affairs is Julius W. Pratt, *A history of United States foreign policy* (New York, Prentice-Hall, 1955) B285.

The reader who acquaints himself with the above-listed books can be certain that he has a well rounded background in history. The object has been to identify works which are authoritative, but the needs of the beginner have been kept in mind too. The list should prove readable and stimulating.

James P. Shenton

History

B286. Adams, Charles K. A manual of historical literature. 3d ed. rev. and enl. New York, Harper, 1889. 720 p.

Superseded by the *Guide to Historical Literature*, 1931, but still useful for well selected older material and excellent critical notes.

B287. American Historical Association. Guide to historical literature. New York, Macmillan, 1961. 962 p.

Resembles the 1931 *Guide*, but is larger. The space allocated to European literature has been restricted to allow fuller coverage for Africa, Oceania, Australasia, and the Americas. Over 20,000 items are grouped into 35 major sections. Certain sections relate to topics (History & related studies, History of religions) while the rest deal with geographical areas and their peoples. The same general scheme of subdivision is used for each section. Most entries are briefly annotated, but the value of the *Guide* lies in the careful selection process exercised by each section editor, a recognized specialist. The reference value of this valuable new tool would have been greatly enhanced by a fuller index. The 1931 *Guide* is still useful for its depth in some areas, for older works not included in the new edition and for fuller annotations.

B288. Franz, Günther, *ed.* Bücherkunde zur Weltgeschichte vom Untergang des römischen Weltreiches bis zur Gegenwart. München, Oldenbourg, 1956. 544 p.

A valuable supplement for current material to the comparable Herre, Hofmeister and Stübe *Quellenkunde zur Weltgeschichte* work of 1910 (B290) and the *American Guide to Historical Literature* of 1931 (B287). Contains over 17,000 selected references. Omits treatment of ancient history. Includes titles in all European languages but emphasizes German language titles. Relatively little space given to countries with good national bibliographies. Evaluative annotations are fewer and briefer than those in the 1931 *Guide to historical literature*.

B289. Harvard guide to American history, by Oscar Handlin, *et al.* Cambridge, Belknap Press of Harvard Univ. Press, 1954. 689 p.

Follows the general plan of its predecessor Channing, Hart and Turner's *Guide to the study and teaching of American history* (Rev. ed. Boston, Ginn, 1912, 650 p.), but is more extensive especially in social and intellectual history. Chapters i-v consist of 66 essays dealing with methods, resources and materials of American history. Chapters v-xxx contain detailed reading lists arranged by historical periods. Each is prefaced by a summary which outlines the topics treated and then cites general and special works as well as sources, maps and relevant bibliographies. An extensive index

(143 p.) facilitates the use of the work. Terminal date for publications included is Dec. 31, 1950. The listings are carefully selected, well organized, but contain little critical or explanatory information.

B290. Herre, Paul. Quellenkund zur Weltgeschichte; ein Handbuch, unter Mitwirkung von Adolf Hofmeister und Rudolf Stübe, bear. und hrsg. von Paul Herre. Leipzig, Koehler, 1910. 400 p.
A well selected list, without comment, of significant historical works on all countries (3,923 items). Emphasis is on secondary works; occasional citation of primary sources and bibliographies. Indicates the existence of German translations. Supplemented to some extent by Günther Franz's *Bücherkunde zur Weltgeschichte* (B288).

B291. Humphreys, Robert A. Latin American history; a guide to the literature in English. Issued under the auspices of the Royal Institute of International Affairs. London, Oxford Univ. Press, 1958. 197 p.
This small, but important, guide achieves with distinction its purpose of unlocking the doors to the literature of Latin American history in the English language. The 2,089 references to books and periodical articles organized by topic, period and geographical area embrace besides history such supplementary areas as economics, politics and sociology. There is a "Biographical index" as well as a general index to authors, editors and translators. Plans have been renewed by the American Council of Learned Societies, the Social Science Research Council and the Hispanic Foundation for a comprehensive Guide to Latin American history.

B292. Langlois, Charles V. Manuel de bibliographie historique. Paris, Hachette, 1901-04. 2 v.
A fundamental work in historical studies which is still valuable for its comments on books cited and valuable suggestions and discussions of bibliographical method. Pt. 1, "Instruments bibliographiques." Pt. 2, "Histoire et organisation des études historiques."

B293. Paetow, Louis J. Guide to the study of medieval history. Rev. ed. Prepared under the auspices of the Medieval Academy of America. New York, Crofts, 1931. 643 p.
1st ed. 1917. 2d ed. adds material published between 1917 and 1928. A true "guide," this scholarly and critical work is divided into three main parts: (1) the most important general works in the study of medieval history (bibliographical works; books of reference; some auxiliaries to the study of medieval history, and a large collection of original sources); (2) general history of the Middle Ages, 500-1,500, and (3) medieval culture, 500-1,300. Pts 2 & 3 are arranged by topic and include an outline of the topic, special recommendations for reading and a bibliography which refers to pt 1. Under each heading the material is listed in order of importance. All the best works in English, French and German are noted with a more limited selection in Spanish and Italian. English history is not treated fully because of the bibliographical guidance for the medieval period found in Gross' *The sources and literature of English history* (B348). Includes extensive index of authors, editors, translators, subjects and titles of large collections. Completion of the revised and enlarged edition, directed by Prof. Gray C. Boyce, has been delayed and may have to be abandoned in favor of a "Guide to the literature of medieval history, 1930-1960."

B294. Sauvaget, Jean. Introduction à l'histoire de l'Orient musulman: éléments de bibliographie, rev. and enl. by C. Cahen. Paris, Adrien-Maisonneuve, 1961. 257 p.
A guide to Islamic history in the

Near East divided into three main sections: (1) problems and sources of Islamic history; (2) reference works and collections of documents; and (3) a basic bibliography of Islamic history. Locates copies (with call numbers) in 4 French libraries. Omits East and West Africa and India.

B295. U.S. *Library of Congress. General Reference and Bibliography Division.* A guide to the study of the United States; representative books reflecting the development of American life and thought. Washington, Govt. Print. Off., 1960. 1,193 p.

An impressive array of 6,487 titles arranged in 32 chapters with such headings as: literature; geography; diplomatic, military, intellectual and local history; economic life; politics; science and technology. The annotations, for nearly all entries, have been written to assist the reader in judging what the book contributes to an understanding of the country and they frequently cite and evaluate related works not included in the numbered entries. Terminal date for some sections is 1955; for others, 1958. Index of authors, subjects and titles. A supplement, to be published in 1966, is in preparation.

Geography

B296. Wright, John K. and Elizabeth T. Platt. Aids to geographical research; bibliographies, periodicals, atlases, gazetteers and other reference books. 2d ed. completely rev. New York, published for the American Geographical Society by Columbia Univ. Press, 1947. 331 p. (American Geographical Society. Research series no. 22)

Comprehensive guide of 1,174 geographical reference materials in various languages. In three main sections: (1) General aids, (2) Topical aids, (3) Regional aids and general geographical periodicals. Includes references to bibliographies in standard or important monographs.

Annotations are descriptive rather than critical. Author, subject and title index. Elio Migliorini's *Guida bibliografica allo studio della geografia.* (Napoli, Pironti, 1945. 265 p.) brings together an excellent selection of important general and specialized works (938 titles) which supplement those of Wright for the countries of Europe.

Biography

B297. Stevenson, Noel C. Search and research; the researchers handbook . . . rev. ed. Salt Lake City, Deseret, 1959. 364 p.

An experienced geneologist supplies a guide to official records and library resources. Main portion of book is arranged by state. Includes, besides the U.S. and its territories, briefer treatment of Canada, Philippine Islands, Cuba, and the British Isles. For each state gives information on historical societies and libraries, reference books, military rosters, rolls and records, official records, federal and state census material. First part of the book analyzes research procedure and problems and list general aids under such topics as pension files, church records, use of newspapers, etc. Some descriptive annotation.

REVIEWS OF THE LITERATURE

History

B298. American historical review. v. 1+ Oct. 1895+ New York. quarterly.

More than half of this 300-page quarterly is devoted to the literature of all periods. The main review section includes 200-250 signed reviews (500-2,000 words) of current publications. This is followed by short notices (150-350 words) on books, 300-400 a year, and a listing of periodical articles. Both sections are classified and international in scope.

The annual index (July issue) includes all books in both sections.

B299. English historical review. v. 1+ 1886+ London, Longmans Green. quarterly.

This major British historical journal devotes about one half of its 200 pages each quarter to book reviews. 60-80 major reviews (1,000-1,700 words) and 200-400 "Short notices" (100-600 words) are included annually. All are signed and all periods of history are covered. The July issue also contains "Notices of periodicals and occasional publications," which is a selective classified descriptive listing of some 400 articles appearing during the previous year. International in scope, but British writing emphasized. Annual index includes "List of reviews of books."

B300. Historical Association, London. Annual bulletin of historical literature. v. 1+ 1911+ London, 1912+.

Survey articles by specialists on the years output of historical works. Highly selective and best for British and other English language materials. General index, v. 1-12. 1911-22 (1923).

B301. Historische Zeitschrift. v. 1+ 1859+ Munich, Oldenbourg. bi-monthly.

A long respected source which devotes about half of each issue to a review of significant historical writing. "Buchbesprechungen" contains 100-200 long (500-2,500 words, critical reviews a year. "Anzeigen und Nachrichten" contains 200-300 brief notices (100-500 words) of books, and periodical articles. "Neue Bücher" is an uncritical classified list of recent books which runs to 1,500-2,500 items a year. Scope of all three sections is international. Annual index lists all book reviews and notices.

B302. Journal of modern history.

v. 1+ 1929+ Chicago, Univ. of Chicago Press. quarterly.

Devoted to the study of history since 1,500. International in scope. Affords short (500-1,500 words), critical, signed reviews for 200-300 works a year. A select, classified bibliography of current book publication in all countries is included in many issues (2-3 a year; 300-500 items). In addition longer review and bibliographical articles are a regular feature. All reviews are included in the annual index.

B303. Revista de historia de America. v. 1+ 1938+ Mexico, D.F. Instituto Pan Americano de Geografía e Historia. semi-annual.

Approximately one half of this historical review is devoted to bibliographical description of recent publications. "Reseñas de libros" contains critical, signed book reviews (250-2,000 words). Limited to Latin American publications on the history of Latin America or America as a whole, but outstanding works in other languages are often included. Each issue contains a section of the "Bibliographia de historia de America," an annotated bibliography of books and periodical articles published in the preceding 3 years. To date it includes over 20,000 numbered items. Bibliographical articles on special topics are an occasional feature.

B304. Revue historique. v. 1+ Jan-Jun., 1876+ Paris, Presses Universitaires de France. quarterly.

Resembles other outstanding quarterlies as a source on current literature of international importance. "Compte rendues critiques" contains long (400-2,000 words), signed, critical reviews (100-200 a year); "Notes bibliographiques," short single paragraph appraisals (200-300 a year). "Recueils périodiques et Sociétés Savantes" is a classified list of periodical articles and society publications. Bibliographical articles on special topics are a regular feature.

Special annual "Index bibliographique."

B305. Speculum; a journal of medieval studies. v. 1+ 1925+ Cambridge, Medieval Academy of America. quarterly.

Each issue includes over 100 (500-4,500 words) valuable critical reviews of the significant books in all languages that deal with any aspect of medieval civilization; also includes "A bibliography of American periodical literature," which lists 50-80 items an issue. An extensive "Books received" section (300-350 a year) affords a concise survey of recent publications. Annual index includes only major book reviews.

Geography

B306. Geographical journal. v. 1+ 1893+ London, Royal Geographical Society. quarterly.

This major British geographical journal carries 4-8 major review articles a year (600-1,800 words) and its "Review" section evaluates over 200 current publications in short (100-600 words) but concise reviews. Less important materials receive short notices (70-100 items a year). All books reviewed are included in annual index.

B307. Petermanns geographische Mitteilungen. v. 1+ 1855+ Gotha, VEB Herman Haack. quarterly.

The sections of this periodical devoted to geographical literature and especially to maps, are of exceptional importance. The section "Geographische Literaturbericht" is divided into 2 parts: (1) "Besprechungen" contains 100-150 critical signed reviews (200-1,000 words); (2) "Neuerscheinunger Bucher und Schriften" lists 150-200 recent publications. "Neuerscheinunger Zeitschriftenschau" lists the tables of contents of recent geographical journals. "Kartenbibliographie," an irregular feature, lists recent books on cartography, atlases and maps. International in scope.

ABSTRACTS AND DIGESTS

B308. Historical Abstracts; a quarterly covering the world's periodical literature, 1775-1945, ed. by Eric H. Boehm. v. 1 + March, 1955+ Santa Barbara, Calif., Clio Press, 1955+ quarterly.

An attempt to provide abstracts in English of articles on the political, diplomatic, economic, social, cultural and intellectual history of the period 1775-1945 appearing in periodicals throughout the world, from June 1954. Particularly useful for those who wish to know what is being written in the less familiar languages of Eastern Europe. In addition to scholarly journals it covers "peripheral" journals which carry occasional historical articles. Does not cover local history. Annual subject and author indexes.

BIBLIOGRAPHIES—CURRENT

History

B309. L'Année philologique; bibliographie critique et analytique de l'antiquité gréco-latine, publiée sous la direction de J. Marouzeau. 1924/26+ Paris, Société d'Édition "Les Belles Lettres," 1928+ annual.

Each of these valuable annual surveys is divided into 2 parts: classical authors and works (arranged by author A-Z); a classified subject section which covers the whole field of history and culture of the classical world. (Literary history, linguistics, antiquities, history, law, philosophy, etc.) Lists recently published books, with their reviews, and periodical articles with some indication of their contents, indexes to collections, ancient authors, humanists, and modern authors. Continues Jules Marouzeau's *Dix années de bibliographie classique . . . 1914-1924* (Paris, 1927) and S. Lambrino's *Bibliographique classique des années 1896 à 1914* (Paris, 1951 +).

B310. Bibliografia storica nazionale. v. 1 + 1939 + Rome, Scalia Editore, 1942 + annual.

Classified listing of books and articles on Italian history published in Italy since 1939. Foreign publications are included only if they are reviewed in Italian periodicals. Regional history is fully covered. Occasional citation of reviews. Name index.

B311. Bibliographie annuelle de l'histoire de France du cinquième siécle à 1939. 1955 + Paris, Éditions du Centre National de la Recherche Scientifique, 1956 + annual.

The newest work in the succession of annual bibliographies of French history. Intended as a continuation of the *Répertoire bibliographique de l'histoire de France* by P. Caron and H. Stein (B340) but with the terminal date extended from 1914 to 1939. The classified listing follows the plan of Caron and Stein and the items included (5,000-6,000 a year) are drawn from all European languages and include books and periodical articles. No annotations. Subject and author index.

B312. Indice historico español. Barcelona, Ed. Teide. v. 1 + 1953 + quarterly.

This comprehensive bibliography has as its objectives (1) to register, both for Spain and foreign countries, all books, pamphlets, articles and significant book reviews dealing with the history of Spain and Spanish America, Asia, Oceania and Africa and (2) to make this information available to scholars within 3 months of the item's appearance. Titles are annotated and evaluated by experts and references to critical reviews are often given. Republished in bound form with title *Bibliographía histórica de España e Hispanoamerica*. v. 1, 1953-1954, v. 2, 1955-56, v. 3, 1957 (to appear annually beginning with vol. 3). Full author and subject indexes.

B313. International bibliography of historical sciences, ed. for the International Committee of Historical Sciences. v. 1 + 1926 + Paris, Colin, 1930 +

Publisher varies. v. 15 (1940-1946 not yet published). An attempt to bring under control major historical contributions, without reference to place or language of origin. Each volume consists of selected classified lists, noting book reviews but otherwise uncritical, of books and articles in most languages. History is interpreted broadly to include political, economic, constitutional, religious and other cultural and social developments. Quality of the selection has varied, but it is of particular value for countries without national bibliographies. The gap in coverage is somewhat met by L.B. Frewer *Bibliography of historical writings published in Great Britain and the Empire, 1940-1945* (B347), P.F. Palumbo, *Bibliografia storica internazionale, 1940-1947* (B332) and W. Holtzmann and G. Ritter *Die deutsche Geschichtswissenschaft im zweiten Weltkrieg* (B329).

B314. International guide to medieval studies; a quarterly index periodical literature. v. 1 + 1961 + Darien, Conn., American Bibliographic Service. quarterly.

A selective mimeographed listing of current periodical articles and book reviews on medieval subjects published in western languages. Two major parts: an alphabetical author listing of articles (400-500 a year) with a subject index; and the book review index (900-1,000 reviews annually listed by author) with indices of authors, editors, translators and reviewers. Cumulative annual indexes. Another valuable current listing is the quarterly bibliography in *Cahiers de civilisation médiévale*. v. 1 + 1958 + (Poitiers, Centre d'Études Superieures de Civilisations Médiévale), a classified arrangement of 1,700-2,000 books and articles a year with a cumulative author index.

B315. Jahresberichte für deutsche Geschichte. v. 1-15/16, 1925-1939/1940. Leipzig, Koehler, 1927-1942; Neue Folge. v. 1+ 1949+ Berlin, Akademie-Verlag, 1952+

An annual bibliography which in effect brings Dahlmann-Waitz (B343) up to date. The first part of each volume lists material by period up to 1919. The second part is an evaluation of the items in Pt. 1, each section being written by a specialist. To date the "Neue Folge" consists only of the bibliography. It lists writings in all major European languages of general interest for German history through 1945. It omits items of purely provincial or local significance. The index of authors and the topical index are excellent. The years between 1941 and 1948 have not yet been covered.

B316. Writings on British history, 1934+ London, Cape, 1937+ annual.

1939 vol. published in 1953. 2 vols. covering 1940-1945 published in 1960. A comprehensive bibliography of books and articles on the history of Great Britain from about 450 A.D. to 1914 with an appendix containing a select list of publications on British history since 1914. Entries are grouped under "general works" and then under periods with subject subdivisions. No annotations are included but entries for books refer to reputable reviews. Emphasis is upon English titles, but many European language materials are included. Subject and author indexes. Volumes covering 1901-33 are being planned.

B317. Writings on American history, 1906+ New York, 1908-10; Washington, 1911-13; New Haven, 1914-19; Washington, 1921+

Publisher and subtitle vary. An excellent annual, classified bibliography with author, title, and subject index. With gaps for writings published in 1904-05 and 1941-47, the series goes back to 1902. From 1906-35 the scope included Canada, the West Indies and the Pacific Islands. Beginning in 1936, the scope narrows to works dealing with the territory and foreign relations of the U.S. All volumes go back to "primitive times," but terminal dates vary and preface of each volume should be checked for its limitations. Includes many contents and descriptive notes and refers to critical reviews. In postwar volumes the citation of reviews has been dropped and the index has been expanded. A long-standing need of a cumulative index to supplement the indexes of the annual volumes was partially remedied in 1956 with the publication of a 1,115 page author, subject and occasional title index for the years 1902-1940. Most valuable for locating material by and about historians. Subject approach is difficult to use and often misleading. There are many typographical errors and some deadend cross references.

Geography

B318. Acta geographica. Supplément bibliographique. 1949+ Paris, Société de Geographie, 1949+ quarterly.

This mimeographed list was published monthly from 1949-1959. Lists all books and series publications received by the library and gives for nearly all of them a short critical evaluation. Does not include periodical articles. Lists over 600 items a year.

B319. American Geographical Society of New York. Current geographical publications; additions to the research catalogue of the American Geographical Society. v. 1+ 1938+ New York. monthly except July and August.

A classified index covering books (with some analytical entries for chapters or sections) and periodical articles. Each issue contains approximately 600 references. Arranged first by general subjects and then by regions and countries. Annual author, subject (using classified groups), and regional indexes.

B320. Bibliographie cartographique internationale, 1936+ Paris, Colin, 1938+ annual.
Irregular to 1948 with varying title and publishers. Presently published under the auspices of the Comité National de Géographique Français and the Union Geographique Internationale. An extensive annual listing of all types of maps, charts and atlases arranged by area. Author index and brief subject index.

B321. Bibliographie géographique internationale. v. 1+ 1891+ Paris, Colin, 1894+ annual.
Title varies slightly; v. 1-24 issued with *Annales de geographie*. This is the most convenient, comprehensive and most important of the annual geographical bibliographies. All aspects of geography are covered. Arrangement is primarily by continent and country, with subject subdivisions, preceded by a general section. The material included is critically selected and to most items brief critiques are appended. Author index only.

B322. Geographisches Jahrbuch. 1866+ Gotha, Perthes. 1 or 2 v. yearly.
An important bibliographical yearbook. Each volume contains a series of reports on the status and progress of study in various fields of geography, the fields covered varying from year to year. The items cited (books and periodical articles) are not annotated, but each section has an introductory survey. An index for the years 1866-1935 was published in v. 40 and 52. For a convenient key to the reports in this series (v. 1-58, 1866-1943) see Wright and Platt *Aids to geographical research*, p. 52-57 (B296).

B323. Royal Geographical Society. New geographical literature and maps. n.s. v. 1+ 1951+ London. semi-annual.
A select, unannotated list of additions to the library, including all new atlases and maps received. Continues *Recent geographical literature, maps and photographs . . .* published as a supplement to the *Geographical journal*, 1918-1940. Periodical articles listed are now drawn from approximately 130 periodicals. Titles in non-western languages are given in translation only. Lack of indexes is a drawback.

Biography

B324. Biography index. v. 1+ 1946+ New York, Wilson. quarterly with annual and triennial cumulations.
An index to all types of biographical material appearing in 1,500 current periodicals and in books of individual or collected biography published in English. Obituaries of natural and international interest are included. Portraits are indicated where they appear in connection with indexed material. Arrangement is alphabetical by biographee with an index by profession.

BIBLIOGRAPHIES—CURRENT

General

B325 Boehm, Eric H. and Lalit Adolphus, *eds*. Historical periodicals; an annotated world list of historical and related serial publications. Santa Barbara, Calif., Clio Press, 1961. 618 p. (Clio reference publications no. 1)
Planned as a successor to the work of Caron and Jayre (B326). Over 5,000 current titles in history and related fields are grouped by country and then arranged alphabetically by title. Includes transactions, acts, and irregular publications not ordinarily classed as periodicals and interprets history in its widest sense. Specifically historical journals are given "long entries" including full biblio-

graphic data, description of contents and occasional notes on special features. Titles in related fields receive abbreviated entries. Foreign titles translated into English. Cross references and an index of titles. A much enlarged edition to be issued in fasicules and including monographic series and bibliographical publications is planned.

B326. Caron, Pierre and Marc Jayre. World list of historical periodicals and bibliographies. New York, Wilson, 1939. 391 p.

An alphabetical list of 3,103 periodicals used in preparing the *International bibliography of historical sciences* (B313). Broad interpretation of history to include allied subjects, *e.g.*, palaeography, genealogy, ethnography, etc. Indexes of editors, subjects and abbreviations. Supplemented and somewhat superseded by *Historical periodicals.* (B325). See also, Heinrich Kramm, *ed. Bibliographie historischer Zeitschriften, 1939-1951* (Marburg, Rasch, 1952-1954. 3 v.) which provides details (from their first issue) of periodicals current between 1939-1951 in 25 European countries.

B327. Chevalier, Cyr U. Répertoire des sources historiques du Moyen Âge. Nouv. éd. refondue, corr. et augm. Paris, Picard, 1894-1907 2v. in 4.

Contents: Bio-bibliagraphie, 1905-07. 2 v.; Topo-bibliographie, 1894-1903. 2 v. Far from complete, contains no evalution, but useful because the number of sources is so voluminous. Part one deals with people and is arranged alphabetically by the French form of the name. For each entry brief biographical data are given plus references to books, periodicals, society publications, etc., which contain information on the person dealt with. Part two supplies similar information for places and topics of medieval history.

B328. Coulter, Edith M. and Me-

lanie Gerstenfeld. Historical bibliographies; a systematic and annotated guide. Berkeley, Univ. of California Press, 1935. 206 p.

Carefully selected and well annotated list of important retrospective and current bibliographies of printed (but not archival) materials for each country. Periodicals are recommended to supplement the retrospective bibliographies. Entries are mainly in English, French and German with occasional citation to reviews. Out of date in many sections. For English language material *Bibliographic index: a cumulative bibliography of bibliographies* (A69), is a useful supplementary tool.

B329. Holtzmann, Walther and Gerhard Ritter. Die deutsche Geschichtswissenschaft im zweiten Weltkreig; Bibliographie des historischen Schrifttums deutscher Autoren 1939-1945. Marburg/Lahn, Simmons Verlag, 1951. 2 v.

Covers German historical writing on all phases of history produced during the war years and thus helps supplement the *International bibliography of the historical sciences* (B313) and the *Jahresberichte für deutsche Geschichte* (B315) which were suspended for those years.

B330. Jahresberichte der Geschichtswissenschaft; im Auftrage der Historischen Gesellschaft zu Berlin. v. 1-36, 1878-1913. Berlin, Mittler, 1880-1916. annual.

International in scope this work is a comprehensive and accurate classified list of historical studies published in each year. It includes both books and periodical articles in the leading European languages. A valuable record for the period covered. Continued for Germany only by the *Jahresberichte der deutschen Geschichte*, v. 1-7, 1918-1924. (Breslau, 1920-26.) See B315.

B331. Kerner, Robert J. Slavic Europe; a selected bibliography in the Western European languages, comprising history, languages, and literature. Cambridge, Harvard Univ. Press, 1918. 402 p. (Harvard bibliographies. Library series v. 1).

A basic list of fundamental works on various aspects of Slavonic life published in Western languages to 1914. Arrangement is by six large ethnic groups (Russians, Poles, Bohemians and Slovaks, etc.) each of which is subdivided into history, language and literature. Author index. No annotations.

B332. Palumbo, Pier F. Bibliografia storica internazionale, 1940-1947; con una introduzione sullo stato degli studi storici durante e dopo la seconda guerra mondiale. Rome, Edizioni del Lavoro, 1950. 241 p.

Along with Frewer's work (B347) this work partially fills the period not covered by the *International bibliography of historical sciences* (B313). Lists 3,572 items by broad topic (storia generale, storia antica, storia bizantina; storia medievale e moderna), subdivided by subject. Major emphasis is on Italian materials but works in all major European languages are included.

B333. Potthast, August. Bibliotheca historica Medii Aevi. Wegweiser durch die Geschichtswerke des europäischen Mittelalters bis 1500. 2. verb. und verm. Aufl. Berlin, Weber, 1896. 2 v.

Sometimes inaccurate but the most complete source available for printed materials on Medieval Europe. Pt. 1 includes lists of the great general collections and the collected "Scriptores" for each country. Pt. 2 is an alphabetical list of medieval writers with, when possible, characterizing phrase and dates indicating manuscripts editions and commentaries. Sometimes inaccurate. A completely new *Repertory of medieval history sources* which will entirely replace Potthast is in preparation under the auspices of the International Scientific Committee for the Edition of a Collection of Sources of European Medieval History.

B334. Rule, John C., *ed.* A select bibliography for students of history. Cambridge, Mass., [Printed by the College of General Education, Boston University] 1957. 215 p. (processed)

Extensive, discriminating selections made by the Harvard Graduate History Club for the use of graduate students of history. The entries are classified under: American, Canadian & Latin American history; Modern European history; Ancient and Medieval History; and Eurasian history. Emphasis on more recent publications; special attention has been given to periodical literature. For the non-familiar language areas works in western languages have been emphasized. No annotations or index.

Asia

B335. Association of British Orientalists. A select list of books on the civilizations of the Orient, ed. by W.A.C.H. Dobson. Oxford, Clarendon Press, 1955. 76 p.

A brief, but authoritative, bibliography of basic materials prepared by members of the Association. Covers Egypt, the Middle East, India, Southeast Asia and the Far East, from ancient to modern times. Primarily English language titles. Some items annotated.

B336. Kerner, Robert J. Northeastern Asia: a selected bibliography. Berkeley, Univ. of California Press, 1939. 2 v.

Nearly 14,000 printed works in Oriental and European languages relating to China, Manchuria, Mongolia, Tibet, Central Asia, Japan, Korea and Asiatic Russia. Titles in oriental languages are transliterated and translated. Scope is wide, but treatment is uneven. Lack of author index a handicap.

Europe

B337. Mayer, Hans E. Bibliographie zur Geschichte der Kreuzzüge. Hannover, Hahnsche, 1960. 271 p.

An extremely valuable and detailed historical bibliography of the period of the Crusades. Aids in bringing Paetow (B293) up to date in this area. 5,362 entries (books and periodical articles in all languages) arranged under a detailed classification scheme with an index of authors, editors and translators. Includes: auxiliary subjects, especially geography; primary sources by medieval authors; and secondary sources through 1959. No annotations but most important works are starred.

B338. Ragatz, Lowell J. A bibliography for the study of European history, 1815 to 1939. Ann Arbor, Mich., Edwards, 1942. 272 p.

A classified bibliography of over 10,000 items emphasizing books and articles in English, German and French. Three main sections: (1) Europe as a whole, (2) Individual countries, and (3) International relations. No annotations. Detailed table of contents but no index. Supplements issued in 1943, 1945 and 1957.

France

B339. Caron, Pierre. Bibliographie des travaux publiés de 1866 à 1897 sur l'histoire de la France depuis 1789. Paris, Cornély, 1912. 831 p.

A valuable bibliography continuing, chronologically, the work of Saulnier and Martin (B342). It is a classified arrangement of 13,496 titles of books, periodical articles, pamphlets and society publications. References to book reviews are made for important items. It is continued for material published since 1897 by Répertoire méthodique de l'histoire moderne et contemporaine de la France (B341).

B340. Caron, Pierre and Henri Stein. Répertoire bibliographique de l'histoire de France. Paris, Picard, 1923-38. 6 v.

A biennial classified bibliography of books and articles on the history of France from earliest times until 1914. The standard current work for the period. Cites book reviews and gives explanatory notes when necessary. v. 7-9, 1932-1945 in preparation. Continued by Bibliographie annuelle de l'histoire de France. (B311).

B341. Répertoire méthodique de l'histoire moderne et contemporaine de la France pour les années 1898-1913. Paris, Rieder, 1899-1932. 11 v.

Continues P. Caron's work covering the period 1866-1897. An annual, subject arranged bibliography of books and articles published during the period concerning French history since 1500. Some entries have explanatory annotations and references to book reviews are included. Vols. for 1907/09 and 1913/-19 in preparation. Continued by P. Caron's Répertoire bibliographique de l'histoire de France (B340).

B342. Saulnier, Eugene and A. Martin. Bibliographie des travaux publiés de 1866 à 1897 sur l'histoire de la France de 1500 à 1789. Paris, Presses Universitaires de France, 1932-38. 2 v.

A classified list of books and articles, in various languages, with references to critical reviews. Continued by Pierre Caron's Bibliographie des travaux publiés de 1866 à 1897 sur l'histoire de la France depuis 1789 (B339).

Germany

B343. Dahlmann, Friedrich C. and Georg Waitz. Quellenkunde der deutschen Geschichte. 9. Aufl. Hrsg. von Hermann Haering. Leipzig, Koehler, 1931-32. 2 v.

The standard bibliography of German history in all its phases through

1919. Classifies virtually all works of any importance on German history in the German language. It is less complete in listing non-German works. Minor titles are printed in smaller type; otherwise there is no evaluation of the works cited. Volume 2; index. A new edition is in preparation.

Great Britain

B344. Bibliography of British history; Tudor period, 1485-1603, ed. by Conyers Read. 2d ed. Oxford, Clarendon Press, 1959. 624 p.

B345. ———; Stuart period, 1603-1704, ed. by Godfrey Davies. Oxford, Clarendon Press, 1928. 459 p.

B346. ———; The eighteenth century, 1714-1789, ed. by Stanley Pargellis and D.J. Medley. Oxford, Clarendon Press, 1951. 642 p.
These 3 volumes provide a continuation of Gross (B348). As selective, annotated bibliographies, they cover both primary and secondary source material, pamphlets and periodical articles. History is interpreted in a wide sense. Author and subject indexes. Mary F. Keeler has begun work on a revision of the Stuart period and plans are being made for further volumes to continue the work where Pargellis and Medley left off at 1789.

B347. Frewer, Louis B. Bibliography of historical writings published in Great Britain and the Empire, 1940-1945. Oxford, Blackwell, 1947. 346 p.
Intended to partially fill the gap in the International bibliography of historical sciences, this work is edited in the same manner and format. Includes 5,315 items (books, articles and reviews), an index of places and an index of persons. Continued by Bibliography of historical works issued in the United Kingdom, 1946-1956. (London, Institute of Histor-

ical Research, Univ. of London, 1967. 388 p.) and the volume for the years 1957-1960 (London, 1962. 236 p.)

B348. Gross, Charles. Sources and literature of English history from the earliest times to about 1485. 2d ed. New York, Longmans, 1915. 820 p.
Best bibliography for its period. A systematic survey of the more useful sources on political, constitutional, legal, social and economic history of England, Wales and Ireland. Scotland is omitted. Covers books, pamphlets and papers in collected essays, journals, and transactions of societies. Only incidental attention to manuscripts. Includes all continental material of any value to students of English history. Critical and descriptive annotations for many entries. General index. A revised edition, under the direction of Prof. Edgar B. Graves, is in preparation.

B349. London University. Institute of Historical Research. Guide to the historical publications of the societies of England and Wales, ed. by E.L.C. Mullins. London, Univ. of London, Athlone Press (In preparation)
Has been coordinated with the Bibliographies of British history (B344-346) and Writings on British history (B316) and will cover 1901-1933 only. For Scotland see Charles S. Terry Catalogue of the publications of Scottish historical and kindred clubs and societies . . . 1780-1908. (Glasgow, MacLehose, 1909. 253 p.) and its continuation by Cyril Matheson, covering the period 1908-1927 (Aberdeen, Milne and Hutchinson, 1928. 323 p.)

Spain

B350. Sánchez Alonso, Benito. Fuentes de la historia española e hispanoamericana. 3 ed. corr. y puesta al día. Madrid, Consejo Superior de Investigaciones Científicas, 1952. 3 v.

The most comprehensive modern guide to the printed sources and secondary works of Spanish history arranged by chronological divisions and including both books and articles. Material has been included to about 1950. Many of the 2,300 entries carry short annotations; sometimes references to reviews. Supplemented by *Indice histórico español* (B312).

United States

B351. Beers, Henry P. Bibliographies in American history; guide to materials for research. New York, Wilson, 1942. 487 p.

A comprehensive, classified list of over 11,000 bibliographies published separately and included in other works. Covers political, diplomatic, religious, cultural and educational history. No limitation as to language or national origin of the bibliography. Chap. 3 lists bibliographies of all federal department publications. Chap. 14 lists individual state bibliographies. No annotations. Author and subject index.

B352. Griffin, Appleton P.C. Bibliography of American historical societies. 2d ed. rev. and enl. Washington, Govt. Print. Off., 1907. 1374 p. (American Historical Association. Annual report, 1905. v.2)

Index to reports, proceedings, transactions, historical records and studies, historical collections, diaries, and other publications emanating from ca. 500 American and Canadian historical societies from the time of their commencement to 1905. Included are university historical series such as the *Harvard historical studies*. National societies are listed first, followed by local societies, arranged by state, and then the Canadian section. Subject, author, biography, and society indexes. Continued informally in *Writings on American history* (B317).

Geography

B353. Harris, Chauncy D. and and Jerome D. Fellmann. International list of geographical serials. Chicago, Univ. of Chicago Press, 1960. 194 p. (Univ. of Chicago. Dept. of Geography. Research paper no. 63)

New edition of the senior author's work of 1950. Essentially an inventory of those periodicals (current and noncurrent) which are primarily geographic in content. The 1,637 entries are arranged by country of issue. Entry includes reference to the title's page location in the *Union list of serials, New serial titles* or the British *Union catalogue of periodicals*. Introductory material printed in English, German, French and Russian.

B354. Logan, Marguerite. Geographical bibliography for all the major nations of the world; selected books and magazine articles. Ann Arbor, Mich., Edwards, 1959. 396 p.

Over 7,000 recent items chosen to give students and general readers "accurate facts with which to think geographically about the area being dealt with." (Pref.) Arrangement is by area and the entries are unannotated. Lack of an index is a handicap.

B355. Pelzer, Karl J. Selected bibliography on the geography of Southeast Asia. New Haven, Conn., Southeast Asia Studies, Yale Univ., 1949-56. 3 v.

A companion to *Bibliography of the peoples and cultures of mainland Southeast Asia* by J.F. Embree (E160) and *Bibliography of Indonesian peoples and cultures* by R. Kennedy (E164). Intended as a selective reference and reading guide to the physical, cultural, economic and political geography of Southeast Asia. V. 1 deals with Southeast Asia in general; v. 2, with the Philippines; v. 3, with Malaya. Entries are arranged under broad subject headings with some subdivision. V. 3, Malaya, was expanded beyond the scope of the first two parts to devote far greater attention to anthropology. Includes books and articles. Lacks an index. Subsequent volumes will cover other Southeast Asian countries.

B356. Salinari, Marina E. Bibliografia degli scritti di geografia urbana, 1901-1954. Roma, Consiglio Nazionale delle Ricerche, 1948-56. 2 v. (Consiglio Nazionale delle Ricerche. Centro di Studi per la Geografia Antropica. Memoire di geografia antropica, v. 2 and v. 11)

A bibliography of writings on urban geography published in all countries from 1901-1954. Following a section on general works the 3,950 entries are arranged by geographical areas with an index of authors. Includes books and articles. Some brief annotations.

B357. Syracuse University. *Dept. of Geography*. Basic readings in geography; an annotated list of important materials and reference sources recommended especially for the Doctoral Candidate in geography. Rev. ed. Syracuse, N.Y., 1959. 56 p.

A classified listing (345 items) which presents a minimum number of standard works in each of the major fields that contain the substance of geographical research. Includes major reference sources. Brief annotations. No index.

Biography

B358. American genealogical-biographical index to American genealogical, biographical and local history materials, ed. by Fremont Rider. Middletown, Conn., Godfrey Memorial Library, 1952+ (In progress).

Continues as "Series two" the work begun under the title *American genealogical index* (Middletown, Conn., 1942-52. 48 v.). These two works represent a monumental index to genealogical material. It is estimated that "Series two" will contain

references to over twelve million "un-traceable" Americans. Indexes not only genealogies and family histories but also books of early vital records of towns, churches, sects, etc. Exact bibliographic citation is given for the works indexed. In the main index the entries are arranged alphabetically giving name, year of birth, state where the person lived, profession and citation to references in key form.

B359. Biographical information; where to find it. Detroit, Gale Research Company. (In preparation)

A bibliography of published biographical data (Who's whos, directories, yearbooks, etc.) as well as unpublished collections such as alumni association files, professional society records. Primary emphasis is on U.S. sources but some international, multi-national and foreign sources are included. Ca. 2,500 entries arranged by country. Each item is fully annotated. Title, author and subject index.

B360. Dargan, Marion. Guide to American biography. Albuquerque, Univ. of New Mexico Press, 1949-52. 510 p.

Arranged chronologically by generation and then by geographical area this bibliography locates material on 380 outstanding or representative Americans. For each individual biographical information is listed under original sources and separately published biographies, as well as references to collective biography and historical works containing biographical or cognate information. Many entries annotated and occasional reviews are cited. Subject index by occupation or field of activity. Alphabetical biographee index.

B361. Kaplan, Louis. A bibliography of American autobiographies. Madison, Univ. of Wisconsin Press, 1961. 372 p.

A comprehensive compilation of 6,377 autobiographies published from the colonial period to 1945. For each autobiography there is given: a brief statement giving the author's main experience; dates and locale in which he lived. Excludes "episodic accounts, journals, diaries, collections of letters, autobiographies serially published, manuscript autobiographies, fictional and spurious works." Locates copies in one library. Especially valuable for the rare material included. The subject index reveals (1) the occupations of the autobiographers, (2) where they lived, and (3) the important historical events in which they played a part.

B362. Matthews, William. American diaries; an annotated bibliography of American diaries written prior to the year 1861. Berkeley, Univ. of California Press, 1945. 383 p. (Univ. of California. Publications in English, v. 16).

Includes diaries written in, or translated into English by Americans or by foreign visitors between the years 1629 and 1861. Manuscript diaries are excluded. Separately published works which include diaries (histories, genealogies, biographies, etc.) are fully cited. Brief biographical information given for each diarist with descriptive notes and occasional evaluation of the diary. Arranged chronologically according to date of first entry. Alphabetical index of diarists.

B363. Matthews, William. British autobiographies; an annotated bibliography of British autobiographies published or written before 1951. Berkeley, Univ. of California Press, 1955. 376 p.

Includes 6,654 entries for persons born in the British Isles and naturalized British subjects. Autobiographies relating wholly to life in Canada, South Africa, New Zealand, Australia and the U.S. are omitted. Arranged alphabetically by author with subject index. Annotations give brief summary of topics covered.

B364. Matthews, William. British diaries; an annotated bibliography of British diaries written between 1442 and 1942. Berkeley, Univ. of California Press, 1950. 339 p.

A list of ca. 2,000 diaries in published and manuscript form written during the last five centuries by Englishmen, Scotsmen, Welshmen and Irishmen. Includes diaries of foreign travelers in England which were published in England. Many of the diaries are included in biographies, histories, genealogies and other works. The entries are arranged chronologically by date of first entry. There is a brief identifying statement for each diarist and a concise description of the contents of the diary as well as occasional notes of evaluation. Diaries which extend over a period of 10 years or more are listed chronologically in a special index. Location of manuscript material is indicated. Index of diarists, but no subject index.

B365. O'Neill, Edward H. Biography by Americans, 1658-1936; a subject bibliography. Philadelphia, Univ. of Pennsylvania Press, 1939. 465 p.

Attempts to record all biographical material written by Americans. Includes ca. 7,000 separately published items dealing with peoples of all nationalities. Autobiographies, diaries and journals are excluded and in the case of more famous people only the more important works have been mentioned. Arranged alphabetically by subject of the biography. Special section for collective biography. Locates copies in 8 libraries. No index.

B366. Riches, Phyllis M. Analytical bibliography of universal collected biography, comprising books published in the English tongue in Great Britain and Ireland, America and the British Dominions. London, Library Association, 1934. 709 p.

Aims to index every volume of collected biography that could be traced up to the end of 1933. The particulars of some 56,000 biographies are arranged alphabetically by the names of the persons, giving for each: date, brief 2 or 3 word description, and a brief citation to books in which biographies appear. This is followed by an alphabetical list of books indexed giving fuller citations. Three indexes: (1) chronological list by century of biographies; (2) a list arranged by profession or occupation; and (3) author and subject index of biographical dictionaries. Useful for obscure biography.

DICTIONARIES

B367. British Association for the Advancement of Science. *Research Committee.* A glossary of geographical terms, ed. by L. Dudley Stamp. London, Longmans, 1961. 539 p.

The first comprehensive glossary of terms used in current English language geographical literature. Foreign words are included only if they are used in their original untranslated form. Where the meaning of a term is clear a short definition from the *Oxford English dictionary* or some standard work is quoted. Where a term has undergone an evolution in meaning a series of quotations from original and standard sources is given. New terms are traced whenever possible to their first use. Includes many terms drawn from such related areas as geology, climatology, biogeography and ecology. Appendices include: Greek and Latin roots commonly used in the construction of terms; Lists of words in foreign languages which have been absorbed into English literature (grouped by language); and some stratigraphical terms.

B368. Fischer, Eric and Francis E. Elliott. A German and English glossary of geographical terms. New York, American Geographical Society, 1950. 118 p.

A useful bi-lingual dictionary which presents terms likely to be encoun-

tered in German geographical literature but not usually found in the standard dictionaries.

B369. Kende, Oskar. Geographisches Wörterbuch; Allgemeine Erdkunde. 2. Aufl. Berlin, Tuebner, 1928. 238 p. (Tuebner's kleine Factwörterbucher, 8)

Though somewhat out of date this dictionary is extremely important for its definitions of German geographical terms, especially in physical and mathematical geography. References are given to publications where the concepts expressed by the various technical terms are explained more fully. Articles on places and regions are excluded. Includes entries on peoples and races and short biographies of eminent geographers.

B370. Moore, Wilfred G. A dictionary of geography; definitions and explanations of terms used in physical geography. 2d ed. rev. and enl. Harmondsworth, Middlesex, Penguin Books, 1952. 191 p.

Reprinted with minor revisions in 1958. This small volume contains brief but clear definitions of over 1,200 terms, including those peculiar to certain countries. Although primarily restricted to physical geography, it does include some climatological and meteorological terms. Line drawings and plates to illustrate some terms. An older work, A. Knox's *Glossary of geographical and topographical terms* (London, Stanford, 1904. 432 p.) still has value.

ENCYCLOPEDIAS AND
ENCYCLOPEDIC SETS

B371. American nation; a history, ed. by Albert B. Hart. New York, Harper, 1904-08. 26 v. plus index.

A comprehensive, well proportioned survey by 24 scholars of the history of the country from the discovery to 1907. Economic, social and diplomatic aspects of history receive attention as well as the political and military. Volumes are divided into 5 chronological groups and each volume, covering a specific phase of history, is complete in itself, having its own index, maps and bibliography. General analytical index. A supplementary volume by F.A. Ogg, *National Progress* (N.Y., 1918) continues the work to 1917. When completed in 43 volumes, *The new American Nation series,* edited by Richard B. Morris and Henry S. Commager (New York, Harper, 1954+) will supplement rather than fully supersede the earlier work. Topical volumes are planned in addition to the chronological ones.

B372. Cambridge ancient history. New York, Macmillan, 1923-1939. 12 v. and 5 v. of plates.

A standard, comprehensive history of the occidental world from early Egyptian and Babylonian history to 324 A.D. and the Roman Empire. Each volume is a self-contained unit comprised of chapters written by specialists and includes an extensive bibliography. Maps and line drawings included in text. The volumes of plates are particularly valuable. Each plate carries a reference to the relevant page of text. Each volume has an individual index, but there is no general index in the set. New editions of volume 1-2 are in preparation. Corrected impressions of volumes 3-11 were issued 1951-54.

B373. Cambridge medieval history. New York, Macmillan, 1911-36. 8 v.

A standard work of reference for the history of the medieval world, based upon the same plan as the *Cambridge ancient history.* Each chapter is an authoritative statement by a scholar of repute. Illustrations and maps are included in a separate portfolio for each volume. There is a full bibliography and general index in each volume. No general index for the set. *The shorter Cambridge medieval history,* by C.W. Previte-

Orton (Cambridge, Eng., University Press, 1952. 2 v.) incorporates some up-to-date material.

B374. Cambridge modern history. New York, Macmillan, 1902-26. 13 v. and atlas.

The third of the "Cambridge sets" the modern history covers the Renaissance period to the early 20th century. It is primarily limited to Europe and its colonies. Chapters are written by competent specialists, and each volume contains an extensive bibliography. An important feature of this set, lacking in the other two, is a comprehensive general index in v. 13. The first volumes of the *New Cambridge modern history* appeared in 1957. Not a revision of the original but a completely new work it will attempt to present a complete social picture rather than just a political account. Major differences are the inclusion of material on art and literature and the elimination of bibliographies. To be complete in 14 vols. covering 1493 to 1945. V. 1-12 will contain the text. V. 13, the "Companion to modern history", will include a general index, chronological tables, and lists of rulers as well as articles on such subjects as bibliography and chronology. V. 14 will be the atlas volume.

B375. Chronicles of America, ed. by Allen Johnson. New Haven, Conn., Yale Univ. Press, 1918-1921. 50 v.

A popular history of America with each volume centered on a specific topic rather than a strict chronological period. A short bibliographical essay and index is appended to each volume. Six supplementary volumes edited by Allen Nevins (New Haven, 1950-51) continue the account to 1945.

B376. Gebhardt, Bruno. Handbuch der deutschen Geschichte..., 8. Aufl. hrsg. von H. Grundman.

Stuttgart, Union Deutscher Verlags-Gesellschaft, 1954-60. 4 v.

Arranged by period and subject the articles in this very useful compendium provide an invaluable bibliography and framework of facts for German history from prehistoric times to present.

B377. Handbuch der Altertumswissenschaft; begründet von I. V. Müller, erweitert von W. Otto, fortgeführt von H. Bengtson. München, Beck 1887- (In progress)

A massive cooperative work of the highest importance. It is made up of a series of scholarly treatises which cover the whole field of classical antiquity. Many of the volumes have appeared in several editions and many others have new editions in preparation. Some of the treatises are the most comprehensive and definitive works in their field, others are more brief. Earlier title *Handbuch der klassischen Altertumswissenschaft*.

B378. Histoire générale des civilisations, éd. by Maurice Crouzet. Paris, Presses Universitaires de France, 1953-1957. 7 v.

This excellent standard French series stresses the origin and development of civilization in its economic, demographic and cultural aspects. It presents for each historical period, alongside a study of Europe and the Middle East, a study of the civilization of the Far East and New World. Includes brief bibliographies and chronological tables.

B379. History of American life, ed. by Dixon R. Fox and Arthur M. Schlesinger. New York, Macmillan, 1927-28. 13 v.

The best general social history of America with emphasis upon the social, cultural and economic life, each volume by a specialist. Each volume contains illustrations, a "critical essay on authorities" and an index. Treatment is loosely chronological from earliest times to 1928.

Not all volumes are of equal value. No general index.

B380. James, Preston E., ed. American geography; inventory and prospect. Syracuse, N.Y., Association of American Geographers, 1954. 590 p.

A cooperative work which assesses the development of American geography and indicates the prospects and needs for the future. Its 26 chapters, each prepared by a group of specialists, deal with all phases of geographical study. Each chapter contains a bibliography and, in all, over 1,300 references are cited. Index includes references to more important items in the bibliographies.

B381. Langer, William L., ed. The rise of modern Europe. New York, Harper, 1934+ 20 v.

An excellent series covering the history of Europe from 1250 A.D. through World War II. Each volume is prepared by an expert and contains a thorough bibliographical essay on the period covered. Several of these bibliographies have been revised in reprintings.

B382. The Oxford history of England, ed. by Sir George N. Clark. Oxford, Clarendon Press, 1936+ 14 v.

The standard introduction to the history of England from Roman times to 1914. Each volume is prepared by a specialist and is equipped with valuable critical bibliographies. Largely supersedes older series—Methuen's *History of England* (1910-34, 8 v.) and Longman's *Political history of England* (1905-15, 12 v.). Revised editions of some volumes.

B383. Paulys Realencyclopädie der classischen Altertumswissenschaft. Neue Bearbeitung begonnen von Georg Wissowa *et al.* Stuttgart, Metzler, 1893+ (In progress)

The standard encyclopedia for classical studies in general. Articles are authoritative, with adequate bibliographies. Published in 2 series running concurrently covering the

letters A-P and R-Z respectively.
Supplement volumes have enabled it
to keep generally up to date. Completion is planned with 4 more volumes in several years.

B384. Peuples et civilisations: histoire générale, éd. by Louis Halphen
and Philippe Sagnac. Paris, Presses
Universitaires de France, 1926+
20 v.

An excellent example of the syn-
thesizing genius of the French. Covers the period from ancient times to
1939. Some of the volumes are unsurpassed. Each contains an excellent
bibliography for the period covered.
Many volumes have been revised or
are currently being revised.

B385. Propyläen Weltgeschichte:
eine Universalgeschichte, hrsg. von
Golo Mann. Berlin, Propyläen Verlag, 1960+ 10 v. (In progress)

First published in 1930-33, this
beautifully executed general history
emphasizes the cultural development
of mankind. Excellent photographs,
reproductions and maps. This new
edition is the work of many specialists and covers the whole range of
Western history from prehistoric
times to the present.

B386. The University of Michigan history of the modern world,
ed. by Allan Nevins and Howard
M. Ehrmann. Ann Arbor, Univ. of
Michigan Press, 1958+ (In progress)

An up-to-date comprehensive history of the leading nations and areas
of the world with major emphasis
upon the 19th and 20th centuries.
Each volume, devoted to a single
country or geographical area, is a distinct unit prepared by a recognized
specialist and contains its own bibliographic essay.

B387. Vidal de la Blache, P.M.J.
and Lucien Gallois. Géographie universelle. Paris, Colin 1927-1946. 15
v. in 23.

The standard French work in regional geography, notable for the
skillful selection and arrangement of
the materials as well as the fine
quality of maps and illustrations.
The work of leading French geographers these volumes cover all regions of the earth and are intended
for general reader as well as the specialist. Bibliographical references are
given.

B388. Winsor, Justin, ed. Narrative and critical history of America.
Boston, Houghton, 1884-89. 8 v.

Represents one of the best early
attempts to prepare a general cooperative synthesis of the history of
the Americas from earliest times to
1850. Its major usefulness today lies
in its wealth of bibliographic information. Each chapter carries "Editorial notes" by Winsor which include bibliographical references and
notes on sources which are available nowhere else. Additional bibliographic data on specific topics is
supplied in the appendices of each
volume. Many illustrations, charts,
maps and portraits.

DIRECTORIES AND BIOGRAPHICAL INFORMATION

B389. American Association for
State and Local History. Historical
societies of the United States and
Canada; a handbook, comp. and ed.
by Christopher Crittenden and Doris
Godard. Washington, 1944. 261 p.

Lists 904 societies. National and
general societies are followed by local societies arranged by state. Information supplied, where available,
on: (1) name, (2) address, (3) date
founded, (4) officers, (5) size,
(6) financial and literary resources,
and (7) publications and activities.
Names and addresses plus limited
information on resources and publications are brought up to date in
Directory of historical societies and
agencies in the United States and
Canada, 1959+ (Madison, Wis.,
1959+ biennial).

B390. Association of American Geographers. Handbook-directory, 1960. Washington, 1961. 192 p.

The handbook portion of this work includes information on the history, constitution, officers, publications, committees, etc. of the Association. Deceased members are listed with references to biographical information in 5 publications. The directory portion lists 2,004 members with a geographical index and an index of subject area specialties. For each entry information is given on: name, birth place and date, education, degrees and honors, fields of research or professional interest, present occupation and address.

B391. Orbis geographicus 1960; world directory of geography, compiled by E. Meynen. Wiesbaden, Steiner, 1960. 605 p. (Special supplement to Geographisches Taschenbuch 1960/61)

This comprehensive directory supersedes the *World directory of geographers* published in 1952. The first section includes (1) medals awarded by geographical societies and learned institutions for services in connection with geography and (2) information on the history, statutes, personnel and organization of the International Geographical Union. The second section lists (1) the major geographical and cartographical societies by countries (2) professional chairs and university institutes of geography, official agencies of general or regional geography, hydrographic offices, and cartographic and topographic surveys. Section three, "Directory of geographers" lists 4,003 geographers by country (with an alphabetical index) giving for each entry name, date of birth, university degrees, academic honors or appointments, present position, publishing or editorial activity, and address.

B392. Pan American Institute of Geography and History. *Commission on History.* Guía de instituciones que cultivan la historia de America.

Alcuidado de Carlos Bosch García. Mexico, D.F., 1949. 231 p. (It's publication 9. Guías 1.; Pan American Institute of Geography and History. Publication, 94)

Gives name, address, officers, special functions, and publications for 835 organizations located in Latin America, the United States and Europe. Name and geographical index. While listings are not complete for each country information is made available which is hard to locate elsewhere. A second edition in preparation.

B393. Pan American Institute of Geography and History. *Commission on History.* Guía de personas que cultivan la historia de America. Alcuidado de Juan Almela Meliá. Mexico, D.F., 1951. 507 p. (It's publication 34. Guías 2. Pan American Institute of Geography and History. Publication, 121)

Not complete, but gives nationality, field of interest, age, education, professional activities, position occupied, honors received, and publications for 1,400 historians from 26 American and 13 European countries. Index by country. New edition in preparation.

B394. Progress of medieval and renaissance studies in the United States and Canada. Bulletin no. 1 + 1923 + Boulder, Colo. Annual v. 1-12, 1923-1934; biennial v. 13 + 1937 +

Each number contains a list of medievalists and for each gives present position, institutional affiliation, and a list of publications.

B395. Répertoire des Médiévistes européens. Poitier, France, Centre d'Études Superieures de Civilisations Médiévale, 1960. 271 p.

An alphabetical listing of 1,662 European medievalists. Information given includes: name, occupation and address, special fields of study and publications since 1954. Indexes by city of residence and specialty. A list of institutes and centers of medieval study is included.

ATLASES AND PICTORIAL WORKS

Geographical Atlases

Geographical atlases in general can be divided into 5 broad categories: (1) Universal reference atlases, (2) general reference atlases, (3) school atlases, (4) national and regional atlases, and (5) atlases devoted to special topics. The universal reference atlas attempts to give, in relatively large scale, as complete an image as possible of all the regions of the world and has the corresponding defect of the virtue of being too general. The national and regional atlases, though general in nature, deal with smaller areas and can therefore treat in more detail a wide variety of subject matter. The general reference atlases and school atlases attempt to fulfill the comprehensiveness of the universal reference atlas but on a smaller scale and, at the same time, try to include as wide a variety of subject information as possible. There are atlases devoted to depicting in graphic form a wide range of special topics. Hence we find economic, climatological, meteorological, oceanographic agricultural, mineralogical and demographic atlases.

Universal Reference Atlases

B396. Russia (1923-   U.S.S.R) *Glavnoe Upravlenie Geodezii i Kartografii.* Atlas mira. Moscow, 1962. 284 p.
This fine Russian atlas devotes 27% of its content to the U.S.S.R. and is the most detailed atlas of Russia to date. The cartographic methods are excellent.

B397. The Times, London. Atlas of the world, ed. by John Bartholomew. Mid-century ed. Boston, Houghton-Mifflin, 1955-1959. 5 v.

The completion of the 2d ed. of this excellent atlas provides the English speaking world with a superb up-to-date and detailed universal reference atlas.

B398. Touring Club Italiano. Atlante internazionale. Ed. del sessantennio. Milano, 1956. 2 v.
One of the best universal reference atlases, ranking equally with *Atlas mira* and the Times *Atlas*. Published in loose-leaf form to facilitate keeping it up-to-date.

General Reference Atlases

B399. Bayer, Herbert. World geographic atlas, a composite of man's environment. Chicago, privately printed for Container Corporation of America, 1953. 368 p.
Often called the first "American" atlas among world atlases. A German edition was published by W. Goldmann Verlag (*Grosser Weltatlas*. Munich, 1955) with some changes.

B400. Visintin, Luigi. Grande Atlante geographico. 5 ed. Novara, Istituto Geografico De Agostini, 1959. 232 p.
A beautifully executed general atlas.

School Atlases

B401. Goode, John P. World atlas; physical, political and economic, ed. by Edward B. Espenshade. 11th ed. Chicago, Rand McNally, 1960. 288 p.

B402. Williams, Joseph E., *ed.* Prentice-Hall world atlas. 2d ed. Englewood Cliffs, N.J., Prentice-Hall, 1963. 137 p.

National and Regional Atlases

B403. Amorin Girão, Aristides de. Atlas de Portugal. 2d ed. Coimbra, Instituto de Estudos Geográficos, 1958. 135 p.
English and Portuguese.

B404. Atlas östliches Mitteleuropa, hrsg. von Theodore Kraus *et al.* Bielefeld, Velhagen & Kasing, 1959. 1 v. (loose-leaf) 68 plates.

B405. Brazil. *Conselho Nacional de Geografia. Divisão de Geografia.* Atlas do Brasil (Geral e regional). Rio de Janeiro, Instituto Brasileiro de Geografica e Estatistica, 1956. 163 maps.

B406. Canada. *Dept. of Mines and Technical Surveys. Geographical Branch.* Atlas of Canada. Ottawa, 1957. 1 v. (loose-leaf) 110 map plates.

B407. France. *Comité national de Géographie.* Atlas de France (Métropole). 2 éd. Paris, Société Française de Cartographie, 1953+ (In progress)

B408. India (Republic) *National Atlas Organization.* National atlas of India, ed. by S.P. Chatterjee. Calcutta, 1957. 26 plates. In Hindi with English summaries. English ed. in preparation.

B409. Svenska Sällskapet för Antropologi och Geografi. Atlas över Sverige. Stockholm, Generalstabens litografiska anstalt, 1953+ (In progress)
English summary.

Special Topics

B410. Van Royen, William. Atlas of the world's resources. New York, published by Prentice-Hall for the Univ. of Maryland, 1952+
v. 1 Agricultural Atlas of the world.
v. 2 Mineral resources of the world.
v. 3 Forestry and Fishery resources. (In preparation)

B411. Visher, Stephen S. Climatic atlas of the United States. Cambridge, Harvard Univ. Press, 1954. 403 p.

B412. Welt - Bevölkerungs - Atlas; Verteilung der Bevölkerung der Erde um das Jahr 1950. Hamburg, Falk-Verlag, 1955+ (In progress)
See entry at D282.

Historical Atlases

B413. Adams, James T. Atlas of American history. New York, Scribner, 1943. 360 p.
Designed to supplement and accompany the *Dictionary of American history* (B428). Its 147 black-and-white line drawings show the internal history of the United States from the discovery of America to 1912. The maps, in their chronological sequence, are designed to show growth, expansion, military history, etc. Each map gives the names of places as they existed at the time (with some indication of present day names, if important for clarity). Spelling of names is according to the most used form over a period of time. Some variant spellings are cross referenced in the index of place names. Little duplication with Paullin (B417).

B414. Grosser historischer Weltatlas, hrsg. vom Bayerischen Schulbuch-Verlag. München, 1954-1957. 3 v.
An exceptionally fine historical atlas covering from prehistoric times to the present day. For v. 1 (in 2 vols.: atlas and text), covering ancient history to the 5th century A.D., there is no comparable English language publication. The maps are extremely clear and detailed with full indexing in vols. 1 and 3.

B415. Lord, Clifford L. and Elizabeth H. Lord. Historical atlas of the United States. Rev. ed. New York, Holt, 1953. 238 p.
A useful, inexpensive historical atlas with 312 outline maps. Not intended as a reference atlas, it supplements but does not replace Paullin (B417) or Adams (B413). The rev. edition has brought some sections, but not all, up to 1950. Divided into four sections: general maps; Colonial period; 1775-1865; 1865-1950. The maps, arranged by topic within each section deal with all aspects of American development.

Appendices include statistical tables of population, presidential elections, immigration, railroad mileage, etc. Indexed by subject and place name.

B416. Meer, Frederic van der. Atlas of western civilization. English version by T.A. Birrell. 2d, rev. ed. Princeton, N.J., Van Nostrand, 1960. 240 p.

Originally published as *Atlas van de Westerse Beschaving* (Amsterdam, Elsevier). Skillful, handsome combination of maps, well chosen illustrations and text. Provides concise, illuminating picture of the development of Western culture from early Greek world to the twentieth century. "The 52 maps form a starting point. Each one represents an epoch, or a particular aspect of Western culture, with emphasis on the centers, the frontiers, the points of contact and the intellectual currents . . ." (Pref.) The text and 977 illustrations provide a running commentary on the maps. The index fully treats maps, text, illustrations, place names, personal names and historical concepts. There are references in the text to appropriate maps and illustrations. Companion volumes to this work and executed in similar fashion are: Frederic van der Meer and Christine Mohrmann *Atlas of the early Christian world* (London, Nelson, 1958); L.H. Grollenberg, *Atlas of the Bible* (London, Nelson, 1956); A.A.M. van der Heyden and H.H. Scullard, *Atlas of the classical world* (London, New York, Nelson, 1959). Using the same format with similar success but for France only is Jacques Boussard, *Atlas historique et culturel de la France* (Paris, Elsevier, 1957). For Russia see Pierre Kovalevsky, *Atlas historique et culturel de la Russie et du monde slave* (Paris, Elsevier, 1961).

B417. Paullin, Charles O. Atlas of the historical geography of the United States. Washington, Carnegie Institution of Washington, 1932. 162 p. 688 maps. (Carnegie Institution Publication, 401)

An authoritative, comprehensive atlas of the history of the United States from earliest times to the late 1920's. Part 1 contains the descriptive text which gives for each map, the sources of information on which it was based, and an explanation of its limitations and historical significance, but no historical interpretations. Part 2 contains the maps, which are chronologically arranged under major topic. These topics include: natural environment, settlement, population and towns, political parties and opinions, military history, boundaries, etc. A very complete index appended to Part 1.

B418. Poole, Reginald L. Historical atlas of modern Europe, from the decline of the Roman Empire; comprising also maps of parts of Asia, Africa and the New World connected with European history. Oxford, Clarendon Press, 1896-1902. 30 pts in 1 v. 90 maps.

An excellent historical atlas based to some extent on Menke's edition of Spruner's *Handatlas* (1880), with additional material from Longnon's *Atlas historique de la France* (1885-89), with fuller treatment for the British Isles. Each map is accompanied by explanatory notes and text prepared and signed by a specialist. In some cases bibliographies are included. Deals with the period A.D. 285-1897. No index.

B419. Rand McNally and Company. Atlas of world history, ed. by R.R. Palmer. Chicago, 1957. 216 p.

A successful attempt toward a genuine "world" approach to world history, as opposed to the "European-centered" or regional focus of many other historical atlases. Despite this wide approach it treats of more than political history. Its maps of economic and social subjects are excellent. Compiled by six experts, this volume of clear well produced maps is arranged chronologically with alternating pages of text which gives explanatory or background material for each map or each series of maps. Seven pages of tables are appended to the main work giving for various periods estimates of population, mortality, disease and migration figures, statistics on commodity production and transportation. In addition to place names the index covers ethnic and state names, explorers' routes, etc.

B420. Roolvink, Roelof. Historical atlas of the Muslim peoples. Amsterdam, Djambatan, 1957. 40 p.

In 52 maps, this attractive small atlas, presents the first overall historical and geographical picture of the entire Islamic world from 617 B.C. to the present. Contains much useful information for quick reference but is not definitive in scope and detail. Lack of an index is a handicap.

B421. Shepherd, William R. Historical atlas. 8th ed. Pikesville, Md., Colonial offset; distributed by Barnes and Noble, N.Y., 1956. 115 p. 226 maps.

An outstanding one volume atlas covering all periods and continents from 145 B.C. to 1955. The 8th ed. reprints all maps contained in 7th ed. (1929) and adds a section of maps for the period since 1929 prepared by C.S. Hammond & Co. These supplement maps (plates 218-226) are very general and do not measure up to the quality of the basic work. The arrangement is chronological with no text. Major emphasis is on political history. A very full index of names (some 25,000 entries) includes classical and medieval Latin names which do not appear on the maps with cross reference to modern or accepted form. The index supplement picks up names omitted in main index and adds names for the period 1911-29 but does not include the new section 1929-1955.

Pictorial Works

B422. Album of American history, ed. by James Truslow Adams, *et al.* New York, Scribner, 1944-1961. 5 v. and index.

Authentic and pertinent illustrations covering American history, by periods, from colonial times to 1953. Text is subordinated to the illustrations. A part of the survey of American life conceived by Dr. Adams and which includes *Atlas of American history* (B413), *Dictionary of American history* (B428) and the *Dictionary of American biography.*

B423. Pageant of America, ed. by Ralph H. Gabriel. New Haven, Conn., Yale Univ. Press, 1925-1929. 15 v.

Each volume deals with a specific subject of American life, e.g. lure of the frontier, American spirit in art, winning of freedom. The narrative is illustrated with nearly 12,000 pictures, portraits, maps, old charts and photographs. The volumes often contain rare and inaccessible material rather than depicting ordinary events. Each volume is indexed and includes a section "Notes on the pictures" to assist in their evaluation. V. 15, in addition, contains a select bibliography and topical index for v. 1-15.

B424. Parmentier, André É.E. Album historique. Paris, Colin, 1907-10. 4 v.

Covers European history from the medieval age to the end of the 19th century. The brief text is supplemented by illustrations of costumes, weapons, architecture, manners and customs. It is chronologically arranged; each volume contains an index of place, names and an index of proper names as well as an alphabetical subject index.

HANDBOOKS, MANUALS, COMPENDIA

B425. Burke, Sir John B. Genealogical and heraldic history of the peerage, baronetage and knightage. London, Burke, 1826+ irregular.

The standard handbook of the British nobility published as a rule annually. Since 1949, it has been issued at intervals of three years (102nd ed., 1959). The main section, "Peerage and baronetage," gives the full family history of every peer and baronet as far back as can be ascertained. Entries are alphabetical by title. In addition, the contents include: royal lineage, tables of precedence, orders, decorations and medals, the spiritual lords; other titled nobility of the British Empire; foreign titles and knightage; General index. Companion volume is Burke's *Genealogical and heraldic history of the landed gentry* (17th ed. London, 1952).

B426. Carruth, Gorton, *ed.* The Encyclopedia of American facts and dates. 3d ed. New York, Crowell, 1962. 758 p.

Chronologically arranged from 986-1961, this work presents its information in four parallel columns; (1) politics and government, war, disasters, vital statistics; (2) books, paintings, drama, architecture, sculpture; (3) science, industry, economics, education, religion, philosophy; (4) sports, fashion, popular entertainment, folklore, society. Includes a 117-page index which covers all items and refers back to the appropriate year and column.

B427. Columbia Lippincott gazetteer of the world, ed. by Leon Seltzer . . . New York, Columbia Univ. Press, 1952. 2148 p.

The major English language world gazetteer. It lists in one alphabet the political subdivision and geographic features of the world giving variant spelling, pronunciation, population (with date) altitude, historical, economic, social and cultural information and other pertinent facts. Places are generally located by straight line distances (in miles) from a larger feature. Occasionally geographical coordinates are given. Lists some 130,000 names with 30,000 cross references. The 1962 printing includes a supplement which adds and updates information through 1961.

B428. Dictionary of American history. James T. Adams, editor in chief. 2d ed. rev. New York, Scribner, 1942. 5 v. and index.

Covers American history in its widest sense (political, economic, social, industrial and cultural history). 6,688 brief, compact articles each dealing with a separate and definite aspect of American history, are signed with full name of the contributor. A few articles covering broad topics. Biographical articles are omitted. Includes many catch words and popular names of bills and laws. Brief bibliographic appendix to most articles. Extensive cross references. Excellent analytical index. *Supplement I, 1940-1960* (New York, Scribner, 1961. 311 p.), also numbered as vol. 6 of the set, brings the original work up to date, by adding new subjects, revising some major articles and expanding some topics. A new index including this material is in preparation. An excellent abridgment of the basic work is *Concise dictionary of American history*, ed. by Thomas C. Cochran and Wayne Andrews (New York, Simon and Schuster, 1962. 1156 p.) in which many of the original articles have been updated.

B429. Geographisches Taschenbuch und Jahrweiser zur Landeskunde . . . , hrsg. E. Meyhen. Wiesbaden, Steiner, 1949+ biennial.

Successor to the *Geographen-Kalendar* (Gotha, Perthes, 1903-1914. annual) this new publication is a compendium of varied and useful information. Included are such things as: chronological tables of events, past and present, of geographical interest; information on maps and publications, including geographical bibliographies and source books; statistical data of all kinds on all parts of the world; information concerning important geographical, geological and related institutions in Germany and other countries; and the names and addresses of more than 1,000 German geographers.

B430. Helps for the students of history. London, Society for Promoting Christian Knowledge, 1918-1924; Historical Association, 1950+

A valuable series of booklets, written by specialists, each giving an outline of the subject treated, selective bibliographies and critical appraisals. New editions and additional titles are being issued by the Historical Association. Similar to the American series published by the Service Center for Teachers of History (B442).

B431. Keller, Helen R. Dictionary of dates. New York, Macmillan, 1934. 2 v.

An outline of events and a digest of information from many sources recording by date the history of the world from earliest times through 1930. Major emphasis is upon political, military and diplomatic history. V. 1 covers the old world (Europe, Africa, Asia, Australasia, and Oceania) and v. 2 covers the Western hemisphere and the Polar regions. Countries are arranged alphabetically. For each country an introductory paragraph describes its geographical location and gives selected statistical information. This is followed by the chronology. The lack of an index limits the usefulness of this work.

B432. Kull, Irving S. and Nell M. Kull. A short chronology of American history, 1492-1950. New Brunswick, N.J., Rutgers Univ. Press, 1952. 388 p.

10,000 short factual entries of social, political and economic interest, chronologically arranged by year and date. A very comprehensive index facilitates quick reference to dates of special events.

B433. Langer, William L. Encyclopedia of world history; ancient, medieval and modern, chronologically arranged. Rev. 3d ed. Boston, Houghton-Mifflin, 1952. 1243, ixxxix p.

Essentially a handbook of historical facts which gives a telescoped narrative treatment to the historical material, thus providing a quick survey of any topic or period. Major emphasis is upon political, military and diplomatic history. The main section which carries information through 1950 is supplemented by a list of events from Jan. 1, 1951 to April 30, 1952. Ten appendices list historical figures under such headings as Roman emperors, British Ministries since Walpole, Holy Roman emperors, etc. The main section includes outline maps and genealogical tables. Comprehensive index.

B434. Larned, Josephus N. New Larned history for ready reference, reading and research . . . Rev. ed. Springfield, Mass., Nichols, 1922-24. 12 v.

A universal history cast in dictionary form. History is used broadly to denote not only "past politics" but also literary, economic, social and scientific history. Under each subject is given one or more quoted articles or extracts from "recognized sources." An exact citation accompanies each reference. Larned relies exclusively on materials already printed in English which excludes many excellent historians whose works were not available in translation. Many cross-references. Text is supplemented by charts, maps and illustrations.

B435. Low, Sir Sydney and Frederick S. Pulling. Dictionary of English history. New ed., rev. and enl. by F.J.C. Hearnshaw and others. London, Cassell, 1928. 1154 p.

A compact, well-edited (33 principal contributors) dictionary. The alphabetically arranged articles deal with persons, events and topics in English history. The articles vary in length according to the importance of the subject. Some are signed and brief bibliographies are usually included.

B436. Martin, Michael R. and Gabriel H. Lovett. An Encyclopedia of Latin-American history. New York, Abelard-Schuman, 1956. 392 p.

A compact, concise tool bringing to the student of Latin American history the indispensable information concerning the history, society and culture of Latin America from pre-Columbian times to the present. The material is alphabetically arranged with adequate cross references. Special entries are made for chief cities, geographical features, industry, military events, etc. Biographical information provided for a large number of major and minor personages. A particularly useful feature is the inclusion of definitions of Spanish and Portuguese terms which have historical significance.

B437. Mayer, Alfred. Annals of European civilization, 1501-1900. London, Cassell, 1949. 457 p.

This topical chronology stresses non-political, cultural history. The major section is a year-by-year treatment of the developments in learning and the civilized arts, subdivided by country. The second section "Summaries," briefly recapitulates this information by arranging the events chronologically under large subject or class, e.g., academics, chemistry, history, religious life, travels, etc. Includes indexes of names and of places.

B438. Morris, Richard B. Encyclopedia of American history. Rev. and enl. ed. New York, Harper, 1961. 840 p.

A reliable chronological manual rather than an encyclopedia as usu-

ally understood. Covering from earliest times to January 20, 1961, the work includes political and non-political topics as well as biography. The chronological listings are supplemented by 38 maps and charts including economic graphs and sketches of transportation networks. Divided into 3 sections: (1) basic political chronology listing major political and military events, using large readings defined by date span; (2) topical chronology presenting the nonpolitical aspects of American life under such general headings as: American economy; thought and culture; science and invention, with subdivision by specific topic and date; (3) biographical sketches of 400 notable Americans. Subject and name index.

B439. Powicke, Frederick M. and E.B. Fryde. Handbook of British chronology. 2d ed. London, Royal Historical Society, 1961, 565 p. (Royal Historical Society. Guides and handbooks, no. 2)

A standard work. Includes: lists of independent rulers of England, Ireland and Scotland; English and Scottish officers of state; Bishops of England, Scotland and Wales; Dukes, marquesses and earls (1066-1714); tables of parliaments and councils. Sources are cited in many cases. Also includes a 261-item guide to the available lists of English office holders (to ca. 1800).

B440. Ronart, Stephan and Nandy Ronart. Concise encyclopaedia of Arabic civilization. The Arab East. Amsterdam, Djambatan, 1959. 589 p.

Useful for quick information, this work contains brief articles, arranged alphabetically, dealing with topics in the cultural development of the Arab Middle East. Emphasis is upon historical material. Cross references are adequate, but the lack of an index is a handicap, especially for variant spelling of names. A companion volume treating the Arab

West (Morocco, Algeria, Tunis, Libya and the Sudan) is planned.

B441. Sandys, Sir John E., *ed.* A companion to Latin studies. 3d ed. Cambridge, Eng., University Press, 1921. 891 p.

An encyclopedic handbook for Latin studies which, despite its age, is still valuable. Separate chapters by specialists on geography, history, religion, antiquities, languages, etc. Good bibliographies. Maps, line drawings, reproductions of ancient art. Four indexes: persons, deities and races; places, rivers and mountains; scholars and modern writers; Latin words and phrases.

B442. Service Center for Teachers of History. Publications. Washington, 1957+. irregular.

Designed as an aid to secondary school teachers this series of pamphlets makes available in concise form a review, summary and analysis of significant contributions in recent writings and pertinent trends in historical study. Each is prepared by a specialist. Illustrative titles are: *Chinese history, a bibliographic review; American revolution: a review of changing interpretations; The Progressive Movement 1900-1920; recent ideas and new literature.*

B443. Strakhovsky, Leonid I., *ed.* Handbook of Slavic studies. Cambridge, Harvard Univ. Press, 1949. 753 p.

An introduction to Slavic history and literature written by specialists. The essays cover the origins, medieval and modern history of Poland, Russia, Czechoslovakia, and the Balkans, and the literatures of the Slavic countries. Each essay is followed by a carefully selected bibliography and the entire work is concluded by a comprehensive chronology.

B444. United States. *Board on Geographic Names.* Gazetteer . . . official standard names. Washington, Govt. Print Off., 1955+

This world series of gazetteers of official standard names, each volume devoted to a country or area identifies and locates, to date, over 2,500,-000 places and geographic features. Entries give geographic coordinates, general identification of the feature (*e.g.*, island, mountain, swamp, region, cove, etc.) and map source from which the name was taken. Each volume contains a list of generic geographical terms. Cross references made from non-official variant spelling.

B445. Virkus, Frederick A. Compendium of American genealogy; the standard genealogical encyclopedia of the first families of America. Chicago, Institute of American Genealogy, 1925-42. 7 v.

Lists 54,000 lineages and approximately 425,000 names of ancestors. The family tree of the paternal and maternal trunk line as well as collateral lines are traced back to colonial times. At the end of each lineage a brief biography of the subject is given. Following the main section in each volume is an alphabetical list of "Immigrant ancestors" to which cross references are supplied from the main section. Illustrations, mostly portraits and coats of arms.

B446. Webster's geographical dictionary; a dictionary of names and places with geographical and historical information and pronunciations. Rev. ed. Springfield, Mass., Merriam, 1962. 1,293 p.

Includes in one alphabet more than 40,000 geographical names. Cross references are given for equivalent and alternative spellings. Gives the usual gazetteer information, location, area, population, description, etc. For the largest cities, important countries, and each state in the United States fuller descriptive and historical information is given. Maps included in text.

B447. Whibley, Leonard. A companion to Greek studies. 4th ed. rev.

Cambridge, Eng., University Press, 1931. 790 p.

An old but still valuable comprehensive handbook designed primarily for the student of Greek literature. Separate chapters on Greek life, art, thought, and physical environment, each prepared by a specialist and including a bibliography. Four indexes: persons, deities, and races; places; scholars and modern writers; Greek words and phrases. Illustrations and maps.

YEARBOOKS

B448. Almanach de Gotha; annuaire généalogique, diplomatique et statistique. Gotha, Perthes, 1763-1944. annual.

For nearly 200 years, the standard source on the nobility in European and non-European countries. Two main sections: Part 1, "Annuaire généalogique" lists genealogies of the royal and princely houses including those dispossessed in the 19th and 20th centuries. Part 2, "Annuaire diplomatique et statistique," gives a descriptive account about various countries, listing their principal executive and legislative officials as well as foreign diplomatic corps. Indexed. Publication suspended by order of the Soviet occupation authorities. Part 1 continued by *Handbuch des Adels* (Limberg a.d. Lahn, C.A. Starke, 1951+ irreg.) The *Handbuch* is in four series: Fuerstliche Hauser, Grafliche Hauser, Freiherrliche Hauser and Adelige Hauser. The arrangement of the four series and the information supplied for each entry are the same as in the original *Almanach*. The "Fuerstliche Hauser" covers the princely families of all European countries while the other three series are chiefly concerned with German nobility.

B449. Current History review of 1959, prepared by the editors of

Current History. Chicago, Rand McNally, 1960+ annual.

Based upon the monthly reviews of current events throughout the world published in *Current History*, this work is arranged alphabetically by country and chronologically under country. The United States is further classified under agriculture, civil rights, foreign policy, etc. Also includes a special section on international affairs. Brief descriptive information for each country includes size, population, religion, language, and other pertinent socio-economic data. The analytical and subject index adds to its reference value.

ORIGINAL SOURCES

B450. Commager, Henry S. Documents of American history. 6th ed. New York, Appleton-Century-Crofts, 1958. 842 p.

A judicious selection of basic sources of American history from the age of discovery to 1957. The 633 "documents" are limited to official or quasi-official publications. Many entries are complete and in others the omissions are usually repetitive phrases. Each document prefaced by a paragraph giving title, date, reference to source used, a note on its historical significance and brief references to information. Arrangement is chronological. Limited index.

B451. English historical documents, ed. by David C. Douglas. London, Eyre & Spottiswoode, 1953+ (In progress)

A comprehensive selection spanning the years 500 to 1915, to be completed in 13 volumes. Each volume has a lengthy general introduction and a select bibliography; each of its parts carries its own introduction and bibliography. All documents are translated into English with the text being well footnoted. Includes maps, tables and statistical data from official and private sources.

B452. Hakluyt Society, London. Publications. London, 1847+

This series, now over 200 volumes, prints the texts of rare and valuable voyages, travels, naval expeditions and other geographical records. The works are not confined to Englishmen and frequently descriptions of some region by several travelers are included in one volume. Each volume is edited by a specialist and include maps, facsimiles, introductory statement, and notes.

B453. Monumenta Germaniae Historica, hrsg. von Georg H. Pertz. Hanover and Berlin, 1826-1925. 120 v.

The most famous 19th century collection of medieval sources. It assembles all the principal sources for the history of medieval Germany from the time of the Germanic invasions until the 14th century. Many volumes have gone through additional editions and some new editions are currently in progress.

B454. Morison, Samuel E. Sources and documents illustrating the American Revolution, 1764-1788, and the formation of the federal constitution. 2d ed. Oxford, Clarendon Press, 1929. 378 p.

B455. Nordenskiöld, Nils Adolf E. Facsimile-Atlas to the early history of cartography with reproductions of the most important maps printed in the XV and XVI centuries. Stockholm, Norstedt, 1889. 147 p. and 51 double plates.

B456. ——— Periplus: An essay on the early history of charts and sailing directions. Stockholm, Norstedt, 1897. 217 p. and 60 plates.

These two volumes, virtually two parts of the same work, constitute one of the most useful single studies in the field of historical geography since they furnish a compendium of material otherwise practically unobtainable. The first deals with printed maps of the period 1475-1592, while the second covers both manuscript and printed coast charts from ancient Greek times to the close of the 18th century.

B457. Original narratives of early American history, ed. by J. Franklin Jameson. New York, Scribners, 1906-1917. 18 v. in 19.

A comprehensive, well rounded collection of classic narratives, from the Norse voyages to ca. 1700. Material consists of: letters, official governmental documents and reports, travel accounts, explorations, chronicles, contemporary history, and literature. Many of the entries are extracts, but in some cases entire books are reprinted. The dates of materials in some volumes overlap but the material in any single volume is arranged chronologically. Each volume has its own editor, introduction, bibliography, notes, maps and facsimiles. All material is translated into English. No general index.

B458. Portugaliae monumenta cartographica, ed. by Armando Cortesão and Avelino Teixera da Mota. Lisbon, 1960+ 5 v. (In progress)

Aim is to present as complete a collection as possible of early Portuguese manuscript charts from about A.D. 1500 to the 17th century. Includes much which is unobtainable elsewhere. Reproductions are mainly in colotype, although some are in color. Each plate is accompanied by an historical and critical commentary. The text is in Portuguese and English and includes extensive bibliographical references.

B459. Royal Historical Society, London. Camden series. 3d series v. 1+ London, 1900+

Series 1 and 2 were published by the Camden Society from 1838 to 1897. This extensive series publishes chronicles, letters and other documents significant to English history. Each volume is edited by an expert and includes an introductory statement, notes in the text and an index. There is no general index for the series, but the titles are listed in the Royal Historical Society's *Transactions.*

B460. Snyder, Louis L. Documents of German history. New Brunswick, N.J., Rutgers Univ. Press, 1958. 619 p.

Provides the texts of the more significant documents on the general course of German history from the early days to the Bonn Republic. Emphasis on the modern era. Includes: constitutions, treaties, pacts, speeches, letters, laws, narratives, etc. All aspects of history covered. Chronologically arranged. The introductory notes for each section give historical background and indicate the origin and importance of the document. Appendices include tables, statistical data and recommended reading. Maps in the text. Index.

SOURCES OF SCHOLARLY
CONTRIBUTIONS

B461. *Journals.*

American historical review. v. 1+ Oct. 1895+ New York, American Historical Association. quarterly.
Bibl Fremd Zeit; Hist Abst; Int Ind; 19 RG; Poole.

Annales de géographie: Bulletin de la Société de Géographie. v. 1+ 1891+ Paris, Colin. bi-monthly.
Bibl Fremd Zeit; Biol Abst; Bull Anal; Bull Sig; UN Lib.

Association of American Geographers. Annals. v. 1+ 1911+ Washington. quarterly.
Bibl Fremd Zeit; Biol Abst; Bull Sig; Int Ind.

Current history; a magazine of world affairs. v. 1+ 1914+ Philadelphia. monthly.
Bibl Fremd Zeit; Bull Anal; Hist Abst; PAIS; RG; UN Lib.

Economic geography. v. 1+ 1925+ Worcester, Mass., Clark University. quarterly.
Bibl Fremd Zeit; Biol Abst; Bull Anal; Bull Sig; Hist Abst; Int Ind; PAIS; Soc Abst.

English historical review. v. 1+ 1886+ London, Longmans, Green. quarterly.
Bibl Fremd Zeit; BR Subj Ind; Hist Abst; Int Ind; 19 RG; Poole.

Erdkunde; Archiv für wissenschaftliche Geographie. v. 1+ 1947+ Bonn, Ferd. Dümmler. quarterly.
Bibl Deut Zeit; Bull Sig.

Geografiska annaler. v. 1+ 1919+ Stockholm, Svenska Sällskapet för Antropologi och Geografi. quarterly.
Text in: English, French, German, Swedish.
Bibl Fremd Zeit; Bull Sig.

Geographical journal. v. 1+ 1893+ London, Royal Geographical Society. quarterly.
Bibl Fremd Zeit; Biol Abst; BR Subj Ind; Bull Anal; Bull Sig; Hist Abst; Int Ind; PAIS; Poole.

Geographical review. v. 1+ 1916+ New York, American Geographical Society. quarterly.
Bibl Fremd Zeit; Biol Abst; Bull Anal; Engr Ind; Hist Abst; Int Ind; PAIS.

Geography; journal of the Geographical Association. v. 1+ 1901+ London, Philip. quarterly.
Bibl Fremd Zeit; Biol Abst; Br Ed Ind; PAIS.

Hispanic American historical review. v. 1+ 1918+ Durham, N.C., Duke Univ. Press. quarterly.
Bibl Fremd Zeit; Hist Abst; Int Ind.

Historische Zeitschrift. v. 1+ 1859+ Munich, Oldenbourg. bi-monthly.
Bibl Deut Zeit; Hist Abst.

Journal of modern history. v. 1+ 1929+ Chicago, Univ. of Chicago Press. quarterly.

Bibl Fremd Zeit; Hist Abst; Int Ind.

Mississippi Valley historical review; a journal devoted to American history. v. 1+ 1914+ Lincoln, Nebr., Mississippi Valley Historical Association. quarterly.
Hist Abst; Int Ind.

Petermanns geographische Mitteilungen. v. 1+ 1855+ Gotha, VEB, Hermann Haack. quarterly.
Bibl Deut Zeit; UN Lib.

Revista de historia de America. v. 1+ 1938+ Mexico, D.F., Instituto Panamericano de Geografia e Historia. semi-annual.
Text in Spanish and English.
Bull Sig; Hist Abst.

Revue d'histoire moderne et contemporaine. v. 1+ 1954+ Paris, Presses Universitaires de France. quarterly.
Bibl Fremd Zeit; Bull Sig; Hist Abst.

Revue historique. v. 1+Jan.-Jun. 1876+ Paris, Presses Universitaires de France. quarterly.
Bibl Fremd Zeit; Bull Sig; Hist Abst.

Revista geografica italiana. v. 1+ 1893+ Florence, Societá di Studi Geografici. quarterly.
Bibl Fremd Zeit; Bull Anal.

Rivista storica italiana. v. 1+ 1884+ Naples, Edizioni Scientifiche Italiane. quarterly.
Bibl Fremd Zeit; Hist Abst.

Speculum; a journal of medieval studies. v. 1+ 1925+ Cambridge, Mass., Medieval Academy of America. quarterly.
Art; Bibl Fremd Zeit; Bull Sig; Int Ind.

Vierteljahrshefte für Zeitgeschichte. v. 1+ 1953+ Stuttgart, Deutsche Verlags-Anstalt. quarterly.
Bibl Fremd Zeit; Bull Anal; Hist Abst.

B462. *Organizations*

American Geographical Society. New York, N.Y. Founded 1852.

American Historical Association. Washington, D.C. Founded 1919.

Hakluyt Society. London. Founded 1846.

Historical Association. London. Founded 1869.

Institute of British Geographers. London. Founded 1933.

International Committee of Historical Sciences. Lausanne, Switzerland. Founded 1926.

International Geographical Union. Zurich, Switzerland. Founded 1923.

Medieval Academy of America. Cambridge, Mass. Founded 1925.

National Geographic Society. Washington, D.C. Founded 1888.

Pan American Institute of Geography and History. Mexico, D.F., Founded 1928.

Société de Géographie. Paris. Founded 1821.

Société de l'Histoire de France Paris. Founded 1833.

B463. *Monograph Series*

American Geographical Society. Special publications. v. 1+ 1915+ New York.

Columbia University. *Dept. of history.* Records of civilizations. v. 1+ 1915+ New York.

Harvard University. Historical studies. v. 1+ 1896+ Cambridge.

London University. Historical studies. v. 1+ 1954+ London.

Northwestern University. Studies

in Geography. v. 1+ 1952+ Evanston, Ill.

Princeton University. Studies in history. v. 1+ 1944+ Princeton, N.J.

Smith College. Studies in history. v. 1+ 1915+ Northampton, Mass.

Société de l'Histoire de France. Publications. v. 1+ 1834+ Paris.

University of California. Publications in geography. v. 1+ 1913+ Berkeley.

University of California. Publications in history. v. 1+ 1911+ Berkeley.

University of Chicago. *Dept of Geography.* Research paper. no. 1+ 1948+ Chicago.

Yale University. Historical publications. v. 1+ 1912+ New Haven.

SOURCES OF CURRENT INFORMATION

B464. Focus. v. 1+ 1950+ New York, American Geographical Society. monthly (except July and August)
Designed to provide background facts and geographical interpretations of current world problems and problem areas. *Indexed in:* PAIS; UN Lib.

B465. Professional geographer. n.s. v. 1+ 1949+ Washington, Association of American Geographers. bimonthly.
Serves as an outlet for short scholarly articles, as a forum for the expression of professional opinion, and as a journal for reports on the activities of the association.

B466. Progress of medieval and renaissance studies in the United States and Canada. Bulletin no. 1+ 1923+ Boulder, Colo. Annual v. 1-12, 1923-1934; biennial v.13+ 1937+

Primarily a directory of medievalists (see B404). This journal also includes news of special interest to medieval scholars—projects, publications, conferences, etc.

B467. Renaissance news. v. 1+ 1947+ New York, Renaissance Society of America. quarterly.
The official organ of the Society which has as its purpose the advancement of learning in the field of Renaissance studies, and especially the promotion of interchange among the various fields of specialization. Articles, book reviews, news of publications, projects, conferences, etc.

SOURCES OF UNPUBLISHED
INFORMATION

B468. Carnegie Institution, Washington. [Guides to manuscript materials for the history of the United States] Washington, 1906-43. 23 v.
Individual monographs which provide guides, inventories, calendars and lists of archives, manuscripts and other unpublished materials in American and European repositories. Indispensible tools, especially the 19 volumes which give information on British, British American, European, Spanish and Spanish American archives. Supplemented by A *guide to manuscripts relating to America in Great Britain and Ireland,* ed. by B.R. Crick and Miriam Alman. (London, published for the British Associations for American Studies by the Oxford Univ. Press, 1961. 667 p.) which lists materials not listed in the Guides or acquired subsequent to their publication.

B469. Columbia University. *Oral History Research Office.* The Oral history collection of Columbia University. New York, 1960. 111 p.
The Oral History Research Office was founded to gather materials in the field of recent American and

world history by means of interviews with "living Americans who have led significant lives." These interviews are then transcribed, edited and indexed. The collection now totals some 65,000 pages with about 35,000 more in progress or awaiting clearance. It is planned to add 20,000 pages annually. This catalog offers a brief description of 195 manuscripts, ⅔ of which are available to qualified researchers. It is arranged alphabetically by interviewee with an added section for special projects and an index. Each entry briefly characterizes the subject matter dealt with and indicates availability of the material for research. A supplement covering 1960-61 adds 44,000 pages of material.

B470. "Graduate theses in Canadian history and related subjects," *Canadian historical review.* 1928+ Toronto, Univ. of Toronto Press.

This compilation appears annually in the Sept. issue and lists Ph.D. and masters' theses completed in Canada, the Commonwealth and the United States.

B471. Hale, Richard W., Jr., *ed.* Guide to photocopied historical materials in the United States and Canada. Ithaca, N.Y., published for the American Historical Association by Cornell Univ. Press, 1961. 241 p.

A union list for nearly 300 libraries of photocopies of 11,137 groups of historical manuscripts (not individual items). Each entry gives the name of the author, compiler, collector, or holder of the original material, followed by the title of the collection, the dates, amount and present location of the original materials and the type of photocopy. International in coverage, including material from ancient to modern times. Geographical arrangement with topical subdivisions. Name index.

B472. Hamer, Philip M. A Guide to archives and manuscripts in the

United States. New Haven, Conn., Yale Univ. Press, 1961. 775 p.

A complete guide to all depositories of archives and manuscripts in the United States with summary descriptions of their major holdings. Covers 1,300 depositories and 20,000 collections of personal papers and archival groups. Includes citations to more extensive published information on individual collection. Excellent 132 page index.

B473. List of doctoral dissertations in history in progress or completed at colleges and universities in the United States since 1958. Washington, American Historical Association, 1961. 61 p.

Series originally initiated by John F. Jameson in 1906. Published by the Carnegie Institution of Washington for the years 1909-1911 with the title *List of doctoral dissertations in history now in progress at the chief universities in the United States.* The 1912 list was published in *The history teachers magazine* (v. 4, 1913). For the years 1913-1917 it appeared in the *American historical review* (v. 19-23, 1914-1918). Carnegie resumed publication for the period 1918-1938. The lists for 1939 and 1940 were issued as supplements to the *American historical review* (v. 45-46, 1940-1941). The 1941 list appeared as vol. 3 of the *Annual report* of the association. None published 1942-1946. The 1947 list published separately. Beginning in 1952 it is issued every three years in its present form. A classified list, with an author index of dissertations reported from 86 colleges and universities as being in progress or completed since the October 1958 edition. See also: "A list of doctoral dissertations" a regular feature in *Progress of medieval and renaissance studies in the United States and Canada.* v. 1+ 1923+ (Boulder, Colo. annual v. 1-12, 1923-1934; biennial v. 13+ 1937+); and "A survey of investigations, in progress and contemplated, in the field of

Hispanic American history" which appeared in the August issue of *Hispanic American historical review* in 1927, 1931, 1935, 1939 and 1947.

B474. London. University. *Institute of historical research*. Historical research for university degrees in the United Kingdom. 1930+ London, 1931+ annual.

Issued since 1932 as "Theses supplement" to the Institute's *Bulletin*. Covers all universities in the United Kingdom. Since 1954 includes only theses completed. Theses in progress now issued in stencilled form. For earlier listings of theses in progress see annual listing in *History* from 1920-1929 and in the Institute *Bulletin* from 1930-1932.

B475. "Recent geography theses completed and in preparation." *Professional geographer*. 1950+ Washington, Association of American Geographers.

Theses titles were published in the March and November issues, 1950-1960. Beginning in 1961 the listing will be annual in the November issue. Lists, by author, Ph.D. dissertations completed and in progress and masters' theses completed. Each entry gives title, university, indication of publication (including microfilming) and availability on interlibrary loan. The lists in 1950 and 1951 are retrospective to 1946. Continues two previous works: (1) Whittlesey, Derwent. "Dissertations, in geography accepted in the United States for the degree of Ph.D. as of May, 1935." *Annals of the Association of American Geographers*, v. 25, Dec. 1935: 211-237. (2) Hewes, Leslie. "Dissertations in geography accepted by universities in the United States and Canada for the degree of Ph.D., June 1935-June 1946, and those currently in progress." *Annals of the Association of American Geographers*, v. 36, Dec. 1946: 215-254.

Thompson M. Little
Carl M. White

3

Economics and Business Administration

Economics may conveniently be described as the study of the production, distribution and consumption of material goods and services destined to fulfill the needs of persons and groups in human societies. This definition of economics is both too wide and too narrow, depending upon one's point of view, but it describes rather well the common concern of most persons who regard themselves as economists. In the course of its development since the eighteenth century, when the first systematic attempt was made to treat economics in its entirety, students of economics have given major stress to different parts of the discipline at different times. But at all times economists have been concerned with four main problems: (1) They have attempted to develop a body of general principles of human behavior in the realms of production, distribution, and consumption of goods and services. This is economic theory. (2) They have attempted to find ways and means of measuring more or less accurately the performance of an economic system and the magnitude of certain rates of change which seemed significant. This is methodology and measurement in economics. (3) They have attempted to discuss the steps which should be taken by governments or private groups and individuals to bring about certain desired results within the realm of economic activity. This is economic policy. (4) They tried to explain the state of the economy of their time as a result of developments in the past, with the hope of adding thereby to their insight into theoretical, methodological and policy prescriptions. This is economic history.

In the course of development of economics as a discipline many attempts were made to provide all-embracing systematic surveys of the field. Some of these were attempts at encyclopedic treatments of the field, covering several volumes and penetrating sometimes deeply into neighboring sciences. But, on the whole, these were less successful than the more compact textbooks or volumes on the general principles of economics, of which we list some of the most representative works pertaining to different periods since the mid-19th century.

C1. Boulding, Kenneth. Economic analysis. 3d ed. New York, Harper, 1955. 905 p.
C2. Marshall, Alfred. Principles of economics. 8th ed. London, Macmillan, 1936. 871 p.
C3. Mill, John Stuart. Principles of political economy. London, Longmans, Green, 1909. 1013 p.
C4. Samuelson, Paul. Economics. 5th ed. New York, McGraw-Hill, 1961. 853 p.
C5. Samuelson, Paul. Foundations of economic analysis. Cambridge, Harvard Univ. Press, 1947. 447 p.
C6. Smith, Adam. An inquiry into the nature and causes of the wealth of nations, ed. by Edwin Cannah. New York, Modern Library, 1937. 976 p.
C7. Taussig, Frank W. Principles of economics. 4th ed. New York, Macmillan, 1939. 2 v.

HISTORICAL DEVELOPMENT OF ECONOMICS

Though comprehensive treatments of economics do not antedate the late 18th century, economic problems have been made the subject of literary efforts long before that time. The catalogue of the Kress Collection, for example, mentions several hundred tracts and pamphlets, as well as books, which appeared long before Adam Smith's, *Wealth of nations*. Some of these publications have extremely interesting contents, not merely from an antiquarian standpoint, but also as contributions to history, to the development of theoretical ideas, and—in some instances—even as guides for policy. This and, of course, the later economic literature have been dealt with descriptively and analytically in a number of ways. First there is a series of general histories of economic thought. Many of these productions are textbooks and were occasioned by the fact that courses in this field are common in American colleges and universities. But we also have some highly original works in this field. The books range from compilations of titles, scarcely more than annotated bibliographies, to highly original analyses. Some treat the whole sweep of economic history from its earliest manifestations in the writings of some authors of antiquity to the present century.

C8. Cossa, Luigi. An introduction to the study of political economy. London, Macmillan, 1893. 587 p.
C9. Hoselitz, Bert F., *et al.* Theories of economic growth. Glencoe, Ill., Free Press, 1960. 344 p.
C10. Schumpeter, Joseph A. History of economic analysis, ed. by Elizabeth B. Schumpeter. New York, Oxford Univ. Press, 1954. 1260 p.
C11. Spiegel, Henry W., *ed.* The development of economic thought: great economists in perspective. New York, Wiley, 1952. 811 p.
C12. Stigler, George J. Production and distribution theories: the formative period. New York, Macmillan, 1941. 392 p.

Other works deal with special periods or "schools" in economics. The period before the crystallization of economics as a discipline has proven very attractive to many students, and there are proportionally more publications available on economic thought before the year 1800 than on the period during which economic thought grew to full stature. The best works in this literature cover a broader area than merely technical economics. In tracing through the development of economic ideas, it is often necessary to include the general political and philosophical thought of a period. Some of these works, though principally in economics, should be considered general intellectual histories of a particular period or movement.

C13. Cannan, Edwin. A history of the theories of production and distribution in English political economy from 1776 to 1848. London, P.S. King, 1924. 422 p.
C14. Dorfman, Joseph. The economic mind in American civilization. New York, Viking, 1946-59. 5 v.
C15. Gruchy, Allan G. Modern economic thought: The American contribution. New York, Prentice Hall, 1947. 670 p.
C16. Halévy, Eli. The growth of philosophic radicalism. London, Faber & Faber, 1949. 554 p.
C17. Heckscher, Eli F. Mercantilism. New York, Macmillan, 1955. 2 v.
C18. Johnson, Edgar A.J. Predecessors of Adam Smith. New York, Prentice Hall, 1937. 426 p.
C19. Robbins, Lionel. The theory of economic policy in English classical political economy. London, Macmillan, 1952. 217 p.
C20. Stephen, Leslie. The English utilitarians. London, Duckworth, 1900. 3 v.
C21. Weulersse, Georges. Le mouvement physiocratique en France. Paris, Alcan, 1910. 2 v.

COLLECTED WORKS AND COLLECTED TRACTS

All these works are secondary sources, i.e., although they discuss the development of economic ideas and theories, they present only excerpts from the works of the authors of these ideas, and in many cases they discuss, question, alter, and interpret these ideas in ways which would have surprised or even shocked the original writers. Yet the continuing concern with these works consisted, in large measure, of the challenge which these older writers presented and the many instructive lessons which could be learned from them. Hence it is not surprising that, at various times, the collected writings of the great economists were published in order to provide as full and comprehensive a documentation as possible of their own words and reasoning. In some instances nationalistic or other political considerations played a role. For example, the publication of the writings of Friedrich List was motivated, in part, by the urge to present to the German public the challenging ideas of a great German economist, and the plan to bring out a complete edition of the works of Karl Marx and Friedrich Engels was plainly motivated by the need, on the part of the intellectual leaders of the Soviet Union, to present the full corpus of the works of their apostles. But many of these editions of works are produced on thoroughly scholarly lines, and several of them may be regarded as constituting the *editio princeps* of the writings of several great economists. We list here a series of the most interesting sets of these collected works. All of them comprise the writings of great and important economists, and some have brought to light various previously unknown manuscripts, letters, and other ephemera and thus have greatly enriched our knowledge of the writings of these authors.

C22. Bentham, Jeremy. Jeremy Bentham's economic writings, ed. by W. Stark. London, Allen & Unwin, 1952-1954. 3 v.
C23. Law, John. Oeuvres, completes, éd. by Paul Harsin. Paris, Recueil Sirey, 1934. 3 v.
C24. List, Friedrich. Schriften, Reden, Briefe, hrsg. von Erwin V. Beckerath *et al.* Berlin, Hobbing, 1932-1935. 12 v.
C25. Marx, Karl and Friedrich Engels. Historisch-kritische Gesamtausgabe: Werke, Schriften, Briefe, hrsg. von D. Riazanov, *et al.* Frankfurt, Marx-Engels-Archiv Verlagsgesellschaft, 1927-1932. 8 v.
C26. Menger, Carl. The collected works of Carl Menger. London, London School of Economics, 1934-1936. 4 v.
C27. Petty, William. The economic writings of Sir William Petty, ed. by Charles H. Hull. Cambridge, Eng., University Press, 1899. 2 v.
C28. Quesnay, François. Ouevres économiques et philosophiques de F. Quesnay, éd. by August Oncken. Frankfurt, J. Baer, 1888. 814 p.
C29. Ricardo, David. The works and correspondence of David Ricardo, ed. by Piero Sraffa and M.H. Dobb. Cambridge, Eng., University Press, 1953-1955. 10 v.
C30. Turgot, Anne R.J. Oeuvres de Turgot et documents le concernant, ed. by Gustave Schelle. Paris, Felix Alcan, 1913-23. 5 v.

In addition to making available for the general student the works of the masters in convenient new editions, some of the scarce older tracts have been collected and reprinted. Here again, some antiquarianism, some pride in the early achievements of a national culture, some search for intellectual origins, and some competition for finding priorities of theories have played a role. But, as in the case of reprints of collected works, the republication of scarce tracts and other books in economics had the additional advantage of making more readily available to the general student works which attracted his interest and which were often of great scarcity. It is eloquent testimony to the utility and value of these reprints that several series are again out of print and that several reprints had to be made of some items. Among the more interesting collections and series of this kind are the following:

C31. Custodi, Pietro. Scrittori classici italiani di economia politica. Milan, Destefanis, 1803-1816. 50 v.
C32. Dubois, A., *ed*. Collection des économistes et des réformateurs sociaux de la France. Paris, Librairie Paul Geuthner, 1911-1913. 12 v.
C33. Hollander, Jacob H. Reprints of economic tracts. Baltimore, Johns Hopkins Univ. Press, 1903 and later years; several vols., many now out of print.
C34. McCulloch, John R., *ed*. Old and scarce tracts on money. London, King, 1933. 637 p.
C35. McCulloch, John R., *ed*. Early English tracts on commerce, Cambridge, Eng., Economic History Society, 1952. 663 p.

METHOD IN ECONOMICS

The works described so far may be regarded as providing a general survey of economics and its problems as a field, of the history of economic ideas, and the main components of the great corpus of economic writings by the most famous and most widely reputed scholars in the field. These works are the backbone of any collection of books in economics, and it is on the basis of these volumes that more specialized aspects of the literature should be considered.

The first specialized topic to which we turn is the consideration of method in economics. Although there is a rather high degree of unanimity today on the most appropriate methods in economics, this has not always been the case. One of the most memorable quarrels in the history of economics has been the so-called "Methodenstreit" or "battle of methods" between Carl Menger and Gustav Schmoller, which turned around the primacy of generalizing theoretical, versus particularizing historical method in economics. It also touched upon the degree of empirical support for economic propositions, and emphasized the need for economists to either accept current psychological theories or make their own assumptions about relevant aspects of human behavior. Most of these conflicts have been resolved, although even today there are somewhat different approaches, and the "model-builders" do not always see eye to eye with the strict "simple-minded empiricists." But the conflicts have become greatly mitigated and must be regarded mainly as differences of emphasis rather than differences of basic approach.

In general, economists favor an empirical approach. They go out to collect factual data or use those collected by others (e.g. statistical offices, census bureaus, etc.). They have developed methods of determining factual data from indirect evidence, and have participated in adding greatly to the knowledge and sophistication of the statistical treatment of mass phenomena. On the basis of factual data, various generalizations are attempted and sets of generalizations are built into theories. Until very recently most of these theories were stated in ordinary language, but it has become customary to state theories in mathematical form. Various branches of mathematics have been further elaborated by economists, since these formulations appeared to be of great utility to the solving of economic problems. For example, economists have made some contribution to matrix theory, and linear programming was developed almost entirely by mathematical economists. Economists have also developed the mathematical theory of games, and have made contributions to the mathematical treatment of difference equations.

But not all the progress of method has been in mathematical or semi-mathematical fields. There has been clarification in language and in specialized economic terms, and there has also been some clarification about the over-all assumptions of human nature and human behavior on which economic propositions are built. Whereas the early economists were utilitarians, and later economists assumed an inbred hedonism and rationality, modern economics has dropped these restrictive assumptions of human nature and merely assumes that human beings act reasonably consistently, i.e. that they continue a given behavior pattern until they make an explicit change.

There has also been a third field in which economic method has progressed—that is, the integration of historical and contemporary comparative study. Until very recently, economic history was regarded by many economists as a separate branch of study having scarcely any relationship with economics proper. For example, in many British universities economic history is split off in a special academic department without close contact with economics proper. This split is now disappearing. Economists discover that many facts which are true about the past of some societies are found in the present of some other societies. Certain institutions in historical settings have analogies or similarities in the present. It has thus become increasingly common to combine certain historical and comparative studies. At the same time, many of the statistical and mathematical procedures which were developed in economics have been applied to historical problems. In fact, some exercises of this kind have, perhaps somewhat jokingly, been referred to as "Cliometrics."

In brief, the spirit impinging upon method in economics is strongly influenced by positivism. Economics has ceased to be speculative and based on *a priori* reasoning—though old habits die slowly, and every now and then a thoroughly speculative book does appear. In its theoretical formulations it is slowly giving up the less accurate, purely linguistic statements and replacing them by rigorously mathematical ones. In collecting its data it applies the various forms of empirical method employed in the social sciences generally, and it processes the data by means of often quite complex statistical methods. Finally, it tends to encompass historical and institutional materials and treat them in a comparative approach. Thus most of the differences between "schools" have diminished and, in large measure, been abolished.

Finally, economic method has become both narrower and broader as concerns its interrelation with other social sciences. In its assumption on human behavior it has greatly reduced the emphasis on hedonistic or rational behavior. On the other hand, economists have become increasingly aware that interrelations with other fields of social research are in many instances indispensable practices of furthering adequate knowledge, and hence they look with more sympathy on interdisciplinary treatments of certain problems. The development, in the other social sciences, of methods similar to those in economics has helped greatly in this process. Although it is premature to expect that this interdependence will lead to a unified social science, a surer command of method in economics and a more modest interpretation of present achievements goes a long way toward laying the groundwork for further elaboration of more refined methods in economics and the other social sciences.

Much of the literature on method is not contained in special monographs or treatises, but appears incidental to substantive contributions. However, we list here a number of works which concern themselves primarily with method in economics and which represent, on the whole, the present state of methodology in the field.

C36. Allen, Roy G.D. Mathematical analysis for economists. New York, Macmillan, 1939. 548 p.
C37. Dorfman, Robert, et al. Linear programming and economic analysis. New York, McGraw-Hill, 1958. 527 p.
C38. Fraser, Lindley M. Economic thought and language. London, Black, 1937. 411 p.
C39. Haavelmo, Trygve The probability approach in economics. Chicago, The Econometric Society, 1944. 118 p.
C40. Keynes, John N. The scope and method of political economy. London, Macmillan, 1891. 359 p.
C41. Klein, Lawrence R. A textbook of econometrics. Evanston, Ill., Row Peterson, 1953. 355 p.
C42. Koopmans, Tjalling. Three essays on the state of economic science. New York, McGraw-Hill, 1957. 231 p.
C43. Robbins, Lionel. An essay on the nature and significance of economic science. London, Macmillan, 1935. 160 p.
C44. Theil, Hans. Linear aggregation of economic relations. Amsterdam, North-Holland Publishing Co., 1954. 205 p.
C45. Von Neumann, John, and Oskar Morgenstern. Theory of games and economic behavior. 3d ed. Princeton, N.J., Princeton Univ. Press, 1953. 641 p.

ECONOMIC THEORY

As already pointed out, the core of economics is economic theory. Theory formed the core of Adam Smith's work and has maintained this position in economic writings since that time. The various "schools" of economic thought are distinguished by the variations in theoretical concepts they use, and the growth of economics as a science is measured by the progress made in theory.

The theoretical literature may be classified according to several principles, but the easiest classification is by fields of concentration in the academic curriculum. It is around these divisions that certain clusters of literature have grown up, and even the more advanced monographic works may, on the whole, be divided by these criteria.

Theories of Value and Price

Since most of economics deals with the study of quantitative relationships which tend to become established on the market, one of its main theoretical concerns is the analysis of values and prices. The problem of value, which at first sight appears a puzzle, is brought into stark focus when it is observed that some of the most necessary things in life often have little economic value and some of the most "useless" ones have high value. Water and diamonds are the two objects whose value is often compared. Since it was so obvious that the more useful of the two had less value than the other, any theories of value which were based on utility were rejected at first. For many decades economists adhered to a labor theory of value which took various expressions and which was stated most clearly and unambiguously by David Ricardo and later by Karl Marx. But by that time the theory was almost 200 years old.

It was replaced within a generation of its ultimate formulation by a value theory based on utility, which remained in force for many decades and still forms the basis of our present theorizing on value. Utility was seen not as an indivisible entity, but as something which could be split into many small portions. To return to our example of water and diamonds, it was shown that the choice of the person assigning a value to each of these objects was not to decide between all the water and all the diamonds, but merely between small quantities of each. If a cup of water is lost, scarcely anything is lost. Hence the decisive unit is this marginal unit, i.e., the last cup of water. Therefore, the theory came to be called the marginal utility theory of value. Since it was first stated almost 100 years ago still further developments have taken place; and the emphasis on marginal utility has been replaced by analysis of situations of preference and indifference, mainly because we come closer to measurable and empirically observable relations. Among the more stimulating works on theory of value in its various aspects are the following:

C46. Edgeworth, Francis Y. Mathematical psychics. London, Kegan Paul, 1881. 150 p.
C47. Hicks, John R. Value and capital. Oxford, Clarendon Press, 1939. 331 p.
C48. Kaldor, Nicholas. Essays on value and distribution. Glencoe, Ill., Free Press, 1960. 238 p.
C49. Knight, Frank H. The Ethics of competition and other essays. New York, Harper, 1935. 363 p.
C50. Walras, Léon. Elements of pure economics, tr. by William Jaffe. London, Allen & Unwin, 1954. 620 p.
C51. Wieser, Friedrich von. Natural value. New York, A.M. Kelley, 1956. 243 p.

Price is closely related to values, in fact it has sometimes been said that price is the monetary expression of value. Some economists have recognized this and have puzzled over the fact that fluctuations in prices from hour to hour and day to day are, in many circumstances, more violent than fluctuations in intrinsic value. Surely a chair which is being sold for $10 for many weeks, and suddenly is put in a clearance sale and offered for $5, has not lost half its value in the few minutes in which the clearance sale is decided upon. It is recognized, therefore, that the external forces of the market influence prices, and that conditions of supply and demand, the openness of entry to markets, the smoothness with which markets function, the pattern of governmental regulation of markets, the presence or absence of monopoly or partial monopoly, all play a role. Prices may be subject to competition, but it has been found that competition sometimes is caused not by changing prices, but by the offer of more services in connection with a purchase or by a change in the quality of a good. In other words, competition can be less than perfect, it can depend upon the relative location of competitors, upon the influence exerted upon people through advertising, and other factors. Finally, it has been recognized that the stark dichotomy between competition and monopoly (i.e., the presence of only one seller or one buyer in a given market) was too extreme, that there is sometimes competition among the few. This has led to the elaboration of the theory of oligopoly, a situation recognized to be applicable in many markets in modern free enterprise economies. The variety of these patterns of price determination is exhibited in the following books. In addition to purely theoretical contributions, one or two monographs concentrating on methods of empirical measurement of prices have been added. Though these do not belong strictly in the field of price "theory," they are clearly relevant in this context.

C52. Chamberlin, Edward. The theory of monopolistic competition. 7th ed. Cambridge, Harvard Univ. Press, 1956. 350 p.
C53. Friedman, Milton. Essays in positive economics. Chicago, Univ. of Chicago Press, 1953. 328 p.

C54. Robinson, Joan. The economics of imperfect competition. London, Macmillan, 1933. 352 p.
C55. Schultz, Henry. The theory and measurement of demand. Chicago, Univ. of Chicago Press, 1938. 817 p.
C56. Stigler, George J. The theory of price. New York, Macmillan, 1946. 340 p.
C57. Triffin, Robert. Monopolistic competition and general equilibrium theory. Cambridge, Harvard Univ. Press, 1940. 197 p.

Theory of Production

As we have seen, the theory of price concentrates on the process of exchange. But economists are also interested in production and hence have developed extensive theories of production. To some extent these theories are attempts at determining the theoretical relationships between inputs into a production process and outputs from it. They imply certain given technologies, but they sometimes consider technology to be one of the variables that needs to be explicitly analyzed. Research and development of new technologies, both in the productive and the organizational fields, are now recognized to be costs of production comparable to other costs, e.g., of raw materials, labor, etc. But the principal inputs in any production process are inputs of labor and capital, and it is in the field of wage theory and capital theory that the most important contributions to the literature of theories of production have been made. It would lead us too far into technical economics to discuss the detailed theories of wages and capital, particularly since each set of theories has its own peculiarities. But it should be quite easy to see that wage theories tend to be affected by the fact that wages are sticky, that an absolute minimum level of wages is essential for survival, even if the value of labor should be lower than that level, and that great differences in a worker's skill, his initiative, his intelligence, and the power of the labor union of which he is a member, may affect the wage he receives.

On the side of capital, the problems which have cropped up find their ultimate basis in the fact that capital assets, though perishable in the long run, have different degrees of durability, that capital as such is therefore consumed over a long time in the form of the services it renders. Moreover, the durability of capital goods is affected by the outlays made on maintenance, and, depending on the span of time one has in mind, the distinction between fixed and circulating capital tends to become blurred. All these aspects—as well as the fact that in modern societies capital appears in the form of cash, securities, inventories, machines, buildings and land, and that these objects have different degrees of liquidity—have complicated the theory of capital. Among the more valuable monographs in the field of theory of production are the following:

C58. Böhm von Bawerk, Eugen. Capital and interest. South Holland, Ill., Libertarian Press, 1959. 3 v.

C59. Carlson, Sune. Study on the pure theory of production. New York, Kelley, 1939. 128 p.

C60. Clark, John B. The distribution of wealth. New York, Macmillan, 1899. 445 p.

C61. Clark, John M. Studies in the economics of overhead costs. Chicago, Univ. of Chicago Press, 1923. 502 p.

C62. Douglas, Paul H. The theory of wages. New York, Macmillan, 1934. 639 p.

C63. Fisher, Irving. The nature of capital and interest. New York, Macmillan, 1906. 427 p.

C64. Hicks, John R. The theory of wages. London, Macmillan, 1932. 247 p.

C65. Leontief, Wassily W. The structure of American economy. 2d ed. New York, Oxford Univ. Press, 1951. 264 p.

C66. Robinson, Joan. The accumulation of capital. Homewood, Ill., Irwin, 1956. 440 p.

The Theory of Income and Employment

The theories discussed so far turn around the behavior of single individuals or firms. In other words, the primary question asked by someone studying the theory of prices is to find out how a firm or a consumer will behave on the market and how, through his behavior, prices will be determined. The study of various forms of competition implies some aggregation, but the basic object of study is still the single economic unit rather than the mass of persons or firms seen in their entirety. The study of income and the theory of employment, on the other hand, turns around mass behavior; the entities with which these studies deal are the whole society or a sizeable portion of it. Hence, whereas the theory of value and price and market transactions, including theories of the firm, are referred to usually as micro-economics, the theory of income and employment, as well as the theory of savings and investment—which are sub-topics of the theory of income—are referred to as macro-economics. Whereas economics began with paying primary attention to macro-economic problems—let us remind ourselves that Adam Smith wrote a book on the *Wealth of Nations*—it turned under the impact of marginal utility theory to pay special attention to problems of micro-economics. In the last twenty years, partly under the impact of the great depression of the 1930's, it once again focussed extensively on macro-economic problems and paid particular attention to income analysis, the study of investment and savings, the theory of consumption, and, as a consequence, the theory of employment and fluctuations in employment.

This change in principal interest was due primarily to the theories of John Maynard Keynes and the subsequent "Keynesian Revolution" in economics which was carried on by his students. But Keynes not only stressed the importance of aggregates such as income, investment, and savings, but he also related these to new interpretations in the field of monetary theory. Hence on the macro-economic level a more intimate relationship was achieved between branches of economics which previously had been treated as rather separate parts. Monetary theory, business cycle theory, and ultimately the theory of secular economic growth was brought within the general context of general economic theory; and a more uniform body of economic theory emerged. This, as well as the stress on the aggregate entities, was the chief merit of Keynesianism.

C67. Baumol, William J. Business behavior, value and growth. New York, Macmillan, 1959. 164 p.
C68. Beveridge, William H. Full employment in a free society. New York, Norton, 1945. 429 p.
C69. Goldsmith, Raymond W. A study of savings in the United States. Princeton, N.J., Princeton Univ. Press, 1955-56. 3 v.
C70. Keynes, John M. The general theory of employment, interest and money. London, Macmillan, 1936. 403 p.
C71. Kuznets, Simon. National income and its composition, 1919-1938. New York, National Bureau of Economic Research, 1941. 2 v.
C72. Lerner, Abba P. The economics of control. New York, Macmillan, 1944. 428 p.
C73. Lundberg, Erik. Studies in the theory of economic expansion. London, P.S. King, 1937. 265 p.
C74. Shackle, George L. S. Expectations, investment, and income. London, Oxford Univ. Press, 1938. 119 p.
C75. Studenski, Paul. A study of the income of nations: theory measurement and analysis, past and present. New York, New York Univ. Press, 1958. 554 p.

Monetary Theory

As we have seen, recent developments in economics have brought about a closer integration of monetary theory with macro-economics. But even before this happened, considerations about money were intimately linked to the theory of prices and to market analysis. For the distinction between natural price and actual prices, which goes back to the classical economists of the early 19th century, was called forth by the fact that under certain circumstances the actual prices paid for given commodities fluctuated widely and were subjected to easily discernible trends. There were periods when all prices rose or declined more or less uniformly, and this phenomenon could only be explained by the general loss or gain in the value of money. Another difficulty required explanation as long as the value of money was tied to some metallic standard, and especially when it was tied to more than one metal, since the price relation between the two metals was also subject to change. Monetary theory was further complicated when near-moneys were invented and tended to be used widely. Banks could create money, either by printing banknotes or by establishing deposits, and the circulation of actual means of exchange could vary greatly, depending upon the amount of loans banks were willing to make or the rights of overdraft they were willing to authorize. Hence, such phenomena as inflation and deflation, the determination of the "adequate and proper" amount of bank credit, the practice of divorcing the circulation of currencies from monetary metals, and sometimes the indiscriminate use of the printing press were all developments which brought attention to the conditions regulating the value of money. As the value of money fluctuated, certain persons gained and others lost. Money as a store of value tended to lose its significance if money gradually lost its value through slow inflationary trends. Men began to speculate in money as they had speculated in other things, and in periods of serious hyperinflation—as for example in post-World War II Germany—they turned to other means of exchange than money. Foreign currencies and even such objects as cigarettes acquired the status of a general means of exchange.

Attention was drawn to such points as the quantity of money in circulation, the velocity of circulation, considerations which induced people to hold stocks of money, and reasons for and against their preference for liquidity. Modern monetary theory takes account of all these features, as well as of the impact which a generally rising or a generally falling price level has on over-all economic prosperity, and the monographs listed here contain extensive discussions of these various aspects of money.

C76. Copeland, Morris A. A Study of moneyflows in the United States. New York, National Bureau of Economic Research, 1952. 338 p.
C77. Fisher, Irving. The purchasing power of money, its determination and relation to credit, interest, and crises. New and rev. ed. New York, Macmillan, 1925. 515 p.
C78. Keynes, John M. Monetary reform. New York, Harcourt, Brace, 1924. 227 p.
C79. Keynes, John M. A treatise on money. London, Macmillan, 1958. 2 v.
C80. Marget, Arthur W. The theory of prices. New York, Prentice-Hall, 1939-1942. 2 v.
C81. Patinkin, Don. Money, interest, and prices. Evanston, Ill., Row Peterson, 1956. 510 p.
C82. Robertson, Dennis H. Money. New ed. rev. New York, Harcourt, Brace, 1929. 202 p.
C83. Robertson, Dennis H. Essays in monetary theory. London, Staples Press, 1946. 234 p.

Theory of Economic Fluctuations

As was noted, one of the peculiarities of economic systems is the fact that they experience periodic fluctuations in the general price level. It was soon observed that these fluctuations are associated with fluctuations in output and employment, and that they appeared to reoccur with a certain periodicity. Though the peaks and troughs of these fluctuations did not always reach the same height or depth, there were periods during which business activity tended to become increasingly sluggish and others in which it picked up again and became quite buoyant. This led to various attempts at explaining the causes of these fluctuations. Among the factors made responsible for the business cycles, (as these fluctuations were soon called), were such events as changes in the harvests due to changing reappearance of sunspots, alterations between optimism and pessimism of business leaders, and differences in the rate of growth of production and of consumption. These latter were often referred to as overproduction or underconsumption theories. There are probably few fields in economics which have produced such a superabundance of attempts at theoretical reasoning and such variation in assigning causes for an economic phenomenon, as the field of business cycles. In part this was due to the sharpness of some depressions, to the apparent inability of finding adequate remedies for the depressed state of business, and to the widespread concern with growing unemployment, falling prices, business failures, and an apparent general loss of vigor in the economy.

In this field, as in others, recent developments have brought some tightening of theoretical understanding. The power of fiscal policy possessed by governments in alleviating, and perhaps even avoiding, depressions is one of the instruments which may be used. Also monetary policies, by the central bank, are instruments of maintaining the economy on a more even keel. The distribution of public works, over time and in space, is another instrument, and various relaxations of other regulatory measures, e.g. in the foreign trade field, are still others. We may not yet have learned how to avoid fluctuations in a free enterprise economy completely, but we probably know the ways and means of avoiding deep depressions and of guarding against runaway inflations.

C84. Clark, John M. Strategic factors in business cycles. New York, Wolff, 1934. 238 p.
C85. Fellner, William. J. Trends and cycles in economic activity. New York, Holt, 1956. 411 p.
C86. Haberler, Gottfried. Prosperity and depression, a theoretical analysis of cyclical movements. New rev. and enl. ed. Cambridge, Harvard Univ. Press, 1958. 520 p.
C87. Hansen, Alvin H. Fiscal policy and business cycles. New York, Norton, 1941. 462 p.
C88. Hicks, John R. A contribution to the theory of the trade cycle. Oxford, Clarendon Press, 1950. 201 p.
C89. Mitchell, Wesley C. Business cycles, the problem and its setting. New York, National Bureau of Economic Research, 1927. 489 p.
C90. Schumpeter, Joseph A. Business cycles. New York, McGraw-Hill, 1939. 2 v.

Theories of Economic Growth

There is only one step from theories of economic fluctuations to theories of secular economic growth. Whereas the former are concerned with the determination of the variables which are responsible for the periodic ups and downs of an economy, the latter try to explain why economies, from a certain point on, tend to progress to higher and higher levels of performance. For even though there are depressions and periods of downturn, the subsequent upturn tends to lead to higher levels of income and output than any peak reached before. In other words, many economies have proven that they experience decided secular growth. These economies may be contrasted with others which have stagnated for a long time, which have apparently been unable to overcome their inherently low productivity, and which do not seem to be able to progress to a point of self-sustained economic growth.

If advancing and stagnating economies are contrasted with one another, the crucial question immediately arises as to what factors determine the point of "take-off." This is merely another way of asking what factors differentiate advancing from stagnant economies, and is equivalent to pointing to the practical policy problem of what changes must be made in stagnating economies in order to push them to a level of output where a self-sustained process of growth will begin. The debate on this question is by no means resolved. Some writers assign predominant importance to the supply of capital, others to the skill and level of education of the labor force, and still others to non-economic factors which have their primary basis in the culture, social structure or political affairs of the societies concerned. The study of economic growth has also prominently concerned itself with the re-examination of the economic history of countries which are among the leaders in the world economy. This has been done in the hope that, by examining this history, often from a new point of view, certain strategic factors could be singled out which would point to the most appropriate policies which poor and "underdeveloped" countries could embrace in order to enter the stage of economic growth.

The study of economic growth represents, in a certain sense, the general state of studies in contemporary economics: it has a theoretical core around which are built considerations stretching into the applied, the historical, and the non-economic areas. It is concerned primarily not with a static equilibrium or even a temporary equilibrium in the short run, but with a situation into which change is built which is in long-run dynamic movement. Finally, it accepts the variability of economic institutions and explicitly recognizes their differentiation in time and space.

C91. Clark, Colin. The conditions of economic progress. 3d ed. London, Macmillan, 1957. 720 p.
C92. Domar, Evsey D. Essays in the theory of economic growth. New York, Oxford Univ. Press, 1957. 272 p.
C93. Frankel, Sally H. The economic impact on under-developed societies. Cambridge, Harvard Univ. Press, 1953. 179 p.
C94. Hirschman, Albert O. The strategy of economic development. New Haven, Conn., Yale Univ. Press, 1958. 217 p.
C95. Hoselitz, Bert F. Sociological aspects of economic growth. Glencoe, Ill., Free Press, 1960. 250 p.
C96. Kuznets, Simon. Six lectures on economic growth. Glencoe, Ill., Free Press, 1959. 122 p.
C97. Kuznets, Simon. Economic change. New York, Norton, 1953. 333 p.

C98. Leibenstein, Harvey. Economic backwardness and economic growth. New York, Wiley, 1957. 295 p.

C99. Lewis, William A. The theory of economic growth. Homewood, Ill., Irwin, 1955. 453 p.

C100. Nurkse, Ragnar. Problems of capital formation in underdeveloped countries. 5th ed. Oxford, Blackwell, 1957. 163 p.

C101. Rostow, Walt W. The stages of economic growth. Cambridge, Eng., University Press, 1960. 178 p.

Time and Space in Economic Theory

The consideration of business cycles and of secular economic growth has made abundantly clear the need to "date" observations in economics. The earlier economists did not explicitly date their observations, though they assumed, of course, relationships which would undergo change over time. But this practice led gradually to the very central position which the analysis of equilibrium situations achieved in economics. All processes were supposed to be temporary, except certain cases of equilibrium, which could be either stable or unstable. Unstable equilibrium, as its very name implies, was not assumed to be permanent, and economists studied the paths that led from one unstable equilibrium position to another, until finally a situation of stable equilibrium was reached.

Gradually, this conception of the functioning of the economy was replaced by a conception of dynamic equilibrium, i.e., equilibrium was not assumed to be a point in time, but a path through time; and the various economic variables were thought to fluctuate around this path. Problems were posed as to whether certain deviations from the equilibrium path would lead to stable or to "explosive" solutions, i.e., whether the variables could be expected to return to some point on the equilibrium path or whether they would move farther and farther away from it. In the former case, the model which resulted in the tracing of the equilibrium path was considered confirmed, in the latter case it was considered in need of replacement.

Of course, there are numerous reasons why certain economic variables may diverge from equilibrium situations. They are subject to various shocks, some of them systematic shocks, but many random shocks, i.e., shocks which come from outside the economic system. The election of a new President may be such a shock. A war in some foreign country, some natural disaster, etc., may all exert shocks on an economic system and prevent the variables from reaching, or even moving closer to, their equilibrium positions. Hence it becomes important not only to analyze the positions which different economic magnitudes (income, prices, etc.) may take over time, but also what shocks they are subject to and what behavior they exhibit when exposed to certain shocks from outside or inside the economic system.

The consideration of location of economic activity, i.e., the role of space in economics, has gone through a similar process of clarification.

In early writings, space was almost assumed out of existence, except in theories relating to the international division of labor. Gradually, economic considerations of location were introduced explicitly into general theorizing, and at present they have come to assume such an important role in the eyes of some students that a separate field of enquiry, "regional science," has become crystallized. Interest in regionalism is not confined to economists but is also found, above all, among geographers and ecologists. But the economics of transportation, of differential pricing depending upon the location of the producer and consumer, and the problems arising out of the fact that shipments between two points may require different transport facilities and different quantities of transport equipment, have been combined with regional studies, and thus are providing a more rounded picture of the place of space and location in economic theory. Some of the more outstanding monographs on dynamics, static equilibrium theory and location theory, including regionalism are listed below:

C102. Harrod, Roy F. Towards a dynamic economics. London, Macmillan, 1948. 168 p.
C103. Isard, Walter. Methods of regional analysis. New York, Wiley, 1960. 748 p.
C104. Lösch, August. The economics of location. New Haven, Conn., Yale Univ. Press, 1954. 520 p.
C105. Perloff, Harvey. Regions, resources and economic growth. Baltimore, Johns Hopkins Univ. Press, 1960. 716 p.
C106. Pigou, Arthur C. The economics of stationary states. London, Macmillan, 1935. 326 p.
C107. Schumpeter, Joseph A. The theory of economic development. Cambridge, Harvard Univ. Press, 1934. 255 p.
C108. Shackle, George L.S. Time in economics. Amsterdam, North-Holland Publishing Co., 1958. 111 p.

Theories of Consumption

So far, we have been concerned primarily with production and distribution, and have paid relatively little attention to consumption. To be sure, the subjective value theories, based on considerations of utility, are concerned with the consumer; so are theories of demand and even theories of business fluctuation. We have seen, for example, that some business cycle theories are based upon assumptions of underconsumption. But, on the whole, consumption and welfare have so far entered into consideration only accidentally or in a subordinate fashion. Yet it may be argued that all production is ultimately destined for the satisfaction of human needs, through consumption either by individuals or by collectivities, e.g., the state. The purchase of armaments and similar objects is also a form of consumption, only these objects are consumed not by private individuals but by a nation, i.e., its citizens as a collective group.

In the past not too much explicit attention was given to the economics of consumption. Most of the studies which dealt with consumption were centered around a specific commodity or group of commodities, (e.g., food), and the main purpose of these studies was to find the nature of demand for these commodities and their place in the consumer's budget. Yet, even at a fairly early stage a number of rather general propositions were made, and quite common relations were discovered. The best known among them is perhaps Engel's law, which states that as the income of a household rises the proportion of its expenditure on food declines. This generalization was shown to be quite widely applicable by the German statistician Engel in the middle of the 19th century. Since then it has been confirmed numerous times.

More modern research in the field of consumption has gone beyond the problem of expenditure on food, and students have discovered relations between a household's income and its expenditures on various perishable, semi-durable (clothes, etc.) and durable (furniture and other household equipment) consumer goods. These studies tend to be summarized in works dealing with the function of consumption as a whole, in which various generalizations relating to changes in the level and type of consumption and changes in income are discussed. The literature on consumption, both on the theoretical and empirical level, is one of the fastest growing branches of modern economics.

C109. Ferber, Robert. A study of aggregate consumption functions. New York, National Bureau of Economic Research, 1953. 72 p.

C110. Ferber, Robert and Hugh G. Wales, *eds.* Motivation and market behavior. Homewood, Ill., Irwin, 1958. 437 p.

C111. Friedman, Milton. A theory of the consumption function. Princeton, N.J., Princeton Univ. Press, 1957. 243 p.

C112. Katona, George and Eva Mueller. Consumer expectations. Ann Arbor, Univ. of Michigan Press, 1957. 144 p.

C113. Reid, Margaret G. Consumers and the market. 3d ed. New York, Crofts, 1942. 617 p.

Welfare Economics

Considerations of consumption problems lead us straight to the consideration of welfare. The classical economists had their philosophical roots in utilitarianism, and some of them, e.g., John Stuart Mill, explicitly applied utilitarian principles to economics. The question was raised as to how economics could contribute to the utilitarian ideal of attaining the greatest happiness for the greatest number. This background may be discerned throughout economic reasoning in later periods also. For example, F. Y. Edgeworth was very much concerned with this problem in the late 19th century. In the period since the end of the first world war, welfare as an objective of economic activity and economic organization has again become a prominent concern of economists. In this area, as in others, the problem is now posed in a new fashion. Instead of attempting an aggregation of individual satisfaction or "happiness," welfare economics takes into account the fact that every person's welfare depends not only upon the "happiness" he achieves himself, but also on that of his family, neighbors and others in his community—i.e., that the concept of a "community welfare" function must be developed. Here economic reasoning comes close to social philosophy and a discussion of the problem of societal values, and is clearly influenced by the assumptions made about these values. In the field of welfare economics we reach, so to speak, the limits of pure economics, and come close to politics, philosophy, and the analysis of social psychology.

C114. Arrow, Kenneth J. Social choice and individual values. New York, Wiley, 1951. 99p.
C115. Little, Ian M.D. A critique of welfare economics. 2d ed. Oxford, Clarendon Press, 1957. 302 p.
C116. Pigou, Arthur C. The economics of welfare. 4th ed. London, Macmillan, 1938. 837 p.
C117. Reder, Melvin W. Studies in the theory of welfare economics. New York, Columbia Univ. Press, 1947. 208 p.

THE APPLICATION OF ECONOMIC THEORIES

In the preceding discussion we have covered all the fields in which economic theories have been developed, with the exception of theories relating to the international division of labor. These theories have found application in several areas of practical concern, and we shall now turn to a few such applications. We shall deal first with agriculture, labor, banking and business management, then with applications of economic theory to the activities of governments, and will finally arrive at a general consideration of economic policies and planning.

Agricultural Economics

Agricultural economics is an area in which a literature has developed which in scope and quantity equals, or perhaps even exceeds, that of all other fields combined. Agricultural economists in the United States have their own professional organization, their own journal, and, in most universities, are organized in their own departments. Hence there are probably more available data on various aspects of economic matters pertaining to agriculture than in any other field of production. This proliferation of research and publication in the field of agricultural economics has taken place in spite of the fact that an increasingly smaller percentage of the labor force in the United States is employed in agriculture. This has had the effect, however, to bring to the attention of many agricultural economists the importance of farming in foreign countries, especially the poorer countries of Asia, Africa, and Latin America. There the majority of the labor force is engaged in agriculture, and a sizeable proportion of the total output of these nations is produced in agriculture.

Moreover, the techniques of farming are primitive, the organization of agricultural production is backward and clumsy, and the applications of modern methods are lagging behind. There are important needs for changes in the structure of landholding, and there are profound changes needed in the patterns of farm management and agricultural marketing. Though the literature does not yet fully represent these concerns, there is a growing stream of articles and pamphlets devoted to these problems, and even the official agencies of the United States Department of Agriculture are becoming increasingly concerned with the problems of the poorer countries.

It would be impossible within a reasonable space to enter into all the ramifications of empirical, theoretical, and applied studies in the field of agricultural economics. We therefore list only a few of the monographs which appear to be of most general interest and of widest applicability. But it should be pointed out that such organizations as the U. S. Bureau of Farm Economics, the Food Research Institute at Stanford University, and many agricultural extension stations and departments of agriculture, especially at the land-grant colleges, supply an abundance of valuable special materials on all aspects of farming, land economics, agricultural marketing and agricultural management.

C118. Benedict, Murray R. Farm policies of the United States 1790-1950. New York, Twentieth Century Fund, 1953. 548 p.
C119. Black, John D. Economics for agriculture. Cambridge, Harvard Univ. Press, 1959. 719 p.
C120. Ely, Richard T. and Edward W. Morehouse. Elements of land economics. New York, Macmillan, 1924. 363 p.
C121. Heady, Earl O. Economics of agricultural production and resource use. New York, Prentice-Hall, 1952. 850 p.
C122. Johnson, David G. Forward prices for agriculture. Chicago, Univ. of Chicago Press, 1947. 259 p.
C123. Schultz, Theodore W. The economic organization of agriculture. New York, McGraw-Hill, 1953. 374 p.
C124. Schultz, Theodore W., ed. Food for the world. Chicago, Univ. of Chicago Press, 1945. 352 p.
C125. Tostlebe, Alvin S. Capital in agriculture: its formation and financing since 1870. Princeton, N.J., Princeton Univ. Press, 1957. 232 p.

The Industrial Labor Force

With agriculture declining in importance in the most advanced countries, there has been an increase in the attention given to industrialism and its associated phenomena. At one time, principal attention was paid to the standard of living of the laborer, but, with increasing capacity of the more highly developed economies to afford a rising standard of comfort for the average worker, the main attention has turned to other problems, principally the question of the size and composition of the labor force, the impact and strategy of trade unions and the conditions of work on the job, including the problem of labor-management relations.

At first sight, the problem of the determination of the labor force appears easiest and most straightforward. Superficially one would assume that the study of the labor force turns around a primarily statistical problem, that of counting the number of workers in a series of industries and of determining fluctuations and changes of that number over time. But once one penetrates beneath the reasons for these fluctuations one observes that many difficult and complex social problems are involved. For example, if we witness a sharp, sudden change in the labor force in a given industry, is this due to technical change, to different social views on the part of the population, to changes in wages or general working conditions, to changes in the requirements of skill in the industry, or to some combination of these forces? What determines the participation of women, especially married women, in the labor force? The income of a household is one factor, its aspirations another; cultural and social attitudes regarding women's work a third, the conditions under which a job may be performed a fourth, hours, wages, wage differentials, a fifth, sixth, seventh and so on. Whether we are interested in the participation of women in industrial and related work, or whether we ask what impact the age of leaving school exerts, whether we study the consequences of automation or the problem of unemployment, we are concerned with some aspect of the analysis of the labor force. Hence, studies in the field have appeared in growing number and have become oriented towards an increasing variety of questions and problems.

C126. Bancroft, Gertrude. The American labor force: its growth and changing composition. New York, Wiley, 1958. 256 p.
C127. Long, Clarence D. The labor force under changing income and employment. Princeton, N.J., Princeton Univ. Press, 1958. 440 p.
C128. Palmer, Gladys. Labor mobility in six cities. New York, Social Science Research Council, 1954. 177 p.
C129. Parnes, Herbert S. Research on labor nobility. New York, Social Science Research Council, 1954. 205 p.
C130. Reynolds, Lloyd G. The Structure of labor markets. New York, Harper, 1951. 328 p.

The Economics of Trade Unionism

Of equally great importance as the problems of size, quality and composition of the labor force is the problem of trade unions. Probably little needs to be said in substantiating the importance of the subject, and so we will list merely a few of the major economic problems associated with the growth and changing structure of labor unionism.

Unions appear most prominently in the public eye as organizations whose internal structure is under scrutiny. When congressional committees investigate unions or racketeering in labor organizations, they are concerned with the degree of internal democracy and representative government within a given local or national trade union. They ask basically whether the leadership is autocratic and whether it uses the resources of the union for the proper purposes of the organization. This is not a strictly economic, but primarily a political, problem.

The properly economic purpose of labor organizations is collective bargaining, and it is this aspect of unionism to which economists have paid most attention. To be sure, the internal structure of a union, the degree of free determination of its policies and objectives by the membership, its centralization, and the weight of its financial control play a role; but the major economic problems relate to the methods the union uses in determining wages and associated working conditions. In this context there is a whole set of further considerations, since determination of wages and working conditions by unions has extensive effects upon the economy as a whole. We have all heard of the inflationary tendencies inherent in a wage-price spiral, and this development is possible only in an economy in which most wages are subject to negotiation by unions.

Of equal seriousness is the problem of negotiations with management. The confrontation of a labor union with the heads of a large enterprise is, economically speaking, an instance of bilateral monopoly. The negotiations under these conditions can best be analyzed by application of principles of the theory of games. Here again the non-achievement of consensus may lead to strikes or work stoppages which, in the case of some basic industries, may have far-reaching effects upon a country's economy. Hence it is not surprising that most modern nations have passed extensive legislation designed to regulate the organization, internal structure, and activities of labor unions.

C131. Dunlop, John T. Wage determination under trade unions. New York, Macmillan, 1944. 231 p.
C132. Harbison, Frederick H. and John R. Coleman. Goals and strategy in collective bargaining. New York, Harper, 1951. 172 p.
C133. Hoxie, Robert F. Trade unionism in the United States. New York, Appleton, 1917. 426 p.
C134. Lipset, Seymour M., et al. Union democracy. Glencoe, Ill., Free Press, 1956. 455 p.
C135. Perlman, Selig. A theory of the labor movement. New York, Macmillan, 1928. 321 p.
C136. Sayles, Leonard R. and George Strauss. The local union. New York, Harper, 1953. 269 p.
C137. Seidman, Joel I., et al. The worker views his union. Chicago, Univ. of Chicago Press, 1958. 299 p.
C138. Ulman, Lloyd. The rise of the national trade union. Cambridge, Harvard Univ. Press, 1955. 639 p.
C139. Webb, Sidney and Beatrice. Industrial democracy. Edition of 1920. London, Longmans Green and Co. 1926. 899 p.
C140. Wolman, Leo. Ebb and flow in trade unionism. New York, National Bureau of Economic Research, 1936. 251 p.

Labor-Management Relations

Negotiations between management and unions about wages and conditions of work also have an impact upon general labor-management relations. The work situation for an individual is not confined to a day's work in a completely impersonal environment and departure after work is done, without the factory or the office having any impact whatsoever.

It was discovered early, at first by efficiency experts, that the environment in which work was performed has an impact upon productivity. It was discovered later that in many instances workers formed informal groups which cooperated and that if these groups were disturbed productivity declined. In brief, it was shown that the internal organization and layout of the work process, the flow of tasks, and the informal social relations which became established between workers had an effect upon the economic results of an enterprise.

But the relations between management and the workers also played a role. Here such problems as grievance procedures, the possibilities of advancement in pay and in rank, considerations of seniority and rights derived therefrom, and the barriers which exist between the blue-collar and the white-collar portions of the work force are paramount. Labor-management relations have passed through various phases. They began with emphasis on strong paternalistic features, developed to a situation in which the two parties faced one another as "enemies," and gradually developed into more or less impersonal business relations. It is becoming increasingly recognized that the injection of some added ingredients which will enhance the worker's interest in his job, his company, and his industry may have beneficial effects upon productivity. A job, it is increasingly recognized, is not merely a means of earning a living; it is part of a man's life.

C141. Kerr, Clark, et al. Industrialism and industrial man. Cambridge, Harvard Univ. Press, 1960. 331 p.

C142. Mayo, Elton. The human problems of an industrial civilization, 2d ed. Boston, Graduate School of Business Administration, Harvard University, 1946. 194 p.

C143. Moore, Wilbert E. and Arnold S. Feldman. Labor commitment and social change in developing areas. New York, Social Science Research Council, 1960. 378 p.

C144. Roethlisberger, Fritz J. and William J. Dickson. Management and the worker. Cambridge, Harvard Univ. Press, 1939. 615 p.

C145. Slichter, Sumner H., et al. The impact of collective bargaining on management. Washington, D.C., Brookings Institution, 1960. 982 p.

C146. Whyte, William Foote. Industry and society. New York, McGraw-Hill, 1946. 211 p.

Theories of Management

The trends which have been observed in the study and research on labor problems have their parallels in the field of management research. On the one hand, there has been a growth of interest in the social position of persons in management jobs, and studies have become extended to cover the psychological pressures and personality characteristics—creativity, achievement orientation, and others—which contribute to the performance of their jobs. On the other hand, there has been the development of scientific management and the growing interpretation of business administration as a system of decision-making processes. Decisions of varying importance under varying constraints are made on different levels in a management structure, and the organization of a decision-making machinery which entails both vertical and horizontal lines of interconnection has become a fascinating field of study.

At the same time, the place and role of business, its structural aspects, and its evolution have become points of interest. Thus the literature may be divided into three parts. The first, which will not be discussed here, is the rather old-fashioned set of studies and texts on technical aspects of business administration, such as accounting practice, advertising, salesmanship, etc. The second part is literature devoted to management as a set of decisions and considerations underlying this interpretation of management. The third is the interpretation of business leadership as the performance of the entrepreneurial function and the history and present challenge to entrepreneurship. A few of the more important works on management proper are listed here.

C147. Berle, Adolf A. and Gardiner C. Means. The modern corporation and private property. New York, Macmillan, 1932. 396 p.
C148. Carlson, Sune. Executive behaviour. Stockholm, Strömberg, 1951. 122 p.
C149. Chapple, Eliot D. and Leonard R. Sayles. The measure of management. New York, Macmillan, 1961. 218 p.
C150. Drucker, Peter F. The practice of management. New York, Harper, 1954. 404 p.
C151. Mack, Ruth P. The flow of business funds and consumer purchasing power. New York, Columbia Univ. Press, 1911. 400 p.
C152. March, James G. and Herbert A. Simon. Organizations. New York, Wiley, 1958. 262 p.
C153. Simon, Herbert A. The new science of management decisions. New York, Harper, 1960. 50 p.

Entrepreneurship

As we have seen, the various studies of the human element in productive activity—labor, management, salaried officials—have begun to stress increasingly the motivational and general psychological background of economic performance in these areas. Of all the types of economic activity, entrepreneurship has been studied most intensively with the personality angle in view, and it was with primary consideration of the performance of entrepreneurship that some students have written monographs which are explicitly devoted to both economics and psychology.

Enterpreneurship has been differently defined, i.e., its main characteristics have been given different weight. J. B. Say defined it as the performance of the act of combining productive factors, i.e., of drawing together labor, capital, and science for purposes of production. Later writers have stressed primarily the risk element characteristic of entrepreneurs; but Joseph Schumpeter has stressed the innovating activity of enterprisers, and this interpretation has become more or less generally accepted. In a private enterprise economy it is the entrepreneur who performs the crucial function of pushing the system along to higher and better standards of performance, who introduces innovations in technology, organization, and marketing activities. But since not every person has the innate or even acquired propensities for entrepreneurship, it is not strange that the question should have been asked: what personality traits are associated with the performance of entrepreneurial functions? The life histories and activities of past entrepreneurs have been examined to determine whether any useful generalizations can be derived from this study.

C154. Beard, Miriam. A history of the business man. New York, Macmillan, 1938. 779 p.
C155. Cochran, Thomas C. The American business system, a historical perspective, 1900-1955. Cambridge, Harvard Univ. Press, 1957. 227 p.
C156. Cole, Arthur H. Business enterprise in its social setting. Cambridge, Harvard Univ. Press, 1959. 286 p.
C157. Lane, Frederic C. and Jelle C. Riemersma. Enterprise and secular change. Homewood, Ill., Irwin, 1953. 556 p.
C158. McClelland, David C. The achieving society. Princeton, N.J., Van Nostrand, 1961. 512 p.
C159. Weisskopf, Walter A. The psychology of economics. 2d ed. Chicago, Univ. of Chicago Press, 1957. 266 p.

Invention and Innovation

If entrepreneurship is defined as consisting primarily of the introduction of innovations, the role of invention in economics becomes crucial. Here is a field which is still too little explored for us to have really useful theories. Yet some work has been done both along historical lines and in an analytical direction. Here, as in the general field of business management, the haphazard accidental practices of earlier days are shown to have been replaced by the much more orderly procedures of research and development departments and the planned execution of inventive activity. The economics of the modern research laboratory have not yet been explored as exhaustively as those of the family farm or the industrial plant, but the principles applicable to them in terms of performance and profitability differ little, if at all, from those applied to other business entities.

C160. Jewkes, John, *et al.* The sources of invention. London, Macmillan, 1958. 428 p.
C161. Meier, Richard L. Science and economic development. Cambridge, Technology Press of M.I.T., 1956. 266 p.
C162. National Bureau of Economic Research. The rate and direction of inventive activity; economic and social factors. Princeton, N.J., Princeton Univ. Press, 1962. 635 p.
C163. Strassman, W. Paul. Risk and technical innovation. Ithaca, N.Y., Cornell Univ. Press, 1959. 249 p.

Banking

Although innovation and entrepreneurship are customarily thought of in connection with industry, an important area of entrepreneurial innovation has been the field of finance and banking. The very ordinary commercial bank, with which we are all familiar, is an invention of medieval Europe. In later periods, specialized investment banks have been founded; and, in the course of the evolution of banking, central banks or central banking systems, like the Federal Reserve System, have come into prominence. Today the central banks are by far the most important portions of the banking systems of the various countries, since they not only perform functions of credit supply, but also assist the fiscal authorities in the implementation of policies of monetary and price stability.

In the course of time, banks have developed many new techniques and new functions; and various banks have specialized in such aspects of business as small loans, mortgage lending, savings deposits, investment trusts, and other financial practices. But the major business of banks has been commercial banking, i.e., the granting of loans to merchants and manu-facturers and the acceptance of deposits against which checks can be drawn. Since checks circulate in place of cash, and since banks can, by granting loans, influence the amount of checks in circulation at any time, they have the power to influence indirectly the quantity of money in circulation, and with it the level of prices. Since banks receive interest on loans, their profit motive gives them an incentive to aug-ment the amount of loans outstanding as much as possible; but at the same time they must impose self-restraints, since, if all outstanding checks were presented at once for payment in cash, the banks could not make these payments. Hence they can expand their loaning activities only up to a certain level and must watch that this does not exceed a cer-tain multiple of their cash reserves. This ratio between outstanding de-posits and cash reserves is the reserve ratio which is sometimes regulated by government; in some countries a customary limit is self-imposed by the banks. Another incentive for banks to expand loans is the rate of in-terest they charge, and the central bank may regulate this by imposing a so-called rediscount rate, which is the rate at which it will loan to banks against certain drafts or bills of exchange as security. The lower the rediscount rate, the easier it will be for banks to make loans. Rediscounting, reserve requirements, and other measures, e.g., open market sales and purchases of certain securities, are the main practices employed by central banks to control the expansion and contraction of bank credit and thus to regulate the effective currency in circulation. It is clear that an understanding of banking practices is closely related to the analysis of monetary phenomena and prices.

C164. Bagehot, Walter. Lombard Street, a description of the money market. London, H.S. King, 1873. 359 p.
C165. Gurley, John G. and Edward S. Shaw. Money in a theory of finance. Washington, D.C., Brookings Institution, 1960. 371 p.
C166. Hawtrey, Ralph G. The art of central banking. London, Longmans, Green, 1932. 464 p.
C167. Hawtrey, Ralph G. Currency and credit. 4th ed. London, Longmans, Green, 1950. 475 p.
C168. Mints, Lloyd W. A history of banking theory in Great Britain and the United States. Chicago, Univ. of Chicago Press, 1945. 319 p.
C169. Robertson, Dennis H. Banking policy and the price level. 3d ed. London, P.S. King, 1932. 106 p.
C170. Sayers, Richard S. American banking system. Oxford, Clarendon Press, 1948. 130 p.
C171. Sayers, Richard S. Modern banking. 5th ed. Oxford, Clarendon Press, 1960. 294 p.

Public Finance

In a modern nation, the policies in the monetary field are closely related to those in the fiscal field. In the present period of the world's development, a large proportion of a nation's income is transferred to government by means of taxes and spent by the government. Through the budgetary process the government can withdraw or add to the purchasing power among the public, and can affect the level of employment and prosperity in the community. Deficit financing may be a blessing when the economy at large is sluggish, and may be a curse in a situation of full or nearly full employment. The instrumentality of raising revenue and spending it on public works or other projects hence becomes— together with the monetary policy of the central bank—an important regulator of general economic activity.

Among all the features of public finance, the problem of taxation is the most hotly debated and controversial. It is not so much the fact of taxation, but rather the economic impact of taxes, the kinds of taxes, and the distribution of the burden of taxation which is under discussion. Among the most important and controversial subjects are the question of indirect versus direct taxes, the problem of proportionality versus progressivity of taxation, and the question of how easy it is to shift taxes onto the shoulders of someone else, e.g., by price changes or by alteration of wage payments. In addition, there are problems of cost of collection, of the possibility of tax evasion and tax avoidance, and, above all, of the equity and justice of a tax system. It should be remembered that modern societies all have a multiplicity of taxes and that what affects each person is not the impact of a single selected tax, but of the tax system as a whole. These and many related problems are discussed in the monographs cited below:

C172. Blough, Roy. The Federal taxing process. New York, Prentice-Hall, 1952. 506 p.
C173. Blum, Walter J. and Harry Kalven, Jr. The uneasy case for progressive taxation. Chicago, Univ. of Chicago Press, 1953. 107 p.
C174. Clark, John M. Economics of planning public works. Washington, Govt. Print. Off., 1935. 194 p.
C175. Dalton, Hugh, et al. Unbalanced budgets. London, Routledge, 1934. 468 p.
C176. Pigou, Arthur C. A study in public finance. 3d ed. London, Macmillan, 1947. 285 p.
C177. Seligman, Edwin R.A. The shifting and incidence of taxation. 5th ed., rev. and enl., New York, Columbia Univ. Press, 1927. 431 p.
C178. Simons, Henry C. Personal income taxation. Chicago, Univ. of Chicago Press, 1938. 238 p.
C179. Simons, Henry C. Federal tax reform. Chicago, Univ. of Chicago Press, 1950. 161 p.

The General Role of Government in the Economy

Although the fiscal policies of the government are the most clearly discernible impact of governmental functions in the economy, modern governments enter in many different ways into the economy. In the preceding paragraphs we have discussed government expenditures as though they were undertaken merely or mainly as a means of economic stabilization. But it will be recalled that at an earlier stage we talked about government consumption. Certain outlays of governments are made precisely for the purchase of goods and services arising from the independent needs of providing the customary government services, rather than from the desire to carry out economic stabilization. In fact, some of the heaviest expenditures undertaken by central and local governments stem from these needs. For example, the expenditure on armaments or on education, on the dispensing of justice and on general administration, are autonomous expenses; only such expenses as certain relief payments, or expenditures on certain public works have primarily a stabilizing function. It is proper, therefore, to study the general level of government activity as it has developed over time, and to look into the problems of such governmental activities as the provision of materials and services for defense, education, etc.

C180. Fabricant, Solomon. The trend of government activity in the United States since 1900. New York, National Bureau of Economic Research, 1952. 267 p.
C181. Hitch, Charles J. and Roland N. McKean. The economics of defense in the nuclear age. Cambridge, Harvard Univ. Press, 1960. 422 p.

C182. Mendershausen, Horst. The economics of war. New York, Prentice-
Hall, 1940. 314 p.

Economic Policy and Economic Planning

Fiscal measures, as well as other steps taken by the government, are all
part and parcel of the over-all economic policy of the government. This
policy may have varying objectives; it may be directed primarily toward
welfare of the people, or toward defense, or toward the maximization
of the rate of economic growth. In all instances there will be efforts to
bring about some degree of equity in the distribution of goods and services, at least in the more modern nations. The steps taken toward these
ends may be fiscal or regulatory; they usually will be combinations of
both.

In all instances in which the intervention of government is not inspired by a general production plan we customarily speak of economic
policy, or sets of economic policies. Whenever the quantity or degree of
regulation is ordered according to a systematic comprehensive schedule
we speak of economic planning. Dahl and Lindblom have shown that
the limits between economic policy and economic planning are often
blurred and that certain policies shade into planning and certain plans
into measures of somewhat disjointed policies. In the literature, somewhat sharper distinctions are drawn; and one may list separately studies which concern themselves primarily with economic policies, the ra-
tionale for certain policies, and the consequences—intended or not—of
economic policies. A few of the more challenging books in this vein are
listed here:

C183. Clark, John M. Social control of business. 2d ed. New York, McGraw-
Hill, 1939. 537 p.
C184. Dahl, Robert A. and Charles E. Lindblom. Politics, economics and
welfare. New York, Harper, 1953. 557 p.
C185. Downs, Anthony. An economic theory of democracy. New York,
Harper, 1957. 310 p.
C186. Simons, Henry C. Economic policy for a free society. Chicago, Univ.
of Chicago Press, 1948. 353 p.
C187. Walker, Edward R. From economic theory to policy. Chicago, Univ.
of Chicago Press, 1943. 273 p.

Other books concentrate on planning. At some point the possibility of
planning as such is questioned, at another its wisdom, and at some points
its efficiency. To all these questions answers have been given, but the debate continues. But the proponents of some form of planning are likely
to win out. Whether this results from the economic temper of our time,
or from the greatly improved capacity of planners to draw up realistic
plans, or whether it shows an over-all trend toward collectivism is difficult to say. But the inclination toward planning has become ubiquitous,
and anyone advocating it appears to be following the wave of the future.

C188. Hayek, Friedrich A., *ed*. Collectivist economic planning. London, Routledge, 1935. 293 p.

C189. Lange, Oskar and Fred M. Taylor. On the economic theory of socialism. Minneapolis, Univ. of Minnesota Press, 1938. 143 p.

C190. Lewis, William A. The principles of economic planning. London, Dobson, 1949. 128 p.

C191. Wootton, Barbara. Freedom under planning. Chapel Hill, Univ. of North Carolina Press, 1945. 163 p.

INTERNATIONAL ECONOMICS

Apart from a few stray comments, our discussion so far has been concerned with economic relations in general, i.e., in a situation in which abstraction was made of the existence of different nations, or in which economic relations were confined to one country. But a large body of economic theory, applied economics, and thinking on economic policy relates explicitly to the problems of international exchanges and international interaction between sovereign nations.

We shall briefly take up the various aspects of this part of economics. The study of international economics may be divided into several branches. First there is general theory, then there are problems of international monetary economics, (e.g., questions of exchange rates), next there are problems of applied economics and of economic policy, and finally there is a literature beginning to deal with questions of international economic planning.

One of the main producers of works and sponsors of research in international economics is the United Nations and its specialized agencies. The United Nations itself publishes statistical and general works on international economic relations between all countries. The various regional Economic Commissions bring out annual reports and additional occasional studies on the international economic relations pertaining to the region they serve. The Food and Agriculture Organization publishes works on international aspects of farm production and trade in agricultural commodities, the International Labour Organization on international migration and comparative studies on wages, etc. In addition, some special agencies, such as the Organization of American States, or NATO, or the Organization for European Economic Cooperation also sponsor international economic research and bring out publications falling into the field of regional or world-wide international economics.

Basic to all this study are works on the general theories of international economics and international trade. The most general works deal with the international, and sometimes also the inter-regional, exchange of goods and services, particularly finished goods. But some studies concentrate on the international movement of productive factors, i.e., of labor and capital. The basic works in the field are the following:

C191a. Angell, James W. The theory of international prices. Cambridge, Harvard Univ. Press, 1926. 571 p.
C192. Haberler, Gottfried. The theory of international trade. New York, Macmillan, 1937. 408 p.
C193. Meade, James E. Trade and welfare. London, Oxford Univ. Press, 1955. 2 v.
C194. Myrdal, Gunnar. An international economy. New York, Harper, 1956. 381 p.
C195. Ohlin, Bertil. Interregional and international trade. Cambridge, Harvard Univ. Press, 1933. 617 p.
C196. Taussig, Frank W. International trade. New York, Macmillan, 1927. 425 p.
C197. Viner, Jacob. Studies in the theory of international trade. New York, Harper, 1937. 650 p.

Balance of Payments and Exchange Rate Problems

The most general treatises in international economics deal primarily with questions of the international exchange of goods and services and the problem of the prices of goods and services that are exchanged. However, as the economists before Adam Smith already knew, what may matter for a country is not so much the items which enter into trade or their prices, but the over-all impact of international exchanges. In other words, does a country come out as a net exporter or a net importer? In the former case it gains currency; in the latter case it loses currency. The mercantilist writers, to whom the acquisition of gold through international trade appeared as a highly favored objective, all wished a positive balance of payments, i.e., a situation in which exports exceeded imports. A government which is welfare-oriented may well take a less extreme view, since an excess of imports over exports may, at certain times, contribute greatly to the over-all level of welfare in a country. But ultimately the most desirable policy is one of equilibrium in a country's international accounts. In general, a net inflow of foreign funds, as well as a net outflow of domestic funds abroad, may have inflationary or deflationary results, just as a governmental budgetary deficit or surplus may have these effects. It is not always easy to insulate the domestic economy against the impact of balance of payments problems, and so policies designed to bring about equilibrium in the international accounts have certain obvious advantages.

One of the mechanisms by which a country's international indebtedness may be settled is the outflow of currency, especially of gold. Another mechanism is the alteration of its rate of exchange, i.e., the alteration of the price of foreign currencies in terms of its domestic currency. Depreciation is an alternative to gold outflows; and usually, if a country's balance of payments worsens, both of these adjustments may take place. In contemporary nations a great deal of effort is spent to influence the balance of payments and the exchange rates by means of various forms of governmental regulation, but before we can consider these we must first gain clarity about the monetary and payments mechanisms involved.

Finally, an important regulatory device may be the international flow of capital, and, in fact, capital flows often have played a stabilizing role in the past. In the more recent post-war period the major stabilizing influence has come from foreign aid, although capital flows in certain cases have also been of significance.

C198. Buchanan, Norman S. International investment and domestic welfare. New York, Holt, 1945. 249 p.
C199. Feis, Herbert. Europe: the world's banker. New Haven, Conn., Yale Univ. Press, 1930. 469 p.
C200. Iversen, Carl. Aspects of the theory of international capital movements. Copenhagen, Levin & Munksgaard, 1935. 536 p.
C201. Kindleberger, Charles P. The dollar shortage. New York, Wiley, 1950. 276 p.
C202. Letiche, John M. Balance of payments and economic growth. New York, Harper, 1959. 378 p.
C203. Williams, John B. International trade under flexible exchange rates. Amsterdam, North-Holland Publishing Co., 1954. 332 p.

Protectionism

As already pointed out, it is rare in our day that the free play of the market is allowed to exert its influence upon international transactions. The regulatory activity employed may be unilateral or multilateral, i.e., it may be imposed by one country without regard to the interests of others, or it may be imposed by some mutual agreement between the countries concerned.

The first policy is protectionism. It consists in the imposition of tariffs, quotas, exchange controls, and various other measures designed to protect the domestic producers and consumers against foreign competition. Although different protective measures have different degrees of effectiveness, the most appropriate measures vary from country to country and from commodity to commodity. In one country, a tariff may be a very effective means of reducing foreign competition, whereas in another country—owing to geographical, or transportation, or institutional factors—the same degree of protection can only be achieved by harsher means, e.g. quotas. Since protectionism is a form of governmental regulation, most of the considerations apply to it which may be applied to other governmental economic policies. To what extent are considerations of equity, or considerations of national power, or of economic growth prevailing. Depending upon differences in objectives, different forms of regulation of international economic transactions will be employed. Finally, it should be remembered that, just as economic policies, in general, have become highly refined and specialized, so have measures of international economic policy, and especially protectionist devices. The ingenuity which has gone into the development of new and more highly dis-

criminating measures has been great, and one might well have hoped
that it would have been applied to a somewhat worthier cause.

C204. Beveridge, William H., *et al.* Tariffs, the case examined. London,
       Longmans Green, 1931. 300 p.
C205. Bidwell, Percy W. The invisible tariff: a study of the control of
       imports into the United States. New York, Council on Foreign
       Relations, 1939. 286 p.
C206. Ellis, Howard S. Exchange control in central Europe. Cambridge,
       Harvard Univ. Press, 1941. 413 p.
C207. Graham, Frank D. Protective tariffs. New York, Harper, 1934. 176 p.
C208. Heuser, Heinrich. Control of international trade. Philadelphia, Blak-
       iston, 1939. 282 p.
C209. Taussig, Frank W. Some aspects of the tariff question. Cambridge,
       Harvard Univ. Press, 1915. 374 p.

International Economic Co-operation

The alternative to regulation of international economic transactions
by unilateral action is regulation by bilateral or multilateral action, i.e.,
the arrangement of controls of international exchanges and the international flow of persons, capital, goods and services by means of various
types of bilateral or multilateral treaties. The place of commercial treaties in the history of international economic relations has often been
studied, with special reference to the place of discrimination which these
treaties were intended to eradicate. A specially favored topic is the study
of the most-favored-nation clause, that is, of a provision in commercial
treaties designed to insure to each signatory partner the same treatment
given to any most highly favored third nation. The struggle against discrimination has been a long and arduous one and is by no means finally
overcome.

Recently, the major effort of finding multilateral patterns of regulating international economic relations has been the formation of customs unions and various other forms of economic union. The European
Economic Community (the so-called "Common Market") is only the
first such device. It is being imitated already in Latin America, and there
are other regional organizations and economic blocks under discussion
or in formation. The main problems of the formation of these unions are
political; but, to the extent to which they extend the territory of common
trade and related economic actions, they have economic results. It is to
these economic results that the more serious literature has been devoted.
Most of the more popular treatments do not come to the heart of the economic problem, but discuss mainly or exclusively the political questions
involved.

C210. Benoit, Emile. Europe at sixes and sevens. New York, Columbia
       Univ. Press, 1961. 275 p.
C211. Hirschman, Albert O. National power and the structure of foreign
       trade. Berkeley, Univ. of California Press, 1945. 170 p.

C212. Meade, James E. Problems of economic union. Chicago, Univ. of Chicago Press, 1953. 102 p.
C213. Meade, James E. The theory of customs unions. Amsterdam, North-Holland Publishing Co., 1955. 121 p.
C214. Viner, Jacob. The customs union issue. New York, Carnegie Endowment for International Peace, 1950. 221 p.
C215. Wilcox, Clair. A charter for world trade. New York, Macmillan, 1949. 333 p.
C216. Wolf, Charles, Jr. Foreign aid: theory and practice in Southern Asia. Princeton, N.J., Princeton Univ. Press, 1960. 442 p.

ECONOMIC HISTORY

We have completed our survey of the major branches of economics in the preceding discussion, but we must touch briefly upon one more topic: the explicit study of economic institutions in countries of different culture. In the customary economics curriculum these problems are usually taught in courses on "comparative economic systems"; but this is a restrictive interpretation, and it is more suitable to think of differences in economic institutions on a quite general level.

Institutions differ either because they belong to different culturally oriented societies or because they belong to different time periods in the same society. Hence the study of economic history—to the extent to which it has economic, rather than historical or antiquarian objectives—is really a study of comparison of economic institutions. Some of the most distinguished writings in economic history (which has a vast literature and hence cannot be discussed extensively), are strictly limited in conception and objectives. Those works are not of interest in the present context. But some monographs on economic history are explicitly devoted to the examination of changing institutions in the field of production, distribution, or exchange and the relation of these changes to the historical evolution of certain societies. These studies are thus devoted to an examination of comparative economic institutions within the historical context. They may be matched by a series of similar studies performing the same function of comparison on a cross-cultural basis. We list here a few of the broadest and most general studies in economic history, some of which are based on viewpoints and methods developed originally by the German historical school in economics.

C217. Bücher, Karl. Industrial evolution. New York, Holt, 1901. 393 p.
C218. Clapham, John H. An economic history of modern Britain. Cambridge, Eng. Cambridge Univ. Press, 1959. 3 v.
C219. Nef, John U. War and human progress. Cambridge, Harvard Univ. Press, 1950. 464 p.
C220. Pirenne, Henri. Economic and social history of medieval Europe. New York, Harcourt Brace, 1937. 243 p.
C221. Polanyi, Karl. The great transformation. New York, Farrar & Rinehart, 1944. 305 p.

C222. Sombart, Werner. The quintessence of capitalism, tr. and ed. by
       M. Epstein. London, Unwin, 1915. 400 p.
C223. Weber, Max. General economic history. Glencoe, Ill., Free Press,
       1950. 419 p.
C224. Wright, Chester. Economic history of the United States. 2d ed. New
       York, McGraw-Hill, 1949. 941 p.

Institutional Economics

One of the consequences of the research of the German historical
school in economics was the development of institutional economics,
which experienced its main flowering in the United States in the early
20th century. Its main representatives were Thorstein Veblen and
John R. Commons in the United States and John A. Hobson in Great
Britain. The institutionalists had no real quarrel with the then prevailing
economic theory, though in some of the less friendly reviews of their
ideas this opinion is sometimes expressed. They tried to do what some
of the more thoughtful members of the German school of historical economics had already attempted i.e., they tried to examine the social role
played by economic institutions and the way in which these institutions
exerted a feedback on the functioning of the economic system itself.
They tried to provide answers to questions which general theory had not
been able to solve. These answers were not to be found in the economic
system as such, but in the social relations, the psychology of the partici-
pants in the economic process, and in the distribution of political power
throughout a given society.

In its period of flowering, i.e., during the first three decades of this century, institutional economics made a very real contribution; but by now
many of the suggestions proffered by the institutional economists have
been incorporated into the general body of economics. In the postwar
period this has been facilitated by the growing interest in the economics
of underdeveloped countries, and the fact that the cultural and social
conditions, as well as the economic institutions of these countries, were
patently different from those of western nations. Hence contemporary
economics, though still predominantly "theoretical and analytical," has
become much more "institutional" than the economics of even a generation ago. Thus the books by the leading institutional economists have
more interest as contributions to the history of economic ideas than to
the analysis of contemporary economic problems.

C225. Ayres, Clarence E. The theory of economic progress. Chapel Hill,
       Univ. of North Carolina Press, 1944. 317 p.
C226. Commons, John R. Institutional economics. New York, Macmillan,
       1934. 921 p.
C227. Hobson, John A. Work and wealth: a human valuation. New York,
       Macmillan, 1914. 367 p.
C228. Veblen, Thorstein. The theory of business enterprise. New York,
       Scribner's, 1904. 400 p.

C229. Veblen, Thorstein. The theory of the leisure class. New York, The
Modern Library, 1934. 404 p.

Cross-Cultural Comparison of Economic Institutions

Some of the work which has incorporated suggestions originally made
by the institutional economists relates, as already suggested, to cross-
cultural comparisons of economic institutions. The number of studies in
this field has been greatly expanded in recent years, and research in this
branch of economics has become very popular. A large number of field
reports has been made available on the economic institutions of peoples
with cultures very different from those of the west; and some steps have
been taken to develop a field of "economic anthropology." It would be
impossible to provide an adequate listing of all the case studies in this
field which are now available.

On the basis of these field studies, and through cooperation of several
researchers, some comparative studies have been produced. These tend
to incorporate the results of field research from various sources. The economist in search for generalizations of some kind is better served by the
comparative studies than by the special field studies, since the former already contribute a certain effort at generalization. Moreover, comparative studies tend to select the major variables from several field studies
and place primary emphasis on them. In an area in which institutional
variety is so large this is an important step forward.

In the following we present a few studies which may properly be said
to fall into the area of the comparative cross-cultural study of economic
institutions. Some are case studies, others are more genuine comparative
studies. Some deal with relatively simple and primitive societies, others
with more advanced societies, notably those in which extensive planning
of the socialist variety is practiced. These are merely samples of a rapidly
growing literature, which in the not-too-distant future is likely to supply
us with extensive descriptive and analytical accounts of the economic relations in most countries and societies of the world.

C230. Aitken, Hugh G.J., ed. The state and economic growth. New York,
Social Science Research Council, 1959. 389 p.
C231. Bergson, Abram. Soviet economic growth: conditions and perspec-
tives. Evanston, Ill., Row Peterson, 1953. 376 p.
C232. Li, Cho-Min. Economic development of Communist China. Berk-
eley, Univ. of California Press, 1959. 284 p.
C233. Moore, Wilbert E. Industrialization and labor. Ithaca, N.Y., Cornell
Univ. Press, 1951. 410 p.
C234. Tax, Sol. Penny capitalism, a Guatemalan Indian economy. Wash-
ington, Govt. Print. Off., 1953. 230 p.
C235. Udy, Stanley G. The organization of work. New Haven, Conn.,
Human Relations Area Files Press, 1959. 182 p.

Bert F. Hoselitz

GUIDES TO THE LITERATURE

C236. Coman, Edwin T., Jr. Sources of business information. New York, Prentice-Hall, 1949. 406 p.

Although some material is out of date, this guide provides a good introduction to business information. Suggests works which are basic, describes simple research methods and points out the uses of resources such as libraries, trade associations, chambers of commerce. Each chapter deals with one phase of business (i.e. finance, management, basic industries) and includes a bibliography as well as a general discussion of sources. Good index. A new edition is in preparation.

C237. Manley, Marian C. Business information: how to find and use it. New York, Harper, 1955. 265 p.

Based on the author's experience as head of the Newark Business Library, this comprehensive guide is of use both to the layman and to the librarian. Part I approaches sources by types; directories, periodicals, associations, "services", and points out various applications of the information. Part II is a bibliography of publications arranged by specific topics (business conditions, administration, production, distribution communication, personal economics) with detailed information on each publication. Extremely good detailed index.

C238. Wasserman, Paul. Information for administrators; a guide to publications and services for management in business and government. Ithaca, N.Y., Cornell Univ. Press, 1956. 375 p.

On the theory that all administrative processes are universal, the author presents sources of information of interest to both business and public administrators. Descriptive treatment of information sources by type (statistics, etc.) and source (associations, "services", etc.). The last two chapters provide a bibliography of basic publications. A good analytical index. Appendices include a list of depository libraries, field offices of the U.S. Department of Commerce and Small Business Administration and information services in foreign countries.

REVIEWS OF THE LITERATURE

C239. American Economic Association. A survey of contemporary economics. Volume I, ed. by Howard S. Ellis. Philadelphia, Blakiston, 1948. 490 p.; Volume II, ed. by Bernard F. Haley. Homewood, Ill., Irwin, 1952. 474 p.

Essays on trends in contemporary economic thinking with extensive references to recent economic literature.

C240. Cole, Arthur H. The historical development of economic and business literature. Boston, Baker Library, Harvard Univ. Graduate School of Business Administration, 1957. 56 p.

A scholarly discussion of economico-business literature as it developed from scattered pamphlets, sermons and occasional books of the 16th century complexity and variety of business and economic publications.

C241. Accountants' digest. v. 1+ Sept. 1935+ Burlington, Vt., L.L. Briggs, Univ. of Vermont. quarterly.

Abstracts of selected important articles in English language accounting journals.

C242. American economic review. v. 1+ March 1911+ Evanston, Ill., American Economic Association. quarterly.

Lengthy book reviews. New book notes, listings of periodical articles and doctoral disertations are arranged by subject.

C243. American Institute of Certified Public Accountants. Journal of accountancy. v. 1+ Nov. 1905+ New York. monthly.
Book reviews and a bibliography of periodical literature.

C244. Business books (of the year or half-year). Library journal.
A carefully prepared list of about fifty of the best or most significant business books.
Short descriptive annotations.

C245. Economic journal, the journal of the Royal Economic Society. v. 1+ March 1891+ London, Macmillan. quarterly.
International list of periodical articles and an annotated list of new books.

C246. The executive; a guide to reading for top management. v. 1+ June 1957+ Boston, Baker Library, Harvard Univ. Graduate School of Business Administration. monthly.
A selection, aimed at business leaders, of significant books, pamphlets, speeches and periodical articles which illuminate current social, political and economic conditions. Lengthy abstracts.

C247. Harvard business review. v. 1+ 1922+ Boston, Harvard Univ. Graduate School of Business Administration. bi-monthly.
"Looking Around" is a frequent bibliographical essay on selected business topics.

C248. Management review. v. 1+ March 1914+ New York, American Management Association. monthly.
Digest of leading articles and reports. Reviews of new books.

ABSTRACTS

C249. Documentation économique; revue bibliographique trimestrielle, publie les analyses classées par sujets des articles parus dans les principales revues économiques. 1934-38, 1947+ Paris, Presses Universitaires de France. quarterly.
Abstracts of selected economic books and articles appearing in some 180 journals of all countries are arranged by subject and annotated in French. Almost a year's lag between publication of articles and the appearance of its abstract here.

C250. Economic abstracts: semi-monthly review of abstracts on economics, finance, trade and industry, management and labour, ed. by the Library of the Economic Information Service, Ministry of Economic Affairs in collaboration with the Library, Netherlands School of Economics and the Library, Ministry of Social Affairs. v. 1+ June 1, 1953+ The Hague, Nijhoff. semi-monthly.
Abstracts of pamphlets, books and periodical articles in the language in which the item is written. Not to be confused with *Economic abstracts* published by New York University Graduate School of Arts and Sciences (1952-1960) which was undertaken by graduate students to carry on the economic part of *Social science abstracts*.

BIBLIOGRAPHIES—CURRENT

C251. Accountants' index; a bibliography of accounting literature. New York, American Institute of Accountants, 1921-1961 (In progress)
A basic index of English-language accounting literature appearing in periodicals, proceedings, reports, books and parts of books. Author, subject and title entries, showing bibliographic information only, appear in a single alphabet. Addresses of publishers are listed separately. The initial volume, published in 1921, referred to literature in print in 1912 and published since that year. Supplements have been issued as necessary; the latest is the 14th dated

1959/60. Extremely complete coverage for a specialized field, although supplements tend to be late in appearing.

C252. American Management Association. Management bookshelf; a catalog of A.M.A. publications and films. New York, 1932+ annual.

Formerly the *Management index* (1932-1955).

C253. Business and technology sources: bulletin of the Business and Technology Department. v. 1+ January 1930+ Cleveland, Ohio, Cleveland Public Library. frequency varies.

Each issue lists magazine articles and books on specific topics (i.e. scientific research and development, building and construction industry, business and technology handbooks), showing bibliographic information, price and brief annotation. Title has varied (1930-1938, *Bulletin*; 1939-1956, *Business information sources*).

C254. Business literature. v. 1+ April 1928+ Newark, N.J., Newark Public Library. 10 times a year.

Issued by one of the finest public business libraries, this monthly covers a specific topic in each number (i.e. records management, industrial site selection, dollars and sense in money management). Material is up-to-date and well described bibliographically. Descriptive and often evaluative annotations.

C255. Business periodicals index; a cumulative subject index to periodicals in the fields of accounting, advertising, banking and finance, general business, insurance, labor and management, marketing and purchasing, office management, public administration, taxation, specific businesses, industries and trades. v. 1+ 1958+ New York, H.W. Wilson. monthly, with semi-annual and annual cumulations.

Successor to the business portion of *Industrial arts index*. Subject headings are constantly revised to correspond with current business nomenclature and include sub-classes and cross references. Best index to business periodical literature, although there is a few months' lag between publication of the article and indexing.

C256. Business service checklist. Washington, U.S. Department of Commerce. weekly.

New government publications and releases of interest to businessmen.

C257. Canadian business and technical index. v. 1+ 1959+ Toronto, Canada, Toronto Public Library. bi-monthly with semi-annual and annual cumulations.

Indexes Canadian publications only.

C258. Employment relations abstracts. 1959+ Detroit, Information Service. semi-annual.

Formerly *Labor personnel index* (1952-1958). A loose leaf service that indexes periodicals and a few books of current interest in the fields of manpower management and labor economics. Entries are arranged under broad categories and a subject index gives the location of specific subjects. Semi-annual with yearly cumulations.

C259. Financial index. v. 1+ May 9, 1960+ New York, The Financial Index Co. weekly with quarterly cumulations.

An index of investment services, financial magazines, brokerage house reports. In the first section articles on industries as a whole are arranged under the industry; in the second section securities and companies are arranged alphabetically. A phrase describes the contents of articles (i.e., acquisition, split, prospects). Covers publications of U.S., Canada, Japan and Great Britain.

C260. Index of corporations and industries. 1960+ Detroit, Funk and Scott Publishing Co. weekly with monthly cumulations.

Indexes financial publications,

stock brokers reports, talks before the Society of Security Analysts. Similar to *Financial index* but much less comprehensive.

C261. Index to labor union periodicals, a cumulative subject index to material from a selected list of newspapers and journals published by major labor unions. Jan., 1960+ Ann Arbor, Bureau of Industrial Relations, Univ. of Michigan. monthly.

A classified, annotated list of material in the field of labor relations. Cross references aid in locating articles.

C262. International bibliography of economics. v. 1-8, 1952-1959. Paris, UNESCO, 1955-1961; v. 9+ 1960+ Chicago, Aldine, 1962+ annual.

Part of a Unesco program to supply basic bibliographic tools of an international scope for each social science. Bibliographic information on books, periodical articles and reports distributed in duplicated form appears under a classified arrangement in both English and French. Separate author and subject indexes. Issued two or three years after publication date of material included.

C263. Johns Hopkins University. *Department of Political Economy.* Economic library selections.

Series I: New books in economics. no. 1+ March 1954+ Baltimore. quarterly.

Classified list of new books, pamphlets, government documents and journals designed to assist college and university libraries in selecting economic material. Each entry includes bibliographic information, a descriptive annotation and an indication of the size of library (by economics book budget) for which purchase is recommended. Entry index to each issue and cumulative index every ten issues. This publication and the following one offer invaluable aid to a library which must

keep its collection well rounded and up to date at a minimum cost.

C264. Series II: Basic lists in special fields. Baltimore, 1954+ irregular.

Designed to assist librarians in "building up basic collections in the several major fields of economics and in appraising their existing collections," these lists are similar in format to "New books in economics" described above. To date six numbers have appeared: (1) International economics (1954), (2) Statistics and econometrics (1955), (3) Selected economic reference works and Professional journals (1956), (4) Business fluctuations (1957), (5) Economic theory and history of thought (1960), and (6) Economics of labor (1961).

C265. Marketing information guide. v. 1+ March 1954+ Washington, U.S. Business and Defense Services Administration. monthly.

Classified listing of current government and non-government publications of interest to the fields of marketing and distribution. Includes books, pamphlets, reports and articles, and gives a brief descriptive annotation as well as bibliographic information. Index supplements are issued semi-annually. From 1954-1961 the title was *Distribution data guide.*

C266. Princeton University. *Industrial Relations Section.* Selected references. no. 1+ January 1945+ Princeton, N.J. bi-monthly.

Annotated list of new books, articles and reports on selected topics in the industrial relations field. "Outstanding Books in Industrial Relations," a section which appears yearly, and other lists on specific topics bring up to date two earlier Princeton publications: *The office library of an industrial relations executive* (1951), and *A trade union library* (6th edition. 1955) see C291. Recent issues have covered such topics as management in the Soviet Union and the cost and financing of health care for the aged.

C267. Public Affairs Information Service. Bulletin. See (A82).

C268. Technical book review index, comp. and ed. in the Technology Dept. of the Carnegie Library of Pittsburgh. v. 1+ 1935+ New York, Special Libraries Association. quarterly.

This is the *Book review digest* of technical literature. The original publication covered the years 1917-1928 and was published by the Technology Dept. of the Carnegie Library. In 1935 S.L.A. revived the project. Material included falls mostly into the 500 and 600 Dewey classification. Bibliographical information, taken from reviews, is followed by review excerpts. A cumulative author index appears annually. While extremely useful in a technical library, this index does not cover all books of interest to business.

C269. Wall Street journal index. December, 1957+ New York, Dow Jones & Co. monthly with annual cumulations.

BIBLIOGRAPHIES—RETROSPECTIVE

C270. American Economic Association. Index of economic journals. Homewood, Ill., Irwin, 1961-62. 5 v.

A classified index of English language articles appearing in the world's major professional economic journals published between 1886 and 1959. Personal author index.

C271. American labor union periodicals; a guide to their location, comp. by Bernard G. Naas and Carmelita S. Sakr. Published for the Committee of University Industrial Relations Librarians by the New York State School of Industrial and Labor Relations. Ithaca, N.Y., Cornell Univ., 1956. 175 p.

A union list of over 1,700 publi-

cations of national and international unions and locals.

C272. American Library Association. *Joint Committee on Library Service to Labor Groups.* Selected list of materials and resources. In its *Guide for developing a public library service to labor groups.* Chicago, 1958. pp. 9-23.

A brief listing of bibliographies and indexes, statistical handbooks, directories and dictionaries, periodicals and organizations which furnish information.

C273. Associated University Bureaus of Business and Economic Research. Index of publications of bureaus of business and economic research, 1950-1956. Eugene, Ore., 1957. Supplements.

Divided into two sections: the first arranges publications (separate works only, no periodicals) by institution and the second arranges publications (including periodicals) by subject. The supplements include periodical articles. For publications through 1949 consult Fern Wilson's *Index of publications by university bureaus of business research* (Cleveland, Ohio, Press of Western Reserve University, 1951).

C274. Batson, Harold E., *comp.* A select bibliography of modern economic theory, 1870-1929. London, Routledge; New York, Dutton, 1930. 224 p. (Studies in Economics and Political Science. No. 6 in the series of bibliographies by writers connected with the London School of Economics and Political Science)

An annotated bibliography of books and articles arranged in two parts, the first a classified section and the second an author section. Separate parts for English, German and French authors. Excellent for the period covered.

C275. Blum, Albert A. An annotated bibliography of industrial relations and the small firm. Ithaca, N.Y., Cornell Univ., 1960. 45 p.

(Cornell University. New York State School of Industrial and Labor Relations. Bibliography series, no. 3)

C276. Braeuer, Walter. Handbuch zur Geschichte der Volkswirtschaftslehre: ein bibliographisches Nachschlagewerk. Frankfurt am Main, Klostermann, 1952. 224 p.
A bibliography of the history of economic doctrine with emphasis on continental European economists. Arrangement is chronological by school. Includes biographical material as well as bibliographies of the works of separate economists.

C277. Clark, Charles T. Selected and annotated bibliography of personnel administration. Austin, Bureau of Business Research, Univ. of Texas, 1958. 27 p. (Bibliography series, no. 1)

C278. Dartmouth College. *Amos Tuck School of Business Administration.* A reading list on business administration. 7th rev. ed. Hanover, N.H., 1958. 68 p.
A classified list of books, periodicals and business reports (including government publications) in business and related fields for the businessman, student and teacher. Originally compiled in response to requests from alumni and others for a basic list, this bibliography covers mainly introductory works. The new revision touches on topics such as automation, quantitative methods and probability, linear programming, game and decision theory and operations research. Short critical annotations are extremely helpful in book recommendations. A title and author index offers quick access to the list.

C279. Downey, Bernard. Free and inexpensive U.S. government publications for labor. In American Library Association. Joint Committee on Library Service to Labor Groups. *Newsletter,* v. 13, no. 2, Fall 1960: 1-6.

C280. Harvard University. *Graduate School of Business Administration. Baker Library.* Business forecasting for the 1960's, a selected annotated bibliography. Boston, 1960. 41 p. (Its Reference list no. 20)

C281. Harvard University. *Graduate School of Business Administration. Baker Library.* Business literature; a reading list for students and businessmen. Boston, 1959. 31 p. (Its Reference list no. 17)
An unannotated bibliography of the most useful books and periodicals in various fields of business. Topics covered include business in the American society, management, employee relations, finance, accounting, marketing, and transportation. The appendix contains a list of reference works and periodicals for the business executive, a list of case books by the members of the Harvard Business School faculty and a directory of publishers. A new revision is in preparation.

C282. Harvard University. *Graduate School of Business Administration. Baker Library.* Executive compensation: selected references. Boston, 1960. 11 p. (Its reference list no. 19)

C283. Harvard University. *Graduate School of Business Administration. Baker Library.* A guide to selected reference sources in Baker Library. Boston, 1961. 19 p. mimeographed.
Although intended for use in Baker Library, this annotated list is useful as a quick reference. It will be issued as part of the Reference list series.

C284. Harvard University. *Graduate School of Business Administration. Baker Library. Kress Library of Business and Economics.* Catalogue; with data upon cognate items in other Harvard libraries. Boston, 1940-1957. 3 v.
A chronological, unannotated list

of economic works, some dating from pre-16th century incunabula. Detailed author and anonymous title index. V. 1 and its supplement cover to 1776; v. 2, 1777-1817.

C285. Harvard University. *Graduate School of Business Administration. Baker Library.* Studies in enterprise; a selected bibliography of American and Canadian company histories and biographies of businessmen. Boston, 1957. 169 p. (Reference list no. 4)

The 2,080 books and articles of over 20 pages, which appear in this bibliography, present an over-all history of a company or an individual "that has been in business in the hope of making a profit." Arranged by industry, each item gives the bibliographical information with a brief explanation only when necessary. Supplements, slightly expanded in scope, appear in the summer issue of *Business history review*.

C286. Hasse, Adelaid R. Index of economic material in documents of the states of the United States. Washington, Carnegie Institution, 1907-1922. 13 v. in 16.

For the thirteen states covered, this is a comprehensive indexing of material on American economic history in printed reports of administrative officers, legislative committees, special commissions of the states and governors' messages.

C287. Larson, Henrietta M. Guide to business history; materials for the study of American business history and suggestions for their use. Cambridge, Harvard Univ. Press, 1948. 1181 p. (Harvard studies in business history, v. 12)

An outstanding compilation of books and periodical articles for the study of business history. Some 4,904 annotated entries are arranged under topics and indexed by author and title. Broad topics include historical background and setting of American business, business admin-istrators, history of individual business units. A section on research and reference materials covers business manuscript records, business and technical museums, trade associations, publications, government materials, doctoral dissertations, biographical collections and state and local histories.

C288. Manpower management five-foot shelf. Minneapolis, Industrial Relations Center, Univ. of Minnesota, 1956. 29 p. (Bulletin no. 19, Nov. 1956)

A well annotated minimum list for libraries on personnel management and industrial relations. Covers books, magazines and miscellaneous sources of information such as newsletters, labor services, pamphlets and indexing services.

C289. Neufeld, Maurice F. A bibliography of American labor union history. Ithaca, N.Y., New York State School of Industrial and Labor Relations, Cornell Univ., 1958. 64 p. (Bibliography series, no. 2).

In an attempt to present all points of view, this unannotated bibliography lists books (from popular novels to scholarly monographs), Ph.D. theses, government reports, union documents, management publications and articles in both professional journals and mass circulation media. Items are arranged under broad headings with no index.

C290. Pittsburgh University. *Bureau of Business Research.* Small business bibliography. 2d ed. Pittsburgh, 1958. 209 p.

A selective list of books, government publications, pamphlets, periodical articles and unpublished material (i.e., dissertations) of particular interest to the small business executive.

C291. Princeton University. *Industrial Relations Section.* A trade union library. 6th ed. Princeton, N.J., 1955. 58 p. (Bibliographical series, no. 84)

Compiled as a guide to a working library for information on labor and unions. Entries are arranged under topics, i.e., trade unions and collective bargaining, personnel problems, reference books, with an author index.

C292. Wasserman, Paul. Decision making; an annotated bibliography. Ithaca, N.Y., Graduate School of Business and Public Administration, Cornell Univ., 1958. 111 p.

C293. Wasserman, Paul. Measurement and evaluation of organizational performance; an annotated bibliography. Ithaca, N.Y., Graduate School of Business and Public Administration, Cornell Univ., 1959. 110 p.

HANDBOOKS, MANUALS, COMPENDIA

Business handbooks are rich sources of quick, factual information. From time to time bibliographies of handbooks appear in *Business and technology sources* (Cleveland Public Library) and in *Business literature* (Newark Public Library). The following list is neither comprehensive nor definitive; it merely cites some of the most useful handbooks and manuals.

C294. Accountants' handbook, ed. by Rufus Wixon. 4th ed. New York, Ronald Press, 1956. various paging.

C295. Advertising handbook, ed. by Roger Barton. New York, Prentice Hall, 1950. 1015 p.

C296. Angel, Juvenal L. Why and how to prepare an effective job résumé. 3d ed. rev. and enl. New York, World Trade Academy Press, 1961. 105 p.

C297. Corporate secretary's encyclopedia, ed. by Lillian Doris. New York, Prentice Hall, 1959. 4 v.
Legal approach to corporation management.

C298. Corporate treasurer's and controller's encyclopedia, ed. by Lillian Doris. New York, Prentice Hall, 1958. 4 v.

C299. Encyclopedia of accounting systems, ed. by Robert L. Williams and Lillian Doris. New York, Prentice Hall, 1956-57. 5 v.

C300. Encyclopedia of corporate meetings, minutes and resolutions, ed. by Lillian Doris and Edith J. Friedman. New York, Prentice Hall, 1958. 3 v.

C301. Financial handbook, ed. by Jules I. Bogen. New York, Ronald Press, 1952. 1289 p.

C302. Foreign commerce handbook. 14th ed. Washington, Chamber of Commerce of the U.S., 1960. 142 p.

C303. Handbook of employee relations, ed. by John C. Aspley. New York, Dartnell, 1955. 1391 p.

C304. Handbook of industrial engineering and management, ed. by W.G. Ireson and E.L. Grant. New York, Prentice Hall, 1955. 1204 p.

C305. Handbook of public relations, ed. by Howard Stephenson. New York, McGraw Hill, 1960. 855 p.

C306. Marketing handbook, ed. by Paul H. Nystrom and Albert W. Frey. New York, Ronald Press, 1948. 1321 p.

C307. Office management handbook, ed. by Harry L. Wylie. 2d ed. New York, Ronald Press, 1958. various paging.

C308. Printing and promotion handbook, ed. by Daniel Melcher and Nancy Larrick. 2d ed. New York, McGraw Hill, 1956. 438 p.

C309. Production handbook, ed. by George B. Carson. 2d ed. New York, Ronald Press, 1958. various paging.

C310. Public relations handbook, ed. by John C. Aspley. 3d rev. ed. Chicago, Dartnell, 1961. 992 p.

C311. Purchasing handbook, ed. by George W. Aljian. New York, McGraw Hill, 1958. various paging.

C312. Sales manager's handbook, ed. by John C. Aspley. 9th ed. Chicago, Ill., Dartnell, 1962. 1008 p.

C313. Standard industrial classification manual. Washington, U.S. Bureau of the Budget, 1957. 433 p.

C314. Systems and procedures; a handbook for business and industry, ed. by Victor Lazzaro. New York, Prentice Hall, 1959. 464 p.

C315. Top management handbook, ed. by Harold B. Maynard. New York, McGraw Hill, 1960. 1236 p.

C316. U.S. *Dept. of Labor.* American worker's factbook. 2d ed. Washington, 1960. 355 p. plus appendix.

C317. U.S. *Bureau of Labor Statistics.* Guide to labor management relations in the U.S. Washington, 1958. (Bulletin no. 1225, March 1958.) Supplement no. 1, November 1958. Supplement no. 2, July 1959.
Originally prepared as a guide to labor management relations in the U.S. for visiting trade unions and management representatives. Good bibliography in Suppl. no. 1.

DICTIONARIES

C318. Benn, Alice E. The management dictionary: standardization of definitions and concepts of the terminology in the field of personnel management. New York, Exposition Press, 1952. 381 p.
Over 4,000 short, clear definitions of terms (phrases as well as words). Wherever necessary for clarity formulas are introduced and explained.

The compiler, head of the Ford Motor Company's Public Relations Research Library, extracted verbatim definitions from periodicals, newspapers, reports, books, radio speeches, etc., issued since 1945. All definitions that were not established as common interpretations of at least five primary sources were rejected, and the selected definitions were then submitted to a specialized group for approval.

C319. Clark, Donald T. and Bert A. Gottfried. Dictionary of business and finance. New York, Crowell, 1957. 409 p.
Compiled by the Librarian of Harvard University Graduate School of Business and a specialist in business management problems. Scope is broad and definitions are given for both general categories and specific examples, i.e., bonds and types of bonds, mortgages and types of mortgages. "See" and "see also" references expand the definitions. An appendix includes tables of equivalents, interest tables and foreign exchange rates.

C320. Encyclopedic dictionary of business, prepared by the editorial staff of Prentice Hall. New York, Prentice Hall, 1952. 704 p.
Non-technical, encyclopedic-type treatment of the language of business. When necessary for clarity of explanation, diagrams are included and methods and formulas are explained (i.e., subject of "overhead" includes samples of how to figure by direct labor method, direct labor-hour method, direct materials and direct labor and machine hours method. Sources are carefully cited. This is the most comprehensive of the strictly business dictionaries.

C321. Encyclopedic dictionary of business finance. New York, Prentice Hall, 1960. 658 p.

C322. Henius, Frank. Dictionary of foreign trade. 2d ed. New York, Prentice Hall, 1947. 959 p.

C323. Horton, Byrne J., *et al.* Dictionary of modern economics. Washington, Public Affairs Information Press, 1948. 365 p.

A non-technical modern economics dictionary, American-oriented, which gives only current meanings. Emphasis is on everyday business terms, societies, laws and biographical material. Some bibliographical references to parts of and entire books.

C324. Kohler, Eric L. Dictionary for accountants. 3d ed. Englewood Cliffs, N.J., Prentice-Hall, 1963. 523 p.

The author of this encyclopedic-type dictionary has previously been associated with the Committee on Terminology of the American Institute of Accountants. Many of the terms defined have been appropriated from other fields; here only the meaning for accounting is given. Entries are quite complete, with examples where necesary and "see" references. An excellent tool for a specialized field.

C325. Munn, Glenn G. Encyclopedia of banking and finance. 6th ed., by F.L. Garcia. Boston, Bankers Publishing Co., 1963. 788 p.

Encyclopedic information on American finance field—banking, investment, economic, financial and related legal terms, over 3,200 in all. Some entries contain bibliographies and explanations with tables and charts. Special features include important acts concerning banking and finance and a list of New Deal agencies. Definitions are explicit and clear.

C326. Palgrave, Sir Robert H.J. Palgrave's dictionary of political economy. London and New York, Macmillan, 1923-26. 3 v.

The first edition of this work appeared in 1894-96; it was reprinted in 1910 without text change but with the addition of a supplement of new articles. The 1915-18 reprint

contained the same supplement but with cross references to the supplement from the main sections. This edition is a reprinting of the 1915-18 edition with some changes and an expanded and enlarged supplement. The original purpose was to provide information for students in understanding the contemporary position of economic thought. Articles are complete and authoritative with bibliographies; each one is signed by a specialist. Oriented largely toward economic developments in the English-speaking world. Much of the information is now out of date, but it is a useful tool for historical and biographical information in economics.

C327. Sloan, Harold S., and Arnold J. Zurcher. A dictionary of economics. 4th ed., rev. New York, Barnes and Noble, 1961. 371 p.

Edited by two professors of economics, this collection of brief definitions in current usage covers a wide field from economic history to industrial organization. Includes digests and brief descriptions of "more important American statutes and judicial decisions of American and international regulatory agencies." If authorities differ on the exact usage, all versions are given. Some cross references and illustrations.

C328. Schwartz, Robert J. The dictionary of business and industry. New York, B.C. Forbes, 1954. 561 p.

With the aid of 1,100 various trade associations, industries and government agencies the author, a practicing attorney, prepared this dictionary. The 45,000 brief definitions include many that have never been published before. Special sections give miscellaneous tables such as weights and measures, weight of building material, hardness conversion numbers for steel. Especially useful for specific industrial terms.

C329. U.S. *Employment Service. Division of Occupational Analysis.*

Dictionary of occupational titles. 2d ed. Washington, Govt. Print. Off., 1949. 2 v.

Originally developed in 1939 to provide a major source of occupational information for the public employment service worker. Volume I covers the job definitions. These are brief descriptions of the work performed, including what the worker does, how he does it and the skill required. A coded number refers to the occupational classification structure developed in volume II. Definitions are arranged alphabetically by title; and in cases where one job may have several different titles, all titles appear. Volume II presents occupational classifications numerically. Broad classifications indicate major groups (i.e., professional and managerial, sales and clerical, service, agriculture); further expansion of the number shows minor groups (i.e., baker, carpenter, weaver); and a still further extension indicates the skill required. An index of commodities is also included to assist in classifying sales personnel. A 341-page supplement was published in March 1955, containing new and revised definitions and new code numbers.

DIRECTORIES

Directories of Directories

C330. Davis, Marjorie V. Guide to American business directories. 2d ed. Washington, Public Affairs Press, 1948. 242 p.

Directories of manufacturing and business concerns (from funeral services to information services) which appear as books or as parts of books are listed with bibliographical information and descriptive annotations. A list of related directories follows each classified section and a title index completes the work. May be supplemented by "Selected business directories" in Newark Public Library's *Business literature*, v. 26, Dec. 1953 and Jan.-Feb. 1954. Needs to be brought up to date.

C331. Guide to American directories. 5th ed. New York, B. Klein, 1962. 448 p.

Designed as an aid in building dependable mailing lists through major United States directories. Includes a separate section for foreign directories.

C332. Trade directories of the world. New York, Croner Publications, 1952 + loose leaf.

Until 1957 the title was *Croner's world register of trade directories*. A listing of commercial directories kept up to date by frequent revisions. Items are arranged geographically by country of publication with two indexes, geographical and trade or profession. These two indexes may be used to cross check against each other to locate a specific trade in a specific country.

Biographical Directories

C333. American Economic Association. Handbook of the American Economic Association . . . 1890/91 + New York, 1890 + irreg.

Biographical information on members covers: range of activities and interests, field of concentration, doctoral dissertation subject and publications. There are references to other directories in which the person is listed. Latest is the 1956 Handbook (*American economic review*, v. 47 no. 4, July 1957) with a 1957 Supplement listing names and addresses of new members.

C334. Directory of directors in the city of New York. New York, Directory of directors, 1898 + annual.

Initiated by a group of accountants and auditors familiar with the *London directory of directors*, this directory lists individuals who have at least one directorship in a company located in New York City and capitalized at $100,000 or over. Brief sketches include name, business and home address, and directorships. A second section covers important companies whose boards of directors include a New York City director or which maintain principal offices in New York City. Information in this section includes names and titles of officers and directors and business type. Such directories are available for many large cities and supplement the more comprehensive *Who's who* volumes.

C335. Poor's register of directors and executives, United States and Canada. New York, Standard and Poor's Corp., 1928+ annual with supplements three times a year.

Essentially a directory of executives, directors, products and services of manufacturing and mining companies, utilities, railroads, banks, insurance companies and partners of financial and investment institutions and law firms. The main section, arranged alphabetically by corporation, is supplemented by a product index, a classified industrial index, a register of directors with brief sketches, an obituary section and a new names section. One of the quickest and best means of locating names of officers or directors of specific companies or of locating company affiliation of a given individual.

C336. World who's who in commerce and industry. 12th ed. Chicago, Marquis, 1962. 1358 p.

Ed. 1-11, *Who's who in commerce and industry.* A roster, mostly American, of best-known men and women in industry and commerce who have achieved something special in their field or hold prominent positions in well-known, large companies. The usual "who's who" type of information. In addition to the alphabetical biographical section, there is a section for additions and changes received after the initial pages were made up. An "Index catalog of selected principal businesses" refers from individual firms to biographees associated with them. Extremely useful as a special-

ized biographical tool when the user keeps in mind the criteria for inclusion.

C337. Who's who in insurance. New York, Underwriter Press and Publishing Co., 1948+ annual.

A complete and up-to-date alphabetical listing of persons prominent in insurance. Biographical information covers position, address, education, memberships and professional experience. Each issue contains a death roll for the previous year. Prior to 1948 information appeared in *Insurance almanac.* An excellent specialized tool.

Directories of Associations and Corporations

C338. American register of exporters and importers, 1945/46+ New York, American Register of Exporters and Importers, Inc., 1947+ annual.

A product index, with text in English, Spanish and French, to sources of materials, products and services.

C339. Angel, Juvenal L., *comp.* Directory of American firms operating in foreign countries, 1955/56+ New York, World Trade Academy Press, annual.

Covering more than 2,300 American corporations controling and operating over 7,500 foreign business enterprises. One section lists the firms under countries in which they do business either through branches, subsidiaries or investments: and a second section is an alphabetical arrangement of companies with U.S. addresses, president and executive in charge of foreign operations.

C340. Bradford's survey and directory of marketing research agencies in the U.S. and the world. 9th ed. New Rochelle, N.Y., 1960. 142 p.

Arranged in three parts (alphabetical, geographical and classified by type of research), this directory describes each agency and when available lists staff members. Supplements.

C341. Dunn and Bradstreet, Inc. Million dollar directory. New York, 1959+ annual.

Intended to show size and potential of industrial companies, utilities, transportation companies, banks and trust companies doing over a million dollars worth of business. There are four parts: alphabetical company directory, geographical company directory, classified directory arranged in accordance with standard industrial classification, and directory of individuals. Similar to *Poor's register of directors and executives.* (C355)

C342. Directory of shopping centers in the U.S. and Canada. v. 1+ 1957-58+ Chicago, National Research Bureau. annual.

C343. Judkins, Clavert J. Directory of national associations of businessmen. Washington, D.C., U.S. Department of Commerce, 1961. 81 p.

Supplements *National associations of the United States.* Lists more than 2,000 national associations of business firms with names, addresses, chief executives, year formed, number of members and size of staff. Key word index.

C344. Kelly's directory of merchants, manufacturers and shippers for Great Britain and the British Empire, with a supplement for other countries. London, Kelly's Directory, 1880+ annual.

Alphabetical and classified list of firms primarily covering the British Empire. Information mostly limited to name, address and type of business or product.

C345. Liggett, Ronald R. Small industry development organizations, a worldwide directory. Glencoe, Ill., Free Press, 1959. 137 p.

Directory of agencies who, through program or research, are concerned with the development of small businesses.

C346. Lloyd's register of shipping. London, Lloyd's, 1834+ annual.

Directory of merchant ships giving tonnage, owners, equipment (i.e., refrigeration services) and builders.

C347. McKittrick directory of advertisers. v. 1+ 1899/1900+ New York, George McKittrick & Co. annual.

Consists of a geographical list of advertisers with information on methods of advertising, agency carrying the account, etc., and an alphabetical agency list showing personnel, accounts held and recognition and membership. The agency list is issued three times a year. Supplemented by a *Weekly correction service* and a *Weekly news bulletin.*

C348. National Research Council. Industrial research laboratories of the United States. 11th ed. Washington, National Academy of Sciences, 1960. 698 p.

"Limited to non-government laboratories devoted to fundamental and applied research, including development of products and processes." Arranged alphabetically by title, each entry gives address, research staff and administration and field. Subject, geographical and personal name indexes.

C349. Plant and product directory, 1961+ New York, Time, Inc. annual.

Issued by the Market Research Department of *Fortune magazine.* Shows products, plants, sales, assets and profits for the 500 largest U.S. industrial companies.

C350. Polk's bankers encyclopedia; the bank directory, 1898+ New York, Polk's Bankers Encyclopedia Co., 1895+ semi-annual, March and September, with monthly supplements.

A comprehensive, geographical listing of banks all over the world showing corporate title, address, telephone number, date of establishment, stock par value and last dividend rate, officers and directors, correspondents and latest financial information. Also covers national and state banking associations, state bank officials and bank examiners, banking hours and holidays. Useful for checking names of persons in office or on the board of directors of various banks because of up-to-date information.

C351. Sheldon's retail trade of the United States, listing department, dry goods and specialty stores, arranged by states and cities giving location of office in New York and names of resident and department buyers, 1884+ New York, J.S. Phelon & Co., 1884+ annual.

C352. Special Libraries Association. National insurance organizations in the United States and Canada. New York, 1957. 65 p.

C353. Standard advertising register. v. 1+ 1915+ New York, National Publishing Company. annual.

This list of national advertisers, arranged by industry, shows officers and executives of the companies, product advertised, agency connections, advertising appropriations and type of media used. Separate geographical index and an agency list. A weekly bulletin keeps the annuals up to date. *Standard advertising register* is best used as an approach to leading advertisers in specific fields, whereas McKittrick's (C347) provides the best geographical approach.

C354. Thomas' register of American manufacturers. New York, Thomas Publishing Co., 1906+ annual.

Designed as a product finding list for purchasing agents, this directory lists over 70,000 products. In volumes 1 to 3 manufacturers are listed under their products; volume 4 lists large manufacturers alphabetically and also carries a list of trade names showing what company uses each name. Information for each firm given in volumes 1 to 3 includes

address, company officers, capital investment and commercial association. Useful for locating makers of unusual products and an indispensable source of directory-type information.

C355. U.S. *Bureau of Labor Statistics.* Directory of national and international labor unions in the United States, 1961. Washington, Govt. Print. Off., 1962. 82 p.

C356. Wiesenberger (Arthur) and Co. Investment companies. New York, Arthur Wiesenberger, 1941+ annual.

Published as a source of factual information on investment companies, merits of their management and status of their securities. Reports of companies are arranged alphabetically under "Open End Investment Companies" and "Closed End Investment Companies." Information includes comparison of management results (by changes in net assets and income), individual firm's background, policy and results. Also included is a list of the 50 most favored stocks for investment trusts.

Other important sources of information are the regional industrial directories (i.e., *Greater New York industrial directory* and *Directory of New England manufacturers*), the many state manufacturers directories and trade directories (i.e., Lockwood's *Directory of the paper and allied trades*).

ATLASES AND PICTORIAL WORKS

C357. Official airline guide. Washington, American Aviation Publications, 1944+ monthly.

A compact guide to airline routes and schedules. The main section is a reproduction of schedules and fares of the world's scheduled airlines. A green section is a quick reference index showing connections from principal cities. This city index gives airlines serving each area and refers to the pages on which the schedules and fares of those airlines appear. Also includes airline maps, a list of military posts and army camps and airlines serving them, international air travel requirements, local taxes and exchange rates and world-wide hotel/motel directory.

C358. Official guide of the railways and steam navigation lines of the United States, Puerto Rico, Canada, Mexico and Cuba, also time-tables of railroads in Central America. New York, National Railway Publishing Company, 1868+ monthly.
Schedules of railways, airlines and sailings. Maps of areas served and index of railroad stations showing on what road the station is located. Additional information includes a list of military posts and camps showing railroad passenger stations and a list of hospitals maintained by the U.S. government.

C359. Oxford economic atlas of the world; prepared by the Economic Intelligence Unit and the Cartographic Department of the Clarendon Press. 2d ed. Oxford, Univ. Press, 1959. 152 p.
Presents basic information about the economics of world commodities. The first section consists of world commodity maps with information on production and consumption; the second section is an index, arranged by country, giving statistical information on the importance of various commodities in each country's economy. All information is from official statistical sources. A series of area atlases to complement the Economic Atlas is being prepared; the first to appear was U.S.S.R. and Eastern Europe (Oxford, University Press, 1956).

C360. Rand McNally and Co. Rand McNally commercial atlas and marketing guide. ed. 94. New York, Rand McNally, 1963. 566 p.

Comprehensive maps, mostly of the United States, giving commercial information and accompanied by an index which shows for each town or city railway facilities, mail addresses and population. Information in tabular form accompanies each map and gives retail and wholesale trends, marketing analysis of the population, agriculture and industries, analysis of market information for principal business centers, standard metropolitan areas and a list of principal cities, county population and area. Also includes transportation maps and information on mining manufacturing, etc. Information is much less complete for foreign countries. The detail shown on the maps and the complete index makes these maps invaluable for locating obscure towns. Revised annually.

C361. Russell's official national motor coach guide. Cedar Rapids, Iowa, Russell's Guides, 1927+ monthly.
Bus schedules.

C362. U.S. *Library of Congress. Map Division.* Marketing maps of the United States, an annotated bibliography. 3d rev. ed. Washington, 1958. 147 p.

YEARBOOKS

C363. Custom house guide. New York, Import Publications Inc., 1862+ annual with monthly supplements.
A guide to U.S. customs regulations containing such information as tariff schedules, rates for handling and storage at American ports, internal revenue codes relating to imported items. There is a directory section of firms and organizations concerned with marine transportation. A subscription to the monthly *American import and export bulletin* is included in the annual subscription.

C364. Editor and Publisher. Market guide. v. 1+ 1924+ New York. annual.

Annual presentation of data on newspaper markets covering cities and towns in the U.S. and Canada. Arranged alphabetically by state or province and then alphabetically by name of town or city, information includes transportation facilities, population, housing facilities, savings banks, auto registration, gas meters, telephones, types of industry, average weekly wages, colleges and universities, retail outlets, store hours, heaviest buying day, chain food stores, newspapers, local contact for newspaper advertising, climate, tap water, agricultural products and mining. This is the only available source for much of this information. Of use to businessmen for market research and plant relocation and useful to individuals who plan to make a move to a new city.

C365. Insurance almanac: who, what, where and when in insurance; an annual of insurance facts. New York, Underwriter Printing and Publishing Co., 1912+ annual.

Primarily a directory of companies (arranged by type of insurance written), organizations, state departments of insurance, agents and brokers, adjusters, the insurance press, etc. Also includes recent laws and a list of historical conflagrations. Until 1948 contained Who's who in insurance (C337) which has since become a separate publication. Lists officers and directors of companies and organizations and gives a brief history. For companies indicates type of insurance written and states in which companies are licensed. There is an index by title of the organization. Answers many quick reference questions.

C366. United Nations. *Dept. of Economic and Social Affairs.* World economic survey. No. 1+ 1945/47+ New York, Published for the United Nations by Columbia Univ. Press, 1948+ annual.

A "comprehensive review of world economic conditions . . . intended to meet the requirements of the Economics and Social Council and other organs for an appraisal of world economic situation prerequisite for recommendations in the economic field . . ." One part traces recent developments in several types of economies (industrial countries, primary exporting countries and centrally planned economies), and a second section is devoted to an examination of a special world problem, i.e., inflation, international commodity problems. Tables and charts are added where necessary for clarity of the text. Data is from governmental, intergovernmental or United Nations sources and is presented in text form.

STATISTICAL SOURCES

Guides

C367. Cole, Arthur H. Measures of business change. Homewood, Ill., Irwin, 1952. 444 p.

A comprehensive listing of various business indicators, both government and private. Information includes compiler, frequency, current and historical data, period covered and any necessary additional description.

C368. Hauser, Philip M. and William R. Leonard. Government statistics for business use. 2d ed. New York, Wiley, 1956. 440 p.

A guide to statistics published by the federal government for management, production and marketing needs. Each chapter, written by an expert in the field, deals with specific topic (i.e., national income, manufacturing, agriculture, population, labor) and indicates where more detailed information may be secured.

C369. Snyder, Richard M. Measuring business changes. New York, Wiley, 1955. 382 p.

Detailed description of the more important business indicators. More selective than Cole's work but offers fuller analysis of each series.

C370. Statistics sources, ed. by Paul Wasserman *et al.* Detroit, Gale Research Co., 1962. 288 p.

A classified listing of current statistical data designed to identify primary sources. Some secondary sources are included. Emphasis is on national American publications and organizations. Includes a few non-published sources, i.e., trade associations, governmental agencies, etc. Very brief annotations. Index of publishers' addresses.

Bibliographies

C371. Chamber of Commerce of the United States. *Committee on Business Statistics.* What's the answer? A brief guide to sources of business statistics. Washington, 1959. 34 p.

Arranged by subject, sources of important types of economic data are briefly discussed. Also contains suggestions for a minimum collection of basic statistical sources and a short list of outside sources.

C372. Johns Hopkins University. *Dept. of Political Economy.* Statistics and econometrics. Baltimore, 1955. 29 p. (Economics library selections II, no. 2)

An annotated list of 167 books which form a working collection of statistical material for economists.

Selected Sources

C373. Bank for International Settlements. Annual report. 1st+ 1930/-31+ Basel, Switzerland. annual.

Statistics on and analysis of economic conditions in various countries. Information covers prices, wages, production, trade, interest rates and credit.

C374. Commodity yearbook. v. 1+ 1939+ New York, Commodity Research Bureau. annual.

Statistical information, arranged alphabetically by product, on supply, demand, consumption, prices and exports of raw and semi-finished products. Special studies of timely interest appear, i.e., in 1960 "The long term outlook for petroleum." Numerous charts illustrate statistics.

C375. Current industrial reports. Washington, U.S. Bureau of the Census. monthly, quarterly and annually.

Formerly *Facts for industry.* More than 75 separate reports cover major manufacturing (textile mill products, apparel, pulp and paper, primary metals, machinery, etc.). Statistical data on production, shipments, orders and inventories.

C376. Economic almanac for 1940+; a handbook of useful facts about business, labor and government in the United States and other areas. New York, National Industrial Conference Board, 1940+ annual.

A quick reference source for economic and business statistics which, judged by the National Industrial Conference Board, are most useful in current economic and management problems. Arranged by topics, i.e., population, resources, agriculture, banking, with a general index. Special features are a Canadian statistical section (with separate index) and a section on international economic statistics. Much of the statistical material is the direct result of research undertaken by the Conference Board and is not found in other sources. Always includes sources of figures and often points up limitations or qualifications of material.

C377. Economic indicators, May 1948+ Washington, U.S. Council of Economic Advisers. monthly.

Charts and tables summarize current economic series in such areas as income and spending, employment and wages, production and business activity, prices, credit and security markets as well as Federal finance. The 1960 *Historical and descriptive supplement* gives data back to 1939 (in some cases further) and an explanation of each series, showing relations to other series, limitations and uses. A concise review of important economic series, current and historical.

C378. Federal reserve bulletin. v. 1+ 1915+ Washington, U.S. Board of Governors of the Federal Reserve System. monthly.

Comprehensive presentation of economic and business developments pertaining to banking and finance. Statistics cover information on Federal Reserve Banks, department store trade, consumer credit, production indexes and international finance. Most statistics are based on reports made to the Board or come from the Treasury Department. An index provides access to the statistical tables.

C379. Handbook of basic economic statistics; a manual of basic economic data on industry, commerce, labor and agriculture in the United States. 1947+ Washington, Economic Statistics Bureau of Washington, D.C. monthly, quarterly and annually.

A compact, centralized source of significant government-compiled statistical series covering all major aspects of the national economy. Statistics for previous years are shown as far back as possible and any adjustments in the series base is pointed out. Each series is well documented as to source.

C380. Industrial Marketing. Market data and directory, 1917+ Chicago, Industrial Marketing Magazine. annual.

Marketing information, arranged by industry, covers current trends, basic statistics, what the industry buys, how the industry buys, available market data (studies), associations and publications and additional data pertinent to that particular field. Tables and charts illustrate statistics; and sources are always given. There is an index to U.S. publications mentioned and a separate Canadian publications index.

C381. International financial statistics. 1948+ Washington, International Monetary Fund. monthly.

Statistics for various countries on exchange rates, gold and foreign exchange, balance of payments, government finance, industrial production, etc. Summary tables by subject are followed by country section with detailed tables and a review of the financial situation of the country. All information is from official publications of the respective countries, from direct communication and from international agencies. For comparison, statistics are given by ten-year intervals for the last 20 years, by years for the last five years and by quarters and months for the current year. Extremely useful because of recentness of information.

C382. International Labor Office. Yearbook of labour statistics, 1930+ Geneva, International Labor Office, 1931+ annual.

Labor statistics for various countries are arranged by subject matter (i.e., employment, hours of work, wages, family living studies, social security, industrial injuries, industrial disputes). An introduction to each chapter explains characteristics of principal types of statistics found in the tables and points out limitations of the international comparability of data. Figures are shown for the latest year; and some statistical series are kept up to date in the monthly *International labour review*. Text appears in English, French and Spanish. Extremely useful for locating internationally comparable figures.

C383. Monthly labor review. v. 1+ 1915+ Washington, U.S. Bureau of Labor Statistics. monthly.

Detailed statistics on employment, work stoppages, payrolls and other labor topics, as well as statistics on consumer and wholesale prices and building and construction. The Bureau of Labor Statistics' *Handbook of labor statistics, 1950* (Washington, Govt. Print. Off., 1951) and its 1951 Supplement give earlier statistics.

C384. Publishers' Information Bureau, Inc. PIB; analysis of advertising. v. 1+ Nov. 1940+ South Norwalk, Conn., Leading National Advertisers, Inc. monthly.

An analysis of advertising space and revenue in general and national magazines and newspapers.

C385. Sales Management survey of buying power. Annual (May 10) and interim supplement (November 10) in *Sales management*.

A statistical presentation of population, effective buying income and retail sales for United States and Canada in various types of markets (city, county, metropolitan, state, regional). Special sections show figures on TV homes and farm data. Statistics presented are *Sales management's* own figures based on government figures and local information.

C386. Standard Rate and Data Service. Consumer markets. Chicago, 1919+ annual.

Statistics useful for market surveys arranged in state, country and city groupings. Information covers such items as income data, household data and trading areas. Other Standard Rate and Data Service publications give excellent information on rates and advertising facilities of radio and TV stations, newspapers and magazines.

C387. Survey of current business. v. 1+ August 1921+ Washington, U.S. Office of Business Economics. monthly with weekly statistical supplements.

Analysis of current business trends is followed by statistical series on national income, gross national prod-

uct, personal and farm income; expenditures for new plant and equipment, retail and wholesale sales, manufacturers' sales, orders and inventories; estimates of balance of international payments; and production, prices and shipment for various commodities. Important issues are: February, covering a review of the previous year; and July, covering national income. Special supplements have been issued; the most important of these are:

Business statistics (biennial, published in odd numbered years). Historical data on each series back to 1929 if possible and extremely valuable explanatory notes.

National income supplement (1954). Statistics on national income and product from 1929 to 1953. Brought up to date by:

U.S. income and output (1959). Revised national income and product statistics for the postwar period.

C388. United Nations. *Statistical Office.* Statistics of national income and expenditures. no. 1-10, New York, 1952-1957 semi-annual. (Statistical papers. Series H)

Each issue supersedes previous issues by carrying the series back to 1938. This publication continued the survey of national income begun in *National income statistics of various countries* (League of Nations, 1938-1947). Superseded by the *Yearbook of national accounts statistics* (New York, 1957+ annual).

C389. United Nations. *Statistical Office.* Yearbook of international trade statistics, 1950+ New York, 1951+ annual.

Trade statistics for over 100 countries with some series going back to 1934. Carries on League of Nations' *International trade statistics* issued from 1925-1939.

C390. U.S. *Bureau of the Census.* Census of business, 1958. Washington, Govt. Print. Off., 1961. 6 v.

The 1948 census legislation provided for complete census of business (as well as of mineral industries and manufacturers) every five years covering statistics for the years ending in 3 and 8. The first census of business was postponed a year to 1954. Previous statistics may be found in the decennial census of 1930 and 1940. The six volumes present summary and area statistics for wholesale, retail and selected service trades. Data covers number of establishments, sales, employment payrolls and legal form of organization.

C391. U.S. *Bureau of the Census*. Census of manufacturers, 1958. Washington, Govt. Print. Off., 1962. 3 v.

Taken decennially from 1810 to 1900, at five-year intervals from 1904 to 1919 and from 1921 to 1939 at two-year intervals. With the 1948 census legislation, these statistics began appearing every five years for years ending with 3 or 8. Information, arranged by industry and by area, includes quantity and value of product made, material used, value added, employment, payrolls, capital expenditure, fuel and electric energy consumer. The *Annual survey of manufacturers*, based on data from a sample representative manufacturers, brings the figures up to date between each census.

C392. U.S. *Bureau of the Census*. Census of mineral industries, 1958. Washington, Govt. Print. Off. 2 v.

From 1840 through 1940 the census of mineral production appeared every ten years. With the 1948 census legislation, the census appears every fifth year ending in 3 or 8. The final report is published in two volumes, one covering general summary statistics and the other showing county and state statistics. Information on the quantity and value of minerals produced, operating companies and employees. Annual statistics appear in the *Minerals yearbook*.

C393. U.S. *Bureau of the Census*. County and city data book, 1956: a supplement to the Statistical abstract of the United States. Washington, Govt. Print. Off., 1957. 565 p.

See entry at A179.

C394. U.S. *Bureau of Old Age and Survivors Insurance*. County business patterns, 1946+ Washington, Govt. Print. Off. annual.

Based upon information obtained by the Social Security Administration directly from employers. Data on number of business establishments, employment and payroll is shown by state and county as well as by industry group and employee-size class.

C395. U.S. *Bureau of Labor Statistics*. Consumer price index. Jan., 1953+ Washington, Dept. of Labor. monthly.

Index numbers measuring changes in prices of goods and services purchased by the average consumer.

C396. U.S. *Bureau of Labor Statistics*. Employment and earnings, 1954+ Washington, Govt. Print. Off. monthly.

Latest statistics on weekly hours, employment trends, turnover rates, hourly and weekly earnings payroll and man-hour indexes, most of which also appear in the *Monthly labor review* (C380).

C397. U.S. *Bureau of Labor Statistics*. Wholesale prices and price indexes. Jan. 1952+ Washington, Govt. Print. Off. monthly.

Index numbers indicating the changes in primary market prices of various commodities. Also appears in the *Monthly labor review* (C380).

C398. U.S. *Dept. of Agriculture*. Agricultural statistics, 1936+ Washington, Govt. Print. Off. annual.

Presents detailed statistics on crops and livestock (acreage, prices, foreign trade, etc.), farm income, and other agricultural economic data.

C399. U.S. *President*. Economic report of the President to the Congress. 1st+ January, 1947+ Washington, Govt. Print. Off. annual.

Annual review of the national economy with statistical appendices covering employment, income and production.

BUSINESS SERVICES

C400. Moody's Investor's Services. Moody's manual of investments—American and foreign. New York, 1909+ 5 annual volumes with semi-weekly supplements.

One of the two most comprehensive U.S. investment services (see also *Standard corporation description*, C403). Each of the five volumes is supplemented by a semi-weekly loose-leaf service and by cumulative indexes. For individual companies financial and operating information is given; general idustry statistics appear also. The five volumes are:

Moody's bank and finance manual; banks, insurance and finance companies, investment trusts, real estate—American and foreign.

Moody's industrial manual—American and foreign.

Moody's municipal and government manual—American and foreign.

Moody's public utility manual—American and foreign.

Moody's public utility manual—railroads, airlines, shipping, traction, bus and truck lines—American and foreign.

C401. Moody's Investor's Services. Moody's bond survey. v. 28+ Jan. 6, 1936+ New York. weekly.

Suggestions for purchase, sale and retention. Monthly cumulative index includes cumulative bulletin of ratings. Supersedes the Bond Section of *Moody's investment survey* and continues its numbering.

C402. Moody's Investor's Services. Moody's stock survey. v. 28+ Jan. 6, 1936+ New York. weekly.

Suggestions for purchase, sale and retention of stock. Supersedes the Stock Section of *Moody's investment survey* and continues its numbering.

C403. Standard and Poor's Corp. Standard corporation description. May, 1914+ New York. 6 volumes with bi-monthly additions.

Prior to 1954 called *Standard corporation records*. The second of the most comprehensive U.S. investment services (see Moody's manuals, C400), the six volumes of this loose-leaf service give statistical and descriptive information on individual companies. Bi-monthly additions are made to each volume. Includes cumulative indexes, and lists of subsidiaries. *Daily news section* and *Daily dividend section* supplement the service.

C404. Standard and Poor's Corp. Industry surveys.

A two-volume loose-leaf service analyzing industries and their leading companies. Every three or four months a "current analysis" gives recent statistics and projections for industries and companies. A "basic analysis" appears annually. Index to industries and companies.

C405. Standard and Poor's Corp. The outlook. v. 1+ Feb. 15, 1937+ New York. weekly.

Weekly analysis of business and market trends.

C406. Standard and Poor's Corp. Stock reports; over-the-counter and regional exchanges. 1916+ New York.

A four-volume, loose-leaf service giving financial information, recent developments, market positions, etc., for stocks traded over-the-counter and on regional exchanges.

C407. Standard and Poor's Corp. Trade and securities statistics. v. 1+ 1917+ New York.

Comprehensive compilation of business, financial and industry statistics.

The quantity of business and economics services makes a complete listing impossible here. Those listed above are the services most commonly used by libraries. More detailed listings may be found in the guides to the literature (Coman, Manley and Wasserman, C236-C238) and in:

C408. McNierney, Mary A., ed. Directory of business and financial services. 6th ed. New York, Special Libraries Assoc., 1963. 187 p.
Kept up to date by listings in the *Bulletin* of the Business and Financial Division, Special Libraries Association.

SOURCES OF SCHOLARLY
CONTRIBUTIONS

C409. *Journals*

American economic review. v. 1+ 1911+ Evanston, Ill., American Economic Association. quarterly.
Bibl Fremd Zeit; Bull Anal; Bull Sig; Doc Econ; Econ Abst; Empl Rel Abst; Hist Abst; Int Ind; PAIS; UN Lib.

Business horizons. v. 1+ 1958+ Bloomington, Bureau of Business Research, School of Business, Indiana Univ. quarterly.
Empl Rel Abst; PAIS.

California management review. v. 1+ 1958+ Berkeley and Los Angeles, Graduate Schools of Business, Univ. of California. quarterly.
Econ Abst; Empl Rel Abst; PAIS.

Econometrica. v. 1+ 1933+ Chicago, Econometric Society. quarterly.
Bibl Fremd Zeit; Doc Econ; Econ Abst; Int Ind.

Economic journal. v. 1+ 1891+

London, Royal Economic Society. quarterly.
Bibl Fremd Zeit; Br Subj Ind; Bull Anal; Doc Econ; Econ Abst; Int Ind; PAIS; Poole; UN Lib.

Economica. v. 1+ 1921+ London, London School of Economics and Political Science. quarterly.
Bibl Fremd Zeit; Bull Anal; Doc Econ; Econ Abst; Int Ind; PAIS; UN Lib.

Harvard business review. v. 1+ 1922+ Boston, Graduate School of Business Administration, Harvard Univ. bi-monthly.
Bibl Fremd Zeit; Bull Anal; Bus Per; Econ Abst; Empl Rel Abst; PAIS; RG; UN Lib.

Industrial and labor relations review. v. 1+ 1947+ Ithaca, N.Y., New York School of Industrial and Labor Relations, Cornell Univ. quarterly.
Bull Anal; Bus Per; Econ Abst; Empl Rel Abst.

Journal of accountancy. v. 1+ 1905+ New York, American Institute of Certified Public Accountants. monthly.
Bus Per; Econ Abst; Engr Ind; Ind Leg Per; Int Ind; PAIS.

Journal of business. v. 1+ 1928+ Chicago, Univ. of Chicago Press. quarterly.
Bus Per; Econ Abst; Empl Rel Abst; Int Ind; PAIS.

Journal of economic history. v. 1+ 1941+ New York, Economic History Association. quarterly.
Bibl Fremd Zeit; Econ Abst; Empl Rel Abst; Hist Abst; PAIS; UN Lib.

Journal of political economy. v. 1+ 1892+ Chicago, Univ. of Chicago Press. quarterly.
Bibl Fremd Zeit; Bull Anal; Bull Sig; Doc Econ; Econ Abst; Hist Abst; Ind Leg Per; Int Ind; PAIS; Poole; UN Lib.

Manchester school of economic

and social studies. v. 1+ 1930+
Manchester, Eng., Manchester
School, Economics Dept. 3 a year.
Econ Abst; Hist Abst; PAIS; UN
Lib.

Oxford economic papers. v. 1+
1937+ Oxford, University Press. 3
a year.
Br Subj Ind; Doc Econ; Econ
Abst; Hist Abst; PAIS; UN Lib.

Quarterly journal of economics.
v. 1+ 1806+ Boston, Harvard University. quarterly.
Bibl Fremd Zeit; Bull Anal; Bull
Sig; Doc Econ; Econ Abst; Empl
Rel Abst; Int Ind; 19RG; PAIS;
Poole; UN Lib.

Review of economics and statistics. v. 1+ 1919+ Boston, Harvard
Univ. quarterly.
Bibl Fremd Zeit; Bull Anal; Bus
Per; Doc Econ; Econ Abst; Empl
Rel Abst; Int Ind; PAIS; UN Lib.

Schmollers Jahrbuch für Gesetzgebung, Verwaltung und Volkswirtschaft. v. 1+ 1877+ Berlin,
Duncker and Humblot. bi-monthly.
Bibl Deut Zeit; Bull Anal; Doc
Econ; Econ Abst; Hist Abst; Int Pol
Sci Abst; Soc Abst; UN Lib.

Schweizerische Zeitschrift für
Volkswirtschaft und Statistik. v. 1+
1865+ Basel, Schweizerische Gesellschaft für Statistik und Volkswirtschaft. quarterly.
Bibl Deut Zeit; Bull Anal; Doc
Econ; Int Pol Sci Abst;
Soc Abst; UN Lib.

Southern economic journal. v. 1+
1933+ Chapel Hill, Univ. of North
Carolina Press. quarterly.
Econ Abst; Int Ind; PAIS.

Soviet studies; a quarterly review
of the social and economic institutions of the USSR. v. 1+ 1949+
Oxford, Eng., Basil Blackwell. quarterly.
Bibl Fremd Zeit; Br Subj Ind;
Bull Anal; Econ Abst; Hist Abst; Int
Pol Sci Abst; PAIS; UN Lib.

C410. *Organizations*

American Economic Association.
Evanston, Ill. Founded 1885.

American Management Association. New York. Founded 1923.

Brookings Institution. Washington. Founded 1927.

Committee for Economic Development. New York. Founded 1942.

Econometric Society. New Haven,
Conn. Founded 1930.

Economic Research Council. London. Founded 1943.

Gesellschaft für Wirtschafts- und
Sozial wissenschaften (Verein für
Sozialpolitik) Frankfurt am Main.
Founded 1872; refounded 1948.

Institute of Asian Economic Affairs (Ajia Keizai Kenkyusho) Tokyo.
Founded 1958.

International Economic Association. Paris. Founded 1949.

National Bureau of Economic Research. New York. Founded 1920.

National Industrial Conference
Board. New York. Founded 1916.

Royal Economic Society. London.
Founded 1890.

Twentieth Century Fund. New
York. Founded 1919.

C411. *Monograph Series*

Cambridge Univ. *Dept. of Applied
Economics.* Monographs, no. 1+
1948+ Cambridge, Eng.

Contributions to economic analysis. v. 1+ 1952+ Amsterdam, North
Holland Publishing Co.

Committee for Economic Development. Research study. 1944+
New York, McGraw-Hill.

Conference on Research in Income and Wealth. Studies in income and wealth. v. 1+ 1937+ New York, National Bureau of Economic Research.

Cowles Foundation for Research in Economics. Monographs. v. 1+ 1934+ New York, Wiley.

Economic handbook series. 1948+ New York, McGraw-Hill.

Harvard economic studies. v. 1+ 1906+ Cambridge, Harvard Univ. Press.

Harvard studies in business history. v. 1+ 1931+ Cambridge, Harvard Univ. Press.

International Association for Research in Income and Wealth. Income and wealth series 1+ 1949+ Cambridge, Eng., Bowers and Bowers.

London. Univ. London School of Economics and Political Science. Studies in economics and commerce. v. 1+ 1933+ London.

National Bureau of Economic Research. General series. v. 1+ 1921+ New York.

National Bureau of Economic Research. Occasional papers. v. 1+ 1940+ New York.

National Bureau of Economic Research. Special conference series. v. 1+ 1949+ New York.

National Bureau of Economic Research. Studies in business cycles. v. 1+ 1946+ New York.

Yale studies in economics. v. 1+ 1950+ New Haven, Conn., Yale Univ. Press.

In addition, the various bureaus of business and economic research of universities execute and publish results of important studies. See the annotation for Associated University Bureaus of Business and Economic Research. *Index of publications of* *bureaus of business and economic research* (C273).

SOURCES OF CURRENT INFORMATION

C412. Advanced management/ Office executive. v. 1+ 1962+ Evanston, Pa., Society for the Advancement of Management and the National Office Management Association. quarterly.
Carries on *Advanced management* and *Office management*. Bibl Fremd Zeit; Bus Per; Econ Abst; Empl Rel Abst; Int Ind.

C413. Barron's national business and financial weekly. v. 1+ 1924+ New York, Barron's Publishing Co. weekly.
Bus Per; Fin Ind; Funk & Scott; Int Ind.

C414. Business week. v. 1+ 1929+ New York, McGraw-Hill. weekly.
Bus Per; Econ Abst; Empl Rel Abst; Fin Ind; Funk & Scott; Int Ind; PAIS; RG; UN Lib.

C415. Commercial and financial chronicle. v. 1+ 1865+ New York, William B. Dana Co. semi-weekly.
Bus Per; Empl Rel Abst; Fin Ind; Funk & Scott; Int Ind; PAIS.

C416. Dun's review and modern industry. v. 2, no. 68+ Nov. 17, 1894+ New York, Dun and Bradstreet. monthly.
Bus Per; Fin Ind; Funk & Scott; RG.

C417. Economist. v. 1+ 1843+ London. weekly.
Bibl Fremd Zeit; Br Subj Ind; Bull Anal; Bus Per; Econ Abst; Fin Ind; Int Ind; PAIS; UN Lib.

C418. Federal reserve bulletin. v. 1+ 1915+ Washington, Board of Governors of the Federal Reserve System. monthly.
Bibl Fremd Zeit; Bull Anal; Bus

Per; Doc Econ; Econ Abst; PAIS; UN Lib.

C419. Fortune. v. 1+ 1930+ New York, Time. monthly.
Bull Anal; Bus Per; Econ Abst; Empl Rel Abst; Fin Abst; Funk & Scott; PAIS; Rysch Abst; QC Ind Med; RG; UN Lib.

C420. International labour review. v. 1+ 1921+ Geneva, International Labour Office. monthly.
Bibl Fremd Zeit; Econ Abst; Empl Rel Abst; Int Ind; PAIS; UN Lib.

C421. Journal of commerce. v. 1+ 1827+ New York. daily.
Fin Abst.

C422. Labor law journal. v. 1+ 1949+ Chicago, Commerce Clearing House. monthly.
Bibl Fremd Zeit; Empl Rel Abst; Ind Leg Per; PAIS.

C423. Monthly labor review. v. 1+ 1915+ Washington, Bureau of Labor Statistics. monthly.
Bibl Fremd Zeit; Bull Anal; Bus Per; Econ Abst; Empl Rel Abst; Engr Ind; PAIS; RG; UN Lib.

C424. Nation's business. v. 1+ 1912+ Washington, Chamber of Commerce of the United States. monthly.
Bus Per; Engr Ind; PAIS; RG.

C425. Survey of current business. v. 1+ 1921+ Washington, Office of Business Economics. monthly.
Bibl Fremd Zeit; Bull Anal; Bus Per; Econ Abst; Int Ind; PAIS; UN Lib.

C426. Wall Street journal. Jan. 1, 1899+ New York, Dow Jones. daily.
Empl Rel Abst; Fin Ind; Funk & Scott; PAIS; WSJ Ind.

SOURCES OF UNPUBLISHED INFORMATION

C427. "Abstracts of doctoral dissertations," *Journal of finance.* v. 7+ 1952+ Chicago, American Finance Assoc.

C428. Clarke, George T. Bibliography of advertising and marketing theses for the doctorate in United States universities and colleges, 1944-1959. New York, Advertising Educational Foundation, 1961. 28 p.
A classified listing of 393 theses prepared at 38 institutions from 1944 to 1959. Cross references but no author index.

C429. Industrial relations theses and dissertations . . . 1950/51+ Berkeley, Institute of Industrial Relations, Univ. of California, 1951+ annual.
Lists 300-400 master's theses and doctoral dissertations a year reported from 38 institutions in the U.S. Arranged alphabetically by author with a subject index.

C430. "List of doctoral dissertations in political economy in American universities and colleges." 8th+ 1911+ *American economic review,* v. 1+ 1911+ Evanston, Ill., American Economic Assoc.
An annual classified listing of theses in preparation and degrees conferred. Covers all fields of economics including price theory, money and banking, public finance, industrial organization, land economics, labor economics and population. List 1-4, 1904-1907, appeared in American Economic Association *Publications,* third series; list 5-6, 1908-1910, in its *Bulletin.*

C431. New York University. *Graduate School of Business Administration.* Bibliography of graduate theses in the field of marketing written at United States colleges and universities 1950-1957. New York, 1958. 92 p.

C432. "Ph.D. degrees conferred in agricultural economics," *Journal of farm economics,* v. 34+ 1952+

Menasha, Wis., American Farm Economic Assoc.

C433. "Research projects in accounting," *Accounting review*, v. 12+ 1937+ Columbus, Ohio, American Accounting Assoc.

An annual classified listing of master's theses and doctoral dissertations. v. 26 (1951) contains a listing for the period 1941-1950/51.

C434. Rosen, Ned and Ralph E. McCoy. Doctoral dissertations in labor and industrial relations, 1933-1953. Urbana, Institute of Labor and Industrial Relations, Univ. of Illinois, 1955. 86 p.

An alphabetical author listing of 1031 items with a subject index.

C435. U.S. *Civil Service Commission. Library.* Dissertations and theses relating to personnel administration accepted by American colleges and universities, 1955+ Washington, 1957+ annual.

Leatrice Kemp
Thompson M. Little
Carl M. White

4

Sociology

Sociology, in the literal sense of the word, is knowledge of society. While this definition might impress laymen, it is of no use to anyone who has to separate sociology from other social sciences. The traditional focus of sociology, however, has been contemporary, complex societies, leaving to historians the study of past societies, and to anthropologists the study of primitive societies. While this division of labor is only approximate, it contains a good rule of thumb for classifying the literature of sociology, anthropology, and history according to its manifest content. In using this rule one should be aware that some authors may be misclassified. Some of the best sociologists have devoted much attention to past societies, studying the same problems as historians; many anthropologists have turned their attention to their own civilized society, studying the same problems as sociologists; and some sociologists have joined anthropologists in the study of the modernization of developing countries. (The shared topics, however, have not necessarily resulted in shared outlooks. Historians tend to describe events and institutions using the language of their sources, while the sociologist would tend to use a generic terminology. Anthropologists seem to pay more attention to culture; sociologists tend to focus on social structure. The professional training and allegiance of the author thus remain informative clues to the more subtle differences in the treatment of similar topics.)

A further complication arises when sociology is to be delineated from those social sciences which happened to be already in existence when sociology emerged: *viz.* economics and political science. At the time sociology emerged, some institutional realms in society, economy and polity, were subjects of special social sciences; while others, *e.g.*, religion, art, and science, were not. The same is true for some types of organizations; for example, legal institutions were already studied by faculties of law, but no academic discipline dealt with families or mass-media. Thus sociology, in practice if not in principle, took only those parts of society for its subject-matter that were not claimed by other departments. This could have resulted in a rather jerrymandered science, but the developing knowledge of society provided its own powerful corrective: over and over again it was found that events in one institutional realm or organization have consequences in another. An amazing interdependence prevails between different parts of society, and in accounting for it one has to cross the borders between institutional realms, and thus, in many cases, between disciplines. Sociology has come to specialize not so much in the inside story, the internal workings, of any organization or institutional realm, as in the outside story, the relations to other organizations and other realms. In this sense sociology covers the entire society. Thus sociology today may be seen as the study of societies and their constituent parts—human encounters, social structures (organizations and markets), institutional realms, communities, cultures—with particular attention to how each one relates to the others, and with particular emphasis on complex contemporary societies.

The Scope of Sociology Illustrated by a Minimum Library

Formal definitions like the one above, of the field of sociology are rather meaningless. A more telling way of conveying what enters into this field is to indicate what would constitute a minimum book shelf in sociology. Such a shelf would have to contain at least one book in each of six areas. The first would would be a selection from *sociological classics* which would convey what has emerged over the last one hundred years as a somewhat distinct and unique outlook on society. The second would be a theoretical title in *micro-sociology*, summarizing laws and social processes within and between groups and within and between market-like structures, a field in which American sociologists have excelled. The third would be a theoretical title in *macro-sociology*, containing conclusions about processes within and between institutional realms and processes of cultural change. The fourth would be a work of *sociological taxonomy* containing lists of general categories which sociologists have found useful in ordering their descriptions of societal life. The fifth book would be a title of *descriptive sociology*, one that gives a survey of one total society (or a part thereof) at one point in time. The sixth should be a book about *sociological methodology*, the accepted procedures for research and theorizing.

In choosing these or other titles in sociology one cannot automatically apply the rule that recent works are better than older ones. Only in micro-sociology is there a sufficient cumulation to warrant acquisition of a recent treatise without much hesitation. However, all sociology has its fair share of fads and fashions; rather than acquiring a library with the latest academic fads one should attempt to acquire at least a minimum library of lasting quality. It is also worth noting that there is no rule that good sociology books become reprinted in cheap paper bindings. Estimates of the number of impulse buyers from paperback racks and estimates of what teachers of elementary college courses might want to assign to their students as readings outside their textbooks determine whether a sociology book reaches the mass market as a paperback, not its scholarly merits.

As an anthology of classical passages of sociology, *Theories of society* edited by Talcott Parsons and others, serves well. (One should not be misled by the word "theories" in the title; many sociologists tend to call all better writing of older vintage in their field "theory." In a still broader sense "social theory" is a discipline acting as custodian of both old and new insights about society: many of these insights have to be studied in their original title, since sociology to date lacks a systematic theoretical synthesis.) Here are Weber, Durkheim, Pareto, Sorokin, Cooley, and a host of others in excerpts which do not merely highlight the history of the discipline, but which continue to serve as inspiration for fruitful ideas in contemporary sociology.

A title in micro-sociological theory that seems to me most attractive and profound in its simplicity is George C. Homans, *Social behavior: its elementary forms.* It demonstrates how fundamental laws of psychology can be re-formulated and extended to account for a large number of regularities in human interaction. It marks in this sense a break with sociological tradition; early sociologists, anxious to establish their field as an independent enterprise, tried repeatedly to show that sociological subject-matter was unique and that sociological laws were irreducible to laws of other sciences. (The somewhat half-hearted acceptance of Homans' work by the older generation of sociologists reflects their concern with this break of tradition, and does not affect its scientific merits.) While the book adds substantially to theoretical sociology, it is well written and quite accessible to a layman.

A macro-sociological work of scope—the largest ever undertaken by a scholar in America—is P. A. Sorokin's *Social and cultural dynamics.* It reviews the flow of events in art, science, law, religion, and ethics from the beginnings of civilization and tabulates the products of culture in terms of the mentality they exhibit. It then relates the results to other analyses and tabulations of the fluctuations in types of social relationships: wars, revolutions, and other aspects of social structure. The boldness of this undertaking, first published between 1937 and

1941, somewhat stunned the field, and several reviews at the time were questioning the work simply because the author stated a preference for a certain balanced, integrated, cultural mentality (and thus had a "bias") and because his macro-sociological statistics were not as precise as ordinary micro-sociological statistics (as if this were usually the case). Only years later does it seem that others in the macro-sociological enterprise begin to experience a rapprochement to its major distinctions and propositions. While still controversial, the work to date remains essentially without serious competing alternatives in sociology.

However, sociology is not only a theoretical science that identifies recurrent problems and sums up social and cultural events in law-like propositions. It is also, and perhaps primarily, a descriptive science that gives systematic accounts of specific cultures, societies, institutional realms, organizations, markets, social relations, positions, and individual encounters. The question of what should enter into any routine sociological description of such phenomena has received much attention, and sociological taxonomies are much in evidence. Since it is fairly easy to draw up abstract categories of doubtful usefulness for sociological descriptions, I think it is wise to select taxonomies which have emerged parallel with important empirical studies, and whose worth has been repeatedly proven by other scholars. An eminent one is the "Kategorienlehre" that Max Weber kept developing at the same time he wrote his famous empirical studies. He never quite finished this work, but it is nevertheless the best we have of its kind. Unfinished portions have been fitted into the finished ones, first by his widow, and later by Johannes Winkelmann in Max Weber's posthumous *Wirtschaft und Gesellschaft* (*Economy and society*.) It is important to acquire a fourth (or a later) edition of this work, since much of Weber's political sociology is not included in the earlier editions. The system of formal definitions in the beginning of this work represent the most successful and most widely used terminology of sociology. But even more valuable is the analytical panorama of all major organizations and markets in economy, polity, and religion that constitute the bulk of the work. One might say that he who knows this work is already a learned man, immune to the easy and sweeping generalizations about human society that plague much of popular intellectual debate, yet aware of the relatively simple forces that shape human society. No single work I know of in sociology provides an education of comparable value.

As mentioned, detailed sociological descriptions are legion, and it is hard to select one that stands above others. If we restrict ourselves to accounts of total societies or communities the choice is simpler, since the titles are fewer. The two books on Middletown by Robert and Helen Lynd, although now some thirty years old, are still ranking titles here.

In the field of sociological methodology I recommend an anthology with superb editorial comments: Paul F. Lazarsfeld and Morris Rosenberg, *The language of social research*. It conveys the very substantial advances in quantitative research methodology of recent decades. It is perhaps less adequate for qualitative analyses and macro-sociological and historical methodology (where standards are not so precise and strict), but so far no standard work has appeared in these areas.

D1. Homans, George C. Social behavior: its elementary forms. New York, Harcourt, Brace & World, 1961. 404 p.
D2. Lazarsfeld, Paul F. and Morris Rosenberg, *eds.* The language of social research. Glencoe, Ill., Free Press, 1955. 590 p. (Revised edition in French in preparation.)
D3. Lynd, Robert S. and Helen M. Lynd. Middletown: a study in American culture. New York, Harcourt, Brace, 1929. 550 p.
D4. Lynd, Robert S. and Helen M. Lynd. Middletown: a study in cultural conflicts. New York, Harcourt, Brace, 1937. 604 p.
D5. Parsons, Talcott, *ed.* Theories of society. New York, Free Press of Glencoe, 1961. 2 v.
D6. Sorokin, Pitirim A. Social and cultural dynamics. New York, Bedminster Press, 1962. 4 v. (Abridged version available from Porter Sargent.)
D7. Weber, Max. Wirtschaft und Gesellschaft. 4. Aufl. Tübingen, Germany, J.C.B. Mohr, 1956. 2 v. (Several partial translations into English available; a full translation is in preparation by The Bedminster Press.)

The above selection should serve to remind us of the wide range of sociological literature.

In setting up a sociological library that goes beyond a shelf or two, it is of course helpful to order the titles in sub-groups. Unfortunately the groupings of the widely-used Dewey decimal system are rather inadequate for sociology. The categories used below are recommended for departmental, private, or other libraries that can operate their own system of classification.

Precursors of Systematic Sociology

Sociology became a somewhat cumulative endeavor about a hundred years ago. Prior to this, much had been written of sociological value. Any good selection from the history of social, political, and economic thought is likely to contain this material. Let us mention here only Aristotle's *Politics,* Ibn Khaldûn's *Muqaddimah,* and Hegel's *Philosophy of history.*

D8. Aristotle. Politics, ed. by Ernest Barker. New York, Oxford Univ. Press, 1946. 411 p. (Many other editions available, including The Modern Library, no. 228.)
D9. Hegel, Georg Wilhelm Friedrich. Vorlesungen über die Philosophie der Weltgeschichte. Leipzig, Miner, 1920-1923. 3 v. (English translation available from The Humanities Press.)
D10. Ibn Khaldûn. The Muqaddimah: an introduction to history, tr. by Franz Rosenthal. New York, Pantheon Books, 1958. 3 v.

Histories, Biographies, Explications of Classical Works

A history of sociology organized in terms of schools of thought has been written by Sorokin, and a more chronologically organized one by Barnes and Becker. Among the several text-book treatments for undergraduates is one by Timasheff. Of histories restricted to particular schools or themes, I hope no one will miss Popper's fascinating account of the autocratic and democratic trends in Western social thought. An anthology of writings containing much of the historical perspective on sociology has been edited by Becker and Boskoff. Strangely enough, no one has written a history of social research; all available histories focus on social theory.

D11. Becker, Howard and Harry Elmer Barnes. Social thought from lore
        to science. New York, Dover, 1961. 3 v.
D12. Becker, Howard and Alvin Boskoff, *eds.* Modern sociological theory
        in continuity and change. New York, Dryden, 1957. 756 p.
D12a. Popper, Karl R. The open society and its enemies. 4th rev. ed. Lon-
        don, Routledge and Kegan Paul, 1962. 2 v.
D13. Sorokin, Pitirim A. Contemporary sociological theories. New York,
        Harpers, 1928. 785 p.
D14. Timasheff, Nicholas S. Sociological theory: its nature and growth.
        Garden City, N.Y., Doubleday, 1955. 328 p.

Biographies of sociologists are not common; several explications of works by particular sociologists can, however, be recommended. Among them is Reinhard Bendix's review of Weber's sociology. Another important summary covers the writings of Durkheim, Pareto, and Weber and is written by Talcott Parsons. Pareto has also been well presented by Henderson. David Riesman has made a keen interpretation of Veblen.

D15. Bendix, Reinhard. Max Weber: an intellectual portrait. Garden City,
        N.Y., Doubleday, 1960. 480 p.
D16. Henderson, Lawrence J. Pareto's General Sociology: a physiologist's
        interpretation. Cambridge, Harvard Univ. Press, 1937. 119 p.
D17. Parsons, Talcott. The structure of social action: a study in social
        theory with special reference to a group of recent european writers.
        Glencoe, Ill., Free Press, 1949. 817 p.
D18. Riesman, David. Thorstein Veblen: a critical interpretation. New
        York, Scribners, 1953. 221 p.

Works that Made History

Of all sociologists the world has seen the marjority are still alive. This fact attests both to the newness of the field and to its recent expansion. A selection of titles that have made sociological history is rather easy to compile, but to select those titles that have made history and still are cited and consulted is a more risky enterprise. The founding father of systematic sociology, Comte, is rarely consulted today. Laubier's short selections from his sociological writings are likely to suffice for any library that is willing to forego the accommodation of historians of sociology.

Spencer, who did so much for the creation and acceptance of sociology as a science, has suffered a similar fate, and one cannot in good faith recommend that every sociological library shall own his multi-volume work on *The principles of sociology*. However, considerable interest still attaches to some of the contemporaries of those pioneers of sociology who were marginal to sociology as a profession. Foremost among them is Karl Marx; but one may also mention some early historians of the French revolution: von Stein in Austria, and de Tocqueville in France. The latter is, of course, known among sociologists mostly for his book on the young equalitarian America. The sociological writings by Marx are scattered throughout his voluminous writings but have recently been brought together in one book by Bottomore and Rubel.

D19. Comte, Auguste. Sociologie. Texts chosen by Jean Laubier. Paris, Presses Universitaires de France, 1957. 212 p.
D20. Marx, Karl. Selected writings in sociology and social philosophy, ed. by T.B. Bottomore and M. Rubel. New York, Humanities Press, 1956. 268 p.
D21. von Stein, Lorenz. Geschichte der soziale Bewegung in Frankreich von 1789 bis auf unsere Tage. 2. Aufl. Leipzig, Wigand, 1855. 3 v. (Several later reprintings. Partial English translation available from The Bedminster Press.)
D22. Tocqueville, Alexis de. Oeuvres, papiers et correspondances. Éd. définitive. Paris, Galimard, 1951-59. 9 v. Volumes 1 and 2 contain *Democracy in America* and *The Ancient Regime and the Revolution* (Both are available in several English editions).

The two decades preceding World War I were particularly glorious ones in the sociological annals. There were several good journals published in Europe and one in America. A list of European monographs and general works from this period can count upon contributions by Durkheim, Tönnies, Sorel, Simmel, Weber, Michels, Pareto.

D23. Durkheim, Emile. De la division du travail social. 5. éd. Paris, Alcan, 1926. 416 p.
D24. Durkheim, Emile. Les formes élémentaires de la vie religieuse: le système totémique en Australie. Paris, Alcan, 1912. 647 p.
D25. Durkheim, Emile. Le suicide: étude de sociologie. Paris, Alcan, 1897. 462 p. (English translations of all these books by Durkheim available from The Free Press.)
D26. Michels, Robert. Zur Soziologie des Parteiwesens in der modernen Demokratie: Untersuchungen ub. d. oligarchischen Tendenzen d. Gruppenlebens. 2. verm. aufl. Leipzig, A. Kroner, 1925. 528 p. (English translation from an Italian version of the first edition available from Collier.)
D27. Pareto, Vilfredo. Trattato di sociologia generale. Florence, G. Barbera, 1916. 3 v. (The English translation reprinted by Dover Press.)
D28. Simmel, Georg. Soziologie: Untersuchungen über die Formen der Vergesellschaftung. 4. aufl. Berlin, Dunker & Humblot, 1958. 578 p. (Partial English translation available from The Free Press.)
D29. Sorel, Georges. Réflexions sur la violence. 11. éd. Paris, M. Riviere, 1950. 458 p. (English translation available from Allen & Unwin.)

D30. Tönnies, Ferdinand. Gemeinschaft und Gesellschaft: Grundbegriffe
       der reinen Soziologie. 7. aufl. Berlin, Curtius, 1926. 254 p. (Eng-
       lish translation available from Michigan State Univ. Press.)

After World War I the sociological center of gravity moved slowly toward America. The outstanding monographs on Middletown by the
Lynds—mentioned before—were published in 1929 and 1937. Around
the University of Chicago grew the new "interactionist" school of sociology, inspired by the social philosophy of G. H. Mead, and many
empirical works such as the magnificent *Polish peasant* by Thomas and
Znaniecki, and the varied inquiries by Robert E. Park.

D31. Mead, George Herbert. Mind, self and society: from the standpoint
       of a social behaviorist, ed. with introduction, by Charles W.
       Morris. Chicago, Univ. of Chicago Press, 1934. 401 p.
D32. Thomas, William I. and Florian Znaniecki. The Polish peasant in
       Europe and America. New York, Dover Press, 1958. 2 v.

Early American sociology is much pre-occupied by Darwinism, and
with few exceptions it shuns the critical problems of class, power, and
social integration which make the continental sociology of the time so
interesting. I would select Veblen's sociological writings as most stimulating and Cooley's social psychology as most appealing; the works of
Sumner, Ross, Ward and others seem less rewarding today.

D33. Cooley, Charles H. Human nature and social order. New York, Scrib-
       ner, 1902. 460 p.
D34. Veblen, Thorstein B. The theory of the leisure class. New York, The
       Modern Library, 1934. 404 p.

The Present State of Sociology

There are several anthologies indicating the state of the arts in the various fields of sociology. *Sociology today* gives a good interpretation of
the advances made by the end of the 1950's, and *Sociology: progress of a
decade* contains a representative selection of articles from the 1950's. Sociology in Europe has also developed at a remarkable pace after the war.
The German anthology edited by René König might serve as a reminder
of this. Sociological writings on a par with that produced at the major
American universities appear every year in Holland, Norway, Poland and
other countries. The days are gone when one turned automatically to the
United States to find the best sociological literature.

D35. König, René, ed. Handbuch der empirischen Sozialforschung. Stutt-
       gart, F. Enke, 1962. 649p. (Second volume in preparation.)
D36. Merton, Robert K. *et al.* Sociology today. New York, Basic Books,
       1959. 623 p.
D37. Lipset, Seymour M. and Neil J. Smelser, *eds.* Sociology: the progress
       of a decade. A collection of articles. Englewood Cliffs, N.J.,
       Prentice-Hall, 1961. 635 p.

SOCIOLOGICAL THEORY

Contemporary Schools

After World War II the University of Chicago did not dominate sociological research and graduate training as before. But the interactionist school which, as mentioned, originated there continued strong. A representative anthology of its achievements has been edited by Arnold Rose. A survey of its precursors, as well as an extension of its theoretical scope into a general dramatic model of society, has been written by H. D. Duncan. One of the leading interactionist sociologists, Herbert Blumer, had a major part during the 1950's in organizing the Sociology Department at the University of California at Berkeley into the newest center of advanced sociology in the United States. In this Department is Erving Goffman, a social theorist in the interactionist tradition, and his ingenious insights are an inspiration to many.

D38. Duncan, Hugh D. Communication and social order. New York, Bedminster Press, 1962. 475 p.
D39. Goffman, Erving. Presentation of self in everyday life. Garden City, N.Y., Doubleday, 1959. 255 p.
D40. Goffman, Erving. Encounters: two studies in the sociology of interaction. Indianapolis, Ind., Bobbs-Merrill, 1961. 152 p.
D41. Rose, Arnold M., *ed.* Human behavior and social processes: an interactionist approach. Boston, Houghton Mifflin, 1962. 680 p.

One weakness of the symbolic interactionist school is the informal methodology that is often employed in its writing. The work of George A. Lundberg and his group at the University of Washington in Seattle has attempted to counterbalance this by a more orthodox operationalism. A useful series of exercises for students has been developed there by Larsen and Catton.

D42. Larsen, Otto N. and William R. Catton, Jr. Conceptual sociology: a manual of exercises relating concepts to specimens, principles, and definitions. New York, Harper & Row, 1962. 276 p.
D43. Lundberg, George A. Foundations of sociology. New York, Macmillan, 1939. 556 p.

At Harvard a new school emerged, identified sometimes as "structuralist-functionalist." Talcott Parsons and his able and loyal body of students made this school dominant during the 1950's, and Parsons made history by being the first to receive substantial foundation grants in support of purely theoretical work in sociology. Parsons' system so far has been presented in a series of working drafts; a more finished version with detailed references to research findings and with discussions of how the system is related to alternative theories is eagerly awaited. The empirical usefulness of the system can, however, already be illustrated by studies made by Parsons' students, e.g. Smelser.

D44. Parsons, Talcott. The social system. Glencoe, Ill., Free Press, 1951. 575 p.
D45. Smelser, Neil J. Social change in the Industrial Revolution: an application of theory to the British cotton industry. Chicago, Univ. of Chicago Press, 1959. 440 p.

A more modest and more empirically oriented version of functional theory (and more conventionally launched) has flourished at the Sociology Department at Columbia University. Here Robert K. Merton, a student of Sorokin's and Parsons', emerged as a leading theoretician through his remarkable ability to take fragments of social thought and revise and refine them into sociological gold. Of the many theoretical advances made under his inspiration are the monographs by Coser and Hopkins.

D46. Coser, Lewis. The functions of social conflict. Glencoe, Ill., Free Press, 1956. 188 p.
D47. Hopkins, Terrence K. The exercise of influence in small groups. Totowa, N.J., Bedminster Press, 1964. 205 p.
D48. Merton, Robert K. Social theory and social structure. 2d ed. Glencoe, Ill., Free Press, 1957. 645 p.

However useful it might be to identify contemporary work in sociology by reference to one of these schools, one should not forget that most contemporary sociology does not fall neatly into either one or the other, and that their differences lie often more in speech habits employed than in facts expounded. The following survey of titles of interest to theoretical sociology will, therefore, ignore the allegiance of the authors to schools and simply group them according to the recurrent problems to which they address themselves.

Theoretical Sociology

1. Social Psychology is the foundation for micro-sociology and should be represented in any sociological library by a summary work, such as the outstanding *Handbook of social psychology,* and by an anthology, such as *Readings in social psychology.* A valuable, somewhat more systematic treatment is also found in the textbook for undergraduates by Newcomb.

D49. Maccoby, Elinor E., *et al.* Readings in social psychology. 3d ed. New York, Holt, Rinehart & Winston, 1958. 686 p.
D50. Newcomb, Theodore M. Social psychology. New York, Dryden Press, 1950. 690 p.
D51. Lindzey, Gardner. Handbook of social psychology. Cambridge, Mass., Addison-Wesley, 1954. 2 v.

2. Groups and Encounters are popular subjects for theory. The most widely read title here is George Homans' *The human group.* The systematic review by Thibaut and Kelly, two psychologists of the small groups field, supplements the other work by Homans already cited: *Social be-*

havior: its elementary forms. Both these works are anchored in psychological learning theory. Contributions based on psychological perception theory are included in the symposium edited by Tagiuri and Petrullo. The books by Goffman (already mentioned) offer many valuable insights in inter-personal processes and collections of research studies from this field are available in two good anthologies which do not overlap appreciably with one another. Very satisfactory mathematical models in this area have been developed by Simon.

D52. Cartwright, Dorwin and Alvin Zander, *eds.* Group dynamics: research and theory. 2d ed. Evanston, Ill., Row, Peterson, 1962 826 p.
D53. Hare, A. Paul, *et al.* Small groups: studies in social interaction. New York, Knopf, 1955. 666 p.
D54. Homans, George C. The human group. New York, Harcourt-Brace, 1950. 484 p.
D55. Simon, Herbert A. Models of man: social and rational. New York, Wiley, 1957. 287 p.
D56. Tagiuri, Renato and Luigi Petrullo, *eds.* Person perception and interpersonal behavior. Stanford, Calif., Stanford Univ. Press, 1958. 390 p.
D57. Thibaut, John W. and Harold H. Kelley. The social psychology of groups. New York, Wiley, 1959. 313 p.

3. Organizations are constituted by rather stable social relations coordinated by a more or less central leadership, and are the focus of many theoretical analyses. In addition to the work by Merton, much of which belongs in this area, one might mention the books by Chester Barnard, Neal Gross and Amitai Etzioni. There are several anthologies dealing with organizational sociology, and many monographs have lately been published, some of which will be mentioned in connection with the institutional order to which they relate.

D58. Barnard, Chester I. The function of the executive. Cambridge, Harvard Univ. Press, 1956. 334 p.
D59. Etzioni, Amitai. A comparative analysis of complex organizations: on power, involvement, and their correlates. New York, Free Press of Glencoe, 1961. 366 p.
D60. Gross, Neal, *et al.* Explorations in role analysis: studies of the school superintendency role. New York, Wiley, 1958. 379 p.

4. Markets are constituted by fairly stable social relations which, unlike organizations, do not have a common leadership. Studies of market-like structures are rather common in sociology; here we may mention only *Personal influence* by Katz and Lazarsfeld which bridges the thinking in the field of small groups to the field of market and media research. It is perhaps noteworthy that no modern sociologist has written a theoretical treatise on market behavior; for example, one has to go back to Weber and Pareto to find discussions of the sociology of the stock market. The work by Smelser on collective behavior can also be cited in this context.

D61. Katz, Elihu and Paul F. Lazarsfeld. Personal influence: the part played by people in the flow of mass communications. Glencoe, Ill., Free Press, 1955. 400 p.
D61a. Smelser, Neil J. Theory of collective behavior, New York, Free Press of Glencoe, 1963. 436 p.

5. Social stratification is the subject of some of the best sociological thinking. In addition to the titles by Marx, Pareto, Veblen, and Weber, most of which have been cited already, the contributions of Schumpeter, Geiger, and Dahrendorf have considerable theoretical interest. An early study of social mobility that also contains much valuable theory was written by Sorokin; a later summary of the same area has been written by Bendix and Lipset.

D62. Dahrendorf, Ralph. Class and class conflict in industrial society. Stanford, Calif., Stanford Univ. Press, 1959. 336 p. (An earlier edition was written in German and published by Enke, Stuttgart.)
D63. Geiger, Theodor. Die Klassengesellschaft im Schmelztiegel. Köln, Kiepenheuer, 1949. 228 p.
D65. Lipset, Seymour M. and Reinhard Bendix. Social mobility in industrial society. Berkeley, Univ. of California Press, 1959. 309 p.
D66. Pareto, Vilfredo. The rise and fall of elites. Totowa, N.J., Bedminster Press, in prep.
D67. Schumpeter, Joseph A. Aufsätze zur Soziologie. Tübingen, J.C.B. Mohr, 1953. 232 p. (One essay on social classes is available in English translation from Meridian Books.)

6. Institutional realms, many sociologists say, constitute the prime sociological concern. However, this preaching is rarely translated into practice. An elementary exposé, relating micro-sociological considerations to those of institutional realms, is found in Gerth and Mills, *Character and social structure*. In the area of institutional realms, however, descriptive case studies begin to dominate. It is hard to cite outstanding theoretical titles beyond the ones by Weber and Sorokin which already have been discussed. The attempt by Parsons and Smelser to integrate the former's theory with macro-economics is one of the few developments here since World War II.

D68. Gerth, Hans and C. Wright Mills. Character and social structure. New York, Harcourt, Brace, 1953. 490 p.
D69. Parsons, Talcott and Neil J. Smelser. Economy and society. Glencoe, Ill., Free Press, 1956. 322 p.

TOPICS OF SOCIOLOGY

Human and Non-Human Resources

The size of the population of a society and the number of individuals in various pursuits are basic items of information for many sociological studies. The field of demography thus becomes part of sociology. The best sociological works in this field, however, tend to go beyond sheer estimates of population size and use characteristics of the population as indicators of social structure. The books by Bogue on the United States, Davis on India and Pakistan, Lorimer on the Soviet Union, Taeuber on Japan, and Thomas on Sweden are outstanding in this respect. They view basic demographic variables such as birth, death and migration both as causes and consequences of variations in social structure and culture. The analysis by the staff of the Population Division of the United Nations brings an invaluable comparative perspective to the key problems in this kind of research.

D70. Bogue, Donald J. The population of the United States. Glencoe, Ill., Free Press, 1959. 873 p.
D71. Davis, Kingsley. The population of India and Pakistan. Princeton, N.J., Princeton Univ. Press, 1951. 263 p.
D72. Lorimer, Frank. The population of the Soviet Union: history and prospects. Geneva, League of Nations, 1946. 289 p.
D73. Taeuber, Irene B. The population of Japan. Princeton, N.J., Princeton Univ. Press, 1958. 461 p.
D74. Thomas, Dorothy S. Social and economic aspects of Swedish population movements 1750-1933. New York, Macmillan, 1941. 487 p.
D75. United Nations. *Department of Social Affairs. Population Division.* The determinants and consequences of population trends: a summary of the findings of studies on the relationships between population changes and economic and social conditions. New York, 1953. 404 p.

The raw material for such analyses are contained in reports by various national and international agencies. In terms of cost per item of information, the *Demographic yearbook* of the United Nations and the *Statistical abstract* of the United States are probably the best bargains for a sociological library. An effort to select the bare minimum of facts and figures from these and other sources (including public opinion polls) and to interpret them for beginning students is made in the *Sociological almanac*. (This essay, incidentally, is organized along the same lines as the *Almanac*.)

D76. Gendell, Murray and Hans L. Zetterberg, *eds.* A sociological almanac for the United States. Totowa, N.J., Bedminster Press, 1961+ triennial.
D77. United Nations. *Statistical Office.* Demographic yearbook, 1948+ New York, 1949+ annual.
D78. United States. *Bureau of the Census.* Statistical abstract of the United States. V.1+ 1878+ Washington, Govt. Print. Off., 1879+ annual.

Research papers in demography have been brought together in three anthologies which give an excellent representation of the field. It may, however, be worthwhile to supplement them by a larger treatment of at least one topic: the population growth in underdeveloped countries. Of the books on this topic one may select the one by Coale and Hoover as the most advanced.

D79. Coale, Ansley J. and Edgar M. Hoover. Population growth and economic development in low-income countries. Princeton, N.J., Princeton Univ. Press, 1958. 389 p.
D80. Hauser, Philip M. and Otis Dudley Duncan, *eds*. The study of population: an inventory and appraisal. Chicago, Univ. of Chicago Press, 1959. 864 p.
D81. Spengler, Joseph J. and Otis Dudley Duncan, *eds*. Demographic analysis: selected readings. Glencoe, Ill., Free Press, 1956. 819 p.
D82. Spengler, Joseph J. and Otis Dudley Duncan, *eds*. Population theory and policy: selected readings. Glencoe, Ill., Free Press, 1956. 522 p.

The widespread manipulation of the human resources of a society through medical and biochemical devices has not yet been subject to a sociological monograph. (There are, however, books on alcohol and society.)

The role of non-human resources for society has been discussed by Cotrell, and the Twentieth Century Fund has begun what we hope is to become a long-lasting habit of compiling periodic reviews of *America's needs and resources* and *Europe's needs and resources*.

D83. Dewhurst, J. Frederic, *et al*. America's needs and resources: a new survey. New York, The Twentieth Century Fund, 1955. 1148 p.
D84. Dewhurst, J. Frederic, *et al*. Europe's needs and resources: trends and prospects in eighteen countries, 1961. New York, The Twentieth Century Fund. 1152 p.

Family Sociology

Much basic material about family structure—marriage, birth, and divorce rates, residence patterns, etc.—are obtained from demography; a book containing much of this material for the contemporary United States has been authored by Paul Glick. A comprehensive history of the American family has been written by Arthur Calhoun; a simple but lucid summary is provided by Sirjamaki.

D85. Calhoun, Arthur W. A social history of the American family. New York, Barnes & Noble, 1960. 3 v.
D86. Glick, Paul C. American families. New York, Wiley, 1957. 240 p.
D87. Sirjamaki, John. The American family in the twentieth century. Cambridge, Harvard Univ. Press, 1953. 227 p.

The family structure of less advanced societies is studied through anthropological records. Of the work done in this latter tradition, sociologists have found Murdock's *Social structure* most rewarding. A treatise that gives a comprehensive description and analysis of family life in various advanced civilizations has been written by William J. Goode. Zimmerman's book and *The family: its function and destiny* might also be of interest here. Among the many monographs focusing on particular family structures, one may mention the ones by Blake on the Jamaican family, Levy on the Chinese family, Wikman on the rural Scandinavian family, and Frazier on the American Negro family. The impact of modern technology on the Western family is the theme of the book by Ogburn and Nimkoff.

D88. Anshen, Ruth N., *ed.* The family: its function and destiny Rev. ed. New York, Harper, 1959. 538 p.
D89. Blake, Judith. Family structure in Jamaica: the social context of reproduction. New York, Free Press of Glencoe, 1961. 262 p.
D90. Frazier, Edward F. The Negro family in the United States. Rev. ed. New York, Dryden Press, 1948. 374 p.
D91. Goode William J. World revolution and family patterns. New York, Free Press of Glencoe, 1963. 432 p.
D92. Levy, Marion J. The family revolution in modern China. Cambridge, Harvard Univ. Press, 1949. 390 p.
D93. Murdock, George P. Social structure. New York, Macmillan, 1949. 387 p.
D94. Ogburn, William F. and Meyer F. Nimkoff. Technology and the changing family. Boston, Houghton Mifflin, 1955. 329 p.
D95. Wikman, Karl R. V. Die Einleitung der Ehe. Åbo, Åbo Akademi, 1937. 395 p.
D96. Zimmerman, Carle C. Family and civilization. New York, Harper, 1947. 829 p.

Interaction and adjustment in the modern family have been frequently studied. Georg Karlsson's monograph summarizes the theories in this field and interprets many of these findings. Important recent monographs in this area have been written by Foote and Cottrell, Goode, and Winch.

D97. Foote, Nelson N. and Leonard S. Cottrell. Identity and interpersonal competence. Chicago, Univ. of Chicago Press, 1955. 305 p.
D98. Goode, William J. After divorce. Glencoe, Ill., Free Press, 1956. 381 p.
D99. Karlsson, Georg. Adaptability and communication in marriage. Uppsala, Almquist & Wiksell, 1951. 215 p. (Abridged, revised edition from The Bedminster Press, 1963.)
D100. Winch, Robert F. Mate selection: a study of complementary needs. New York, Harper, 1958. 349 p.

Economic Sociology

In classifying books as economic or political sociology, one must have some conception of how these fields differ from economics and political science. Generally speaking, we deal with a sociological problem whenever its determinants lie in one institutional realm and its result in another. Thus Weber's *The Protestant ethic and the spirit of capitalism* falls in the area of sociology rather than theology or economics, since it links events in religion (the Protestant Ethic) to events in the economy (the spirit of capitalism). By contrast, a book indicating how capital investments vary with long-term interest rates would fall clearly in economics since it relates some events in the economy to other events in the economy. (It is also useful to make it a rule to classify the sociology books which link events in different realms of society to each other by the resultant events. Thus Weber's book will be listed in economic sociology, not in sociology of religion, since economic events are depicted as the resultant ones. It must be admitted, however, that this cannot always be done, due to the interrelatedness of determinants and results in macrosociology.)

Max Weber's previously mentioned work on *Economy and society* contains much relevant material, as do his analyses of the world religions, since he was very much interested in tracing their effect on economic life. A monograph in Weber's vein but with a limited focus is Nelson's *Idea of usury*.

How events in the body politic and the ideologies of the governing of men tie in with industrial systems is the subject of an excellent comparative study by Bendix, entitled *Work and authority in industry*. In general, however, today's sociological literature is shallow when it comes to monographs linking events in polity to events in the economy. The situation today contrasts sharply with the times of social Darwinism, when the sociological literature was full of statements, albeit value-loaded, on the accommodation of politics and business.

It is also striking that there are hardly any recent monographs available about the interrelations of science and economy. Yet events in science have had the greatest impact on modern economy. Ogburn's work some thirty years ago on *Social change* is hardly the most viable one possible in this area. One may mention the monograph by Fourastié as a suggestive source, but this field is still wide open for a first major contribution.

D101. Bendix, Reinhard. Work and authority in industry: ideologies of management in the course of industrialization. New York, Wiley, 1956. 466 p.
D102. Fourastié, Jean. Machinisme et bien-être. Paris, Editions de Minuit, 1951. 255 p. (English translation available from The Free Press.)
D103. Nelson, Benjamin N. The idea of usury: from tribal brotherhood to universal brotherhood. Princeton, N.J., Princeton Univ. Press, 1949. 257 p.
D104. Ogburn, William Fielding. Social change: with respect to culture and original nature. New York, B.W. Huebsch, 1922. 365 p.
D105. Weber, Max. Gesammelte Aufsätze zur Religionssoziologie. Tübingen, J.C.B. Mohr, 1922-23. 3 v. (Partial English translation of vol. 1 on The Protestant Ethic available from Scribner. English translation of vol. 2 on Hinduism and Buddhism available from The Free Press and English translation of vol. 3 on Ancient Judaism also available from The Free Press.)

The composition and origin of the business elite has been the subject of many studies; the monograph by Warner and Abegglen is the most ambitious of these. A study of union leaders and their origin has been made by Mills. The changing composition of the American labor force has been treated by Jaffe and Carleton; the facts of this book are now outdated, but it illustrates a mode of analysis that remains valid.

D105a. Jaffe, Abram J. and R.O. Carleton. Occupational mobility in the United States, 1930-1960. New York, Columbia Univ. Press, 1954. 105 p.
D106. Mills, C. Wright. The new men of power: America's labor leaders. New York, Harcourt, Brace, 1948. 323 p.
D107. Warner, Lloyd W. and James Abegglen. Occupational mobility in American business and industry, 1928-1952. Minneapolis, Univ. of Minnesota Press, 1955. 315 p.

Blue-collar workers in "dead end" jobs have been studied by Chinoy; it would be interesting to get a similar monograph on the many white-collar workers who lack chances for advancement. A general survey of the sociology of work has been written by Caplow, and a summary of numerous studies of workers' morale has been made by Viteles. One may also recommend Hughes' perceptive essays on the sociology of work.

D108. Caplow, Theodore. The sociology of work. Minneapolis, Univ. of Minnesota Press, 1954. 330 p.
D109. Chinoy, Ely. Automobile workers and the American dream. Garden City, N.Y., Doubleday, 1955. 139 p.
D110. Hughes, Everett C. Men and their work. Glencoe, Ill., Free Press, 1958. 184 p.
D111. Viteles, Morris S. Motivation and morale in industry. New York, Norton, 1953. 510 p.

Most of the recent works in economic sociology are focused on economic organizations (business enterprises or unions) or on markets (mostly consumer behavior). Of the studies of firms and factories and their relations with the outside community, one may mention the pioneering one by Roethlisberger and Dickson, and the later ones by Gouldner, Jacques, Touraine, and Segerstedt and Lundquist. The union study by Lipset and his co-workers is considered one of the best sociological monographs of the 1950s.

D112. Gouldner, Alvin W. Patterns of industrial bureaucracy. Glencoe, Ill., Free Press, 1954. 282 p.
D113. Jacques, Elliot. The changing culture of a factory. New York, Dryden Press, 1952. 341 p.
D114. Lipset, Seymour M., *et al*. Union democracy: the internal politics of the International Typographical Union. Glencoe, Ill., Free Press, Press, 1956. 455 p.
D115. Roethlisberger, Fritz J. and William J. Dickson. Management and the worker: an account of a research program conducted by the Western Electric Company, Hawthorne Works, Chicago. Cambridge, Harvard Univ. Press, 1950. 615 p.
D116. Segerstedt, Torgny T. and Agne Lundquist. Människan i industrisamhället. Stockholm, SNS, 1952-55. 2 v.
D117. Touraine, Alain. L'evolution du travail ouvrier aux usines Renault. Paris, Centre National de la Recherche Scientifique, 1955. 202 p.

Market research findings about consumer decisions and some parallel
findings about executive decisions are analyzed in Lazarsfeld's contribution to the symposium on business and the social sciences. Katona's work
is interesting, both in its comprehensive description of the American as a
consumer, and in its ability to make findings from social research bear
upon problems in economic theory. While much attention has been
given to the consumer, very little serious sociological research has been
done on the salesman, dealer, and broker.

D118. Dahl, Robert A., *et al.* Social science research on business: product
    and potential. New York, Columbia Univ. Press, 1960. 185 p.
D119. Katona, George. The powerful consumer. New York, McGraw-Hill,
    1960. 276 p.

Political Sociology

Sociologists have, unfortunately, rather effectively avoided the topic of
power, that is, the creation and maintenance of a chosen version of
order. The best ideas on this topic are probably still found in Weber's
and Pareto's fifty-year-old treatises, previously mentioned. Here indeed
is a major topic in search of an author. Max Weber's political sociology
(in *Economy and society*) has remained untranslated until recently. A
representative monograph in his tradition about the German socialists
has been written by Guenther Roth.

A sociological perspective on the body politic was furnished some years
ago in America by Robert McIver. The essays written by his students in
his honor and collected in *Freedom and control in modern society* give
an indication of the varieties of political sociology he has inspired. Other
inspirations to American political sociology have come from Robert
Lynd's *Knowledge for what?*, a persuasive plea for an active role of sociology in the shaping of the future of society. A third and different inspiration for political sociology has come from public opinion research, and
the detailed election studies initiated by Paul F. Lazarsfeld which cul-
minated with the publication of *Voting* in 1954. A very good book that
unites several of these approaches is called *Political man.*

D120. Berelsen, Bernard R., *et al.* Voting: a study of opinion formation in
    a presidential campaign. Chicago, Univ. of Chicago Press, 1954.
    395 p.
D121. Berger, Morroe, *et al.* Freedom and control in modern society. New
    York, Van Nostrand, 1954. 326 p.
D122. Lipset, Seymour M. Political man: the social bases of politics. Garden
    City, N.Y., Doubleday, 1960. 432 p.
D123. Lynd, Robert S. Knowledge for what? Princeton, N.J. Princeton
    Univ. Press, 1939. 268 p.
D123a Roth, Guenther. The Social Democrats in Imperial Germany, To-
    towa, N.J., Bedminster Press, 1963. 348 p.

There is much recent work in the area of comparative political sociology; it has not yet been summarized into a comprehensive treatise but

some is available in an anthology edited by Almond and Coleman (A38). An effort to confront ideas of freedom with facts and findings from social psychology has been made by Bay. A more conventional confrontation of the ideas of democracy, with both logic and sociological realities, has been made by Tingsten. Kornhauser has analyzed marginal and extremist groups in modern societies.

D124. Bay, Christian. The structure of freedom. Stanford, Calif., Stanford Univ. Press, 1958. 419 p.
D125. Kornhauser, William. The politics of mass society. Glencoe, Ill., Free Press, 1959. 256 p.
D126. Tingsten, Herbert. Demokratiens problem. Rev. ed. Stockholm, Aldus, 1960. 157 p. (English translation from Bedminster Press.)

No standard work exists in the field of sociology of law but an excellent book focusing on the sanctions used by legal institutions has been written by Vilhelm Aubert. (Aubert's thinking about social control is also summarized in his textbook *Sosiologi* of which there is an English translation forthcoming from Scribners.)

D127. Aubert, Vilhelm. Om straffens sosiale funksjon. Oslo, Akademisk Forlag, 1954. 241 p.

Books on military sociology are not abundant, but it is easy to locate outstanding titles. The works by Speier and Janowitz are important. American experiences in World War II are skillfully analyzed by Stouffer *et al.* and Ginsberg *et al.*

D128. Ginsberg, Eli, *et al.* The ineffective soldier: lessons for management and the nation. New York, Columbia Univ. Press, 1959. 3 v.
D129. Janowitz, Morris. The professional soldier: a social and political portrait. Glencoe, Ill., Free Press, 1960. 464 p.
D130. Speier, Hans. Social order and the risk of war; papers in political sociology. New York, G.W. Stewart, 1952. 497 p.
D131. Stouffer, Samuel A. The American soldier. Princeton, N.J., Princeton Univ. Press, 1949. 2 v.

The impact of non-party voluntary associations on the body politic has been analyzed by Hausknecht. C. Wright Mills has written a much debated book on the impact by various elites on the process of government in America. At the level of the local community, similar problems have been dealt with by Hunter. Hyman has analyzed how political allegiances develop when children grow into adults, and Lane has summarized what is known about the ways in which people become engaged in political pursuits. Political apathy is one of the subjects in Bell's *End of ideology*. All these books deal with the United States; for a perspective, one should also consult studies in different settings, e.g. Mayntz' book on the organization of a political party in Berlin, and Selznick's analysis of the methods of international communism.

D132. Bell, Daniel. The end of ideology: on the exhaustion of political ideas in the fifties. Glencoe, Ill., Free Press, 1960. 416 p.

D133. Hausknecht, Murray. The joiners: a sociological description of vol-
untary association membership in the United States. New York,
Bedminster Press, 1962. 141 p.
D134. Hunter, Floyd. Community power structure: a study of decision
makers. Chapel Hill, Univ. of North Carolina Press, 1953, 297 p.
D135. Hyman, Herbert H. Political socialization. Glencoe, Ill., Free Press,
1959. 175 p.
D136. Lane, Robert E. Political life: why people get involved in politics.
Glencoe, Ill., Free Press, 1959. 374 p.
D137. Mayntz, Renate. Parteigruppen in der Gross-Stadt. Cologne, West-
deutscher Verlag, 1959. 159 p.
D138 Mills, C. Wright. The power elite. New York, Oxford Univ. Press,
1956. 423 p.
D139. Selznick, Philip. The organizational weapon: a study in Bolshevik
strategy and tactics. New York, McGraw-Hill, 1952. 350 p.

The composition of the political parties gauged by election statistics
and public opinion polls are revealed in several books. For the United
States one might consult *The American voter*; systematic international
comparisons were first used by Tingsten in 1937; many others have followed.

D140. Campbell, Angus, *et al*. The American voter. New York, John Wiley,
1960. 573 p.
D141. Tingsten, Herbert. Political behavior; studies in election statistics.
Totowa, N.J., Bedminster Press, 1963 231 p.

Public opinion is subject to numerous sociological studies. In addition
to the classic book by Lippman, perhaps the best titles to acquire here
are the anthologies edited by Berelson and Janowitz, and by Schramm.
They also contain many references to mass-media research. Of the many
specialized monographs in the latter area, one may select the one by
Janowitz on the function of the neighborhood newspaper in a big city.

D142. Berelson, Bernard and Morris Janowitz, *eds*. Reader in public opin-
ion and communication. Glencoe, Ill., Free Press, 1953. 611 p.
D143. Janowitz, Morris. The community press in an urban setting. Glen-
coe, Ill., Free Press, 1952. 256 p.
D144. Lippmann, Walter. Public opinion. New York, Macmillan, 1922.
323 p.
D145. Schramm, Wilbur L., *ed*. Mass communications; a book of readings.
Urbana, Univ. of Illinois Press, 1960. 695 p.

Sociology of science and education

A history of science that appeals to sociologists has been written by
Price. A critical look at the world of learning in today's America is found
in Barzun's *The house of intellect*. Some effects of other institutions on
the world of knowledge are subject to speculation and study by Mannheim. Barber and Hirsch have edited an anthology which gives a good
indication of the status of sociology of science.

D146. Barber, Bernard and Walter Hirsch. The sociology of science: a
        reader. New York, Free Press of Glencoe, Ill., 1963. 662 p.
D147. Barzun, Jacques. The house of intellect. New York, Harper, 1959.
        276 p.
D148. Mannheim Karl. Ideology and utopia: an introduction to the soci-
        ology of knowledge. New York, Harcourt, Brace, 1953. 318 p.
D149. de Solla Price, Derek J. Science since Babylon. New Haven, Conn.,
        Yale Univ. Press, 1961. 149 p.

Higher education has recently become a more frequent topic for sociological investigation. The book by Wilson entitled *The academic man*
can be selected as a comprehensive treatise that opened up this field for
sociological research. The book with the somewhat similar title of *The
academic mind* deals with reactions of social scientists in colleges and
universities to recent issues of academic freedom but contains also a
wealth of information about professors in general. The job market for
professors has been critically examined by Caplow and McGee.
   Professional schools are also becoming objects of sociological curiosity.
A book by Merton *et al.* on medical schools is already available; Good-
man's careful look at a teacher's college is a finished but unpublished
Ph.D. thesis (Columbia University); and it should not be long before we
have good studies published about law schools, library schools, military
academies, and other institutions of higher learning, including research
institutes. A comprehensive sociological study of libraries and librarians
has never been done; however, the survey by Fiske contains material
of interest beyond the rather special situation that prompted the study.
In spite of the now large and serious interest recently in sociology of professions, no comprehensive treatise on this topic is available.

D150. Fiske, Marjorie. Book selection and censorship; a study of school
        and public libraries in California. Berkeley, Univ. of California
        Press, 1959. 145 p.
D151. Lazarsfeld, Paul F. and Wagner Thielens, Jr. The academic mind:
        social scientists in a time of crisis. Glencoe, Ill., Free Press, 1958.
        460 p.
D152. Merton, Robert K., *et al.* The student-physician. Cambridge, Har-
        vard Univ. Press, 1957. 351 p.
D153. Wilson, Logan. The academic man; a study in the sociology of a
        profession. New York, Oxford Univ. Press, 1942. 248 p.

The values of college and high school students have been carefully examined in the books by Goldsen *et al.* and by Coleman. Hollingshead's
Elmtown's youth continues to hold its position as the best study of the
impact of the community stratification system on the students of a high
school. We still await a comprehensive sociological analysis of the recruit-
ment of students to higher education, and the meaning of higher education for career, marriage, and style of life in today's society; in the meantime the book by Haveman and West, *They went to college*, fills a gap
in the literature.

D154. Coleman, James S. The adolescent society: the social life of the teenager and its impact on education. New York, Free Press, 1961. 368 p.
D155. Goldsen, Rose K., *et al*. What college students think. Princeton, N.J., Van Nostrand, 1960. 240 p.
D156. Haveman, Ernest and Patricia Salter West. They went to college: the college graduate in America today. New York, Harcourt, Brace, 1952. 277 p.
D157. Hollingshead, August B. Elmtown's Youth: The impact of social classes on adolescents. New York, Wiley, 1949. 480 p.

Sociology of Art

The sociology of fine art is not far advanced. Tastes in different strata of American society are reviewed in an amusing vein by Russell Lynes. Among more professional monographs one may mention Silbermann's work on music, which is comprehensive in context but short in bulk. A specialized topic—how community factors influence the repertoire played by symphony orchestras—is treated in the book by Mueller. Lowenthal's work on the sociology of literature benefits from historical knowledge. Duncan's work on sociology of literature benefits from a general theory of symbols which is applied to fiction and criticism.

D158. Duncan, Hugh D. Language and literature in society. New York, Bedminster Press, 1961. 262 p.
D159. Lowenthal, Leo. Literature and the image of man: sociological studies of the European drama and novel, 1600-1900. Boston, Beacon Press, 1957. 242 p.
D160. Lynes, Russell. The taste-makers. New York, Harper, 1955. 262 p.
D161. Mueller, John H. The American symphony orchestra: a social history of musical taste. Bloomington, Indiana Univ. Press, 1951. 437 p.
D162. Silbermann, Alphons. Wovon lebt die Musik: Die Prinzipien der Musiksoziologie. Regensburg, Gustav Bosse Verlag, 1957. 235 p. (An English translation, *The sociology of music* is available from Routledge and Kegan Paul.)

Popular culture is a favorite sociological topic; the anthology edited by Rosenberg and White gives an impression of this field, which, in spite of much research and thought, remains largely without established principles.

D163. Rosenberg, Bernard and David M. White, *eds.* Mass culture: the popular arts in America. Glencoe, Ill., Free Press, 1957. 561 p.

Sociology of Religion

Max Weber's writings in the sociology of religion still command interest, as does Durkheim's study of the cohesive force of religion, both of which have already been cited. Surprisingly, however, even these celebrated works in sociology of religion are variations of an old and still unverified theory that religion is somehow essential to the functioning of society. This view has been very congenial to the American pragmatic image of religion as something that can be socially advantageous. A later work that distills and refines the best of Durkheim's lines of thought is *Religion among the primitives* by Goode. None of the many attempts to apply his theory of religion in contemporary society is as successful.

D164. Goode, William J. Religion among the primitives. Glencoe, Ill., Free Press, 1951. 321 p.

A sociologically slanted survey of religious phenomena in history and around the world, giving the right balance between detailed and general features, has been made by Widengren. This book reflects the modern break with traditional evolutionary approach to the sociology of religion in which all religious development ends in monotheism. For a more conventional view one might consult Wach's work.

D165. Wach, Joachim. Sociology of religion. Chicago, Univ. of Chicago Press, 1951. 418 p.
D166. Widengren, Geo. Religionens värld. 2 ed. Stockholm, Svenska Kyrkans Diakonistyrelse, 1956. 534 p.

The contemporary religious composition of the United States is well analyzed by Herberg. The book by Clark is of interest beyond its Canadian locale.

D167. Clark, Samuel D. Church and sect in Canada. Toronto, Univ. of Toronto Press, 1948. 458 p.
D168. Herberg, Will. Protestant, Catholic, Jew: an essay in American religious sociology. Rev. ed. Garden City, N.Y., Doubleday, 1960. 309 p.

A close sociological look at a Catholic parish has been made by Fichter. There is no very adequate study of Protestant congregations in print. Lenski has traced the effects of religion on attitudes toward phenomena in other institutional realms. A sociologist might also find useful the book by Argyle, which summarizes what interview surveys and psychological tests reveal about individual religiosity.

The lack of sociological studies of ethics is noted with regret.

D169. Argyle, Michael. Religious behavior. Glencoe, Ill., Free Press, 1959. 196 p.
D170. Fichter, Joseph H. The dynamics of a city church. Chicago, Chicago Univ. Press, 1951. 283 p.
D171. Fichter, Joseph H. Social relations in the urban parish. Chicago, Univ. of Chicago Press, 1954. 263 p.
D171a. Lenski, Gerhard. The religious factor. Rev. ed. Garden City, N.Y., Doubleday, 1963. 414 p.

Urban and Rural Life, Communities and Societies

The *Sourcebook of rural sociology* remains the outstanding collection of data and synthesis of principles in rural sociology. A sociological analysis of ancient city life has been written by Sjoberg, and the medieval

city is the subject of a minor classic by Pirenne. For other centuries there
is Mumford's readable survey, a work of art as well as science.

D172. Mumford, Lewis. The city in history. New York, Harcourt, Brace,
World, 1961. 657 p.
D173. Pirenne, Henri. Les villes du moyen âge; essai d'histoire écono-
mique et sociale. Brussels, Lamertin, 1927. 203 p. (English trans-
lation available from Doubleday.)
D174. Sjoberg, Gideon. The pre-industrial city, past and present. Glencoe,
Ill., Free Press, 1960. 353 p.
D175. Sorokin, Pitirim A., et al. A systematic source book in rural sociology.
Minneapolis, Univ. of Minnesota Press, 1930-32. 3 v.

There is a wealth of sociological monographs depicting a rural or an
urban setting. With few exceptions, e.g. Angel's study of the integration
of cities, these monographs are case studies with a richness of local detail.
Most of them make good and easy reading. The following stand out in
my memory as particularly astute in their observations.
About rural life:

D176. Arensberg, Conrad M. and Solon T. Kimball. Family and community in Ireland. Cambridge, Harvard Univ. Press, 1940. 322 p.
D177. Tumin, Melvin M. Caste in a peasant society: a case study in the
dynamics of caste. Princeton, N.J., Princeton Univ. Press, 1952.
300 p.

About suburban life:

D178. Seeley, John R., et al. Crestwood Heights: the culture of suburban
life. New York, Basic Books, 1956. 505 p.

About city life:

D179. Angell, Robert C. The moral integration of American cities. Chicago,
Chicago Univ. Press, 1951. 140 p.
D180. Caplow, Theodore et al. The urban ambience: a study of San Juan,
Puerto Rico. Totowa, N.J., Bedminster Press, 1963. 250 p.
D180a. Dollard, John. Caste and class in a Southern town. Garden City,
N.Y., Doubleday, 1957. 446 p.
D181. Drake, St. Clair and Horace R. Cayton. Black metropolis: a study of
Negro life in a Northern city. Rev. ed. New York, Harper, 1962.
2 v.
D182. Warner, William D. The social life of a modern community. New
Haven, Conn., Yale Univ. Press, 1941. 460 p.
D183. Whyte, William F. Street corner society· the social structure of an
Italian slum. 2d ed. Chicago, Univ. of Chicago Press, 1961.
364 p.

Sociological libraries should also have represented a rarer kind of book
attempting a sociological analysis of an entire society. The work by
Hughes on French Canada, by Bauer et al. on the Soviet Union, and
Wallerstein on Africa are typical books of this kind. One may also mention Max Lerner's America as a civilization, whose author, while not a

professional sociologist, is sensitive to sociological problems and views and draws upon a large number of sociological studies.

D184. Bauer, Raymond A., *et al.* How the Soviet system works. Cambridge, Harvard Univ. Press, 1957. 274 p.
D185. Hughes, Everett C. French Canada in transition. London, K. Paul, Trench, Trubner & Co., 1946. 227 p.
D186. Lerner, Max. America as a civilization: life and thought in the United States today. New York, Simon and Schuster, 1957. 1036 p.
D187. Wallerstein, Immanuel. Africa: the politics of independence. New York, Vintage Books, 1961. 173 p.

Social Problems

The literature on social problems is large, and it is not easy to decide what titles to select. Some classical titles have already been mentioned—namely, Durkheim on suicide and Thomas and Znaniecki on the adjustment of immigrants.

Of the many social problems sociologists have studied, crime and delinquency have received the most attention. Vold has surveyed the many attempts made in the past and present to explain criminal behavior. A popular text in criminology is the one by Sutherland and Cressey (now in its 6th edition). Among the many books on juvenile delinquency there is none which is clearly superior or which has become outstandingly popular. However, the text by Shulman is suggested for its broad coverage and recent publication. In the sociological study of delinquency there have been, in the past few years, some stimulating theoretical formulations. See particularly the books by Cohen and Cloward and Ohlin. In the study of adult law-breaking, Sutherland's two monographs, *White-collar crime* and *The professional thief*, have become minor classics. Ohlin has also written a pamphlet on the use of sociology in the field of correction.

D188. Cohen, Albert K. Delinquent boys: the culture of the gang. Glencoe, Ill., Free Press, 1955. 202 p.
D189. Cloward, Richard A. and Lloyd E. Ohlin. Delinquency and opportunity: a theory of delinquent gangs. Glencoe, Ill., Free Press, 1960. 220 p.
D190. Ohlin, Lloyd E. Sociology and the field of corrections. New York, Russell Sage Foundation, 1956. 58 p.
D191. Sutherland, Edwin H. The professional thief. Chicago, Univ. of Chicago Press, 1937. 257 p.
D192. Sutherland, Edwin H. White-collar crime. New York, Dryden Press, 1949. 272 p.
D193. Vold, George B. Theoretical criminology. New York, Oxford Univ. Press, 1958. 334 p.

A large number of other social problems are most competently reviewed in the anthology edited by Merton and Nisbet. One topic that is not covered in this anthology is gambling, which receives its first sophisticated sociological analysis in a book by Tec. Race relations is, of course, well represented in the anthology, but Myrdal's *An American dilemma* remains the ranking entry in this field. Applied social research is a modern phenomenon almost everywhere present. (See, for example, the previously mentioned works by Lazarsfeld and Thielens, and by Fiske.) Applied social theory is rare; Zetterberg's *Social theory and social practice* represents this promising field.

D194. Merton, Robert K. and Robert A. Nisbet, *eds.* Contemporary social problems: an introduction to the sociology of deviant behavior and social disorganization. New York, Harcourt, Brace & World, 1961. 754 p.
D195. Myrdal, Gunnar. An American dilemma. New York, Harper, 1944. 1483 p.
D196. Tec, Nechama. Gambling in Sweden: a sociological inquiry into gambling behavior. Totowa, N.J., Bedminster Press, 1964. 139 p.
D197. Zetterberg, Hans L. Social theory and social practice. New York, Bedminster Press, 1962. 191 p.

METHODS OF SOCIOLOGY

The philosophical foundation for social science inquiry has been treated by McEwen, who has reviewed a common question from almost a century ago: how is social-scientific knowledge possible? He has answered it by an examination of the procedures of social scientists, a method hardly feasible at the time the issue was first raised. Problems of explanation in the social sciences are compared with related problems in the physical and biological sciences in Nagel's excellent book.

D198. McEwen, William P. The problem of social-scientific knowledge. Totowa, N.J., Bedminster Press, 1963. 590 p.
D199. Nagel, Ernest. The structure of science: problems in the logic of scientific explanations. New York, Harcourt Brace, & World, 1961. 618 p.

Books on the methodology of theory construction in sociology are rare. A symposium edited by Gross, however, contains several papers about the logical structure of sociological theories, and the second edition of Zetterberg's monograph deals with the problem on a somewhat more practical level. Still closer to actual practices of scientists is the book by Berger *et al.* which is restricted to conclusions drawn from microsociological experiments.

D200. Berger, Joseph, *et al.* Types of formalization in small-group research. Boston, Houghton Mifflin, 1962. 159 p.
D201. Gross, Llewellyn, *ed.* Symposium on sociological theory. Evanston, Row Petersen, 1959. 642 p.
D202. Zetterberg, Hans L. On theory and verification in sociology. Rev. ed. Totowa, N.J., Bedminster Press, 1963. 84 p.

There are a few books which present research techniques often used by sociologists: for example, quantitative content analysis; demographic analysis; and techniques for compiling life histories. There are several textbooks which attempt to teach sociologists the statistical methods most useful or adaptable to their research problem. However, I do not know of any adequate manual for field methods in sociology, nor any book that adopts historical methods for sociological use.

D203. Barclay, George W. Techniques of population analysis. New York, Wiley, 1958. 311 p.
D204. Berelson, Bernard. Content analysis in communication research. Glencoe, Ill., Free Press, 1952. 220 p.
D205. Dollard, John. Criteria for the life history. Gloucester, Mass., Peter Smith, 1949. 228 p.
D206. Zeisel, Hans. Say it with figures. 4th ed. New York, Harper, 1957. 257 p.

The most distinct sociological research tool is that of the sample survey. Sampling has been treated both theoretically and practically by Dahlenius, interviewing and survey analysis by Hyman. Both principles and tricks of the trade as developed at Columbia's Bureau of Applied Social Research are dealt with in *The Language of social research,* an outstanding book mentioned earlier. The discussions of indices and indicators in this anthology cover this important topic until we get a modern monograph on sociological measurements. The selection of Stouffer's research papers can serve as illustration of survey research at its best.

D207. Dalenius, Tore. Sampling in Sweden: contributions to the methods and theories of sample survey practice. Stockholm, Almquist & Wiksell, 1957. 247 p.
D208. Hyman, Herbert H. Interviewing in social research. Chicago, Univ. of Chicago Press, 1954. 415 p.
D209. Hyman, Herbert H. Survey design and analysis: principles, cases and procedures. Glencoe, Ill., Free Press, 1955. 425 p.
D210. Stouffer, Samuel A. Social research to test ideas. New York, Free Press, 1962. 314 p.

Hans L. Zetterberg

GUIDES TO THE LITERATURE

No separate general guide to the literature of sociology is available.

REVIEWS OF THE LITERATURE

D211. American journal of sociology. v. 1+ 1895+ Chicago, Univ. of Chicago Press. bi-monthly.

One of the oldest American sociological journals this periodical contains 175-200 critical, signed book reviews of medium length (400-1,300 words) each year. The section "Current books" lists 400-500 titles a year with brief explanatory statements for many. The July issue contains two sections on doctoral dissertations completed and in progress. See (D297).

D212. American sociological review. v. 1+ 1936+ New York, American Sociological Association. bi-monthly.

The official publication of the American Sociological Association, this journal surveys current publication in three sections: (1) "Book reviews"; medium length (400-900 words) critical, signed reviews of 200-250 books a year, (2) "Book notes"; short notices (125-400 words) on 50-100 additional titles, (3) "Publications received"; lists 750-1,000 items per year. Occasional review articles. Annual index of book reviews, book notes and reviewers.

D213. L'Année sociologique. v. 1-12, 1896-1912; n.s. v. 1-2 no. 2 1923-24, 1924-25; 3d series v. 1+ 1948+ Paris, Alcan, 1896-1925; Presses Universitaires de France. 1948+.

More than one half of each volume of this respected publication founded by Emile Durkheim is devoted to a selective survey of the significant literature of sociology. The 200-300 reviews a year vary in length from brief analyses to lengthy essays surveying the significant contributions in a given subject area. Scope is international, but emphasis is upon developments in French sociology. The signed reviews are grouped under 6-8 major areas (general sociology, social morphology, social systems and civilizations, sociology of religion, etc.) with an author index. The gap between 1925 and 1948 was partially filled by *Annales sociologiques* v. 1-4, 1934-1941, which was issued in 5 series: (a) Sociologie générale, (b) Sociologie religieuse, (c) Sociologie juridique et morale, (d) Sociologie économique, (e) Morphologie sociale, language, technologie, esthetique. Format the same as *L'Année*.

D214. British journal of sociology. v. 1+ 1950+ London, London School of Economics and Political Science. quarterly.

In addition to 2-4 review articles this journal carries 75-100 critical reviews (450-1,800 words) a year. 25-50 other works are noted with briefer reviews (125-300 words) and 250-300 publications are listed as books received. Book reviews are included in annual index.

D215. Current sociology, v. 1+ 1952+ Paris, UNESCO, 1952-1957; London, Blackwell, 1958+. quarterly.

Conceived as a periodical which would deal in alternate issues with a world bibliography and trend reports on special subjects. In 1955 the *International bibliography of sociology* (D223) became a separate publication. Each issue now contains an analysis of trends shown by published research on some aspect of sociology, supported by a lengthy (300-1,000 items) annotated bibliography. Recent issues covered: Caste; Sociology of ageing; Rural sociology in Southeast Asia; Sociology of education; Political sociology; Social factors in economic growth.

D216. Gittler, Joseph B., *ed.* Review of sociology; analysis of a decade. New York, Wiley, 1957. 588 p.

22 specialists survey the most significant literature and developments in all areas of sociological inquiry for the period 1945-1955. Each of the 14 essays (Sociological theory, Population research, Collective behavior, Marriage and the family, Racial and cultural relations, etc.) is followed by a bibliography. A total of 2,158 items are listed. Five annotated bibliographical appendices (Sociology of education, politics, religion, art and culture change) list an additional 423 titles.

D217. Kölner Zeitschrift fur Soziologie und Sozialpsychologie. v. 1 + 1949 + Cologne, Westdeutscher Verlag. quarterly.

An important German journal which reviews 150-200 monographs a year. Long (1,000-2,000 words) critical single reviews are supplemented by extensive essays reviewing groups of books.

D218. Population. v. 1 + 1946 + Paris, Institut National d'Études Démographiques. quarterly.

One half of each issue is devoted to surveying current literature. "Analyses" carries 150-200 short critical reviews (150-600 words) of monographs in all fields of population study. "Notes" analyzes in short reviews (100-300 words) between 200 and 250 periodical articles selected from major scholarly journals. Reviews included in general index.

D219. Social service review. v. 1 + 1927 + Chicago, Univ. of Chicago Press. quarterly.

This journal, devoted to the scientific and professional interests of social work, surveys the current literature in long (385-2000 words), critical, signed reviews. The 100-150 reviews a year are generally restricted to English language titles but included are reviews of important government reports and public docu-

ments. Annual index of book reviews. Since 1954 "Doctoral dissertations in social work" has been a regular feature. See (D298)

See also: F256

ABSTRACTS AND DIGESTS

D220. Excerpta criminologica. v. 1 + 1961 + Amsterdam, Excerpta Criminologica Foundation. bimonthly.

Abstracts articles from criminological periodicals and pertinent material from related fields. International in scope. Some books (manuals, texts, etc.) are abstracted as well as composite monographic studies. Abstracts are classified under 14 major headings with an author index in each issue and annual author and subject indexes. 1,655 items included in 1961.

D221. Sociological abstracts. v. 1 + 1952 + New York. 5 times a year.

An important journal which abstracts 200-250 books and 1,500-2,000 articles a year appearing in ca. 250 periodicals. 31 major sociological journals from 12 countries are indexed in full, the remaining journals in cognate areas are partially abstracted for articles of significance to sociologists. The entries are classified under 42 major subject areas with annual indexes of authors, subjects, and periodicals. Category 42 abstracts current texts, readers and reference books. All titles in foreign languages are translated into English.

D222. Tumin, Melvin M. Segregation and desegregation. New York, Anti-Defamation League of B'nai B'rith, 1957. 112 p.

Comprises one page reviews and digests of 107 significant articles from professional journals (1951-1956) classified under 12 general subject headings including, segregation and integration, factors affecting the process of desegregation, attitudes and their measurement, theoretical issues in the analysis of prejudice, etc. A supplement carries work through 1959: *Segregation and desegregation: a digest of recent research 1956-1959* (N.Y. Anti-Defamation League of B'nai B'rith, 1960. 32 p.) Revised edition in preparation.

See also: A51; F258.

BIBLIOGRAPHIES—CURRENT

D223. International bibliography of sociology. v. 1-9, 1951-1959. Paris, UNESCO, 1952-61; v. 10+ 1960+ Chicago, Aldine, 1962+ annual.

A current record of significant scientific publications without limitation as to country of origin, language or form (books, articles, duplicated reports, etc.). The 3,000-5,000 entries a year are arranged by a very detailed classification scheme with author and subject indexes. No coverage for demography or social psychology. No annotations. Time lag about two years. Vols. 1-4, 1951-54 appeared as issues of *Current sociology* (D215).

D224. Population index. v. 1+ 1935+ Princeton, N.J., Office of Population Research, Princeton Univ. and Population Association of America. quarterly.

An annotated bibliography of books and periodical literature (ca. 5,000 items a year) on all phases of population problems, classified according to broad aspects—general studies and theory, regional studies, spatial distribution, mortality, etc.—with detailed subdivisions. A section devoted to official statistics is classified by country. Three monthly indexes: subject index; author index; and geographical index. Cumulated

annual indexes for authors and countries.

D225. "Topical bibliography of current technical literature." *International review of criminal policy* no. 1+ 1952+ New York, United Nations, Dept. of Social Affairs. semi-annual.

A classified bibliography which aims to give a comprehensive survey of technical literature relating to the prevention of crime and the treatment of offenders currently being published throughout the world. Coverage begins with Jan., 1950 and to date over 10,000 books, pamphlets, periodical articles and reports have been listed. No annotations. Author index for each volume.

D226. United Nations. *Department of Economic and Social Affairs.* Social welfare information series, current national literature and conferences. V. 1-11 no. 3, 1948-1953. New York, 1949-1955. semi-annual.

Each issue is a select classified bibliography of the current social welfare literature of one of the 29 participating countries. Some items annotated. Occasional special issues dealing with a single topic. Over 10,000 items. Continued by the bibliography in each issue of the *International social service review* v. 1+ 1956+ (New York, U.N., Dept. of Economic and Social Affairs. semi-annual.) These bibliographies are devoted to a single topic but arrangement is by (1) international organization and (2) by country.

D227. U.S. *Children's Bureau. Clearinghouse for Research in Child Life.* Research relating to children; an inventory of studies in progress. Bulletin no. 1+ 1949+ Washington, Govt. Print. Off. annual.

An annual survey of research in progress classified under the following headings: long term research; growth and development; personality and adjustment; educational process; exceptional children; family; social, economic and cultural influences; health services; and social services. For each entry information given includes: title, purpose, subject, methods, finding, publication references or plans; duration of the study and the principal investigators. Index of organizations and index of investigators.

BIBLIOGRAPHIES—RETROSPECTIVE

D228. Anderson, Walfred A. Bibliography of researches in rural sociology. Ithaca, N.Y., New York State College of Agriculture, 1957. 186 p. (It's Rural sociology publication 52)

A selective bibliography of over 2,500 items (books, articles, reports, documents) which brings together research completed by rural sociologists in the U.S. from the early 1900's to 1956. The unannotated entries are arranged in 46 subject areas with an author index. The first of these, Background publications, has 15 subdivisions. The remaining 45 are arranged alphabetically and include: class and caste, cooperatives, ecological studies, labor, migration and mobility, population, school, social trends, stratification, values, etc. Does not include all research reported in *Rural sociology* as a separate index of these is being published.

D229. Barbano, Filippo and Mario Viterbi. Bibliografia della sociologia italiana: 1948-1958. Turino, Ramella, 1959. 168 p. (Turin Univ. Istituto di Scienze Politiche. Publications vol. 6)

A classified bibliography of 1,624 items from journals and other sources surveying the postwar development of Italian sociological research. The entries are arranged under 12 major areas: science, methodology, sociological research; phenomenological sociology; sociology of politics; sociology of education; sociology of eco-

nomics; industrial sociology; human relations; public relations; rural sociology; and urban sociology. Author index. Kept up-to-date by annual listings in *Bollettino delle ricerche sociali* (A187).

D230. Benedict, Burton. A short annotated bibliography relating to the sociology of Muslim peoples. Montreal, Institute of Islamic Studies, McGill Univ., 1955. 115 p.

A select collection of materials useful to the sociologist or social anthropologist. Covers all Muslim countries and areas with a large Muslim population. Includes books and articles (in French and English) arranged alphabetically by country covering demography, social structure, social and economic change, socialization, family kinship, etc. Annotations are either short descriptive passages or contents notes. No index.

D231. Cabot, Phillippe S. de Q. Juvenile delinquency; a critical annotated bibliography. New York, Wilson, 1946. 166 p.

A select, annotated bibliography of 973 items of American authorship from 1914 to 1944, compiled to bring together scattered source material of major significance to research. All items, books, periodical articles, reports, are fully abstracted, giving authors' views but no criticism. The entries are arranged alphabetically by author with a subject index.

D232. California. University. *Bureau of Public Administration.* Bibliography of crime and criminal justice, 1927-1931, 1932-1937, comp. by Dorothy C. Culver. New York, Wilson, 1934-39. 2 v.

A continuation of Kuhlman's *Guide to material on crime and criminal justice* (D246). The volume for 1927-31 is international in scope and includes published and manuscript materials appearing in major western languages. This feature was dropped in the 1932-37 volume which lists only English language material. The classification of the 23,606 items (books, articles, reports) is based on the Kuhlman work with some modification. Coverage includes: crime and criminal statistics; administration of criminal justice; offenders; police; probation; institutional treatment; crime prevention, etc. General index. Continued by: Tompkins, Dorothy C. *Sources for the study of the administration of criminal justice* (Sacramento, Calif., Special Crime Study Commission and California State Board of Corrections, 1949. 294 p.) which covers 1938-1948 and emphasizes material pertinent to conditions in California; California. University. Bureau of Public Administration. *Administration of criminal justice, 1949-1956; a selected bibliography*, comp. by D.C. Tompkins. (Berkeley, Calif., 1956. 351 p.) which provides a selection of materials which reflect the developments in the U.S. for the period covered.

D233. Chambers, Merritt M. and Elaine Exton. Youth-Key to America's future; an annotated bibliography. Washington, American Council on Education, 1949. 117 p.

A select, annotated bibliography of 240 works representative of the vast amount of material published in the U.S. from 1943-48 about the problems and prospects of the nation's youth. Supplements Menefee and Chambers *American youth* (D242). The entries are arranged under 18 general subject areas (e.g., adolescence, child labor, employment, negro youth, youth in rural America, etc.). Annotations are exceptionally complete. Author index.

D234. Cummings, *Sir* John G. A contribution towards a bibliography dealing with crime and cognate subjects. 3d ed. London, printed by the Receiver for the Metropolitan Police District, New Scotland Yard, 1935. 107 p.

A classified bibliography of books and some articles. The 1,900 titles are arranged under some 200 subject headings. Coverage is international although the majority of works are in English and the general point of view is British. Combined geographical and subject index and an index of authors.

D235. Eldridge, Hope T. The materials of demography; a selected and annotated bibliography. New York, International Union for the Scientific Study of Population and the Population Association of America, 1959. 222 p.

A selective, well annotated bibliography of 411 English language items intended to identify and describe significant published works in the field of population analysis. Compiled with the needs of the teacher of demography in mind. The entries (books and articles) are arranged under 10 general areas, *e.g.*, population problems and theories, problems and methods of demographic analysis, studies of mortality and morbidity, etc. A companion volume for French material is Jean-Claude Chasteland's *Démographie: bibliographie et analyse d'ouvrages et d'articles en français* (Paris, Institut Nationale d'Études Démographiques et Union Internationale pour l'Étude Scientifique de la Population, 1961. 181 p.) which lists 850 works. Similar compilations in Italian and Spanish are planned.

D236. Haskett, Richard C. "An introductory bibliography for the history of American immigration, 1607-1955." In George Washington University. *A report on world population migrations as related to the United States of America*. Washington, 1956. p. 85-295.

A classified bibliography compiled as the first step in a survey and research project in the field of American immigration. Over 3,000 items deal with all aspects of immigration to the U.S., internal migration movements, racial groups, and the immigrants effect upon all aspects of American life. Covers 1607-1921 with a final chapter dealing with the period 1921-1955. No index, but detailed table of contents. Some brief annotations.

D237. International Society of Criminology. Selected documentation on criminology. Paris, UNESCO, 1961. 114 p. (International Committee for Social Sciences Documentation. Reports and papers in the social sciences, no. 14)

Essentially a comparative international bibliographical guide intended to facilitate research studies in comparative criminology. Its 1,158 monographic items, including "classics" as well as newer works of major significance, are arranged first by country and then by subject. Each of the 25 national bibliographies is supplemented by a list of criminological periodicals, statistical source material and a list of institutions which specialize in the study of criminal phenomena. A future volume will contain similar information on Eastern European, Asiatic and African nations. General index. No annotations.

D238. International Sociological Association. The nature of conflict; studies on the sociological aspects of international relations. Paris, UNESCO, 1957. 314 p. (Tensions and technology series)

A comprehensive survey and evaluation of research by sociologists and social psychologists into the nature, conditions and implications of human conflict and particularly the conflict between nations. Excludes by definition research in family conflict, culture conflict, crime, ideological conflict, etc. Consists of 4 essays surveying current knowledge with references to a 1,160 item bibliography which is arranged under 4 major headings: (1) Sociology and psycho-sociology of intergroup conflicts, (2) International relations, (3) Racial conflicts, and (4) Industrial and agrarian conflicts. Includes books, articles, reports, etc. in all languages generally published since 1945. Many items fully annotated. No index.

D239. Inventory of research in racial and cultural relations. Chicago, 1948-1953. 5 v.

Issued by the Committee on Education, Training and Research in Race Relations, Univ. of Chicago. For the period covered, a valuable bibliography of research (published and unpublished) in intergroup relations. Each quarterly issue arranged alphabetically by author. The last issue (v. 5, no. 4) is a cumulative author and subject index. Each of the 4,912 items is fully annotated. Includes books, articles, theses, dissertations and unpublished reports. Restricted to English language materials. (Unesco is presently trying to resurrect this work).

D240. Joint University Council for Social and Public Administration. Bibliography of social work and administration; a classified list of articles from selected British periodicals, 1930-1952. London, 1954. 117 p.

This listing of some 6,000 items from 39 periodicals covers population, labor, social work, criminology, social psychology, leisure and specific social services. Kept up to date by annual supplements. No index.

D241. Lavell, Carr B. and Wilson E. Schmidt. "An annotated bibliography on the demographic, economic and sociological aspects of immigration." In George Washington University. *A report on world population migrations as related to the United States of America*. Washington, 1956. p. 296-499.

750 monographs and periodical articles are arranged under 7 major headings with subdivisions: (1) General works, (2) International migration, (3) Immigration to the U.S., (4) The immigrant in the U.S., (5)

Immigration and the nation, (6) Immigration control, and (7) Immigration policy. No index. Annotations are very complete. See also (D236).

D242. Menefee, Louise A. and Merritt M. Chambers. American youth; an annotated bibliography. Washington, American Council on Education, 1938. 492 p.

A comprehensive survey and digest of the literature of youth problems. The 2,500 titles (articles, books, pamphlets, reports, etc.) were largely written between 1930-1938 and hence afford a panorama of youth problems during the depression period. The entries are arranged under 19 major categories with a detailed general index. Chapter 18 lists 137 works dealing with the youth in other countries. Annotations are quite full. Supplemented by Chamber's *Youth-Key to America's future* (D233).

D243. Shock, Nathan W. A classified bibliography of gerontology and geriatrics. Stanford, Calif., Stanford Univ. Press, 1951. 599 p.

———. Supplement one, 1949-1955. Stanford, Calif., Stanford Univ. Press, 1957. 525 p.

———. Supplement two, 1956-1961. Stanford, Calif., Stanford Univ. Press, 1963. 624 p.

A standard bibliography which attempts to cover the subject from biochemistry and medicine to social science and social work as they concern the aged. 51,861 items (books, articles, reports, etc.), in all languages, are classified under 7 major headings with detailed subdivision. Abstracts of articles are cited when available. Subject index refers to classification topics rather than individual references. Supplemented by lists prepared by the author for the *Journal of gerontology*.

D244. Smith, Bruce L. and Chitra M. Smith. International communication and political opinion; a guide to the literature. Princeton, N.J.,

Princeton Univ. Press, 1956. 325 p.

Designed to continue but not replace Smith, Lasswell and Casey's *Propaganda, communication and public opinion* (D245). Concentrates on the political aspects of international propaganda and promotional activities. The 2,563 annotated entries (in French, German and English) are classified under 7 major headings with detailed subdivisions. Includes books, periodical articles, government documents and some unpublished material. Author and subject index.

D245. Smith, Bruce L., *et al.* Propaganda, communication and public opinion; a comprehensive reference guide. Princeton, N.J., Princeton Univ. Press, 1946. 435 p.

Continues *Propaganda and promotional activities; an annotated bibliography* by H.D. Lasswell, et al. (Minneapolis, Univ. of Minnesota Press, 1935. 450 p.). Contains 4 essays on "the science of mass communications" and a selective, annotated bibliography of 2,558 books and articles which appeared between 1934 and 1943. Material is drawn from all social science disciplines. Author and subject index. Continued by *International communication and political opinion* (D244).

D246. Social Science Research Council. *Committee on Survey of Research on Crime and Criminal Justice.* Guide to material on crime and criminal justice . . . prepared by Augustus F. Kuhlman. New York, Wilson, 1929. 633 p.

"A descriptive, classified, union catalog of books, monographs, and pamphlets in thirteen selected libraries, and of articles listed in the leading periodical indexes relating to all phases of crime and criminal justice in the United States." (Pref.) 13,276 entries are arranged under 17 broad headings with detailed subdivisions. The object was to be inclusive rather than selective, but all materials of value for research purposes have received descriptive annotations. Continued by D.C. Culver's *Bibliography of crime and criminal justice* (D232).

D247. Stoetzel, Jean. Sociology and social psychology, 1945-1958. New York, Cultural Center of the French Embassy, 1960. 86 p. (French bibliographical digest. Series II, no. 33)
A select, annotated review of postwar French literature. 469 items (monographs and articles) are classified under 6 main headings with an index of authors. The annotations are descriptive.

D248. Thompson, Edgar T. and Alma M. Thompson. Race and region; a descriptive bibliography. Chapel Hill, Univ. of North Carolina Press, 1949. 194 p.
Briefly annotates books and articles dealing with the Negro and race relations with special emphasis upon Negro-White relations in the U.S. Samples taken from all varieties of race literature, but major emphasis is upon more serious studies by social scientists. Entries arranged alphabetically by author under 32 main headings with an author index.

D249. Tighe, Leo W. A classified bibliography for the field of social work. Santa Clara, Calif., Premier Publishers, 1959. 235 p.
5,500 books, articles, dissertations, government publications, and audiovisual materials classified under 2 main headings: Counseling and guidance, and Social work. The second is the major part of the work and its 57 sections cover all aspects of social work drawn almost entirely from U.S. sources published in the last 25 years. Contents notes for audio-visual material only. No index.

D250. Tompkins, Dorothy C. Drug addiction; a bibliography. Berkeley, Univ. of California, Bureau of Public Administration, 1960. 130 p.
A select bibliography of materials relating to the legal, medical, psycho-logical and regulatory aspects of drug addiction published since 1930. Entries arranged under 15 major headings with an author index and some brief annotations. See also New York Academy of Medicine. *Narcotic addiction; a bibliography* (New York, 1952. 39 p.) for selected works prior to 1930 and some foreign titles.

D251. United Nations. *Dept of Economic and Social Affairs.* Analytical bibliography of international migration statistics, 1925-1950. New York, 1955. 195 p. (It's Population studies, no. 24)
A compilation of official sources for emigration and immigration data for 24 countries. The entry for each country is in 3 parts: (1) a list of the primary official sources and other publications containing statistical data; (2) a summary in tabular form of the information available in each of the primary sources, indicating the major categories of arrivals and departures and the years for which the data is available; (3) a more detailed table indicating the specific classifications and cross-classifications for which statistics are available, e.g., sex, nationality, country of origin, age group, occupation, etc.

D252. U.S. *Dept. of Health, Education and Welfare. Library.* Juvenile delinquency, causes, prevention, treatment; an annotated bibliography. Rev. ed. Washington, 1953. 45 p.
A selective listing of 282 items published primarily during the 1940's and early 1950's. Books and articles are arranged under 8 main headings with subdivisions and an author index.

D253. U.S. *Dept. of Health, Education and Welfare. Library.* Selected references on aging; an annotated bibliography. Washington, Govt. Print. Off., 1959. 110 p.
Lists 800 items selected to reflect the most recent basic thinking and research conclusions (since 1949)

in all of the major aspects of aging. The books, articles and pamphlets are arranged under 3 major headings with subject subdivision: (1) Social aspects of aging; (2) Economic aspects of aging; and (3) Aging process, health and medical care. Author Index.

D254. U.S. *Library of Congress. Census Library Project.* Catalog of United States census publications, 1790-1945. Washington, Govt. Print. Off., 1950. 320 p.

A comprehensive annotated listing of all material issued by the Bureau of the Census and its predecessors beginning with the first decennial census in 1790. Supplemented by: U.S. Bureau of the Census. *Census publications; catalog and subject guide.* v. 1+ 1945+ (Washington, Govt. Print. Off., + quarterly with annual cumulations).

D255. U.S. *Library of Congress. Census Library Project.* General censuses and vital statistics in the Americas. Washington, Govt. Print. Off., 1943. 151 p.

The first of a series of compilations giving general descriptions of published official statistics of population and related subjects. An annotated bibliography of the past censuses and current vital statistics of the 21 American republics and colonial territories.

The other works in the series include: *National censuses and vital statistics in Europe, 1918-1939.* (Washington, Govt. Print. Off., 1948. 215 p. and Supplement 1940-1948 published in 1948.); *Population census and other official demographic statistics of British Africa* (Washington, Govt. Print. Off., 1950. 78 p.

D256. Work, Monroe N. A bibliography of the Negro in Africa and America. New York, Wilson, 1928. 698 p.

A basic and carefully selected list of 17,000 documents, books, maps, articles and pamphlets in various languages tracing the known career of the Negro, showing his achievements as well as the problems encountered in his history. Entries are grouped under 2 main headings, "Africa" and "America" with 74 detailed subdivisions. Occasional explanatory notes. Author index. A typed supplement brings the listings to 1935. Supplemented by the quarterly bibliography appearing in the *Journal of Negro education* v. 1+ 1932+ (Washington, Howard Univ. Press. quarterly), a classified listing of 1,000-1,500 books, articles, theses, dissertations and pamphlets a year on all aspects of Negro culture.

See also: D284; D291; E165; F267.

DICTIONARIES

D257. Bernsdorf, Wilhelm and Friedrich Bülow. Wörterbuch der Soziologie. Stuttgart, Enke, 1955. 640 p.

An encyclopedic dictionary of sociological terms with signed contributions by 84 German specialists. Entries vary from short paragraphs to full length essays. The latter usually include bibliographies. Biographies are omitted. No index, but abundant use is made of cross references.

D258. Elsevier's dictionary of criminal science in eight languages. Compiled and arranged on an English alphabetical base by Johann A. Adler. New York, Elsevier, 1960. 1460 p.

A multilingual glossary which interprets criminal science in its widest sense covering criminal law, criminology and criminolistics as well as auxiliary sciences. Part I consists of 10,930 English/American terms (with indication of British or American usage and field of application, *e.g.*, law, medicine, psychology, etc.)

with translations into French, Italian, Spanish, Portuguese, Dutch, Swedish and German. Part II is made up of alphabetical glossaries for each of the languages above with references to Part I.

D259. Fairchild, Henry P., *ed.* Dictionary of sociology. New York, Philosophical Library, 1944. 342 p.

An alphabetical dictionary of some 500 sociological terms compiled with the aid of 93 specialists. The entries are signed and vary from brief definitions to lengthier comments. Numerous cross-references. Biography is excluded.

D260. König, Rene. Soziologie. Frankfurt am Main, Fischer Bücherei, 1958. 364 p. (Das Fischer Lexikon, 10)

The work of 8 German sociologists this lexikon comprises a series of 40 essays of varying length on the major concepts of current sociology. The concepts are listed alphabetically and the design of each essay follows the same general pattern: the concept as used in presociological literature; changes in meaning; critical analyses; empirical research; cross classification with other concepts; and assessment and current status. A highly selective bibliography is appended to most essays in addition to references cited in the essay itself.

D261. Mihanovich, Clement S., *et. al.* Glossary of sociological terms. Milwaukee, Bruce, 1957. 36 p.

Not a straight alphabetical list but a classification of about 475 terms under 54 general categories or basic concepts. Terms related to, associated with or emanating from the basic terms are defined under the basic term. Each definition is brief with adequate cross references. Some items are defined more than once. The glossary index includes all defined terms in alphabetical order. For similar treatment see Emory S. Bogardus "Selected sociological concepts for beginning students in so-

ciology." *Sociology and social research*, v. 44, Jan.-Feb. 1960; 200-08, which presents brief analyses of 52 concepts (accommodation, communication, social mobility, socialization, etc.) as they are treated by sociologists.

D262. United Nations. *Dept. of Social Affairs.* Multilingual demographic dictionary, prepared by the Demographic Dictionary Committee of the International Union for the Scientific Study of Population. New York, 1958+ (In progress)

The English edition is paralleled in the first instance by French and Spanish editions published by the U.N., and German and Italian editions published separately. A Russian edition is in preparation. Organized, not as an alphabet of terms, but as a series of chapters on demographic topics that include the technical terms in a running text. All terms defined are numbered and listed in an alphabetical index. Equivalent terms in the various language volumes receive the same reference number. The problem of non-equivalent terms is handled by notes in the various texts. German edition: Winkler, Wilhelm. *Mehrsprachiges demographischen Wörterbuch.* (Hamburg, Deutsche Akademie für Bevölkerungswissenshaft an der Universitat Hamburg, 1960. 147 p.); Italian edition: *Dizionario demografico multilingue; volume italiano.* (Milan, Dott A. Gruffre, 1959, 166 p.)

D263. Willems, Emilio. Dictionnaire de sociologie, adaptation française par Armand Cuvillier. Paris, Rivière, 1961. 272 p.

Originally published in Portuguese in 1950, the French translation has been revised and brought up to date. Contains succinct and precise definitions of basic sociological concepts. 538 of its 1,055 main entries are brief biographical sketches of important world social scientists (not limited to sociologists). Gives for each: profession, dates, present position or major contribution, and a select bibliography. Includes people not in *Internationales Soziologenlexikon* (D277).

D264. Young, Earl F. Dictionary of social welfare. New York, Social Science Publishers, 1948. 218 p.

Designed as a tool for social workers in the field who do not have a variety of technical dictionaries at hand. In addition to general social work and social casework terms, it includes sociological, legal, psychological, psychiatric, medical, biological, chemical and statistical terms as well as slang expressions, racial and cultural colloquialisms. Definitions are brief with cross references.

D265. Zapf, Karl. Wörterbuch der Sozialarbeit. Dictionary of social work. Dizionario del lavoro sociale. Woordenboek vor maatschappelijk. Diccionario de trabajo social. Lexilogion horoñ koinōnikēs prononias. Köln, Heymann, 1961. 463 p.

A multilingual glossary of 2,972 technical terms connected with social work. Part I is a parallel column listing of the terms in German, English, Dutch, French, Italian and Spanish. Each term is numbered. Parts 2-7 are alphabetical glossaries in each of these languages plus Greek with reference numbers to the main list.

ENCYCLOPEDIAS AND
ENCYCLOPEDIC SETS

D266. Gurvitch, Georges, *ed.* Traité de sociologie. Paris, Presses Universitaires de France, 1958-60. 2 v.

Aims to give as objective and comprehensive an image as possible of the field and the present situation of sociology. Many French specialists have contributed essays on statistics, sociological research, geographical, urban, rural, economic and industrial sociology, sociology of religion, art,

law and knowledge, criminology, social psychology and the problems in relations between the so-called "archaic" societies and the historical societies. Also examines the ties of sociology with other social sciences, e.g. psychology, history and ethnology. International in scope, but emphasizes contemporary French thought. Select bibliographies for each chapter. No index.

D267. Hauser, Philip M. and Otis D. Duncan, *eds.* The study of population; an inventory and appraisal. Chicago, Univ. of Chicago Press, 1959. 864 p.

28 scholars have contributed to this volume, offering a comprehensive survey of the field of demographic study. 4 main parts: Part 1 reviews demography's current status as a science; Part 2 reviews demography's historical background and surveys the current status of development in France, Great Britain, Germany, Italy, Brazil, India, the Pacific area and the U.S.; Part 3 is an exhaustive study of demography's components (fertility, mortality, migration, population growth, composition, distribution, etc.) appraising the topics, research methods, hypotheses and theories of each; Part 4 considers the relations of demography with other natural and social sciences. All articles have select bibliographies. General index.

D268. Tibbitts, Clark, *ed.* Handbook of social gerontology; societal aspects of aging. Chicago, Univ. of Chicago Press, 1960. 770 p.

One of 3 volumes sponsored by the Inter-University Council in Social Gerontology which together attempt to present an encyclopedic account of the physiological, psychological, sociological and medical aspects of aging. In this volume 23 scholars present a comprehensive statement of the field of social gerontology. Each of the 19 chapters contains an extensive bibliography. The second volume edited by James E.

Birren, *Handbook of aging and the individual; biological, social, and psychological bases of aging in individuals.* (Chicago, Univ. of Chicago Press, 1959. 939 p.) is a comprehensive presentation by 30 specialists. The final volume edited by Ernest W. Burgess, *Aging in western culture; a survey of social gerontology* (Chicago, Univ. of Chicago Press, 1960. 492 p.) is a review of major trends and developments in aging in several countries of western Europe and Great Britain.

D269. Vierkandt, Alfred, *ed.* Handwörterbuch der Soziologie. Stuttgart, F. Enke, 1931. 690 p.

An older work, but still important for its survey of pre-Nazi German sociology. Contains 62 long articles on large subjects and concepts. Brief bibliographies. Index of names and smaller subjects.

D270. Ziegenfuss, Werner, *ed.* Handbuch der Soziologie. Stuttgart, F. Enke, 1956. 2 v.

Collected essays by German specialists covering all fields of sociology and allied fields including social anthropology, social psychology, demography, and political science. Especially notable is Heinz Maus' essay on the history of sociology which has been published separately in English (*A short history of sociology.* London, Routledge and Kegan Paul, 1962. 226 p.) International in scope, but with emphasis upon recent German developments. Bibliographies vary in length. Name and subject indexes.

DIRECTORIES AND BIOGRAPHICAL
INFORMATION

D271. American Sociological Association. Directory. New York, 1959. 199 p.

An alphabetical listing of the 6,346 members of the Association giving for each entry: highest degree granted, subject specialties, occupational history, present affiliation and address. Student members are listed in a special section. Geographical list of members. Issued every three years.

D272. American University, Washington, D.C. *Bureau of Social Research.* Directory of organizations in opinion and related research outside the United States. Washington, 1956. 1 v.

Lists over 200 organizations and private individuals who conduct research on public opinion, consumer behavior and attitude in 45 countries. Information includes: name, address, foreign and domestic affiliates, staff, types of research conducted, types of clients, sampling and data gathering techniques and publications. Arranged by country with an alphabetical name index.

D273. Chambers, Merritt M. Youth-serving organizations; national non-governmental associations. 3d ed. Washington, American Council on Education, 1948. 162 p.

Lists ca. 250 organizations that are concerned directly or indirectly with youth and youth problems. Arranged under 19 major subject headings with an alphabetical list of organizations. Gives information on membership, officers, purposes, activities, publications, staff and finances. Includes youth membership organizations.

D274. Directory of member agencies of the Family Service Association of America. New York, 1911+ annual.

D275. International directory of opinion and attitude research, ed. by Laszlo Radvanyi. Mexico, D.F., Social Sciences, 1948. 1 v.

A dated but still useful directory of 548 people in the fields of (1) public opinion measurement, (2) attitude measurement and (3) the measurement of information, habits and customs. Each entry gives full directory information.

D276. International repertory of institutions conducting population studies. Paris, UNESCO, 1959. 240 p. (International Committee for Social Sciences Documentation. Reports and papers in the social sciences, no. 11)

The first attempt to compile a listing of all institutions conducting studies in the field of population research. Lists 16 international organizations and 393 institutions in 84 countries. Arranged alphabetically by country and for each country three categories are given: (1) governmental agencies; (2) universities and university institutes; and (3) autonomous bodies. A brief outline of the main research projects is given for each entry with a list of publications issued since 1954. No index.

D277. Internationales Soziologen-Lexikon, hrsg. von Wilhelm Bernsdorf. Stuttgart, F. Enke, 1959. 662 p.

A companion volume to *Wörterbuch der Soziologie* (D257), this biographical dictionary lists more than 1,000 sociologists or those whose work is closely connected with sociological knowledge in a broad sense. International in scope. Includes the "fathers" of sociology (Condorcet, Comte, Smith) as well as those of the most recent generation. Each entry has three parts: (1) a brief biographical sketch; (2) analysis of the man's work and an appraisal of the importance of his contribution to sociology; and (3) a listing of the titles and dates of his principal books and articles, as well as works written about him. Each entry is signed by one of the 50 specialists who collaborated on this work. No index.

D278. National Social Welfare Assembly. Service directory of national organizations affiliated and associated with the National Social Welfare Assembly. New York, 1951+ annual.

D279. Public welfare directory. Chicago, Public Welfare Association, 1940+ annual.

Provides information concerning the programs, administrative practices and staff of national, state and local public welfare agencies in the U.S. and Canada. Includes brief synopses of each state's public assistance program.

D280. United Nations. *Dept. of Social Affairs.* International directory of nation-wide organizations concerned with family, youth and child welfare. New York, 1952. 289 p.

Contains the names and addresses of more than 1,800 governmental agencies and voluntary organizations in 48 countries concerned exclusively with family and child welfare or having special services dealing with these areas. Local or regional agencies are omitted.

D281. White House Conference on Aging, *Washington, D.C.*, 1961. Handbook of national organizations . . . with plans, programs and services in the field of aging. Washington, Govt. Print. Off., 1960. 117 p.

A directory of 298 national organizations including fraternal organizations, unions, service clubs, religious organizations, professional groups, public welfare agencies, etc. For each information is given on membership, purpose, present and future programs and services for the aged, official policy position in behalf of the welfare of the aged, and cooperative activities with other groups. Does not attempt to be all inclusive. Supplemented by U.S. Congress. Senate. Committee on Labor and Public Welfare. *Directory of voluntary organizations in the field of aging.* (Washington, Govt. Print. Off., 1961. 365 p.) a classified listing of 225 national, regional and local organizations, listing 59 national organizations not included above.

See also: D263; D287.

ATLASES AND PICTORIAL WORKS

D282. Welt-Bevölkerungs-Atlas; Verteilung der Bevölkerung der Erde um das Jahr 1950. World atlas of population; distribution of population on the earth about the year 1950, hrsg. von F. Burgdörfer. Hamburg, Falk-Verlag, 1955+ (In progress)

Based upon the results of the first world population census. To be complete in 10 maps. The maps are physical and population density is indicated by dots with towns being graded in some 13 sizes, from 1,000 upwards.

HANDBOOKS, MANUALS, COMPENDIA

D283. Cantril, Hadley. Public opinion, 1935-1946. Princeton, N.J., Princeton Univ. Press, 1951. 1191 p.

An extensive compilation of over 12,000 public opinion polls collected from 23 organizations in 16 countries covering the period 1935-1946. Classified arrangement utilizing Library of Congress subject headings. Includes only those polls based upon a national cross section. Entry includes: place of poll and date; the question and the results; and the organization conducting the poll. No index, but a 45 page table of contents with extensive cross references. From 1940 to 1951 *Public opinion quarterly* reported all available polls from major U.S. polling organizations and occasional foreign polls. This section was reinstated in the Spring 1961 issue.

D284. Cuvillier, Armand. Manuel de sociologie avec notices bibliographiques. 4. éd. Paris, Presses Universitaires de France, 1962. 2 v.

Designed as a student manual giving an extensive survey of the history, systems, methods and principal trends of sociological thought and research. Prefaced by a general bibliography of 300 items. Each of its 11 chapters contains a detailed bibliography.

D285. Ogburn, William F. and Meyer F. Nimkoff. A handbook of sociology. 4th ed. rev. London, Routledge & Kegan Paul, 1960. 584 p.

A basic textbook considered by many as a "classic handbook" of the subject covering in 7 major sections a general introduction, society, group behavior, personality, human ecology and population, social institutions and social change. General index and lists of selected readings. The third American edition is entitled *Sociology* (Boston, Houghton Mifflin, 1958. 756 p.)

D286. U.S. *Dept. of Health, Education and Welfare. Office of Program Analysis*. Handbook on the program of the U.S. Department of Health, Education and Welfare. Washington, Govt. Print. Off., 1960+ annual.

A useful source which brings together information about the program objectives of each major unit of the Department and about the extent of the problem toward which each program is directed, the scope of the program, its legal basis, and related information. In addition a 5 year statistical summary of each program is included giving information on finance, personnel, etc. Major units included: Public Health Service; Food and Drug Administration; Office of Education; Social Security Administration; and the Office of Vocational Rehabilitation.

YEARBOOKS

D287. Social work yearbook. 14th ed. New York, National Association of Social Workers, 1960. 767 p.

Issued biennially from 1929-1951. Since 1951 editions have appeared every three years. A valuable work describing organized activities in social work and related fields. 3 main sections: (1), three articles on the development, status and trends of social work and social security in the U.S.; (2), 86 topical articles on all aspects of social work written by authorities in each field; (3), a directory listing 33 international organizations, 65 national governmental agencies, 337 voluntary organizations in the U.S. and 40 Canadian agencies. The articles in Parts 1 and 2 contain footnote references and select bibliographies. General index.

STATISTICAL SOURCES

D288. Bogue, Donald J. Population of the United States. Glencoe, Ill., Free Press, 1959. 873 p. (Studies in population distribution, 14)

Originally intended as an up-dating of Warren Thompson's *Population trends in the United States* (New York, McGraw-Hill, 1933. 415 p.) this volume evolved into a completely new work which aims to describe and interpret U.S. population changes from 1950-1960 and to summarize available knowledge about recent changes and trends in each of the main fields of population analysis. Statistics are drawn from hundreds of books, special government reports and unpublished tabulations. 392 tables are included in its 26 chapters. An additional 69 tables appear in the appendix. Sources are cited for each table, often with critical comment. General index.

D289. California. University. *International Urban Research*. The world's metropolitan areas. Berkeley, Univ. of California Press, 1959. 115 p.

Attempts to establish the real demographic boundaries of metropolitan communities and not the arbitrary figures obtainable from census data. The problems of delineating the unit of measurement—the metropolitan area—are explained and followed by a lengthy set of tables giving the population of each major city in the world and its metropolitan area (over 100,000 inhabitants). Figures are given for two dates, that of the most recent census year and that of one later year usually 1954, 1955 or 1956. An appendix lists the component units of each metropolitan area and sources of data.

D290. Gendell, Murray and Hans L. Zetterberg. A sociological almanac for the United States. Totowa, N.J., Bedminster Press, 1961+ biennial.

Designed to supply recent and comparable historical statistics for those interested in contemporary American society but who do not need information on latest short-term fluctuations. Draws statistical information for about 100 selected tables on population, family, politics and government, science and education, economy, religion, art ethics and the community from a wide range of sources, both governmental and nongovernmental, both books and articles, each with an exact citation to source. Each topic is presented both in text and tables. Some tables of international comparisons.

D291. United Nations. *Statistical Office*. Demographic yearbook, 1948+ New York, 1949+ annual.

A compilation of official population statistics with accompanying technical notes and explanation. General tables presenting annual series on total population and vital statistics are repeated and carried forward in each issue. The remaining tables, varying from year to year, present detailed information on selected characteristics. These special topics have been: general demography, 1948, 1953; natality, 1949-50, 1954, 1959; mortality, 1951, 1957, 1961; population distribution, 1952; population trends, 1960; population censuses, 1955; ethnic and economic characteristics, 1956; marriage and divorce, 1958. In certain issues the introductory text includes an analysis of some aspect of world population trends. Each issue from 1948 to 1955 contains a bibliography of recent national and international publications containing official demographic statistics. The 1953 bibliography cumulates all previous ones; those for 1954 and 1955 add new titles.

D291a. U.S. *Department of Health Education and Welfare*. Indicators, 1961+ Washington, D.C. 1961+ monthly.

Charts and tables dealing with latest fluctuations of standard indicators on U.S. population, prosperity, health, radioactive fallout, school construction, pensions and insurance, unemployment, and public assistance, vocational rehabilitation. Each issue contains one or two interpretative articles and a list of recent statistical publications.

D292. U.S. *Federal Bureau of Investigation*. Uniform crime reports for the United States and its possessions. v. 1+ Aug. 1930+ Washington, Govt. Print. Off.

An annual statistical compilation of crime in the U.S. Tables include: classification of offenses (27 items); index to crime by geographic division; index to crime by state; index to crime in standard metropolitan areas; city crime trends by population group; offenses in individual areas (over 25,000 pop.); arrests by age group; and police employment statistics. Published quarterly, 1932-1942; semi-annually, 1942-1958; annually, 1958+.

SOURCES OF SCHOLARLY
CONTRIBUTIONS

D293. *Journals*

Acta sociologica. Scandinavian review of sociology. v. 1+ 1955+ Copenhagen, Munksgaard. quarterly.
PAIS; Soc Abst.

American journal of sociology. v. 1+ 1895+ Chicago, Univ. of Chicago Press. bi-monthly.
Bibl Fremd Zeit; Biol Abst; Bull Anal; Bull Sig; Chem Abst; Doc Econ; Int Ind; Int Pol Sci Abst; Psych Abst; Soc Abst; UN Lib.

American sociological review. v. 1+ 1936+ New York, American Sociological Association. bi-monthly (Preceded by *Papers of the American Sociological Society*, 1906-1935).
Bibl Fremd Zeit; Bull Anal; Bull Sig; Int Ind; Int Pol Abst; PAIS; Psych Abst; Soc Abst.

British journal of criminology, delinquincy and deviant social behavior. v. 1+ 1950+ London, Institute for the Study and Treatment of Delinquency. quarterly. (Title 1950-1959; British journal of delinquency).
Bibl Fremd Zeit; Br Ed Ind; Br Subj Ind; Bull Sig; Psych Abst; Soc Abst; UN Lib.

British journal of sociology. v. 1+ 1950+ London, London School of Economics and Political Science. quarterly.
Bibl Fremd Zeit; Br Ed Ind; Br Subj Ind; Bull Anal; Bull Sig; Hist Abst; Int Ind; PAIS; Psych Abst; Soc Abst.

Cashiers internationaux de sociologie. v. 1+ 1946+ Paris, Presses Universitaires de France. semi-annual.
Bibl Fremd Zeit; Bull Anal; Bull Sig; Soc Abst.

International review of criminal policy. v. 1+ 1952+ New York, United Nations, Dept. of Social Affairs. semi-annual.
Bibl Fremd Zeit; Bull Anal; PAIS; UN Lib.

International social service review. v. 1+ 1956+ New York, United Nations, Dept. of Economic and Social Affairs. semi-annual.
UN Lib.

Journal of gerontology. v. 1+ 1946+ St. Louis, Mo., Gerontological Society. quarterly.
Bibl Fremd Zeit; Biol Abst; Bull Sig; Chem Abst; Med Lit; Nutr Abst; PAIS; Psych Abst; QC Ind Med.

Kölner Zeitschrift für Soziologie un Sozial Psychologie. v. 1+ 1948+ Cologne, Westdeutscher Verlag. quarterly. (New series of *Kölner Vierteljahrshefte für Sociologie,* 1921-1934).
Bibl Deut Zeit; Bull Anal; Bull Sig; Psych Abst; Soc Abst.

Phylon quarterly; a review of race and culture. v. 1+ 1940+ Atlanta, Ga., Atlanta Univ. quarterly.
Bibl Fremd Zeit; Bull Anal; Bull Sig; Ind Sel Per; Int Ind; PAIS; Psych Abst; Soc Abst.

Polish sociological bulletin. v. 1+ 1962+ Warsaw, Ossolineum. quarterly.
Soc Abst.

Population. v. 1+ 1946+ Paris, Institut National d'Études Démographiques. quarterly.
Bibl Fremd Zeit; Bull Anal; Bull Sig; Doc Econ; Soc Abst; UN Lib.

Population bulletin. v. 1+ 1945+ Washington, Population Reference Bureau. 8 times a year.
PAIS; UN Lib.

Population studies. v. 1+ 1947+ London, London School of Economics and Political Science. 3 times a year.

Br Subj Ind; Bull Anal; Bull Sig; Hist Abst; PAIS; Soc Abst; UN Lib.

Public opinion quarterly. v. 1+ 1937+ Princeton, N.J., Princeton Univ. Press. quarterly.
Bibl Fremd Zeit; Bull Anal; Int Pol Sci Abst; Int Ind; PAIS; Psych Abst; UN Lib.

Quarterly journal of studies on alcohol. v. 1+ 1940+ New Haven, Conn. quarterly.
Biol Abst; Bull Sig; Chem Abst; Med Lit; PAIS; Psych Abst; QC Ind Med; Soc Abst.

Revista internacional de sociologia. v. 1+ 1943+ Madrid, Instituto Balmes de Sociologia. quarterly.
Bibl Fremd Zeit; Bull Anal; Bull Sig; Int Pol Sci Abst; Soc Abst; UN Lib.

Revue française de sociologie. v. 1+ 1960+ Paris, Centre d'Études Sociologiques. quarterly.
Bull Anal; Bull Sig.

Rural sociology; devoted to the scientific study of rural life. v. 1+ 1936+ Ithaca, N.Y., Dept. of Rural Sociology, Cornell Univ. quarterly.
Agr Ind; Bibl Fremd Zeit; Bull Anal; Bull Sig; PAIS; Psych Abst; Soc Abst.

Sociological quarterly. v. 1+ 1960+ Carbondale, Illinois, Midwest Sociological Association. quarterly.
Psych Abst; Soc Abst.

Sociological review. v. 1+ 1908+ Keele, Staffordshire, Eng., University College of North Staffordshire. semi-annual.
Br Subj Ind; Bull Anal; Bull Sig; Hist Abst; Int Ind; Soc Abst; UN Lib.

Sociology and social research; an international journal. v. 1+ 1916+ Los Angeles, Univ. of Southern California. bi-monthly to v. 44; quarterly, v. 45+
Bibl Fremd Zeit; Bull Anal; Bull Sig; Int Ind; PAIS; Psych Abst; Soc Abst.

Sociologus; Zeitschrift für empirische Soziologie, Sozialpsychologische und ethnologische Forschung. n.s. v. 1+ 1951+ Berlin, Duncker and Humblot. semi-annual (Old series v. 1-9, 1925-1933).
Bibl Deut Zeit; Soc Abst.

D294. *Organizations*

American Sociological Association. Washington, D.C. Founded 1905.

British Sociological Association. London. Founded 1951.

Centre d'Études Sociologiques. Paris. Founded 1945.

Columbia University. Bureau of Applied Social Research, New York. Founded 1935.

Deutsche Akademie für Bevölkerungs-Wissenschaft. Hamburg. Founded 1953.

Deutsche Gesellschaft für Soziologie. Berlin. Founded 1910.

Gerontological Society. St. Louis, Mo. Founded 1945.

International Society of Criminology. Paris. Founded 1934.

International Sociological Association. Geneva, Switzerland. Founded 1949.

International Union for the Scientific Study of Population. Paris. Founded 1928.

National Conference on Social Welfare. Columbus, Ohio. Founded 1874.

Population Association of America. Providence, R.I. Founded 1932.

Princeton University. Office of Population Research. Princeton, N.J. Founded 1936.

Roper Public Opinion Research Center. Williamstown, Mass. Founded 1957.

Russell Sage Foundation. New York. Founded 1907.

Scripps Foundation for Research in Population Problems. Miami University, Oxford, Ohio. Founded 1922.

University of Chicago. National Opinion Research Center. Chicago. Founded 1941.

Westermarck Society. Helsinki, Finland.

D295. *Monograph Series*

Centre d'Études Sociologiques. Travaux. v. 1+ 1955+ Paris.

Duke University. Sociological series. No. 1+ 1939+ Durham, N.C.

France. Institut Nationale d'Études Démographiques. Travaux et documents. v. 1+ 1946+ Paris, Presses Universitaires de France.

Frankfurter Beitrage zur Soziologie. v. 1+ 1955+ Frankfurt am Main, Instituts fuer Sozialforschung.

Harvard University. Harvard sociological studies. No. 1+ 1935+ Cambridge.

National Conference on Social Work. Proceedings. v. 1+ 1804+ New York, Columbia Univ. Press.

UNESCO. Population and culture series. No. 1+ 1954+ Paris.

University of California. Publications in sociology and social institutions. v. 1+ 1951+ Berkeley, Calif.

University of Colorado. Studies: Series in sociology. v. 1+ 1945+ Boulder, Colo.

Westermarck Society. Transactions. v. 1+ 1947+ Helsinki, Finland. (Distributed by Munksgaard, Copenhagen)

Yale University. Yale studies in

attitude and communication. v. 1+
1957+ New Haven.

SOURCES OF UNPUBLISHED
INFORMATION

D296. American Sociological Association. Current sociological research, 1953+ New York. annual.

This compilation of research in
progress is based upon questionnaires
sent to members of the Association.
Entries are listed alphabetically by
author under 25 broad headings
(community, criminology, public
opinion, social change, small group
analysis, etc.) with an author index.
Items are listed twice or more when
the topic covers more than one category.

D297. [Dissertations and theses
in sociology] *American journal of
sociology.* v. 22+ 1916-17+ Chicago, Univ. of Chicago Press.

This annual listing is in two parts:
Part I, "Higher degrees in sociology," lists Ph.D. and M.A. degrees
conferred during the past year in the
U.S. and Canada arranged by degree
and school; Part II, "Doctoral dissertations in progress," is a current
listing of work in progress in colleges
and universities in the U.S. and
Canada.

D298. "Doctoral dissertations in
social work." *Social service review.*
v. 28+ 1954+ Chicago, Univ. of
Chicago Press.

This annual listing includes abstracts of dissertations completed
during the year ending June 30 and
a list of dissertations in progress in
schools of social work offering doctoral programs. Vol. 28 includes dissertations completed from July, 1952
to June, 1954.

Thompson M. Little
Carl M. White

5

Anthropology

Anthropology, which may be characterized broadly as the study of human variation, has been nurtured in three scholarly traditions: natural science, social philosophy, and social, or behavioral, science. The first tradition produced the subfields of physical anthropology (somatology), ethnology, prehistoric archaeology, and anthropological linguistics, with the bulk of their technical literature in serials of governmental and private institutions, including museums. The second, becoming systematized in 19th-century speculations about origins, progress, and differences in custom, was essentially a humanistic tradition. These ideas became disciplined as anthropology entered the universities, and became associated primarily with the social sciences. The third tradition is seen most fully in a new subfield called social anthropology. This survey will be primarily concerned with the fields and problems of anthropology, rather than reports of research.

The following is a selection of works giving a broad overview of anthropology:

E1. Beals, Ralph L. and Harry Hoijer. An introduction to anthropology. 2d ed. New York, Macmillan, 1959. 711 p.
E2. Firth, Raymond W. Human types: an introduction to social anthropology. Rev. ed. London, Nelson, 1956. 224 p.
E3. Keesing, Felix M. Cultural anthropology: the science of custom. New York, Holt, Rinehart and Winston, 1958. 477 p.

E4. Kroeber, Alfred L. Anthropology. New ed. rev. New York, Harcourt, Brace, 1948. 856 p.
E5. Kroeber, Alfred L., *ed.* Anthropology today: an encyclopedic inventory. Chicago, Univ. of Chicago Press, 1953. 966 p.
E6. Siegel, Bernard J. Biennial review of anthropology. Stanford, Calif. Stanford Univ. Press, 1959+
E7. Thomas, William L., *ed.* Current anthropology: a supplement to anthropology today. Chicago, Univ. of Chicago Press, 1956. 377 p.

HISTORY OF ANTHROPOLOGY

Anthropological studies were anticipated in the writings of Greek, Chinese, and other scholars of classic times, as is perhaps best seen in the compilation of translations by Lovejoy and Boas listed below. The first scholarly use of "anthropology" as a label was perhaps by Magnus Hundt in 1501. Early writers variously defined it as "a description of body and soul" with "the laws of their union," or the "history of human nature," as seen in "philosophical and anatomical collections."

Information on man's physical differences was systematized from the second half of the 18th century (the "age of the naturalists"). In much of continental Europe, "anthropology" still means what English speakers call physical anthropology. Ethnology traces back to increasingly systematic compendiums of custom, in the late 18th century and the first half of the 19th century, by French, British, and German scholars, including social philosophers. Archaeology had scope to grow from the 1840's, when geologists established the great age of the earth. By that time, folklorists, linguists, and students of comparative law, religion, marriage, art, and other topics were busily searching the records of explorers, travelers, missionaries, and others for bits and pieces of information, accurate or otherwise.

The first permanent scientific societies and serials bearing anthropological titles date from around the mid-19th century. Museums, while representing an older tradition (the Ashmolean collection at Oxford dates from 1683), were by then systematizing their materials and sending collectors throughout the world. Some of the early anthropologists not only organized exhibits of artifacts for the great fairs and expositions but also brought groups of Indians, Ainus, and others for display. German scholars gave a general term "culture" within which all of human custom could be comprehended.

Scholars in many fields interested themselves in anthropology, and it gained from the work of devoted amateurs. By the 1880's, however, a hard core of full-time professionals gave it shape as a science. In the United States, a milestone was the creation in 1879 of the Bureau of American Ethnology as an offshoot of the U.S. Geological Survey. In Germany, a so-called "geographic school" built up systematic knowledge of cultures in terms of regional distributions and relations. What anthro-pologists call "field work" became the growing front of the science. In recognition of the spread of anthropology international organizations were established under governmental or other auspices to many countries, e.g., the International Congress of Anthropology and Prehistoric Ar-chaeology, the International Congress of Americanists, the Polynesian Society.

Near the end of the 19th century, a few universities, particularly ones with museum staffs, developed some teaching and professional training in the subject, as at Oxford, Cambridge, Harvard, Paris, Berlin, and Utrecht. In 1896, Columbia University appointed the German-trained scholar Franz Boas as a full-time teacher, and the first department of anthropology, in the modern sense, took form. The initial teaching of the subject was done in only a few universities and almost wholly at the graduate level. Since the 1920's, however, anthropology has spread down to the undergraduate curriculum, and its dynamic extension into university and college programs at large is still under way.

Although no complete history of anthropology as a field of knowl-edge has been written, the following provide substantial coverage:

E8. Haddon, Alfred C. History of anthropology. Rev. ed. London, Watts, 1934. 146 p.
E9. Lovejoy, Arthur O., ed. A documentary history of primitivism and related ideas. Baltimore, Johns Hopkins Univ. Press, 1935+
E10. Lowie, Robert H. History of ethnological theory. New York, Farrar & Rinehart, 1937. 296 p.
E11. Mead, Margaret, ed. The golden age of American anthropology. New York, Braziller, 1960. 630 p.
E12. Spencer, Robert F., ed. Method and perspective in anthropology. Minneapolis, Univ. of Minnesota Press, 1954. 323 p.
E13. Royal Anthropological Institute of Great Britain and Ireland. Notes and queries on anthropology. 6th ed. rev. London, Routledge, 1951. 403 p.
E14. Yearbook of anthropology, 1955. New York, Wenner-Gren Founda-tion for Anthropological Research, 1955. 836 p.

THE ORIGINS AND EVOLUTION OF CULTURE

Students of early man and comparative custom were inevitably tempted to formulate some grand laws which could explain human progress. Placing the behaviors of the educated 19th century man (themselves) unquestioningly at the top, they fitted the customs of "sav-ages" (those most different from themselves) into supposed earlier stages of development. According to their predilections, they pictured determining forces as geographic (climate, soil, etc.), biological-psychological (race, instinct, etc.), economic (diet, labor, etc.) or socio-logical (struggle, conquest, etc.). When Darwin formulated his evolutionary theory, it offered what seemed an obvious unifying frame of reference.

For physical anthropology there has been a long haul to get from the crude Darwinian concepts to what Washburn called, in 1951, "The New Physical Anthropology" (*Transactions, New York Academy of Sciences,* Series II, 8 pp. 298-304) which takes account of studies of animal behavior, fossil finds, and the genetic, ecological, demographic, and cultural dynamics involved in man's biological variation. By the 1860's, the evolutionary frame was also being applied analogously to culture and society. Unfortunately, few of these earlier scholars exercised the critical sense shown by Edward Tylor which led him to be called the "father of modern ethnology." Library shelves became cluttered with theoretically naive works, purporting to explain the origins of custom, and equating the behaviors of non-Western peoples with stages of unilinear evolution. Works of this kind still find publishers. Some are anthropological classics, as with those cited below by Morgan and Frazer. Lowie and other text writers tell how such non-historical and simplistic schemes broke, partly under their own weight, partly through telling blows by Boas in the United States and by W.H.R. Rivers in England. A whole generation of anthropologists, indeed, was to view the terms "cultural evolution" or "social evolution" with deep suspicion.

Following are some examples of the earlier evolutionary approaches:

E15. Buckle, Henry T. History of civilization in England. London, Parker, 1857-61. 2 v.
E16. Frazer, *Sir* James G. The golden bough; a study in magic and religion. Abridged ed. New York, Macmillan, 1922. 752 p.
E17. Maine, *Sir* Henry J.S. Ancient law; its connection with the early history of society and its relation to modern ideas. London, J. Murray, 1861. 415 p.
E18. Morgan, Lewis H. Ancient society; or, researches in the lines of human progress from savagery, through barbarism to civilization. New York, Holt, 1877. 560 p.
E19. Tylor, *Sir* Edward B. Primitive culture. London, J. Murray, 1871. 2 v.

Recently there has been a resurgence of interest in social and cultural evolution, as indicated by the following recent publications. This development will be discussed further under the heading "Culture Change."

E20. Anthropological Society of Washington. Evolution and anthropology: a centennial appraisal. Washington, 1959. 172 p.
E21. White, Leslie A. The evolution of culture. New York, McGraw Hill, 1959. 378 p.
E22. Goldschmidt, Walter R. Man's way; a preface to the understanding of human society. New York, Holt, Rinehart & Winston, 1959. 253 p.

CULTURAL DEVELOPMENT AND DIFFUSION

Late 19th century science turned to an emphasis on empirical study, objectivity, and laboratory observation of specific units of phenomena. Boas, from 1896 on, wrote insistently that the specific history of cultural development in time and place must be in hand before generalizations could be made about culture processes, evolutionary or otherwise. What he called the "historical method" produced not only extensive information on cultures in their temporal and spatial settings, but also an encyclopedic type of anthropologist who might write on all phases of the science. Giants such as Alfred Kroeber, Clark Wissler, Roland Dixon, and Robert Lowie exemplify this.

Boas contributed theory largely by the oppositional method of attacking fallacies and naivetes of his day, such as racism, geographic and economic determinism, and psychological explanations of cultural differences. Other scholars, such as those mentioned, made frontal attacks on the problem of accounting for cultural growth. In the mood of scientific objectivity, they looked at human behavior as a "superorganic" heritage of cultural elements or "traits," each a product of "invention" and distributed through "diffusion." A culture was viewed as a localized cumulation of traits; such traits also tended to cluster in related "complexes" (the maize-complex, the African cattle-complex); and, as Wissler pointed out from setting up museum cases, every culture has a similar frame or "universal culture pattern." This approach did not need a psychology, so to speak, since the individual could be viewed as an anonymous carrier of his culture, or at most an occasional innovator.

The dilemma of the American historicalists was that they wanted to document cultural growth and distribution factually, yet the peoples they described were mostly non-literate; written documents were lacking until recently. At most, there were the artifacts and attendant inferences of archaeology to give time depth. Elaborate ground rules were therefore devised for cultural reconstruction, such as application of the so-called age-area hypothesis (that an older item is likely to be more widely spread than a newer one), or awareness that formal likenesses could be products of independent invention, or parallelism (e.g., pyramidal structures in the Near East and Middle America). Scientific accuracy was seemingly fostered by counting and correlating traits in mathematical fashion, as in elaborate "culture element distribution" studies. This historicalist picture of culture, however, came under criticism as being too reified, atomistic, and mechanistic, with little resemblance to the rich texture of human behavior.

E23. Boas, Franz. Race, language and culture. New York, Macmillan, 1940. 647 p.
E24. Dixon, Roland B. The building of cultures. New York, Scribner, 1928. 312 p.

E25. Kroeber, Alfred L. Anthropology. New York, Harcourt Brace, 1923.
523 p.
E26. Lowie, Robert H. Selected papers in anthropology, ed. by Cora Du-
bois. Berkeley, Univ. of California Press, 1960. 509 p.
E27. Sapir, Edward. Time perspective in aboriginal American culture.
Ottawa, Government Ptg. Bureau, 1916. 87 p. (Canada. Geologi-
cal Survey. Memoir 90)
E28. Wissler, Clark. Man and culture. New York, Crowell, 1923. 371 p.

American scholars stressed regional approaches to culture growth, not
least of all because of their absorption with how the diversified, aboriginal
American cultures developed separately from those of the Old World
except for a postulated trickle of peoples and traits across the Bering
Strait region. In Europe, scholars looking at maps visualized much more
easily various boatmen crossing the open Pacific or Atlantic. Even with
the breakdown of unilinear evolution, many continued to be absorbed
with building a unified world history of culture. The invention-diffusion
approach gave them a new frame of reference.

In England, a physical anthropologist of sorts, Elliott Smith, became
impressed with the finds of Egyptologists to a point where he postulated
that all the essential "higher" cultural elements were diffused throughout the world from Egypt. This approach, followed up by his main
disciple, William Perry, is variously called "English diffusionism," the
"heliocentric theory," or the Manchester School, after Smith's university
attachment. Allegedly related categories such as sun worship, kingship,
mummification of the dead, and building megalithic structures are traced
uncritically back to Egypt. No follower of this school seems to survive,
though its literature, often with catchy titles, still tempts the reader in
public libraries. Amateur scholars, however, may purport to "retrace" the
pathways of supposed early travelers of this ilk, Egyptian and otherwise.

A Continental "diffusionist" approach had a much more rigorous
definition of its assumptions and methods. Building on the earlier German geographic ideas, its spokesmen called it a "culture historical" approach; and the main presentation in English, by Father Wilhelm
Schmidt, has this rubric in its title. It is also called the Vienna or Anthropos School, having been developed by scholars of the Anthropos
Institut, a Roman Catholic study center originally in Vienna but now in
Switzerland. Its central feature has been to isolate from human custom,
particularly of the remoter "primitives," a series of *kulturkreis* (culture
"circles," "complexes," or "strata") which emerged chronologically, and
out of which the regional cultures of later times have supposedly been
compounded. Never gaining any following in the United States, this approach has been criticized as non-historical, even mystical. Its principal
surviving adherents have acknowledged its inadequacies, so that what remains is a rich body of descriptive materials collected by missionary fathers and other workers under its stimulus.

E29. Graebner, Fritz. Methode der Ethnologie. Heidelberg, Winter, 1911.
      192 p.
E30. Perry, William J. Growth of civilization. London, Methuen, 1924.
      224 p.
E31. Schmidt, Wilhelm. The culture historical method of ethnology. New
      York, Fortuny's, 1939. 383 p.
E32. Smith, Grafton E. Human history. New York, Norton, 1929. 472 p.

FUNCTIONALISM

By the 1920's, anthropologists who were taking the trouble to read into
science and philosophy found a yeast of new ideas: concern with phenomena as wholes, the relativity of parts to one another, operationalism,
complementarity, the stability and dynamism of structures or systems.
Such thinking gave new frames of reference within which culture, society, and the individual could be viewed. Four creative scholars are usually given most credit for leadership here: Bronislaw Malinowski and
A. R. Radcliffe-Brown in the British setting, and Edward Sapir and Ruth
Benedict in the American setting.

In 1910, at a meeting of the leading anthropologists in England, it was
decided that those primarily interested in ethnohistory and museum
work would call themselves "ethnologists," while those interested in
theories about custom and society would call themselves "social anthropologists." Radcliffe-Brown took university posts in South Africa, Australia, and Chicago before he was appointed to an anthropology chair at
Oxford just prior to World War II. Meantime, Malinowski, a Polish
scholar turned Englishman, held an influential professorship in anthropology at the London School of Economics and Political Science. Mali-
nowsky wrote prolifically for audiences in and out of anthropology.
Radcliffe-Brown was primarily a teacher, writing occasional articles. Malinowski's ideas tended to make their impact first. Both emphasized what
they called a "functional" approach to the study of custom.

Put in somewhat simplified form, Malinowski saw his Trobriand island
culture, on which he wrote most, as comprising a meaningful totality of
institutions or activities, each functionally interrelated to all the rest, and
each essential in meeting needs. More widely, culture has universal aspects—economic, social, political, legal, religious, aesthetic, recreative,
linguistic, educational—because such needs motivate all humans. Malinowski brushed aside chronological studies of culture, and his "need"
lists were over-simple. He gained no slavish followers, but his functional
concept and his often brilliant writings on religion, law, and other matters provided springboards for the ideas of others.

Radcliffe-Brown and Malinowski sedulously avoided using each other's
concepts, so that the former approaches functionalism with a different

schema. With no English school of sociology to protest, he called his approach "comparative sociology" interchangeably with "social anthropology." His concepts, too, are drawn largely from the early 20th-century Durkheim school of French sociology. Stressing "society" rather than "culture," he saw his Andaman islanders, and others he studied, as interrelated by a "social structure" and their customs as functionally contributing to their "social integration." A society could be well integrated ("eunomic") or poorly integrated ("dysnomic"), with resulting malaise, conflict, and other telltale signs. Radcliffe-Brown's frame of reference was so broad, and at the same time so rigid, that he gained no slavish followers. Yet his social structure terminology set the pattern for continuing British social anthropology. A resulting sharp terminological rift has come about between Americans. For most of them "culture" continued to be the key concept in studying behavior.

E33. Firth, Raymond. Man and culture; an evaluation of the work of Bronislaw Malinowski. London, Routledge, 1957. 292 p.
E34. Malinowski, Bronislaw. Argonauts of the western Pacific. New York, Dutton, 1922. 527 p.
E35. Malinowski, Bronislaw. A scientific theory of culture and other essays. Chapel Hill, Univ. of North Carolina Press, 1944. 228 p.
E36. Radcliffe-Brown, Alfred R. The Andaman Islanders. Cambridge, Eng., University Press, 1933. 510 p.
E37. Radcliffe-Brown, Alfred R. Structure and function in primitive society. London, Cohen & West, 1952. 219 p.

CONFIGURATIONALISM

In the United States, holistic thinking also entered anthropology during the 1920's, but in quite different ways. Sapir, one of Boas' students, developed brilliant linguistic studies which showed languages as unities "unconsciously patterned" by grammar and style. He applied these insights to the personalities of individuals and to cultures looked at as wholes. He also saw the conventional delineations of cultures and of traits as generalized abstractions from the behavior of individuals, who had learned and so were sharing through communicative acts a series of common symbols—that is, culture is a "symbolic system." A particular tradition, he suggested in an early paper, might be compounded of such variegated and inconsistent elements that it might lack the unity of a "genuine" culture; later he took interest in the "abnormal" individual as seen in psychiatric-anthropological perspectives. Teaching between 1925 and 1939 at Chicago and Yale, he anticipated most phases of later theory.

Benedict, another Boas student, developed an interest in the "psychological" contrasts between the Pueblo "town-dwellers" and their American Indian neighbors in the Southwest United States. Inventories of

separate traits, she said, failed to bring out the pervasive integrating factors which made a given culture more or less unique: the purposes, goals,
orientations, mainsprings of action, or dominant configurations, to list
some of the terms she tried out to express her ideas. The Zuni Pueblo
people were group-minded, disciplined, and ritualistic, or—a term bor-
rowed from Spengler and other philosophers—"Apollonian." The Navajo and Plains Indians were individualistic and violent, or of the philosophers' "Dionysian" type. In the same way, what is important for
understanding other cultures is to delineate the configurations which give
them wholeness. Critics attacked her interpretations as selecting those
elements which fitted her picture, her methods as being subjective and
intuitive, her work as "art, not science." Nevertheless, her classes at
Columbia became workshops for further creative approaches to what became known as "configurationalism," and a whole generation of anthropologists was set to work upon ways of delineating the basic or pervasive premises, values, goals, orientations of cultural systems.

E38. Benedict, Ruth. An anthropologist at work: writings of Ruth Benedict,
    ed. by Margaret Mead. Boston, Houghton Mifflin, 1959. 583 p.
E39. Benedict, Ruth. Patterns of culture. Boston, Houghton Mifflin, 1934.
    290 p.
E40. Sapir, Edward. Language. New York, Harcourt Brace, 1921. 258 p.
E41. Sapir, Edward. Selected writings of Edward Sapir in language, cul-
    ture, and personality, ed. by David G. Mandelbaum. Berkeley,
    Univ. of California Press, 1949. 617 p.

CULTURE AND PERSONALITY

Benedict's first graduate student at Columbia was Margaret Mead.
When, after some orthodox museum work, Mead went to Samoa to make
a field study, she took with her a problem then interesting educational
psychologists—the supposedly universal storm and stress of adolescent
experience. A small book on which she reported the relaxed adolescence
of Samoan girls opened up exciting vistas for understanding how children have the adult traditions transmitted to them.
    Most standard monographs to this time had included a few formal
paragraphs on the birth, naming, training, and possible initiation of children. Several anthropologists had also written biographies or autobiographies of their informants; the "life history" approach is one of the central methods of anthropological field study. But Mead followed by probing child rearing and the roles of individuals, male and female, within
various Melanesian cultures and in Bali. Her theory was built particularly around the concept of "character": the distinctive characteristics
which individuals acquire as a result of training by parents and others,
and which consistently pervade the adult cultural tradition, even including interpretations of Deity. More than any other anthropologist to her

time, Mead talked to educators, psychologists, psychiatrists, psychoan-alysts, doctors and to the public audience at large.

Anthropologists had criticized with relish Freud's *Totem and taboo* and similar psychoanalytic writings which purposed to equate tensions and abnormalities in Western behaviors with primitive customs and supposed early states of cultural growth. Essentially they contained the same naivetes as had the evolutionary speculations. Malinowski in the 1920's had seemingly given the coup de grâce to the universality of the Oedipus complex by pointing out that in Trobriand society the predomi-nant male in the child's life was not the father but the mother's brother. By the time Mead and her followers were at work, psychologically ori-ented scholars had a ready fund of searching questions with cross-cultural reference for the anthropologists, and anthropologists were conditioned especially by Sapir to respond positively. The way was opened to develop a strong though sprawling field now usually termed "culture and per-sonality," or "ethnopsychology."

In 1936, Ralph Linton published an anthropological text embodying his introductory class lecture materials at the University of Wisconsin. Hitherto known for good museum and field work, he presented in lucid English an integrated interpretation of culture, society, and personality. His central idea was that the individual from birth assumes a whole series of statuses, some by ascription (sex, age, possible caste, and perhaps other statuses) and others by achievement, as through competition or choice. Personality may be looked at as a sum of all the statuses in which an in-dividual participates. No one individual carries in his experience the whole culture, though there are "universals" which all individuals share. A society comprises the people who together carry a culture.

Boas retired at this time, and Linton was brought to Columbia in his place. As one of the varied activities in progress there, another creative woman anthropologist, Cora DuBois, was working in a graduate seminar with a psychoanalyst, Abram Kardiner, probing anthropological and psychoanalytic approaches to culture. The former went to Malaysia to undertake a field test of various leads. Linton took her place. A notable Kardiner-Linton collaboration ensued, with culture after culture laid out descriptively by anthropologists for combined psychoanalytic and cul-tural analysis. Kardiner's prime concern was the manner in which a "basic personality structure" pertaining to each culture was transmitted to the child. Linton noted this, but beat the drums for his own concept of "status personality," which represented a life-long process of dynamic adjustment. Because the "basic personality" is a mode around which the behaviors of individuals tend to cluster it they receive normal culturally patterned training, many anthropologists now prefer DuBois' term: "modal personality."

Early in the 1930's, an Institute of Human Relations was formed at Yale with the hope of bringing psychologists, sociologists, anthropologists, and other students of behavior into fruitful association. A central theme of experimental work was learning by humans and animals. An influential body of theory developed concerned with "drives," "responses," "rewards," and "punishments." When applied to human behavior, it pictured culture as a set of acquired habits maintained by tension-relieving rewards; personality as the habit system of the individual; and cultural change as the unlearning of old habits as a result of punishments and the learning of new habits through trial and error. This precise yet sparse apparatus of thought about behavior, often known as the "Yale learning theory" weaves through the writings of a number of prominent anthropologists, such as G. P. Murdock, A. I. Hallowell, J. Gillin, and J. Whiting, as it does in psychological literature. Yet because the scholars concerned treat many other problems to which learning theory is marginal, their work is mellowed by additional concepts generated more within their profession, and leavened by inclusion of the less extreme psychoanalytic concepts. Following are selected works representing this broad personality and culture field in anthropology.

E42. Cohen, Yehudi. Social structure and personality. New York, Columbia Univ. Press, 1961. 544 p.
E43. DuBois, Cora A. The people of Alor. Minneapolis, Univ. of Minnesota Press, 1944. 654 p.
E44. Gillin, John P. The ways of men. New York, Appleton-Century, 1948. 649 p.
E45. Hallowell, Alfred I. Culture and experience. Philadelphia, Univ. of Pennsylvania Press, 1955. 434 p.
E46. Honigmann, John J. Culture and personality. New York, Harper, 1954. 499 p.
E47. Kaplan, Bert, ed. Studying personality cross-culturally. Evanston, Ill., Row, Peterson, 1961. 687 p.
E48. Kardiner, Abram. Psychological frontiers of society. New York, Columbia Univ. Press, 1945. 475 p.
E49. Kluckhohn, Clyde. Personality in nature, society and culture. 2d ed., rev. and enl. New York, Knopf, 1953. 701 p.
E50. Linton, Ralph. The cultural background of personality. New York, Appleton-Century, 1945. 157 p.
E51. Linton, Ralph. Study of man. New York, Appleton-Century, 1936. 503 p.
E52. Mead, Margaret. Coming of age in Samoa. New York, W. Morrow, 1928. 297 p.
E53. Mead, Margaret. Sex and temperament in three primitive societies. New York, W. Morrow, 1935. 335 p.
E54. Whiting, John W.M. and Irvin L. Child. Child training and personality; a cross-cultural study. New Haven, Conn., Yale Univ. Press, 1953. 353 p.

NATIONAL CHARACTER

Studies of character and personality type were dramatically put to use during World War II, when the majority of professional anthropologists were absorbed into the work of military and civilian agencies. Often teamed up with other social scientists, they were asked questions concerning the morale, vulnerability, and other characteristics of the enemy peoples, of friendly nations with whom working relations were needed, and of immigrant minorities whose attitudes might be in question. What were usually termed "natural character" studies were notably featured, as with Benedict's study of dualities in Japanese culture. Information of this kind was also imparted by anthropologists in various area-training programs for military personnel conducted at the university.

After the war, Benedict had military financing for extensive studies of national behaviors by teams of scholars in a Columbia University program of research on contemporary cultures. Other studies of this kind were developed at the Russian Research center at Harvard, directed by Kluckhohn, by United Nations specialized agencies, and in other institutional settings. Among the cultural traditions notably documented are those of the United States, China, France, and the East European countries, especially the Soviet Union. Broad characterizations in this manner have also been severely criticized for their great generality of statement and the uncertainties of how far the broad models of conduct apply to regional sub-groups, classes, and so on down to the motivations of individuals.

The following selections represent both the strengths and weaknesses of this area of inquiry:

E55. Benedict, Ruth. The chrysanthemum and the sword; patterns of Japanese culture. Boston, Houghton Mifflin, 1946. 324 p.
E56. Gorer, Geoffrey. The American people, a study in national character. New York, Norton, 1948. 246 p.
E57. Gorer, Geoffrey and John Rickman. The people of great Russia. London, Cresset, 1949. 235 p.
E58. Hsu, Francis L.K. Americans and Chinese: two ways of life. New York, Schuman, 1953. 457 p.
E59. Mead, Margaret. And keep your powder dry. New York, W. Morrow, 1942. 274 p.
E60. Mead, Margaret and Rhoda Metraux, eds. The study of culture at a distance. Chicago, Univ. of Chicago Press, 1953. 480 p.
E61. Zborowski, Mark and Elizabeth Herzog. Life is with people. New York, International Universities Press, 1952. 456 p.

COMMUNITY AND SOCIAL STRUCTURE

The tradition of ethnology was to study non-Western cultures, usually those counted in popular language "primitive." Robert Redfield of Chicago, influenced by the community studies of sociologists, made a Mexican village a unit for analysis. Meantime, Lloyd Warner, an American anthropologist who had studied with Radcliffe-Brown in Australia, had joined the faculty at Harvard and was stimulating his students to investigate with him the "social structures" of Western communities. A research team went to Ireland, tracing families who had come to the Boston area. Next a major study was launched of industrial organization, class structure, and other features of "Yankee City," or Newburyport, Massachusetts, reported in a series of publications. Another study was made by white and Negro research teams of "Southern Town" (Natchez, Mississippi), reported in another publication series. Warner was also drawn into structural studies of work organization by the Elton Mayo group in the Harvard School of Industrial Relations.

Warner shifted to Chicago, where his continuing interest in studying American community structure yielded the popular "high," "middle," and "low" brow, and "upper-upper" etc. Class system concepts. A social structure, to him, comprises a system of formal and informal groupings by which the social behavior of individuals is regulated. The individual must therefore be studied in terms of the total system of interaction and society as a total system of interdependent statuses. Here the line between anthropology and sociology is thin indeed, and Warner was as much at home with sociologists and students of industry as he was among his intellectual progenitors, the anthropologists.

At Harvard, meanwhile, Warner's ideas were followed up by a group headed by a young instructor, Eliot Chapple. Chafing at the lack of precision in studies of social relations, Chapple decided that measurement could be applied to them by timing the interaction of individuals. With Conrad Arensberg, he used stop watches to record the interaction behavior of Boston shipyard workers. Then, in a book co-authored by the physical anthropologist Carlton Coon, came a completely novel reinterpretation of virtually the whole data of anthropology in terms of equilibria and disequilibria of interaction among the individuals composing a society. Moving from the university to found an industrial consultant firm, Chapple Associates, he developed an "interaction chronograph" comprising a structured interview through which the interaction habits of individuals can be scored mechanically. Those buying the chronograph service use it to place individuals in the job that fits their habits, e.g., ability to originate interaction, speed or slowness in response, extreme behaviors ranging to abnormalities. The writings of Chapple and others who followed his leads are found particularly in the journal of the Society for Applied Anthropology, *Human organization*.

Interaction theory has continued to be influential in behavioral science analysis. Starting from the minimal interaction of two individuals —pair events, or social dyads—it looks at group behavior as a structuring of such interactions, involving various types of transactions, and charged with different emotions. The gains and losses of viewing the rich tapestry of human custom through such a sharp yet simplified focus can be argued at length.

E62. Arensberg, Conrad M. and Solon T. Kimball. Family and community in Ireland. Cambridge, Harvard Univ. Press, 1940. 322 p.

E63. Chapple, Eliot D. and Carleton S. Coon. Principles of anthropology. New York, Holt, 1942. 718 p.

E64. Dollard, John A. Caste and class in a southern town. 2d ed. New York, Harper, 1949. 502 p.

E65. Oliver, Douglas L. A Solomon Island society. Cambridge, Harvard Univ. Press, 1955. 533 p.

E66. Redfield, Robert. Tepoztlan; a Mexican village. Chicago, Univ. of Chicago Press, 1930. 247 p.

E67. Warner, William L. The living and the dead. New Haven, Conn., Yale Univ. Press, 1959. 528 p.

E68. Warner, William L. and Paul S. Lunt. The social life of a modern community. New Haven, Conn., Yale Univ. Press, 1941. 460 p.

THE CULTURE CONCEPT AND CULTURAL VALUES

In the 1940's, as one aspect of continuing holistic approaches to culture, some anthropologists began to probe the concept of "values," the emotionally charged expectancies and preferences which may unconsciously or consciously pervade a people's way of life. Outstanding early theorists here were Kroeber, Redfield, and Clyde Kluckhohn of Harvard. Kluckhohn worked with a notable group of students, now influential in anthropology, in a values project laboratory based both in Cambridge and at Ramah, New Mexico, where comparative investigations were made of the value systems or "philosophy," of Pueblo and Navajo Indians, Spanish Americans, Mormons, and frontier American homesteaders. Kluckhohn also worked with Kroeber in trying to reduce the scattered terminology of anthropology, including the label "culture" itself, to operationally meaningful order. Among the scholars of philosophy who integrated their work closely with the interested anthropologists were F. S. C. Northrop of Yale, M. Singer of Chicago, and David Bidney and Ethel Albert, both of whom have subsequently associated themselves professionally with anthropology.

Controversies emerged at this time as to whether anthropologists should or should not throw their weight behind a philosophical approach called "ethical relativism," or "cultural relativism." Some insisted that the "tough minded" scholar must see values or ethics as relative to culture, eschewing value absolutes. Others believed that the anthropologist as a scientist could do no more than study values objectively, leaving value judgments to the humanists. Others, acknowledging that each society sets up its own value system through its cultural apparatus, pointed out that there could be universal values shared in all cultures, and that human problems had been better solved by some means than by others.

Redfield of Chicago was among those who argued the case against extremes of cultural relativism. With Singer, mentioned above, he also launched a major series of comparative studies of "Cultures and Civilizations." A very broad typology of peoples was set up—the "little community," "peasant societies," the "great traditions," "urban communities"; and the common characteristics of each type were delineated. Of the great traditions, India has been a principal target of study for this group.

E69. Bidney, David. Theoretical anthropology. New York, Columbia Univ. Press, 1953. 506 p.
E70. Kluckhohn, Clyde. Mirror for man: the relation of anthropology to modern life. New York, Whittlesay House, 1949. 313 p.
E71. Kluckhohn, Florence R. and Fred L. Strodtbeck. Variations in value orientations. Evanston, Ill., Row, Peterson, 1961. 437 p.
E72. Kroeber, Alfred L. and Clyde Kluckhohn. Culture: a critical review of concepts and definitions. Cambridge, Mass., Peabody Museum, 1952. 223 p. (Papers of the Peabody Museum of American Archaeology & Ethnology, Harvard Univ. v. 47, no. 1)
E73. Kroeber, Alfred L. The nature of culture. Chicago, Univ. of Chicago Press, 1952. 437 p.
E74. Redfield, Robert. The primitive world and its transformations. Ithica, N.Y., Cornell Univ. Press, 1953. 185 p.
E75. White, Leslie A. Science of culture. New York, Farrar, Straus, 1949. 444 p.

LANGUAGE AND CULTURE

Going back to the period 1939-42, three influential essays appeared written by a business man turned anthropologist, Benjamin Whorf, who had studied with Sapir because of his interest in languages. A people's language, Whorf claimed, shaped the way a people categorized its "view of the world," through its formal characteristics of grammar and style. Whorf died before he could defend his thesis, but it stimulated research into the relationship between language and culture, often called "metalinguistics." As shown in the volume edited by Harry Hoijer, anthropologists feel that language forms do not determine culture, but that each people has built up a way of viewing the world (time, space, motion, power, human identification, and so on) which is expressed in the components of its language—that is, the verbal and other symbols of communicating and storing experience. A number of linguists are now advancing the study of semantic systems, while social anthropologists, along with psychologists, are interesting themselves in the study of "cognitive systems" and also investigating other cultural phenomena by way of linguistic taxonomies.

E76. Hoijer, Harry. Language in culture. Chicago, Univ. of Chicago Press, 1954. 286 p.

E77. Lounsbury, Floyd. "Language." In Siegel, Bernard J., *ed.* Biennial review of anthropology, 1959. Stanford, Calif., Stanford Univ. Press, 1959. p. 185-209.
E78. Sebeok, Thomas A., *ed.* Style in language. Cambridge, Mass., Technology Press of M.I.T., 1960. 470 p.
E79. Whorf, Benjamin L. Language, thought and reality; selected writings, ed. by John B. Carroll. Cambridge, Mass., Technology Press of M.I.T., 1956. 278 p.

CULTURAL CHANGE

Throughout the world, the anthropologist in the field found changes going on around him, and indeed he could not avoid being an agent of change. At first he recorded such happenings, sentimentally or otherwise, as a kind of contamination of aboriginal culture, and if he published his observations it was mainly to show how the new had to be stripped off to get at the old. Occasionally, however, notable movements of change were recorded for their own sake, as with a report by James Mooney on the "Ghost Dance Religion" among Western Indian tribes.

Around the turn of the century, the term "acculturation" came into some use among American anthropologists to express the changing of a culture through outside contact, particularly the impact of Western civilization on isolated systems of life. By the 1930's, this was formally recognized as a legitimate phase of anthropological study, filling in the contexts of the historicalist terms "invention" and "diffusion." British anthropologists, however, preferred to speak of "culture contact" or "social change" rather than acculturation. A literature rapidly began to accumulate covering American Indians, Pacific Islanders, Africans, and other groups undergoing recent changes; the gradual impacts of Hispanic traditions upon Middle and South America were explored; and theory relating to cultural dynamism was given some formulation.

By the early 1940's, some American scholars were also returning to the older problem of long term cultural growth, and even the term "evolution" was beginning to reappear in generalized statements about culture process. Leslie White undertook at this time a vigorous campaign to rehabilitate and expand the unilinear evolutionary concepts of Tylor and Morgan, particularly meaning "culturological" progress in terms of increasingly efficient use of energy. Julian Steward particularly emphasized study of the processes inherent in the multilinear development of culture, including the generally parallel courses of the food-producing revolutions in the Near East and nuclear America. Kroeber and Linton were among other notable writers who took part in this revival of interest in longer-term cultural dynamism.

A survey by Keesing of the literature on culture change shows it shifting by the 1950's from a marginal to a central place in cultural theory.

American scholars now generally treat change itself as part of a larger tapestry of behavioral dynamics. This covers both the dynamics of adapting cultural systems and "steady states,": that is, the factors of persistence; innovation, or resistance to innovation; obsolescence and loss; reformulation of old and new cultural elements in situations of change; differential rates of change; cultural drift (slow directional changes) and cultural stress, shock, revolution, and breakdown (massive changes); reformulative movements and cults; psychological process and culture change; and the dynamics of external intervention or non-voluntary change, as in cultural planning and forceful manipulation.

E80. Barnett, Homer G. Innovation; the basis of cultural change. New York, McGraw-Hill, 1953. 462 p.
E81. Herskovits, Melville J. Acculturation: the study of culture contact. New York, Augustin, 1938. 155 p.
E82. Keesing, Felix M. Culture change; an analysis and bibliography of anthropological sources to 1952. Stanford, Calif., Stanford Univ. Press, 1953. 242 p.
E83. Kroeber, Alfred L. Configurations of cultural growth. Berkeley, Univ. of California Press, 1944. 882 p.
E84. Linton, Ralph. Acculturation in seven American Indian tribes. New York, Appleton-Century, 1940. 526 p.
E85. Linton, Ralph. Tree of culture. New York, Knopf, 1955. 692 p.
E86. Spindler, George D. Sociocultural and psychological processes in Menomini acculturation. Berkeley, Univ. of California Press, 1955. 271 p. (Univ. of California. Publications in culture and society, v. 5)
E87. Steward, Julian H. Theory of culture change. Urbana, Univ. of Illinois Press, 1955. 244 p.

APPLIED ANTHROPOLOGY

The last point mentioned above, external intervention, is the characteristic feature of applying anthropology to practical situations. In essense, the anthropologist is presented by a planner, policy maker, or action specialist with some problem relating to administration, development, or welfare. He applies his professional skills just as rigorously as he would to a problem on the growing front of his science, providing technical information relevant to the necessary decisions, venturing predictions on the possible results of different courses of action, or the most likely way to reach a desired goal.

Governments with overseas territories in which indigenous populations had to be administered found anthropologists useful in training programs for their personnel conducted at such centers as Oxford, Cambridge, Paris, Berlin, Leiden, and Utrecht. The foundation for such administration had to be the customs of the governed, rather than those of the governors. Some territories employed anthropologists on their staffs to provide technical information and to act as troubleshooters and policy advisers.

References have been made to other applications of anthropology, including studies of industrial structures and the needs of World War II. Physical anthropologists have contributed in matters requiring knowledge of bodily structures, as in designing prosthetic devices and, most recently, the planning of equipment for space travel. Linguists have designed orthographies for the unwritten languages, improved language learning methods, and taught languages to personnel going to the under-developed countries. Ethnologists and social anthropologists have worked on a wide range of training programs and research problems, including community development and resettlement schemes, overseas and minority administration, and health, industrial, educational, and other practical affairs. Cultural anthropologists have analyzed the processes of education and cultural transmission. One of the most active fronts is represented in "medical anthropology," with work going on in medical, public health, and nursing schools, veterans hospitals, community and state organizations, and other relevant settings. The socio-cultural problems of potential colonies of men living beyond the earth are also challenging thought.

E88. Barnett, Homer G. Anthropology in administration. Evanston, Ill., Row, Peterson, 1956. 196 p.
E89. Leighton, Alexander H. Governing of men. Princeton, N.J., Princeton Univ. Press, 1945. 404 p.
E90. Linton, Ralph, *ed.* Science of man in the world crisis. New York, Columbia Univ. Press, 1945. 532 p.
E91. Mair, Lucy P. Studies in applied anthropology. London, Univ. of London, Athlone Press, 1957. 81 p. (Monographs on social anthropology, no. 16)
E92. Mead, Margaret, *et al.* Man in space; a tool and program for the study of social change. In New York Academy of Sciences. Annals, v. 72, April 1958: 165-214.
E93. Opler, Marvin K. Culture and mental health. New York, Macmillan, 1959. 533 p.
E94. Paul, Benjamin D., *ed.* Health, culture and community. New York, Russell Sage Foundation, 1955. 493 p.
E95. Spicer, Edward H. Human problems in technological change. New York, Russell Sage Foundation, 1952. 301 p.
E96. Spindler, George D. Education and anthropology. Stanford, Calif., Stanford Univ. Press, 1955. 302 p.
E97. World Federation for Mental Health. Cultural patterns and technical change; a manual, ed. by Margaret Mead. Paris, UNESCO, 1953. 348 p.

SOCIAL STRUCTURE, ECONOMIC BEHAVIOR,
PHYSICAL ANTHROPOLOGY, LINGUISTICS

Anthropologists have continued their more traditional studies of the different aspects of culture. By far the most systematically worked field has been the study of marriage, family, descent, and other aspects of kinship. This has been central in the British studies of social structure, theoretical work by Fortes, Evans-Pritchard, and Leach, being especially notable. In France, Claude Lévi-Strauss has developed a social structural approach which is widely influential. In the United States, Murdock used the vast ethnographic compilations of an inter-university "Human Relations Area File," which he first developed at Yale, to elucidate the typology and dynamics of kinship; and younger scholars such as K. Romney, W. Goodenough, and D. Schneider are experimenting with, and refining, methods and categories of study.

Economic behavior has been discussed from the anthropological viewpoint particularly by Firth, Herskovits, and Arensberg. Political behavior has been treated sporadically, with most attention focused on law, leadership, factionalism, and conflict. The study of religion, always a strong interest for German scholars, has been in the doldrums for English-speaking anthropologists until recently; but through the Harvard Values Project and other points of interest, it is gaining some new life. Art, however, still remains marginal to anthropological study except in the museums, particularly those of European countries, and, along with play and recreation, calls for new attention. Folklore studies are gaining in vitality through newer linguistic approaches. Technology studies tend to be in the museums and scientific laboratories.

The field of physical anthropology, though marginal to this discussion, is in a particularly vigorous state of reformulation today, and its newer frame of reference touches cultural anthropology at many more points than did the older structural-anthropometric approach. The small breeding isolates among modern men can provide models though which the dynamics of early human populations may be inferred. As culture accumulates, it is seen as providing complex forces of selection, of interaction, and of population growth; the body (phenotypic) growth of the individual involves a complex play of sociocultural factors; and studies of animal behavior are throwing exciting light on the nature of culture. The theoretical interplay between the biological and the cultural approaches, indeed, are providing an embarrassment of riches for the practitioner in each field.

Archaeology, too, has escaped from the stereotypes created earlier by interpreting world culture history in terms of the European finds only —the standard scheme from eoliths upward still found in so many works. It is now systematizing data from all the continents to give creative new vistas of cultural growth and relationship. With new finds announced in rapid-fire succession, with new dating methods which can show amazingly accurate occupation dates of caves and other sites back to 40,000 years, and with vigorous controversies among the specialists, no one is up to date without reading the standard current journals.

The vigor of linguistics, and its importance for cultural anthropology more generally, has already received reference. The study of speech, together with the wider matrix of communication, bids fair to assume a role in the behavioral sciences comparable to the role of statistics in science at large. Structural linguistics is now a highly technical field of research. Historical linguistics has exciting new leads relevant for culture history, including glottochronology, or lexicostatistics. It is significant that anthropologists with linguistically oriented problems are further along in effectively utilizing computers for research than any other group within the profession.

The various interests referred to above are represented in part by the selections listed below, particularly the *Scientific American* reprints representing an excellent selection of articles based on current knowledge in physical anthropology, archaeology and linguistics. The frontiers of these fields are expanding so rapidly, however, that much of the significant new material can be found only in professional journals, such as the *American anthropologist, Southwestern journal of anthropology, Behavioral science,* and *Current anthropology.*

E98. Boas, Franz. Primitive art. Cambridge, Harvard Univ. Press, 1927. 376 p.
E99. Firth, Raymond W. Elements of social organization. London, Watts, 1951. 257 p.
E100. Fried, Morton H. Readings in anthropology. New York, Crowell, 1959. 2 v.
E101. Goldschmidt, Walter R. Exploring the ways of mankind. New York, Holt, Rinehart and Winston, 1960. 700 p.
E102. Herskovits, Melville J. Economic anthropology, a study in comparative economics. 2d ed. New York, Knopf, 1952. 547 p.
E103. Hoebel, Edward A. Law of primitive man; a study in comparative legal dynamics. Cambridge, Harvard Univ. Press, 1954. 357 p.
E104. Human species. Scientific American, v. 60, Sept. 1960; 62-217. (Also issued as a separate reprint series).
E105. Lévi-Strauss, Claude. Les structures élémentaires de la paternité. Paris, Presses Universitaires de France, 1949. 639 p.
E106. Murdock, George P. Social structure. New York, Macmillan, 1949. 387 p.
E107. Nadel, Siegfried F. Theory of social structure. Glencoe, Ill., Free Press, 1957. 159 p.
E108. Shapiro, Harry L. Man, culture and society. New York, Oxford Univ. Press, 1956. 380 p.

THE TEACHING OF ANTHROPOLOGY

As a corollary to the accelerated development of anthropology in both graduate training programs and undergraduate education, a new self-consciousness about teaching has emerged during the past decade. Several brief papers on this subject appeared in the *American anthropologist*, before 1950. In 1952, a whole issue of this journal was devoted to the training and education of anthropologists. During the past two years, conferences have been held both abroad and in the United States, under the sponsorship of the Wenner-Gren Foundation, on the teaching of anthropology; and the scope of concern has broadened to include attention to the undergraduate curriculum. The need for reading material for large undergraduate courses has resulted in a proliferation of books of readings, some of which have been listed elsewhere (Kluckhohn, Murray and Schneider, E49; Fried, E100; Goldschmidt, E101), numerous paperback editions of standard works, and one new series of short culture case studies.

E109. Mandelbaum, David G., *et al.* Resources for the teaching of anthropology. Berkeley, Univ. of California Press, 1963. 316 p.
E109a. Mandelbaum, David G., *et al.* The teaching of anthropology. Berkeley, Univ. of California Press, 1963. 611 p.
E110. [Papers presented at the Symposium on the training of the professional anthropologist, Chicago, Nov. 15-17, 1951] *American Anthropologist*, v. 54, July-Sept. 1952: 313-346.
E111. Spindler, George, and Spindler, Louise, *eds.* Case studies in cultural anthropology. New York, Holt, 1960. 5 v.

CONCLUSION

The survey presented here has been concerned with the literature which reveals the fields and problems of anthropology. Additionally, the solid work of the science is reported in numerous field studies of particular peoples and cultures. Basic, therefore, to library building is the assembly of perhaps two hundred first-class books and monographs of this type, representative of regions, culture types, and field study approaches. No carefully chosen listing of this kind seems yet available; but it could be compiled with profit.

In conclusion, it may be said that anthropology today has a seat on the stock exchange of ideas. The anthropologist may talk the language of many other intellectual skills beside his own, and is increasingly finding a place in interdisciplinary teamwork. The profile of anthropology courses fits in usefully with many other subjects in the biological and social sciences and in the humanities. As one result, the anthropology shelves of a library are widely drawn upon by other university departments, and the staff and students of anthropology are plagued, typically, by shortages, empty shelves, and waiting lists on desired books.

Felix M. Keesing

GUIDES TO THE LITERATURE

No separate general guide to the literature of anthropology is available.

REVIEWS OF THE LITERATURE

E112. Africa; journal of the International African Institute. v. 1+ 1928+ London, Oxford Univ. Press. quarterly.

An excellent example of a regional journal which assists in providing current control and review of the literature. It critically reviews in 350-2,500 words some 40-50 items a year and includes a quarterly classified bibliography (anthropology and sociology, linguistics, native administration, etc.) of 1,000-1,500 books and articles a year.

E113. American anthropologist. v. 1+ 1888+ Menasha, Wis., American Anthropological Association. bi-monthly.

The major American anthropological journal. Reviews 200-300 titles a year in critical, signed reviews of 350 to 3,000 words. Arranged by author under six major headings: general, ethnology, archaeology, linguistics, physical anthropology, and other. The items listed in "Publications received" number from 300-400 a year. All books reviewed are included in the annual index.

E114. Anthropologie. v. 1+ 1890+ Paris, Masson et Cie. bi-monthly.

"Mouvement scientifique" con-tains 100-250 critical, signed reviews (250-2,000 words) under three headings: prehistory, physical anthropology, and ethnography. "Bulletin bibliographique" briefly abstracts the contents of ca. 100 periodicals a year. Included is a section devoted to articles of anthropological interest published in other journals. All book reviews included in the index.

E115. Anthropos; revue internationale d'ethnologie et de linguistic. v. 1+ 1906+ Fribourg, Switz., Anthropos-Institut. 3 a year.

Devotes one-third of each number to a survey of recent publications. "Bibliographia" contains 175-250 critical reviews a year (100-1,300 words). "Publicationes recentes" lists alphabetically by author ca. 400 items annually. "Periodica" reviews the contents of over 100 journals of anthropological interest. Scope is international. All book reviews indexed by author, subject and geographical area.

E116. Biennial review of anthropology, ed. by Bernard J. Siegel. Stanford, Calif., Stanford Univ. Press, 1959+ biennial.

The first volume of a series devoted to periodic reviews of published anthropological research. The bibliographical essays in this initial volume cover research published since 1955 in five fields of current interest: social and cultural change, physical anthropology, linguistics, social organization, and the psychological dimensions of culture.

Cultural history (archeology, ethno-history, historical ethnology) is excluded. Each issue will include a critical review of recent anthropological research outside the U.S. Each essay is prepared by a specialist and some 1515 works are cited. General index. V. 2 (1961) lists 1713 items.

E117. Buck, Peter H. An introduction to Polynesian anthropology. Honolulu, Bernice P. Bishop Museum, 1945. 133 p. (Bernice P. Bishop Museum. Bulletin 187)

An appraisal of research and publication on Polynesian anthropology concerned primarily with native culture prior to foreign contact. Each chapter is followed by an excellent bibliography. A second volume *Specialized studies in Polynesian anthropology* (Honolulu, Bernice P. Bishop Museum, 1947. 88 p. Bernice P. [Bishop Museum. Bulletin 193]) deals with subjects which are more concerned with developments after foreign contact (missionary contributions, acculturation, education, government, psychological studies). Both volumes have general subject indexes. See also Keesing's *Social anthropology in Polynesia* (E120).

E118. Elkin, Adolphus P. Social anthropology in Melanesia; a review of research. London, Oxford Univ. Press, 1953. 166 p.

One unit of a research project initiated by the South Pacific Commission to provide a comprehensive survey of the work done to date in social anthropology and to suggest areas for future research. Three main sections: (1) Types of ethnological records and research up to 1950, (2) Survey of anthropological knowledge of the region with suggestions for research projects, and (3) Principles for a plan of anthropological research in Melanesia. Part 2, the longest section, cites over 650 items in the text and lists of refer-

ences. See also Keesing's *Social Anthropology in Polynesia* (E120).

E119. Keesing, Felix M. Culture change; an analysis and bibliography of anthropological sources to 1952. Stanford, Calif., Stanford Univ. Press, 1953. 242 p. (Stanford anthropological series, 1)

Part I is a chronological analysis of the progress of anthropological thought written in the fields variously called cultural dynamics, culture change, culture growth, culture process, culture contact and acculturation. The last section of Part I gives a critical assessment of the present status and future needs of thought in this area. Part II is a chronological listing (4,212 items) of the works discussed. Most items appear after 1865.

E120. Keesing, Felix M. Social anthropology in Polynesia; a review of research. London, Oxford Univ. Press, 1953. 126 p.

The second unit of the South Pacific Commission project mentioned above (E118). A short introductory chapter on the nature of social anthropology is followed chapters on health, economic and social development. The final chapter deals with research needs and possibilities. References in the text refer to the select bibliography of 950 items arranged geographically. The period covered is roughly 1890-1950. Does not include some Polynesian groups (i.e., the Hawaiian, Maoris, Easter and Pitcairn Islands). See also (E117).

E121. Man; a monthly record of anthropological science. v. 1+ 1900+ London, Royal Anthropological Institute. monthly.

The 150-250 critical, signed book reviews (100-1,000 words) included in this journal are arranged geographically by continent with one section for general material. Annual index contains an author list of book reviews. Also includes a month-by-month classified accessions list for the Library of the Institute.

ABSTRACTS AND DIGESTS

E122. Abstracts of New World archaeology. v. 1+ 1959+. Washington, Society for American Archaeology, 1960+ annual.

This annual aims to publish short abstracts of all published titles dealing expressly with New World archaeology, as well as masters' theses and doctoral dissertations. The 676 items in vol. 1 are arranged by author under 26 regional headings. Each abstract is signed and presents only the ideas of the author of the work. When editorial comments are included they have been set off in brackets. Author index and cross references. Vol. 2 (1960) lists 1026 items.

E123. African abstracts; a quarterly review of ethnographic, social, and linguistic studies appearing in current periodicals. v. 1+ 1950+. London, International African Institute. quarterly.

Abstracts 500-600 articles a year from over 100 periodicals published primarily in Europe and Africa. The abstracts are in French or English. Under two main headings (1) Ethnographic and social studies and (2) Linguistic studies, the items are arranged geographically. Annual index includes a general index, an ethnic and linguistic index, an author index and an index of periodicals abstracted.

E124. Siegel, Bernard J. Acculturation; critical abstracts, North America. Stanford, Calif., Stanford Univ. Press, 1955. 231 p. (Stanford anthropological series, 2)

"In this volume an effort is made to abstract all the major empirical studies reported by anthropologists in the setting of North America which are of importance in analyz-

ing the processes of socio-cultural change under conditions of cultures in contact." (Pref.). 39 monographs, including unpublished Ph.D. dissertations, and 55 periodical articles, published through 1951, are extensively summarized. Future volumes dealing with Middle and South America, Africa, the Middle East, Asia and the Pacific are planned.

BIBLIOGRAPHIES—CURRENT

E125. "Annual bibliography of folklore," *Journal of American folklore. Supplement.* v. 68+ 1955+. Philadelphia, American Folklore Society. annual.

Beginning in 1955 the Supplement has contained an annual bibliography of ca. 1,000 items arranged alphabetically by author under 14 main headings (e.g., folkart, customs, folk narrative, folkdance, etc.). Includes some books and monographic series publications, but primarily lists articles from over 200 periodicals. International in scope. Some brief explanatory notes. No index. Supplement also contains a periodic survey of "Work in progress."

E126. "Bibliographie américaniste," *Journal de la Société des Américanistes.* n.s. v. 10+ 1919+. Paris, Musée de l'Homme. annual.

This important annual bibliography, particularly useful for its European material, gives a comprehensive listing of anthropological publications for North and South America and the West Indies. Major emphasis upon anthropology, ethnography, linguistics, and archaeology, but includes some history and geography. The 1,500-2,000 items listed a year include books, periodical articles and society publications in all languages. Scope is international. No annotations. Author index.

E127. "Bibliographie africainiste,"

Journal de la Société des Africainistes.
v. 1+ 1931+. Paris, Musée de
l'Homme. annual.

This important current bibliography of 1,000-1,500 items a year
emphasizes archaeology, prehistory,
anthropology, ethnography and linguistics but includes items of historical and geographical interest.
Scope is international and includes
monographs, articles, society, publications, documents, etc. in all languages. No annotations.

E128. "Bibliographie de l'Océanie," *Journal de la Société des
Océanistes.* v. 2+ 1946+ Paris,
Musée de l'Homme. annual.

This selective, classified bibliography covers geographically, Polynesia, Micronesia, Melanesia and
Australia (excludes the Philippines,
Japan and Indonesia). Major emphasis upon anthropology, ethnology, acculturation and linguistics
with some entries for history, colonization, economics, art and literature. The 1,000-1,500 items a year
include books, articles, society publications, documents, theses and
newspaper articles which are significant sources of documentation or
information on the Pacific Islands.
Scope is international. No index. No
annotations.

E129. Bibliographie ethnographique de l'Afrique sud-saharienne,
1925+ Tervuren, Belgium, Musée
Royal de l'Afrique Centrale, 1932+
annual.

Title 1925-1959, *Bibliographie ethnographique du Congo Belge et regions avoisinantes.* Author list of
books and articles with a subject
index. Most items annotated. Cites
reviews for more important items.

E130. Bibliographie linguistique
de l'année 1939+ Utrecht, Spectrum, 1949+ annual.

Although containing much material beyond the scope of anthropology, this international bibliography
contains much of importance to an-

thropologists. Lists books and articles
from over 700 world periodicals (including 40 major anthropological
journals). The material is grouped
under large classes (language groups
or area) with subdivisions. Cites
book reviews. Author index.

E131. Boletin bibliográfico de antropologiá Americana. v. 1+ 1937+
Mexico, D.F., Instituto Panamericano de Geografiá e Historia. annual.

Issued in 2 parts since 1949 this
bibliography provides an excellent
guide to current literature on anthropology in the Americas. Part I
contains news items, reviews of research projects and special articles.
Part II contains: (1) "Crítica bibliográfica," a classified listing of over
100 critical, signed reviews (150-3,500 words). Most reviews are of
books, but some significant articles
are also covered; (2) "Revista de
libros," a classified bibliography of
current book publication (250-700
items); (3) "Revista de revistas," a
listing of tables of contents of over
120 periodicals arranged by country
and title. The majority are published
in the Americas, but certain European titles are included. Another
regular feature is a bibliography of
the works of a prominent anthropologist. Occasional appendices present bibliographies of special topics,
e.g., Rafael H. Valle "Bibliografia
maya" appendix to v. 1-5, 1937-1941. 404 p. Ca. 3800 items.

E132. "Bibliography of Canadian
anthropology," National Museum of
Canada. *Contributions to anthropology,* 1954-55+ Ottawa, 1956+ annual. (Canada National Museum Bulletin, 142+)

Continues "Recent publications
relating to Canada: ethnology, anthropology and archeology" formerly published in the *Canadian
historical review* v. 1-35, 1920-55.
An annual listing of 150-350 monographs and articles published in various languages dealing with all aspects
of Canadian anthropology. Arranged

by author, the entries carry short critical or descriptive annotations. No index.

E133. COWA surveys and bibliographies. series I+ 1958+ Cambridge, Mass., Council for Old World Archeology. biennial.

The primary purpose of the Council is to aid scholars in keeping abreast of the latest activities and publications in the prehistory and archeology of the Old World. The biennial series, a means to this end, is divided into 22 booklets each covering some convenient area of Europe, Africa, Asia and Oceania. Each covers the last 2 or 3 years of archeological activity in the area and consists of a survey of current work and an annotated bibliography of the more important books and articles. References are made from the survey to the bibliography as well as to the preceding issue when required.

E134. "Folklore bibliography," *Southern folklore quarterly*. v. 2+ 1938+ Gainesville, Fla., Univ. of Florida. annual. (March issue)

A classified bibliography compiled from 1938-1959 by R.S. Boggs. Contains ca. 800 items a year. International in scope, but with major emphasis upon U.S. and Latin American publications and subjects. Some brief descriptive annotations. Lack of an index is inconvenient.

E135. India. *Dept. of Anthropology*. Cumulative index to current literature on anthropology and allied subjects, 1955+ Calcutta, 1956+ semi-annual.

A cumulation of the monthly indexes which the Department's Library has issued since January, 1955, listing articles appearing in some 200 current journals in anthropology and allied fields. Entries are arranged alphabetically by author under subjects with author and subject indexes. V. 1 covers 1955; subsequent vol-

umes appear semi-annually. International in scope.

E136. International bibliography of social and cultural anthropology. v. 1-5, 1955-1959. Paris, UNESCO, 1958-1961; v. 6+ 1960+ Chicago, Aldine, 1962+ annual.

This important work includes references to all books and articles published throughout the world, in any language, which represent a definite contribution to the science of anthropology. Material covered includes ethnology, archeology, linguistics, folklore, and applied anthropology as well as historical and geographical material of anthropological relevance. 3,500-5,000 items a year are arranged systematically under nine general headings with author and subject indexes. Entries are brief but include an English or French translation of any title not in either of these languages. Must be used in conjunction with more specialized bibliographies.

E137. Internationale Volkskundliche Bibliographie; International folklore bibliography; Bibliographie internationale des arts et traditións populaires, années 1939-41+ Bâle, Commission Internationale des Arts et Traditións Populaires, 1949+ annual.

A comprehensive current bibliography of folklore which continues *Volkskundliche Bibliographie, 1917-1938* (v. 1-13 Berlin, de Gruyter, 1919-41; v. for 1937-38 Berlin, Akademie Verlag, 1957). Each annual volume contains 6,000-8,000 entries for books and articles (from over 1,000 journals) arranged under 22 main headings with detailed subdivisions. Major headings include: folklore in general; objects; signs; technology, arts and crafts, industries; manners and customs; popular beliefs and folkliterature. Especially valuable for European writings. English and American material is not fully represented to date. Subject and author index.

General

E138. Beckham, Rexford S. A basic list of books and periodicals for college libraries. In Mandelbaum, David G., et al. Resources for the teaching of anthropology. Berkeley, Univ. of California Press, 1963. pp. 77-316.

A basic classified listing of 1714 books and periodicals suitable for undergraduate teaching of anthropology. Emphasis upon English language materials and titles in print. Older material and foreign titles of intrinsic importance are included. Author index and extensive cross references. No annotations.

E139. Bloxam, George W. Index to the publications of the Anthropological Institute of Great Britain and Ireland, 1843-1891. London, Anthropological Institute, 1893. 301 p.

An author and subject index to the *Journal* and *Transactions* of the Ethnological Society of London (1843-1871); *Journal* and *Memoirs* of the Anthropological Society of London (1863-1871); *Anthropological review*, 1863-1870; and the *Journal* of the Anthropological Institute, 1871-1891.

E140. Boggs, Ralph S. Bibliography of Latin American folklore. New York, H.W. Wilson, 1940. 109 p.

A standard work of 643 items selected as a partial guide to the field. Supplemented by the section on folklore in the *Handbook of Latin American studies* (A75). The entries are classified by types of folklore and then arranged by country. Some brief annotations. General index. See also (E189).

E141. Comas, Juan. Historia y bibliografía de los congresos internacionales de ciencias antropológicas: 1865-1954. Mexico, D.F., Dirección General de Publicaciones, 1956. 409 p. (Universidad Nacional Autónoma de Mexico. Publicaciones del Instituto de Historia, 1 ser., no. 37)

Surveys the activities and the publications of 4 major international anthropological organizations. Several less active bodies are also treated, but less extensively. The first half is concerned with the history, charters, programs, etc. of the organizations. The second and major part is a classified bibliography of some 3,000 papers which have been published in the reports and transactions of the more important congresses. Author index. A similar publication by the same author, *Los Congresos Internacionales de Americanistas; síntesis histórica e índice bibliográfico general, 1875-1952* (Mexico, D.F. Instituto Indigenista Interamericano, 1954. 224 p.) is a classified bibliography of papers published in the proceedings of the Congresses of Americanists.

E142. Centralblatt für Anthropologie, Ethnologie und Urgeschichte. Jena, Kern, 1896-1912. 17 v.

Title, place and publisher vary. Each volume covers material published during the year of issue. Divided into two sections, comprising reviews of books and periodical articles and a bibliographical survey of current anthropological literature. In each section the material is classified under four broad headings: (1) general; (2) anthropology; (3) ethnology and ethnography (geographical subdivision); and (4) prehistory. Author and subject indexes.

E143. Haywood, Charles. A bibliography of North American folklore and folksong. New York, Greenberg, 1951. 1292 p.

An extensive bibliography of over 40,000 books, articles, sets, recordings etc. The entries in Book I, "American people north of Mexico," are arranged by subject under regional, ethnic and occupational headings. Book II, "American Indians north of Mexico," is classified first by cultural area, then by Folklore,

Music and Tribes, A-Z. Music in printed form and on records is given equal importance with other forms of folklore. Annotations are mainly descriptive. Author and subject index with title entries for individual songs and songs in collection. A supplement of material since 1948 is in preparation. A 2 vol. reprint (New York, Dover, 1961) adds an index of composers, arrangers and performers not found in the original work.

E144. International catalogue of scientific literature . . . P, Anthropology, 1900-1914. Published for the International Committee by the Royal Society of London. London, 1903-17. 13 v.

A valuable record of major contributions, books and articles, in 17 subject areas, each having its separate annual volume. Section P is devoted to anthropology. Each annual volume contains: (a) a schedule of the detailed classification scheme in English, German, French & Italian; (b) an alphabetical index to the classification scheme; (c) author catalog; and (d) subject catalog. The author catalog contains the full citation for the entry. Entries in the subject catalog or index include only authors name and brief title. The 13 anthropological volumes contain over 43,000 references.

E145. Klieneberger, H.L. Bibliography of Oceanic linguistics. London, Oxford Univ. Press, 1957. 143 p. (London Oriental Bibliographies, v. 1)

A useful bibliography of 2,100 references to books and periodical articles covering the whole of Oceania. Emphasizes linguistic works as such (dictionaries, grammars, individual and comparative studies) leaving aside the extensive literature published in many South Sea languages. The entries are arranged by region subdivided by language. Some entries include references to reviews. Locates rare material. No annota-

tions. Index of personal and corporate authors.

E146. Miller, Mamie T. An author, title and subject checklist of Smithsonian Institution publications relating to anthropology. Albuquerque, N.M., Univ. of New Mexico Press, 1946. 218 p. (Univ. of New Mexico. Bulletin, 405; Bibliographical Series, v. 1, no. 2)

This work is best described as an index of all Smithsonian contributions to anthropology, contained in 9 series excluding the publications of the Bureau of American Ethnology (see E159). Specifically it indexes by author, title and 94 broad subjects the following series: Smithsonian *Annual report*, 1848-1941; *Annual report* of the U.S. National Museum, 1848-1942; *Contributions from the U.S. National Museum Herbarium*, 1891-1929, v. 1-29 (complete); *Contributions to knowledge*, 1848-1916, v. 1-35 (complete); Explorations and field work, 1927-1940; *Miscellaneous collections*, 1862-1942, v. 1-103; Scientific series, 1929-1932, v. 1-12 (complete); U.S. National Museum *Bulletin*, 1875-1942; U.S. National Museum *Proceedings*, 1878-1942.

E147. Smithsonian Anthropological bibliographies. v. 1+ 1960+ Washington, Smithsonian Institution. irregular.

An experimental series for use in answering inquiries from the public, and for teachers, students and the profession. It will include bibliographies of varying length and technicality, both areal and topical, in all fields of anthropology. No. 1 is "A selected bibliography on the Plains Indians" by John C. Ewers.

E148. Steinmetz, Sebald R. Essai d'une bibliographie systématique de l'ethnologie jusqu'à l'année 1911. Bruxelles, Misch et Thron 1911. 196 p. (Instituts Solvay. Institut de Sociologie. Monographies bibliographiques, 1)

One of the earliest "select bibliographies" of the whole subject of ethnology. Over 2,100 older books and articles in French, German and English are classified in a scheme which gives a wide interpretation to ethnology, including such subjects as psychology, economics, religion and material culture (quite unique for its time). Ethnology is strictly interpreted as the "comparative theoretical study of primitive peoples" and hence descriptions of things concerning only one people or one group of peoples is excluded. Most entries date from 1870. Author index.

Africa

E149. French Equatorial Africa. *Service de la statistique générale.* Bibliographie ethnographique de l'Afrique équatoriale française, 1914-1948. Paris, 1949. 107 p.

E150. Jones, Ruth. Africa bibliography series; ethnology, sociology, linguistics and related subjects. London, International African Institute, 1958+ (In progress)
This series of volumes is based upon the classified card index of the Institute's library. The main source of this card index has been the annual bibliography appearing in *Africa* (E112) and hence this present series represents a type of cumulation from 1929 to the present. Aims to include all significant works rather than to produce an exhaustive bibliography. The classification is primarily geographical. Each volume is devoted to a specific area. It in turn is subdivided territorially and then by subjects. Ethnology and linguistics in addition to general works are the only subjects included in the present series. It is hoped that other subjects will be dealt with later as well as up-to-date supplements. The volumes issued to date contain over 10,000 references. Some brief annotations. An ethnic and linguistic index and an author index are included in each volume.

E151. Mylius, Norbert. Afrika Bibliographie, 1943-1951. Wien, Verein Freunde der Völkerkunde, 1952. 237 p.
Serves as a supplement to H.A. Wieschhoff's *Anthropological bibliography of Negro Africa* (E153), but does not include periodical articles. The 2,500+ items are arranged geographically and subdivided by subjects and large tribal groups with a place and tribal index. Two general sections list bibliographies (92 items) and periodicals (239 titles) dealing exclusively or in large part with Africa. Includes some material on history, law, race relations, colonial policy, economics and missionary activities. Index of places and tribes.

E152. Schapera, Isaac. Select bibliography of South African native life and problems. London, Oxford Univ. Press. 1941. 249 p.

E153. Wieschhoff, Heinrich A. Anthropological bibliography of Negro Africa. New Haven, Conn., American Oriental Society, 1948. 461 p. (American oriental series, v. 23)
A voluminous bibliography (over 12,000 entries) of books and periodical articles to the year 1942. Arranged alphabetically by tribal name, language and geographical area the material primarily covers ethnographic and linguistic topics, but also includes personal narratives and memoirs, travel accounts, geographical studies and some historical items. Not limited as to country of publication or date. Cross references in text, but no index. Norbert Mylius' *Afrika Bibliographie, 1943-1951* (E151) serves as a supplement.

America

E154. "A bibliography of anthropological bibliographies: the Americas," compiled under the direction of Gordon D. Gibson. *Current Anthropology*, v.1, Jan. 1960; 61-73.

A compilation of the most significant anthropological bibliographies pertaining to the Americas originally published before 1955. Includes separately published bibliographies and those appearing as journal articles. General anthropological bibliographies, personal bibliographies of a particular anthropologist, lists of references cited in books and articles, bibliographies in related fields, and book review series are generally omitted. The 290 items are arranged geographically with general index of authors, general subjects and major regions. Each entry gives full bibliographic information with an indication of number of items included, classification scheme, kind of indexes, and type of annotation, if any. Locates copies in Library of Congress or one of 12 other major U.S. libraries.

E155. Comas, Juan. Bibliografía selectiva de las culturas indígenas de América. Mexico, D.F., Instituto Pan-Americano de Geographía e Historia, 1953. 292 p. (It's Publicación núm. 166; Comisión de Historia, 64. Bibliografiás, I)

A classified arrangement of 2,014 books, monographic series and some periodical articles, including works in various languages with a preponderance of English titles. The main division of material is between a historical part (235 items), containing the classics of the ethnographical literature on the Americas, and a second part (1,779 items) which includes the more recent literature dealing with the different primitive peoples. The major portion of part two is classified by 11 cultural areas. Major sub-areas and ethnic groups are indicated. Indexes to indigenous groups and authors. Short but useful annotations given for the most important entries. Includes maps.

E156. Parra Germán, Manuel and Wigberto Jiménez Moreno. Biblio-

grafía indigenista de Mexico y Centro-América (1850-1950) Mexico, D.F., Instituto Nacional Indigenista, 1954. 342 p. (It's Memorias, v. 4)

6,445 items (books, articles, reports, etc.) classified under 31 subject headings (geography, physical anthropology, ethnography, mythology, folklore, music, demography, etc.) with indexes of persons, institutions, places, tribes, and languages.

E157. Murdock, George P. Ethnographic bibliography of North America. 3d ed. New Haven, Conn., Human Relations Area Files, 1960. 393 p.

A classified bibliography of 17,300 items covering all of North America (including Greenland) north of Mexico. The work is organized by 16 cultural areas and within each area by tribal groups. Under the areal headings are included regional studies, geographical and historical sources, travel accounts, etc. Under tribal headings are included works pertaining directly to the particular group or subgroup. The attempt has been made to make the tribal bibliographies as complete as possible on all ethnographical subjects. "Works on physical anthropology and linguistics and on archaeology where pertinent to a known historical culture, have been listed whenever obtained in the search for ethnographic items . . ." (Pref.). Cut-off date is 1958 but important material published in 1959-1960 is included. Restricted to published material. Index of tribal names. A companion volume, *An ethnographic bibliography of South America* by Timothy J. O'Leary, containing ca. 23,000 entries is in press.

E158. Rouse, Irving A. and John M. Goggin. An anthropological bibliography of the eastern seaboard. New Haven, Conn., Yale Peabody Museum, 1947. 174 p. (Eastern States Archeological Federation. Research publication no. 1)

An extensive bibliography of the archeology, ethnology and indian history of the states which drain into the Atlantic Ocean. Over 3,200 entries (books, articles, reports, etc.) are grouped under the three headings listed above with geographical and/or tribal subdivisions. Prefaced by a tribal key (classification and synonyms). No index. Vol. 2 is being prepared at the University of Oklahoma Research Institute.

E159. U.S. *Bureau of American Ethnology.* List of publications of the Bureau of American Ethnology, with index to authors and titles. Rev. to Dec. 31, 1961. Washington, Govt. Print. Office, 1962. 130 p.

Lists the contents of 77 *Annual reports* and 186 *Bulletins,* 16 publications of the Institute of Social Anthropology, 9 vols. of *Contributions to North American ethnology,* 4 vols. of *Introductions* and 14 miscellaneous publications. Author and title indexes.

Asia

E160. Embree, John F. and Lillian O. Dotson. Bibliography of the peoples and cultures of mainland Southeast Asia. New Haven, Conn., Yale Univ., 1950. 821 p.

An extensive bibliography conceived in order to provide a base for future research. Material includes books and articles in English and in European languages retrospective to the earliest studies. The area covered includes Assam, Chittagong, Burma, Thailand, Laos, Cambodia and Vietnam. Malaya is not included. For Malayan material see Pelzer, K.J. *Selected bibliography, on the geography of Southeast Asia.* v. 3 (B-365). The entries are arranged first by general area then by tribal group and finally by subject. The subject matter includes: race, racial history and migration, ethnology, cultural history, social organization and law, religion, folklore, language and writing. Detailed table of contents but no indexes. For recent material reference should be made to the *Bibli-*

ography of Asian studies (A71). Some items have brief descriptive annotations.

E161. Field, Henry. Bibliography on Southwestern Asia. Coral Gables, Fla., Univ. of Miami Press, 1953-1962. 10 v.

Extensive listing of books and articles published in all languages from 1940 to 1959. Two major sections: (1) Anthropogeography and (2) Natural history. The first includes anthropology, ethnology, sociology, linguistics, demography, archeology, geology, agriculture, cartography, astronomy, medicine, art, literature and music. The 31,254 references for this section are arranged alphabetically by author with a cumulative subject index for v. 1-5. No annotations.

E162. Fürer-Haimendorf, Elizabeth von. An anthropological bibliography of South Asia, together with a directory of recent anthropological field work. Paris, Mouton, 1958. 748 p.

Deals with India, Pakistan, Nepal, Sikkion, Bhutan and Ceylon rather than the whole of South Asia as the title indicates. The 5,316 entries (books, articles, dissertations, theses, etc.) are first divided into 19 geographical areas with a 20th division for general works. Each area is further divided into three parts: Part A is a bibliography of works published prior to 1940 and is based largely upon David G. Mandelbaum's *Materials for a bibliography of the ethnology of India* (Berkeley, Dept. of Anthropology, Univ. of California, 1949. 200 l. mimeo); Part B includes publications issued 1940-1954; Part C is not bibliographical but consists of data on field research carried out from 1940-1954. A and B cover all phases of Anthropology; C is restricted to social and cultural anthropology. A supplement with subsequent biennial bibliographies is projected. No annotation. Author index. See also Calcutta. National

Library. *Bibliography of Indology.*
v. 1 Indian anthropology. (Calcutta,
1960. 290 p.) which contains 2,067
entries arranged geographically under
10 regions. 1,004 entries are annotated. Author and subject indexes.

E163. Jakobsen, Roman *et al.* Pa-
leosiberian peoples and languages; a
bibliographical guide. New Haven,
Conn., Human Relations Area Files,
1957. 222 p. (Behavior science bibliographies)
An extensive bibliography dealing
with the peoples (Gilyak, Chuk-
chee, Yukaghir and Yenisei) who in-
habit NE Asiatic Russia. The 1,898
entries include a large number of
Russian titles (which are translated)
as well as material in other western
languages. Two general chapters are
followed by one devoted to each of
the 4 groups. Some brief explanatory
annotations. No index.

E164. Kennedy, Raymond. Bibliography of Indonesian peoples and
cultures. Rev. ed. New Haven,
Conn., Human Relations Area Files,
1955. 2 v. (Behavior science bibliographies).
An extensive classified bibliography of monographs and articles arranged first by islands and then by
peoples or tribes with a special subdivision for Dutch language publications under each heading. Main
focus of the rev. ed. is anthropology
and sociology, including ethnography, archeology, linguistics and acculturation. Other subjects have
been included because of their pertinence to the anthropology of the
area (less so than in ed. 1, 1945).
No evaluation of items listed and
the lack of an index is a handicap.
Includes some material on Malaya.
Reprinted in 1962 as 2d rev. ed.
Changes in format only.

Europe

E165. Halpern, Joel, *ed.* Bibliography of anthropological and sociological publications on Eastern Eu-

rope and the USSR (English language sources). Los Angeles, Univ.
of California at Los Angeles, 1961.
142 p. (Russian and East European
Study Center series, v. 1, no. 2)
A preliminary but extensive bibliography of the most easily available
books and articles in the English
language. The entries are arranged
geographically covering: the Slavs in
general, Eastern Europe, Balkans,
Albania, Bulgaria, Czechoslovakia,
Hungary, Poland, Roumania, Yugoslavia and the USSR. For each area
the entries are classified by subject,
e.g. archeology and history, ethnology, geography, linguistics, religion,
demography, social change, etc. No
index.

E166. Ripley, William Z. Selected
bibliography of the anthropology
and ethnology of Europe. Boston,
Public Library, 1899. 160 p.
Very full bibliography of over
2,000 older books and articles arranged alphabetically by author with
subject and regional indexes. Especially strong in prehistoric archeology, historical or philological ethnology, and physical anthropology.

Oceania

E167. Taylor, Clyde R.H. A Pacific bibliography; printed matter
relating to the native peoples of Polynesia, Melanesia and Micronesia.
Wellington, N.Z., Polynesian Society, 1951. 492 p. (Memoirs of the
Polynesian Society, v. 24)
A basic bibliography (over 10,000
items) of books and periodical articles in various languages dealing
with peoples of the Pacific Islands.
Intended for specialist and general
reader. Material is grouped by subject (bibliography, ethnology, culture contacts, tribal organization,
language, folklore, dress, etc.) under
geographical area (island group).
General index includes only those
items which are not specifically related to some segment of the classi-

fication scheme. Some brief explanatory annotations. A revised and enlarged edition is in preparation. Supplemented by F.M. Cammack and S. Saito, *Pacific island bibliography* (New York, Scarecrow Press, 1962. 421 p.).

DICTIONARIES

E168. Bosi, Roberto. Dizionario di etnologia. Milano, A. Mondadori, 1958. 364 p.
Short definitions with good cross-referencing covering the whole field of ethnography including tribal names, concepts, etc.

E169. Dictionary of anthropology, ed. by Wolfgang H. Lindig. (In preparation)
A cooperative project to be undertaken under the auspices of *Current anthropology*, this new work is intended as a dictionary of anthropology for anthropologists. See also (E171). Initially the contributions to this new project will be published in *Current anthropology*, then commented upon by others and finally the revised and synthesized articles and comments will be published in book form. Each article will include diagrams and/or photographs, when necessary, as well as a bibliography of the most important publications on the subject. To be included are articles on (1) terms and concepts used in anthropological fields, including prehistory, linguistics and ethnology; (2) designations and descriptions of prehistoric and modern cultures; and (3) biographies of anthropologists.

E170. International dictionary of regional European ethnology and folklore. Copenhagen, published for the International Commission on Folk Arts and Folklore by Rosenkilde and Bagger, 1960+ (In progress)

Intended as a reference work in English providing definitions of ethnological and folkloristic technical terms and concepts. To be complete in 12 main sections. The first two "General ethnological concepts" and "Folk literature" are now complete. Preference given to terms created by European regional ethnologists but American contributions are extensive. Each term is given in English, French, Spanish, German and a Scandinavian language (usually Swedish). The definitions include citations to the literature.

E171. Multilingual glossary of anthropological terms, ed. by Grete Mostny. (In preparation)
A second cooperative project to be undertaken under the auspices of *Current anthropology*, this work will bring together, in 4 or more languages, all the words and technical terms needed for their research by anthropologists. Publication will be handled similarly to (E169) above. The glossary will consist of 2 parts: (1) A topical section of 24 chapters, e.g., weapons, agriculture, social organization, art, etc., with more detailed subdivisions; (2) a lexicon with 4 or more independently alphabetically arranged vocabularies, each headed by one of the languages (4-6), with each term translated into the other languages used. Simple diagrams will be included in part I to facilitate understanding.

E172. Winick, Charles. Dictionary of anthropology. New York, Philosophical Library, 1956. 579 p.
A moderately successful attempt to help the layman rather than the student or the specialist, containing some 7,000 entries with numerous cross references. Includes some biographical information and many proper names. The technical definitions are adequate, but the many errors of fact or interpretation detract from the usefulness of the work.

ENCYCLOPEDIAS AND
ENCYCLOPEDIC SETS

E173. Anthropology today; an encyclopedic inventory, prepared under the chairmanship of Alfred L. Kroeber. Chicago, Univ. of Chicago Press, 1953. 966 p.
Extensive survey of present anthropological knowledge presented by 50 specialists. Each "Inventory" or "Background" paper presents a systematic overview of the methods employed and substantive results obtained by research in a particular area of anthropological study. The material is divided into 3 major sections dealing with (1) problems of the historical approach; (2) problems of process; and (3) problems of application. Bibliographic references and a general index. These papers were presented at the Wenner-Gren Foundation International Symposium on Anthropology (1952). Discussion of these papers by scholars attending the symposium is reported in *An appraisal of anthropology today*, ed. by Sol Tax. (Chicago, Univ. of Chicago Press, 1953. 395 p.) Together these works form a statement of the status of anthropology in 1952 and a synthesis of what is expected to be done in the future. See also (E204).

E174. Biasutti, Renato. Le razze e i popoli della terra. 3 ed. Turin, Unione Tipografica-editrice Torinese, 1959. 4 v.
A comprehensive account of the physical and cultural anthropology of the world arranged on a regional basis. Each chapter has a good bibliography. Many illustrations, photographs and maps. One of the best general, not overly condensed surveys available to date. General index in v. 4. See also Hugo A. Bernatzik's *Die neue grosse Völkerkunde: Völker und Kulturen der Erde in Wort und Bild.* (Frankfurt am Main, Herkul, 1954. 3 v.)

E175. Ebert, Max. Reallexikon der Vorgeschichte, unter Mitwirkung zahlreicher Fachgelehrter, hrsg. von M. Ebert. Berlin, De Gruyter, 1924-32. 15 v.
The extensive and authoritative work on prehistory, each article prepared by a specialist. More important articles carry lengthy bibliographies and shorter entires have selected references. Each volume has ca. 130 plates and maps with the text referring to these in detail. Includes the ancient history of various countries. V. 15 is a general index.

E176. Ethnographic survey of Africa, ed. by Daryll Forde. London, International African Institute, 1950+ (In progress)
Aim of the survey is to present a concise, critical and accurate account of our present knowledge of the tribal groupings, distribution, physical environment, social conditions, political and economic structure, religious beliefs, cult practices, technology and art of the African peoples. Published as a series of separate studies each prepared by an expert and devoted to a particular people or cluster of peoples. Includes bibliographies.

E177. Steward, Julian H. Handbook of South American indians. Washington, Govt. Print. Off., 1946-1959. 7 v. (Bureau of American Ethnology. Bulletin no. 143)
A comprehensive synthesis of present knowledge of the aboriginal population of South America, indicating deficiencies in this knowledge and the needs of future research. The *Handbook* centers attention on the culture of each tribe at the time of its first contact with Europeans. V. 1, Marginal tribes; v. 2, Andean civilizations; v. 3, Tropical forest tribes; v. 4, Circum-Caribbean tribes; v. 5, Comparative ethnology; v. 6, Physical anthropology, linguistics, and cultural geography; v. 7, General index. Each volume contains a bibliography of all references cited in the

text. Many useful maps and photographs.

E178. Wauchope, Robert, *ed.* Handbook of Middle American indians. (In progress)

The area to be included in this work is Mexico and Central America. Thus it covers the area south of Hodge's *Handbook of North American indians* (E192) and will update recent developments in the southern Central American area also described in Steward's *Handbook of South American indians* (E177). The 11 volumes will cover natural environment, archaeology, ethnohistory, ethnology, social and physical anthropology, and language and linguistics. V. 6-7 will provide a guide to the sources and materials for ethnohistory; v. 6 covering general and chronological materials with listings of institutions, archives, periodical publications, primary sources, etc.; v. 7 consisting of specialized, annotated bibliographies for each of the major cultural areas of Middle America.

DIRECTORIES AND BIOGRAPHICAL INFORMATION

E179. "Associates in Current Anthropology as of April 1, 1962." *Current anthropology*, v. 3, June 1962: 319-368.

Lists over 2,300 world anthropologists giving for each: name, address, position and institution, field of specialization, areas of interest (by topic and geographical area). Useful supplement to the *International directory of anthropologists* (E181) until edition 4 is published.

E180. International directory of anthropological institutions, ed. by William L. Thomas, Jr. and Anna M. Pikelis. New York, Wenner-Gren Foundation for Anthropological Research, 1953. 468 p.

"The *Directory* is a handbook of world resources for research and education in anthropology conceived as a stocktaking supplementary to that inventory of the achievements of anthropology since published as *Anthropology today . . ."* (Pref.). Anthropology is broadly defined to include archaeology, prehistory, folk lore, linguistics, physical anthropology, ethnography, ethnology, social anthropology, and cultural anthropology. Gives for each country or area an outline of the history, scope, and status of anthropological research, followed by detailed information about individual educational institutions, research institutions and museums, professional associations, and subsidizing agencies. Basic geographic arrangement is supplemented by an alphabetical index of cities and towns, and another of institutions. A new edition is in the planning stage.

E181. International directory of anthropologists. 3d ed. Washington, Division of Anthropology and Psychology, National Research Council, 1950. 210 p.

A biographical directory of 2133 living anthropologists who returned questionnaires (137 who did not are listed in a separate section). Those included are mostly professionals (i.e., anthropologists who earn their living in the field, have earned higher degrees in anthropology and have made scholarly contributions, especially through research and publication). Information for each entry includes (when provided) address, education, degrees, fellowships, positions and offices held, brief description of research in progress and the location of his field research. Alphabetically arranged. No index. Edition 4 is currently in preparation.

ATLASES AND PICTORIAL WORKS

E182. Driver, Harold E., *et al.* Indian tribes of North America. Bal timore, Waverly Press, 1953. 30 p. and map. (Indiana University publications in anthropology and linguistics. Memoir 9)

This publication consists essentially of a map together with explanatory notes, a bibliography of sources, and an index of tribal names. It is the third attempt to provide a continental map assigning definite tribal territories to 238 tribes. The earlier maps were included in Alfred L. Kroeber's *Cultural areas of native North America* (Berkeley, Univ. of California Press, 1939. 242 p. [California publications in American archaeology and ethnology, v. 38]) and George P. Murdock's *Ethnographic bibliography of North America* (E157).

E183. Duggan-Cronin, A.M. The Bantu tribes of South Africa; reproductions of photographic studies done by A.M. Duggan-Cronin. Cambridge, Deighton, Bell, 1927+ (In progress)

A series of volumes each containing a collection of photographs focusing on the landscape, homesteads, scenes of daily life, costumes, ornaments or portraits of one or more tribes, together with notes on the photographs and an introductory essay by a specialist describing the culture of the people. A beautifully executed anthropological record.

E184. Fundaburk, Emma L. Southeastern indians: life portraits, a catalogue of pictures, 1564-1860. Luverne, Ala., Author, 1958. 135 p.

E185. Fundaburk, Emma L. and Mary D. Foreman. Sun circles and human hands; the southeastern indians—arts and industries. Luverne, Ala., Author, 1957. 232 p.

These two works are collections of illustrations depicting the life and customs of the indians of Southeastern United States, with descriptive and historical notes.

E186. LaFarge, Oliver. A pictorial history of the North American in-

dian. New York, Crown, 1956. 272 p.

A valuable summary for the specialist and introduction for the general reader. Follows the common pattern of describing the coming of man to the New World, followed by chapters on the cultural areas and finally one on the Indian in the modern world. Emphasis is on arts and crafts and way of life rather than social and political structure. Illustrations are well chosen from many sources including museum specimens and early drawings. Accompanying text is clear and concise. See also the important, but not always easily accessible, work of Edward S. Curtis, *The North American indian; being a series of volumes picturing and describing the indians of the United States and Alaska*, written, illustrated and published by Edward S. Curtis, ed. by Frederick W. Hodge. Seattle, 1907-1930. 20 v.

E187. Spencer, Robert F. and Elden Johnson. Atlas for anthropology. Dubuque, Iowa, W.C. Brown, 1960. 52 p.

A purposefully simplified students' manual of tribal, linguistic and social groupings. Cultural areas (maps 1-5); Language families (maps 6-10); Prehistory (maps 11-14); Racial distribution of mankind (map 15). Includes an alphabetical listing of ca. 500 tribal and ethnic groups with map references.

HANDBOOKS, MANUALS, COMPENDIA

E188. Bernatzik, Hugo A. Afrika; Handbuch der angewandten Völkerkunde. München, Bruckmann, 1951. 2 v.

This handbook of applied anthropology covers North Africa, Sudan, West Africa, East Africa, Congo, Angola-Zambesi area, South Africa and Madagasgar. For each area information is given on geography, history and ethnography in relation to problems of applied anthropology. Each chapter has a select bibliography.

E189. Coluccio, Felix. Diccionario del folklore americano (contribución). Buenos Aires, El Ateneo, 1954+ (In progress)
An alphabetical dictionary of Latin American folklore. The main section is preceded by a 3,394 item bibliography. References in each article refer to this bibliography.

E190. Funk and Wagnalls standard dictionary of folklore, mythology and legend, ed. by Maria Leach. New York, Funk & Wagnalls, 1949-50. 2 v.
A valuable compilation of information relative to the folklore of the world. It is selective in the sense that it attempts "to gather together a representative sample of the gods of the world, the folk heroes, the festivals, rites, etc." The entries range from very brief definitive statements to review articles (50) dealing with national folklore or subjects of central importance— folklore, ballad, dance, etc. Many entries are signed and contain references to the literature. The index and bibliography, as yet not published, will increase the general usefulness of the work.

E191. Hambly, Wilfrid D. Source book for African anthropology. Chicago, 1937. 953 p. (Field Museum of Natural History. Anthropological series, v. 26. Publication 394, 396)
A general synthesis and description of the cultures of Africa which discusses the significant results of anthropological work in Africa. Section I is a broad introduction to the salient facts of physiography, biology, archaeology, physical anthropology and linguistics. Section II views the continent in terms of culture area concepts. Section III discusses the basic nature of Negro culture (e.g., sexual life, education of children, religion, etc.). Section IV surveys the European period of African development. Selective but extensive bibliography listing over 2,600 book and periodical references. General index. A supplement to the bibliography was published in 1952 covering the years 1937-1949. *Bibliography of African anthropology, 1937-1949.* (Chicago, Natural History Museum, 1952. 292 p. [Fieldiana: Anthropology, v. 37, no. 2]).

E192. Hodge, Frederick W. Handbook of American indians north of Mexico. Washington, Govt. Print. Off., 1907-10. 2 v. (U.S. Bureau of American Ethnology. Bulletin 30)
An extensive compilation of authoritative information arranged alphabetically with a large number of cross references. Aims to give a brief description of every linguistic stock, confederacy, tribe, subtribe or tribal division, and settlement, with information concerning ethnic relations, history, languages, manners and customs, arts and industries. Each entry includes the origin and derivation of the name treated as well as a record of variant forms of the name with references to the authorities. These "synonyms" are assembled, in alphabetical order, in vol. 2 as cross references. All sources cited are listed in an extensive bibliography in vol. 2. Many articles include illustrations.

E193. Jenness, Diamond. The Indians of Canada. 3d ed. Ottowa, National Museum, 1955. 452 p. (National Museum Bulletin, 65)
A standard source of information on Canadian indians. Part I treats the various aspects of indian life under such headings as economic conditions, dwellings, social and political organization, religion, art and music, etc. Part II treats the various tribes individually. The work is well documented and includes 132 illustrations. General index. Maps.

E194. Kroeber, Alfred L. Handbook of the indians of California. Washington, Govt. Print. Off., 1925.

995 p. (Bureau of American Ethnology. Bulletin 78)

An encyclopedic guide to the culture and civilization of the Californian indians arranged in a series of 50 tribal descriptions. Includes 161 illustrations, maps, and a 415 item bibliography. Classified subject index and general index.

E195. Lowie, Robert H. Indians of the Plains. New York, published for the American Museum of Natural History by McGraw-Hill, 1954. 222 p. (Anthropological handbook no. 1)

A general summary of the culture of those indians who inhabited the area between the Mississippi and the Rocky Mountains. Chapters on material culture, social organization, recreation, art, supernaturalism, prehistory and history, and acculturation are supplemented by 105 illustrations, a brief bibliography and a general index.

E196. Meillet, A. and Marcel Cohen, eds. Les langues du monde. Nouv. éd. Paris, Centre National de la Recherche Scientifique, 1952. 1294 p.

The main reference work in linguistics covering upwards of 10,000 languages and dialects. Under each language group are given sections on classification, features, syntax, the various dialects and a comprehensive bibliography. For individual languages information is given on phonology, grammar, phraseology, morphology, etc. There is an annotated bibliography on classification and general linguistics. Appended is Atlas des langues du monde, containing 21 maps. Index of languages. A less detailed and more popular treatment is Mario A. Pei's The world's chief languages (5th rev. ed. New York, S.F. Vanno, 1960. 663 p.). See also: Atlas linguisticus, ed. by Albert Drexel. (Innsbruck, Austria, Druck und Verlag, 1934. 1 v.)

E197. Murdock, George P. Out-

line of world cultures. 3d ed. rev. New Haven, Conn., Human Relations Area Files, 1962. 227 p. (Behavior science outlines, no. 3)

Companion volume to the Outline of cultural materials (E198) prepared as a tool for the HRAF cross-cultural survey, this volume classifies by geographical region all known cultures in the world including extinct historical and prehistoric peoples.

E198. Murdock, George P. et al. Outline of cultural materials. 4th rev. ed. New Haven, Conn., Human Relations Area Files, 1960. 164 p. (Behavior science outlines, no. 1)

Originally developed as a tool for the cross-cultural survey instituted at Yale University in 1937, this classification scheme has as its ultimate purpose the organization into "readily accessible form the available data on a statistically representative sample of all known cultures, primitive, historical and contemporary, for the purpose of testing cross-cultural generalizations, revealing deficiencies in the descriptive literature, and directory corrective research." (Pref.) It is now the basic scheme used for the Human Relations Area Files. The scheme divides all cultural and background information into 79 major divisions and into 619 minor divisions. Following the number and title of each category is a descriptive statement of the type of information included along with cross references to other categories. Index.

E199. Royal Anthropological Institute. Notes and queries on anthropology. 6th ed., rev. London, Routledge and Kegan Paul, 1951. 403 p.

A valuable handbook giving concise and illuminating descriptions of the various factors and elements of the social life of non-literate peoples. Essentially a handbook of anthropological method. Excellent definitions of technical terms. Four major sections: (1) Physical anthropology, (2) Social anthropology, (3) Material culture and (4) Field antiquities. Analytical index.

E200. Seligman, Charles G. Races of Africa. 3d ed. London, Oxford Univ. Press, 1957. 236 p.

A concise treatment of the 9 major races indigenous to the African continent. Includes Bushmen, Hottentots, Negrillos, Negro, Hamites, Nilo-hamites, Nilotes, Bantu and Semites.

E201. Swanton, John R. Indian tribes of North America. Washington, Govt. Print. Off., 1952. 726 p. (Bureau of American Ethnology. Bulletin 145)

A useful compilation of information on indian tribes of North America. Major emphasis is upon indians of the states within the U.S., but some consideration is given to the tribes of Alaska, Canada, Greenland, Mexico, Central America and the West Indies. The tribal entries are arranged alphabetically under each state. Information includes: origin of tribal name and a brief list of important synonyms, tribal connections, the linguistic stock, location, history, population, and the "connection in which has become noted." 1650 is roughly the base date used in mapping tribal locations. References to the more important sources of information are included. Index of names and places.

E202. Thompson, Stith. Motif-index of folk-literature; a classification of narrative elements in folk-tales, ballads, myths, fables, medieval romances, exampla, fabliaux, jest-books and local legends. Rev. and enl. ed. Bloomington, Ind., Univ. of Indiana Press, 1955-58. 6 v.

This comprehensive and detailed classification scheme is based upon 23 main divisions (e.g., mythological motifs, animals, tabu, deceptions, chance and fate, society) each of which is minutely subdivided. Many of the motifs have extensive bibliographical references, while the rest have at least one instance of its appearance. Extensive cross references. Over 40,000 motifs are listed and indexed. V. 6 is an alphabetical index of motifs.

E203. Tischener, Herbert, *ed.* Völkerkunde. Frankfurt am Main, Fischer Bücherei, 1959. 370 p. (Das Fischer Lexikon, 13)

A concise but authoritative handbook of the ethnology of the Americas, Asia, Africa, Oceania and the Arctic regions arranged under 27 geographical headings. Each essay treats the material culture and technology, social organization, religion, magic and art of the primitive peoples of the area concerned. Illustrations. Index. A second work in the same series, dealing primarily with physical anthropology, contains much additional information, Gerhard Heberer, ed. *Anthropologie* (Frankfurt am Main, Fischer Bücherei, 1959. 362 p. [Das Fischer Lexikon, 15]).

YEARBOOKS

E204. Yearbook of Anthropology, 1955. New York, Wenner-Gren Foundation for Anthropological Research, 1955. 836 p.

Intended to be as complete a record as possible of the accomplishments in anthropology during the period 1952-54, emphasizing particularly the common interests of all engaged in anthropological research. The volume is divided into 6 parts each consisting of essays by specialists with bibliographies for each: 1) an essay on cultural and biological evolution; 2) 10 essays discussing "Man's Past"; 3) 8 essays on current theory; 4) 6 essays reporting on new developments in applied anthropology; 5) 13 essays reviewing work in Europe and Southwest Asia; 6) Reference data. The last includes a list of over 1,400 Ph.D. dissertations awarded at 61 institutions from

1870-1954. Only one issue of the *Yearbook* appeared. In 1956 19 of its essays were reprinted under the title *Current anthropology: a supplement to Anthropology today,* ed. by William L. Thomas, Jr. (Chicago, Univ. of Chicago Press, 1956. 377 p.) See also (E173). In 1957 the Foundation established the bimonthly journal *Current anthropology* to carry out the basic idea of interchange of information and the survey of progress expressed in the *Yearbook* and its predecessors. See (E208). The first issue appeared January, 1960.

ORIGINAL SOURCES

E205. Archives of archaeology. v. 1+ 1960+ Madison, Wis., published jointly by the Society for American Archaeology and the Univ. of Wisconsin Press.

A new series of occasional publications on microcard of primary documentation of archaeological investigations and related materials. Hopes to make available the primary data from archaeological sites which rarely is published in any form.

E206. Primary records in culture and personality, ed. by Bert Kaplan. Madison, Wis., Microcard Foundation, 1956+

The purpose of this microcard series is to make available for interpretation and further research hitherto unpublished source material and field data collected by anthropologists and psychologists. Primarily the materials pertain to individuals living outside the mainstream of western culture. Each volume consists of a number of separate contributions, each containing a set of data from a single culture. These data are of several types: Rorschachs, TATS, dreams, life histories. In addition each contribution includes an explanatory introduction by the contributor describing in general the nature of the study being conducted at the time the material was collected, the locale and characteristics of the culture group concerned, the methods used and conditions under which the samples were taken. Classified according to Murdock's *Outline of world cultures* (E197).

SOURCES OF SCHOLARLY CONTRIBUTIONS

E207. *Journals*

Africa. v. 1+ 1928+ London, International African Institute. quarterly. (Text in English, French and German)
Bibl Fremd Zeit; Bull Anal; Bull Sig; Soc Abst.

American anthropologist. v. 1+ 1888+ Menasha, Wis., American Anthropological Association. bimonthly.
Bibl Fremd Zeit; Bull Anal; Bull Sig; Int Ind; Psych Abst; Soc Abst.

American antiquity. v. 1+ 1935+ Madison, Wis., Society for American Antiquity. quarterly.
Bibl Fremd Zeit; Biol Abst; Bull Sig; Int Ind.

Anthropological quarterly. v. 1+ 1928+ Washington, D.C., Dept. of Anthropology, Catholic University of America. quarterly.
Bibl Fremd Zeit; Cath Ind.

Anthropologie. v. 1+ 1890+ Paris, Masson et Cie. bi-monthly.
Bibl Fremd Zeit; Biol Abst; Bull Sig.

Anthropos; revue internationale d'ethnologie et de linguistique. v. 1+ 1906+ Fribourg, Switz., Anthropos Institut. 3 a year. (Text in English, French and German)
Bibl Fremd Zeit; Bull Sig.

Arts et traditions populaires. v.

1+ 1953+ Paris, Société d'ethnographie française. quarterly.
Bull Sig.

Ethnology; an international journal of cultural and social anthropology. v. 1+ 1962+ Pittsburgh, Univ. of Pittsburgh. quarterly.

Ethnos. v. 1+ 1936+ Stockholm, Statens Etnografiska Museum. quarterly. (Text in German and English)
Bibl Fremd Zeit; Bull Sig.

Human Organization. v. 1+ 1941+ Ithaca, N.Y. Society for Applied Anthropology. quarterly.
Biol Abst; Int Ind; Psych Abst; Soc Abst.

International journal of American linguistics. v. 1+ 1917+ Bloomington, Ind. Indiana University. quarterly.
Bibl Fremd Zeit; Bull Sig; Psych Abst.

Journal of American folklore. v. 1+ 1888+ Philadelphia, American Folklore Society. quarterly.
Bibl Fremd Zeit; Bull Sig; Int Ind.

Man; a record of anthropological science. v. 1+ 1901+ London, Royal Anthropological Institute of Great Britain and Ireland. monthly.
Bibl Fremd Zeit; Biol Abst; Br Subj Ind; Bull Sig; Soc Abst.

Oceania; devoted to the study of the native peoples of Australia, New Guinea and the islands of the Pacific Ocean. v. 1+ 1930+ Sydney, Australia, Univ. of Sydney. quarterly.
Aust PAIS; Bibl Fremd Zeit; Bull Sig; Trop Abst.

Polynesian Society. Journal; a study of the native peoples of the Pacific area. v. 1+ 1892+ Wellington, N.Z. quarterly.
Bull Sig; N.Z. Ind; Soc Abst.

Royal Anthropological Institute of Great Britain and Ireland. Journal. v. 1+ 1871+ London. semi-annual.
Bibl Fremd Zeit; Biol Abst; Br Subj Ind; Bull Sig; Soc Abst.

Southwestern journal of anthropology. v. 1+ 1945+ Albuquerque, N.M., Univ. of New Mexico. quarterly.
Biol Abst; Bull Sig; Int Ind; Psych Abst; Soc Abst.

Zeitschrift für Ethnologie. v. 1+ 1869+ Braunschweig, Germany. Deutschen Gesellschaft für Völkerkunde. semi-annual.
Bibl Deut Zeit.

E208. *Organizations*

American Anthropological Association. Washington, D.C. Founded 1902.

American Ethnological Society. New York. Founded 1842.

American Folklore Society. Philadelphia. Founded 1888.

Bernice P. Bishop Museum. Honolulu, Hawaii. Founded 1889.

Bureau of American Ethnology. Washington, D.C. Founded 1879.

The Folk-lore Society. London. Founded 1878.

Human Relations Area Files. New Haven, Conn. Founded 1949. For a general description of this organization and its unique collection see Gladys W. White, "The Human Relations Area Files," *College and research libraries*, v. 19, March 1958: 111-117

International African Institute. London. Founded 1926.

International Union of Anthropological and Ethnological Sciences. Paris. Founded 1948.

Peabody Museum of Archaeology

and Ethnology, Harvard University. Cambridge, Mass. Founded 1866.

Polynesian Society, Inc. Wellington, N.Z. Founded 1892.

Rhodes-Livingstone Institute. Lusaka, Northern Rhodesia. Founded 1937.

Royal Anthropological Institute of Great Britain and Ireland. London. Founded 1843.

Société des Africanistes. Paris. Founded 1931.

Société des Américanistes. Paris. Founded 1895.

Société des Océanistes. Paris. Founded 1937.

Society for American Archaeology. Ann Arbor, Mich. Founded 1934.

Society for Applied Anthropology. New York. Founded 1941.

Wenner-Gren Foundation for Anthropological Research, Inc. New York. Founded 1941.

E209. *Monograph Series*

American Anthropological Association. Memoirs. v. 1+ 1905+ Menasha, Wis.

American Ethnological Society. Monographs. no. 1+ 1940+ New York.

American Ethnological Society. Publications. v. 1+ 1907+ New York.

American Folklore Society. Memoirs. v. 1+ 1894+ Philadelphia.

American Museum of Natural History. Anthropological Papers. v. 1+ 1907+ New York.

Bernice P. Bishop Museum. Memoirs. v. 1-12, 1899-1949. Honolulu.

Bernice P. Bishop Museum. Bulletin. no. 1+ 1922+ Honolulu.

Chicago Natural History Museum Fieldiana; Anthropology. v. 1+ 1895+ Chicago.

Columbia University. Contributions to Anthropology. v. 1+ 1913+ New York.

Etnografiska Museet. Etnografiska studier. v. 1+ 1935+ Göteborg, Sweden. (Text in English)

Kölner Ethnologische Mitteilungen. v. 1+ 1960+ Köln, Seminar für Völkerkunde, Universität Köln.

London University. London School of Economics and Political Science. Monographs in social anthropology. v. 1+ 1940+ London.

Peabody Museum of American Archaeology and Ethnology. Papers. v. 1+ 1888+ Cambridge, Mass.

Société d'Anthropologie de Paris. Bulletins et memoires. v. 1+ 1860+ Paris.

Society for Applied Anthropology. Monograph no. 1+ 1959+ Ithaca, N.Y.

U.S. *Bureau of American Ethnology.* Bulletin. no. 1+ 1886+ Washington, Govt. Print. Off.

Université de Paris. Institut d'Ethnologie. Travaux et memoires. v. 1+ 1926+ Paris, Musée de l'Homme.

Universiteti Uppsala. Studia ethnographica Upsaliensia. v. 1+ 1950+ Uppsala, Sweden. (Text in English, French and German)

University of California. Folklore studies. v. 1+ 1953+ Berkeley.

University of California. Publications in American archaeology and ethnology. v. 1+ 1903+ Berkeley.

University of Oklahoma. Civilization of the American indian. v. 1+ 1940+ Norman.

Wenner-Gren Foundation for Anthropological Research. Viking Fund publications in anthropology. v. 1 + 1943 + New York.

Yale University. Publications in anthropology. v. 1 + 1936 + New Haven, Conn.

SOURCES OF CURRENT INFORMATION

E210. International Committee on Urgent Anthropological and Ethnographical Research. Bulletin. no. 1 + 1959 + Vienna, Institut für Völkerkunde. irreg.

Reports on localities, cultures, languages, ethnic groups, etc., where research is urgently needed in order to save data which might otherwise be lost.

E211. Current anthropology; a world journal of the sciences of man. v. 1 + 1960 + Chicago, Univ. of Chicago. 6 a year.

Designed to supplement on a current and continuing basis the concepts established in the *Yearbook of Anthropology* (E204). Aims to be a forum for world-wide interchange of ideas and a vehicle for surveying current progress in anthropology. Includes short articles, news items, and a directory issue (E179).

E212. Fellow newsletter. v. 1 + 1947 + Washington, D.C. American Anthropological Association. monthly except July and August.

The major news and information medium of the Association. Includes Association news, a meeting calendar, grants and fellowships, field training programs, information on new journals, and news of individual anthropologists and the profession.

E213. Katunob; a newsletter bulletin on Mesoamerican anthropology. no. 1 + 1960 + Magnolia, Arkansas,

Dept. of Sociology and Anthropology, Southern State College. quarterly.

A source of current information on all aspects of Middle American Anthropology, linguistics and archaeology. Reports new projects, research, publications etc., as well as news of interest originally published elsewhere.

SOURCES OF UNPUBLISHED INFORMATION

E214. "Dissertations in anthropology," *Kroeber Anthropological Society Papers*. Berkeley, Calif., 1956 + irreg.

List masters' theses and Ph.D. dissertations, beginning in no. 15 for the year 1955-56, from 25 American institutions (some of which do not participate in *Dissertation abstracts*). For each entry gives author, title, degree, month and year award, pages, and when applicable plans for publication. This same series also publishes, beginning with no. 14, abstracts of dissertations done at Univ. of Calif. from 1946+

E215. Dockstader, Frederick J. The American indian in graduate study; a bibliography of theses and dissertations. New York, Museum of the American Indian, Heye Foundation, 1957. 399 p. (It's Contributions, 15)

A listing of 3,684 theses and dissertations which deal in any way with New World aborigines, including the Eskimo, done at 203 institutions in the U.S. (191), Canada (9) and Mexico (3) between 1890 and 1955. "The criterion has been the selection of all graduate studies which consider the indian to the extent of at least one chapter . . ." (Preface). The bibliography does not attempt to be critical but about half the entries have brief informative annotations. Arrangement is alphabetical by author, giving for each entry the degree, date, institution, title, pages, and reference to the published version (if any). The 35 page index includes topics, tribes, archaeological sites, geographical names, etc.

Thompson M. Little
Carl M. White

6

Psychology

Psychology, the scientific study of behavior and experience, has shown in relatively recent years a considerable surge of growth with an attendant diversity. The problems psychologists are interested in, the methods they use, and the implicit assumptions they make vary both within national boundaries and from country to country. In some countries, especially the United States, many scholars have left the academic scene to turn to the practice of psychology. The scientific field itself makes contact on one side with its biological neighbors, particularly physiology, and, on the other, with those in the social sciences, especially sociology. Since much psychology is quantitative, there is another direction of relationship, that with mathematics through use of statistics. In France and Germany, much psychological endeavor is still consciously rooted in philosophical speculation, creating still another dimension. Psychology as a profession makes contact with the general public, with physicians and psychoanalysts, with industrial personnel, with teachers, counselors and school children, to name but a few. Consequently, books by physiologists, statisticians, psychoanalysts and the like, if they have been appropriated by psychologists, must be considered. Only in the case of sociology, for which another account is available, is rigid exclusion practiced.

Today over half of the world's psychologists are found in English-speaking countries. It should come as no surprise that books in English predominate; but attention is also paid to psychological works in German and French. Books in other languages have not been considered. Analysis shows that, of the 249 books included, 181 originally appeared in English (22 from Great Britain and Canada), 49 in German, 17 in French and 2 in other languages. Whenever feasible, an edition in English is given. Nevertheless, 13 books in French and 29 in German are included.

The organizational scheme used for the books that follow throws some light on the major subdivisions of the field of psychology. General and experimental psychology is considered first, followed by a discussion of the tool subject of statistics. The history of psychology is then taken up. Specific subdivisions of general psychology are then examined—systems of psychology, personality theories, learning, feeling, feeling and emotion, thought and language, and sensation. This last-mentioned topic is so intimately related to physiological psychology that the two are discussed together. It is at this point that perspective shifts from subdivisions of general psychology to the various branches of psychology. Aside from physiological psychology, they are grouped in order: social psychology, abnormal psychology, animal psychology, developmental psychology, testing and individual differences, and applied psychology.

GENERAL AND EXPERIMENTAL PSYCHOLOGY

General textbooks serve to introduce the field of psychology. The ones that follow are among those that have in common the characteristics of solid scholarship, wide adoption, some depth in coverage, and no blatant appeal to popularization. Although not a textbook, an excellent introduction to the present state of German psychology is the volume edited by Hofstätter in the famous "Fischer Lexikon" series.

F1. Hilgard, Ernest R. Introduction to psychology. 2d ed. New York, Harcourt, Brace, 1957. 653 p.
F2. Hofstätter, Peter R., *ed.* Psychologie. Frankfurt am Main, Fischer, 1957. 367 p. (Fischer Lexikon, 6)
F3. Morgan, Clifford T. Introduction to psychology. New York, McGraw-Hill, 1956. 676 p.
F4. Munn, Norman L. Psychology: the fundamentals of human adjustments. 4th ed. Boston, Houghton Mifflin, 1961. 812 p.
F5. Rohracher, Hubert. Einführung in die Psychologie. 5. Aufl. Wien, Urban and Schwarzenberg, 1953. 568 p.
F6. Thouless, Robert H. General and social psychology: a textbook for students of psychology and the social sciences. 4th ed. London, University Tutorial Press, 1958. 464 p.

The core of psychology is general experimental psychology. Over fifty years ago Titchener published a manual of experimental psychology which is still a major reference work for the early literature, especially that on sensory experience and psychophysics. Murchison's manual is also out-of-date, but some among the twenty chapters are still valuable. The volume edited by Stevens is indispensable as a modern reference work. Each of its sections has several chapters. The sections are concerned with psychological mechanisms, growth and development, learning, motivation, cognitive and speech processes, sensory process and performance.

F7. Katz, David and Rosa Katz, *eds.* Handbuch der Psychologie. 2. Aufl. Basel, Schwabe, 1960. 666 p.
F8. Murchison, Carl. A handbook of general experimental psychology. Worcester, Mass., Clark Univ. Press, 1934. 1125 p.
F9. Stevens, Stanley S., *ed.* Handbook of experimental psychology. New York, Wiley, 1951. 1436 p.
F10. Titchener, Edward B. Experimental psychology; a manual of laboratory practice. New York, Macmillan, 1901-05. 2 v. in 1.

Textbooks in experimental psychology are written with a laboratory course in mind. They try to present the experiments on the traditional topics of psychophysics, sensation, perception, learning, motivation, emotion and the "higher mental processes." Fraisse supplies a French, and Pauli a German manual of experiments to be performed. To some extent they are parallel to American manuals which are also available.

F11. Fraisse, Paul. Manual pratique de psychologie experimentale. Paris, Presses Universitaires de France, 1956. 316 p.
F12. Osgood, Charles E. Method and theory in experimental psychology. New York, Oxford Univ. Press, 1953. 800 p.
F13. Pauli, Richard. Psychologisches Praktikum. 6. Aufl. Stuttgart, Fischer, 1957. 325 p.
F14. Underwood, Benton J. Experimental psychology; an introduction. New York, Appleton, 1949. 638 p.
F15. Woodworth, Robert S. and Harold Scholsberg. Experimental psychology. Rev. ed. New York, Holt, 1954. 948 p.

Although the above-mentioned books devote some attention to experimental methods, they tend to emphasize content rather than method. Other books are more concerned with the question of how research in experimental psychology is conducted. This group of books varies in amount of statistical material, and, hence, in the degree of overlap with books in that section. In terms of direct concern with experimental design to the relative exclusion of statistics, they can be ordered as follows: Underwood, Fisher, Edwards, and Cochran and Cox.

F16. Cochran, William G. and Gertrude M. Cox. Experimental designs. 2d ed. New York, Wiley, 1957. 611 p.
F17. Edwards, Allen L. Experimental design in psychological research. Rev. ed. New York, Rinehart, 1960. 398 p.
F18. Fisher, Ronald A. The design of experiments. 7th ed. New York, Hafner, 1960. 248 p.
F19. Underwood, Benton J. Psychological research. New York, Appleton, 1957. 298 p.

Series of handbooks are being written which attempt in systematic fashion to encompass psychology in general. The seven volumes of *Psychology; a study of a science*, edited by Koch, four of which have appeared, will be the most comprehensive handbook series in English when completed. A German series, edited by Lersch and Thomae, is also in process. Since the volumes in both series deal with segments of the field, each of those volumes which have appeared is mentioned later in its appropriate place.

STATISTICS

Statistical procedures are important tools of psychological research. In this area American and British workers have taken the lead. In the books that follow there is but one translation from the German, the rest having been written in English. There are introductory (Edwards, Underwood), intermediate (McNemar, Vernon, and Yule and Kendall), and an advanced general text (Kendall). There are also specialized books on factor analysis (Burt, Harman and Thurstone), probability theory and practice (von Mises), psychometric and psychological methods (Guilford), nonparametric statistics (Siegel), sampling (Cochran), elementary (Torgerson) and advanced scaling (Gulliksen and Messick). Statistics as a tool is used in all branches of psychology, but in other sections the books with which there is greatest direct overlap are those on tests and experimental design.

F20. Burt, Cyril L. The factors of the mind: an introduction to factor analysis in psychology. New York, Macmillan 1941. 509 p.
F21. Cochran, William G. Sampling techniques. New York, Wiley, 1953. 330 p.
F22. Edwards, Allen L. Statistical analysis. Rev. ed. New York, Holt, Rinehart and Winston, 1958. 234 p.
F23. Guilford, Joy P. Psychometric methods. 2d ed. New York, McGraw-Hill, 1954. 597 p.
F24. Gulliksen, Harold and Samuel Messick, *eds.* Psychological scaling: theory and applications. New York, Wiley, 1960. 211 p.
F25. Harman, Harry H. Modern factor analysis. Chicago, Univ. of Chicago Press, 1960. 469 p.
F26. Kendall, Maurice G. The advanced theory of statistics. 3d ed. London, Griffin, 1947-48. 2 v.
F27. McNemar, Quinn. Psychological statistics. 3d ed. New York, Wiley, 1962. 468 p.
F28. Mises, Richard von. Probability, statistics and truth. 2d ed. New York, Macmillan, 1957. 244 p.
F29. Siegel, Sidney. Nonparametric statistics for the behavioral sciences. New York, McGraw-Hill, 1956. 312 p.
F30. Thurstone, Louis L. Multiple factor analysis. Chicago, Univ. of Chicago Press, 1947. 535 p.
F31. Torgerson, Warren S. Theory and methods of scaling. New York, Wiley, 1958. 460 p.

F32. Underwood, Benton J. Elementary statistics. Rev. ed. New York, Appleton-Century-Crofts, 1954. 239 p.
F33. Vernon, Philip E. The measurement of abilities. 2d ed. London, University of London Press, 1956. 276 p.
F34. Yule, George U. and Maurice G. Kendall. An introduction to the theory of statistics. 14th ed. London, Griffin, 1950. 701 p.

HISTORY OF PSYCHOLOGY

Psychology can lay claim to at least three books which may be considered as classics. *The principles* by William James, originally published in 1890, shows the greatest continuity with the earlier philosophical tradition from which psychology emerged. Its charm, its penetration, and its scope have lifted it to a position as one of the great books in the world literature. Early editions of books by psychology's most prolific writer, Wilhelm Wundt, preceded that of James. It is generally agreed that the *Grundzüge*, which went through many German editions between 1874 and 1911, is his most important work. The monograph by Ebbinghaus, first published in 1885, concerned with learning and memory, was psychology's most memorable early research study.

F35. Ebbinghaus, Hermann. Memory: a contribution to experimental psychology, tr., by H.A. Ruger. New York, Teachers College, Columbia University, 1913. 193 p.
F36. James, William The principles of psychology. New York, Holt, 1890. 2 v.
F37. Wundt, Wilhelm. Grundzüge der physiologischen Psychologie. 6. Aufl. Leipzig, Engelmann, 1908-11 3 v.

First-rate books about the history of psychology are not numerous. The abridged Brett's *History* is the only one which attempts to say anything about the period extending from the Pre-Socratic Greeks through the Middle Ages; but this part was written over fifty years ago. Of the two standard general histories of the modern experimental period, that by Boring is the more detailed and authoritative.

F38. Boring, Edwin G. A history of experimental psychology. 2d ed. New York, Appleton-Century-Crofts, 1957. 777 p.
F39. Boring, Edwin G. Sensation and perception in the history of experimental psychology. New York, Appleton, 1942. 644 p.
F40. Brett, George S. History of psychology, ed. and abridged by R.S. Peters. New York, Macmillan, 1953. 742 p.
F41. Dennis, Wayne, ed. Readings in the history of psychology. New York, Appleton-Century-Crofts, 1948. 587 p.
F42. Murphy, Gardner. Historical introduction to modern psychology. Rev. ed. New York, Harcourt, 1951. 466 p.

SUBDIVISIONS OF GENERAL PSYCHOLOGY

Systems of Psychology

There is considerable agreement among psychologists on the nature of their science as exemplified by the books in general and experimental psychology. Nevertheless, there have been, and will continue to be, attempts to stress some area within a larger framework, such as personality or learning, some principle such as Gestalt, some goal such as behaviorism, or some method such as psychoanalysis. It is in this context that one can speak of systems of psychology and theories of personality and theories of learning. Systems of psychology on the one hand, and theories of personality and of learning on the other, differ in emphasis. Systems are more extensive, and may have subsumed under them narrower theories of personality and theories of learning. For example, psychoanalysis and Gestalt psychology include a personality theory. In contrast, theories of both personality and of learning make central that particular issue, while treating other aspects of psychology as peripheral. The books concerned with the broader systems, behaviorism, Gestalt psychology, psychoanalysis and related systems, and a small miscellaneous group, will be examined at this juncture, leaving for later discussion personality and learning theories.

Inclusive secondary accounts are available. Woodworth discusses various systems, behaviorism, Gestalt psychology, psychoanalysis and the like, while Chaplin and Krawiec organize their presentation around such topics as sensation, learning and motivation as they are dealt with by the systems.

The book edited by Marx, and that by Feigel and Scriven contain papers on the theoretical foundations for psychology, many of which deal with the systems but also include those concerned with a host of other problems, such as operationism, theoretical constructs, and the like, which cut across the theories and systems. Brunswik logically analysed modern psychological systems. In many books Piaget has given a statement of his use of logic as a technique for analysing behavior and a model for his thinking. A representative account is listed.

F43. Brunswik, Egon. The conceptual framework of psychology. Chicago, Univ. of Chicago Press, 1952. 102 p.
F44. Chaplin, James P. and Theophile S. Krawiec. Systems and theories of psychology. New York, Holt, Rinehart and Winston, 1960. 473 p.
F45. Feigl, Herbert and Michael Scriven *eds*. The foundations of science and the concepts of psychology and psychoanalysis. Minneapolis, Univ. of Minnesota Press, 1956. 346 p.
F46. Marx, Melvin H., *ed*. Psychological theory: contemporary readings. New York, Macmillan, 1951. 585 p.
F47. Piaget, Jean. Logic and psychology. New York, Basic Books, 1957. 48 p.

F48. Woodworth, Robert S. Contemporary schools of psychology. Rev. ed. New York, Ronald, 1948. 279 p.

First expressed in talks and articles, the behaviorism of John B. Watson rapidly gained acceptance from many American psychologists during the second and third decades of this century. Watson advocated psychology conceived as a purely experimental science and the banishment of introspection and mentalistic thinking as a relic of the Middle Ages. One of his two most influential books, *Psychology from the standpoint of a behaviorist,* first appeared in 1919. His views changed over the years, making authoritative the third revised edition. This book needs supplementation by a second statement, written in more popular terms, called *Behaviorism.*

F49. Watson, John B. Behaviorism. Rev. ed. Chicago, Univ. of Chicago Press, 1930. 308 p.
F50. Watson, John B. Psychology from the standpoint of a behaviorist. 3d rev. ed. Philadelphia, Lippincott, 1929. 458 p.

In 1910 Gestalt psychology came into being in Frankfurt, as the result of an experiment conducted by Max Wertheimer, with Wolfgang Köhler and Kurt Koffka as subjects. These three psychologists were destined to maintain leadership in the work of this system. In the twenties and thirties, they all migrated to the United States where their work became well known. The Gestalt movement was characterized by a vigorous attack on the view that would have mental life reducible to elements such as sensory qualities. It espoused a phenomenological approach, recognizing that there are psychological properties of wholes not reducible to parts. Wertheimer wrote no detailed, complete, systematic statement of his views. In addition to the books by Koffka and Köhler, a current German statement of Gestalt psychology is to be found in Metzger. It is hard reading, but it is perhaps the most orthodox systematic treatise that is available. Gestalt publications on specialized topics are mentioned later.

F51. Koffka, Kurt. Principles of Gestalt psychology. New York, Harcourt, 1935. 720 p.
F52. Köhler, Wolfgang. Gestalt psychology: an introduction to new concepts in modern psychology. Rev. ed. New York, Liveright, 1947. 369 p.
F53. Metzger, Wolfgang. Psychologie: die Entwicklung ihrer Grundannahmen seit der Einführung des Experiments. 2. Aufl. Darmstadt, Steinkopff, 1954. 407 p.

As a psychological system or theory, psychoanalysis is a more or less distinct field, with many of its practitioners and theorists allied with fields other than psychology. Psychoanalysis grew out of Freud's work with neurotic adults. In the course of this work, he developed a method of diagnosis and treatment called free association; a conviction of the importance of unconscious functions, particularly sexual, as determinants of an individual's behavior; a theory of personality, based upon Id, Ego and Superego functioning; and a theory of stages of psychosexual development.

Sigmund Freud was a productive writer for many years. His *Collected works* has appeared in English and German. If a selection must be made, his *Interpretation of dreams*, first published in 1900, is a classic of the highest magnitude. His *Introduction*, and the supplement of many years later, *The new introductory lectures*, give a reasonable coverage of his views.

Even during Freud's lifetime, changes within orthodox psychoanalysis were taking place. Emphasis on so-called ego functioning was a major development. Anna, Freud's daughter, published a major work in this area, as did Heinz Hartmann.

The volume edited by Levitt has chapters contributed by various experts on psychoanalytic theory. An examination of the scientific status of psychoanalysis by Pumpian-Mindlin, Hilgard and Kubie is valuable. Munroe presented not only orthodox psychoanalysis but also the related systems discussed next. Other volumes in the psychoanalytic tradition are found in sections dealing with more specialized topics.

F54. Freud, Anna. The ego and the mechanisms of defense. New York, International Universities Press, 1946. 196 p.
F55. Freud, Sigmund. The interpretation of dreams, tr. and ed. by John John Strachey. New York, Basic Books, 1955. 692 p.
F56. Freud, Sigmund. A general introduction to psychoanalysis. New York, Boni and Liveright, 1920. 406 p.
F57. Freud, Sigmund. New introductory lectures on psychoanalysis. New York, Norton, 1933. 257 p.
F58. Hartmann, Heinz. Ego psychology and the problem of adaption, tr. by David Rappaport. New York, International Universities Press, 1958. 121 p.
F59. Levitt, Morton, *ed*. Readings in psychoanalytic psychology. New York, Appleton-Century-Crofts, 1959. 413 p.
F60. Munroe, Ruth L. Schools of psychoanalytic thought; an exposition, critique, and attempt at integration. New York, Dryden, 1955. 670 p.
F61. Pumpian-Mindlin, Eugene, *ed*. Psychoanalysis as science. Stanford, Calif., Stanford Univ. Press, 1952. 174 p.

Views related to the psychoanalytic, but sufficiently distinct to warrant separate mention, have been expressed by the so-called Neo-Freudians. The Neo-Freudians tend to assimilate a considerable amount of Freudian theory into a more distinctively social framework which could have justified later mention in connection with social psychology.

F62. Fromm, Erich. Escape from freedom. New York, Farrrar and Rinehart, 1941. 305 p.

F63. Horney, Karen. The neurotic personality of our time. New York, Norton 1937. 299 p.
F64. Sullivan, Harry S. The interpersonal theory of psychiatry. New York, Norton, 1953. 393 p.

Alfred Adler, who originally worked with Freud, developed his own distinctive point of view, individual psychology. He placed specific emphasis upon inferiority feelings and upon man's inherent social interest, along with a general emphasis upon social factors. He published a great deal, but much of it was not systematically organized. The Ansbachers reorganized selections from his writings and published them along with annotations. An authoritative account is also given by Dreikurs.

F65. Adler, Alfred. The individual psychology of Alfred Adler; a systematic presentation in selections from his writings, ed. by Heinz L. Ansbacher and Rowena R. Ansbacher. New York, Basic Books, 1956. 503 p.
F66. Dreikurs, Rudolf. Fundamentals of Adlerian psychology. New York, Greenberg, 1950. 117 p.

Carl Gustave Jung, another Freudian collaborator, was also prolific. His theory, referred to as *analytic psychology*, stressed unconscious factors as did Freud's, but made the postulated energy of the libido nonsexual in nature, including a large collective component, and depended heavily for evidence upon myths, legends, and cultural history, along with exploration of the mental life of disturbed individuals. Jung's complete works are being published volume by volume. His style and topical organization make it very difficult to arrive at a representative selection. His work having the most appeal to psychologists is that on word association and psychological types. A broader representative statement of his theory of the unconscious is contained in *The structure and dynamics of the Psyche*. A secondary account is given by Jacobi.

F67. Jacobi, Jolan. The psychology of C.G. Jung. Rev. ed. New Haven, Conn., Yale Univ. Press, 1951. 244 p.
F68. Jung, Carl G. Studies in word association. London, Heinemann, 1918. 575 p.
F69. Jung, Carl G. Contributions to analytic psychology. New York, Harcourt, Brace, 1928. 410 p.
F70. Jung, Carl G. The structure and dynamics of the psyche. New York, Pantheon, 1960. 596 p. (His Collected works, v. 8)

There are three other systems that must be mentioned at this point, even though they bear no relation to one another. In his account of how behavior is organized, Hebb emphasized the use of neurological concepts. In the Continental tradition of Dilthey, Spranger and Jaspers, Gruhle writes on "Verstehende" psychology, Wellek supplies an intuitive, holistic development of the approach of Felix Krueger which owed part of its inspiration to Gestalt psychology.

F71. Gruhle, Hans W. Verstehende Psychologie (Erlebnislehre). 2. verb.
    Aufl. Stuttgart, Thieme, 1956. 633 p.
F72. Hebb, Donald O. The organization of behavior; a neuropsychological
    theory. New York, Wiley, 1949. 335 p.
F73. Wellek, Albert. Ganzheitspsychologie und Strukturtheorie. Bern,
    Francke, 1955. 258 p.

Theories of Personality

Although narrower than systems, theories of personality are still relatively broad in scope. Most often a psychologist advancing a personality
theory attempts to account for the uniqueness of the individual, the relation of broad patterns of his behavior to his experiences and his com-
monality with other men. Other psychological topics, for example, the
other sub-divisions of general psychology are minimized, if dealt with at
all. This serves to distinguish a personality theory from a psychological
system which, by definition, must come to grips with these other aspects
of psychology.

In a secondary source, Hall and Lindzey bring together the Freudian,
Neo-Freudian, Adlerian and Jungian systems, along with many of the
theories to be considered later. The volume edited by Kluckhohn and
Murray is valuable, not only for giving their specific views on personality, but also for the inclusion of articles by others on the formation of
personality and on the influence of constitutional, group-membership,
role, and situational determinants upon personality formation. A handbook on personality, edited by Hunt, is supposed to appear shortly in a
new revision. Meanwhile, the original 1944 edition is still a standard
source for an account of personality and its theories. The second volume,
most of which is devoted to the behavior disorders, is valuable for its account of abnormal psychology as well. A volume in the Koch edited
series is concerned with a somewhat disconnected array of worthwhile
articles most directly related to personality but also peripherally related
to social psychology. The textbook by Stagner on personality is meant to
present a systematic survey of facts about personality, irrespective of
their particular theoretical origin. In a sense, this eventuated in an
eclectic theory. McClelland, too, has written an eclectic book, using the
device of relating each theoretical construct to the personality of the
same individual. This gives added coherence to his presentation.

F74. Hall, Calvin S. and Gardner Lindzey. Theories of personality. New
    York, Wiley, 1957. 572 p.
F75. Hunt, Joseph M., ed. Personality and the behavior disorders; a hand-
    book based on experimental and clinical research. New York,
    Ronald, 1944. 2 v.
F76. Kluckhohn Clyde, ed. Personality in nature, society, and culture. 2d
    rev. ed. New York, Knopf, 1953. 701 p.
F77. Koch, Sigmund, ed. Psychology; a study of a science. Study I: Con-
    ceptual and systematic. Vol. 3: Formulations of the person and
    social context. New York, McGraw-Hill, 1959. 837 p.

F78. McClelland, David C. Personality. New York, Dryden, 1951. 634 p.
F79. Stagner, Ross. Psychology of personality. 3d ed. New York, McGraw-
      Hill, 1961. 586 p.

Certain theories of personality are influential in the United States. Allport, influenced by Gestalt psychology, William Stern, and William James among others, has worked out a theory of development and organization of the personality that is of relatively wide scope. While doing so, he managed to encompass much eclectic material by making basic the concept of trait. A factor analysis of personality trait measures characterizes the approach of Cattell. A volume representative of his several books is listed. Based upon a wide and deep acquaintance with the psychological literature, the personality theory of Murphy is eclectic and yet reasonably consistent throughout. Sheldon has intensively studied physique as related to temperament and thereby developed a theory of personality.

F80. Allport, Gordon W. Pattern and growth in personality. New York,
      Holt, Rinehart and Winston, 1961. 593 p.
F81. Cattell, Raymond B. Descriptions and measurement of personality.
      Yonkers, N.Y., World Book, 1946. 602 p.
F82. Murphy, Gardner. Personality; a biosocial approach to origins and
      structure. New York, Harper, 1947. 999 p.
F83. Sheldon, William H. The varieties of human physique; an introduc-
      tion to constitutional psychology. New York, Harper, 1940. 347 p.
F84. Sheldon, William H. The varieties of temperament; a psychology of
      constitutional differences. New York, Harper, 1942. 520 p.

In Great Britain, Eysenck has used a rigorous operational approach to research on personality. A representative book on his dimensional theory of the behavior of neurotic and non-neurotic individuals is listed.

F85. Eysenck, Hans J. The scientific study of personality. London, Rout-
      ledge and Kegan Paul, 1952. 320 p.

In Germany there is wide-spread interest in personality. A volume in the new German handbook series, edited by Lersch and Thomae, is devoted to the problem. The work of Spranger on types is well known both in Europe and in the United States (There is an earlier edition to his work available in English). Kretschmer's work on physique and character is, if anything, better known. In this instance, the available English translation is so out of date as to give a grotesque picture of his work. The most famous book on graphology, a subject in which interest is widely current on the Continent, is that of Klages. Typological systems and character structures in the German tradition are described by Helwig, while an introductory statement of characterology is supplied by Rohracher. Theories of the stratification of personality are held by many German psychologists. Complimentary views are given by Lersch and by Rothacker, while a synthesis is attempted by Thiele.

F86. Helwig, Paul. Charakterologie. 2. veränderte Aufl. Stuttgart, Klett, 1952. 311 p.

F87. Klages, Ludwig. Handschrift and Charakter. 24. Aufl. Bonn, Bouvier, 1956. 259 p.

F88. Kretschmer, Ernest. Körperbau und Charakter. 21 und 22. wesentlich verb. und verm. Aufl. Berlin, Springer, 1955. 444 p.

F89. Lersch, Philipp. Aufbau der Person. 7. Aufl. München, Barth, 1956. 590 p.

F90. Lersch, Philipp and Hans Thomae, *eds.* Persönlichkeitsforschung und Persönlichkeitstheorie. Göttingen, Verlag für Psychologie, 1960. 612 p. (Handbuch der Psychologie. Band 4)

F91. Rohracher, Hubert. Kleine Charakterkunde. 7. Aufl. Wien, Urban & Schwarzenberg, 1956. 254 p.

F92. Rothacker, Erich. Die Schichten der Persönlichkeit. 5. Aufl. Bonn, Bouvier, 1953. 184 p.

F93. Spranger, Eduard. Lebensformen. 8. Aufl. Tübingen, Neomarius-Verlag, 1950. 450 p.

F94. Thiele, Rudolf. Person und Charakter. Leipzig, Thieme, 1940. 43 p.

French and Belgian views of personality warrant summarization. Wallon's system of characterology is empirically based and highly respected on the Continent. Based upon LeSenne's speculative philosophical system of characterology, Berger prepared a manual of character analysis, while Caille combined LeSenne's system with graphology. A self-realization theory of personality is advanced by Nuttin.

F95. Berger, Gaston. Traité pratique d'analyse du caractère. Paris, Presses Universitaires de France, 1950. 250 p.

F96. Caille, Emile. Caractères et écritures. Paris, Presses Universitaires de France, 1957. 292 p.

F97. Nuttin, Jozef. Psychoanalysis and personality; a dynamic theory of normal personality. New York, Sheed and Ward, 1953. 310 p.

F98. Wallon, Henri. Les origines du caractère chez l'enfant. 2. éd. Paris, Presses Universitaires de France, 1949. 233 p.

Learning

Learning is the single most dominant field of research in American psychology today. It is of secondary interest on the Continent, as exemplified by the inclusion here of hardly any European work. On the basis of experimental evidence, many prominent psychologists have promoted a general, over-all, theoretical point of view in which learning is made central. They hope there will eventually be a broader system. With commendable caution it is assumed that if one works thoroughly with the central issue of learning, then the other problems in psychology, relatively neglected for the moment, will be seen in the perspective of the research findings of learning, making it possible to cope with them thereafter. Research workers on learning do not deny that there are other problems in psychology. They merely insist that learning is a strategically appropriate place to start work on building the science of psychology.

The current major points of view are represented by Bush and Mosteller's linear operator probability model, Estes' statistical association model, Guthrie's contiguous conditioning, Hull's systematic behavior theory, Skinner's operant conditioning, Spence's modification of systematic behavior theory, Thorndike's connectionism and Tolman's sign-Gestalt, cognitive theory. Related to more inclusive systems of the kind mentioned earlier are Pavlovian conditioning and Köhler's Gestalt approach to learning. Some of these points of view are brought together in the handbook series edited by Koch.

Although these various points of view are sufficiently distinct to warrant the terms that have been applied, there is actually a considerable body of agreement about the results of research studies in learning. Major secondary accounts of learning have been prepared by Hilgard and by Hilgard and Marquis. A phenomenological analysis of memory and forgetting in the European tradition is supplied by Gurdorf.

F99. Bush, Robert R. and Frederick Mosteller. Stochastic models for learning. New York, Wiley, 1955. 365 p.

F100. Estes, William K., *et al.* Modern learning theory. New York, Appleton-Century-Crofts, 1954. 379 p.

F101. Gusdorf, Georges Memoire et personne. Paris, Presses Universitaires de France, 1951. 2 v.

F.102. Guthrie, Edwin R. The psychology of learning. Rev. ed. New York, Harper, 1952. 310 p.

F103. Hilgard, Ernest R. Theories of learning. 2d ed. New York, Appleton-Century-Crofts, 1956. 563 p.

F104. Hilgard, Ernest R. and Donald G. Marquis. Conditioning and learning, rev. by Gregory A. Kimble. 2d ed. New York, Appleton-Century-Crofts, 1961. 590 p.

F105. Hull, Clark L. A behavior system; an introduction to behavior theory concerning the individual organism. New Haven, Conn., Yale Univ. Press, 1952. 372 p.

F106. Hull, Clark L. Principles of behavior; an introduction to behavior theory. New York, Appleton-Century-Crofts, 1943. 422 p.

F107. Koch, Sigmund, *ed.* Psychology; a study of a science. Study I: Conceptual and systematic. Vol. 2: General systematic formulations, learning, and special processes. New York, McGraw-Hill, 1959. 706 p.

F108. Köhler, Wolfgang. The mentality of apes. New York, Harcourt, Brace, 1925. 342 p.

F109. Pavlov, Ivan P. Conditioned reflexes; an investigation of the physiological activity of the cerebral cortex. London, Oxford Univ. Press, 1927. 430 p.

F110. Skinner, Burrhus F. Science and human behavior. New York, Macmillan, 1953. 461 p.

F111. Skinner, Burrhus F. The behavior of organisms; an experimental analysis. New York, Appleton-Century, 1938. 457 p.

F112. Spence, Kenneth W. Behavior theory and conditioning. New Haven, Conn. Yale Univ. Press, 1956. 262 p.

F113. Thorndike, Edward L. Human learning. New York, Century, 1931. 206 p.

F114. Thorndike, Edward L. The fundamentals of learning. New York,
Teachers College, Columbia Univ., 1932. 638 p.
F115. Tolman, Edward C. Purposive behavior in animals and men. New
York, Century, 1932. 463 p.

Motivation and Emotion

Motivation and emotion as topics of intrinsic psychological interest
show a certain diversity and lack of definite direction, although a fair
amount of work is being done. Reymert edited a volume on the emotions
with 47 contributors, most of whom are of major stature. Young presented a survey of both motivation and emotion.

F116. Reymert, Martin L., ed. Feelings and emotions; the Mooseheart
symposium. New York, McGraw-Hill, 1950.
F117. Young, Paul T. Motivation and emotion, a survey of the determinants of human and animal activity. New York, Wiley, 1961.
648 p.

Emotion and motivation in the service of some other major interest is
characteristic of much present work as shown by certain prominent publications. Bindra considers motivation as goal directed behavior, not as a
mechanism in itself but as an aspect of learning. The use of projective
techniques for the investigation of motivation is the theme of the volume by McClelland, et al. Rapaport deals with emotions as related
to memory, with emphasis upon psycoanalytic interpretation, while
Luria considers conflict as related to motivation. Lewin, who worked in
a field theory tradition derived from Gestalt psychology, is represented
by a collection of papers concerning motivation as related to personality
and social psychology. A flourishing school of comparative ethology
has produced a considerable number of studies of instinct and learning
in animals. Tinbergen and Thorpe, each a leading investigator, have
published accounts. Mierke wrote in a phenomenological tradition on
needs, imprinting, habits and conscience as factors of motivation, along
with an account of a series of experiments. Emotion (and personality)
from a phenomenological-stratigraphic point of view has been the
concern of Strasser.

F118. Bindra, Dalbir. Motivation; a systematic reinterpretation. New York,
Ronald, 1959. 361 p.
F119. Lewin, Kurt. A dynamic theory of personality; selected papers. New
York, McGraw-Hill, 1935. 286 p.
F120. Luriya, Aleksandr R. The nature of human conflicts; or emotion, con-
flict and will. New York, Liveright, 1932. 431 p.
F121. McClelland, David C., et al. The achievement motive. New York,
Appleton-Century-Crofts, 1953. 384 p.
F122. Mierke, Karl. Wille und Leistung. Göttingen, Verlag für Psycholo-
gie, 1955. 295 p.
F123. Rapaport, David. Emotions and memory. Baltimore, Williams and
Wilkins, 1942. 282 p.
F124. Strasser, Stephen. Das Gemüt: Grundgedanken zu einer phäno-

menologischen, Philosophie und Theorie des menschlichen Ge-
fühlslebens. Freiburg, Herder, 1956. 291 p.
F125. Thorpe, William H. Learning and instinct in animals. Cambridge,
Harvard Univ. Press, 1956. 493 p.
F126. Tinbergen, Nikolaas. The study of instinct. London, Oxford Univ.
Press, 1951. 228 p.

Thinking and Problem-Solving and Communication

Closely intertwined are theory and research on thought and problem
solving on one hand, and speech and language on the other. They are,
nevertheless, separable for present purposes.

More general statements of thinking and problem solving are given
by Bruner et al., by Johnson and by Vinacke. The early work on thinking
is summarized very ably by Humphrey. Thinking in the Gestalt tradition
is the theme of Wertheimer, and Rapaport edits a volume concerned
with both normal and abnormal thought, especially strong in translations
of the European literature. A phenomenological approach to problem
solving from the Netherlands is contained in Van de Geer. Peel, in
Britain, and Russell, in the United States, deal with children's thinking.

F127. Bruner, Jerome S., *et al.* A study of thinking. New York, Wiley,
1956. 330 p.
F128. Humphrey, George. Thinking: an introduction to its experimental
psychology. New York, Wiley, 1951. 331 p.
F129. Johnson, Donald M. The psychology of thought and judgment.
New York, Harper, 1955. 515 p.
F130. Peel, Edwin A. The pupil's thinking. London, Oldbourne, 1960.
200 p.
F131. Rapaport, David, *ed.* Organization and pathology of thought: se-
lected sources. New York, Columbia Univ. Press, 1951. 786 p.
F132. Russell, David H. Children's thinking. Boston, Ginn, 1956. 449 p.
F133. Van de Geer, Johan P. A psychological study of problem solving.
Haarlem, Netherlands, De Toorts, 1957. 216 p.
F134. Vinacke, William E. The psychology of thinking. New York, Mc-
Graw-Hill, 1952. 392 p.
F135. Wertheimer, Max. Productive thinking. Enl. ed. New York, Harper,
1959. 302 p.

Psychologists and individuals from related fields have been concerned
with communication, language and meaning, and information theory.
A standard book on the applications of information theory is supplied by
Miller. Osgood and his associates carried on research on meaning
through his technique of the semantic differential. Communication in its
mathematical aspects is the concern of Shannon and Weaver. Whorf, as
edited by Carroll, has presented a stimulating and controversial account of the relation of thought to the structure of language.

F136. Miller, George A. Language and communication. New York, McGraw-
Hill, 1951. 298 p.

F137. Osgood, Charles E., *et al.* The measurement of meaning. Urbana, Univ. of Illinois Press, 1957. 342 p.
F138. Shannon, Claude E. and Warren Weaver. The mathematical theory of communication. Urbana, Univ. of Illinois Press, 1949. 117 p.
F139. Whorf, Benjamin L. Language, thought and reality: selected writings, ed. by John B. Carroll. Cambridge, Mass., Technology Press of M.I.T., 1956. 278 p.

Perception

Perception is an international field of research with authorities in many countries. The nine books that follow originate from five countries.

An account of the theories of perception and the evidence on which they are based has been given by Allport. Perception in the Gestalt tradition is the theme of Metzger. With emphasis upon research design, Brunswik discusses the perception of objects. Space perception as arising through the primacy of a monocular factor is a major theme of Gibson. An account of visual perception is given by Carr. A phenomenological analysis of pain has been made by Buytendijk (a French edition is also available, *De la doleur*. Paris, Presses Universitaires de France, 1951.). Fraisse has produced the major works on the perception of time and of rhythm, topics neglected in the United States. In Belgium, Michotte has worked on the perception of causality. His book is classic. Stevens, cited earlier, and Koch, cited in the next listing, contain valuable accounts of modern, rigorously disciplined theories of perception.

F140. Allport, Floyd H. Theories of perception and the concept of structure. New York, Wiley, 1955. 709 p.
F141. Brunswik, Egon. Perception and the representative design of psychological experiments. 2d ed. rev. and enl. Berkeley, Calif., Univ. of California Press, 1956. 154 p.
F142. Buytendijk, Frederic J. J. Über den Schmerz. Bern, Huber, 1948. 182 p.
F143. Carr, Harvey A. An introduction to space perception. New York, Longmans Green, 1935. 413 p.
F144. Fraisse, Paul. Les structures rhythmiques: étude psychologique. Louvain, Publications Universitaires de Louvain, 1956. 124 p.
F145. Fraisse, Paul. Psychologie du temps. Paris, Presses Universitaires de France, 1957. 326 p.
F146. Gibson, James J. The perception of the visual world. Boston, Houghton Mifflin, 1950. 235 p.
F147. Metzger, Wolfgang. Gesetz des Sehens. 2. Aufl. Frankfurt, Kramer, 1953. 470 p.
F148. Michotte, Albert E. La perception de la causalite, 2d éd. Louvain, Publications Universitaires de Louvain, 1954. 306 p.

Sensory and Physiological Psychology

Sensory psychology is so intimately related to physiological psychology that it is preferable to discuss them together. The more general books will be considered first. One of the Koch edited volumes in the handbook series is devoted to physiological, sensory, and perceptual topics. Morgan and Stellar have written the standard text in physiological psychology. A standard handbook in physiology, as differentiated from physiological psychology, is that of Howell, as edited by Fulton. Piéron's book on the senses, with emphasis on sense physiology, is an indispensable standard reference. It was brought more nearly up to date in 1955, thus superseding the English translation of an earlier edition. Psychologists are in considerable debt to Geldard for his presentation of psychological material about all the senses, not merely that on audition and vision.

F149. Geldard, Frank A. The human senses. New York, Wiley, 1953. 365 p.
F150. Howell, William H. Textbook of physiology, ed. by John F. Fulton. 16th ed. Philadelphia, Saunders, 1949. 1258 p.
F151. Koch, Sigmund, *ed.* Psychology; a study of a science. Study I: Conceptual and systematic. Vol. I: Sensory, perceptual and physiological formulations. New York, McGraw-Hill, 1959. 710 p.
F152. Morgan, Clifford T. and Eliot Stellar. Physiological psychology. 2d ed. New York, McGraw-Hill, 1950. 609 p.
F153. Piéron, Henri. Aux sources de la connaissance: la sensation, guide de vie. 3. éd. Paris, Librarie Gallimard, 1955. 626 p.

Vision is a field which interests specialists from a considerable number of disciplines other than psychology. Neurophysiologists, physicists, neurologists and anatomists make major contributions, as the following books attest. The only book by a man primarily a psychologist is that by Bartley. One of the three volumes by Le Grand has been translated into English (*Light, color and vision.* New York, Wiley, 1957).

F154. Bartley, Samuel H. Vision: a study of its basis. New York, Van Nostrand, 1941. 350 p.
F155. Granit, Ragnar. Receptors and sensory perceptions; a discussion of aims, means, and results of electrophysiological research into the process of reception. New Haven, Conn., Yale Univ. Press, 1955. 369 p.
F156. Helmholtz, Hermann L. F. von. Treatise on physiological optics, ed. by James P. Southall. Rochester, N.Y., Optical Society of America, 1924-25. 3 v.
F157. Judd, Deane B. Color in business, science and industry. New York, Wiley, 1952. 401 p.
F158. LeGrand, Yves. Optique physiologique. 2. éd. rev. et augm. Paris, Editions de la "Revue d'optique," 1952-1956. 3 v.
F159. Polyak, Stephen L. The vertebrate visual system. Chicago, Univ. of Chicago Press, 1957. 1390 p.

Audition is also an area where individuals other than psychologists have made major contributions, but psychologists are represented in the work of Stevens and of Wever. Von Békésy gives the definitive statement of the biophysics of the inner ear, studies which gained him the Nobel Prize for work carried on since 1949 in Harvard's Psycho-Acoustic Laboratory.

F160. Fletcher, Harvey. Speech and hearing in communication. New York, Van Nostrand, 1953. 461 p.
F161. Helmholtz, Hermann L. F. von. On the sensations of tone as a physiological basis for the theory of music. 3d ed. New York, Longmans Green, 1895. 576 p.
F162. Stevens, Stanly S. and Hallowell Davis. Hearing: its psychology and physiology. New York, Wiley, 1938. 489 p.
F163. Von Békésy, George. Experiments in hearing. New York, McGraw-Hill, 1960. 745 p.
F164. Wever, Ernest G. Theory of hearing. New York, Wiley, 1949. 484 p.

As suggested by their very titles, there are more specialized volumes on various aspects of physiology and physiological psychology.

F165. Adrian, Edgar D. The physical background of perception. London, Oxford Univ. Press, 1947. 95 p.
F166. Delafresnaye, Jean F., *ed.* Brain mechanisms and consciousness. Oxford, Blackwell, 1954. 556 p.
F167. Eccles, John C. The neurophysiological basis of mind: the principles of neurophysiology. Oxford, Clarendon Press, 1953. 314 p.
F168. Lashley, Karl S. Brain mechanisms and intelligence: a quantitative study of injuries to the brain. Chicago, Univ. of Chicago Press, 1929. 186 p.
F169. Sherrington, Charles S. The integrative action of the nervous system. New Haven, Conn., Yale Univ. Press, 1947. 433 p.

BRANCHES OF PSYCHOLOGY

Social Psychology

Social psychology is a hybrid in that both sociologists and psychologists quite legitimately lay claim to being social psychologists. It is prophetic that the same year, 1908, saw the appearance of the first books bearing the title of social psychology, one by a psychologist, McDougall, and the other by a sociologist, Ross. The books by psychologists need supplementation by those of sociologists, cited in an earlier chapter.

The standard handbook of social psychology was edited by Lindzey with the aid of many authorities, and gives a broad coverage, including its history; systematic positions held; research methods followed; the motivation perception and socialization of the individual in a social context; group psychology, including problem solving, social structure, mass phenomena and leadership; and the applications of social psychology to the problems of prejudice, communication, industry, and political behavior. A more specialized volume devoted to the various methods of research in social psychology is that edited by Festinger and Katz. A valuable collection of a large number of papers on various aspects of social psychology, theoretical and contentual, has been edited by Maccoby.

F170. Festinger, Leon and Katz, Daniel, *eds*. Research methods in the behavioral sciences. New York, Dryden, 1953. 660 p.
F171. Lindzey, Gardner, *ed*. Handbook of social psychology. Cambridge, Mass., Addison-Wesley, 1954. 2 v.
F172. Maccoby, Eleanor E., *et al*. Readings in social psychology. 3d ed. New York, Holt, Rinehart and Winston, 1958. 674 p.

Three quite different American textbooks are available. Although representative, all of them are necessary if one is to appreciate the full gamut of the field. Asch emphasized a Gestalt approach; Kretch, Crutchfield and Ballackey are influenced by field theory and cognitive principles applied to social psychology; Murphy and his associates, within the limits of the publication date, gave a thorough analysis of the experimental literature. A British account by Argyle, although short, remains close to the research evidence.

F173. Argyle, Michael. The scientific study of social behavior. London, Methuen, 1957. 239 p.
F174. Asch, Solomon E. Social psychology. New York, Prentice Hall, 1952. 646 p.
F175. Krech, David, *et al*. Individual in society; a text-book of social psychology. New York, McGraw-Hill, 1962. 564 p.
F176. Murphy, Gardner, *et al*. Experimental social psychology. Rev. ed. New York, Harper, 1937. 1121 p.

Some conception of the extensiveness of social psychology can be gleaned by examining the topics of the more specialized books. They are concerned with prejudice, memory as influenced by meaning and cultural factors, group dynamics, leadership, cognitive dissonance, interpersonal relations, public opinion and propaganda, social learning and imitation, and social norms, and group functioning. This list by no means exhausts all possibilities. These fields flourish in the United States work on the Continent is more or less derived from it. Unique to Germany is the presence of an interest in so-called folk psychology, a tradition deriving directly from the time of Wundt. This is represented here by Hellpach.

F177. Allport, Gordon W. The nature of prejudice. Cambridge, Addison-Wesley, 1954. 551 p.
F178. Bartlett, Frederic C. Remembering: a study in experimental and social psychology. New York, Macmillan, 1932. 317 p.
F179. Bass, Bernard M. Leadership, psychology, and organizational behavior. New York, Harper, 1960. 548 p.
F180. Cartwright, Dorwin and Zander, Alvin, *eds*. Group dynamics: research and theory 2d ed. Evanston, Ill., Row, Peterson, 1960. 826 p.
F181. Festinger, Leon. A theory of cognitive dissonance. Evanston, Ill., Row, Peterson, 1957. 291 p.
F182. Heider, Fritz. The psychology of interpersonal relations. New York, Wiley, 1958. 322 p.
F183. Hellpach, Willy H. Einführung in die Völkerpsychologie. 3. Aufl. Stuttgart, F. Enke, 1954. 204 p.

F184. Katz, Daniel, *et al.* Public opinion and propaganda; a book of
     readings. New York, Dryden, 1954. 779 p.
F185. Miller, Neal E. and Dollard, John. Social learning and imitation.
     New Haven, Conn., Yale Univ. Press, 1941. 341 p.
F186. Sherif, Muzafer. The psychology of social norms. New York, Harper,
     1936. 209 p.
F187. Thibaut, John W. and Harold H. Kelley. The social psychology of
     groups. New York, Wiley, 1959. 313 p.

Abnormal Psychology

Abnormal psychology and psychiatry are closely related fields, but
they exhibit the differences to be expected when considering a scientific and a medical specialty. In abnormal psychology there is more
stress on research findings as differentiated from clinical observation,
more emphasis on understanding the person than on treating the patient, and more emphasis upon psychological functioning within the
rubrics of psychology than on diagnoses. Two handbooks—one in abnormal psychology, published in 1961 and the other in psychiatry, published in 1959—bring out these differences clearly.

British authors, under the editorship and direction of Eysenck, prepared a *Handbook of abnormal psychology* divided into three sections—
one concerned with abnormalities grouped as those of psychomotor functions, expressive movements, perception, intellectual abilities, cognitive
abilities, motivation and ego functions; another with heredity and constitutional factors, child upbringing, conditioning and the like as they
determine abnormal behavior; and the third with the experimental
study of the psychological effects of brain damage, drugs, electroshock
and psychotherapy.

Arieti and his collaborators consider the history of psychiatry, personality, community factors, genetics of mental disorder, interview and examination techniques, the psychoneuroses, the functional psychoses,
psychopathy, psychosomatic medicine, child disorders, organic conditions, the various therapies, contributions from related fields, and legal
and administrative problems.

F188. Arieti, Silvano, *ed.* American handbook of psychiatry. New York,
     Basic Books, 1959. 2 v.
F189. Eysenck, Hans J., *ed.* Handbook of abnormal psychology: an ex-
     perimental approach. New York, Basic Books, 1961. 816 p.

Textbooks in abnormal psychology have been written by Cameron
and Margaret, Maslow and Mittelmann, and White. They bear in
varying degrees the impress of Neo-Freudian thinking. A more orthodox statement of this view is to be found in Fenichel. Kretschmer's conception of abnormal psychology, clinical psychology, and psychotherapy is influential in Germany. Shaffer and Shoben, in a textbook, have
dealt with problems of adjustment of a less severe nature.

F190. Cameron, Norman A. and Ann Margaret. Behavior pathology. Boston, Houghton Mifflin, 1951. 645 p.
F191. Fenichel, Otto. The psychoanalytic theory of neurosis. New York, Norton, 1945. 703 p.
F192. Kretschmer, Ernst. Medizinische Psychologie. 11. verb. und verm. Aufl. Stuttgart, Thieme, 1956. 382 p.
F193. Maslow, Abraham H. and Béla Mittelmann. Principles of abnormal psychology: the dynamics of psychic illness. Rev. ed. New York, Harper, 1951. 665 p.
F194. Shaffer, Laurence F. and Edward J. Shoben. The psychology of adjustment: a dynamic and experimental approach to personality and mental hygiene. 2d ed. Boston, Houghton Mifflin, 1956. 672 p.
F195. White, Robert W. The abnormal personality: a textbook. 2d ed. New York, Ronald Press, 1956. 644 p.

Animal Psychology

Most psychological studies of animals are carried on in the service of some branch of psychology, e.g., motivation and learning. Consequently, much of the research with animals is absorbed in other areas, but two books should be mentioned. One is devoted to the psychologist's favorite animal subject, the white rat, and the other stresses a comparative approach to the animal behavior of the various species.

F196. Munn, Norman L. Handbook of psychological research on the rat: an introduction to animal psychology. Boston, Houghton Mifflin, 1950. 598 p.
F197. Stone, Calvin P., *ed*. Comparative psychology. 3d ed. New York, Prentice Hall, 1951. 525 p.

Developmental Psychology

Interest in the sweep of development from infancy through childhood, adolescence and maturity through old age, has characterized the work of a considerable number of psychologists. More interest has been shown in infancy and childhood than in older ages, although in relatively recent years gerontological problems have been receiving increasing attention. The handbook volumes edited by Carmichael and by Birren represent modern summaries to which most of the leading American authorities on their respective specialties contributed. One of twelve volumes in a German handbook series, edited by Thomae, is devoted to developmental psychology. The volume edited by Mussen, as the title implies, is concerned with methods of study of the child. The research efforts of Gesell, Piaget and Sears, although very different in nature, are outstanding. When dealing with the research work of these three men, it is difficult to find from their many works something even approaching representativeness. This is especially the case with Piaget. The work of his that is mentioned not only deals with logical thinking in children; it also throws light on Piaget's use of logico-mathematical models. Koffka approached child psychology from a Gestalt point of view, Remplein used stratification theory, while Erikson employed a psychoanalytic approach. A classic German account of development is given by Bühler. Goodenough and Tyler, Jersild, Kuhlen, McCandless, Mussen and Conger, and Watson supply standard American textbooks.

F198. Birren, James E., *ed.* Handbook of aging and the individual. Chicago, Univ. of Chicago Press, 1959. 939 p.

F199. Bühler, Karl. Abriss der geistigen Entwicklung des Kindes. 7. Aufl. Heidelberg, Quelle & Meyer, 1949. 180 p.

F200. Carmichael, Leonard, *ed.* Manual of child psychology. 2d ed. New York, Wiley, 1954. 1295 p.

F201. Erikson, Erik H. Childhood and society. New York, Norton, 1950. 397 p.

F202. Gesell, Arnold L. and Frances L. Ilg. Child development: an introduction of the study of human growth. New York, Harper, 1949. 2 v. in 1.

F203. Goodenough, Florence L. and Leona E. Tyler. Developmental psychology: an introduction to the study of human behavior. 3d ed. New York, Appleton-Century-Crofts, 1959. 552 p.

F204. Inhelder, Bärbel and Jean Piaget. The growth of logical thinking: from childhood to adolescence. New York, Basic Books, 1958. 356 p.

F205. Jersild, Arthur T. Child psychology. 5th ed. Englewood Cliffs, N.J., Prentice Hall, 1960. 506 p.

F206. Koffka, Kurt. The growth of the mind: an introduction to child psychology. 2d ed. rev. London, Routledge and Kegan Paul, 1928. 426 p.

F207. Kuhlen, Raymond G. The psychology of adolescent development. New York, Harper, 1952. 675 p.

F208. McCandless, Boyd R. Children and adolescents: behavior and development. New York, Holt, Rinehart and Winston, 1961. 521 p.

F209. Mussen, Paul H., *ed.* Handbook of research methods in child development. New York, Wiley, 1960. 1061 p.

F210. Mussen, Paul H. and John J. Conger. Child development and personality. New York, Harper, 1956. 569 p.

F211. Remplein, Heinz. Die seelische Entwicklung des Menschen im Kindes- und Jungendalter. 7. Auf. München, Reinhardt, 1959. 693 p.

F212. Sears, Robert R., *et al.* Patterns of child rearing. Evanston, Ill., Row, Peterson, 1957. 549.

F213. Thomae, Hans, *ed.* Entwicklungspsychologie. Göttingen, Verlag für Psychologie, 1959. 622 p. (Handbuch der Psychologie. Band 3.)

F214. Watson, Robert I. Psychology of the child: personal social and disturbed child development. New York, Wiley, 1959. 662 p.

Tests and Individual Differences

Interested as he was in individual difference among men, Sir Francis Galton in England began working with various ingenious psychological tests in the decade of the seventies. It is prophetic that his interests in individual differences and the use of tests went hand in hand with his furthering the advance of the use of statistics through development of a measure of correlation. Since that time, there has been an intimate relation. In fact, some of the statistical books mentioned earlier are closely related to the present topic. Books by Spearman and Thurstone bring this out clearly.

F215. Spearman, Charles E. The abilities of man. New York, Macmillan, 1927. 415 p.
F216. Spearman, Charles E. and Llewellyn W. Jones. Human ability. London, Macmillan, 1950. 198 p.
F217. Thurstone, Louis L. The measurement of values. Chicago, Univ. of Chicago Press, 1959. 322 p.

After the turn of the century, Binet in France developed the first major practicable device for measuring intelligence. L. M. Terman at Stanford University published the first edition of the Stanford-Binet in 1916. The third revision is now extant. The ink blots of Hermann Rorschach were described in a book first appearing in 1920. Many related projective techniques subsequently made their appearance. They are described in the volume edited by the Andersons. A test designed expressly for the testing of adults, the Wechsler Bellevue Scale, made its appearance in a 1939 standardization. A new revision and an accompanying monograph were published in 1958. E. K. Strong, Jr. devoted much of his research efforts to sutdying vocational interests resulting in the so-called Strong Vocational Interest Blank.

More general books about tests have appeared. Those by Cronbach, Gulliksen, and Thorndike and Hagen complement one another, covering somewhat different aspects of the problem. French, German and Swiss clinical psychologists predominate as contributors to the volume edited by Stern, making it a valuable account of continental practice in the use of psychological tests. Diagnostic testing in a French setting is the theme of Delay and his collaborators.

F218. Anderson, Harold H. and Gladys L. Anderson, eds., An introduction to projective techniques: and other devices for understanding the dynamics of human behavior. New York, Prentice Hall, 1951. 720 p.
F219. Cronbach, Lee J. Essentials of psychological testing. 2d ed. New York, Harper, 1960. 650 p.
F220. Delay, Jean, et al. Méthodes psychométriques en clinique; tests mentaux et interpretation. Paris, Masson, 1955. 327 p.
F221. Gulliksen, Harold. Theory of mental tests. New York, Wiley, 1950. 486 p.
F222. Rorschach, Hermann. Psychodiagnostics; a diagnostic test based on perception. New York, Grune and Stratton, 1942. 226 p.
F223. Stern, Erich, ed. Handbuch der klinichen Psychologie: I. Die Tests in der klinischen Psychologie. Zürich, Rascher, 1954-55. 2 v.
F224. Strong, Edward K., Jr. Vocational interests of men and women. Stanford, Calif., Stanford Univ. Press, 1943. 746 p.
F225. Terman, Louis M. and Maud A. Merrill. The Stanford-Binet Intelligence Scale; manual for the third revision. Boston, Houghton Mifflin, 1960. 363 p.
F226. Thorndike, Robert L. and Elizabeth Hagen. Measurement and eval-

uation in psychology and education. 2d ed. New York, Wiley,
1961. 602 p.

F227. Wechsler, David. The measurement and appraisal of adult intelligence. 4th ed. Baltimore, Williams and Wilkins, 1958. 297 p.

The standard account of differential psychology is by Anastasi. Since
mental retardation is a matter of individual differences, and since tests
are used in its study, it is convenient to mention at this point the book on
this topic by Sarason.

F228. Anastasi, Anne. Differential psychology. 3d ed. New York, Macmillan, 1958. 664 p.

F229. Sarason, Seymour B. Psychological problems in mental deficiency.
3d ed. New York, Harper, 1959. 678 p.

Applied Psychology

Applications of psychology to various areas of human problems characterizes the field. Psychologists work in a variety of settings in which
they apply the principles of psychology. Workers in these areas would
also insist that the settings in which they work afford them opportunities to do research which serves to advance psychology as a pure science.
Some of the major fields in which these effects are carried out include industrial psychology and human engineering, clinical psychology, and
educational psychology. A handbook edited by Fryer and Henry shows
the scope of these applications.

F230. Fryer, Douglas H. and Edwin R. Henry, *eds.* Handbook of applied
psychology. New York, Rinehart, 1950. 2 v.

Industrial psychology and human engineering is an international subject, as is the case with industry itself. An account of industrial psychology edited by Herwig and Mayer appeared in the new German handbook series. Henri Piéron is editing a multi-volumed series on psycho-
technology in France. It is difficult to choose one particular volume, but
the one devoted to methodology is selected rather than one from the
various content areas. Human engineering in the relation of man and
machine, as expressed through the influence, say, of motivation or fa-
tigue upon performance, is the theme of Chapanis and his associates.
Textbooks on industrial psychology are supplied by Gilmer and his associates, and by Maier. The book by Roe on the psychology of occupations has implications not only for industrial but also for counseling
psychology.

F231. Chapanis, Alphonse R. E., *et al.* Applied experimental psychology;
human factors in engineering design. New York, Wiley, 1949.
434 p.

F232. Gilmer, Beverly von H., *et al.* Industrial psychology. New York,
McGraw-Hill, 1961. 513 p.

F233. Herwig, Bernhard and Arthur Mayer. Betriebspsychologie. Göttingen, Verlag für Psychologie, 1960. 664 p. (Handbuch der Psychologie. Band 3)

F234. Maier, Norman R.F. Psychology in industry; a psychological approach to industrial problems. 2d ed. Boston, Houghton Mifflin, 1955. 678 p.

F235. Piéron, Henri, *et al.* Methodologie psychotechnique. Paris, Presses Universitaires de France, 1951. 339 p. (Traité de psychologie appliquée. Livre 2)

F236. Roe, Anne. The psychology of occupations. New York, Wiley, 1956. 340 p.

In educational psychology, standard American textbooks are those of Cronbach, Skinner and his associates, and Stephens. Under the editorship of Zazzo, a large number of authors discuss educational psychology in France. In the German handbook series, Hetzer edited a volume on educational psychology.

F237. Cronbach, Lee J. Educational psychology. New York, Harcourt, Brace, 1954. 628 p.

F238. Hetzer, Hildegard, *ed.* Pädagogische Psychologie. Göttingen, Verlag für Psychologie, 1959. 544 p. (Handbuch der Psychologie. Band 10)

F239. Skinner, Charles E., *ed.* Educational psychology. 4th ed. Englewood Cliffs, N.J., Prentice-Hall, 1959. 755 p.

F240. Stephens, John M. Educational psychology. Rev. ed. New York, Holt, 1956. 717 p.

F241. Zazzo, René and Hélène Gratiot-Alphaniery. La psychologie scolaire. Paris, Presses Universitaires de France, 1953. 194 p.

The tasks of clinical psychologists tend to differ from country to country. In the United States and, to some extent, on the Continent, the clinical psychologist engages in both diagnosis and therapy, while in England he is likely to be limited to testing. In all countries he carries on research. The literature on psychological tests is discussed elsewhere. Textbooks conceived in varying degrees with diagnosis and therapy, along with professional problems of clinical psychology, are those of Garfield, Hadley, Pennington and Berg, and Wallen.

F242. Garfield, Sol L. Introductory clinical psychology. New York, Macmillan, 1957. 469 p.

F243. Hadley, John M. Clinical and counseling psychology. New York, Knopf, 1958. 682 p.

F244. Pennington, Leon A. and Irwin Berg, *eds.* An introduction to clinical psychology. 2d ed. New York, Ronald, 1954. 709 p.

F245. Wallen, Richard W. Clinical psychology; the study of persons. New York, McGraw-Hill, 1956. 388 p.

Although there were a few lonely pioneers, clinical psychologists, as a group, first began to practice psychotherapy during and after World War II. There is an extensive psychiatric literature on the subject which must be neglected here. Psychologists, too, have made distinctive contributions. The so-called client-centered approach of Rogers to psychotherapy is important in this regard. A contrasting, eclectic approach by Thorne is also influential. Dollard and Miller, less task-oriented than these two,

present a more theoretical analysis of psychotherapy in terms of rein-
forcement, learning theory, and psychoanalysis. Psychoanalytic influences are important upon the thinking and practice of the clinical
psychologist, making relevant the books mentioned in the section devoted to psychoanalysis.

F246. Dollard, John and Neal E. Miller. Personality and psychotherapy;
      an analysis in terms of learning, thinking and culture. New York,
      McGraw-Hill, 1950. 488 p.
F247. Rogers, Carl R. Counseling and psychotherapy; newer concepts in
      practice. Boston, Houghton Mifflin, 1942. 450 p.
F248. Rogers, Carl R. Client-centered therapy; its current practice, impli-
      cations, and theory. Boston, Houghton Mifflin, 1951. 560 p.
F249. Thorne, Frederick C. Principles of personality counseling. Brandon,
      Vt., Journal of Clinical Psychology, 1950. 491 p.

                                                    Robert I. Watson

GUIDES TO THE LITERATURE

F250. Daniel, Robert S. and Chauncey M. Louttit. Professional problems in psychology. New York, Prentice-Hall, 1953. 416 p.

In part a revision and expansion of Louttit's *Handbook of psychological literature* this work is a manual for the student and practicing psychologist. Part I provides an orientation to psychology and a brief resume of its development as a profession. Part II is concerned with the problems of psychological literature. In addition to general characteristics of the literature, information is given on sources of original contributions, reference works, bibliographies and library problems and classification. Part III deals with problems of reporting psychological research, and Part IV with professional organizations, responsibilities and problems. Appendices include: (1) an annotated list of 306 reference books classified under 11 major headings, e.g., experimental, developmental, social, clinical, abnormal, educational and industrial psychology; (2) an alphabetical listing of 331 psychological journals, and (3) sources of books, tests, apparatus and equipment recommended for purchase as well as a glossary of abbreviations. Index of names and index of subjects.

F251. Louttit, Chauncey M. Handbook of psychological literature. Bloomington, Ind., Principia Press, 1932. 273 p.

A pioneer effort to systematize treatment of the "scattered" literature of psychology. Now largely superseded (see F250), it is still useful for its appendices: a bibliography of 1,000 journals in psychology and related fields; a list of psychological publications in series; and a list of American and British library collections.

REVIEWS OF THE LITERATURE

F252. L'Année psychologique. v. 1+ 1894+ Paris, Presses Universitaires de France. annual.

Each annual volume has 2 main sections: the first consists of original articles, subject and literature surveys; the second, "Analyses bibliographiques," provides signed abstracts of 400-500 periodical articles and 75-100 critical book reviews which attempt to be expository rather than evaluative. Scope is extremely wide and coverage is international. Index of authors, and more recently of subjects as well. Since 1953 issued in two fasicules a year.

F253. Annual review of psychology. v. 1+ 1950+ Stanford, Calif., Annual Reviews. annual.

Contains 13-18 reviews of the literature in various topical areas of contemporary psychology prepared by prominent specialists. The editorial plan developed in 1958 calls for the presentation of certain topics each year, other topics on alternate years, still others every third or fourth year, and a few at irregular intervals. Thus over a period of 5 years some 34 topics would be covered. (For the outline of this plan see Preface of vol. 11, 1960). The major areas of coverage include developmental psychology, learning and motivation, comparative psychology, receptor processes, personality, psychological psychology, social psychology, industrial psychology, statistics and abnormal psychology. The bibliographical essays, covering noteworthy publications (2714 items in v. 14, 1963) emphasize interpretation and evaluation. Author and subject indexes.

F254. Contemporary psychology; a journal of reviews. v. 1+ 1956+ Washington, American Psychological Association. monthly.

An effort to concentrate book reviews in one place, this journal serves as the review medium for the 11 journals published by the Association. 200-250 long (1,200-3,500 words) critical reviews published

each year. 500-600 books are listed as "Books received." One section "Instructional media" reviews instructional materials including films and other audio-visual materials. Author and subject indexes.

F255. Psychological bulletin. v. 1+ 1904+ Washington, American Psychological Association. bimonthly.

Took over the literature review section of the *Psychological review*. It published the proceedings for many years, as well as book reviews and abstracts of periodical literature. In 1927 the abstracts were taken over by *Psychological abstracts* and since then the *Bulletin* has been devoted to evaluative reviews of research literature in various areas of psychology.

F256. Rehabilitation literature. v. 1+ 1940+ Chicago, National Society for Crippled Children and Adults. monthly.

As a reviewing and abstracting journal *Rehabilitation literature* identifies and describes current books, pamphlets, and periodical articles pertaining to the care, welfare, education and employment of handicapped children and adults. Through v. 19 (1958) it consisted of abstracts of current literature. Its new format consists of the Article of the month, Review of the month, Other books reviewed, Digest of the month (a journal article, a chapter of book, or research report) and Abstracts of current literature. The 1,000-1,500 items a year are arranged by subject with annual author indexes. Another abstracting tool with emphasis upon medical aspects is *Excerpta medica. Section 19. Rehabilitation* (v. 1+ 1958+ Amsterdam, Excerpta Medica Foundation. monthly.)

See also: D217

ABSTRACTS AND DIGESTS

BIBLIOGRAPHIES—CURRENT

F257. Psychological abstracts. v. 1+ 1927+ Washington, American Psychological Association. bimonthly. (Issued monthly through 1953).

The leading abstracting journal in the field. 9,000-12,000 items a year are classified under 12 major headings with annual author and subject indexes. (One major section is Social psychology). Coverage includes monographs, pamphlets, documents, articles, analytics, films, psychological tests and unpublished doctoral dissertations (the last is not a regular feature). Over 550 English and foreign language journals are searched regularly for items of psychological interest. The signed abstracts are evaluative and noncritical. Time lag of about one year, between publication of the original item and its abstract. See also (F261). Cumulative author index published separately (F264). A cumulated subject index has been announced for publication by G. K. Hall.

F258. Society for Research on Child Development. Child development abstracts and bibliography. v. 1+ 1927+ Lafayette, Ind., Purdue Univ. bi-monthly.

Includes abstracts of 600-700 periodical articles a year on physical and mental health areas, as well as environmental factors, education, growth, heredity, social welfare, and psychological development of the child. Classified arrangement with annual author and subject indexes. Includes some foreign language articles. Critical reviews of books about children (80-100 per year) are included in a separate section of each issue.

See also: A51

F259. Mental health book review index. v. 1+ 1956+ Flushing, New York. semi-annual.

Lists references to signed book reviews appearing in 150 English language journals. Book titles are listed with references to 3 or more reviews when the reviews (1) appear in psychological, psychiatric or psycho-analytical journals; (2) when the journals represent at least 3 fields in the behavioral sciences as a whole; (3) when at least 3 of the journals originate outside the U.S. or (4) when the books reviewed are in a foreign language. Over 2,000 books (and 10,000 reviews) have been listed to date. Some 7,000 titles with at least one review are on file until they can be listed under the criteria above. Titles are arranged alphabetically by author and number consecutively. Titles listed previously and having 3 or more additional reviews are repeated using the original item number. No index.

F260. Psychological index, 1894-1935, an annual bibliography of the literature of psychology and cognate subjects. Princeton, N.J., Psychological Review Corp., 1894-1936. 42 v.

Begun as a supplement to the *Psychological review* this annual bibliography continues Rand's *Bibliography of philosophy, psychology and cognate subjects* (F272) and provides an extensive coverage of all the literature of psychology and allied fields (150,844 items). Lists original publications in all languages, books, and articles, and translations and new editions in English, German, French, and Italian. Includes about 5,000 titles per year arranged in a classified subject list with an alphabetical author index. Ca. 350 periodicals indexed a year (for this list see vol. 30). Discontinued after vol. 42, its work being carried on by *Psychological abstracts* (F257).

F261. Psychological index. Abstract references, ed. by H.L. Ansbacher. Columbus, Ohio, American Psychological Assoc., 1940-41. 2 v.

A backward extension of *Psychological abstracts*. It is composed of a list of the item numbers of those titles listed in *Psychological index* from 1894-1928 for which one or more abstracts could be located in the journals examined. References to abstracts have been located for 43% of the 107,000 titles listed through 1928. Multiple listing places the number of actual abstracts listed at over 75,000. Must be used with *Psychological index*.

F262. Voutsinas, Dimitri. Documentation sur la psychologie française. Paris, Groupe d'Études de Psychologie de l'Université de Paris, 1957+ Fasc. 1+ (in progress)

A current and retrospective survey of the literature. Vol. 1, entitled "Dix années de psychologie française," is a classified bibliography of French articles appearing from 1947-56. Vol. 2 lists articles published in 1957 and books published since 1947. Vol. 3 lists books and articles of 1958 plus a retrospective listing of significant articles published from 1843-1946. Vol. 4 lists books and articles for 1959 plus additional items 1947-1959. Vol. 5 lists major publications for 1960. Author indexes. The French bibliographical digest no. 5, *Psychologie* (New York, Cultural Center of the French Embassy, 1950. 95 p.) lists 469 books and articles published between 1940-1948. See also Jean Stoetzl *Sociology and social psychology* (D247).

F263. Zeitschrift für Psychologie und Physiologie der Sinnesorgane. v. 1-156, 1890-1944. Leipzig, Barth. irregular.

In addition to 100-150 critical book reviews (200-1,500 words) this journal includes an annual classified bibliography. From 1890-1916 it covered world psychological literature, from 1925-1944 it indexed German literature only. For the years 1926-1929 psychological literature published outside Germany was indexed in the *Archiv für die Gesamte Psychologie* (v. 62-79; 1928-1931). Beginning in 1911 the *Zeitschrift* followed closely the pattern of the *Psychological index* (F260). Ca. 1,000 items (books, articles, disertations) are listed under 3 main areas with 33 subdivisions with an author index. In 1954 after a lapse of ten years the *Zeitschrift* merged with Abteilung I of the *Zeitschrift für angewandte Psychologie und Charakterkunde* (v. 157+ 1954+) but the bibliography has not been continued.

See also: D227

BIBLIOGRAPHIES—RETROSPECTIVE

F264. Columbia University. *Libraries. Psychology Library*. Author index to Psychological index, 1894 to 1935, and Psychological abstracts, 1927 to 1958. Boston, G.K. Hall, 1960. 5 v.

The publication of a card index compiled at Columbia. Every item included in PI and PA since their inception has been arranged alphabetically by author. The 5 volumes contain an estimated 350,000 entries. Supplements Murchison (F271) for material published since 1932 and provides bibliographies of psychologists who were excluded from the *Psychological register*.

F265. Corsini, Raymond J. and Lloyd J. Putzey "Bibliography of group psychotherapy" *Group psychotherapy*, v. 9, Nov. 1956; 177-249.

A chronologically arranged bibliography of all known books, chapters in books, journal articles and theses concerned with group psychotherapy published from 1906 through 1955. Includes 1,700 items and is international in scope. No annotations. Author and subject indexes. Future editions planned for 5 year intervals. For additional material through 1959 see Norman Locke's A *decade of group psychotherapy; the bibliography for 1950-1959* (New York, Group Psychotherapy Center, 1960. 48 1. mimeo.) An alphabetical bibliography of 1,014 items (books, articles, theses) with a subject index. Current material is surveyed annually in the April issue of the *International journal of group psychotherapy*. See also the section on current literature (abstracts and book reviews, American and foreign) in each quarterly issue of the *American journal of psychotherapy* (v. 1+ 1947+).

F266. The fifth mental measurements yearbook, ed. by Oscar K. Buros. Highland Park, N.J., Gryphon Press, 1959. 1292 p.

The eighth publication in a series begun in 1935 with the publication of a 44 page unannotated bibliography of tests entitled *Educational psychological and personality tests of 1933 and 1934.* The present volume covers the period 1952-1958. Two major sections: (1) "Tests and reviews" lists 957 commercially available tests—educational, psychological, and vocational—published in English speaking countries. The tests are arranged by type and each entry includes a description of the test, one or more critical reviews, excerpts from test reviews in professional journals and a bibliography of references (e.g., 1,077 items for Rorschach); (2) "Books and reviews" lists 485 books on measurement and closely related fields published in English. Entries include full bibliographic data and, for most, excerpts from critical reviews. Index of titles. Index of names (author, reviewers and bibliographical references). Classified index of tests. Cross references to earlier editions. See also Oscar K. Buros, *ed. Tests*

in print. (Highland Park, N.J., Gryphon Press, 1961. 1292 p.) A comprehensive classified listing of 2,126 separately published tests in print and 841 out of print. Brief descriptions.

F267. Graham, Earl C. and Marjorie M. Mullen. Rehabilitation literature, 1950-1955. New York, McGraw-Hill, 1956. 621 p.

Indexes and annotates 5,214 periodical articles, pamphlets and books relating to the medical care, education, employment, welfare and psychology of the handicapped. Entries are arranged by subject with authors and brief subject indexes. Annotations are brief. Continues Maya Riviere's *Rehabilitation of the handicapped, a bibliography 1940-1946.* (New York, National Council on Rehabilitation 1949. 2 v.) which includes 5,000 unannotated items arranged alphabetically by author with a general subject index, lists of films, film catalogs and film sources. Current literature is surveyed in *Rehabilitation literature* (F256).

F268. Grinstein, Alexander. The index of psychoanalytic writings. New York, International Universities Press, 1956-60. 5 v.

A revision and modernization of J. Rickman's *Index psychoanalyticus, 1893-1926* (London, Woolf, 1928) this comprehensive index includes books, monographs, periodical articles, reviews and abstracts written by psychoanalysts or concerning psychoanalysis and published in any language from 1900 through 1952. The 37,121 numbered entries are arranged alphabetically by author. Volume 5 contains a detailed subject index. Bibliographic data for translations follows entry for the original publication. For foreign works which did not also appear in English, translation of the title is provided. All known reviews and abstracts are noted for each title. All of Freud's writings which were known at the time of publication are included in a special appendix in vol. I. An *Index* for the years 1953-1960 is in preparation. Current literature is surveyed in the *Annual survey of psychoanalysis* v. 1+ 1950+ (New York, International Universities Press, 1952+ annual.)

F269. Harvard University. The Harvard list of books in psychology. Compiled and annotated by the psychologists in Harvard University. Cambridge, Mass., 1955. 84 p.

A select, annotated bibliography, classified by major subject areas, of 607 books judged to be the most important to psychology and which present a picture of the scope of the profession at the present time. Annotations are very brief. Index of authors. A supplementary list, published in 1958, adds 92 titles.

F270. Louttit, Chauncey M. Bibliography of bibliographies in psychology, 1900-1927. Washington, National Research Council, 1928. 108 p. (National Research Council. Bulletin, 65)

Lists 2,134 bibliographies appearing in books or articles published between Jan. 1, 1900 and Dec. 31, 1927. Four main parts: (1) a list of periodicals and general works searched; (2) "Further bibliographical sources"—indexes, abstracts, review journals; (3) the main list of bibliographies arranged by author; and (4) a subject index with numerous cross-references. Some titles published as early as 1850 are included because of their historical importance.

F271. Psychological register, ed. by Carl Murchison. Worcester, Mass., Clark Univ. Press, 1929-32. v. 2-3.

Includes brief biographies with full bibliographies of living psychologists throughout the world, arranged by country. Vol. 1, planned to include psychologists from ancient times to 1929, was never published. Vol. 2 (1929) includes 1,250 psy-chologists from 29 countries. Standards for inclusion were not very precise. Vol. 3 (1932), a revision and expansion of Vol. 2, includes 2,400 psychologists from 40 countries and is more carefully prepared. Each entry gives name, address, place and date of birth, education and degrees, positions held, professional memberships, and a full bibliography of published contributions. A cumulative name index was never published.

F272. Rand, Benjamin. Bibliography of philosophy, psychology and cognate subjects. New York, Macmillan, 1905. 2 v.

Forms v. 3 of *Dictionary of philosophy and psychology*, ed. by James M. Baldwin (F275). Part I, "History of philosophy," includes works by and about the great philosophical thinkers from Thales to Spencer. Part II, arranged systematically includes psychology (Section G, p. 913-1192) as a separate subject. Over 14,000 items are arranged by author under 43 major subject headings. No index. This section which brings the literature down to 1902 is continued by *Psychological index* (F260). The best source for the older literature in psychology.

F273. Raven, Bertram H. A bibliography of publications relating to small groups. Los Angeles, Dept. of Psychology, University of California, Los Angeles, 1959. 1 v. various paging.

An extensive survey of the literature pertinent to small group research based upon a coded card file established by the author. The 1,445 items (monographs, journal articles, dissertations, published and unpublished reports) are arranged alphabetically by author with a subject index based upon the coding system which itself is outlined in Supplement no. 1. A 653 item supplement was published in May, 1961. Restricted almost wholly to English language items. No annotations. The bulk of the initial bibliography was based upon A.P. Hare's bibliography in *Small groups*. See (F274).

F274. Strodtbeck, Fred L. and A. Paul Hare. "Bibliography of small group research (from 1900 through 1953)" *Sociometry*, v. 17, May 1954; 107-178.

The first comprehensive bibliography on small group research this work lists research reports which place a central emphasis on the nature and consequences of face-to-face interaction in small groups. The 1,407 items are arranged by author and those monographs and articles considered to be important substantive and methodological contributions are starred. Topical cross references or classified arrangement would increase the bibliography's usefulness. 584 of the items dealing most precisely with small groups have been compiled as an annotated bibliography in A. Paul Hare's *Small groups* (N.Y. Knopf, 1955. p. 577-666). A new work by A. Paul Hare, *Handbook of small group research* (New York, The Free Press of Glencoe, 1962. 512 p.), is essentially a "state-of-the-art" review of the study of social interaction in small groups which presents "a catalog of the field" with references in the text to a 1,385 item bibliography of works published between 1900 and 1959.

See also: D243, D253.

DICTIONARIES

F275. Baldwin, James M., *ed.* Dictionary of philosophy and psychology . . . New York, Macmillan, 1901-05. 3 v. in 4.

Developed as an aid toward standardizing definitions of the principal concepts of ethics, logic, aesthetics, philosophy of religion, mental pathology, anthropology, biology, neurology, economics, political and social philosophy, philology, physical science and education. A second object: to interpret the movements of thought which have given significance to these terms and their different meanings. Equivalent terminology given in French, German and Italian. Four categories of articles: concise definitions, definitions with brief historical and other explanatory information, longer topical articles (1,000-5,000 words) and some brief biography. Many bibliographies. Authoritative when first issued although out of date for modern developments.

F276. Dorsch, Friedrich. Psychologisches Wörterbuch. 6th völlig rev. Aufl. Hamburg, Meiner, 1959. 488 p.

The revised and expanded 6th ed. of the dictionary, founded by Fritz Giese and first published in 1920. Encyclopedic in its coverage of current psychological terms. Definitions cite Latin and Greek derivations, refer to original authors and give cross-references to the 1,200 item bibliography. English language terms are cited and translated. Appendix lists and describes over 500 mental tests.

F277. Drever, James. A dictionary of psychology. Harmondsworth, Middlesex, Penguin Books, 1952. 315 p.

An excellent, inexpensive dictionary in which some 4,000 terms are concisely defined with adequate cross-references. Includes foreign terms.

F278. English, Horace B. and Ava C. English, A comprehensive dictionary of psychological and psychoanalytical terms; a guide to usage. New York, Longmans, Green, 1958. 594 p.

An excellent up-to-date dictionary of psychological terms with over 13,000 entries. Attempts to define all terms frequently used in a special or technical sense by psychologists as well as relevant terms from mathematics, medicine, and other related fields. Sources are not routinely identified but specialized terms or usages of a branch of science, school or an individual are so labeled. Extensive cross-referencing. Contains more discussion of moot points and obscure matters than Warren (F282).

F279. Hehlmann, Wilhelm. Wörterbuch der Psychologie. 2. erg. und erw. Aufl. Stuttgart, A. Kröner, 1962. 640 p.
A standard German dictionary with over 3,500 entries. References to the literature accompany all main entries. Includes information on the work of individual psychologists, together with their principal publications. Extensive entries on the schools and branches of psychology. Chronology of significant names and events. Appendix of psychological literature.

F280. Hinsie, Leland E. and Robert J. Campbell. Psychiatric dictionary. 3d ed. New York, Oxford Univ. Press, 1960. 788 p.

F281. Piéron, Henri. Vocabulaire de la psychologie. 3. ed. Paris, Presses Universitaires de France, 1963. 528 p.
An alphabetical listing of over 3,700 terms, briefly defined and assigned to their creators and exponents with dates, but no direct references to the literature. Definitions are signed. Some English terms are included; there are also German and English equivalents, synonyms, antonyms and adequate cross-references. Alphabetical index of 1,160 names cited. Nine appendices deal with abbreviations, symbols, tables, formulae, etc.

F282. Warren, Howard C. Dictionary of psychology. Boston, Houghton Mifflin, 1934. 372 p.
An authoritative earlier work now largely superseded by English (F278) but still useful for foreign equivalents included in many definitions

and also the German and French glossaries included in the appendix.

ENCYCLOPEDIAS AND
ENCYCLOPEDIC SETS

F283. Handbuch der Psychologie, hrsg. von Philipp Lersch *et al.* Göttingen, Verlag für Psychologie, 1959 + (in progress)
An extensive survey of the progress of modern psychology. Each of its 12 volumes deals with a different aspect of the subject and is the work of many scholars. Human behavior, cognition, developmental psychology, are among the topics covered to date. Thorough bibliography supplements each chapter. Author and subject indexes in each volume.

F284. Harriman, Philip L. Encyclopedia of psychology. New York, Philosophical Library, 1946. 897 p.
The only English language encyclopedia of psychology. Unfortunately, the quality of the articles varies widely and the length of the articles frequently has little relation to the importance of the topic. Index of topics. Articles are signed and include brief bibliographies.

F285. Psychology: a study of a science, ed. by Sigmund Koch. New York, McGraw-Hill, 1959+ (in progress)
An extensive inquiry into the status and tendency in psychological science, the end result of the American Psychological Association's "Project A" which had as its purpose to analyze the "methodological, theoretical and empirical status of psychological science." 80 scholars have contributed sustained essays which consider: (Study I, v. 1-3) the fields and systematic formulations within psychology; and (Study II, v. 4-6) the structure, mutual interrelations and associations with other sciences. A final volume by the editor will include commentary on the

significance of the findings. Each volume has name and subject indexes.

See also: D268, D274n.

See also: D268, D274n.

DIRECTORIES AND BIOGRAPHICAL
INFORMATION

F286. American Board for Psychological Services. Directory of American psychological services. 2d ed. Glendale, Ohio, 1960. 214 p.

A directory of 180 clinical, counseling, industrial and research services in the U.S. and Canada which are available to the public.

F287. American Psychiatric Association. Biographical directory of fellows and members, as of May 8, 1963. New York, Bowker, 1963 645 p.

An alphabetical listing of 10,000 American psychiatrists and including a few from foreign countries. Gives for each his professional training, experience, specialty, selection of publications and address. Geographical index.

F288. American Psychological Association. Directory. v. 1+ 1916+ Washington. annual.

Basic directory of American psychologists (1963 ed. lists 20,989 members) giving for each entry date of birth, education, occupation, special fields of interest and address. Geographical and institutional index. Supplementary information on APA history, bylaws, publications, membership requirements and officers.

F289. National Research Council. Committee on an International Directory of Psychologists. International directory of psychologists, exclusive of the U.S.A. Assen, Netherlands, Van Gorcum, 1958. 527 p.

A listing of 7,000 psychologists from 76 countries outside of the U.S. Arrangement is by country. Informa-

tion given on name and title, address, date and place of birth, highest academic degree, professional membership, editorial responsibilities, current occupation and primary fields of interest. Alphabetical index of names. New edition in preparation.

F290. Psychological register, ed. by Carl Murchison. Worcester, Mass., Clark Univ. Press, 1929-32. v. 2-3.
See description under (F271ᵃ).

HANDBOOKS, MANUALS, COMPENDIA

F291. Arieti, Silvano, *ed.* American handbook of psychiatry. New York, Basic Books, 1959. 2 v. (2098 p.)

In these two volumes 111 specialists have presented "the developments, concepts, trends, techniques, problems and prospects of psychiatry today, in a form useful for both the expert and the beginner, in which every leading school of thought and every major approach is included." (Pref.) For social psychologists numerous articles or parts of articles are of special interest, including discussions of personality theory, the family and the community of the psychiatric patient, statistical data on mental illness, juvenile delinquency, social psychology, psychiatric problems of adolescence, etc. Bibliographical references. Name and subject indexes.

F292. Eysenck, Hans J., *ed.* Handbook of abnormal psychology; an experimental approach. New York, Basic Books, 1961. 816 p.

F293. Fryer, Douglas H. and Edwin R. Henry, *eds.* Handbook of applied psychology. New York, Rinehart, 1950. 2 v.

Comprehensive coverage in the form of 115 essays by specialists, each contribution carrying a bibliography. Five major areas dealing with the application of psychology to: (1) group living and individual efficiency, (2) business and industry, (3) education (4) clinical investigation and (5) professional problems. Concludes with a select but extensive classified bibliography of 2,382 items. Subject index.

F294. Lindzey, Gardner, *ed.* Handbook of social psychology. Cambridge, Mass., Addison-Wesley, 1954. 2 v.
Authoritative, critical surveys of the work in every field of social psychology prepared by 45 specialists. Largely supersedes the older work by Murchison (F295). Vol. 1 presents "theoretical convictions, systematic positions and methods" of social psychology. Vol. 2 focuses upon the substantive findings and applications of social psychology. Each chapter is followed by an extensive bibliography. Each volume has its own author and subject index.

F295. Murchison, Carl, *ed.* Handbook of social psychology. Worcester, Mass., Clark Univ. Press, 1935. 1125 p.
The contributions of 24 specialists constitute a useful, but dated, guide to the collected literature on topics in social psychology emphasizing socialization and the social behavior of the individual. Extensive bibliographies. Largely superseded by Lindzey (F294).

F296. Stevens, Samuel S., *ed.* Handbook of experimental psychology. New York, Wiley, 1951. 1436 p.
A comprehensive survey by 44 specialists which systematizes, digests and appraises the mid-century state of experimental psychology. Updates Carl Murchison's *Handbook of general experimental psychology* (Worcester, Mass., Clark Univ. Press, 1934. 1125 p.) Major sections: (1) physiological mechanisms, (2) growth and development, (3) motivation, (4) learning and adjustment, (5) sensory processes, and (6) hu-

man performance. Each chapter has bibliographical references. Name and subject indexes.

SOURCES OF SCHOLARLY
CONTRIBUTIONS

F297. *Journals*

American journal of psychology. v. 1+ 1887+ Austin, Texas, Dept. of Psychology, Univ. of Texas. quarterly.
Bibl Fremd Zeit; Biol Abst; Bull Sig; Chem Abst; Med Lit; Psych Abst; QC Ind Med.

British journal of psychology. v. 1+ 1904+ London, British Psychological Society. quarterly.
Bibl Fremd Zeit; Biol Abst; Br Subj Ind; Br Ed Ind; Bull Sig; Med Lit; Psych Abst.

British journal of social and clinical psychology. v. 1, no. 1+ Feb., 1962+. Cambridge, British Psychological Society. quarterly.

Human relations. v. 1+ 1947+ London, Tavistock Publications. quarterly.
Bibl Fremd Zeit; Biol Abst; Br. Ed Ind; Br Subj Ind; Bull Anal; Bull Sig; Int Ind; PAIS; Psych Abst; Soc Abst.

Journal of abnormal and social psychology. v. 1+ 1906+ Washington, American Psychological Association. bi-monthly through 1961; monthly 1962+.
Bibl Fremd Zeit; Biol Abst; Bull Anal; Bull Sig; Med Lit; Psych Abst; QC Ind Med; Soc Abst.

Journal of applied psychology. v. 1+ 1917+ Washington, American Psychological Association. bi-monthly.
Bibl Fremd Zeit; Bull Sig; Psych Abst.

Journal of social issues. v. 1+ 1945+ New York, Society for the

Psychological Study of Social Issues. quarterly.

Bibl Fremd Zeit; Bull Anal; Bull Sig; Int Ind; Psych Abst; Soc Abst.

Journal of social psychology. v. 1+ 1929+ Provincetown, Mass., Journal Press. quarterly.

Bibl Fremd Zeit; Biol Abst; Bull Anal; Bull Sig; Psych Abst.

Psychological review. v. 1+ 1894+ Washington, American Psychological Association. bi-monthly.

Bibl Fremd Zeit; Biol Abst; Bull Sig; Med Lit; Psych Abst.

Psychologie française. v. 1+ 1956+ Paris, Société Française de Psychologie. quarterly.

Bull Sig; Psych Abst.

Psychologische Beiträge. v. 1+ 1953+ Meisenham am Glan, Deutsche Gesellschaft für Psychologie. quarterly (Summaries in English and French).

Bibl Deut Zeit; Psych Abst.

Psychologische Forschung; Zeitschrift für Psychologie und Ihre Grenzwissenschaften. v. 1+ 1921+ Berlin, Springer Verlag. irregular.

Bibl Deut Zeit; Bull Sig; Med Lit.

Psychologische Rundschau; Überlick über der Fortschritte dr Psychologie in Deutschland, Österreich und der Schweiz. v. 1+ 1949+ Göttingen, Verlag für Psychologie. quarterly.

Bibl Deut Zeit; Bull Sig; Psych Abst.

Rivista di psicologia. v. 1+ 1905+ Firenze, Societa Italiana di Psicologia. quarterly (Summaries in English, French and German).

Bibl Fremd Zeit; Bull Sig; Psych Abst.

Sociometry; a journal of research in social psychology. v. 1+ 1937+ New York, American Sociological Society. quarterly.

Bull Anal; Bull Sig; PAIS; Psych Abst; Soc Abst.

Sociologus; Zeitschrift für empiris-

che Soziologie, Sozial psychologische und ethnologische Forschung. n.s.v. 1+ 1951+ Berlin, Duncker und Humbolt. semi-annual.

Bibl Deut Zeit; Soc Abst.

Zeitschrift für Psychologie und angewandte Psychologie und Charakterkunde. v. 1+ 1890+ Leipzig, Barth. irregular. (Suspended publication 1945-1953).

Bibl Deut Zeit; Bull Sig; Psych Abst.

F298. *Organizations*

American Association for Social Psychiatry. Washington. Founded 1958.

American Group Psychotherapy Association. New York. Founded 1942.

American Psychological Association. Washington, D.C. Founded 1892.

Association for Research in Nervous and Mental Diseases. New York. Founded 1920.

British Psychological Society. London. Founded 1902.

Deutsche Gesellschaft für Psychologie. Mainz. Founded 1903.

Inter American Society of Psychology. Mexico City. Founded 1951.

International Association of Applied Psychology. Paris. Founded 1920.

International Union of Scientific Psychology. Paris. Founded 1951.

Psychometric Society. St. Louis, Mo. Founded 1935.

Société Française de Psychologie. Paris. Founded 1901.

Society for Research in Child Development. Lafayette, Ind. Founded 1933.

Society for the Psychological Study of Social Issues. Ann Arbor, Mich. Founded 1936.

Tavistock Institute of Human Relations. London. Founded 1946.

Université de Paris. Institut de Psychologie. Paris. Founded 1920.

F299. *Monograph Series*

Archives de psychologie. v. 1+ 1901+ Geneva, Switzerland.

Archives of psychology. no. 1-300, 1906-1945. New York, Columbia Univ. Press. (Merged with *Psychological monographs* in 1945).

British journal of psychology (Monograph supplement) v. 1+ 1911+ London, British Psychological Society.

Catholic University of America. Studies in psychology and psychiatry. v. 1+ 1926+ Washington, D.C.

Genetic psychology monographs. v. 1+ 1926+ Provincetown, Mass., Journal Press. quarterly.

Menninger Foundation. Monograph series. v. 1+ 1936+ Topeka, Kansas.

Neue psychologische Studien. Bd. 1+ 1926+ Munchen, C.H. Beck'sche. (Supersedes *Psychologische studien.* v. 1-10, 1905-1918. Leipzig).

Sociometry monographs. v. 1+ 1941+ New York, Beacon House.

Psychodrama and group psychotherapy monographs. v. 1+ 1944+ New York, Beacon House.

Psychological isues. v. 1+ 1959+ New York. International Universities Press.

Psychological monographs; general and applied. v. 1+ 1895+ Washington, American Psychological Assoc. Stanford University. Stanford

studies in psychology. v. 1+ 1959+ Stanford, Calif.

University of California. Publications in psychology. v. 1+ 1910+ Berkeley.

F300. Acta psychologica. European journal of psychology. v. 1+ 1935+ Amsterdam, North Holland Publ. Co. irregular.
Serves as a forum for European psychology and gives a general outline of current psychological research in many European countries. *Indexed in*; Bibl Fremd Zeit; Br Subj Ind; Bull Sig; Psych Abst.

F301. American psychologist; the professional journal of the American Psychological Association. v. 1+ 1946+ Washington. monthly.
The best single source to use to keep up to date with developments in American psychology. Some unsolicited articles, but mostly made up of papers and proceedings of the Association, articles about the profession, news and discussion on current problems, news of new research projects; and occasional articles on the state and progress of current psychology in other countries. *Indexed in*: Bibl Fremd Zeit; Biol Abst; Bull Sig; Chem Abst; Psych Abst; Soc Abst.

F302. Psychologia; an international journal of psychology in the Orient. v. 1+ 1951+ Kyoto, Japan, Psychologia Society. quarterly.
As a channel of communication from East to West and as a forum for international discussions *Psychologia* publishes symposia, general surveys, original materials, discussions, news, etc. from Japan, India and other Asian countries. *Indexed in*: Bull Sig; Psych Abst.

Thompson M. Little
Carl M. White

7

Education

The term *education* has several meanings. The basic one has been defined by John Dewey in 1911 in Paul Monroe's *A cyclopedia of education:* "Speaking generally, education signifies the sum total of processes
by means of which a community or social group, whether small or
large, transmits its acquired power and aims with a view to securing its
own continuous existence and growth." So far as the immature individual is concerned, Dewey defined education "as a process of the continuous reconstruction of experience with the purpose of widening and
deepening its social content, while, at the same time, the individual
gains control of the methods involved." There are other and somewhat
contrasting definitions, both in the present and throughout history, but
all of them usually consider education from the standpoint of the community and of the individual.

Education is also a body of knowledge and technique designed to prepare professional teachers through the study of psychology and its applications to school problems, the history and philosophy of schools and
the learning process, teaching and administrative procedures, and the
like. It is also applied to a scholarly discipline which seeks to discover
new and authenticated knowledge through the various processes of objective scientific research, such as the historical and experimental
methods. Education draws upon other disciplines for its basic content,
but it deals with this material in a way that the other fields do not, that

is, with reference to school learning processes, administration, and problems, as well as to broader issues involving influences on knowledge, attitudes, and behavior of individuals and groups.

The following analysis of educational literature will limit itself to books, although there are numerous articles and pamphlets of considerable reference value. It is too much to expect even a specialized librarian to be familiar with all the important smaller writings in the many branches of education. Familiarity with the bibliographies and indexes will be sufficient, in most instances, to direct the inquiring reader to satisfactory sources of periodical information.

Pedagogical literature is as old as recorded history. The masterworks of thought of all people have either been devoted to education or have contained thoughts on raising children and related questions. Thus, the *Book of proverbs* in the Bible, Plato's *Republic*, Cicero's *Essays and orations*, and many other great books from the remote past to the present have had something of significance to say about the various aspects of education. So far as special pedagogical works are concerned, there is a long list of writings, such as Plutarch's essay on the education of children in his *Moralia*; Quintilian's *Institutes of oratory*; Erasmus' *Education of the Christian prince*; John Locke's *Some thoughts concerning education*; Jean-Jacques Rousseau's *Emile*; the numerous writings by Johann Heinrich Pestalozzi, Johann Friedrich Herbart, and Friedrich Froebel; the annual reports of Horace Mann; the books by Sir Richard Livingstone, John Dewey, Maria Montessori, Anton S. Makarenko, and other educators of many nations. The major works of this nature can be located with little delay in the standard biographies of the writers, books on educational history and theory, the educational encyclopedias, and specialized bibliographies. The educational reference librarian would do well to compile lists of the educators, more or less influential, of the various countries, together with some biographical facts and the titles of the chief works.

In addition to the seminal studies of educational theory which date from ancient times, there is a vast corpus of volumes on different aspects of education intended for the prospective teacher, the practicing teacher, the scholar in education, and the educational research worker. Such books began to appear with increasing frequency from the early 19th century onward, although monographs on educational history go back at least three centuries earlier. Obviously, it is impossible for the most advanced scholar to be familiar, let alone intimate, with this abundance of writings in the field of education. Even the educational historian would find it very difficult to know all the important works of the past and present in his area in the major languages. It is helpful to keep in mind the remark by Professor Will Seymour Monroe in his *Bibliography of education* (New York, Appleton, 1897. p. xi), that "the literature on education is now admittedly large and is growing daily." That was in 1897, and the situation six and one half decades later is even more true. Accordingly, it is clear that the librarian who specializes in education must be selective and critical in his approach toward the mastery of the literature in his field. He must also constantly be reading and scanning to broaden the scope of his knowledge of and acquaintance with the significant books and other source materials.

INTRODUCTORY WORKS

From about the early 19th century onward, there appeared systematic treatises on pedagogy which offered introductions and surveys of the entire field or major portions of it. Among the classic works are Johann F. Herbart's *Allgemeine pädagogik aus dem zweck der erziehung abgeleitet.* (Göttingen, J. F. Röwer, 1806. 482 p.), Tuiskon Ziller's *Vorlesungen über allgemeine pädogogik.* (Leipzig, H. Matthes, 1876. 344 p.), and Alexander Bain's *Education as a science* (New York, Appleton, 1879. 453 p.). These books influenced generations of educators and teachers in their native countries and abroad.

There are some still older works which have much to offer the reader, even if they are outdated with respect to some particular details and statistics. Chapman and Counts treat the interrelationship of education with society, psychology, and the nature of the school. Klapper's approach is to consider education as physical, social, economic, and mental adjustment, while Burton treats some of the same themes and adds much material on the American school system and education as a profession. Wilson and Kandel offer a brief survey of the American educational system but, unlike many other authors of similar books at the time, include a chapter on private and religious schools. The volume edited by Skinner and Langfitt covers the principles, methods, organization, and administration, psychology, history, and other aspects of American education. Of similar scope, but particularly helpful for the understanding of the European backgrounds of American education, is the work by Russell and Judd. Doughton offers a detailed treatment of the philosophy, science, organization, and problems of education from the standpoint of theory and history.

Among the introductory books published since the end of World War II, two are compilations by various contributors. The one edited by Valentine covers educational theory, psychology, sociology, and organization. In this volume proponents of the various schools of thought present their respective views. The Bereday-Volpicelli book, briefer but much more recent, contains essays on various problems and issues in American education. The latter is especially suited for a synoptic view of the current stresses and strains; it is also useful to the foreign student wishing to be familiar with the main developments and pressure points in education in the United States.

The introductory treatises are designed mainly for the prospective teacher but might also be consulted with profit by teachers in service, administrators, and others who wish to obtain a general and fundamental notion of education and of the American school system. All consider similar subject matter to a greater or lesser extent—principles, administration and organization, methods and materials of learning and teaching, the relation to society, and the like. Reeder includes a long section on education as a profession. A special feature of the MacLean-Lee volume is the relation of the United States to international educational activities, while that of French is the relation of American education to foreign school systems. The third edition of De Young's book, which is of considerable value for reference, emphasizes administration and organization and includes a sizable chapter on the educational controversies. At least two-fifths of Thayer's book is concerned with such issues as racial segregation, academic freedom, church and state in relation to school, Federal aid, and criticism of public schools. Lee presents a comprehensive view of the American school system, plus international education and several controversies. Pounds and Bryner analyze the historical and current relationships of the schools to the community, the socio-economic problems of education, contrasting conceptions of the school, and education on an international scale. Hillway discusses the standard content in a brief and elementary but clear manner. Hughes inserts a chapter on the various non-public schools. Chandler's book is a concise survey of the background, nature, and problems of American education, as a prelude to the study of the scholarly and professional preparation of the teacher. Callahan combines textual matter and source readings in his approach to the past, present, and probable future of education.

The librarian should be acquainted with a sampling of the foreign general works on education. Sir Percy Nunn emphasizes philosophical and psychological principles, while Raymont adds curriculum theory and practice. Hughes and Hughes include a detailed chapter on creativity in education. Lester Smith gives attention to the theory, sociology, and organization of education.

Hubert is a standard, comprehensive introduction. Schneider deals mainly with the theoretical structure and problems of education. Morando's book concentrates on the historical, philosophical, and scientific foundations of education, together with current problems in Italy and elsewhere. García Hoz treats these topics and also a variety of other themes, including comparative education. Finally, account should be taken of the introductory books published in the U.S.S.R. The volume edited by Kairov appears to be a revision of the successful text by Yesipov and Goncharov, part of which was published in English as, "I want to be like Stalin." This book discusses principles, theory, organization, and methodology of education.

G1. Bereday, George Z.F. and Luigi Volpicelli, *eds.* Public education in America. New York, Harper, 1958. 212 p.
G2. Burton, William H. Introduction to education. New York, Appleton-Century, 1934. 833 p.
G3. Callahan, Raymond E. An Introduction to education in American society. 2d ed. New York, Knopf, 1960. 467 p.
G4. Chandler, Bobby J. Education and the teacher. New York, Dodd, Mead, 1961. 403 p.
G5. Chapman, James C. and George S. Counts. Principles of education. Boston, Houghton Mifflin, 1924. 645 p.
G6. De Young, Chris A. Introduction to American public education. 3d ed. New York, McGraw-Hill, 1955. 604 p.
G7. Doughton, Isaac. Modern public education: its philosophy and background. New York, Appleton-Century, 1935. 729 p.
G8. French, William M. Education for all. New York, Odyssey, 1955. 383 p.
G9. García Hoz, Victor. Principios de pedagogía sistemática. Madrid, Ediciones Rialp, 1960. 448 p.
G10. Hillway, Tyrus. Education in American society. Boston, Houghton Mifflin, 1961, 530 p.
G11. Hubert, René. Traité de pédagogie générale. Paris, Presses Universitaires de France, 1946. 687 p.
G12. Hughes, Arthur G. and Ethel H. Hughes. Education: some fundamental problems. London, Longmans, Green, 1960. 296 p.
G13. Hughes, James M. Education in America. Evanston, Ill., Row, Peterson, 1960. 496 p.
G14. Kairov, I.A. *et al.* Pedagogika. Moscow, Uchpedgiz, 1956. 436 p.
G15. Klapper, Paul. Contemporary education: its principles and practice, New York, Appleton, 1929. 660 p.
G16. Lee, Gordon C. An introduction to education in modern America. Rev. ed. New York, Holt, 1957. 624 p.
G17. Lester Smith, W.O. Education. Harmondsworth, Penguin Books, 1961. 240 p.
G18. MacLean, Malcolm S. and Edwin A. Lee. Change and process in education. New York, Dryden, 1956. 520 p.
G19. Mason, Robert E. Educational ideals in American society, Boston, Allyn and Bacon, 1960. 337 p.
G20. Morando, Dante. Pedagogia. Brescia, Morcelliana, 1951. 446 p.
G21. Nunn, *Sir* Thomas P. Education: its data and first principles. 3d ed. London, Arnold, 1945. 383 p.
G22. Pounds, Ralph L. and James R. Bryner. The school in American society. New York, Macmillan, 1959. 518 p.
G23. Raymont, Thomas. Modern education: its aims and methods. 4th ed. London, Longmans, Green, 1953. 237 p.
G24. Reeder, Ward, G. A first course in education. 4th ed. New York, Macmillan, 1958. 644 p.
G25. Russell, John D. and Charles H. Judd. The American educational system. Boston, Houghton Mifflin, 1940. 554 p.
G26. Schneider, Friedrich. Einführung in die Erziehungswissenschaft. 2. Aufl. Graz, Verlag Styria, 1953. 427 p.

G27. Skinner, Charles E. and Roy E. Langfitt, *eds.* An introduction to modern education. Boston, Heath, 1937. 491 p.
G28. Thayer, Vivian T. The role of the school in American society. New York, Dodd, Mead, 1960. 530 p.
G29. Valentine, Percy F., *ed.* Twentieth century education. New York, Philosophical Library, 1946. 655 p.
G30. Wilson, Lester M. and Isaac L. Kandel. Introduction to the study of American education. New York, Nelson, 1934. 328 p.

EDUCATIONAL HISTORY

The student of the history of education can find short sketches of the subject in ancient, medieval, and Renaissance writings. Occasionally there are longer treatments, as in the histories prepared by Chinese scholars from the Han Dynasty onward, and in the works of Leonardo Bruni and Flavio Biondo in Italy in the middle of the 15th century. A historical treatise published in 1517 by Robert Goulet on the genesis of the University of Paris represents one of the earliest books devoted exclusively to educational history—in the Western world, at least. During the succeeding three centuries there were several books of broad scope, such as Hermann Conring's *De antiquitatibus academicis dissertationes septem* (three editions—1651, 1674, 1739), on the history of higher education, and Claude Fleury's *Traité des choix et de la méthode des études* (1675) on the general history of education. But there were many more specialized histories of individual universities or schools and biographies of educators. For example, Cotton Mather included a history of Harvard College in the fourth book of his classic, *Magnalia Christi Americana* (1702).

It was toward the end of the 18th century that the writing of the history of education may be said to have begun. During the 19th century, the most comprehensive and most influential general works were by Germans: Karl von Raumer (1847), Karl Schmidt (1860-1862), and K. A. Schmid (1884-1902). The work by the von Raumer appeared in English in Henry Barnard's *American journal of education* and provided the content for some of the leading American books on the history of education. In the United States, there were various writings on educational history, concerned mainly with colleges, prior to the publication in 1842 of the first general treatment, Henry I. Smith's *History of education, ancient and modern.*

As can very well be imagined, there is a plenitude of published material on the history of education, both general and specialized, in a variety of forms and in every literate language. The specialist is at a loss to be acquainted with even a small segment of it. The best that can be done is to select a sampling of books, particularly those that have enjoyed wide circulation. Let the student bear in mind that all branches and sub-branches in the field of education have a history. Some of these historical writings are of greater value than others. In several instances it is still necessary to write the history of a specific area or problem in education.

The literature on educational historiography can be classified in various ways. In the first place, there are the general works which usually cover the development of educational ideas, content, methods, institutions, and personalities from ancient times to the present, particularly in the Western world. Typical of this group are the books by Butts, Cubberley, Eby and Arrowood, and Mulhern. Another group considers the history of education in a specific country or period, the historical development of a single institution, idea, subject of study, or teaching procedure. Then there is a type of educational historiography which traces the origin and growth of one or more educational problems or issues.

The general works in the history of education are usually read as textbooks or are used for broad reference purposes. A *history of education,* by Cubberley, begins with Greece and Rome, concentrates on Western Europe, and concludes with Europe and the United States in the early twentieth century. A *cultural history of Western education,* by Butts, covers similar scope and geographical territory, emphasizing the intellectual role of education. Also concentrating on the West, but paying particular attention to Germany, is the three-volume work by Moog. Considerable detail is presented in the two volumes by Eby and Arrowood. A Catholic approach is furnished by McCormick and Cassidy, who also include chapters on several Asian nations. A special effort to pay adequate notice to Egypt and India is made by Mulhern. A recent work which seeks to balance the history of the education of East and West is Myers' adaptation and extension of Arnold J. Toynbee's historical thesis.

The history of education through an analysis of specific problems and phases, rather than through a direct chronological narration, is the contribution by Brubacher. Curtis and Boultwood confine themselves to the history of educational theory in the West, as does Ulich. Two thorough studies of ancient education deserve special notice—Woody's on Asia, classical Greece and Rome; and Marrou's on Greco-Roman education.

Owing to the richness of all types of specialized writings in educational history, it will be possible to mention only a small number. There is no implication that these are necessarily better than those omitted. Monroe offers a comprehensive, but largely undocumented, analysis of American education until 1865. Curti studies and documents fully the views of the most influential American educators of the 19th and 20th centuries. Lowndes deals with the changes in English education from 1895 to 1935. Bollnow presents the thought of German educators during the 19th century. Glatigny covers briefly French education from the middle ages to the 20th century.

Several collections of historical source materials might be mentioned as examples. Cubberley's readings include documents and extracts on all aspects of education from ancient times onward. The book by Knight and Hall has similar sources on the history of American education. Painter's work contains long passages from educational writings from Plato to the thinkers of the nineteenth century. Ulich adds to these some of the educational classics of the Eastern world.

There are still many varieties of monographs in educational history to which attention might be invited. Only some can be cited however, because of the shortage of space.

G31. Bollnow, Otto F. Geschichte der Pädagogik: Die Pädagogik der deutschen Romantik: Von Arndt bis Froebel. Stuttgart, Kohl-hammer, 1952. 227 p.

G32. Brubacher, John S. A history of the problems of education. New York, McGraw-Hill, 1947. 688 p.

G33. Butts, R. Freeman. A cultural history of Western education. 2d ed. New York, McGraw-Hill, 1955. 645 p.

G34. Cubberley, Ellwood P. The history of education. Boston, Houghton Mifflin, 1920. 849 p.

G35. Cubberley, Ellwood P. Readings in the history of education. Boston, Houghton Mifflin, 1920. 648 p.

G36. Curti, Merle. The social ideas of American educators. New York, Scribner, 1935. 613 p.

G37. Curtis, Stanley J. and Myrtle E.A. Boultwood. A short history of educational ideas. 2d ed. London, Universal Tutorial Press, 1956. 563 p.

G38. Eby, Frederick and Charles F. Arrowood. The history and philosophy of education: ancient and medieval. New York, Prentice-Hall, 1940. 966 p.

G39. Eby, Frederick and Charles F. Arrowood. The development of modern education. New York, Prentice-Hall, 1934. 922 p.

G40. Glatigny, Michel. Histoire de l'enseignement en France. Paris, Presses Universitaires de France, 1949. 128 p.

G41. Knight, Edgar W. and Clifton L. Hall. Readings in American educational history. New York, Appleton-Century-Crofts, 1951. 799 p.

G42. Lowndes, George A.N. The silent social revolution. London, Oxford Univ. Press, 1937. 274 p.

G43. Marrou, Henri I. A history of education in antiquity, tr. by G. Lamb. New York, Sheed and Ward, 1956. 466 p.

G44. McCormick, Patrick J. and Francis P. Cassidy, History of education. 3d ed. Washington, Catholic Education Press, 1953. 688 p.

G45. Monroe, Paul. Founding of the American public school system. New York, Macmillan, 1940. 520 p.

G46. Moog, Willy. Geschichte der Pädagogik. Osterwieck/Harz, Zickfeldt, 1928-1933. 3 v.

G47. Mulhern, James. A history of education. 2d ed. New York, Ronald, 1959. 754 p.

G48. Myers, Edward D. Education in the perspective of history. New York, Harper, 1960. 388 p.

G49. Painter, Franklin V.N. Great pedagogical essays: Plato to Spencer. New York, American Book Co., 1905. 426 p.

G50. Ulich, Robert. History of educational thought. New York, American Book Co., 1945. 412 p.

G51. Ulich, Robert, *ed*. Three thousand years of educational wisdom. 2d
   ed. Cambridge, Harvard Univ. Press, 1954. 668 p.
G52. Woody, Thomas. Life and education in early societies. New York,
   Macmillan, 1949. 825 p.

EDUCATIONAL PHILOSOPHY

   This type of literature comprises general textbooks such as Brubacher's
Modern philosophies of education, which present fundamental principles and the viewpoints of the various schools of thought; an exposition
of a single theory, such as Breed's volume; and collections of statements
by different thinkers. A basic work is Dewey's *Democracy and education*, which represents pragmatism or experimentalism, but which must
be supplemented by his later and critical book, *Experience and education*. Another influential work exemplifying the pragmatic standpoint is
the book by Kilpatrick. The two volumes by Brameld treat contrasting
schools of educational thought as well as the author's own position of
Reconstructionism. Idealism is expressed by Horne, the Catholic educational philosophy is presented by Redden and Ryan, and the principles
of realism are stressed by Broudy. Woelfel analyzes in detail the theories
of seventeen American educators of different shades of thought. Brubacher brings together statements by an experimentalist, a realist, an
idealist and other educational philosophers, in the *41st Yearbook*. Two
symposia, by Brubacher and Scheffler, offer the thinking on education
by general philosophers.

G53. Brameld, Theodore. Philosophies of education in cultural perspective.
   New York, Dryden, 1955. 446 p.
G54. Brameld, Theodore. Toward a reconstructed philosophy of education.
   New York, Dryden, 1956. 417 p.
G55. Breed, Frederick S. Education and the new realism. New York, Mac-
   millan, 1939. 237 p.
G56. Broudy, Harry S. Building a philosophy of education. 2d ed. Engle-
   wood Cliffs, N.J., Prentice Hall, 1961. 410 p.
G57. Brubacher, John S. Modern philosophies of education. 2d ed. New
   York, McGraw Hill, 1950. 349 p.
G58. Brubacher, John S., *ed*. Modern philosophies and education. Chicago,
   National Society for the Study of Education, 1955. 374 p. (*Fifty-
   fourth yearbook, Part I*)
G59. Brubacher, John S., *ed*. Philosophies of education. Bloomington, Ill.,
   National Society for the Study of Education, 1942. 321 p. (*Forty-
   first yearbook, Part I*)
G60. Dewey, John. Democracy and education. New York, Macmillan,
   1916. 434 p.
G61. Dewey, John. Experience and education. New York, Macmillan,
   1938. 116 p.
G62. Horne, Herman H. The philosophy of education. New York, Macmillan, 1904. 295 p.

G63. Kilpatrick, William H. Philosophy of education. New York, Macmillan, 1951. 465 p.
G64. Redden, John D. and Francis A. Ryan. A Catholic philosophy of education. Rev. ed. Milwaukee, Bruce, 1956. 601 p.
G65. Scheffler, Israel, *ed*. Philosophy and education. Boston, Allyn and Bacon, 1958. 311 p.
G66. Woelfel, Norman. Molders of the American mind. New York, Columbia Univ. Press, 1933. 304 p.

EDUCATIONAL PSYCHOLOGY AND MEASUREMENT

As in the other branches of the field of education, there are various types of books in educational psychology and measurement. Some are broad in scope, embracing such topics as intelligence, learning, the individual, physical and social growth, behavior, and the like. Examples of these are the works of Stroud and Stephens. Others concentrate on the different aspects of the learning process, with particular reference to learning in school, but do not omit any of the basic content. Among such books are those by Frandsen and Lindgren. In addition, there are available specialized, scholarly analyses, such as the volume by McGeoch and Irion on the learning process. Some works are compilations of chapters by specialists on various phases of growth and development, learning, personality, and measurement. Typical of this group is the book edited by Skinner and Remmers *et al*. The anthology edited by Fullagar and colleagues contains statements on learning not only by contemporaries but also by historical personalities, such as Edward L. Thorndike and John Dewey.

The book on measurement by Ross and Stanley is a thorough presentation of all aspects of the subject of testing, including its history. Another work of similar scope, but briefer in historical detail, is the one by Noll. The topic of tests and measurements appears, often in more abbreviated fashion, in the general textbooks on educational psychology.

G67. Frandsen, Arden N. How children learn. New York, McGraw-Hill, 1957. 546 p.
G68. Fullagar, William A., *et al*. Readings for educational psychology. New York, Crowell, 1956. 500 p.
G69. Lindgren, Henry C. Educational psychology in the classroom. New York, Wiley, 1956. 521 p.
G70. McGeoch, John A. and Arthur L. Irion. The psychology of human learning. 2d ed. New York, Longmans, Green. 1952. 596 p.
G71. Noll, Victor H. Introduction to educational measurement. Boston, Houghton Mifflin, 1957. 437 p.
G72. Remmers, Hermann H., *et al*. Growth, teaching, and learning. New York, Harper, 1957. 557 p.
G73. Ross, Clay C. and Julian C. Stanley. Measurement in today's schools. 3d ed. New York, Prentice-Hall, 1954. 485 p.

G74. Skinner, Charles E., *ed.* Educational psychology. 3d ed. New York, Prentice-Hall, 1951. 791 p.

G75. Stephens, John M. Educational psychology. Rev. ed. New York, Holt, 1956. 717 p.

G76. Stroud, James B. Psychology in education. Rev. ed. New York, Longmans, Green, 1956. 617 p.

EDUCATIONAL SOCIOLOGY

The field of educational sociology was inaugurated around the turn of the 20th century by sociologists who applied the principles of their discipline to the problems of education. After a period during which it was developed by educators who injected a social emphasis into the study of education, it seems to have attracted, in recent years, more and more attention by professional sociologists. Brown's textbook deals with the individual in relation to social institutions, particularly the school. Of similar scope is the volume by Havighurst and Neugarten, which also introduces the international context of education. Brookover treats education in relation to the social order and the impact of the school on personal and interpersonal development. The book by Rodehaver *et al.* is a brief survey of the school in connection with the individual, groups, and society at large, while Dahlke covers these topics and others in a more thorough form. In a book of readings, Mercer and Carr present discussions by sociologists and educators of the interrelationship of education, culture, and society, and of the role of the school in American society. The compilation by Meltzer *et al.* comprises a similar scope, mainly from the viewpoint of educators. Stanley and his collaborators offer essays by sociologists, educators, and other social scientists on the school as a social institution, the school in relation to the community, the school in American society, and the social apsects of school organization, teaching methods, and the teaching profession. Of the growing literature of a specialized nature two studies might be mentioned. The classic work by Warner *et al.* is a significant analysis of the actual status in America of the concept of equal educational opportunity for all. Knapp considers racial segregation, social class differences, and other problems involved in the administration of education in large cities.

G77. Brookover, Wilbur B. A sociology of education. New York, American Book Co., 1955. 436 p.

G78. Brown, Francis J. Educational sociology. New York, Prentice-Hall, 1947. 626 p.

G79. Dahlke, H. Otto. Values in culture and classroom. New York, Harper, 1958. 575 p.

G80. Havighurst, Robert J. and Bernice L. Neugarten. Society and education. Boston, Allyn and Bacon, 1957. 465 p.

G81. Knapp, Robert B. Social integration in urban communities. New

York, Bureau of Publications, Teachers College, Columbia Univ.,
        1960. 196 p.
G82. Meltzer, Bernard N., *et al.* Education in society: readings. New York,
        Crowell, 1958. 498 p.
G83. Mercer, Blaine E. and Edwin R. Carr, *eds.* Education and the social
        order. New York, Rinehart, 1957. 585 p.
G84. Rodehaver, Myles W., *et al.* The sociology of the school. New York,
        Crowell, 1957. 262 p.
G85. Stanley, William O., *et al.* Social foundations of education. New York,
        Dryden, 1956. 638 p.
G86. Warner, W. Lloyd, *et al.* Who shall be educated? New York, Harper,
        1944. 190 p.

COMPARATIVE EDUCATION

The study of the national system of education or of an educational
problem in the perspective of the development of one or more nations
has achieved some popularity in recent decades, especially during the
1950's. As a field of research and writing, however, it is well over a century and a half old. The literature includes reference books, compilations,
theoretical works, documentary collections, textbooks, yearbooks, periodicals, analyses of observations, and so forth. Among such writings are
the yearbooks of Teachers College of Columbia University and of the
University of London Institute of Education, the yearbooks of the International Bureau of Education, the volumes of the *World survey of
education* issued by Unesco, the *International review of education* and
the *Comparative education review*, and the monographic reports on education in various countries, published by the U.S. Office of Education.

The fundamental theoretical work by Schneider throws light on the
nature of comparative education and on educational questions in international perspective. The classic study, *Comparative education*, by
Kandel, considers eight issues—national character, state and school,
teacher education, etc.—in five European countries and the United
States. To some extent, his later volume is an abbreviated and updated
treatment of these and other problems. Hans, also a pioneer in the field,
deals with language, race, religion, and other factors underlying national
educational systems, and compares the school systems of England,
France, the U.S.S.R., and the U.S.A. Cramer and Browne treat school
administration, organization, and other problems in several countries
in Asia, Europe, Australia, and North America. Mallinson deals comparatively with the traditional subject matter of the field from the standpoint of nine European nations and the United States. King, utilizing
the approach of national systems, devotes attention to four European
countries, the United States, and India.

The more specialized studies include monographs on the school systems of several or single countries, sometimes in comparison with other countries. Many are concerned with one or more educational problems in the context of one or more foreign cultures. An example of the latter is the compilation of reports edited by Hylla and Wrinkle, which covers the various phases and problems of education in the West European countries. DeWitt's study is a careful examination of the educational system of the Soviet Union, with special reference to the training of scientists and engineers, and with consideration of the comparable situation in the United States. Ward indicates the problems in the education of the emergent nations of Africa and Asia. Merriam discusses the approaches and methods of training for citizenship in several European countries and the U.S. The study by Peers emphasizes adult education in England but includes a treatment of America, Germany, and underdeveloped nations.

G87. Cramer, John F. and George S. Browne. Contemporary education: a comparative study of national systems. New York, Harcourt, Brace, 1956. 637 p.
G88. De Witt, Nicholas. Education and professional employment in the U.S.S.R. Washington, Govt. Print. Off., 1962. 856 p.
G89. Hans, Nicholas A. Comparative education. 3d ed. London, Routledge and Kegan Paul. 1958. 333 p.
G90. Hylla, Erich and William L. Wrinkle, eds. Die Schulen in Westeuropa. Bad Nauheim, Christian-Verlag, 1953. 663 p.
G91. Kandel, Isaac L. Comparative education. Boston, Houghton Mifflin, 1933. 922 p.
G92. Kandel, Isaac L. The new era in education: a comparative study. Boston, Houghton Mifflin, 1955. 388 p.
G93. King, Edmund J. Other schools and ours. New York, Rinehart, 1958. 234 p.
G94. Mallinson, Vernon. An introduction to the study of comparative education. 2d ed. New York, Macmillan, 1960. 257 p.
G95. Merriam, Charles E. The making of citizens: a comparative study of the methods of civic training. Chicago, Univ. of Chicago Press, 1931. 371 p.
G96. Peers, Robert. Adult education: a comparative study. London, Routledge and Kegan Paul, 1958. 365 p.
G97. Schneider, Friedrich. Triebkräfte der Pädagogik der Völker. Salzburg, Otto Müller-Verlag, 1947. 503 p.
G98. Ward, William E.F. Educating young nations. London, Allen and Unwin, 1959. 194 p.

GENERAL METHODS OF TEACHING

In recent years, the trend has been away from the writing of treatises on general methods of teaching, as was common several decades ago. The book by the McMurry brothers provided guidance to teachers in the application teaching principles associated with Johann F. Herbart and his followers in Germany. The new procedures in teaching, such as the project method, are described in conversational form in Kilpatrick's classic exposition. Another approach to teaching, based on the practice of the great teachers of history from Socrates to the present, is depicted by Highet. Mort and Vincent offer a compendium of actual classroom methods, which they classify into 21 teaching procedures. Hicks and Walker compile lesson plans for classes on the different scholastic levels and include useful suggestions for the prospective teacher. A thorough-going treatise on teaching practice as derived from the principles of learning is contributed by Burton. Of great value for improving instruction and remedial teaching of reading and other basic subjects in elementary and high schools is the book by Blair.

G99. Blair, Glenn M. Diagnostic and remedial teaching. New York, Macmillan, 1956. 409 p.
G100. Burton, William H. The guidance of learning activities. 2d ed. New York, Appleton-Century-Crofts, 1952. 737 p.
G101. Hicks, William V. and Clare C. Walker. Full-time student teaching. East Lansing, Michigan State Univ. Press, 1958. 146 p.
G102. Highet, Gilbert. The art of teaching. New York, Knopf, 1950. 291 p.
G103. Kilpatrick, William H. Foundations of teaching. New York, Macmillan, 1925. 383 p.
G104. McMurry, Charles A. and Frank M. McMurry. The method of the recitation. New York, Macmillan, 1903.
G105. Mort, Paul R. and William S. Vincent. Modern educational practice: a handbook for teachers. New York, McGraw-Hill, 1950. 437 p.

SPECIAL METHODS OF TEACHING

In this category may be found books of broad and narrow scope, with respect to level of school and subject matter. Heffernan and Todd describe the recommended procedures for teaching in a kindergarten. The instructional methods in the various activities of learning in the elementary school are presented in detail in the works by Ohlsen, Kyte, Stendler, Logan and Logan, and Mehl *et al.* One method, the unit, is discussed in great detail by Hanna and colleagues. In the field of secondary school teaching there have been several books of significance and influence. Among these Morrison's occupies a place of great importance, especially because of its analysis of the unit method. The volumes by Bossing, Butler, and Mills and Douglass are general treatises on teaching procedures in high school. In addition, there are books on the teaching of special subjects in the primary and secondary schools. To this group belong Strickland's teaching of reading, writing, and spelling in the elementary grades; Preston's manual on methods in elementary social studies; and the volume on the procedures for secondary school social studies by Wesley and Wronski. Finally, there are still more specialized works dealing with the teaching of a single subject in the elementary or high school. An example of this type of methodological literature is furnished by Johnson's pioneering and thorough analysis of history instruction on the elementary and secondary school levels. In the past two decades, moreover, there has emerged a trend for the publication of books on methods of teaching in colleges and universities, although systematic and comprehensive books appeared as far back as 1920. Blauch discusses learning principles and teaching methods such as the lecture, discussion, individual study, and the like, with particular attention to the teaching of dentistry. The volume edited by Cronkhite offers essays on general methods, testing, special methods in several subject areas, and guidance for the prospective college instructor. Justman and Mais treat principles, methods, testing, student relations, and other pertinent subjects of importance to teaching in colleges and universities. The volume edited by Cooper deals with many new techniques of teaching which are adaptable in higher education. Finally, Mueller analyzes effective procedures for the teaching of adults.

G106. Blauch, Lloyd E. *et al.* Teaching in colleges and universities. Indianapolis, Ind., American Association of Dental Schools, 1945. 341 p.

G107. Bossing, Nelson L. Teaching in secondary schools. 3d ed. Boston, Houghton Mifflin, 1952. 558 p.

G108. Butler, Frank A. Improvement of teaching in secondary schools. 3d ed. Chicago, Univ. of Chicago Press, 1954. 433 p.

G109. Cooper, Russell M., *ed.* The two sides of the log: learning and teaching in today's college. Minneapolis, Univ. of Minnesota Press, 1958. 317 p.

G110. Cronkhite, Bernice B., *ed.* A handbook for college teachers. Cambridge, Harvard Univ. Press, 1950. 272 p.

G111. Hanna, Lavone A., *et al.* Unit teaching in the elementary school. New York, Rinehart, 1955. 592 p.

G112. Heffernan, Helen and Vivian E. Todd. The kindergarten teacher Boston, Heath, 1960. 419 p.

G113. Johnson, Henry. Teaching of history. Rev. ed. New York, Macmil lan, 1940. 467 p.

G114. Justman, Joseph and Walter H. Mais. College teaching: its practice and its potential. New York, Harper, 1956. 257 p.

G115. Kyte, George C. The elementary school teacher at work. New York, Dryden, 1957. 530 p.

G116. Logan, Lillian M. and Virgil G. Logan. Teaching the elementary school child. Boston, Houghton Mifflin, 1961. 900 p.

G117. Mehl, Marie A., *et al.* Teaching in elementary school. 2d ed. New York, Ronald, 1958. 518 p.

G118. Mills, Hubert H. and Harl R. Douglass. Teaching in high school. 2d ed. New York, Ronald, 1957. 516 p.

G119. Morrison, Henry C. The practice of teaching in the secondary school. Rev. ed. Chicago, Univ. of Chicago Press, 1931.

G120. Mueller, A.D. Principles and methods in adult education. New York, Rinehart, 1958. 382 p.

G121. Ohlsen, Merle M., *ed.* Modern methods in elementary education. New York, Holt, 1959. 688 p.

G122. Preston, Ralph C. Teaching social studies in the elementary school. Rev. ed. New York, Rinehart, 1958. 382 p.
G123. Stendler, Celia B. Teaching in the elementary school. New York, Harcourt Brace, 1958. 541 p.
G124. Strickland, Ruth G. The language arts in the elementary school. 2d ed. Boston, Heath, 1957. 464 p.
G125. Wesley, Edgar B. and Stanley P. Wronski. Teaching social studies in high schools. 4th ed. Boston, Heath, 1958. 628 p.

EDUCATIONAL ADMINISTRATION AND SUPERVISION

Perhaps the best general and bibliographical introduction to the literature of this broad area, as of 1947, is the volume by Sears. Moehlman discusses principles of organization and administration, and then proceeds to analyze the administration of schools on the local, state, and national levels. Miller and Spalding stress the role of decision-making in the community's schools, but also provide the socio-administrative framework for it. Reeder concentrates on the practical administration of teacher and pupil personnel, the plant, and finances, while Hunt and Pierce combine theory and practice with broader concepts of administration. A recent trend has been the production of publications which lay the theoretical groundwork of educational administration. Thus, Mort and Ross deal with values, democracy, prudence, and other basic concepts in working with the variety of human beings involved in the educational enterprise. In a briefer way, the Webers consider the relationship of democracy to leadership and group cooperation in schools. The volume edited by Campbell and Gregg presents chapters on the theory of administrative behavior and the professional development of educational executives. Another book written by Campbell and colleagues adds the lessons of educational history to the theory and practice of school administration. Case studies of administrative problems in education compiled by Sargent and Belisle provide prospective administrators with live material for learning principles and practices. The origins, theory, and practical procedures connected with the administration of a state educational system are presented by Thurston and Roe.

Specialized writings deal with particular forms and levels of administration. The book by Otto comprehensively covers administration, organization, curriculum issues, community relations, and other aspects of elementary education. French and colleagues treat similar questions in relation to the high school. Burton and Brueckner consider the theory, organization and practice of school supervision and the improvement of instruction, together with the evaluation of supervision. In a similar way, but adding a more detailed historical background and stressing the functional approach, Gwynn offers a recent analysis of supervision. The role and functions of members of school boards are adequately described in Tuttle's handbook. The numerous problems of planning and constructing schools are given specific and practical solutions in the volume by Engelhardt and colleagues.

G126. Burton, William H. and Leo J. Brueckner. Supervision: a social process. New York, Appleton-Century-Crofts, 1955. 715 p.
G127. Campbell, Roald F., *et al.* Introduction to educational administration. Boston, Allyn and Bacon, 1958. 434 p.
G128. Campbell, Roald F. and Russell T. Gregg. *eds.* Administrative behavior in education. New York, Harper. 1957. 547 p.
G129. Engelhardt, Nickolaus L., *et al.* School planning and building handbook. New York, F.W. Dodge Corp., 1956. 626 p.
G130. French, Will, *et al.* American high school administration: policy and practice. Rev. ed. New York, Rinehart, 1957. 604 p.
G131. Gwynn, John M. Theory and practice of supervision. New York, Dodd, Mead, 1961. 473 p.
G132. Hunt, Herold C. and Paul R. Pierce. The practice of school administration: a cooperative professional enterprise. Boston, Houghton Mifflin, 1958. 544 p.
G133. Miller, Van and Willard B. Spalding. The public administration of American schools. 2d ed. Yonkers, N.Y., World Book Co., 1958. 605 p.
G134. Moehlman, Arthur B. School administration. 2d ed. Boston, Houghton Mifflin, 1951. 514 p.
G135. Mort, Paul R. and Donald H. Ross. Principles of school administration. 2d ed. New York, McGraw-Hill, 1957. 451 p.
G136. Otto, Henry J. Elementary-school organization and administration. 3d ed. New York, Appleton-Century-Crofts, 1954. 719 p.
G137. Reeder, Ward J. The fundamentals of public school administration. 4th ed. New York, Macmillan, 1958. 625 p.
G138. Sargent, Cyril G. and Eugene L. Belisle. Educational administration: cases and concepts. Boston, Houghton Mifflin, 1955. 474 p.
G139. Sears, Jesse B. Public school administration. New York, Ronald, 1947. 433 p.
G140. Thurston, Lee M. and William H. Roe. State school administration. New York, Harper, 1957. 427 p.
G141. Tuttle, Edward M. School board leadership in America. Danville, Ill., Interstate Printers and Publishers, 1958, 320 p.
G142. Weber, Clarence A. and Mary E. Weber. Fundamentals of educational leadership. New York, McGraw-Hill, 1955. 279 p.

ELEMENTARY EDUCATION

The books on the elementary education comprise presentations of principles and curriculum. Those relating to methods have already been discussed in a previous section. Herrick *et al.* treat the historical background, relations to society, curriculum, and practices. In the symposium edited by Shane are essays on concepts of curriculum, child growth, and administration of elementary education. Caswell and Fosbay review the history of the elementary school, its role in American society, and the contributions of new experimental efforts. Stratemeyer and colleagues consider the contemporary curriculum, mainly of the elementary school, the provisions for individual change. Shane and McSwain offer a detailed analysis of the theory and procedures of evaluating what has been taught in elementary schools.

G143. Caswell, Hollis L. and A. Wellesley Fosbay. Education in the elementary school. 2d ed. New York, American Book Co., 1950. 406 p.
G144. Herrick, Virgil E. *et al.* The elementary school. Englewood Cliffs, N.J., Prentice-Hall, 1956. 474 p.
G145. Shane, Harold G., *ed.* The American elementary school. New York, Harper, 1953. 434 p.
G146. Shane, Harold G. and Eldridge T. McSwain. Evaluation and the elementary curriculum. Rev. ed. New York, Holt, 1958. 436 p.
G147. Stratemeyer, Florence B. Developing a curriculum for modern living. 2d ed. New York, Bureau of Publications, Teachers College, Columbia Univ., 1957. 740 p.

SECONDARY EDUCATION

One of the early comprehensive works in this field, edited by Monroe, discusses the history, principles, organization, curriculum of the American secondary school and provides extensive facts and figures on secondary education in France, Germany, and England. The historical and comparative approaches are also utilized in the more recent work by Franzén, who stresses the relation of objectives to content and methods. Alexander and Saylor follow a similar plan and include treatments of curriculum, methods, and administration. A detailed analysis of the theoretical and practical problems involved in the administration and reorganization of the high school curriculum is given by Leonard. The most thorough and systematic examination of the conflicting theories underlying the American secondary school has been made by Justman. A recent work of importance is the compilation, by Chase and Anderson, of statements by outstanding educators on the historical and comparative contexts of the high school, the national and world conditions affecting it, and the various considerations toward redirection and change. Finally, the single book which has received most attention in some time is the report by Conant on the present status and future needs of the high school in the United States.

G148. Alexander, William M. and John G. Saylor. Modern secondary education: basic principles and practices. New York, Rinehart, 1959. 765 p.
G149. Chase, Francis S. and Harold A. Anderson, *eds.* The high school in a new era. Chicago, Univ. of Chicago Press, 1958. 465 p.
G150. Conant, James B. The American high school today. New York, McGraw-Hill, 1959. 141 p.
G151. Franzén, Carl G.F. Foundations of secondary education. New York, Harper, 1955. 492 p.

G152. Justman, Joseph. Theories of secondary education in the United
       States. New York, Bureau of Publications, Teachers College, Co-
       lumbia Univ., 1940. 481 p.
G153. Leonard, John P. Developing the secondary school curriculum. Rev.
       ed. New York, Rinehart, 1953. 582 p.
G154. Monroe, Paul, *ed*. Principles of secondary education. New York,
       Macmillan, 1914. 790 p.

HIGHER EDUCATION

A brief survey of the history of higher education all over the world
from ancient times to the 20th century is given by Aigrain. The book
edited by Clapp is devoted to universities in Europe and the United
States in the 19th century. The 20th century university in various countries is treated in greater or lesser detail in such works as those of Bradby,
Kotschnig and Prys, Nash, Ducret and Rafe-uz-Zaman, Schairer and
Hoffman, Bereday and Lauwerys, and Cueto Fernandini. Bradby deals
systematically with universities in fourteen countries. Nash pays particular attention to the contrast between democratic and dictatorial conceptions of the university.

The historical development of higher education in the United States
from the colonial period to the present era is clearly and comperhen-
sively, if not exhaustively, covered by Brubacher and Rudy. A more
specialized historical account, stressing the problems of academic freedom and including the European roots, is contributed by Hofstadter and
Metzger. An indispensable collection of significant documents on the
history of American higher education is presented by Hofstadter and
Smith. Flexner's study contrasting American universities with those of
England and Germany is controversial and provocative, but is nontheless
an important classic in the literature. Carmichael furnishes factual data
on universities in the United States and in the British Commonwealth
in a more objective manner, even if he does not comparatively analyze
these higher educational institutions. Two significant reports should be
studied with care—the Harvard Report on general education and the
report of the President's Commission—since both of them were widely
discussed and had an impact on higher education in America.

Henderson scrutinizes the objectives, curriculum, faculty and students
and administration of the college and university. The essays in Frankel's
volume are concerned with the role and problems of the American university at home and abroad, as well as with the principles and values
underlying it. Of the many new works on the sociology of the university, Wilson's book seems to supply the basic framework for analyzing the
academic community. The recent compilation by Sanford of studies on
the social and psychological problems and context of the college in the
United States is a unique and valuable contribution to the literature.

Berelson's report on the graduate school embraces the history, present status, programs, and issues of this type of higher education. A comprehensive study of the nature, problems, and possible future development of the two-year college is made by Medsker.

G155. Aigrain, René. Histoire des universités. Paris, Presses Universitaires de France, 1949. 125 p.
G156. Berelson, Bernard. Graduate education in the United States. New York, McGraw-Hill, 1960. 346 p.
G157. Bereday, George Z.F. and Joseph A. Lauwerys, eds. Higher education: 1959. Yonkers, N.Y., World Book Co., 1959. 520 p.
G158. Bradby, Edward, ed. The university outside Europe. London, Oxford Univ. Press, 1939. 332 p.
G159. Brubacher, John S. and Willis Rudy. Higher education in transition, an American history, 1936-1956. New York, Harper, 1958. 494 p.
G160. Carmichael, Oliver C. Universities; Commonwealth and American. New York, Harper, 1959. 390 p.
G161. Clapp, Margaret, ed. The modern university. Ithaca, N.Y., Cornell Univ. Press, 1950. 115 p.
G162. Cueto Fernandini, Carlos, ed. La universidad en el siglo XX. Lima, Peru, Universidad Nacional Mayor de San Marcos, 1951. 408 p.
G163. Ducret, Bernard and Rafe-uz-Zaman, eds. The university today, its role and place in society; an international survey. Geneva, World University Service, 1960. 333 p.
G164. Flexner, Abraham. Universities, American, English, German. New York, Oxford Univ. Press, 1930. 381 p.
G165. Frankel, Charles, ed. Issues in university education. New York, Harper, 1959. 175 p.
G166. Harvard University. *Committee on the Objectives of a General Education in a Free Society.* General education in a free society. Cambridge, 1945. 267 p.
G167. Henderson, Algo D. Policies and practices in higher education. New York, Harper, 1960. 338 p.
G168. Hofstadter, Richard and Walter P. Metzger. The development of academic freedom in the United States. New York, Columbia Univ. Press, 1955. 527 p.
G169. Hofstadter, Richard and Wilson Smith, eds. American higher edution; a documentary hsitory. Chicago, Univ. of Chicago Press, 1961. 1016 p.
G170. Kotschnig, Walter M. and Elined Prys, eds. The university in a changing world. London, Oxford Univ. Press, 1932. 224 p.
G171. Medsker, Leland L. The junior college; progress and prospect. New York, McGraw-Hill, 1960. 367 p.
G172. Nash, Arnold S. The university and the modern world. London, S.C.M. Press, 1945. 223 p.
G173. Sanford, Nevitt, ed. The American college. New York, Wiley, 1962. 1084 p.
G174. Schairer, Reinhold and Conrad Hoffmann, eds. Die Universitäts-ideale der Kulturvölker. Leipzig, Quelle und Meyer, 1925. 125 p.
G175. U.S. *President's Commission on Higher Education.* Higher education for American democracy. New York, Harper, 1948. 1 v.
G176. Wilson, Logan. The academic man. New York, Oxford Univ. Press, 1942. 248 p.

TEACHER EDUCATION

A comprehensive history of the training, work and status of the teacher in America from the colonial period to the 20th century is offered by Elsbree. Borrowman covers in detail the development of programs for the education of the American teacher from the early 19th century onward, with special reference to the relation of general to professional studies. Monroe traces fully the history of teaching-learning theory in connection with the evolution of the aims and practices in teacher education. Peterson's book is made up of biographical essays of influential teachers and professors, American and foreign, by their pupils. Wesley reviews a century of the National Education Association, while the Commission on Educational Reconstruction summarizes the history of the American Federation of Teachers. American teacher education—its status, administration and organization, programs, and problems—is examined systematically by Stiles *et al.* The volume editited by Cottrell is another comprehensive treatment of the education of the teacher. Hodenfield and Stinnett sum up clearly the deliberations of academic professors and educationists at three national conferences on the proper content of teacher education programs. The volume of essays under the editorship of Stiles investigates the changing situation of the teacher in America, especially the issues involving his functions and professional status. Huggett and Stinnett furnish basic data on the status, rights and obligations of the professional teacher; and the book by Kearney covers about the same scope. Finally, Lieberman analyzes critically, with specific detail, the extent to which teaching is actually a profession in the United States.

G177. Borrowman, Merle L. The liberal and technical in teacher education. New York, Bureau of Publications, Teachers College, Columbia Univ., 1956. 247 p.

G178. Commission on Educational Reconstruction. Organizing the teaching profession: the story of the American Federation of Teachers. Glencoe, Ill., Free Press, 1955. 320 p.

G179. Cottrell, Donald P., *ed.* Teacher education for a free people. Oneonta, N.Y., American Association of Colleges for Teachers Education, 1956. 415 p.

G180. Elsbree, Willard S. The American teacher: evolution of a profession in a democracy. New York, American Book Co., 1939. 566 p.

G181. Hodenfield, G.K. and Timothy M. Stinnett. The education of teachers. Englewood Cliffs, N.J., Prentice-Hall, 1961. 177 p.

G182. Huggett, Albert J. and Timothy M. Stinnett. Professional problems of teachers. New York, Macmillan, 1956. 468 p.

G183. Kearney, Nolan C. A teacher's professional guide. Englewood Cliffs, N.J., Prentice-Hall, 1958. 358 p.

G184. Lieberman, Myron. Education as a profession. Englewood Cliffs, N.J., Prentice-Hall, 1956. 540 p.

G185. Monroe, Walter S. Teacher-learning theory and teacher education: 1890 to 1950. Urbana, Univ. of Illinois Press, 1952. 426 p.
G186. Peterson, Houston, *ed.* Great teachers. New Brunswick, N.J., Rutgers Univ. Press, 1946. 351 p.
G187. Stiles, Lindley J., *ed.* The teacher's role in American society. New York, Harper, 1957. 298 p.
G188. Stiles, Lindley J., *et al.* Teacher education in the United States. New York, Ronald, 1960. 512 p.
G189. Wesley, Edgar B. NEA: the first hundred years. New York, Harper, 1957. 419 p.

ADULT EDUCATION

A history of adult education in the context of various societies from primitive man to the 20th century in America is furnished by Grattan, with the developments during the past century and a half more fully described than those of previous centuries. Grattan also presents a useful collection of documents illustrating the evolution of the theory of adult education in America. Predeek supplies a meticulously documented historical account of libraries in Britain and the United States. Shera offers a scholarly monograph on more than two centuries of the New England public library, while Bode traces the development of the lyceum as an institution of American adult education. The *Handbook of adult education* (G310) provides encyclopedic information on all phases of adult education in the United States. Brunner and colleagues offer a thoroughgoing analysis of the research studies on the various subdivisions of the field. For a well-annotated bibliography of the study of liberal arts subjects in adult education, especially in the universities, the librarian is referred to the comprehensive compilation of Mezirow and Berry. Kempfer's volume treats the aims, content, methods, administration, and organization of adult education.

G190. Bode, Carl. The American lyceum. New York, Oxford Univ. Press, 1956. 275 p.
G191. Brunner, Edmund de S., *et al.* An overview of adult education research. Chicago, Adult Education Association, 1959. 279 p.
G192. Grattan, C. Hartley, *ed.* American ideas about adult education, 1710-1951. New York, Bureau of Publications, Teachers College, Columbia Univ., 1959. 140 p.
G193. Grattan, C. Hartley. In quest of knowledge: a historical perspective on adult education. New York, Association Press, 1955. 337 p.
G194. Kempfer, Homer. Adult education. New York, McGraw-Hill, 1955. 433 p.
G195. Mezirow, Jack D. and Dorothea Berry, *comps.* The literature of liberal adult education: 1945-1957. New York, Scarecrow Press, 1960. 308 p.
G196. Predeek, Albert. A history of libraries in Great Britain and North America. Chicago, American Library Association, 1947. 177 p.

G197. Shera, Jesse H. Foundations of the public library: The Origins of the Public Library Movement in New England, 1629-1855. Chicago, Univ. of Chicago Press, 1949. 308 p.

EDUCATION OF THE TALENTED

Gifted or talented children, especially in the academic sense of the term, have been given increasing attention during the past decade. Freehill treats the identification, teaching, curriculum, and other aspects of the education of the gifted children. De Haan and Havighurst cover similar ground, with special attention to research. Sumption and Luecking add the historical background to the customary content, as well as a chapter on the gifted in college. Shertzer presents a collection of papers on identification, guidance, community, cooperation evaluation, and other phases of educating talented students in high school, and Copley devotes his little book to a careful description of the Advanced Placement Program, whereby qualified students proceed to higher educational courses while still in high school. The book of readings by French contains essays on identification, curriculum, adjustment, and other problems related to educating the academically gifted, plus a sizable group of reports of research studies. Fliegler's volume confines itself to specific analyses of curriculum provisions. The papers edited by Torrance pertain to research on identification, development, and utilization of talented individuals.

G198. Copley, Frank O. The American high school and the talented student. Ann Arbor, Univ. of Michigan Press, 1961. 92 p.
G199. De Haan, Robert F. and Robert J. Havighurst. Educating gifted children. Rev. ed. Chicago, Univ. of Chicago Press, 1961. 363 p.
G200. Fliegler, Louis A., ed. Curriculum planning for the gifted. Englewood Cliffs, N.J., Prentice-Hall, 1961. 414 p.
G201. Freehill, Maurice F. Gifted children: their psychology and education. New York, Macmillan, 1961. 412 p.
G202. French, Joseph L., ed. Educating the gifted: a book of readings. New York, Holt, 1959. 555 p.
G203. Shertzer, Bruce, ed. Working with superior students: theories and practices. Chicago, Science Research Associates, 1960. 370 p.
G204. Sumption, Merle R. and Evelyn M. Luecking. Education of the gifted. New York, Ronald, 1960. 499 p.
G205. Torrance, Ellis P., ed. Talent and education. Minneapolis, Univ. of Minnesota Press, 1960. 210 p.

CRITICISMS OF AMERICAN EDUCATION

Ever since World War II, particularly in the 1950's, the tempo of dissatisfaction with one phase or another of American education, or all of it, has accelerated greatly. Many books and other writings have appeared in response to the interest of the public and the profession. Some of this literature attacks educational abuses, another segment defends and explains education in a better light, and some publications seek to steer a middle course.

The anthology by Scott, Hill, and Burns deals with a number of controversial issues, mainly on the curriculum controversy, from various viewpoints. Ehlers and Lee present a wider selection of issues, likewise from more than one point of view. Bestor, a professor of history, criticizes Progressive education and teacher training in *Educational wastelands* and offers a program in a second volume for the redemption of the "unfulfilled promise of American education." Rickover, a naval vice-admiral, castigates what he conceives to be the faults of American education and urges reforms. A systematic, constructive program of subject matter is offered by several specialists in the volume edited by Koerner. For the defense of American education, Dewey's classic little book rejects the extremists' interpretations of Progressive education and points out the proper path. Thayer represents a Progressive and liberal position on controversial issues in education. Cremin's scholarly history of Progressivism in American education points up the errors of the movement, but it also appreciates its contributions. Woodring takes a middle-of-the-road stand in his analysis of the current controversy in education. Finally, Lieberman's penetrating volume criticizes the critics and theorists of all schools of thought and proposes his own program toward reform.

G206. Bestor, Arthur E. Educational wastelands. Urbana, Univ. of Illinois Press, 1953. 226 p.
G207. Bestor, Arthur E. The restoration of learning. New York, Knopf, 1955. 459 p.
G208. Cremin, Lawrence A. The transformation of the school: progressivism in American education, 1876-1957. New York, Knopf, 1961. 387 p.
G209. Dewey, John. Experience and education. New York, Macmillan, 1938. 116 p.
G210. Ehlers, Henry and Gordon C. Lee. Crucial issues in education. Rev. ed. New York, Holt, 1959. 342 p.
G211. Koerner, James D., ed. The case for basic education. Boston, Little, Brown, 1959. 256 p.
G212. Lieberman, Myron. The future of public education. Chicago, Univ. of Chicago Press, 1960. 294 p.
G213. Rickover, Hyman G. Education and freedom. New York, Dutton, 1959. 256 p.
G214. Scott, Cecil W., et al. The great debate: our schools in crisis. Englewood Cliffs, N.J., Prentice-Hall, 1959. 184 p.
G215. Thayer, Vivian T. Public education and its critics. New York, Macmillan, 1954. 170 p.
G216. Woodring, Paul. Let's talk sense about our schools. New York, McGraw-Hill, 1953. 213 p.

REFERENCE WORKS AND SERIAL PUBLICATIONS

The remainder of the chapter, following this section, will present annotations of reference works, periodicals, and yearbooks, thus giving the reader an opportunity to see the extent of educational literature as a whole.

Those who are engaged in doing educational research or in seeking information on education will want to consult a general educational encyclopedia. Paul Monroe's *A cyclopedia of education* is useful as a starting point, especially for historical orientation, but it needs to be updated. Those who read a foreign language might profit from examining such a work as the Swiss or the German *Lexikon der Pädagogik*. The best single source for research summaries and data is the *Encyclopedia of educational research*, edited by Walter S. Monroe (1941, 1950) and Chester W. Harris (1960). This can be supplemented by the current issue, and many of the past issues, of the *Review of educational research*. For periodical references, the most comprehensive listing can be found in the *Education index*. These titles, of course, are but first steps in the acquisition of information on education. The reader should examine carefully the descriptions of the other works on the following pages.

There is a vast periodical literature (G217) in education. The NEA *journal*, which has the largest circulation in the field in the United States, is a popularly written magazine for the classroom teacher. More advanced publications are the fraternity journals, *Phi Delta Kappan* and *Educational forum*, both of which treat domestic and foreign educational developments. *Teachers College journal*, another general periodical, stresses theory and research, while *School and society* emphasizes educational theory and controversy and higher and foreign education. The *Saturday review education supplement* is concerned with current issues, personalities, and books. On the foreign scene, the reader will be enlightened by the trilingual *International review of education*, the British *journal of educational studies*, and the (London) *Times educational supplement*.

The specialized periodicals are too numerous to mention in this essay. Hence, a sampling will be given from a number of representative branches in the field of education. Philosophies of education are given extensive coverage in *Educational theory*. School administrators find suitable articles, photographs, and diagrams in *Overview*. Teachers of very young children read *Childhood education*, while elementary and secondary teachers obtain reading matter of merit and depth in *Elementary school journal* and *School review*, respectively. In the area of higher education, there are *College and university*, the *Journal of teacher education*, the *Journal of higher education*, the *Junior college journal*, *Liberal education*, *Educational record*, the *Journal of general education*, and the *Bulletin of the American Association of University Professors*.

The various professions have their specialized magazines, such as the *Journal of medical education* and the *Journal of legal education.*

Most subjects that are taught in the elementary and high schools are promoted by magazines which cover content and methodology. Examples of this type include the *Arithmetic teacher, English journal, Science education, Modern language journal, Social education,* and the like. Also of significance are such periodicals as the *Journal of educational research,* the *Review of educational research,* and the *Journal of experimental education.* To be abreast of developments in education all over the world it is desirable to be familiar with *Comparative education review* and *Overseas.* For recent scholarship in the history of education, one might examine the *History of education quarterly* and *Pedagogical historica,* which publishes articles in English, French, German, and other languages.

Obviously, the reader cannot read all of them, and it is not necessary that he do so. What he can do, however, is to scan the contents of representative journals periodically so as to familiarize himself with the general subject matter, trends of interest and concern, and educational news of importance. Moreover, as he gets to know the various magazines, he will be able to decide which of these carry critical book reviews.

Another type of periodical publication is the yearbook. There are several types of yearbooks, some of them having a long consecutive run. The John Dewey Society yearbooks deal with educational problems and issues, often of a theoretical nature. The American Association of School Administrators, which has published yearbooks for about three decades, has covered a variety of topics, such as curriculum, character, buildings, and so forth. The National Council for the Social Studies publishes alternately yearbooks on American history, world history, citizenship, geography, and other specialized subjects. Foreign education can be followed in the International Bureau of Education in Geneva and Unesco in Paris. Another publication in this category is the *Year book of education,* published jointly by the University of London Institute of Education and Teachers College of Columbia University. Whereas the former presents current facts and figures from most countries all over the world, the latter concentrates on a single theme. Thus, recent yearbooks deal with education and economics, the secondary school curriculum, higher education, and communication media and the school, and report developments in many countries located in far-flung areas. The educational reader should also acquaint himself with an older and discontinued series, the *Educational yearbook* published by the International Institute of Teachers College, Columbia University, from 1925 to 1944. Most of these contain articles that are still valuable today.

Special attention should be given to the yearbooks published by the National Society for the Study of Education almost without interruption since 1895. Each year the Society issues two yearbooks dealing with different subjects. Among the topics treated in this long series have been general education, audio-visual education, educational theory, international education, the graduate school, and professional education.

William W. Brickman

GUIDES TO THE LITERATURE

G218. Alexander, Carter and Arvid J. Burke. How to locate educational information and data; an aid to quick utilization of the literature of education. 4th ed. rev. New York, Teachers College, Columbia Univ., 1958. 419 p.

Designed both to guide the individual researcher in the use of the literature and to serve as a text for class instruction, this excellent guide covers basic library techniques as well as more specialized techniques. The 14 chapters in this second division cover such fundamentals on the utilization of the literature as reference books (use and evaluation), government publications, instructional materials, sources for legal and biographical information, news items and statistics. "Library experiences" at the end of each chapter transform this massive introductory work into a textbook. Several devices facilitate the use of the volume. Works described are numbered in order of appearance in the text, and any mention of a work described more fully elsewhere is followed by this reference number. A "Key to locating references" makes it possible to find the master description of a tool no matter where the user may have come upon it in the text. Index to subjects, forms of material, exact titles, authors, editors, compilers, etc. as well as to "Experiences."

G219. Brickman, William W. Guide to research in educational his-

tory. New York, New York University bookstore, 1949. 220 p.

A competent application of historical research methods to educational research. Contains lists of general works, bibliographies, periodicals, and source collections. Discusses special problems of historical analysis and includes practical pointers on note-taking, documentation and organization of written reports.

G220. Seeger, Ruth E. Using library resources in educational research. Columbus, Ohio, Bureau of Educational Research, Ohio State Univ., 1957. 26 p.

An effective first-aid in developing the ability to "do it yourself." Connected discussion of the use of more than a hundred works (listed at the end), with a ratio of about four specialized sources to one not limited to education.

REVIEWS OF THE LITERATURE

G221. Encyclopedia of educational research, ed. by Chester W. Harris. 3d ed. New York, Macmillan, 1960. 1564 p.

As the foreword indicates, the term "encyclopedia" means here the attempt to provide a "critical evaluation, synthesis and interpretation of all pertinent research—early as well as recent," based on the literature embodying the results of research. An unusual conception well executed. Long articles on broad topics, signed and dated by specialists, critically review and sum up the results of educational thought and experience as found in the literature produced by research and conclude with a statement on further research needed. References to the literature in the text of articles are keyed to numbered items in bibliographies, which, because they are at once extensive and well selected, form an important feature of the work. A subject index on yellow paper appears in the middle of the volume. The *Review of educational research* helps to bring this encyclopedia up to date.

G222. Review of educational research. v. 1+ 1931+ Washington, American Educational Research Association, National Education Association.

Appearing five times a year the *Review* covers eleven large subdivisions of education in an approximate three-year cycle. Since each issue contains a review of the literature on one topic for the previous three years, the latest will bring its subject very nearly up to date, while earlier issues, though useful, become correspondingly out of date. A special index for the first 12 years appeared in 1944; thereafter the index appears in the last issue for each year. Tracing a subject back is facilitated by a note in each issue indicating the previous review of that subject. Plan is similar to *Encyclopedia of educational research* which it up-dates. Indexed in *Education index*.

G223. Educational forum. v. 1+ 1936+ Menasha, Wis., Kappa Delta Pi. quarterly.

Signed critical book reviews averaging 300 to 800 words in the field of education psychology and social studies, and one longer review of approximately 1,500 words.

G224. Elementary school journal.

1900+ Chicago, Ill., Univ. of Chicago. 8 times a year.

Signed book reviews of 400 to 600 words, covering the nature, strength, and limitations of the book, and brief abstracts of periodical articles, titled "Selected References on Elementary School Instruction."

G225. Harvard educational review. v. 7, no. 1+ 1937+ Cambridge, Harvard Univ., Graduate School of Education. quarterly.

(Earlier numbers appeared as the *Harvard teachers record*, February 1931-October 1936). Signed critical book reviews on all subjects which might be pertinent to education. Usually short informative reviews and one long (1,500 to 2,500 words) critical essay-type review.

G226. Journal of higher education. 1930+ Columbus, Ohio State Univ. monthly.

Lengthy, signed book reviews.

G227. Social education. v. 1, no. 1+ 1937+ Washington, National Council for the Social Studies. 8 times a year.

Signed book reviews and brief descriptions of pamphlets and government publications.

G228. Teachers College record. 1900+ New York, Teachers College, Columbia Univ. 8 times a year.

Critical reviews of books on subjects of cultural as well as professional value to educators. Reviews are of three kinds: (1) an essay review article, using two or more books on related subjects and discussing the issues raised by them; (2) standard reviews; and (3) short evaluating book notes of 50 to 75 words.

ABSTRACTS AND DIGESTS

G229. Dissertation abstracts; a guide to dissertations and monographs available in microfilm. 1+ 1935+ Ann Arbor, University Microfilms.

See entry at A192.

G230. Education digest. 1935+ Ann Arbor, The Education Digest. 9 times a year.

Independent of association affiliation. Presents digests of periodical articles and portions of books of current interest to workers in education. Full credit is given for each article or book. News notes, some book reviews and a classified list of additional educational materials appear at the end of each issue. An author index appears in the May issue. Indexed in *Education index.*

G231. National business education quarterly. v. 1, no. 1+ 1932+ Washington, United Business Education Association, National Education Association. quarterly.

Since 1953 one issue a year has been devoted to summaries of studies and research in business education having regional or national significance, compiled by Delta Pi Epsilon, graduate professional fraternity in business education. Each research description includes purpose, methods, and sources and summary of findings.

G232. UNESCO. *Education Clearing House.* Education abstracts: educational studies and documents. v. 1+ 1945+ Paris, 1949+ monthly except July and August.

Not to be confused with *Education abstracts,* 1937-1944, published by Phi Delta Kappa educational fraternity. The first three volumes (1949-1951) carried the title *Fundamental education abstracts.* With the change in 1952 to the present title the scope was widened. Individual issues of early volumes were sometimes devoted to one topic or geographic area, but beginning with volume 6 each issue is devoted to publications of various countries on one specific subject, i.e., rural education, adult education, etc. Published in three separate language editions: English, French and Spanish. So far as possible full bibliographical information and price is given for each item. Items are numbered consecutively throughout the year and each issue has a separate author and subject index. Annual cumulated author and subject indexes appear in each December issue.

BIBLIOGRAPHIES

Bibliographies of Bibliographies

G233. Monroe, Walter S. and Louis Shores. Bibliographies and summaries in education to July, 1935; a catalog of more than 4,000 annotated bibliographies and summaries listed under author and subject in one alphabet. New York, H.W. Wilson, 1936. 470 p.

This annotated author-subject bibliography of books, parts of books, magazine articles and publications of the Office of Education was developed from card files at the Library of George Peabody College for Teachers and the Bureau of Educational Research, University of Illinois. The period covered is 1910 to 1935, but some important bibliographies appearing before 1910 are included. The same annotations appear for the entry by subject and by author. "See" and "See also" references are liberally employed. Related to the *Education index* which keeps it up to date. The arrangement is strictly alphabetical except for serial bibliographies which have been entered throughout under special sub-division "Serial bibliographies." Annotation gives number of items in the bibliography described and other pertinent information, i.e., chief emphasis, time coverage, peculiarities of arrangement.

Bibliographies-Current

G234. America's education press; a classified list of educational publications issued in the United States, 1926+ Washington, Educational Press Association, 1926+ biennial.

Geographical list of educational journals with full information about each title. Published in the *Yearbook* of the Association and available also as a reprint. In 1950 the Association attempted to include a section on foreign journals in the 23rd yearbook. With the 26th yearbook (1957) the Education Press Association issued jointly with Unesco an international list covering some 100 countries and titled *International list of educational periodicals*. The 27th Yearbook (1960) described American periodicals only. Another international list, *Educational periodicals*, sponsored jointly by Unesco and the Association, appeared in 1963. Periodicals in the U.S. section include those that are general in scope and circulation, organs of state education associations and state departments of education, journals issued by local, state or regional professional organizations, etc. For the history and purposes of education magazines, *America's education press: fiftieth anniversary yearbook* (Washington, Educational Press Association, 1946) is probably the best source. In addition to specific information for each periodical (i.e., issues per year, size, index, purpose, founding date, etc.) the *Anniversary yearbook* includes a chronological list of magazines to be found in Frank L. Mott's A *history of American magazines*.

G235. Education index, January 1929+ A cumulative subject index to a selected list of educational periodicals. New York, H.W. Wilson, 1932+ monthly, cumulating annually and triennially.

Indexes about 211 titles, American and a few British (periodicals, proceedings, yearbooks, bulletins, monographic series, etc.). Useful supplementary material includes full title, editor, price and address for each periodical indexed, directory of publishers, abbreviations used. Until 1961 *Education index* was also an author index and included books and pamphlets. The basic source for keeping abreast of the literature. Also excellent as a subject heading list.

G236. Educational books of (the year), compiled by Enoch Pratt Free Library, Education Department. In *Educational horizons*, Spring issue. annual.

A thorough listing of books, pamphlets, monographs, yearbooks and issues of magazines which appeared the previous year and are devoted to a single topic in education. Excluded are elementary and secondary textbooks, courses of study and reports of school superintendents. From 1928 to 1947 the list appeared in *School and society*, from 1948 to 1952 in *Phi Delta Kappan*, in 1953 in Pi Lambda Theta *Journal*. Classified arrangement under such broad subjects as history, philosophy, psychology, measurement, methods, administration. Invaluable source for locating obscure books and pamphlets if the year of publication is known and addresses of little-known publishers.

G237. Educational film guide, New York, H.W. Wilson, 1936-1962. annual with cumulative monthly supplements.

Titled *Educational film catalog* until 1945. A cumulative 1953 volume replaces all preceding editions. Includes all 16 mm. motion pictures intended for use in schools, libraries and adult groups as well as all sponsored or "free" religious, travel, music, sports, documentary and experimental films. Also lists some "home movies" and 16 mm. feature films. Does not include professional medical, dental or psychiatric films. Beginning with the 1954-58 cumulative volume, an annotated alphabetical title list and a subject index replaced the Dewey Decimal classified list. Special features include optimal grade level of usefulness, L.C. card numbers, order numbers for Film Evaluation cards available from the Education Film Library Association, notation of reviews from periodicals such as *Educational screen, Saturday review* and *Film news*. A starred evaluation indicates composite rating. Ceased publication in 1962. To be superseded by *Educational media index*, a comprehensive directory of nonbook instructional materials, to be published by the Educational Media Council, New York.

G238. Educators guide to free films, 1941+ Randolph, Wis. Educators Progress Service, 1941+ annual.

Revised annually, this guide has grown from a list of 671 titles in 1941 to a list of 4,479 titles in 1963. In the main section films are arranged by title under broad teaching areas, with cross references to related fields. New titles are starred in each edition. Date, size and running time are given as well as a brief annotation. Separate indexes by title, subject and source and availability are printed on paper of three different colors, a feature which greatly facilitates use. Similar publications by Educators Progress Service are *Educators guide to free filmstrips,* formerly *Free slide films* (1949-1958), and *Educators guide to free tapes, scripts and transcriptions* (1955+).

G239. Elementary teachers guide to free curriculum materials, 1944+ Randolph, Wis., Educators Progress Service, 1944+ annual.

A selective listing of about 1,200 items (bulletins, pamphlets, exhibits, charts, posters and books). A similar publication is *Educators guide to free science materials* (1960+).

G240. Filmstrip guide, September 1948-Spring 1962. New York, H.W. Wilson, 1948-1962. annual with cumulative monthly supplements.

Lists new filmstrips, stripfilms, slidefilms and filmslides. The 1955-1958 supplement supersedes all published since the 3rd edition in 1954. Excluded are professional, medical, dental, public health and psychiatric films; fiction, fairy tale and folklore filmstrips; and U.S. government filmstrips. Beginning with the 1954-1958 cumulation, Part I is arranged alphabetically by title rather than by Dewey Decimal Classification numbers. Part II is a subject index based on Sears headings; Part III is a directory of sources. Main entry information covers title, main source, year of release, number of frames, sound or captions, black and white or color, purchase price, interest levels, sponsor, speed and running time if accompanied by disc and brief content note. For filmstrips prior to 1947 see Vera M. Falconer's *Filmstrips: a descriptive index and user's guide* (New York, McGraw Hill, 1948. 572 p.). Ceased publication in 1962. To be superseded by *Educational media index.* See (G237n).

G241. Master's theses in education, 1951/52+ Cedar Falls, Iowa, State College of Iowa, 1953+ annual.

The first edition covered the period July 1, 1951, through June 30, 1952, and contained 2,607 theses reported by 182 institutions granting master's degrees in education. The latest edition, 1961/62, listed over 3,721 theses. Numbered serially, theses are arranged alphabetically by author under subject headings. A code number directly after each title indicates the institution accepting the theses. All these institutions are in running code number order in the Institutional Index where they are arranged alphabetically first by state and then by name. The serial numbers of the theses granted by them are listed after each institution. There are also author and subject indexes. A useful and unique series weakened by failure to use serial rather than page numbers in the author index.

G242. Outstanding educational books of (the year), 1924+ Compiled by Enoch Pratt Free Library, Education Department. In National Education Association *Journal*, May issue. annual.

A reliable selection, based on composite judgment of specialists, of the most important education books to appear any one year. Includes new editions as well as new titles. Until 1947 titled "Sixty educational books of the year." A varying number of books are listed and briefly annotated. Individual items are keyed to a numbered publisher list at the end. Lack of publisher with each item does create difficulties if the list is clipped, but this deficiency is thoroughly compensated for by the dependability and compactness of the single-sheet listing. Available also as a separate publication from the Enoch Pratt Free Library for a nominal sum as long as the supply lasts.

G243. Research studies in education: a subject index of doctoral dissertations, reports and field studies; and a research methods bibliography, 1953+ Bloomington, Ind., Phi Delta Kappa, 1955+ annual.

Broad in scope, this subject index carries on three predecessor sources: *Research studies in education; a subject index of doctoral dissertations, reports and field studies, 1941-51* (subject list with loose-leaf annual supplements, compiled by Mary Louise Lyda and Stanley B. Brown. Boulder, Colorado, 1953); "Doctor's dissertations under way in education," edited by Carter V. Good (*Journal of educational research*, 1931-46, and thereafter in the *Phi Delta Kappa*); and "Research methods bibliography" (a selected bibliography on methodology in edu-

cational, psychological and social research, edited by Carter V. Good and published in *Journal of educational research*, 1931-46, when it was transferred to *Phi Delta Kappan*). Listed alphabetically by author under headings used by Enoch Pratt in its annual compilation "Educational books," each entry shows title, sponsoring institutions and date. Number of entries under such headings as "administration" or "curriculum" is large. Use of the series as a whole is complicated by lack of a master index of authors (author indexes included first in the 1955 annual) and close-set photo-offset reproduction. The reference staff of Teachers' College Library, Columbia University, has compiled an author index for this publication.

G244. Textbooks in print, 1872+ New York, Bowker, 1872+ annual.

Formerly called *American educational catalog*, this is a useful subject index to elementary and secondary textbooks issued by major firms and reported in *Publishers' weekly*. Gives publisher, price and series (if any) for both new editions and new titles, and arranges them not only by subject but also by grade level. Includes work books and teachers manuals to accompany the texts. Title and subject index. The only source for a relatively complete graded listing of textboks at these levels for the period since 1872.

Bibliographies-Retrospective

G245. Blackwell, Annie M. A list of researches in education and educational psychology, presented for higher degrees in the universities of the United Kingdom, Northern Ireland and the Irish Republic, 1918+ London, Newnes Educational Publishing Co., 1950. 2 v. with supplements.

The title accurately describes purpose and scope. Two main volumes cover 1918-1948 and 1949-1951. Three supplements cover 1952-53,

1954-55 and 1956-57. Entries are classified according to a modification of the Dewey system and within categories are arranged chronologically. The analytical subject index is keyed to class numbers which appear in the upper corners of the main listing. An author index in all except the first volume. Degrees include B.Litt., Ed.B., M.A., M.S., M.Ed. M.Litt., and Ph.D. Continued by *Current researches in education and educational psychology*, 1960/61+ (London, Information Service of the National Foundation for Educational Research in England and Wales, 1961+).

G246. Buros, Oscar K., *ed.* Tests in print; a comprehensive bibliography of tests for use in education, psychology and industry. Highland Park, N.J., Gryphon Press, 1961. 1292 p.
See F266.

G247. Doctoral dissertations accepted by American univesrities, 1933/34-1954/55. New York, H.W. Wilson, 1934-1955. 22 v.
Continued by "Index to American dissertations," no. 13 of *Dissertation abstracts* (see A192). Earlier dissertations may be found in Walter S. Monroe, *Ten years of educational research, 1918-1927.* (Urbana, Univ. of Illinois, 1928. Univ. of Illinois Bulletin, 25) and U.S. Office of Education, *Bibliography of research studies in education 1926/27-1937/38* (Washington, 1929-1940. 12 v.).

G248. Eells, Walter C., *ed.* American dissertations on foreign education. Washington, Committee on International Relations, National Education Association, 1959. 300 p.
Lists ca. 5,700 dissertations and theses written at American universities and colleges on education or educators in foreign countries and on the education of groups of foreign birth or ancestory in the U.S. between 1884 and 1958.

G249. Forrester, Gertrude. Occupational literature: an annotated bibliography. New York, H.W. Wilson, 1958. 603 p.
Since first published in 1946 as *Occupations: a selected list of pamphlets*, the title has varied. In addition to the 3,500 pamphlets and 900 books listed in this 1958 edition, material in charts, posters and visual aids is included. This annotated, up-to-date bibliography provides a well organized approach to material on occupations as well as contributions to the standardization of terminology. Another useful but somewhat less comprehensive bibliography of occupational material is *Guide to career information*, by the New York Life Insurance Company (New York, Harper, 1957. 203 p.). Current material is listed in *Occupational index* (v. 1 + 1936 + Jaffrey, N.H., Personnel Services. quarterly).

G250. George Peabody College for Teachers. *Division of Surveys and Field Services.* Free and inexpensive learning materials. 11th ed. Nashville, Tenn., 1962. 278 p.
A title listing under broad subjects of selected materials costing 50¢ or less. The 1960 edition contained 3,984 items. Generous cross references to related subjects and frequent annotations together with complete information needed for ordering in the main list makes supplementary indexes unnecessary.

G251. Gray, Ruth A. Doctor's theses in education: a list of 797 theses deposited with the Office of Education and available for loan. Washington, Govt. Print. Off., 1935. 69 p.
A numbered list of all the theses deposited prior to September 15, 1934. Arrangement is alphabetical by author, subject and institution. Author, title, institution, date, pages and an indication of whether the work is in manuscript or published form are given for each entry.

G252. McClusky, Frederick D. The A-V bibliography. 2d ed. Dubuque, Iowa, W.C. Brown, 1955. 218 p.

The only consolidated listing of books, parts of books, theses, doctoral dissertations (1921-1954) and magazine articles on audio-visual instruction. Main sections of the second edition include "Philosophy and psychology of teaching with audio-visual materials," "Audio-visual teaching materials and their use," "Elementary schools," "Secondary schools," "Higher education," "Administration of audio-visual instruction," and "Research on value and utilization of audio-visual materials." Table of contents shows multiple subdivisions under these headings and the material is further organized by helpful bibliographical references used to introduce each of these subdivisions. Another audio-visual bibliography, compiled largely in a graduate seminar, is *Bibliography of research in audio-visual education and mass media, 1930-50* by Lawrence C. Larson (Bloomington, Indiana Univ., Audio-Visual Center, 1950), and its 1950-53 Supplement. Although Larson's work indexes masters theses and some research studies, it is less complete.

G253. Monroe, Walter S. Ten years of educational research, 1918-27. Urbana, Illinois, Univ. of Illinois, 1928. 367 p. (Univ. of Illinois, College of Education, Bureau of Educational Research. Bulletin No. 42)

The first part consists of a series of chapters surveying the results of research in education during the period 1918-1927, much in the manner of the later *Encyclopedia of educational research.* Topics include, for example, "General survey of the period 1918-27," "Research in educational measurements," and "Curriculum research." Part I concludes with a summary of activities of the University's Bureau of Educational Research and a list of its printed publications, 1918-1928. Part II is a list of 3,650 research contributions—books, periodical articles, doctors' theses and society, institutional and government publications —with a topical index to this bibliography. "A list of doctors of philosophy in education by Institutions" appears at the end; dissertations by these Ph.D's are listed in Part 2. The only work of its kind for the period covered.

G254. Smith, Henry L. and William I. Painter. Bibliography of literature on education in countries other than the United States of America. Bloomington, Indiana Univ., Bureau of Cooperative Research, 1937. 341 p. (Bulletin of the School of Education, Indiana Univ. v. 13, no. 2)

An annotated bibliography of 3,510 books and magazine articles in English with citation and brief annotations. Publication dates of material listed fall between January 1, 1925 and December 31, 1936.

G255. U.S. *Office of Education.* Index to reports of the Commissioner of Education, 1867-1907. Washington, Govt. Print. Off., 1909. 103 p. (Bulletin, 1909, no. 7)

An irreplaceable boon to the student of the history of education. The *Reports* often included excellent studies of education here and abroad. Confined to *Reports* issued as separate publications. In later years the Bureau or Office report appeared only within the annual report of the parent agency—first the Department of the Interior, then the Federal Security Agency and now the Department of Health, Education and Welfare.

G256. U.S. *Office of Education.* List of publications, 1867-1910. Washington, Govt. Print. Off., 1910. 55 p. (Bulletin, 1910, no. 3)

G257. U.S. *Office of Education.* List of publications, 1910-1936; including those of the former Federal Board for Vocational Education for 1917-1933, with author and subject indexes. Washington, Govt. Print. Off., 1937. 158 p. (Bulletin, 1937, no. 22)

G257a. U.S. *Office of Education.* Publications, 1937-1959. Washington, Govt. Print. Office, 1960. 157 p. (Bulletin, 1960, no. 3)

G258. U.S. *Office of Education. Library.* Bibliography of research studies in education, 1926/27-1939/40. Washington, Govt. Print. Off., 1929-42. 14 v.

An annual annotated classified list of doctoral dissertations, masters' essays and other research studies in all aspects of education. Author, subject and institution indexes appeared regularly. Information for each thesis included author, title, degree, completion date, name of institution granting degree, number of pages, annotation and an indication as to whether the study appears in manuscript or published form. Theses and dissertations on file at the Office of Education are marked with a star. This work carried on the listing of masters' and doctors' theses in education done by Monroe in *Ten years of educational research* (G253). More recent listings of research studies are found in Mary Louise Lyda and Stanley B. Brown's *Research studies in education, a subject index of doctoral dissertations, reports and field studies, 1941-1951* (Boulder, Colorado, Beta Delta Chapter, Phi Delta Kappa, 1953) which became *Research studies in education, 1953+* (G243).

G259. Witmer, Eleanor M. Education books: Significant publications, 1937-1952. New York, Teachers College, Columbia Univ., 1953. 32 p.

A winnowing of educational books for a 15-year period by specialists working under the direction of the Librarian of an outstanding collection in this field. A good idea of the results is conveyed by the prefatory statement, "This highly selective list of writings in the thirty-five areas of education indicates what some experts consider to be currently the more important books published in the last fifteen years." The broad areas in which the literature is classified include: reference books, finance, school plant, history and biography, art, teacher education, foreign education and religion in education. This list supersedes several similar compilations from time to time in the *Teachers College record.* Now out of print and unavailable for purchase.

DICTIONARIES

G260. Good, Carter V. Dictionary of education. 2d ed. New York, McGraw-Hill, 1959. 676 p.

Financed by Phi Delta Kappa, the second edition of this pioneer dictionary contains more than 1,600 words and is the work of more than 100 specialists and numerous assistants. Covers special terms in American education and terms used in the study of comparative education in Canada, France, England, Germany and Italy, as well as terms commonly met in psychology, sociology, philosophy and other cognate fields. Omitted are items to be found in encyclopedias, such as personal names, institutions, school systems, organizations, publications "except where a movement, method or plan is represented." Cross references and synonyms are numerous. Pronunciation is given for difficult words. In this edition many definitions show revision and some new ones are added. Rated high for accuracy and scholarship.

ENCYCLOPEDIAS AND
ENCYCLOPEDIC SETS

G261. Encyclopedia of modern education, ed. by Harry N. Rivlin. New York, Philosophical Library, 1943. 902 p.

Signed articles with bibliographies on modern trends, policies and activities, but information is not always complete or accurate. Brief bibliographies usually limited to English language sources, drawing heavily on secondary sources. Notwithstanding limitations, it is a useful "first place" to look for information on modern education. No first-rate up-to-date encyclopedia in the field available.

G262. Lexikon der Pädagogik. Bern, A. Francke, 1950-52. 3 v.

Signed articles with bibliographies and a biographical section.

G263. Monroe, Paul. Cyclopedia of education. New York, Macmillan, 1911-13. 5 v.

Signed articles by more than 1,000 specialists. Known for its scholarly character, the *Cyclopedia* presents a historically, well-oriented world view of education in all its aspects. Numerous cross references, good illustrations and bibliographies. Handicapped by age, but a sterling work that remains unsurpassed for much historical and biographical material.

G264. Smith, Edward W. The educator's encyclopedia. Englewood Cliffs, N.J., Prentice-Hall, 1961. 914 p.

DIRECTORIES AND BIOGRAPHICAL
INFORMATION

Biographical

G265. Cattell, Jaques, *ed.* Directory of American scholars; a biographical directory. 3d ed. Lancaster, Pa., Science Press, 1957. 836 p.

Includes scholars in the humanities and social sciences. Information on name, present location, specialization, place and date of birth, place and date of degree(s), places of employment and special activities. With this edition scholars working in the social sciences have been transferred to volume three of *American men of science* (A142). R.R. Bowker Co. is preparing a new 4 vol. edition. Vol. I will cover history; vol. II, English, speech and drama; vol. III, foreign languages, linguistics and philology; and vol. IV, philosophy. To appear 1963-64.

G266. Cattell, Jaques and E.E. Ross. Leaders in education: a biographical directory. 3d ed. Lancaster, Pa., Science Press, 1948. 1208 p.

Although rapidly becoming outdated, this directory gives information not found elsewhere. Gives for each of the 17,000 American educators: name, title, address, place and date of birth, education and degrees, positions held, honors, society membership, activities field(s) of specialization, publications. Some names previously included in this volume were transferred in 1948 to *American men of science* and to *Directory of American scholars*. For these subject areas it lists only active administrators such as deans and college presidents.

G267. Who's who in American education: an illustrated biographical dictionary of eminent living educators of the United States. Nashville, Tenn., 1928+ biennial.

Information similar to that contained in *Leaders in education* (G266) with the addition of portraits in recent editions. Two companion works have been published in alternate years: *Trustees, presidents, and deans of American colleges and universities* in 1933, 1952, 1955 and 1957, 1958-59, 1960-61 and 1962-63; and *Leaders in American science* in 1952-54, 1955-56, 1958-59. Frequent complaint of inaccuracy. Whenever possible use in conjunction with other sources. Does contain some information not available elsewhere.

Directories of Institutions and Associations

G268. American Council on Education. American junior colleges. 5th ed. Washington, 1960. 564 p.

This companion volume to *American universities and colleges* (G269) performs a similar service for junior colleges recognized by regional or state accrediting agencies and follows a similar plan in organization of its material. 6th ed. to appear late in 1963.

G269. American Council on Education. American universities and colleges. 8th ed. Washington, 1960. 1212 p.

First published in 1928, this directory has been revised every four years. Information appears in four main sections: 1) survey articles on U.S. higher education; 2) articles on professional education in law, medicine, architecture, etc., signed by specialists and a list of accredited or approved schools in each field; 3) information on accredited colleges and universities in the U.S. and the Canal Zone covering history, organization, resources, equipment, requirements, staff analysis, size, degrees, fees, etc.; 4) appendices (list of accredited colleges, educational associations, degree abbreviations). Coverage of basic data makes it in some ways the most useful of the directories of higher institutions, but it does tend to become outdated between the four year periods of revision. 9th ed. to appear in 1964.

G270. American Council on Education. Guide to graduate study programs leading to the Ph.D. degree. 2d ed. Washington, 1960. 457 p.

A practical aid for the undergraduate, this book attempts to provide a basis for making a selection of graduate school. The first part, entitled "Graduate study and the undergraduate," discusses the character of graduate work and life and the basis for choice of institution and concludes with a selective bibliography. The second part lists alphabetically graduate schools offering programs leading to the Ph.D. and for each gives a brief history, admission requirements, fees and field of study. An appendix chart shows types of doctorates awarded by other institutions. There is an institutional index as well as an index by field of study.

G271. American Council on Education. *Commission on Education and International Affairs*. Sources of information on international educational activities. Washington, 1958. 114 p.

A listing of organizations which provide "continuous and current information" on educational programs in the international field. Such programs may be aimed at U.S. students, foreign students here and foreign and U.S. faculty members. A checklist of organizations gives the "information purpose," information resources and services and a description of publications of each. Concludes with a separate list of foreign government information services in the U.S., a brief bibliography and an index.

G272. College blue book. Yonkers on Hudson, N.Y., Christian E. Burckel, 1923+ (irregular schedule of revisions)

A lithographed work with table of contents at the back whose use is further complicated by space saving devices. Succeeds, however, in amassing much valuable information about "every institution of higher education in the U.S." regardless of accreditation or status in other respects. The main section along with two others on general information, precedes briefer ones on various subjects (art, dentistry, secondary education, etc.), each introduced by a list of institutions offering work in the field (if such exists). This is followed by histories of societies and associations in the field with full information on their functions, publications, etc.

G273. College handbook, 1955/ 56+ Princeton, N.J., College Entrance Examination Board, 1955+ biennial.

Formerly titled *Annual handbook,* this guide to fully accredited colleges which are members of the College Entrance Examination Board gives information for each on location, size, programs of study, terms of admission, financial aid and freshman year. An appendix lists the types of entrance examinations used by members of the Board and gives dates for applicants to take them.

G274. Commonwealth universities yearbook, a directory to the universities of the British Commonwealth and the handbook of their Association. London, Association of Universities of the British Commonwealth, 1914+ annual.

The latest edition covers 200 institutions in the British Commonwealth, both members and nonmembers of the Association. Arranged under countries, with an introductory article on universities in that country, the institutional listings show teaching and administrative staff by name and general information about facilities, degrees and fees. Each listing is dated at time of revision. Index of names.

G275. Directory for exceptional children, 1954+ Boston, Porter Sargent, 1954+ biennial.

Describes schools, homes, hospitals and other services for handicapped or maladjusted children.

G276. Fine, Benjamin. American college counselor and guide, 1958/59. 2d ed. New York, Prentice-Hall, 1957. 240 p.

Oriented toward the student choosing a college, this practical aid begins with a discussion of choice of a college, what college is like and financing an education. Then follows the orientation material on higher education: how it is organized, how the aims of the liberal arts colleges, universities and junior colleges differ from one another. And this leads up to an excellent summary of educational programs for various professions with qualifications sought in recruits, standards of accreditation, tuition, student aid, course of study, subdivisions of the field and a list of major centers of training by state. A more detailed summary in tabular form places information on accredited colleges and universities under 21 headings ranging from size of library to size of ground in acres. Concludes with a brief bibliography and index. Range and organization of the material make this an extremely useful aid in counselling students towards programs to serve their individual needs.

G277. Handbook of private schools. v. 1+ 1915+ Boston, Porter Sargent, 1915+ annual.

A standard reference in the field, this handbook-directory now uses the following scheme of presentation: special articles on private school education (different from year to year) including a review of the "Educational year"; school list arranged by states and locality (name, address, type, tuition, staff and student body size, costs, specialties, etc.); school list classified by type; supplementary list of remedial, tutoring and vocational schools; association list; directory of firms, agencies, bureaus, associations and index of schools.

G278. Herzog, John D. Preparing college graduates to teach in schools. Prelim. ed. Washington, American Council on Education, 1960. 49 p.

Resulting from the work of twenty-nine Eastern liberal arts colleges which organized to recruit for Harvard's 5th year teaching program, this is a directory of 5th year programs preparing students without undergraduate teaching preparation to teach in elementary and secondary schools. For each college gives such information as admission requirements, program, financial aid and application deadline.

G279. Index generalis; general yearbook of universities, and of higher educational institutions, academies, archives, libraries, scientific institutes, botanical and zoological gardens, museums, observatories, learned societies, 1919+ Paris, Dunod, 1919+ annual.

Title and publisher vary, but best known as *Index generalis*. Subtitle indicates broad scope. International coverage is uneven but useful. Dated information indicates functions and organization and lists all university professors by department. A voluminous alphabetical personal-name index follows. Published annually 1919-1939. First post-war edition, 1952/53, includes all countries except the USSR. Plans for a complete 1958 revision were canceled although the "France 1958" section was issued. Future plans uncertain.

G280. International handbook of universities, 1962. 2d ed. Paris, International Association of Universities, 1962. 773 p.

Designed as a companion to *American universities and colleges* (G269) and to *Commonwealth universities yearbook* (G274), this volume presents information in English on higher education in some 84 countries. Information on each institution, obtained from the institution itself or from sources in the possession of the International Association of Universities, covers academic structure and year, admission, degrees, diplomas, academic staff, composition of student body, language or languages of instruction, libraries and publications. Index of institutions in

English and in native language. The same type of information appeared earlier in *Universities of the world outside the U.S.A.* (Washington, American Council on Education, 1950).

G281. Lovejoy's college guide: a complete reference book to . . . American colleges and universities for use by students, parents, teachers and guidance counselors. New York, Simon and Schuster, 1953/54+ biennial.

First published in 1940 under the title *So you're going to college*. Beginning with the 1953/54 edition it became biennial and included non-accredited institutions, junior colleges and professional schools as well as accredited universities and colleges. Special chapters on choosing the college, application for admission, etc., supplement the usual information on each institution, i.e. enrollment, expenses, degrees, scholarships. Easier to use than other reference books containing such quantity and variety of information. Directed towards the same audience as Fine's *American college counselor and guide* (G276).

G282. National Education Association. NEA handbook. v. 1+ 1945/46+ Washington, National Education Association, 1945+ annual.

An annual providing basic facts about the N.E.A., its divisions, commissions, councils and departments. There is an alphabetical list by state of state and local associations and a membership list of the World Confederation of Organizations of the Teaching Profession. For each department or division, etc., provides information on current officers, dues, size of membership, publications, historical background and description of activities. For each affiliated state and local association it gives date of founding, date of most recent or next projected annual meeting, officers, state educational officials and related information. Details vary from year to year but there is little change in essential information.

G283. Patterson's American education. Chicago, Field Enterprises, Inc., 1950+ annual.

Began publication in 1904 as *Patterson's American educational directory*, but took the present title in 1954 when Educational Directories, Inc., took over publication. In 1958 this comprehensive directory of public and private schools, colleges and universities expanded from a one-part work to a two-part, separately paged work. The first volume arranges main listings geographically by state and city. Under each state appear names of personnel of the state education department, state board of education, state education association and county superintendents. Schools and colleges are listed alphabetically by place names; names of officers of local boards of education, superintendents and principals of public schools appear regularly (and heads of high school departments when available). For officers of colleges and universities the user is referred to the appropriate location in the "Schools classified" section. Then follow two parts with information on parochial and Lutheran schools and a directory of education associations. The second volume classes schools, colleges and institutions under field of interest (agriculture, journalism, theology, etc.), and lists them alphabetically under home state, giving names of chief officers. Although information is sometimes out of date and unreliable, it does list more personnel than the U.S. Office of Education *Directory*.

G284. U.S. *Office of Education*. Directory of public secondary day schools, showing accreditation, status, enrollment, classroom teachers and other data, 1958/59. Washington, Govt. Print. Off., 1961. 163 p.

Successor to *Directory of secondary day schools, 1951/52*. Presents in tabular form information on 24,226 secondary public schools in the U.S. as well as schools for American dependents outside the continental U.S. A companion volume, *Nonpublic secondary schools, a directory 1960-61*, listing 4,128 schools, was published in 1963.

G285. U.S. *Office of Education*. Education directory, 1912+ Washington, Govt. Print. Off., 1912+ annual.

An expansion of the directory of school and education officers which appeared as a chapter in the annual report of the U.S. Commissioner of Education from 1895-1911, the *Education directory* was part of the Bulletin series from 1912 to 1941. It is now an independent series. Since 1934 it has been issued in four parts entitled "Federal government and state education," "County and city school officers," "Higher education" (accredited institutions only), and "Educational associations and directories." Number and kinds of school officers have varied from year to year although the titles have been standardized. Since this directory appears each year, it may be used as a check upon information in *American universities and colleges* (G269) and *Patterson's American education* (G283).

G286. World of learning, 1947+ London, Europe Publications, 1947+ annual.

Annual cumulation of information on institutions of learning formerly appearing in *Europa* (London, Europa Publications, 1946+) and *Orbis* (London, Europa Publications, 1938+). A short section gives name, location, purpose, structure, executive officer and chief publications of numerous international organizations, the ranking one being Unesco. Arranged alphabetically under country, the list of learned societies, research institutions, libraries, museums, art galleries, universities and colleges provides information on dates of founding, officers and facul-ties, etc. Names of full professors and other ranking officers in larger organizations are given; but there is no personal-name index. Similar in-formation for earlier years may be found in *Minerva; Jahrbuch der ge-lehrten Welt*, 1891/92+ (publisher varies).

G287. Young, Raymond J. A di-rectory of educational research agen-cies and studies. 2d revision. Bloom-ington, Ind., Phi Delta Kappa, 1962. 75 p.

An invaluable list of research agencies in colleges and universities, state education departments, large city school systems and educational associations. Indicates types of re-search the agency undertakes, and studies completed, including method of publication. Sets forth in handy form much information formerly hidden in college catalogs, state and association directories and hand-books.

G288. Zimmerman, Oswald T. and Irving Lavine. College place-ment directory. 3d ed. Dover, N.H., Industrial Research Service, 1958. 598 p.

A guide to companies and gov-ernment organizations that hire col-lege and technical institute graduates.

Directories of Scholarships and Fellowships

Information on scholarships and fellowships may also be found in many of the directories of institu-tions and associations described in the preceding section and from state and local lists.

G289. Advancement and Place-ment Institute. World wide grad-uate award directory: internships, research grants, scholarships, fellow-ships, student deanships and assist-antships. Brooklyn, N.Y., 1957-1959. 3 v.

A geographically arranged list of opportunities for financial help on the graduate level, both in the United States and abroad.

G290. Angel, Juvenal L. National register of scholarships and fellow-ships. New York, World Trade Academy Press, 1957+

The first volume (Volume I, Scholarships and Loans, 3d ed., 1959) lists by state and type of sponsor scholarships and loans, giv-ing the name, number of scholar-ships and range. The second volume (Volume II, Fellowships and Grants, 2d ed., 1958) classifies fellowships and grants by subject field and gives sponsoring agency, number of fel-lowships, average value and part-time employment possibilities.

G291. Association of American Colleges. Fellowships in the arts and sciences. 1st ed.+ Washington, 1957+ annual.

An annual companion to *Guide to graduate study* (G270). Lists pre-doctoral and postdoctoral fellowships, grants for summer study and loans with information for each about pur-pose of award, qualifications of can-didates, period of award, amount of award, conditions, type of applica-tion, method of reviewing applica-tions, time schedule and deadline for applications.

G292. Feingold, S. Norman. Scholarships, fellowships and loans. v. 1+ Boston, Bellman Pub. Co., 1949+

A guide for vocational counselling and sources of financial assistance, this directory provides an extensive list of agencies, other than colleges and universities, administering schol-arships, fellowships and loans. The first volume stresses undergraduate awards and contains a bibliography for students and counselors. Later volumes add new material on sources of aid, expand and improve the treat-ment of career information. Volume III (1958) contains directions for use, chapters on vocational guidance, an alphabetical list of agencies (location, qualification, funds available, field[s] of interest, how to apply), a 300 item bibliography and a subject-loan-donor index.

G293. Lovejoy-Jones college scholarship guide. v. 1+ New York, Simon and Schuster, 1957+
Arranged alphabetically by donor, the guide gives brief information about scholarships, fellowships, grants, loans and awards. There are cross references and an index.

G294. Mattingly, Richard C. Financial assistance for college students: undergraduates. Washington, Govt. Print. Off., 1962. 360 p.
Information on all types of financial assistance for students in some 1,800 colleges.

G295. UNESCO. Study abroad: international handbook, fellowships, scholarships and educational exchange, 1948+ Paris, 1948+ annual.
The 1963 volume lists over 130,000 opportunities for fellowships, scholarships or travel grants offered by governments, universities and foundations in more than 116 states and territories. Preliminary chapters and all directions are in French, English and Spanish. Subjects for study cover almost every field of learning and the awards permit travel and study in almost every country in the world. The 1963 volume contains information on exchange of persons, results of the 10th annual survey of foreign student enrollment by Unesco, facilities for study abroad, international fellowships and scholarships available in 1963 arranged by donors with an index by beneficiaries.

HANDBOOKS, MANUALS, COMPENDIA

G296. Armstrong, W. Earl and Timothy M. Stinnett. A manual for certification requirements for school personnel in the U.S., including requirements in the fifty states, District of Columbia and Puerto Rico. Washington, National Education Association, 1951+ biennial.
Following a full summary of current certification practices and trends, the alphabetical directory of states and territories shows certification requirements for teachers, supervisors, administrators and special school service personnel. One chapter is devoted to a discussion and listing of teacher education institutions and approved programs. Concludes with an appendix listing the several certificates issued by different states, a bibliography and a glossary of terms.

G297. Baird, William R. Baird's manual of American college fraternities. 17th ed. Menasha, Wis., George Banta Publishing Co., 1963. 834 p.
Revised periodically since the first publication in 1879, this directory of social and professional fraternities and sororities, honor societies and recognition societies of American colleges and universities gives a detailed historical account of each organization listed.

G297a. Botts, L.S. and Jack Solomon, Jr. Complete handbook on educational systems: British, French, Russian, American. Chicago, National Debate Research Co., 1958. 214 p.
Prepared for use in debating the pros and cons of each of these educational systems, this handbook provides a good description of each system and a comprehensive bibliography.

G298. Campbell, William G. Form and style in thesis writing. Boston, Houghton Mifflin, 1954. 114 p.

G299. Engelhardt, Nickolaus L. School planning and building handbook. New York, F.W. Dodge Corp., 1956. 626 p.
Covers all aspects of school build-

ing from public relations, plans, estimates, legal analysis to financing and naming the school.

G300. Handbook of adult education in the United States. 4th ed. Chicago, Adult Education Association, 1960. 624 p.

First published in 1934, this handbook provides the only detailed account in one place of adult education activity in the United States through survey articles by specialists, notes on programs of organization and institutions. Particularly helpful directory information on adult education agencies.

G301. Institute of International Education. Handbook on international study, 1961. 3d ed. New York, 1961. 450 p.

Divided into two parts. The first, orientated towards foreign students in the United States, presents information on awards, organizations for foreign visitors and government regulations; and the second part, orientated towards United States students abroad, gives corresponding information.

G302. Sasnett, Martena T. Educational systems of the world: interpretations for use in evaluation of foreign credentials. Los Angeles, Univ. of Southern California Press, 1952. 838 p.

Information on some 80 educational systems is presented with an outline of the system and an explanation of the degrees or certificates awarded for completion of various phases of work, indicating equivalent in the United States. Sources include foreign ministers, consulates, administrative officers of the institutions checked, educational commissions and publications.

G303. Turabian, Kate L. Manual for writers of term papers, theses and dissertations. Rev. ed. Chicago, Univ. of Chicago Press, 1955. 82 p.

G304. Woellner, Robert C. and M. Aurilla Wood. Requirements for certification of teachers, counselors, librarians, administrators for elementary schools, secondary schools, junior colleges. Chicago, Univ. of Chicago Press, 1935+ annual.

A summary of the requirements necessary to obtain initial certification for the positions noted in all of the fifty states.

G305. World survey of education: handbook of educational organization and statistics. v. 1+ 1951+ Paris, UNESCO, 1952+ triennial.

Originally published under the title *World handbook of educational organization and statistics*. Beginning with the 1954 edition this was projected as a series covering general, primary, secondary and higher education. Information for each country includes organization of primary education, policy and administration and problems and trends. A bibliography and a chart of educational statistics, with source of statistics indicated, rounds out the picture for each country. Index to countries, subjects and institutions.

YEARBOOKS

G306. International yearbook of education. v. 1+ Geneva, Issued jointly by UNESCO and the International Bureau of Education, 1933+ annual.

Issued also in French as *Annuaire international de l'education et de l'enseignement*, the 1961 edition includes reports from 86 countries on current education situations. A lengthy section, "Comparative Study of Educational Progress in 1960/61," summarizes, in a form designed to facilitate ready comparison, advances throughout the world in educational administration, free compulsory education, primary, secondary, vocational and higher education and the manpower situation in education. The national reports which follow elaborate on the subdivisions of the "Progress" section adding pertinent information. There are listings of leading officials in ministries of education with titles, and tables giving the latest available educational statistics in cooperating countries (i.e. enrollments, number and per cent male-female). Publication was suspended from 1940-45.

G307. Educational yearbook of the International Institute of Teachers College, Columbia University, 1924-1944. New York, Macmillan, 1925-27; Teachers College, 1928-44. 20 v.

G308. Yearbook of education. London, Evans; Yonkers-on-Hudson, N.Y., World Book Co., 1932-40, 1948+
Since 1953 this yearbook has been compiled jointly by the Institute of Education, University of London and Teachers College, Columbia University. A good "first place" to go for annual surveys of education in the English-speaking and major European nations of the world. The comparative statistical studies on education, which have appeared since 1935, have covered school population, school finance, costs and teachers' salaries. Each issue is devoted to a specific theme.

G309. Yearbook of school law, 1950+   , ed. by Lee O. Garber. Danville, Ill., Interstate Printers and Publishers, 1950+ annual.
Until 1957 the publisher was the Univ. of Pennsylvania School of Education. Reviews as completely as possible in a limited space decisions of higher courts for a given year that bear on education. Appendix usually deals with a single topic of timely importance. No index but a good analytical table of contents. Continues the *Yearbook*, v. 1-10, 1933-1942, which was indexed in both the *Education index* and the *Index to*

legal periodicals. The present yearbook is indexed only in the latter.

Yearbooks or annual reports of associations, which are devoted to a special subject, are often useful and timely. For example see:

G310. American Association of School Administrators. Yearbook. 1st+ 1923+ Washington.
Since the 11th volume each issue has a distinctive title. The 1960 issue (v. 38) was entitled "Professional administrators for America's schools."

G311. American business education yearbook. v. 1+ 1944+ Somerville, N.J.
The 19th, issued in 1962, was concerned with "Secretarial education with a future."

G312. Claremont College Reading Conference. Yearbook. v. 1+ 1936+ Claremont, Calif.
Beginning with v. 10 each issue has a theme. In 1961 it was "Facing issues in reading."

G313. Educational conference (New York). v. 1+ 1932+ Washington, American Council on Education.
Issues have concerned themselves with such fields as "Measurement and research" (1960), "Curriculum planning" (1959), and "Positive values in the American education system" (1958).

G314. John Dewey Society, Yearbook. v. 1+ 1937+ New York, Appleton Century.
Discusses topics such as "Programs for the gifted" (1961) and "The teacher's role in American society" (1957).

G315. Middle States Council for the Social Studies. Proceedings. v. 1+ 1903+ Philadelphia.
With v. 41 each issue bears a distinctive title. V. 55 1957/58 was concerned with "The challenge of metropolitan development."

G316. National Art Education Association. Yearbook. v. 2+ 1951+ Kutztown, Pa.

G317. National Council for the Social Studies. Yearbook. v. 1+ 1931+ Philadelphia, McKinley Publishing Co.

Recent issues have covered "New viewpoints in geography" (v. 29, 1959), "Citizenship for a free society" (v. 30, 1960) and "Interpreting and teaching American history" (v. 31, 1961).

G318. National Council of Teachers of Mathematics. Yearbook. v. 1+ 1926+ Washington.

Each year the yearbook centers around a topic such as "Growth of mathematical ideas, grades K-12" (1959), "Instruction in arithmetic" (1960), and "Evaluation in mathematics" (1961).

G319. National Education Association. *Dept of Elementary School Principals.* Yearbook. v. 1+ 1922+ Washington.

Recent issues have discussed "Elementary school buildings" (1959) and "The first school years" (1960).

G320. National Education Association. *Dept. of Science Instruction.* Proceedings. v. 1-8, 1936-1943. Washington.

Merged with National Science Teachers Assoc. in 1944 and published *Proceedings* v. 1-3, 1944-1946. No more published.

G321. National Education Association. *Dept. of Supervision and Curriculum Development.* Yearbook. v. 1+ 1944+ Washington.

The latest issues (17th, 1960 and 18th, 1961) carried the titles "Leadership for improving instruction" and "Balance in the curriculum."

G322. National Society for the Study of Education. Yearbook. v. 1+ 1902+ Chicago.

Recent topics have included "Re-

thinking science education" and "Dynamics of instructional groups."

G323. National Society of College Teachers of Education. Studies in education: yearbook. v. 1-24, 1910-1944. Chicago.

G324. New York State Association of Secondary School Principals. Proceedings. 1890+ Syracuse, N.Y.

Since 1950 each issue has carried a distinctive title, *e.g.,* "Fundamentals for today's high schools" (1956).

G325. Western Arts Association. Yearbook. v. 1+ 1893+ Cincinnati, Ohio.

STATISTICAL SOURCES

G326. Health, education and welfare trends. 1961/62 ed. Washington, Office of Program Analysis. Department of Health, Education and Welfare, 1961. 153 p.

The education section of the presentation of statistical trend data gives such information as population by educational age groups, 1900-1980, enrollments, educational attainment, staffing and salaries, facilities and finance.

G327. Research bulletin, 1923+ Washington, National Education Association. 4 or 5 times a year.

Compiled by the Research Department of the N.E.A., this periodical presents and interprets current statistical data, drawn from the U.S. Office of Education, census figures, the research division itself and reliable private sources. Indexed by subject, not author, in *Public Affairs Information Service Bulletin* since 1923 and in *Education index* since 1929.

G328. UNESCO. Basic facts and figures: international statistics relating to education, culture and mass communication, 1952+ Paris.

Statistics, mostly from United Nations sources, are arranged by topics, *i.e.* population, educational institutions, libraries and museums, paper consumption, radio broadcasting, television. Most of the statistics may be found in other U.N. publications, but this is a convenient grouping. See also (A172).

G329. UNESCO. International yearbook of education. Geneva, issued jointly by Unesco and the International Bureau of Education, 1933+ (See annotation at G306).

G330. UNESCO. World survey of education: handbook of educational organization and statistics. v. 1+ 1951+ Paris. (See annotation at G305.)

G331. U.S. *Office of Education.* Biennial survey of education, 1916/18-1957/58 chp. 2. Washington, Govt. Print. Off., 1919-1962.

By statute this Office is directed to collect "such statistics and facts" as are necessary to give an inclusive picture of conditions and progress in education. Absorbing and expanding the statistical service formerly performed by the *Annual report* of the Commissioner, this is the only official, regularly published source for all U.S. educational statistics. Before 1940 it was published as a series of bulletins and later cumulated into a volume which was also in the numbered *Bulletin* series. Since 1940 it has been published in separate chapters: Chapter I, "The Summary," always the last to appear; Chapter 2, "State School Systems"; Chapter 3, "Local School Systems"; Chapter 4, "Higher Education"; and Chapter 5, "Libraries." Date of publication is regularly two or more years later than the biennium covered. Coverage is somewhat incomplete; data are lacking for an unknown number of private, vocational and trade schools, private correspondence schools, etc. Superseded by *Statistics of education in the United States, 1958/59 series.* (Washington,

Govt. Print. Off., 1961+), a new annual numbered series, each volume to cover a particular area of educational statistics for the school year.

SOURCES OF SCHOLARLY
CONTRIBUTIONS

G332. *Journals*

Education forum. v. 1+ 1936+ Menasha, Wis., Kappa Delta Pi. quarterly.
Ed Ind.

Educational record. v. 1+ 1920+ Washington, American Council on Education. quarterly.
Bull Sig; Ed Ind; PAIS; Psych Abst; UN Lib.

Harvard educational review. v. 7+ 1937+ Cambridge, Mass. quarterly. (Title v. 1-6, 1931-1936, *Harvard teachers record.*)
Bibl Fremd Zeit; Ed Ind; PAIS; Psych Abst; Soc Abst.

Journal of education. v. 1+ 1875+ Boston, School of Education, Boston Univ. quarterly.
Ed Ind; Psych Abst.

Journal of educational psychology. v. 1+ 1910+ Washington, American Psychological Association. bimonthly.
Bibl Fremd Zeit; Bull Sig; Ed Ind; Psych Abst; Soc Abst.

Journal of educational research. v. 1+ 1920+ Bloomington, Ill., National Association of Directors of Educational Research. 9 a year.
Bibl Fremd Zeit; Bull Sig; Ed Ind; Psych Abst; Soc Abst.

Journal of educational sociology. v. 1+ 1927+ New York, Payne Educational Sociology Foundation. 9 a year.
Bibl Fremd Zeit; Ed Ind; PAIS; Psych Abst; Soc Abst.

Journal of exceptional children.

v. + 1934+ Washington, International Council for Exceptional Children, National Education Association. quarterly.
Bull Sig.

Journal of experimental education. v. 1+ 1932+ Ann Arbor, Mich., Edwards Bros. quarterly.
Bull Sig; Ed Ind; Psych Abst.

Journal of higher education. v. + 1930+ Columbus, Ohio State Univ. monthly.
Bibl Fremd Zeit; Ed Ind; Soc Abst.

Research bulletin. v. 1+ 1923+ Washington, National Education Association. 4 or 5 a year.
Bull Sig; Ed Ind; PAIS.

Teachers College record. v. 1+ 1900+ New York, Teachers College, Columbia Univ. 8 a year.
Bibl Fremd Zeit; Ed Ind; Psych Abst; Soc Abst.

G333. *Organizations*

American Association of University Professors. Washington. Founded 1915.

American Council on Education. Washington. Founded 1918.

American Educational Research Association. Washington. Founded 1915.

Association of American Colleges. Washington. Founded 1915.

Carnegie Foundation for the Advancement of Teaching. New York. Founded 1905.

Fund for the Advancement of Education. New York. Founded 1951.

Middle States Association of Colleges and Secondary Schools. Philadelphia. Founded 1887.

National Education Association of the United States. Washington. Founded 1857.

National Council for the Social Studies. Washington. Founded 1921.

National Council of Teachers of English. Champaign, Ill. Founded 1911.

Pi Lambda Theta. Washington. Founded 1910.

Phi Delta Kappa. Bloomington, Ind. Founded 1906.

Southern Regional Education Board. Atlanta, Ga. Founded 1948.

G334. *Monograph Series*

Columbia University. Teachers College. Contributions to education. v. 1+ 1950+ New York.

Columbia University. Teachers College. Studies in education. no. 1+ 1951+ New York.

George Peabody College for Teachers. Contributions to education. v. 1+ 1920+ Nashville, Tenn.

Harvard University. Harvard monographs in education. v. 1+ 1922+ Cambridge.

Harvard University. Harvard studies in education. v. 1+ 1914+ Cambridge.

SOURCES OF CURRENT INFORMATION

G335. Adult education. v. 1+ 1950+ Cleveland, Ohio, American Association for Adult Education. quarterly.
Ed Ind.

G336. California journal of secondary education. v. 1+ 1925+ Berkeley, California Association of Secondary School Administrators. quarterly.
Ed Ind.

G337. Educational screen and audio-visual guide. v. 1+ 1922+ Chicago, Educational Screen. 10 times a year.
Ed Ind.

G338. Elementary school journal. v. 1+ 1900+ Chicago, Univ. of Chicago Press. 8 times a year.
Ed Ind; Psych Abst.

G339. High school journal. v. 1+ 1918+ Chapel Hill, School of Education, Univ. of North Carolina. 8 times a year.
Ed Ind; Soc Abst.

G340. Higher education. v. 1+ 1945+ Washington, Office of Education. 9 times a year.
Ed Ind; PAIS; UN Lib.

G341. Higher education and national affairs. v. 1+ 1940+ Washington, American Council on Education. irreg.

G342. Institute of International Education. News bulletin. v. 1+ 1925+ New York. monthly.

G343. National Education Association. Journal. v. 1+ 1913+ Washington. monthly.
Ed Ind; Psych Abst; RG.

G344. Overview for all educational executives. v. 1+ 1960+ New York, Buttenheim Publishing Corp. monthly.
Ed Ind; Soc Abst. Supersedes *School executive* (1881-1959).

G345. School life. v. 1+ 1918+ Washington, Office of Education. 9 times a year.
Ed Ind; PAIS.

G346. School and society. v. 1+ 1915+ New York, Society for the Advancement of Education. biweekly.
Bibl Fremd Zeit; Bull Sig; Ed Ind; Psych Abst; RG; Soc Abst.

The *New York Times,* most local newspapers and the special monthly issues of *Saturday review* offer additional coverage of educational news and opinion.

SOURCES OF UNPUBLISHED INFORMATION

G347. American Council on Education. Office of Statistical Information and Research. Washington.

G348. U.S. Dept. of Health, Education and Welfare. Office of Education. Washington.
Makes available unpublished information from various studies about six months after completion of the study.
See also: G241, G243, G245, G247, G248, G251, G253, G258.

Leatrice Kemp
Thompson M. Little
Carl M. White

8

Political Science

More than is likely to be the case in the other social sciences, the literature of political science is particularly prone to obsolescence. There are a
number of reasons for this. In the first place, government and politics
are forever undergoing rapid change. Second, political science as a science
does not have a stable and agreed upon theoretical structure. And
third, methodological innovations, especially in the years since the
second world war, make for continuous scientific ferment. With its
long and noble tradition in political philosophy on the one hand, and
its incessant need to anticipate the future on the other hand, political science carries the burden of both past and future. It is, of necessity, a historical discipline, and, of equal necessity, a predictive science.
It is concerned with the political behavior of individual persons, and
it is concerned with the functioning of large political systems. Its
theoretical and empirical tasks are, therefore, both complex and difficult.

It is equally difficult to suggest a viable core for a collection of books
in political science. Just what to include or exclude is hardly a matter on
which consensus can be readily attained. The books listed in this essay
are not necessarily the "best," for there is no single criterion of proper
choice. They are, hopefully, representative of different genres of political science research and writing and useful as points of departure in
search for political knowledge.

Political science, broadly defined, is the study of a great number and variety of institutions, processes and behavior patterns by which societies, communities, organizations and groups, as well as individual persons, make decisions in response to common problems requiring collective solutions. Like a giant redwood tree, its roots are both deep and shallow; its densely leaved limbs may be falling away in age, but they are forever replenished at the top; its tall trunk is massive in outline, on close inspection yet minutely grained. Paradoxically, it is easier to identify the branches than the main stem.

Nevertheless, it is possible to identify at least three major traditions which still exert a powerful influence on the contemporary study of "government and politics," as the subject matter of political science is conventionally called. The first is the classical metaphysical and ethical-moral tradition which began with Socrates and Plato in ancient Athens, and which is continued today by some practitioners in the sub-field of "political theory" or "political philosophy." A second tradition originated in Roman jurisprudence, was carried on by the medieval legal scholars, and had its flowering in the 19th century. It continues today in such sub-fields as "constitutional law" or "international law." Finally, modern political science derives from the tradition of empirical science which began with Aristotle, was lost during the Middle Ages, and was rediscovered in the 16th century. It is today the most pervasive and widely practiced of the three traditions. It is characterized by a great variety of approaches, ranging from macrocosmic description and analysis of large political systems—such as the nation-state or even the world system of inter-state relations—to microcosmic description and analysis of individual and small group behavior; from inductive observation and classification of political phenomena to deductive theory-building and hypothesis-testing; from concern with political structures and functions to concern with political issues and public policies.

Within these traditions, political science has given birth to many subfields and formulations which, as scholarly specialization increases, become more numerous and varied. The following recent works present general descriptions or analyses of political science as it is practiced today in colleges and universities:

H1. Easton, David. The political system: an inquiry into the state of political science. New York, Knopf, 1953. 320 p.
H2. Eulau, Heinz. "Political Science." In Hoselitz, Bert F., *ed.* A reader's guide to the social sciences. Glencoe, Ill., Free Press, 1959. pp. 89-127.
H3. Hyneman, Charles S. The study of politics: the present state of American political science. Urbana, Univ. of Illinois Press, 1959. 232 p.
H4. UNESCO. Contemporary political science. Paris, 1950. 713 p.
H5. Van Dyke, Vernon. Political science: a philosophical analysis. Stanford, Calif., Stanford Univ. Press, 1960. 235 p.
H6. Waldo, Dwight. Political science in the United States of America. Paris, UNESCO, 1956. 84 p.

HISTORY OF POLITICAL SCIENCE

Dating origins is always difficult. In political science, setting a date for the beginnings of the discipline hinges largely on the meaning given to "science" in the title by different practitioners. Those skeptical of the possibility of a positive-empirical science of politics, or even hostile to such an enterprise, date the discipline back to Plato and Aristotle. More empirically oriented political scientists find its origins in the writings of Machiavelli, Hobbes, Montesquieu and Vico. Still others, defining the discipline more narrowly, identify its origins with the establishment of independent chairs of "political ethics" or "political economy" in the first part of the 19th century, or with the establishment of independent departments of "political science" in the last quarter of the century.

Whatever date is chosen, it is generally agreed today that politics represents an independent sphere of human activity—independent, analytically at least, from ethics, history, and law—and worthy of disciplined study in its own right. Paradoxically, as political science freed itself from ethics, history and law, it discovered its affinity to some of the other modern social sciences, notably psychology and sociology. However, its primary concern with national, intra-national and inter-national political phenomena has exposed the discipline to the danger of being extraordinarily culture-bound, undermining its status as a *scientific* discipline. It has been argued that political science is a peculiarly American phenomenon, and there is an element, but only an element, of truth in the allegation. Except in the earliest period of American political science, when its leading practitioners received their training principally in continental European universities, and in the most recent past, when students of comparative politics discovered that the analytic concepts of American political science do not fit the facts of non-Western political experiences, little effort was made to transcend cultural limitations. This could only be achieved by developing theoretical concepts and propositions of a generic character capable of coping with state systems and their subsidiary institutions, but also with more primary political units such as the family, the village community, or the tribe; and with secondary units such as the voluntary association or the "state-less" society. Attempts along this line, accompanied by increasing efforts to develop mathematical and purely abstract models of political systems and processes, constitute the frontiers of modern, trans-national political science. Even so, political science as an empirical study remains a predominantly American discipline, though important training and research along lines pioneered in America can now be found in England, France, and Germany, as well as in the Scandinavian countries.

In the United States, then, the institutionalization of political science was largely the work of scholars trained in European universities toward the end of the last century. However, because of its dependence on the tradition of European public law and the theory of state sovereignty, American political science remained for many years excessively legalistic and formalistic in its orientation. Moreover, the early separation of the subject matter of political science into "politics" and "administration" long retarded an integrated discipline. At the same time, political theory was reduced largely to a study of the history of political philosophy and failed to fertilize the growing number of sub-fields. When, after the first world war, international relations became an important area of scholarly interest, it was little more than a quasi-legalistic, quasi-journalistic study of current affairs. Occasional attempts at revolt, as in the work of Arthur F. Bentley or Charles A. Beard, did not bear fruit until many years, if not decades, later. Although political science, in the twenties and thirties, produced a huge body of descriptive and, in a sense, realistic studies of political institutions and processes, it was not until the end of the second world war that the discipline achieved a more self-consciously theoretical and empirical focus. Perhaps most influential in this development were the teachings of Charles E. Merriam at the University of Chicago and the contributions of his most imaginative and brilliant student, Harold D. Lasswell. In the late twenties and thirties the Chicago Department of Political Science produced a great number of gifted scholars who, in due time, introduced intellectual ferment into almost all sub-fields of the discipline.

In the years since the second world war, a number of developments may be noted. In the first place, there has been a rejuvenation of political theory in both its normative-ethical and empirical-systematic aspects. Second, there has been a revitalization in the study of comparative politics, in an attempt to develop categories of analysis transcending cultural myopia and to facilitate genuine comparative analysis. Third, there has been a breaking away from formal and purely institutional descriptions in the direction of behavioral analyses of individual political actors and groups. Finally, there have been attempts to solve the problem of the relationship between fact and value in the study of politics through new formulations of political science as a "policy science." These developments are still under way and will be treated in later sections. The following items give a summary:

H7. Crick, Bernard. The American science of politics: its origins and conditions. Berkeley, Univ. of California Press, 1959. 252 p.

H8. Haddow, Anna. Political science in American colleges and universities, 1636-1900. New York, Appleton-Century, 1939. 308 p.

H9. Heller, Hermann. "Political Science." In Encyclopaedia of the social sciences. New York, Macmillan, 1933. v. 11, pp. 207-24.

H10. Lasswell, Harold D. The analysis of political behavior: an empirical approach. New York, Oxford Univ. Press, 1948. 314 p.

H11. Merriam, Charles E. New aspects of politics. Chicago, Univ. of Chicago Press, 1925. 253 p.

H12. Pollock, Frederick. An introduction to the history of the science of
      politics. New York, Macmillan, 1890. 128 p.

STRUCTURE OF POLITICAL SCIENCE

As an institutionalized academic study, political science is something
like a holding corporation, with more or less dependent affiliates, some of
which have grown out of older forms of inquiry, and some of which have
developed in response to the challenges of changing times. These affiliates constitute a matrix of two major dimensions. On one axis they are
characterized by their substantive concerns—the study of politics, public law, public administration and political values. On the other axis,
they are characterized by spatially defined arenas of action—the national
arena, the cross-national arena and the inter-national arena. In the
American context, for instance, it is possible to locate the sub-fields which
emerge from these classifications in a table, as follows:

RESEARCH TOPICS	RESEARCH ARENAS		
	National	*Cross-national*	*Inter-national*
Politics	American Politics	Comparative Politics	International Politics
Public Law	American Const. Law	Comparative Public Law	International Law
Public Administration	American Administr.	Comparative Administr.	International Organization
Political Values	American Pol. Thought	Comparative Ideologies	International Pol. Theory

While the matrix includes the major sub-divisions of political science,
it by no means exhausts the number of specializations in which courses
are now offered or textbooks written. In the first place, all of the sub-
fields feed into and are fertilized by what may be called "general political philosophy" and "systematic theory," the former concerned with the
great traditions of political thought, the latter with theoretical-empirical
propositions and the conceptual apparatus of the discipline. Second, almost each affiliate has its own subsidiaries, usually based on specific
processes, functions or institutions. By way of just one illustration, under
American politics we find specialized courses and texts on the electoral
process, the legislative institution, and executive functions. Third, depending on the formal structural complexity of a political system, political, legal and administrative processes take place within particular
geographical jurisdictions, giving rise, in the case of the United States,
for instance, to what are called "levels of government"—the federal,

state and local levels, each of which may become areas of specialized research and instruction. Fourth, there are particular "problem areas" which may be sources of institutional specialization, often cutting across the more formal sub-fields, such as "government and the economy," "civil-military relations," "foreign-policy making," or "inter-governmental relations."

It is within this complex framework, then, that research is undertaken, courses are offered and textbooks are written. Indeed, it is the textbook which, perhaps more than any other factor, gives unity to the whole enterprise of political science and its sub-fields. The number of general and special texts is legion, as is the variety of approaches they represent. They differ a great deal both in the quantity of material included and in quality. It would be folly to attempt a listing, even a partial one, of the texts now on the market—partly because they are often written with particular levels of instruction in mind, partly because their selection is a matter of taste and judgment for which no generally valid standards exist. If, in this essay, some texts are listed, it is because they represent a fresh "contribution" to knowledge, and not because they are necessarily the best instruments of instruction.

From the very beginning of the discipline in the present century, and in spite of its structural and functional heterogeneity, attempts have been made to write "introductions" to political science as a whole. In general, these attempts have not been too successful, but their contents give some indication of the changing foci of interest and approach of the discipline. The following list does not purport either to pass judgment on the merits of these works or to be comprehensive. And because its purpose is to present changing orientations, the listings are in terms of date of publication rather than in alphabetic order by author:

H13. Goodnow, Frank J. Politics and administration. New York, Macmillan, 1900. 270 p.
H14. Garner, James W. Introduction to political science. Cincinnati, American Book Company, 1910. 616 p.
H15. Willoughby, William F. An introduction to the study of the government of modern states. New York, Century, 1919. 455 p.
H16. Laski, Harold J. A grammar of politics. London, Allen & Unwin, 1925. 672 p.
H17. Catlin, George E.G. A study of the principles of politics. New York, Macmillan, 1930. 469 p.
H18. Wilson, Francis G. The elements of modern politics. New York, McGraw-Hill, 1936. 716 p.
H19. Sait, Edward M. Political institutions: a preface. New York, Appleton-Century, 1938. 548 p.
H20. Merriam, Charles E. Systematic politics. Chicago, Univ. of Chicago Press, 1945. 349 p.
H21. MacIver, Robert M. The web of government. New York, Macmillan, 1947. 498 p.
H22. De Grazia, Alfred. The elements of political science. New York, Knopf, 1952. 635 p.

APPROACHES IN POLITICAL SCIENCE

Within the complex organizational structure of political science, the practitioners of the discipline approach their subject matter in an almost equally complex manner. By "approach" is meant here not the particular methods of inquiry and research, but the models in terms of which the data of government and politics are analyzed and interpreted. Furthermore, these models and approaches are of quite different character, at times overlapping, and more or less widely accepted. All of them are beset by theoretical, empirical and methodological difficulties. To mention just one example by way of illustration, because it centers in a concept of wide currency: power. It is relatively easy, as many political scientists are inclined to do, to define political science as the study of the acquisition, distribution and transformation of power, and of all that the definition involves. But it is another thing to translate the concept of power into theoretically valid operational procedures, to gain access to the kind of data necessary to construct empirical indicators of power, and, above all, to observe the functioning and consequences of power relationship, not to mention the problem of measurement. Difficulties of this sort, and others, are equally prevalent in other approaches.

The approaches currently used in political science may be categorized in different ways. Some of them involve the specification of a single critical factor, usually expressed in a single concept, which serves as a kind of master orientation in organizing and interpreting the data of politics—in addition to the power approach, the group approach, the elite approach, the conflict approach, or the ideological approach. Another set of models is based on multi-factorial analyses centered in more complex themes, such as decision-making, input-output conceptions, or structural-functional formulations. Finally, approaches differ in terms of the theoretical or empirical units of analysis employed, ranging from the study of micro phenomena—political behavior, motivations, perceptions and attitudes—to macro phenomena, such as large-scale institutions and organizations.

None of these approaches is, of necessity, mutually exclusive. But some are more likely to be found in combination. For instance, institutional analysis has been more often coupled with the power approach than has behavioral analysis, largely because the ambiguity of the concept and ensuing measurement problems can be more readily ignored in the former than in the latter. The same is true of structural-functional analysis, the group approach, or conflict theory. On the other hand, elite analysis, decision-making studies, or input-output models are more easily usable in the treatment of behavioral than of institutional units. However, as work at the frontiers of research proceeds, efforts at integration are likely to be accelerated.

Finally, it is worth noting that, though in theory generic, some approaches are more easily applicable in some sub-fields of political science than in others. For instance, the power approach, most prevalent in the study of international politics, has in recent years been prominently tried in the study of local communities. Structural-functional analysis is particularly congenial to modern institutionalists working with complex variables, but it is increasingly used in behavioral studies as well. The study of international relations, which, more than any other area of research, is troubled by ready access to data, has increasingly used system and decision-making models. On the other hand, the group approach, developed in the pluralistic setting of the United States, has encountered obstacles when attempted in other societies.

Many of these analytical developments in political science are influenced by or related to parallel developments in other social sciences. For instance, system analysis draws a great deal on work done in biology and sociology; structural-functional analysis is indebted to anthropology; decision-making derives from work in economics; behavioral approaches come from psychology and psychoanalysis. However, each approach has its own fountainheads or spokesmen within the profession of political science. The power approach, with a long tradition going back to Machiavelli and Hobbes, has its most prominent spokesman today in Hans Morgenthau, a student of international politics. The group approach, stemming from Arthur E. Bentley, has been given fresh formulation by David B. Truman and Earl Latham. Elite analysis, first advanced by Gaetano Mosca and Vilfredo Pareto, has been reformulated as a neutral instrument of inquiry by Harold Lasswell and others. Decision-making analysis, also promoted by Lasswell, has been refined by Richard Snyder in the field of international politics, and by Robert Dahl in American politics. Conflict analysis, long neglected, has proved useful in Edward Banfield's work on metropolitan politics. System models have been formulated by David Easton and Morton Kaplan. Institutional studies, long purely descriptive and untheoretical, have been given various structural-functional formulations by Gabriel Almond, David Apter, and other students of comparative politics. Role analysis, cast in both systems and structural-functional terms, has been applied to the study of large institutional groups like legislatures by John Wahlke and his associates.

This short survey by no means exhausts the models now being used in political analysis. One might mention communication models, field theory, equilibrium concepts, developmental constructions and others. But this review, superficial as it is, suggests that the entire discipline of political science is in a state of flux—a sign of dissatisfaction with past ways, but also a sign of promise for the future. The fact that the current ferment is not restricted to any one sub-field, but permeates the discipline as a whole, is evidence of the changing character of political science. Some of these changes will be discussed further in later sections.

While there is a growing monographic literature which either presents or applies various approaches, there is much discussion of these matters in the professional journals. Some of these efforts are to be found in different books of "readings" listed elsewhere, but a few of the more important monographs may be listed here:

H23. Almond, Gabriel A. and James S. Coleman, *eds.* The politics of the developing areas. Princeton, N.J., Princeton Univ. Press, 1960. 591 p.

H24. Bentley, Arthur F. The process of government. Evanston, Ill., Principia Press, 1908. 501 p.

H25. Dahl, Robert A. and Charles E. Lindblom. Politics, economics, and welfare. New York, Harper, 1953. 557 p.

H26. Kaplan, Morton A. System and process in international politics. New York, Wiley, 1957. 283 p.

H27. Lasswell, Harold D., *et al.* The comparative study of elites. Stanford, Calif., Stanford Univ. Press, 1952. 72 p.

H28. Leites, Nathan. A study of bolshevism. Glencoe, Ill., Free Press, 1953. 639 p.

H29. Meyerson, Martin and Edward C. Banfield. Politics, planning, and the public interest. Glencoe, Ill., Free Press, 1955. 353 p.

H30. Morgenthau, Hans. Dilemmas of politics. Chicago, Univ. of Chicago Press, 1958. 390 p.

H31. Snyder, Richard, *et al.* Decision-making as an approach to the study of international politics. Princeton, N.J., Foreign Policy Analysis Project, 1954. 120 p.

H32. Truman, David B. The governmental process. New York, Knopf, 1951. 544 p.

H33. Wahlke, John C., *et al.* The legislative system: explorations in legislative behavior. New York, Wiley, 1962. 540 p.

POLITICAL PHILOSOPHY AND POLITICAL THEORY

Political philosophy or political theory—the terms are used interchangeably, though some clarification may be necessary—is the oldest of the sub-fields of political science. That it should be a sub-field at all is, perhaps, unfortunate. For it can be argued, and has been argued, that theorizing of one kind or another takes place throughout the many divisions of political science, and that the separation of theory from the rest of the total enterprise is artificial and detrimental to both. On the other hand, it can also be argued that, in a discipline as complex and heterogeneous as political science, specialization in political philosophy or theory is both necessary and desirable, provided that there be constant contact between the theorists and the specialists in the other sub-fields. However, this virtuous objective has only been approximated rather than achieved. It has not been achieved because, as a sub-field, political theory keeps its own peculiar difficulties and dilemmas.

Needed, first of all, is a clarification of the term "political theory."

The term covers, in fact, at least four clearly distinguishable types of theorizing. First, it refers to what might be properly labeled "philosophy" or "doctrine." This division of political theory—we might call it the classical tree—has its roots in ancient Greece, and its branches have grown through the centuries. It is concerned with inquiries of the most speculative kind into the nature of the good life and the prescription of those norms and institutions best suited to achieving the good life. Its main task is the development of moral and ethical principles for evaluating political institutions and behavior, for appraising the rightfulness of political systems and actions, and for suggesting alternatives. The political theorist, in this sense, is both a creative thinker and a critic who seeks in past political philosophies valid bases for his own thought, or who scrutinizes them from the perspective of his own formulations. His "texts" are the works of Plato and Aristotle, St. Augustine and Thomas Aquinas, Hobbes, Locke and Rousseau, Hume, Kant, Burke, Hegel, Bentham, Marx, Mill, and many others. His "products" are usually commentaries such as the following:

H34. Kendall, Willmoore. John Locke and the doctrine of majority rule. Urbana, Univ. of Illinois Press, 1941. 141 p.
H35. Meisel, James H. The myth of the ruling class: Gaetano Mosca and the elite. Ann Arbor, Univ. of Michigan Press, 1958. 432 p.
H36. Strauss, Leo. Thoughts on Machiavelli. Glencoe, Ill., Free Press, 1958. 348 p.

Second, political theory refers to what has been conventionally called the "history of political ideas," and what, more appropriately, might be called the "sociology of political knowledge." It is probably the most widely practiced branch of political theory in the United States and abroad. Its bias is strongly empirical, in the sense that it is not concerned with formulating moral or ethical criteria of judgment, but seeks to describe and explain the origins and growth of important political concepts and ideas, or ideologies. At their best, these histories are sophisticated analyses of the relationship between political ideas and institutions, social structures and processes, cultural variations, economic conditions, and contemporary assumptions about the nature of man and the needs of the time. At their worst, histories of political theory are arid transcriptions of what past political theorists have said or seriatim presentations of related political ideas.

There has been, in the course of the last sixty years, much progress in this genre of scholarly writing. At the very outset, and for a generation, William A. Dunning's descriptive historicism set the tone for a long series of similar works, of more or less originality, describing the contents of the classical texts and avoiding contextual analysis. In due time, similar histories were written for the development of political ideas in particular periods or individual countries of the Western world; and precedents were traced for particular concepts, such as sovereignty or natural law. One result of this empirical historicism was that political theory, as a sub-field, became increasingly isolated from the rest of political science. And the other sub-fields, themselves in the claws of hyperfactualism, were no longer fertilized by political thought. The following is a very brief list of works in this tradition:

H37. Allen, John W. A history of political thought in the sixteenth century. London, Methuen, 1951. 525 p.
H38. Coker, Francis. Organismic theories of the state. New York, Columbia Univ. Press, 1910. 211 p.
H39. Dunning, William A. A history of political theories. New York, Macmillan, 1902-1920. 3 v.
H40. Emerson, Rupert. State and sovereignty in modern Germany. New Haven, Conn., Yale Univ. Press, 1928. 282 p.
H41. McIlwain, Charles H. The growth of political thought in the West. New York, Macmillan, 1932. 417 p.
H42. Martin, Kingsley. French liberal thought in the eighteenth century. London, Benn, 1929. 313 p.
H43. Merriam, Charles E. A history of the theory of sovereignty since Rousseau. New York, Columbia Univ. Press, 1900. 233 p.

There were, of course, exceptions, especially works by historians or philosophers who tended to view political doctrine as rationalizations rather than as determinants of action. But in political science it was George H. Sabine, publishing in the late thirties, who reversed the trend by bringing methodological rigor into the analysis of political ideas and discriminating between statements of fact and value, between descriptive and causal explanations. The newer orientation was powerfully aided by the work of Karl Mannheim whose *Ideology and utopia* was first published in the United States in 1946. But only in the fifties did the history of ideas as a sociology of knowledge come into its own. The following works of political scientists and others are of particular interest:

H44. Brinton, Crane. Ideas and men: the story of Western thought. New York, Prentice-Hall, 1950. 587 p.
H45. Cassirer, Ernst. The myth of the state. New Haven, Conn. Yale Univ. Press, 1946. 303 p.
H46. Elliott, William Y. The pragmatic revolt in politics. New York, Macmillan, 1928. 540 p.
H47. Hacker, Andrew. Political theory: philosophy, ideology, science. New York, Macmillan, 1961. 612 p.
H48. Jaeger, Werner. Paideia: the ideals of Greek culture. New York, Oxford Univ. Press, 1939-44. 3 v.
H49. Mannheim, Karl. Ideology and utopia. New York, Harcourt, Brace, 1946. 318 p.
H50. Popper, Karl R. The open society and its enemies. London, Routledge and Kegan Paul, 1945. 2 v.
H51. Ruggiero, Guido de. The history of European liberalism. London, Oxford Univ. Press, 1927. 476 p.
H52. Sabine, George H. A history of political theory. New York, Holt, 1937. 797 p.

H53. Wolin, Sheldon. Politics and vision. Boston, Little, Brown, 1960.
     529 p.

Third, political theory refers to a body of writing which is chiefly concerned with the syntactics and semantics of political analysis. This "analytic political theory" does not seek to contribute either to ethical inquiry, the role of political ideas, or empirical politics, but is concerned
with the internal logic and clarity of value statements or causal propositions. It seeks to lay bare, through linguistic analysis, the metaphysical
assumptions of political philosophy and to advance the reformulation of
political problems along operational lines. As a genre, this type of political theory is indebted to logical positivism and the modern philosophy
of science. Its practitioners are few today, but it is likely to be an influential current in the future:

H54. Brecht, Arnold. Political theory: the foundations of twentieth-
     century political thought. Princeton, N.J., Princeton Univ. Press,
     1959. 603 p.
H55. Weldon, Thomas D. The vocabulary of politics: an enquiry into the
     use and abuse of language in the making of political theory. Lon-
     don, Penguin Books, 1953. 193 p.

Finally, political theory refers to "empirical political theory," that is,
theory which avoids value statements and strives for empirically relevant
propositions, be they of a causal, functional, or correlational sort. Propositions of this kind, subject to available scientific tests, are more often
cultivated in other sub-fields of political science than in political theory
as such. This kind of theory, then, consists of operational definitions and
hypotheses about the functioning of political institutions and processes,
and about the behavior of individual political actors. These hypotheses
may be of low generalizable order, medium-gauged, or very general.
They are usually centered in single master-concepts or related to each
other in multi-factorial schemata. The objective of this type of theory is,
ultimately, to formulate generalizations of predictive power about political processes and political behavior. The following is a listing of purely
theoretical works in this genre and does not include theories developed
in connection with empirical research:

H56. Black, Duncan. The theory of committees and elections. Cambridge,
     Eng., University Press, 1958. 242 p.
H57. Dahl, Robert A. A preface to democratic theory. Chicago, Univ. of
     Chicago Press, 1956. 155 p.
H58. De Grazia, Alfred. Public and republic: political representation in
     America. New York, Knopf, 1951. 262 p.
H59. Downs, Anthony. An economic theory of democracy. New York, Har-
     per, 1957. 304 p.
H60. Lasswell, Harold D. and Abraham Kaplan. Power and society. New
     Haven, Conn., Yale Univ. Press, 1950. 295 p.
H61. Simon, Herbert A. Administrative behavior. New York, Macmillan,
     1947. 259 p.

H62. Schubert, Glendon A. The public interest: a critique of the theory of a political concept. Glencoe, Ill., Free Press, 1960. 244 p.

COMPARATIVE GOVERNMENT AND POLITICS

In its search for universal principles of governance, the study of politics, from the Greek thinkers to the present day, has followed essentially two roads. One of these roads, we have seen, involved the pursuit of philosophical or theoretical speculation; the other, we shall see, involved the careful accumulation of governmental and political experiences in different societies which might serve as bases for inference concerning universals. Although Aristotle, with his survey of constitutions in the Greek world, was the first empirical student of comparative government, it was not until the time of the Italian Giovanni Batista Vico, in the first third of the 18th century, that broad-gauged empirical comparison made much headway in the study of government and politics. Vico reacted against the ahistorical, speculative methods and "findings" of the natural law philosophers, and he influenced the French Baron Charles Louis de Montesquieu, whose famous *Spirit of the laws* (1748) revived Aristotle's empirical, historical and comparative approach. Through the next hundred years, well into the second part of the 19th century, the comparative study of government was much concerned with the institutions of Greece and Rome, as well as with contemporary institutions in the "civilized" world, on the assumption that such investigation could reveal the essential and universal characteristics of human governance. In due time, influenced by the emerging discipline of anthropology, the comparative horizon was extended to "simple" societies and the Middle Ages, as in the work of such Englishmen as Henry Maine and Edward A. Freeman, or of the German Otto von Gierke. The approach was predominantly legal and historical, but the objective was to find, through comparison, general principles.

It is quite paradoxical, therefore, that as political science became an independent discipline and provided for a sub-field called "comparative government," the study of "foreign" governments and politics turned ever less comparative and more parochial. In part, this was probably due to the sway of social evolutionism which saw in Western constitutions the quintessence of "advanced" government, and which would treat earlier or more "primitive" forms as curiosities of little relevance to modern problems. In part, it was due to the alienation of political theory from the rest of the discipline, tending to reduce empirical investigation to description of limited generalizability. In part, it was due to the increasing amount of specialization and division of labor among scholars interested in the foreign field.

As a result, the huge bulk of work in comparative government during the first half of the century was concerned with describing, in more or less detail and with more or less coverage, individual state systems, usually those of the Western world, or particular institutions within individual nations. The problems of constitution-making, constitutional interpretation and constitutional change were of primary interest. They were supplemented by descriptive analyses of governmental structures, with particular emphasis on the difference between the presidential and parliamentary forms, or between the federal and unitary modes of territorial organization. With the appearance of communism in Russia and fascism in Italy and Germany, the differences between democratic and totalitarian systems became an object of research. Studies on the origin, nature and structure of representation, the history and activities of political parties, the organization and procedures of legislatures, the functioning of electoral systems, and the workings of executive agencies and civil services in particular countries abounded. Most of these works are now outdated, and to list even a selection would serve no useful purpose.

Moreover, regardless of whether they dealt with whole national systems or particular institutions, most of these works ignored or neglected the social matrix or the cultural context within which governmental and political processes take place. Little, if any, attention was paid to a country's economic conditions, its class structure, cultural traditions and values as important factors influencing political life. Occasionally, these matters might be superficially dealt with in an introductory chapter, but they were not integrated into the substantive analysis, which remained chiefly legalistic and institutional. It is in this respect, however, that more recent single-country studies, still as popular (and, probably, necessary) as ever, differ from their pre-World War II predecessors.

With research concern, over so many decades, being ethnocentric and untheoretical, it is not surprising that the texts in the field reflected the state of research. On the one hand, they presented, in country-after-country fashion, parallel descriptions of institutions; on the other hand, they often compared uncomparables. Moreover, they were often shot through with more or less open bias for the traditional institutions of the writer's own country. American writers were likely to be as partial to the presidential as British writers were to the parliamentary type of representative government. As textbooks came to be written by teams of country specialists, comparison ceased altogether. Low-level propositions based on limited numbers of cases and ignoring contrary evidence were proverbs more useful for reform politics than research purposes. All this is not meant to imply that most of these works, as the research on which they were based, were of low quality. Rather, it is to point out the difficulties besetting the student of comparative politics who wishes to be at all-comprehensive in his treatment of heterogeneous political systems.

There were, of course, exceptions. James Bryce, Harold Laski, Herman

Finer and Carl J. Friedrich, though writing texts, brought fresh, if different, viewpoints to the study of foreign institutions. Although at times intuitive and speculative, their books were less out of line with the earlier comparative tradition. They demonstrated an interest in general political theory and sought universal principles in the particular circumstances they examined. Moreover, they paid attention to the wider social and cultural milieu in which political forms and processes originate, grow, flourish and disappear. As a result, factors such as leadership, public opinion and ideology became part and parcel of their treatment. Although their arenas of interest remained in the West, they were more sensitive to national similarities and differences. Their theoretical orientation was tempered, in the case of Bryce, by the practicing politician's respect for the human variable; in the case of Laski it was colored first by his pluralist and later his Marxist bias; in the case of Finer it was affected by a frankly utilitarian ethos; and in the case of Friedrich by the tradition of German *Staatslehre*. Moreover, all of them retained the concept of the "state" to circumscribe the central object of political analysis.

H63. Bryce, James. Modern democracies. New York, Macmillan, 1921.
2 vols.
H64. Finer, Herman. The theory and practice of modern government. New
York, Dial, 1932. 2 vols.; Rev. ed. New York, Holt, 1949. 978 p.
H65. Friedrich, Carl J. Constitutional government and democracy. Boston,
Ginn, 1946. 695 p.
H66. Laski, Harold J. The state in theory and practice. New York, Viking,
1935. 299 p.

As in other sub-fields, there is today much ferment in comparative government. This ferment, quite apart from dissatisfaction with the intuitive, speculative, and descriptive approaches of the earlier work, has a number of sources. In the first place, the exigencies of the second world war, so much more global than the first, suggested the feasibility of treating national arenas not as isolated systems, but as units of larger areas, such as geographical, economic or cultural areas. Interdisciplinary orientations, stimulated by the war-time cooperation of social scientists, made areal treatment theoretically plausible and practically desirable. However, while the areal approach served to alert students of comparative politics to social and cultural factors previously ignored or neglected, and while it made for more intensive and comprehensive analysis, it did not solve either the conceptual or methodological problems of comparison. Although studies of this sort were superior to the earlier single-country works, they remained essentially descriptive, and their findings could not be readily generalized. For comments and criticisms of the state of comparative politics through the post-war decade, the following may be consulted:

H67. Ehrmann, Henry. Interest groups on four continents. Pittsburgh,
Univ. of Pittsburgh Press, 1958. 316 p.

H68. Heckscher, Gunnar. The study of comparative government and politics. New York, Macmillan, 1957. 172 p.
H69. Macridis, Roy C. The study of comparative government. Garden City, N.Y., Doubleday, 1955. 77 p.

Second, the post-war emergence of the "new states," so-called, alerted students of comparative government to the need for new conceptual categories more appropriate to the new settings than the traditional concepts of Western constitutionalism, such as monarchy, democracy, separation of powers, and so on, or even such distinctions as those between totalitarian, autocratic and democratic systems. The search for new categories of analysis has been profuse and intense, but few of these ingenious analytic inventions have been generally accepted. In general, these efforts at reconceptualization and theory-building in comparable politics do not differ significantly from similar attempts in other subfields. Among recent publications the following are useful as introductions to the newer developments:

H70. Almond, Gabriel A. and James S. Coleman, *eds.* The politics of the developing areas. Princeton, N.J., Princeton Univ. Press, 1960. 591 p.
H71. Beer, Samuel H., *et al.* Patterns of government: the major political systems of Europe. New York, Random House, 1958. 622 p.
H72. Lerner, Daniel. The passing of traditional society. Glencoe, Ill., Free Press, 1958. 466 p.
H73. Lipset, Seymour M. Political man: the social bases of politics. Garden City, N.Y., Doubleday, 1960. 432 p.
H74. Macridis, Roy C. and Bernard E. Brown., *eds.* Comparative politics: notes and readings. Homewood, Ill., Dorsey, 1961. 577 p.
H75. Neumann, Sigmund, *ed.* Modern political parties: approaches to comparative politics. Chicago, Univ. of Chicago Press, 1956. 460 p.
H76. Pye, Lucian W. Guerilla Communism in Malaya: its social and political meaning. Princeton, N.J., Princeton Univ. Press, 1956. 369 p.
H77. Spiro, Herbert. Government by constitution. New York, Random House, 1959. 496 p.

THE AMERICAN ARENA

That American political scientists should pay more attention to the description and analysis of American government and politics than to any other political arena—just as other national academic communities do—is self-explanatory. But it also involves one of the major problems faced by political science as "science"—the danger of being more parochial and culture-bound than any other scientific discipline. As "science," political science should not know of national boundaries. There can be no American, or British, or French political science. From a strictly scientific point of view, therefore, the study of the American arena is really meaningful only in the perspective of a comparative political science.

Though political scientists have produced an enormous amount of writing and research on almost every conceivable institution, process, policy, or action pattern in the American complex of government and politics—national, state, and local—, it was in the nature of the American experience that constitutional law should first claim their attention, and that the legal approach should provide an initial orientation. The great political conflicts in American history had been conflicts over the Constitution—such as those between the President and Congress, or between the federal government and the states. Constitutional problems stemming from the due process, equal protection of the laws, and contract clauses of the Constitution, or such constitutional grants as the commerce and taxing powers, were of interest to political scientists. The pervasiveness of the legal-analytical approach is evident in most of the early work of the profession. This concern with constitutional matters continues to the present day, though new view-points, such as "legal realism" and a more political interpretation of the judicial process, have been widely accepted. Political scientists now take a closer look at what the judges do when they interpret the law, and dissect the semantics, political issues and judicial attitudes of court personnel. The following are either representative of the older or newer interpretations, or noteworthy in their own right:

H78. Carr, Robert K. The Supreme Court and judicial review. New York, Farrar & Rinehart, 1942. 304 p.
H79. Cahill, Fred V. Judicial legislation: a study of American legal theory. New York, Ronald, 1952. 164 p.
H80. Corwin, Edward S. The doctrine of judicial review. Princeton, N.J., Princeton Univ. Press, 1914. 177 p.
H81. Haines, Charles G. The American doctrine of judicial supremacy. New York, Macmillan, 1914. 365 p.
H82. Horn, Robert. Groups and the Constitution. Stanford, Calif., Stanford Univ. Press, 1956. 187 p.
H83. Mendelson, Wallace. The Constitution and the Supreme Court. New York, Dodd, Mead, 1959. 520 p.
H84. Murphy, Walter F. and C. Herman Pritchett. Courts, judges, and politics: an introduction to the judicial process. New York, Random House, 1961. 707 p.
H85. Pritchett, C. Herman. The Roosevelt court: a study in judicial politics, 1937-1947. New York, Macmillan, 1948. 314 p.
H86. Rosenblum, Victor. Law as a political instrument. Garden City, N.Y., Doubleday, 1955. 88 p.
H87. Schmidhauser, John R. The Supreme Court: its politics, personalities, and procedures. New York, Holt, Rinehart & Winston, 1960. 163 p.
H88. Schubert, Glendon. Constitutional politics: the political behavior of Supreme Court Justices and the constitutional policies that they make. New York, Holt, Rinehart & Winston, 1960. 735 p.

Within the framework set by the historical approach and constitutional categories, political scientists have produced a huge body of either descriptive or reform-oriented literature. The problems arising out of the

American federal structure of government, both legal and administrative, has made for sometimes polemical, sometimes remedial, and, more recently, diagnostic analyses:

H89. Benson, George C.S. The new centralization. New York, Farrar and Rinehart, 1941. 181 p.
H90. Bowie, Robert R. and Carl J. Friedrich. Studies in federalism. Boston, Little, Brown, 1954. 887 p.
H91. Clark, Jane P. The rise of a new federalism. New York, Columbia Univ. Press, 1938. 347 p.
H92. Macmahon, Arthur W. Federalism: mature and emergent. Garden City, N.Y., Doubleday, 1955. 557 p.

Of equal interest to political scientists are the problems stemming from the functional separation of powers between the President and Congress, particularly the President's role as a legislative leader. In addition to many earlier works, some recent publications are noteworthy:

H93. Binkley, Wilfred E. President and Congress. New York, Knopf, 1947. 312 p.
H94. Chamberlain, Lawrence H. The President, Congress and legislation. New York, Columbia Univ. Press, 1946. 478 p.
H95. Corwin, Edward S. The President: office and powers. 4th ed. New York, New York Univ. Press, 1957. 519 p.
H96. Fenno, Richard F. The President's Cabinet. Cambridge, Harvard Univ. Press, 1959. 326 p.
H97. Horn, Stephen. The Cabinet and Congress. New York, Columbia Univ. Press, 1960. 310 p.
H98. Neustadt, Richard E. Presidential power: the politics of leadership. New York, Wiley, 1960. 224 p.
H99. Rossiter, Clinton. The American presidency. New York, Harcourt, Brace, 1956. 175 p.

The problems and politics of the Congress, too, have occasioned a spate of works. While earlier studies were concerned with description of legal powers and the procedural maze of the legislative process, later works have dealt with the need for organizational reforms and the political aspects of the legislative process, especially the group nature of legislative conflicts. More recently, using roll-call analyses and interviews, a number of excellent works have concentrated on how Congressmen behave with regard to the issues they must face:

H100. Burns, James M. Congress on trial: the politics of modern lawmaking. New York, Harper, 1949. 224 p.
H101. Bailey, Stephen K. Congress makes a law: the story behind the Employment Act of 1946. New York, Columbia Univ. Press, 1950. 282 p.
H102. Galloway, George B. The legislative process in Congress. New York, Crowell, 1953. 689 p.
H103. Gross, Betram M. The legislative struggle: a study in social combat. New York, McGraw-Hill, 1953. 472 p.
H104. MacRae, Duncan Jr. Dimensions of congressional voting. Berkeley, Univ. of California Press, 1958. pp. 203-390. (University of

California. Publications in sociology and social institutions. v. 1, no. 3)

H105. Matthews, Donald R. U.S. Senators and their world. Chapel Hill, Univ. of North Carolina Press, 1960. 303 p.

H106. Truman, David B. The Congressional Party: a case study. New York, Wiley, 1959. 336 p.

H107. Turner, Julius. Party and constituency: pressures on Congress. Baltimore, Johns Hopkins Press, 1951. 190 p.

H108. Young, Roland. The American Congress. New York, Harper, 1958. 333 p.

Just as constitutionalism has pervaded the writings on government and politics, so the pluralistic quality of American life has made a deep impression on American political science. The influence of groups, especially of the highly organized "pressure groups," became an area of specialized research and writing. Although Arthur F. Bentley had called attention to the "group nature" of politics as early as 1908, his work was neglected for many years, and his general approach had to be independently rediscovered by specialists on administrative and legislative politics twenty years later. Gradually, too, attention came to be directed not only to the external, but also the internal, politics of the great associations whose activities impinge on the political system. The following works are representative:

H109. Garceau, Oliver. The political life of the American Medical Association. Cambridge, Harvard Univ. Press, 1941. 186 p.

H110. Herring, E. Pendleton. Group representation before Congress. Baltimore, Johns Hopkins Press, 1929. 309 p.

H111. Kesselman, Louis C. The social politics of FEPC: a study in reform pressure movements. Chapel Hill, Univ. of North Carolina press, 1948. 253 p.

H112. Latham, Earl. The group basis of politics: a study in basing-point legislation. Ithaca, N.Y., Cornell Univ. Press, 1952. 244 p.

H113. Odegard, Peter. Pressure politics: the story of the Anti-Saloon League. New York, Columbia Univ. Press, 1928. 299 p.

H114. Truman, David B. The governmental process: political interests and public opinion. New York, Knopf, 1951. 544 p.

H115. Schattschneider, Elmer E. Politics, pressures and the tariff. New York, Prentice-Hall, 1935. 301 p.

It is anomalous that the study of the role of political parties in the American political process did not come into its own until fairly recently. One reason is likely to be found in the preoccupation with the extension of the franchise during the 19th and the early 20th centuries. Another is that reform efforts to introduce the devices of direct democracy —initiative, referendum and recall—were based partly on the assumption that parties were detrimental to a truly democratic politics. Above all, the founders of the republic had been hostile to parties, and though Alexis de Tocqueville, writing in the first third of the 19th century, considered parties important components of democratic life, the bias of the founders persisted. It was an Englishman, James Bryce, who presented the first extensive treatment of parties toward the end of the century, and while other writers acknowledged their existence and even, as A. Lawrence Lowell, did some intensive research, it was not until the twenties of the present century that this rigorous study of parties and party behavior reached maturity. By this time, studies of aggregate voting statistics had sufficiently advanced to permit interpretations of American party politics in terms of geographical section and social class. At the same time, inquiries into the origins and growth of the parties added historical depth. Of the now large body of literature, the following are useful:

H116. Beard, Charles A. An economic interpretation of the Constitution. New York, Macmillan, 1913. 330 p.
H117. Binkley, Wilfred E. American political parties: their natural history. New York, Knopf, 1943. 420 p.
H118. David, Paul T., *et al.* The politics of national party conventions. Washington, Brookings Institution, 1960. 592 p.
H119. Heard, Alexander. The costs of democracy. Chapel Hill, Univ. of North Carolina Press, 1960. 493 p.
H120. Herring, E. Pendleton. The politics of democracy. New York, Rinehart, 1940. 468 p.
H121. Holcombe, Arthur N. Political parties of today. New York, Harper, 1924. 399 p.
H122. Key, Valdimer O., Jr. Southern politics in state and nation. New York, Knopf, 1949. 675 p.
H123. Leiserson, Avery. Parties and politics: an institutional and behavioral approach. New York, Knopf, 1958. 379 p.
H124. McDonald, Neil A. The study of political parties. Garden City, N.Y., Doubleday, 1955. 97 p.
H125. Schattschneider, Elmer E. Party government. New York, Farrar and Rinehart, 1942. 219 p.

In addition, the politics of local communities, but especially of the large cities, came to be intensively studied. While the first of these studies were largely limited to the formal and informal activities of the parties on the local scene, more recent research has sought to understand local politics in the broader context of all community decision-making and community power relations. Though begun by sociologists, this last type of interest is now widely shared by political scientists. The following works illustrate the changing focus of research on local politics:

H126. Banfield, Edward C. Political influence. Glencoe, Ill., Free Press, 1961. 354 p.
H127. Dahl, Robert A. Who governs? Democracy and power in an American city. New Haven, Conn., Yale Univ. Press, 1961. 355 p.
H128. Gosnell, Harold F. Machine politics: Chicago model. Chicago, Univ. of Chicago Press, 1937. 229 p.
H129. Janowitz, Morris, *ed.* Community political systems. Glencoe, Ill., Free Press, 1961. 259 p.
H130. McKean, Dayton D. The boss: The Hague machine in action. Boston, Houghton Mifflin, 1940. 285 p.

H131. Peel, Roy V. The political clubs of New York City. New York, Putnam's, 1935. 360 p.

Valuable aid in understanding party politics and the role of parties has come from the many studies of American voting behavior, whether based on electoral statistics or surveys. The earliest of these researches, using aggregate electoral data, were primarily concerned with voter turn-out at the polls and with voting preferences, which were correlated with available demographic data on age, sex, race, education, income, religion, and so on. Most of these studies tested isolated, low-level hypotheses about political behavior. But these studies were inherently incapable of explaining either the individual voter's motivations and perceptions, or the effect of party activities on his behavior. This kind of study was made possible by the emergence, in the mid-thirties, of the interview polls and surveys. The fiasco of the polls in 1948 for a time shattered confidence in their reliability, but they have proved to be useful tools of investigation in the study of elections and electoral behavior. They have made possible multivariate analyses of a great range of factors which seem to influence voting—party identification, issue orientation, candidate image, social class, mass communications, party activities, multiple group memberships, personality attributes, and so on. Of the great mass of books in this field, only a few can be cited here:

H132. Berelson, Bernard, *et al*. Voting: a study of opinion formation in a Presidential campaign. Chicago, Univ. of Chicago Press, 1954. 395 p.
H133. Burdick, Eugene and Arthur J. Brodbeck, *eds*. American voting behavior. Glencoe, Ill., Free Press, 1959. 475 p.
H134. Campbell, Angus, *et al*. The American voter. New York, Wiley, 1960. 573 p.
H135. Eldersveld, Samuel J. Political affiliation in metropolitan Detroit. Ann Arbor, Bureau of Government, Institute of Public Administration, Univ. of Michigan, 1957. 199 p.
H136. Ewing, Cortez A.M. Presidential elections: from Abraham Lincoln to Franklin D. Roosevelt. Norman, Univ. of Oklahoma Press, 1940. 226 p.
H137. Gosnell, Harold F. Grassroots politics. Washington, American Council on Public Affairs, 1942. 195 p.
H138. Janowitz, Morris and Dwaine Marvick. Competitive pressure and democratic consent. Ann Arbor, Bureau of Government, Institute of Public Administration, Univ. of Michigan, 1956. 122 p.
H139. Key, Valdiner O., Jr. American state politics: an introduction. New York, Knopf, 1956. 289 p.
H140. Merriam, Charles E. and Harold F. Gosnell. Non-voting: causes and methods of control. Chicago, Univ. of Chicago Press, 1924. 287 p.
H141. Mosteller, Frederick, *et al*. The pre-election polls of 1948. New York, Social Science Research Council, 1949. 396 p.
H142. Rice, Stuart A. Farmers and workers in American politics. New York, Columbia Univ. Press, 1924. 231 p.

Of all the sub-fields of political science, public administration is most eminently concerned with the relationship between means and ends, facts and values, conduct and the goals of action. Yet, the founders of public administration as a field developed a sharp division between policy (or politics) and administration. This was due, in part, to the demand for an impartial civil service and other governmental reforms unsullied by politics; it was due, in part, to the contemporary scientific management movement, with its emphasis on economy and efficiency. The following are "classics" of this approach:

H143. Goodnow, Frank J. Politics and administration. New York, Macmillan, 1900. 270 p.
H144. White, Leonard D. Introduction to the study of public administration. New York, Macmillan, 1926. 495 p.
H145. Willoughby, William F. Principles of public administration. Washington, Brookings Institution, 1927. 720 p.

As a result of this orientation, the question, "administration for what?," was largely ignored. Goals and values were taken for granted, and research emphasis was on the formal structural aspects of administration or on rather vague "principles" of proper administrative conduct. Though "outsiders" like John Dewey or Felix Frankfurter contributed perceptive statements of the need to relate policy considerations to the conduct of the public business, writers on public administration generally continued to discuss structural matters throughout the thirties. An influential volume, edited in 1937 by Luther Gulick and Lyndall Urwick, once more restated the traditional approach and its magic summary term of administrative functions, POSDCORB, i.e., planning, organizing, staffing, directing, coordinating, reporting, and budgeting. But other writers began to place public administration in its political context by emphasizing the nature of policy-making. Administration came to be viewed as a means to ends which could not be properly evaluated apart from the uses to which the means were put. The new orientation was given near-manifesto form in a series of papers by Gaus, White and Dimock. It was explicitly applied in a volume edited after the second world war by F. M. Marx, and it was given its most complete formulation by Paul Appleby in 1949. These developments were codified by Waldo in a book published in 1948:

H146. Appleby, Paul. Policy and administration. University, Ala. Univ. of Alabama Press, 1949. 173 p.
H147. Gaus, John M., et al. The frontiers of public administration. Chicago, Univ. of Chicago Press, 1936. 146 p.
H148. Gulick, Luther and Lyndall Urwick, eds. Papers on the science of administration. New York, Institute of Public Administration, 1937. 195 p.
H149. Marx, Fritz M., ed. Elements of public administration. New York, Prentice-Hall, 1946. 637 p.

H150. Waldo, Dwight. The administrative state: a study of the political
      theory of American public administration. New York, Ronald,
      1948. 227 p.

Two problems, in particular, have occupied the attention of students
of public administration. One is the problem of "bureaucracy," the
other the problem of "public interest." The former concern involved
initially the issues of administrative discretion and responsibility, and
more recently the problems of bureaucratic behavior, including its pre-
sumed pathology. Less progress has been made in pinning down the
empirical implications of the concept of "public interest"—admittedly a
vague and ambiguous concept which, in fact, may prove to be non-re
searchable. Of works in these two problem areas, the following are illustrative:

H151. Bernstein, Marver H. Regulating business by independent commis-
      sions. Princeton, N.J., Princeton Univ. Press, 1955. 306 p.
H152. Blau, Peter M. Bureaucracy in modern society. New York, Random
      House, 1956. 124 p.
H153. Cushman, Robert E. The independent regulatory commissions.
      New York, Oxford Univ. Press, 1941. 780 p.
H154. Herring, E. Pendleton. Public administration and the public inter-
      est. New York, McGraw-Hill, 1936. 416 p.
H155. Hyneman, Charles S. Bureaucracy in a democracy. New York, Har-
      per, 1950. 586 p.
H156. Landis, James M. The administrative process. New Haven, Conn.,
      Yale Univ. Press, 1938. 160 p.
H157. Leiserson, Avery. Administrative regulation: a study in representa-
      tion of interests. Chicago, Univ. of Chicago Press, 1942. 292 p.
H158. Marx, Fritz M. The administrative state: an introduction to bu-
      reaucracy. Chicago, Univ. of Chicago Press, 1957. 202 p.
H159. Meyerson, Martin and Edward C. Banfield. Politics, planning, and
      the public interest. Glencoe, Ill., Free Press, 1955. 353. p.

Recent developments in public administration stem, on the one hand,
from efforts to relate the field to the more general theories of organization formulated in business administration, sociology and social psychology; on the other hand, the problems of teaching in what some students
consider an "applied field" have led to the study of "cases" involving
policy decisions and administrative implementation of these decisions.
The first line of inquiry was greatly stimulated by the work of Herbert
A. Simon, who not only presented the most radical critique of the
traditional approaches, but broke new ground in two major respects.
First, he sought to cope with the problem of means and ends, suggesting
their linkage in a single chain in which, depending on the level of analysis, ends could be treated as means, and means as ends. Second, he
sought to bring public administrative thinking in line with the psychology of human relations. In recent years, students in disciplines other
than political science have made significant contributions to a more
rigorous and behavioral approach in the field:

H160. Dahl, Robert A. and Charles E. Lindblom. Politics, economics, and welfare. New York, Harper, 1953. 557 p.
H161. Leighton, Alexander. The governing of men. Princeton, N.J. Princeton Univ. Press, 1946. 404 p.
H162. March, James G. and Herbert A. Simon. Organizations. New York, Wiley, 1958. 262 p.
H163. Selznick, Philip. TVA and the grass roots: a study in the sociology of formal organization. Berkeley, Univ. of California Press, 1949. 274 p.
H164. Simon, Herbert A. Administrative behavior: a study of decision-making processes in administrative organization. New York, Macmillan, 1947. 259 p.
H165. Stein, Harold, *ed.* Public administration and policy development: a case book. New York, Harcourt, Brace, 1952. 860 p.
H166. Thompson, Victor A. Modern organization. New York, Knopf, 1961. 197 p.

The literature on American state and local government is legion but very similar in approach to that on the national government. Constitutional questions and the role of the governor as administrator and policy-maker are treated like microscopic cases of the federal pattern. State administrative organization and reorganization, legislative reform, as well as the relations between the federal government and the states, and between the states and the municipalities, appear as concerns of academic study. In general, then, the treatment of state and local government has been and continues to be conventional. However, in recent years there has been a growing and lively literature on the politics of individual states or regions. Moreover, the urgent problems of urban growth and metropolitan balkanization, and the failure of proposals for reform, has occasioned some lively writing on urban problems. The following are some recent works in these areas:

H167. Adrian, Charles R. State and local governments: a study in the political process. New York, McGraw-Hill, 1960. 531 p.
H168. Anderson, William, *et al.* Government in the fifty states. New York, Holt, Rinehart and Winston, 1960. 509 p.
H169. Banfield, Edward C. *ed.*, Urban government: a reader in administration and politics. New York, Free Press of Glencoe, 1961. 593 p.
H170. Epstein, Leon D. Politics in Wisconsin. Madison, Univ. of Wisconsin Press, 1958. 218 p.
H171. Fenton, John H. Politics in the border states. New Orleans, La., Hauser, 1957. 230 p.
H172. Lee, Eugene C. The politics of nonpartisanship. Berkeley, Univ. of California Press, 1960. 232 p.
H173. Lockard, Duane. New England state politics. Princeton, N.J., Princeton Univ. Press, 1959. 348 p.
H174. Williams, Oliver P. and Charles Press, *eds.* Democracy in urban America: readings on government and politics. Chicago, Rand McNally, 1961. 561 p.
H175. Wood, Robert C. Suburbia: its people and their politics. Boston, Houghton Mifflin, 1959. 340 p.

INTERNATIONAL POLITICS AND ORGANIZATION

The relations between and among "states" have been a source of scholarly interest ever since the emergence of the modern nation-state in the sixteenth century. However, the problems involved were not unfamiliar to the city-states of the ancient world, the colonial colossus which was Rome, and even that complicated universal state of the Middle Ages known as "the Holy Roman Empire of the German Nation." But before the first world war "international relations" as a field of study was of interest more to historians concerned with diplomatic history, and to international lawyers concerned with the rights and duties of "sovereign nations," than to political scientists. These aspects of international relations, as well as others such as international trade of communication, remain today as areas of specialization sometimes taught in departments of political science, sometimes in departments of history and economics, or in the law schools. Within political science, the bulk of teaching and research is concerned with "international politics" and "international organization."

Of these two specializations, "international organization" came into its own after the first world war. Stimulated by the establishment of the League of Nations, the study of international relations, if not journalistic in its concern with "current affairs," was motivated by a hopeful moralism which, despite recurring disasters, was intent on suggesting and implementing what were conceived to be the goals of the "international community," largely through legal and institutional means. Writing and research focused on formal structures, techniques of peaceful adjustment of international conflicts, and the need to abide by legal commitments. While these efforts were singularly free of nationalistic bias and technically competent, they lacked methodological rigor and often confused untestable assertions concerning goals with statements of fact. The great body of literature on international relations from ancient times into the thirties was reviewed in the following:

H176. Russell, Frank M. Theories of international relations. New York, Appleton-Century, 1936. 651 p.

Gradually, however, and particularly after the rise of fascism in Italy and Germany, there was a realization that the preoccupation with institutional and legal gadgetry had neglected the realities of international life. While concern with international organization has continued and was, in fact, reinforced by the setting up of the United Nations and its affiliates, making it a matter of continued scholarly effort, the focus shifted to "international politics." International relations was increasingly seen as a "struggle for power" in a world of nationalism and imperialism in which the problems of "national interest" and "security" represented the hard facts of life. International relations was now seen as a function of foreign policies, and there was a growing tendency to examine the motivations of peoples and policy-makers, their capacity and willingness to carry through on commitments, and all those factors— economic, military, geographic, demographic and even psychological—which determine this capacity. In other words, the shift of emphasis was from description of formal international structures and prescriptions on how to cure the world's ills to closer observation of international processes and their determinants. There was a tendency to break down the separation of international from domestic policy, and a new awareness of the close relationship between national ideologies and national objectives. The following works illustrate these shifting foci:

H177. Beard, Charles A. The idea of national interest. New York, Macmillan, 1934. 583 p.
H178. Jessup, Philip C. A modern law of nations. New York, Macmillan, 1948. 236 p.
H179. Lasswell, Harold D. World politics and personal insecurity. New York, McGraw-Hill, 1945. 307 p.
H180 Micaud, Charles. The French Right and Nazi Germany. Durham, N.C., Duke Univ. Press, 1943. 255 p.
H181. Schuman, Frederick L. International politics. New York, McGraw-Hill, 1933. 922 p.
H182. Spykman, Nicholas. America's strategy in world politics. New York, Harcourt, Brace, 1942. 500 p.
H183. Wolfers, Arnold. Britain and France between two wars. New York, Harcourt, Brace, 1940. 467 p.

But the reaction to the reformist orientation in international relations literature in the inter-war years resulted in a new one-sidedness. The tendency to ignore values altogether made for political cynicism and soon gave rise to a debate over "realism versus idealism" as approaches in the study of international politics. If this debate had any useful consequences, it was the realization that concern with values, as long as values are clearly distinguished from facts, need not mean lack of precision in knowledge, but may contribute to the clarification of policy alternatives as they are circumscribed by the facts of the situation. Of the books which took either one line or the other, or which sought to mediate between the two positions, the following are relevant:

H184. Carr, Edward H. Conditions of peace. New York, Macmillan, 1942. 282 p.
H185. Fox, William T.R. The super-powers. New York, Harcourt, Brace, 1944. 184 p.
H186. Herz, John H. Political realism and political idealism. Chicago, Univ. of Chicago Press, 1951. 275 p.
H187. Kennan, George. American diplomacy, 1900-1950. Chicago, Univ. of Chicago Press, 1951. 146 p.
H188. Morgenthau, Hans. Politics among nations. New York, Knopf, 1948. 489 p.
H189. Weldon, Thomas D. States and morals. New York, Whittlesey House, 1947. 301 p.

Sheer exhaustion, probably more than anything else, terminated the debate between realists and idealists. Even while it raged, new approaches came to be formulated. It is difficult, if not impossible, to characterize the newer tendencies in terms of a single, neat formula. If a label is needed, the term "scientific" will do. What it means, in this connection, is that the newer tendencies seek to avoid ideological involvement. This does not mean that they are not "policy-oriented." Indeed, the state of the "international system" is seen as stemming from the foreign-policy behavior of the main actors in the international arena —the nation states. However, the task of analysis is to describe and explain not only these actors and their actions, but also the recurring patterns of behavior which arise out of the properties of the international system itself. The main difference between all the newer tendencies and the older journalistic, institutional and moral approaches lies in their devotion to conceptual clarity, theoretical explicitness, hypothetical formulation of problems and empirical relevance. As a result, there has been in recent years more theoretical development in the study of international politics than in other sub-fields of political science. These developments have been so rapid that empirical research has been unable to keep in step. Moreover, much of this writing has been reported in the learned journals, and the book literature is still relatively small. The following are noteworthy:

H190. Haas, Ernst and Allen S. Whiting. Dynamics of international relations. New York, McGraw-Hill, 1956. 557 p.
H191. Hoffman, Stanley H. *ed.* Contemporary theories in international relations. Englewood Cliffs, N.J., Prentice-Hall, 1960. 293 p.
H192. Rosenau, James N. *ed.* International politics and foreign policy: a reader in research and theory. New York, Free Press of Glencoe, 1961. 511 p.
H193. Wright, Quincy. The study of international relations. New York, Appleton-Century-Crofts, 1955. 642 p.

In general, the newer tendencies seem to fall into three categories: first, theoretical efforts to describe and explain international politics on the highest level of analytic generality; second, studies, both theoretical and empirical, of the foreign-policy process and its determinants; and third, attempts to relate both foreign policies and resulting patterns of international relations to the complex interaction of cultural and personality factors. Of the three categories, the last is probably the oldest. It relies on interviews and the quantitative analysis of mass communications as tools of inquiry. Closely related are studies of important elites and elite behavior in the international arena. The following books are suggestive of the approach:

H194. Almond, Gabriel A. The American people and foreign policy. New York, Harcourt, Brace, 1950. 269 p.
H195. Buchanan, William, and Hadley Cantril. How nations see each other. Urbana, Univ. of Illinois Press, 1953. 220 p.

H196. Deutsch, Karl W. and Lewis J. Edinger. Germany rejoins the powers: mass opinion, interest groups and elites in contemporary German foreign policy. Stanford, Calif., Stanford Univ. Press, 1959. 320 p.

H197. Klineberg, Otto. Tensions affecting international understanding. New York, Social Science Research Council, 1950. 227 p.

H198. Pool, Ithiel de Sola. The "Prestige" papers. Stanford, Calif., Stanford Univ. Press, 1952. 142 p.

H199. Stanton, Alfred H. and Stewart E. Perry, *eds.* Personality and political crisis. Glencoe, Ill., Free Press, 1951. 260 p.

The second group of studies is primarily concerned with the conditions and consequences of the foreign policy-making process and those circumstances which affect the course of policy, such as technological developments, environmental conditions, ideological commitments, and changes in the social structure. The distinction between the ends and means of policy, as well as between the internal and external policies of states, calls attention to such problems as the receptivity of policy makers to communications, or the role of the military in strategic planning in relation to foreign policy. Of the many studies of this genre, the following may serve as illustrations:

H200. Cohen, Bernard C. The political process and foreign policy: the making of the Japanese peace settlement. Princeton, N.J., Princeton Univ. Press, 1957. 293 p.

H201. Herz, John H. International politics in the atomic age. New York, Columbia Univ. Press, 1959. 360 p.

H202. Hilsman, Roger Jr. Strategic intelligence and national decisions. Glencoe, Ill., Free Press, 1956. 187 p.

H203. Huntington, Samuel P. The soldier and the state. Cambridge, Harvard Univ. Press, 1957. 534 p.

H204. Kissinger, Henry A. Nuclear weapons and foreign policy. New York, Harper, 1957. 463 p.

H205. Sprout, Harold and Margaret Sprout. Man-milieu relationship hypotheses in the context of international politics. Princeton, N.J., Center of International Studies, 1956. 101 p.

Finally, there has been increasing realization that, just as in other areas covered by the social sciences, progress in the study of international politics may require more general theories, or at least conceptual schemes of some generality, within which the great number and range of variables of international life can be systematically related and given meaning. A number of such theoretical schemes have been advanced, along with more specific models, among them system analysis schemes, game-theoretical, decision-making and communication models, field theory, and experiments in simulation. At this time, most of these efforts remain unrelated, though there is a growing feeling that integration of diverse theories is the next step. Most of the following works in this genre are concerned with the stability of the international system under varying conditions, with its integrative and disintegrative tendencies, and with efforts to measure "power" and other values of relevance:

H206. Deutsch, Karl. Nationalism and social communication. New York, Wiley, 1953. 292 p.
H207. Kaplan, Morton A. System and process in international politics. New York, Wiley, 1957. 283 p.
H208. Liska, George. International equilibrium. Cambridge, Harvard Univ. Press, 1957. 223 p.
H209. Schelling, Thomas C. The strategy of conflict. Cambridge, Harvard Univ. Press, 1960. 309 p.
H210. Snyder, Richard, *et al.* Decision-making as an approach to the study of international politics. Princeton, Foreign Policy Analysis Project, 1954. 120 p.

POLITICAL SCIENCE AS A BEHAVIORAL SCIENCE

The fact that political science necessarily deals with large collectivities and institutions—nations, governments, mass movements, organizations, and so on—long distracted attention from the role played by individuals or small groups in the drama of politics. Though the classical models of the polity—of a Hobbes, Locke, or Rousseau—had all been explicitly based on assumptions about the nature of man, academic political science, by taking human nature for granted, largely ignored it and, by ignoring it, practically denied it. Early protests by men like Graham Wallas or Walter Lippmann did not impress the profession. When, in 1930, Harold D. Lasswell published his first book on the psychopathology of political behavior and continued his effort to bring political observation back to its moorings in the nature of man through a steady stream of later works, his impact was only gradually absorbed. Only after the second world war was it possible to speak, as one writer did, of "the impact on political science of the revolution in the behavioral sciences." Moreover, Lasswell's main lead—the intensive study of political personality—has not been followed by more than a handful of political scientists, not because of lack of interest, but because of lack of the training and skills needed in personality research. However, a number of psychologists have developed the area of political personality research. The following works deal with the problem:

H211. Adorno, Theodor W., *et al.* The authoritarian personality. New York, Harper, 1950. 990 p.
H212. George, Alexander L. and Juliette L. Woodrow Wilson and Colonel House. New York, John Day, 1956. 362 p.
H213. Lasswell, Harold D. Psychopathology and politics. Chicago, Univ. of Chicago Press, 1930. 282 p.
H214. Lasswell, Harold D. Power and personality. New York, Norton, 1948. 262 p.
H215. Lippmann, Walter. A preface to politics. New York, Kennerley, 1913. 318 p.
H216. Smith, M. Brewster, *et al.* Opinions and personality. New York, Wiley, 1956. 294 p.

H217 Wallas, Graham. Human nature in politics. London, Constable, 1908. 302 p.

But it would be a mistake to think of the "behavioral revolution" as a psychological revolution alone. Though the new tendencies specified as the object of analysis the behavior of individual persons or social groups rather than events or institutions, political behavior is now seen as a function not only of personality, but also of societal and cultural factors. In other words, political science as a behavioral science seeks to explain the phenomena of politics, individual behavior as well as the behavior of aggregates and institutions, in a frame of reference common to all the social sciences—psychology as well as sociology and cultural anthropology. By the end of the second world war, much progress had been made in these disciplines towards more rigorous formulation of theory, hypotheses and research designs, as well as towards more precise and reliable methods and techniques of investigation. Moreover, though not untouched by the "brute facts" approach of an earlier descriptive empiricism, the other social sciences had largely escaped the unfortunate separation of theory and research which had accompanied the emergence of political science as an independent discipline. In short, there was much to be learned by political scientists from the other behavioral disciplines—about the individual as a psychological, sociological and cultural being; about interdisciplinary developments; about the interdependence of theory and research; and about the strategies and tactics of behavioral investigation.

The "behavioral movement" has not gone unchallenged, but, as the forties turned into the fifties, ever increasing numbers of political scientists either re-tooled old concepts, methods and techniques, or acquired new ones. Though a few behavior-oriented books by political scientists such as Almond or Truman appeared in the fifties, the bulk of behavioral research was published in the learned journals, and it was not possible until the second half of the decade to publish collections of theoretical and empirical work on political behavior. In addition to works cited earlier, the following books can serve as introductions to the behavioral approaches:

H218. Butler, David. The study of political behavior. London, Hutchinson, 1959. 128 p.
H219. Eulau, Heinz, *et al.* Political behavior: a reader in theory and research. Glencoe, Ill., Free Press, 1956. 421 p.
H220. Key, Valdimer O., Jr. Public opinion and American democracy. New York, Knopf, 1961. 566 p.
H221. Lane, Robert E. Political life: why people get involved in politics. Glencoe, Ill., Free Press, 1959. 374 p.
H222. Ulmer, S. Sidney, *ed.* Introductory readings in political behavior. Chicago, Rand McNally, 1961. 465 p.
H223. Verba, Sidney. Small groups and political behavior. Princeton, N.J., Princeton Univ. Press, 1961. 273 p.

H224. Wahlke, John C. and Heinz Eulau, *eds.* Legislative behavior: a
      reader in theory and research. Glencoe, Ill., Free Press, 1959.
      413 p.
H225. Young, Roland, *ed.* Approaches to the study of politics. Evanston,
      Ill., Northwestern Univ. Press, 1958. 382 p.

Not surprisingly, and quite in line with the interdisciplinary orientation of the behavioral sciences since 1945, there has been increasing interest in things political on the part of other social scientists. As a result,
political science has been enriched by a variety of contributions from
these "outsiders." In particular, social psychologists and sociologists
have produced important research on electoral behavior, bureaucracy
and public opinion. The following items are suggestive:

H226. Hyman, Herbert. Political socialization: a study in the psychology
      of political behavior. Glencoe, Ill., Free Press, 1959. 175 p.
H227. Janowitz, Morris. The professional soldier: a social and political
      portrait. Glencoe, Ill., Free Press, 1960. 464 p.
H228. Katz, Daniel, *et al.* Public opinion and propaganda. New York,
      Dryden, 1954. 779 p.
H229. Lipset, Seymour M., *et al.* Union democracy: the internal politics
      of the International Typographical Union. Glencoe, Ill., Free
      Press, 1956. 455 p.
H230. Stouffer, Samuel A. Communism, conformity, and civil liberties.
      Garden City, N.Y., Doubleday, 1955. 278 p.
H231. Vidich, Arthur J. and Joseph Bensman. Small town in mass society:
      class, power, and religion in a rural community. Princeton, N.J.,
      Princeton Univ. Press, 1958. 329 p.
H232. Wilensky, Harold L. Intellectuals in labor unions: organizational
      pressures on professional roles. Glencoe, Ill., Free Press, 1956.
      336 p.

POLITICAL SCIENCE AS A POLICY SCIENCE

From its very beginnings, political science, if it was not formalistic and
legalistic, has had a strong therapeutic orientation. In other words, it did
not limit itself to describing, and possibly explaining, things political and
governmental, but sought to change and improve the political order
(depending, of course, on a writer's point of view). In part, this was due
to the discipline's roots in ethics; in part it was due to the coincidence
that, in the United States, its emergence as an independent discipline
came in an era of political dissatisfaction, muckraking and reform. The
outstanding political scientists before the first world war were eminently
reform-minded. But much of the therapy was built on limited and often
irrelevant diagnoses. Moreover, the recommendations for governmental
reforms made by political scientists took the values and goals of democratic society for granted. It was a therapy of the means rather than of
the ends of the polity.

Once the zeal for reform had subsided, political science was "mere" description or, as in the case of public administration, reiterated familiar recipes—the city manager plan on the local level, executive integration on the federal level, and so on. Its bias was essentially conservative, its rationality was procedural, and its goals were increasingly remote from the world revolutionary changes which characterized the epoch between the two wars. There were exceptions, of course, but, on the whole, political science slumbered as either a therapeutic or diagnostic discipline.

Only during and after the second world war did political scientists awake to the new demands made on them by a changing world. At long last it came to be realized that the old values could not be simply taken for granted, that more thorough-going disgnoses were needed and more radical cures required. The clarification of values and goals rather than historical description or textual exegesis was recognized as a much needed task. At the same time, the impact of behavioral approaches tended to deepen and solidify analysis and diagnosis. The new symbiosis of concern with values and goals, on the one hand, and behavioral analysis, on the other hand, has come to be referred to as "policy science."

There are both theoretical and practical difficulties involved in the policy-science approach. The problem of the relationship between facts and values—how to move from scientific analysis to prescription—remains as unsolved as ever. There is the danger that the scientific enterprise may become the handmaiden of dominant ideologies. On the other hand, the policy-science approach assumes that the social sciences, no matter how much they may strive for objectivity, cannot be ethically neutral or value-free, and that it is the better part of wisdom to spell out value biases as a necessary or desirable prerequisite for appraising the validity of scientific analyses. In this regard, then, the policy-science approach sensitizes the political scientist to the problems in the real world of practical affairs where decisions must be made, even if not all is known that should be known. And it sensitizes the policy-maker to the need for valid and reliable analyses of the preferences and behavior patterns of those who are the objects of policy decisions. In any case, policy science is geared to the subtle, if evasive, interpenetration of facts and values, means and ends, behavior and policy. If it is not misused—and there are those who mistrust it because it can be misused and damage the scientific effort—the notion of policy science can be a potent antidote to a valuationally empty political science. Of books self-consciously concerned with the policy orientation, not all by political scientists, the following are suggestive:

H233. Barber, Bernard. Science and the social order. Glencoe, Ill., Free
    Press, 1952. 288 p.
H234. Leighton, Alexander H. Human relations in a changing world: ob-
    servations on the use of the social sciences. New York, Dutton,
    1949. 354 p.

H235. Lerner, Daniel, and Harold D. Lasswell, *eds.* The policy sciences: recent developments in scope and method. Stanford, Calif., Stanford Univ. Press, 1951. 344 p.

H236. Lerner, Daniel, *ed.* The human meaning of the social sciences. New York, Meridian Books, 1959. 317 p.

H237. Lynd, Robert S. Knowledge for what? The place of social science in American culture. Princeton, N.J., Princeton Univ. Press, 1939. 268 p.

H238. Price, Don K. Government and science. New York, New York Univ. Press, 1954. 203 p.

H239. Wolfle, Dael. Science and public policy. Lincoln, Univ. of Nebraska, 1959. 81 p.

INSTRUCTION IN POLITICAL SCIENCE

Just as political science as a theoretical and research enterprise is beset by difficulties, so is political science as a field of instruction, especially on the undergraduate level of teaching. These difficulties stem, in part, from the diverse interests which college students bring into political science classes. For many, political science is part of a liberal education, and only for a few a major part. Most of the students are not interested in political science as science, but in the ideas and practices which shape the world of politics, national and international. They are understandably impatient with subtle problems of theory and method. They wish merely to learn something about the world in which they are living, its past and its future. They like to have the materials of political science pre-digested; the textbook and the exciting classroom orator serve their needs.

Other undergraduates share this orientation, but they come to political science with more specific occupational objectives. For some it is a preparatory course on the road to law school or school of business. For others it is preparation for civil service or foreign service. Again, their objectives constitute important considerations in the development of undergraduate programs. In any case, only relatively few undergraduates are interested in political science as an academic discipline; they are the few who become high school teachers and the even fewer who become professional political scientists.

As a result, the problem of curriculum content has long occupied the profession. Committee recommendations, journal articles and much small-talk at professional meetings are evidence of this concern. The interested reader should turn, first of all, to the report of the Committee for the Advancement of Teaching of the American Political Science Association, listed below. Some of the chapter titles of this report, though ten years old, express the range of problems involved in the teaching of political science:

Goals of Citizenship Education
Teaching International Relations

Education for Public Service
The Field of Concentration
Integration and Cooperation in the Social Sciences
The Beginning Course
Better Teamwork between High Schools and Colleges
Graduate Instruction: A Threshold to Teaching
Modernizing Teaching Methods

In recent years, the new orientations in political science, notably the behavioral approaches and interest in public policy, have had considerable effects on classroom teaching. Increasingly, instructors of the behavioral persuasion have not hesitated to expose their students to field research, especially interviewing of politicians. Greater emphasis, too, has been placed on practical experience in the world of politics and administration; and this tendency has been facilitated by foundation grants for internships with political party organizations, legislative bodies and administrative bureaus. This has brought the student into closer contact with policy-making than he had previously had through reading the *New York Times*. Within the classroom, the abundance of cheap paperbacks has accentuated a tendency to go to the sources, especially in political philosophy and general introductory courses, rather than rely on texts. The development of "case" materials, especially in administration, but also in politics, has made classroom work more vital and meaningful. The production of "readers," some of them not shying away from including difficult material at the frontiers of research, has raised the level of undergraduate sophistication and brought the undergraduate closer to the research concerns of the profession. In general, the scholarly ferment of the post-World War II years has gradually found its way into the classroom. The following works are concerned with these matters:

H240. American Political Science Association. *Committee for the Advancement of Teaching.* Goals for political science. New York, Sloane, 1951. 319 p.
H241. Hyneman, Charles S. The study of politics: the present state of political science. Urbana, Univ. of Illinois Press, 1959. 232 p.
H242. Robson, William A. The university teaching of social sciences: political science. Paris, UNESCO, 1954. 249 p.

Heinz Eulau

H243. Aufricht, Hans. Guide to League of Nations publications; a bibliographical survey of the work of the League, 1920-47. New York,

Columbia Univ. Press, 1951. 682 p.

The most comprehensive bibliographical guide to the documents of the League and its autonomous affiliates. Selective rather than exhaustive in coverage it includes the most significant documents (including those not put on public sale). Arrangement is by large subject with a lengthy introduction prefacing each section. Each entry is annotated in one of three forms: (1) brief commentaries indicating the importance of the document, (2) reproduction of tables of contents and (3) footnotes which contain references to related documents, articles, books or other pertinent information. Includes appendices (241 p.) of basic League documents. Analytical subject index.

To supplement Aufricht there are three other sources: Carroll, Marie J. *Key to League of Nations documents placed on public sale, 1920-29,* and four supplements, 1930-36. (Boston, World Peace Foundation, 1930-36); Breycha-Vauthier, Arthur C. von *Sources of information; a handbook on the publications of the League of Nations.* (London, Allen and Unwin, 1939. 118 p.); League of Nations. *Catalogue of publications 1920-1935* and five supplements 1936-1945. (Geneva, 1935-45).

H244. Bemis, Samuel F. and Grace G. Griffin. Guide to the diplomatic history of the United States, 1775-1921. Washington, Govt. Print. Off., 1935. 979 p.

An important guide (5,811 numbered items) to the printed and manuscript sources for the study of the diplomatic history of the United States. Part I contains the bibliographical chapters, topically and chronologically arranged. Includes documents, histories, letters, maps, and manuscript materials. Part II contains analyses of printed state papers and further manuscript sources. Author index and index to

collections of personal papers. Supplemented by *Foreign affairs bibliography* (H277).

H245. Boyd, Anne M. United States government publications. 3d ed. revised by Rae E. Rips. New York, Wilson, 1949. 627 p.

An extensive and valuable guide to United States government publications originally intended as a library school text but more fully expanded for reference use. Chps 1-7 deal with general points; the nature of government publications, the printing and distribution of United States documents; descriptions of catalogs and indexes, Congressional publications, laws and statutes, and the Federal Courts. The remaining chapters describe the important and typical publications of each federal department and agency. Does not attempt exhaustive coverage. Complemented by: *Subject guide to United States government publications* by Herbert S. Hirshberg and Carl H. Melinat (Chicago, American Library Assoc., 1947. 228 p.) ". . . a selection of those books and pamphlets, most of them published during the past 20 years, believed to be most generally useful in libraries" (Pref.) For guides to more popular materials see: A *popular guide to government publications* by W. Philip Leidy (2d ed. New York, Columbia Univ. Press, 1963. 291 p.) a selection of some 2,500 items published from 1940-50 arranged by broad subject with detailed subject index; and *Guide to popular U.S. government publications* by John L. Androit (Arlington, Va., Documents Index, 1960. 125 p.) Part one is arranged by Departments and Agencies and covers popular periodicals and serials. Part two lists 2,000 titles of popular publications in print arranged by subject.

H246. Brown, Everett S. Manual of government publications; United States and foreign. New York, Appleton-Century-Crofts, 1950. 121 p.

A brief but excellent guide to document publication and bibliography emphasizing American, British, League of Nations and the U.N. with brief summaries for other major countries. One chapter devoted to state and local materials. Very good source for discussion of British and Commonwealth publications. No index.

H247. Burchfield, Laverne. Student's guide to materials in political science. New York, Holt, 1935. 426 p.
Intended as a guide to the more important source materials, finding devices, bibliographies and general reference works. Although out of date no similar work has taken its place and it is still useful for older materials. Covers the whole field of political science and is international in scope. Many titles annotated. Index.

248. Egbert, Donald D. and Stow Persons. Socialism and American life. Princeton, N.J., Princeton Univ. Press, 1952. 2 v. (Princeton studies in American civilization no. 4)
V. 1 is one of the most authoritative studies of the impact of socialism on American life to appear to date. Each essay prepared by a specialist. V. 2 is a comprehensive bibliographical guide, in essay form, to the literature of American socialism and its European antecedents. Six main sections deal with: the historical background of American socialism; its types; doctrinal bases; economic, political and psychological aspects; and its effect upon American art and literature. Each section includes "General readings" and a series of short essays on specific topics. Subject, author, title and editor index.

249. Schmeckebier, Laurence F. and Roy B. Eastin. Government publications and their use. Rev. ed. Washington, Brookings Institution, 1961. 476 p.

"The purpose of this volume is to describe the basic guides to government publications, to indicate the uses and limitations of available indexes, catalogs and bibliographies, to explain the systems of numbering and methods of titling, to call attention to certain outstanding compilations or series of publications, and to indicate how the publications may be obtained." (Foreword). Text arranged in 19 chapters (e.g. Congressional publications, state laws, foreign affairs, periodicals). Strong in field of public administration. Weak on publications of the executive branch.

H250. Tompkins, Dorothy C. Materials for the study of federal government. Chicago, Public Administration Service, 1948. 338 p. (Public Administration Service. Publication, 46)
Provides a guide to materials for the study of selected, domestic aspects of the federal government. This is achieved mainly by a discussion of various agencies, their legislative history and publications dealing with the constitution, laws and codes; publications of the legislative, judicial and executive branches, and the President; the federal budget, government statistics, the New Deal, and World War II. Emphasis is upon official publications of the period 1940-1947. Some chapters include a list of selected references which include unofficial sources of information. Author and subject index.

REVIEWS OF THE LITERATURE

H251. American political science review. v. 1+ 1906+ Washington, American Political Science Association. quarterly.
Significant American source for bibliography on international political science. Since 1950 most issues include a bibliographical article in

a particular subject or area. 50-75 books are critically reviewed (500-2,400 words) by specialists each year. "Book notes and bibliography" provides an extensive classified list of current writing, American and some foreign, including books, selected articles and documents. The book entries (200-250 a year) are given short (50-700 word) annotations. 2-3 issues a year include a "Bibliography of selected articles and documents on methodology and research in the social sciences." "Doctoral dissertations in political science in American universities" is a regular feature. See (H403).

H252. Foreign affairs. v. 1+ 1922+ New York, Council on Foreign Relations. quarterly.

An important source for American study of international affairs, this journal carries in each issue a useful bibliographical section. Part I lists new books (500-600 a year) in various languages, classified by subject and area and annotated with brief evaluative comments. Part II, "Source material," is a selective unannotated list of official documents (250-450 a year) and a list of pamphlets (150-250 a year). The book note sections have been cumulated in *Foreign affairs bibliography* (H277).

H253. International affairs. v. 1+ 1927+ London, Royal Institute of International Affairs. quarterly.

The British counterpart to the American *Foreign affairs*. Its extensive book review section is an important source for the more notable contributions to Western politico-economic literature. The 500-600 books selected for comment each year are grouped by subject and area, and described in short (200-600 words) evaluative notes. Annual index of book reviews.

H254. International review of administrative science. v. 1+ 1928+ Brussels, International Institute of

Administrative Sciences. quarterly.

Technical journal which surveys the developments in public administration throughout the world. The literature of public administration and allied fields is surveyed in 300-400 critical reviews (80-500 words) and 3-5 survey articles a year. International in scope.

H255. Neue Politische Literatur; berichte über das internationale Schrifttum zur Politik. v. 1+ 1956+ Villingsen/Schwarzwald, Ring-Verlag. monthly.

Issued 1952-1955 as *Politische Literatur*. A journal of reviews of international political science literature. 300-500 significant titles a year are critically reviewed (750-2,000 words) by specialists in individual reviews or review articles. "Zeitschriften-Bibliographie," a classified listing of periodical articles, lists ca. 1,000 items a year. Annual author and subject indexes.

H256. Revue française de science politique. v. 1+ 1951+ Paris, Fondation Nationale des Sciences Politiques. quarterly.

About one quarter of each issue is devoted to surveying current literature. "Notes bibliographiques" contains signed reviews (500-3,000 words) of 75-100 significant works a year. "Informations bibliographiques" contains short book notes or abstracts for ca. 900 titles annually Both sections are international in scope and treat all aspects of political science and many cognate areas. In addition each issue carries 1 to 3 review articles dealing with some area of the literature.

See also: H366.

ABSTRACTS AND DIGESTS

H257. Background on world politics; an inter-disciplinary digest. v. 1+ 1957+ Waco, Texas. quarterly.

Digests about 100 articles dealing with the problems of world politics, but which "are scattered through publications not primarily devoted to world politics." The digests are arranged under 9 headings: (1) The U.S. (2) Western Europe (3) U.S.-S.R. & East Europe (4) Middle East & Africa (5) East and South Asia (6) Latin America (7) Scientific & technical potential (8) Processes of international relations (9) Notes on theory. About 250 journals (primarily English language) in many fields (law, psychology, sociology, political science, history, economics, etc.) are "read" for articles to be abstracted for *Bankground*.

H258. Current thought on peace and war. v. 1+ 1960+ Durham, N.C. semi-annual.
A digest of literature and research in progress on the problems of world order and conflict. Its object is to distill from the work of social and natural scientists the thinking directly concerned with the prevention of war. Each issue includes 400-800 items classified under 6 major headings. Within each class are listed (1) published material, (2) current research and (3) supplementary sources. Items listed in (1) are fully abstracted. Research projects are merely listed or carry a brief description. Books, articles and some government document are included. Plans to include foreign material are being considered. The projected annual supplement will be a directory of American and foreign groups involved in research in international relations. Author index.

H259. Digest of the public record of Communism in the United States. New York, Fund for the Republic, 1955. 753 p.
A collection (most comprehensive available to date) of digests or extracts of United States federal and state statutes, administrative regulations, legislation and legislative committee proceedings and court deci-

sions relating directly or indirectly to Communism in the U.S. Part III is a comprehensive annotated bibliography of public documents on the subject published by Congress, by the executive departments of the federal government and the state governments. Good general index. See also its companion volume *Bibliography on the Communist problem in the United States* (H273).

H260. Index digest of state constitutions, ed. by Richard A. Edwards. 2d ed. New York, Legislative Drafting Research Fund of Columbia Univ., 1959. 1132 p.
This comparative analysis and statement by subject of all provisions of state constitutions makes it possible to review and compare pertinent provisions of the fundamental law of the 50 states. The entries are listed under some 200 major titles or subjects arranged alphabetically. These major subjects are subdivided in the text. Each state's provision is given separately under the major heading (or subdivision) except in those cases where identical or nearly identical language is used. Nearly all entries are paraphrases rather than verbatim excerpts. A suplement published in 1962 brings the information to Dec. 31, 1960. Current information appears in the *Book of the states* (H357).

H261. International law reports, 1919-22+ London, Longmans, 1929-1938; Butterworth, 1938+ annual.
From 1919/22-1949 issued as *Annual digest and reports of public international law* with slight variations in title. These important volumes give accurate digests of international law cases under 11 general headings (e.g., states as international persons, jurisdiction, the individual in international law, treaties, war and neutrality, etc.) For each case the facts and the decision are summarized followed by an extensive quotation from the court's opinion. Each volume has an index.

table of cases reported (alphabetical by name and also by country), and a table of cases cited. Time lag is currently 4 years (1956 vol. published 1950).

H262. International political science abstracts. v. 1+ 1951+ Oxford, Blackwell. quarterly.

Abstracts articles from a world list of political science journals as well as selected from journals in related areas. The classified arrangement of the 1,400-1,500 entries per year is a simplified form of that used in the *International bibliography of political science* (H267) with six major headings. The abstracts are short and are in English and French. Current practice abstracts English articles in English, those of other languages in French. Quarterly subject index and list of periodicals. Cumulated annual subject index and author index.

H263. Moore, John B. Digest of international law. Wash., Govt. Print. Off., 1906. 8 v.

Digests and indexes international law (up to 1906) as embodied in diplomatic discussions, treaties and other international agreements, international awards, the decisions of municipal courts, writings of jurists and especially in documents, published and unpublished, issued by U.S. presidents and secretaries of state, opinions of attorneys general, and the decisions of courts, federal and state. v. 8 is a general index. Supplemented for the period 1906-1940 by *Digest of international law* by Green H. Hackworth (Wash., Govt. Print. Off., 1940-44. 8 v.).

H264. U.S. *Library of Congress. Legislative Reference Service.* Digest of public general bills with index, 74th Congress+ 1936+ Wash., Govt. Print. Off., 1936+

Principal section consists of brief digests of bills and resolutions introduced in Congress, with somewhat fuller information for reported measures. Arranged numerically by House

and Senate, with a subject index. Second section presents the status of bills acted upon plus a summary of the law if the bill was passed. The 7-8 issues per session are cumulative.

BIBLIOGRAPHIES—CURRENT

H265. Androit, Jeanne K. and John L. Androit. Checklist and index of congressional hearings. Arlington, Va., Documents Index, 1958+

A current, up-to-date index of committee hearings. Each Congress is to be covered by 4 six-month volumes and a final cumulative volume. Arrangement is by committee and sub-committee with title, subject, bill number and witness indexes. Includes published and unpublished hearings. Bibliographic information for printed hearings includes pagination and descriptive information, the Supt. of Documents, Dewey, Library of Congress classification numbers and the L.C. card number

H266. Gt. Brit. *Stationery Office.* Government publications; catalogue. London, 1923+ annual.

Issued daily, monthly and cumulated annually and quinquennially (since 1936). Includes all priced items sold or published by the Stationery Office. Includes parliamentary and non-parliamentary material. There are no Stationery Office lists of unpriced publications. Preceded by the *Quarterly list* 1897-1921. Three sections (1) Parliamentary publications (2) classified list by department or agency and (3) periodicals. Index.

H267. International bibliography of political science. v. 1+ 8, 1952-1959 Paris, UNESCO, 1954-1961; v. 9+ 1960+ Chicago, Aldine, 1962+ annual.

A part of the Unesco Documentation in the Social Sciences series, this extensive, but selective, annual classified bibliography includes 4,000-5,000 items per year. Political science is broadly interpreted and material in other fields of value to political scientists is included. Attempts to list all published books and periodical articles, national and international documents of "scientific value." Beginning in volume 4 references is made to articles which are analyzed in *International political science abstracts* (H262). Occasional references to book reviews of important or controversial titles. Author and subject indexes.

H268. Literatur-Verzeichnis der politischen Wissenschaften, 1952+ Hrsg. von der Hochschule für Politische Wissenschaften München. München, Isar Verlag. annual.

An important selective survey of German literature in the field of political science, covering the new publications of the West German, Austrian and Swiss press. "Politischen Wissenschaft" has broader meaning than political science. It is more closely akin to "policy sciences" or those aspects of the social sciences which are of immediate significance to public policy making. Thus the classified listing has main headings of society and state, state and organization, business and society, international relations, history and geography, natural sciences and politics. Separate lists of reference works and periodicals. Author and publisher indexes.

H269. United Nations. *Library, N.Y. Documents Index Unit*. United Nations documents index, January, 1950+ Lake Success, N.Y. 1950+ monthly.

List all documents and publications of the U.N. and the specialized agencies, except restricted materials and internal papers. Arrangement is alphabetical by the abbreviated name of the agencies (FAO, Fund, ICAO, etc.) The monthly indexes

are cumulated annually. For documents prior to 1950 see the as yet incomplete United Nations, Secretariat. Dept. of Public Information. Library Services. *Checklist of United Nations documents* (Lake Success, N.Y., 1949+) which covers the period 1946-1949. See also: *Documents of international organizations,* v. 1-3, Nov. 1947-Sept. 1950. (Boston, World Peace Foundation, 1945-1950); a selective quarterly bibliography; and *Index to United Nations documents* (London, Royal Institute of International Affairs, 1947-49. 4 v.); probably the best single index to early U.N. documents 1940-1949).

H270. U.S. *Dept. of State. Library*. International politics; a selective monthly bibliography. v. 1+ 1956+ Washington. monthly.

A select list of articles (300-400 a month) from periodicals which are analyzed regularly by the library. Includes some monographs. Arrangement of entries is geographical. Lists items of immediate practical concern to the understanding of the affairs of other countries in the conduct of U.S. Foreign policy. Primarily English language material. No indexes or annual cumulation. Useful as an up-to-date listing of articles, especially those from periodicals which are not indexed elsewhere.

H271. U.S. *Library of Congress. Processing Dept*. Monthly checklist of state publications. v. 1+ 1910+ Washington, Govt. Print. Off., monthly.

A current bibliography recording those state documents received by the Library of Congress (10,000-13,000 items a year). Includes all publications of the states, territories and insular possessions arranged alphabetically by state. Publications of associations of state officials and regional organizations are included in a special section. Full bibliographic information given including content notes for composite reports.

General annual index refers to these notes as well as main titles.

H272. U.S. *Supt. of Documents.* United States government publications: Monthly catalog. v. 1+ Jan. 1895+ Washington, Govt. Print. Off. monthly.

A monthly subject listing with cumulative annual index of publications issued by all branches of the government, including both congressional and departmental documents. Arrangement of entries is alphabetically by issuing agency. Has included processed material since 1936. No serial set numbers given. These can be obtained from *Numerical lists and schedules of volumes of the reports and documents of the 73rd Congress,* 1933/34+ (Wash., Govt. Print. Off., 1934+) which is the index to the serial set.

BIBLIOGRAPHIES—RETROSPECTIVE

H273. Bibliography on the Communist problem in the United States. New York, Fund for the Republic, 1955. 474 p.

An annotated bibliography "devoted to literature relating to Communism in the U.S. since the birth, in 1919, of the first American parties adopting the Communist label" (Intro.) The main part of the work is an author index of ca. 4,500 books, periodical articles and pamphlets. This is followed by the same material arranged in a topical outline (without annotations). Includes 5 appendices which include select bibliographies on native American radicalism; Communist ideology; theory organization and objectives; and a list of Communist and left-wing periodicals. 1952 was closing date. All public documents are listed in a companion volume *Digest of the public record of Communism in the United States* (H259).

H274. Carnell, Francis. The poli-

tics of the new states; a select annotated bibliography with special reference to the Commonwealth. London, Institute of Commonwealth Studies, 1961. 171 p.

A bibliographic guide to literature on the politics of the new and emerging states, especially the Afro-Asian areas. 1,599 items (books, articles and documents) are classified under 21 major headings with cross references and author and place indexes. Some brief annotations. General political surveys considered "basic reading" are starred. A companion volume to Arthur Hazlewood's *Economics of "Under-developed" areas.* 2d enl. ed. (London, Institute of Commonwealth Studies, 1959. 156 p.).

H275. Deutsch, Karl W. An Interdisciplinary bibliography on nationalism, 1935-1953. Cambridge, Mass., Technology Press of M.I.T., 1956. 165 p.

A selective, classified bibliography which surveys the field of nationalism since Pinson's study (H283). The first of fourteen sections lists major surveys and bibliographies; the second, special works in nationalism. The next eleven sections list relevant material by special fields (political science, cultural anthropology, history, economics, geography, biology, philosophy, etc) The fourteenth and longest section lists material by geographic area, subdivided by the topics of section 1-13. Includes monographs and periodical articles in major European languages. Some brief annotations. Author index.

H276. Dolléans, Edouard and Michel Crozier, *eds.* Mouvements ouvrier et socialiste; chronologie et bibliographie. Paris, Editions Ouvriéres, 1950+ (In progress)

The most recent general bibliography of socialist publications and works about socialism which promises to become the standard guide. The volumes published to date cover: (1) England, France, Germany and the U.S., 1750-1918; (2) Italy to 1922; (3) Spain, 1750-1936; (4) Russia, 1725-1917; and (5) Latin America, 1492-1936. A volume covering Scandinavia is in preparation. Content arrangement varies, but each volume contains chronologies for the period covered and a bibliography of documents, books, articles, pamphlets and a listing of periodicals and reviews published during the years covered. Name indexes and some subject indexes.

H277. Foreign affairs bibliography; a selected and annotated list of books on international affairs, 1919-32; 1932-42; 1942-52. New York, published for the Council on Foreign Relations by Harper, 1933-1955. 3 v.

A comprehensive, but selective, listing of monographs in English and in major western European languages dealing with all aspects of international affairs. The volumes are primarily based upon the bibliographical notes appearing in the quarterly *Foreign affairs* (H252). Three major headings (general international relations, world since 1914, and world by regions) are subdivided by subject and/or by area. Subject matter covers history, politics, diplomacy, economics, international law, world organization, social problems, racial problems, etc. No government documents included. Annotations are very brief. Author index.

H278. Government Affairs Foundation, N.Y. Metropolitan communities; a bibliography with special emphasis upon government and politics. Chicago, Public Administration Service, 1957. 392 p. (Public Administration Service. Publication no. 128)

A comprehensive bibliography on urban development listing over 5,000 separately published monographs issued prior to Sept., 1955. Two main parts, subdivided by area and subject: Part I, Government and

politics, lists major problems of concern to governments in metropolitan areas; Part II, Socio-economic background, lists references to social, economic, demographic, etc. works necessary to the full understanding of the material in part I. A supplement published in 1960 adds 2,524 items appearing from 1955 to 1957. The supplement index is a general index for both volumes. For foreign materials see D. Halász's *Metropolis; a selected bibliography on administration and other problems of metropolitan areas throughout the world.* (Hague, International Union of Local Authorities, 1961. 45 p.) which covers Europe, Australia, India, Japan, Latin America and the Philippines.

H279. Graves, William B. Intergovernmental relations in the United States; a selected bibliography on interlevel and interjurisdictional relations. Prepared for the Commission on Intergovernmental Relations. Washington, 1955. 207 p.

A selective bibliography of books, reports, monographs and articles arranged according to major topic subdivided by subject and form. Emphasis is upon Federal relationships but some information is included upon interstate relations and state-local relationships. Some brief annotations. No index but a detailed table of contents.

H280. Hunt, R.N. Carew. Books on Communism. London, Ampersand, 1959. 333 p.

A very useful, select, classified bibliography giving brief descriptions of some 1,500 books on Communism in the English language (including translations into English) published between 1945 and 1957, as well as revisions of earlier works. Three major works. Three major divisions: (1) Studies of Communism in general and in the USSR; (2) Communism in other countries; and (3) Official documents and publications

(U.S. and Great Britain). Index of authors and titles.

H281. International Committee for Social Sciences Documentation. Etudes des bibliographies courantes des publications officielles nationales; guide sommaire et inventaire. A study of current bibliographies of national official publications; short guide and inventory. Paris, UNESCO, 1957. 260 p. (UNESCO bibliographical handbooks, 7)

The results of a preliminary survey of government publications in more than 90 countries are presented in two major sections: "Summary guide" classifies and specifies the problems involved in establishing a current bibliography for national official publications; "Inventory by countries" is a summary which briefly describes the types of publications issued by each country, the principal lists, catalogs and bibliographies of official documents, and notes the sources of descriptions of official publications and also the agencies for printing and publishing.

H282. Maryland. University. *Bureau of Governmental Research.* Political Science; a selected bibliography of books in print with annotations. College Park, Md., 1961. 97 p.

A classified and briefly annotated bibliography of ca. 250 significant books in the major fields of political science which are currently available. A good representative list generally restricted to American imprints. No index.

H283. Pinson, Koppel S. A bibliographical introduction to nationalism. New York, Columbia Univ. Press, 1935. 71 p.

A selective, annotated bibliography of 431 items published in English, French or German, and arranged under two main topics: (1) Theoretical and analytical studies; and (2) Historical and regional studies. Limited to works which deal specifically with the problems of nationalism. Includes monographs and articles. Index of names. Continued by Deutsch (H275).

H284. Speeckaert, Georges P. International institutions and international organizations; a select bibliography. Brussels, Union of International Associations, 1956. 116 p.

Includes 783 items dealing with the operating methods of international organizations, their legal status and the relationships between inter-governmental and non-governmental organizations. Omits international relations, politics and economy. Especially strong in the history of international bodies and their relationships. No annotations. Author index.

H285. Stammhammer, Josef. Bibliographie des Socialismus und Communismus. Jena, Gustav Fischer, 1893-1909. 3 v.

A standard bibliography for earlier material on Socialism and Communism through 1908. Entries arranged alphabetically by author with subject index.

H286. U.S. *Library of Congress. General Reference and Bibliography Division.* A guide to bibliographic tools for research in foreign affairs, compiled by Helen F. Conover. 2d ed. with supplement. Washington, 1958. 145 p., 15 p.

A carefully selected and well annotated bibliography with 351 main entries and many more titles referred to in the annotations. Includes bibliographies, bibliographical serials, manuals, indexes, encyclopedias, dictionaries, directories, yearbooks, journals, etc. Three main sections: (1) General reference sources; (2) Sources for international studies (various categories of reference tools; (3) Specialized sources (for regional studies, including the U.N.) Index of authors and titles and a subject index. Annotations are exceptionally full and informative.

H287. United Nations. *Office of Legal Affairs*. List of treaty collections. New York, 1956. 174 p.

Designed as a new and simplified successor to Denys P. Myers' *Manual of collections of treaties and of collections relating to treaties* (Cambridge, Harvard Univ. Press, 1922. 685 p.), this publication supplements but does not supersede the older work. The *List* is generally restricted to compilations published since 1780, but important earlier collections are included. Excludes official gazettes or reviews of international law which contain texts of treaties. Three major sections: (1) General collections (86 items), also includes indexes, chronologies, bibliographies and handbooks; (2) Collections by subject matter (59 items); (3) Collections by states (553 items) includes collections in special topics and treaties with separate states. Annotations give nature of contents, types of indexes and explanatory information. Index.

See also: A97, D238, D244, D245.

Documents

H288. Ford, Percy and Grace Ford. A breviate of Parliamentary Papers, 1900-1916. Oxford, Blackwell, 1957. 470 p.

Ford, Percy and Grace Ford. A breviate of Parliamentary Papers, 1917-1939. Oxford, Blackwell, 1951. 571 p.

Ford, Percy and Grace Ford. A breviate of Parliamentary Papers, 1940-1954. Oxford, Blackwell, 1961. 1515 p.

Although all papers dealing with foreign and diplomatic questions, statistical returns, and internal colonial and Dominion reports have been excluded, these "breviates" of the Parliamentary Papers and departmental materials are an indispensible key to the reports of the Royal Commissions and other committees of inquiry in the fields of constitutional, economic, financial

and social policy and of legal administration. For each report covered there is a statement of the terms of reference, argument, conclusions and recommendations made. Reports are classified under 16 major subject headings with topical subdivision. Includes: subject classification, subject list of documents, alphabetical key word subject index, and an index of authors. Together with *Hansard's catalogue and breviate of Parliamentary Papers, 1696-1834* (H291) and *Select list of British Parliamentary Papers, 1833-1899* (H289) the three breviates provide an important key to the Parliamentary Papers from 1696 to 1954.

H289. Ford, Percy and Grace Ford. A select list of British Parliamentary Papers, 1833-1899. Oxford, Blackwell, 1953. 165 p.

A classified list of the most significant reports and other material issued by commissions and similar bodies of investigation on economic, social, constitutional questions and matters of law and administration. Cites and classifies 4,500 papers. Excludes papers in foreign and colonial affairs. Companion volume to *Hansard's catalogue and breviate* (H291).

H290. Gt. Brit. *Parliament. House of Commons*. General index to the bills, reports, estimates, accounts and papers, printed by order of the House of Commons and to the Papers presented by command. 1801+ London, Stationery Office, 1853+.

The basic index of the Parliamentary papers. This material is indexed annually in sessional indexes which are consolidated into Decennial Indexes and these in turn into General Indexes covering a period of 50 years. Three of the latter have been issued to date (1801-1852; 1852-1899; 1900-1949). Excludes the papers of the House of Lords unless they are duplicated in the Commons papers and the publications of bureaus and departments. Arrangement is alphabetical by large subject. Gives full locational information for each paper but has few analytical entries.

H291. Gt. Brit. *Parliament. House of Commons.* Hansard's catalogue and breviate of Parliamentary Papers, 1696-1834. Reprinted in facsimile with an introduction by P. Ford and G. Ford. Oxford, Blackwell, 1953. 220 p.

A classified listing of the most significant Parliamentary Papers under 26 major subject headings. Each entry locates the paper and gives an analytical abstract of its contents. Scope includes those papers on "public" subjects. Routine materials, foreign affairs, etc., are largely excluded. General index. This edition contains "A select list of House of Lords' Papers not in this Breviate."

H292. Hasse, Adelaide R. Index to United States documents relating to foreign affairs, 1828-1861. Washington, Carnegie Institution, 1914-21. 3 v.

An index to published records, documents, papers, correspondence, legislation and judicial decisions on international and diplomatic questions. The index is arranged by names of individuals and subjects. Fills the gap between Class 1 of the *American state papers* (H382) and *Foreign relations of the United States* (H380).

H293. Thomen, Harold O. Checklist of hearings before congressional committees through the Sixty-seventh Congress. Washington, Library of Congress, Legislative Reference Service, 1941-58. 9 v.

A checklist of over 5,000 printed committee hearings of which record has been found in the printed government catalogs, the National Union catalog and in various governmental and research libraries. Arrangement is first by committee and then by congress. As far as possible a location or source for each title is given. No index.

H294. United Nations. *Dept. of Public Information.* Ten years of United Nations publications, 1945-1955; a complete catalogue. New York, 1955. 271 p.

Excellent guide to the printed documents of the U.N. Kept up to date by annual supplements. Includes information about League of Nations publications, documents preparatory to the formation of the U.N., information on mass media services, and visual materials. Does not include mimeographed items or any information on the publication of the specialized agencies. Subject and title index.

H295. U.S. *Congress. House. Library.* Index of congressional committee hearings in the Library of the United States House of Representatives prior to January 1, 1951. Washington, Govt. Print. Off., 1954. 485 p.

An index to the holdings of Congressional committee hearings in the House Library. Arranged in three major sections (1) alphabetically by subject (2) by committee (House, Senate, Joint and Special) and (3) by bill number. Gives dates of each hearing, Congress and session, House or Senate Report, number or other locations of published hearings. Supplement brings index through January 3, 1955.

H296. U.S. *Congress. Senate. Library.* Index of congressional committee hearings (not confidential in character) prior to January 3, 1935 in the United States Senate Library. Washington, Govt. Print. Office, 1935. 1056 p.

An index to the holdings of congressional committee hearings in the Senate Library. The hearings are classified by subject, by committee and by bill number. Gives full information on hearing (date, congress, session, etc.) and location of publication, e.g., House Report, Senate Report, etc. Supplemented by *Cumulative index of congressional committee hearings (not confidential in character) from Jan. 3, 1935 through . . . Jan. 3, 1959 in the United States Senate Library* (Washington, Govt. Print. Off., 1959. 823 p.).

H297. U.S. *Supt. of Documents.* Catalog of the public documents of Congress and of all departments of the government of the United States for the period March 4, 1893-December 3, 1940. Washington, Govt. Print. Off., 1896-1945. 25 v.

A complete and permanent dictionary catalog of government publications, both congressional and departmental. Entries listed under author (corporate and personal), subject and, when necessary, title. Full bibliographical details are given. Includes serial set numbers for Congressional publications. Processed material included from v. 20. Beginning with v. 23 (1935-37) each volume covers two years. Two basic works, despite errors and omissions, for earlier period are: A *descriptive catalogue of the government publications of the United States, September 5, 1774-March 4, 1881* by Benjamin P. Poore (Wash., Govt. Print. Off., 1392 p.) and *Comprehensive index to the publications of the United States government, 1881-1893* by John G. Ames (Washington, Govt. Print. Office, 1905. 2 v.).

H298. U.S. *Supt. of Documents.* Checklist of United States public documents 1789-1909 . . . ed. rev. and enl. Washington, Govt. Print. Off., 1911. 1707 p.

Essentially a shelf list of all the publications in the Supt. of Documents Library. Documents are listed (by department) according to the Supt. of Documents classification system. Full bibliographic details are given including information on various editions of a given publication and its serial set number. Lists the Congressional serial set volumes by serial number and gives a general idea of their contents. Also lists the

Proceedings and miscellaneous publications of Congress, papers of the revolutionary period and the 1st 14 Congresses, bills and resolutions of the Senate and House, journals of the Continental Congress, and Congressional hearings. Also called 1909 checklist. A basic and fundamental tool.

H299. Wilcox, Jerome K. Bibliography of new guides and aids to public documents use, 1953-56. New York, Special Libraries Association, 1957. 16 p.

The latest in a series of compilations originally appearing in *Special libraries* (v. 40, 1949; v. 45, 1954). The 70 entries range over federal, state and municipal documents in the U.S. as well as guides to the documents of foreign governments and international organizations.

Public Administration

H300. Greer, Sarah. Bibliography of public administration; part I—general literature. New York, Institute of public administration, 1933. 90 p.

Originally published in 1926. Only Part I of this revised and enlarged 1933 edition was published. Entries are classified under 13 major headings with detailed subdivision. Covers all aspects of public administration—national, state and local—for the U.S. and foreign countries. Some brief annotations. No index, but a detailed table of contents.

H301. Heady, Ferrell and Sybil L. Stokes. Comparative public administration; a selective bibliography. 2d ed. Ann Arbor, Univ. of Michigan Press, 1960. 98 p.

H302. Seckler-Hudson, Catheryn. Bibliography on public administration; annotated. 4th ed. Washington, American Univ. Press, 1953. 131 p.

A highly selective bibliography of 1,100 English language books primarily in the field of national and international administration. Material is arranged topically by chapter with an index of authors and sponsoring bodies. Each title is annotated. No periodical articles included. Includes a list of public administration periodicals.

H303. United Nations. *Technical Assistance Program.* International bibliography of public administration. New York, 1957. 101 p.

A selective bibiliography of 1,435 separately published monographs intended as a "working list" for public administration experts. The material is international in scope (12 languages) and is arranged by author under 26 main headings which include: general administration and management; technical assistance for economic development; police administration; public finance; local government, etc. No annotations. No index.

State Government

H304. Council of State Governments. State government: an annotated bibliography. Chicago, 1959. 46 p.

A listing of sources of comparative information on all phases of state government and administration, which are published on a regular continuing basis or revised or supplemented at regular or irregular intervals. Part I lists general works. In Part II the entries are grouped under 104 headings (e.g., banking, crime control, elections, housing, liquor, welfare, etc.). Includes books, periodical articles, pamphlets and reporting services primarily published in the U.S. Descriptive annotations including frequency of publication. No index, but adequate cross references.

H305. Graves, William B. *et al.* American state government and administration; a state-by-state bibliography of significant general and special works. Chicago, Council of State Governments, 1949. 79 p.

A selective bibliography which lists (1) general works of some scholarly significance relating to the governments of particular states and (2) a state-by-state listing of separately published monographs and reports relating to constitutions; the executive, legislative and judicial branches of government; the administrative organization, and the general structure of local government. Very few periodical articles included. No index.

H306. Tompkins, Dorothy C. State government and administration; a bibliography. Berkeley, Bureau of Public Administration, Univ. of California, 1954. 269 p. (Public Administration Service. Publication no. 123)

A bibliography of primary sources of information, mostly post-1930, which are essential to the study of state government and administration. The material, half of which is devoted to the legislative process, is arranged under 18 large topics (e.g., state constitutions, state documents, lobbying, laws and codes, etc.) with subdivision by subject and/or state. Brief annotations only to clarify titles, or indicate content. Author and subject index. Useful for locating laws, regulations and reports.

DICTIONARIES

H307. Abraham, Louis A. and Stephen C. Hawtrey. A parliamentary dictionary. London, Butterworth, 1956. 224 p.

An alphabetical guide to expressions in common usage in the Houses of Parliament with definitions and explanations of procedures. Designed to be a practical guide not a definitive source. For the latter see T.E. May, *A treatise on the law, privileges, proceedings and usage of Parliament* (15th ed. London, Butterworth, 1950. 1057 p.)

H308. Black, Henry C. Black's law dictionary, definitions of terms and phrases of American and English jurisprudence, ancient and modern. 4th ed. St. Paul, Minn., West, 1951. 1882 p.

Intended to be of value to the practitioner, judge and law student who require quick and convenient access to the meanings of legal terms as well as the legal meanings of standard English words. Although emphasizing English and American terms it includes a very complete collection of definitions of terms used in old English, European and feudal law. Includes also a considerable vocabulary from the civil, canon, French, Spanish, Scotch, and Mexican law and other foreign systems. Abbreviations and maxims are scattered through the alphabet. Definitions are short and concise, with references to legal decisions and publications having authoritative comments upon the term being defined.

H309. Bouvier, John. Bouvier's law dictionary; Baldwin's student edition, 1934, ed. by William E. Baldwin. Cleveland, Banks-Baldwin, 1934. 1331 p.

H310. Dictionnaire de la terminologie du droit international. Publié sous le patronage de l'Union Académique Internationale. Paris, Sirey, 1960. 755 p.

A dictionary of the terminology of international law giving the technical definitions of terms, their classification, and their different meanings. Terms were selected from treaties, diplomatic correspondence, proceeding of diplomatic congresses, decisions of international tribunals and reports and decisions of international organizations. Each definition is illustrated by one or more accurate quotations from the sources. Includes tables listing the terms in German, English, Italian, and Spanish, giving the French equivalent.

H311. Haensch, Günther. Inter-nationale Terminologie: Diplomatie, Verträge, Internationale Organizationen, Konferezen . . . Stuttgart, Müller, 1954. 180 p.

A German, French, English, Spanish glossary of 1,121 terms arranged in 8 subject groups (e.g., international law, diplomacy, international treaties, war, etc.). Treats the most important vocabulary from international politics and diplomacy. Following the systematic section are alphabetical indexes in each of the four languages.

H312. Hunt, R.N. Carew. A guide to Communist jargon. New York, Macmillan, 1957. 169 p.

Contains 50 articles (2-3 pages) defining the principal terms of the Communist vocabulary, political or semi-political, which are used to explain or defend their position. Terms like aggression, coexistence, dogmatism, practicism, tailism, etc. are concisely explained with examples from the most authoritative Soviet sources.

H313. Landshut, Siegfried and Wolfgang Gaebler. Politisches Wörterbuch. Tübingen, J.C.B. Mohr, 1958. 265 p.

H314. Radin, Max. Law dictionary, ed. by Lawrence G. Greene. New York, Oceana, 1955. 408 p.

H315. Smith, Edward C. and Arnold J. Zurcher. New dictionary of American politics. New York, Barnes and Noble, 1949. 437 p.

This useful dictionary of over 3,500 entries aims "to incorporate all leading ideas and institutions in each of the special areas of American government and politics." Also included are slogans, political slang, nicknames, etc. The entries are short and concise.

H316. White, Wilbur L. White's political dictionary. New York, World Publishing Co., 1947. 378 p.

A popular dictionary, international in scope, which covers the whole

range of political terminology with
emphasis on terms in active use.
Entries are brief. Some variant meanings indicated. Cross references.

ENCYCLOPEDIAS AND
ENCYCLOPEDIC SETS

H318. Handwörterbuch der Staatswissenschaften, hrsg. von Ludwig
Elster, Adolf Weber, Fr. Wieser.
4. gänz. ungearb. Aufl. Jena, Fischer,
1923-29. 8 v. and suppl.

Although somewhat dated this
comprehensive German work remains the leading encyclopedia of
political science. Supplemented to
some extent, but not superseded by,
the *Handwörterbuch der Sozialwissenschaften* (A141). The lengthy
signed articles are prepared by specialists and include excellent bibliographies. Biographical articles give a
full list of works by the writer as
well as material about him. V. 8 includes a subject index. The supplementary volume carries its own
index.

H319. Renouvin, Pierre. Histoire
des relations internationales. Paris,
Hachette, 1954-1958. 8 v.

An excellent synthesis of the development of international relations
from 1815 to 1945, explained in
terms of geographic, economic, demographic and social conditions; of
collective psychology; and the individual acts of leaders. Bibliographies at the end of each chapter.

H320. Staatslexikon; Recht, Wirtschaft, Gesellschaft, hrsg. von Görres-
Gesellschaft. 6., völlig neu bearb. und
erweiterte Aufl. Freiburg, Herder,
1957+ v. 1+ (In progress)

A standard German encyclopedia
written from the catholic point of
view. This new edition to be in 8
volumes will comprise some 4,000
signed articles dealing with basic
problems and special items in the

fields of government, law, economics
and sociology.

H321. Strupp, Karl. Wörterbuch
des Völkerrechts. 2. Aufl. hrsg. von
Hans-Jürgen Schlochauer. Berlin, de
Gruyter, 1960+ (In progress)

An encyclopedia, rather than dictionary, of international law unique
in its approach and comprehensive
in its coverage. To be completed in
3 volumes comprising some 1,200 articles. Each topic followed by a bibliography which is selective for works
prior to 1945 and as complete as
possible for the more recent period.
Historical matters included where
required for full understanding of
the development of international law
and diplomacy. All "causes célèbres"
of international law are treated at
length. Cases appear under names
by which they are generally known,
with extensive cross references. The
multitude of postwar European organizations and treaties is fully
treated. Equal detail is given to
problems and subjects of concern to
the British Commonwealth, America, Africa and Asia.

DIRECTORIES AND BIOGRAPHICAL
INFORMATION

H322. Almanac of current world
leaders. v. 1+ 1958+ Los Angeles,
Calif. quarterly.

An up-to-date listing of major
government officials (cabinet rank
and above) in 124 countries and 15
organizations and alliances. For each
country is listed the seat of the government, its membership in international organizations, and the date of
the next election. For each leader information given includes: full name,
office held and political party affiliation. A system of symbols is used to
indicate qualifications of the position
held, i.e., re-election, unconfirmed,
etc.

H323. American Political Science

Association. Biographical directory. 4th ed. Washington, 1961. 355 p.

A biographical directory of members of the Association giving for each information on: basic biographical data, education, honors, academic career, other career work, publications (limited to 4 items) and fields of interest. Index by field of interest. Appendices include factual material about the Association, its constitution, officers, affiliations and a directory of regional political science associations.

H324. Congressional staff directory. 1959+ Indianapolis, New Bobbs-Merrill. annual.

Designed as a companion to the official *Congressional directory* (H338), this handbook lists the staffs of Senators, Representatives, committees and sub-committees of the House and Senate and brief biographies of key staff personnel. Other useful information includes a listing of committee and sub-committee assignments of congressmen, key federal officials and their liason staffs, and a listing of 4,500 major cities giving their congressional districts and representatives. Index of personal names.

H325. Council on Foreign Relations. American agencies interested in international affairs. Compiled by Ruth Savord and Donald Wasson. 4th ed. New York, 1955. 289 p.

Directory of research and action groups in the U.S. working, directly or indirectly, in the various fields relating to international affairs. Partial or complete information on 363 groups include purpose, date of foundation, organization, finance, directorship, activities, membership, publications. Four separate listings; (1) alphabetical list, (2) chambers of commerce; (3) foreign information bureaus; (4) dormant and discontinued organizations. Subject index to activities and personnel index. New edition in preparation. See also "Directory of voluntary organi-

zations in world affairs." *Intercom.* v. 3, May 1961: 12-61. which gives directory information and brief program descriptions of over 350 American organizations wholly concerned with world affairs and those engaged in major programs of world affairs education or activity.

H326. Dictionnaire des parlementaires français; notices biographiques sur les ministres, sénateurs et députés français de 1889 à 1940, ed. by Jean Jolly. Paris, Presses Universitaires de France, 1960+ (In progress)

Extensive biographical dictionary supplementing *Dictionnaire des parlementaires français* by Adolphe Robert and Gaston Cougny (Paris, Bourloton, 1891. 5 v.) which covered the period 1789 to 1889. The biographical section in v. 1 is proceeded by: (1) a chronological list of ministries of France from 1871-1940 followed by the composition of each cabinet; (2) the presidents of the Senate, 1876-1940; (3) an alphabetical list of senators from 1876-1945; (4) the presidents of the National Assembly and the Chamber of Deputies 1871-1940; (5) an alphabetical list of the members of the National Assembly 1871-76. The biographical entries are quite long emphasizing the political activity of the biographer.

H327. Directory of organizations and individuals professionally engaged in governmental research and related activities, 1935+ New York, Governmental Research Assoc., 1935+ annual.

Arranged in 5 sections. Part I, Local and state agencies includes independently organized research agencies, taxpayers' associations, citizens' and voters' leagues, college and university governmental research divisions, legislative reference agencies, and tax supported agencies all arranged by state and city. Part II, National agencies concerned directly or indirectly with governmental research, listed alphabetically. Part III, Individual Members of GRA. Part IV, index of organizations, and Part V, an index of individuals. For each organization the entry includes founding date, address, telephone, name of the executive officer and the professional research staff.

H328. Dod's Parliamentary review for 1832+ London, Business Directories, 1832+ annual.

Brief biographies of members of the House of Lords and the House of Commons. Lists the constituencies and the votes cast at the most recent elections (including by-elections). Also includes a list of major government offices and officials.

H329. Gt. Brit. *Stationery Office*. British imperial calendar and civil service list, 1809+ London. annual.

British equivalent to the *Official register of the U.S.* (H336) listing administrative officials in the royal households, Cabinet offices and public departments, ministries commissions etc., of England and Wales, Scotland and Northern Ireland. Gives name, official position, degrees, honors and salary. Alphabetical index of names.

H330. Greene, Katrine R.C. Institutions and individuals; an annotated list of directories useful in international administration. Chicago, Public Administration Clearing House, 1953. 59 p.

A list of 215 directories with brief information on scope and contents. Approximately half of the titles published since 1949.

H331. Kosch, Wilhelm. Biographisches Staatshandbuch; Lexikon der Politik, Presse und Publizistik. München, Francke, 1959+ (In progress)

Contains brief sketches of the careers of notable personalities in the political life of the German speaking countries during the last 150 years. Also included are entries for individual newspapers. Excellent source for minor figures. Full bio-

graphical references are cited for each individual.

H332. Public administration organizations; a directory of unofficial organizations in the field of public administration in the United States and Canada. 7th ed. Chicago, Public Administration Clearing House, 1954. 150 p.

"Designed to guide public officials and others concerned with governmental problems to sources of useful information and to identify organizations which impinge upon or affect public administration." (Intro). The 513 organizations fall into 3 main categories: (1) professional and technical societies, (2) organizations of or for public officials and administrators and (3) citizen organizations. For each entry information is given on: name, date of founding and officials, membership, finances, secretariat, activities, affiliations and publications. Classified and geographical indexes. No plans for a new edition.

H333. Repertorium der diplomatischen Vertreter aller Länder seit dem Westfälischen Frieden (1648). Repertory of the diplomatic representatives of all countries since the Peace of Westphalia (1648). Zurich, Fretz & Wasmuth, 1936-1950. v. 1-2 (In progress)

Under each major country the representatives are listed by the country to which they were sent. For each man is given: his name, his capacity, the dates of his mission, and the source of this information. V. 1 covers 1648-1715 and V. 2, c1716-1763. V. 3 (in prep.) will cover 1763-1815 and include the U.S. Each volume has a personal name and country index.

H334. Union of International Associations. Les congres internationaux de 1681 à 1899, Brussels, 1960. 76 p. (It's Publication no. 164)

A chronological listing of 1414 international congresses giving for each the name of the meeting, the city where it was held and the inclusive dates. Preface and analytical index are in French and English. A second volume covering 1900 to 1919 is in preparation.

H335. Union of International Associations. The 1978 organizations founded since the Congress of Vienna; chronological list. Brussels, 1957. 204 p. (It's Documents no. 7)

A chronological listing of all international governmental and nongovernmental organizations established between 1693 and 1956. For each entry the day, month, year and place of founding are given plus indication of those which have ceased to function. Brief notes give information on changes of name, successor organizations, etc. French and English subject indexes.

H336. U.S. *Civil Service Commission*. Official register of the United States, 1933+ Washington, Govt. Print. Off. annual.

Prior to 1861 published by the State Dept.; 1861-1905, Interior Dept.; 1907-1932, Census Dept. Official list of government employees, formerly known as the *Blue book*. Contains name, official title, compensation, legal residence and place of employment for persons occupying administrative and supervisory positions in the legislative, executive and judicial branches of the federal government including the District of Columbia. Classified by branch of government with an index of names.

H337. U.S. *Congress*. Biographical directory of the American Congress, 1774-1961 . . . Rev. ed. Washington, Govt. Print. Off., 1961. 1863 p.

Presents 10,400 short biographies of Senators and Representatives elected or appointed to the Continental Congress and to the Congress of the U.S. from 1789-1961. Also includes: a chronological list of ex-

ecutive officers; a listing of delegates to the Continental Congress, 1774-1789; a listing of Congresses through the 86th with dates, officers and members; and a listing of members of the 87th Congress who are serving their first term.

H338. U.S. *Congress*. Official congressional directory for the use of the United States Congress, 1809+ Washington, Govt. Print. Off., 1809+

To 1864 published irregularly by private firms. Currently issued for each session of Congress. Includes: biographical sketches of members of Congress arranged by state; state delegations; terms of service; committees and commissions; sessions of Congress; governors of states; votes cast for congressmen; biographical sketches of cabinet members and a list of officials in each department; biographies of members of the Supreme Court and a list of courts; officials of independent agencies; international organization delegations; foreign and U.S. diplomatic officers; press galleries; maps of congressional districts; and an index of individuals. Detailed table of contents.

H339. U.S. *Dept. of State*. Biographic register, 1869+ Washington, Govt. Print. Off. annual.

Title varies. To 1942 called *Register of the Department of State*. Contents vary. To 1942 it usually contained sections on organization, historical lists, information about the foreign service and a biographical section. Since 1943 only the biographical section and chronological historical lists are included. Part I contains biographies of the principal officers of the State Dept., the U.S. Mission to the U.N., the International Cooperation Administration, U.S. Information Agency, and the Foreign Agricultural Service. Part II contains biographical sketches of the administrative and professional personnel of these agencies. Part III includes chronological tables of presidents and secretaries of state and a historical list of the diplomatic agents of the U.S., arranged by country.

H340. U.S. *Dept. of State.* Diplomatic list, 1893+ Washington, Govt. Print. Off. bi-monthly.

Lists members of the diplomatic corps and staff members of foreign embassies and legations in Washington. Within each country names are arranged according to personal rank.

H341. U.S. *Dept. of State.* Foreign consular offices in the United States, 1932+ Washington, Govt. Print. Off. annual.

Frequency varies. Contains a complete and official listing of foreign consular offices in the U.S., together with their jurisdictions and personnel. Arranged alphabetically by country.

H342. U.S. *Dept. of State.* Foreign service list, 1929+ Washington, Govt. Print. Off. quarterly.

Published under various titles at varying intervals from 1837. Lists the personnel of each diplomatic post maintained by the U.S. overseas (Embassies, Legations, Missions, Consulates, etc.). Includes personnel of the Foreign Service, U.S. Information Agency, International Cooperation Administration, U.S. Dept. of Agriculture, and the Army, Navy and Air Force. Supplemental lists of personnel assigned to the Dept., on detail as inspectors, on special detail, assigned to the U.N. Mission, assigned to the International Cooperation Administration and the U.S. Information Agency. Index of persons and geographic index.

H343. U.S. *Dept. of State. Division of Biographic Information.* Directory of Soviet officials. Washington, 1960+ v. 1+ (It's Biographic Directory no. 272)

Lists the leading officials and administrators of the Communist party, of the Soviet government and

of "independent" socio-cultural institutions identified by their official title and arranged according to their position in the U.S.S.R. Thus it outlines the structure of the organization and identifies the encumbent officials. Volume I contains 6,900 entries and 5,200 names and covers the U.S.S.R. and R.S.F.S.R. Volume II (to be published) does the same for the 15 union republics. Similar works for Poland and Communist China (*Directory of Polish officials.* B.D. no. 274, 1960; *Directory of party and government officials of Communist China.* B.D. no. 271, 1960). All are periodically revised.

ATLASES AND PICTORIAL WORKS

H344. Boyd, Andrew K.H. An atlas of world affairs. 4th rev. ed. New York, Praeger, 1962. 160 p.

A handy volume which presents 70 simplified maps on the most important aspects of contemporary affairs. A short, concise text accompanies each map giving background information and summarizing the situation. Subject index. See also Andrew Boyd and Patrick Van Rensburg, *An atlas of African affairs* (New York, Praeger, 1962. 133 p.); Norman J.G. Pounds and Robert C. Kingsbury, *An atlas of Middle Eastern Affairs* (New York, Praeger, 1962. 120 p.) and Norman J.G. Pounds, *An atlas of European affairs* (New York, Praeger, 1963. 125 p.).

HANDBOOKS, MANUALS, COMPENDIA

H345. Cyclopedia of American government, ed. by A.C. McLaughlin and A.B. Hart. New York, Appleton, 1914. 3 v.

A dated but still useful encyclopedia dealing with all aspects of American government. The signed articles are arranged alphabetically by small subjects and each carries a brief bibliography. Good for biography. Name and subject index.

H346. Everyman's United Nations; the structure, functions and work of the organization and its related agencies during the years 1945-1958. 6th ed. New York, U.N. Dept. of Public Information, 1959. 607 p.

Official handbook explaining fully and clearly the varied aspects of the U.N. Part I is devoted to the description and purposes of the body; Part II, the major part of the book, surveys the work of the U.N. and Part III gives information about the intergovernmental agencies related to the U.N. Each new edition (first published in 1948) brings the total picture, including changes in responsibility and organization, up to date. General index.

H347. The Municipal Yearbook, 1934+ Chicago, International City Managers' Association. annual.

Chief purpose "is to provide municipal officials with information on the current problems of cities throughout the country, with facts and statistics on individual city activities, and with analyses of trends by population groups." (Foreword) Some of the sections remain the same from year to year with only the statistics brought up to date, while other sections are entirely new. Five major categories: governmental units; municipal personnel; municipal finance; municipal activities; and directories of officials. Selected bibliography appended to each section. Index includes references to selected material in previous issues not repeated in the current edition.

H348. Pfeffer, Karl H. Handwörterbuch der Politik. Darmstadt, Leske Verlag, 1956. 275 p.

An excellent topical encyclopedia of political science providing information and thought on political geography, race, nationality, population, government, international affairs and economic and spiritual problems.

H349. Political handbook of the world; parliaments, parties and press. Jan. 1, 1927+ New York, Published by Harper for Council on Foreign Relations. annual.

Lists for each country: the names of the chief government officials; the composition of the parliament; members of the cabinet; the leaders and the programs of the political parties; notes on the form of government and recent political events; and, the names of the editors and the political affiliation of the chief newspapers and periodicals.

H350. Theimer, Walter. An encyclopedia of modern world politics. New York, Rinehart, 1950. 696 p.

An expansion of his *Penguin political dictionary* (London, Penguin Books, 1939. 256 p.) this edition was prepared especially for American readers and gives wider coverage to American politics. An alphabetically arranged survey of political terms, problems, trends, and catchwords of the contemporary world. Brief explanations. Includes short political sketches of almost all countries with some biographical notes on outstanding political figures. Problems to which special attention is given are those of 1949. A later work of the same nature is Florence Elliott and Michael Summerskill's *A dictionary of politics*. (Baltimore, Penguin Books, 1961. 372 p.). Primarily an encyclopedia for world affairs with special attention given to recent developments.

H351. U.S. *Dept. of State. Office of Intelligence Research and Analysis.* World strength of the Communist party organizations. Washington, 1957+ (It's Intelligence Report 4485 R-10+) annual.

Presents data on the strength of the Communist movement in 120 countries and territories giving for each information on: Communist voting strength (number of votes, per cent of the total vote, number of seats won); total parliamentary representation (non-Communist list, Center, Conservative, other); estimated or claimed party membership; and a brief statement on the overall status, strengths and weaknesses of the Communist organization.

H352. U.S. *National Archives. Federal Register Division*. United States government organization manual, 1935+ Washington, Govt. Print. Off. annual.

Combines the features of a handbook and an organization directory. An official up-to-date source of information on the organization and functions of the principal governmental agencies in the three major branches. In addition it includes: selected boards, committees and commissions having function set by law; quasi-official agencies; major multi- and bi-lateral international organizations; a description of agencies transferred or abolished since 1933; and an annotated list, by agency, of major government publications. For the complex period of World War I and World War II see the Division's publications *Handbook of federal war agencies and their records, 1917-1921* (Washington, 1943. 666 p.) and *Federal records of World War II.* (Washington, 1950-51, 2 v.)

H353. Wilding, Norman W. and Philip Laundy. An encyclopaedia of Parliament. Completely rev. ed. with a supplement including additional material to 31 March 1961. London, Cassel, 1961. 797 p.

Concentrates on the parliaments of the United Kingdom, but includes information on all representative bodies of the Empire and the Commonwealth. The material is arranged in alphabetical order with parliamentary history broken up into short sections under the name of the reigning monarch. Statesmen and politicians are treated separately only if they were directly concerned with parliamentary growth, powers or tradition. Appendices provide a chronological list of parliaments, ministers, secretaries, clerks, etc. and an excellent bibliography.

YEARBOOKS

H354. L'Année politique. 1st series, 1874-1905; 2nd series, 1944-45+ Paris, Presses Universitaires de France, 1876-1906, 1945+ annual.

Chronological review of major political, diplomatic, economic and social events in France and French overseas territories. An invaluable guide for French politics and foreign affairs. Abundant documentary material and French electoral statistics. Good index.

H355. Annuaire européen. European yearbook. v. 1+ 1948+ Published under the auspices of the Council of Europe. The Hague, Nijhoff, 1955+ annual.

The purpose of this valuable yearbook is to give basic documents and information about European organizations accompanied by articles explaining in narrative form their functions and activities. V. 1 covers 1948-1953. The 7 to 10 articles are printed in English or French with summaries in the other language. The documentary section (two thirds of each volume) contains a chronology or summary of events for each of the principal organizations and the basic texts of agreements which they have concluded or their basic constitutional documents (in French and English). Officers are also listed. A bibliography section lists books, pamphlets and articles on European integration. Index of names. V. 5 contains a cumulative index for v. 1-4, a feature to be repeated every 3 years. With the publication of v. 6 in late 1959 the time lag has been reduced from two years to one.

H356. Annuaire français de droit international. v. 1+ 1955+ Paris, Centre National de la Recherche Scientifique, 1956+ annual.

In addition to articles on current legal and international relations questions (and occasional texts of recent documents) this excellent annual contains a chronology, critical book reviews and a systematic bibliography of works on international law published during the year.

H357. Book of the states. v. 1+ 1935+ Chicago, Council of State Governments. biennial.

A comprehensive manual providing information on the structures, working methods, financing and functional activities of the state governments. Issued at the beginning of even numbered years; two supplements appear in odd numbered years. Includes reports on the work of the Council of State Governments and other organizations dealing with inter-governmental problems. Suppl. no. 1 (January) lists elective administrative officials, supreme court justices and members of legislatures. Suppl. no. 2 (July) lists elective officials and includes a comprehensive listing of administrative officials, elective or appointed, classified by functions.

H358. British yearbook of international law. Issued under the auspices of the Royal Institute of International Affairs. v. 1+ 1920-21+ London, Oxford Univ. Press, 1920+ annual.

H359. Die internationale Politik, 1955+ München, Oldenbourg, 1958+ annual.

A survey of international relations with substantial appendices of current literature, notes and documents. A scholarly, reliable source of information prepared by specialists.

H360. Jahrbuch für Internationales Recht. Band 1+ 1950+ Göttingen, Vandenhoeck. annual.

H361. Survey of international affairs, 1920-23+ London, Oxford Univ. Press, 1925+ annual.

A prominent series reviewing events of international importance throughout the world. Subject coverage varies with world events, but in general parts of each volume are devoted to individual areas of the world. Contents consist of detailed factual statements, documented with footnote references. As the volumes are published 3 or more years after the events analyzed, the importance of the series is largely historical. The first volumes covered 4 years; subsequent volumes appeared annually v. 1, 1938. Suspended during the war years, v. 2-3, 1938 were published in 1951 and 1953. Six volumes with distinctive titles were published to cover the years 1939-1946. The postwar series began with a volume for 1947-48, then 1949-50 and is again on an annual basis with the volumes for 1951+.

H362. United Nations. Yearbook 1946/47+ New York, United Nations, Dept. of Public Information. annual.

Record of activities of the United Nations, its 13 specialized agencies and GATT during the year covered. The various subjects (political and security questions, economic and social questions, trusteeship, legal questions, administrative questions) are treated in detailed essays to which are appended documentary references and in many cases the text of (and vote on) the relevant resolutions. Information of a more general nature is provided for the specialized agencies. There are tables and lists of informational data (especially offices and officers) and a comprehensive index of persons, countries and subjects.

H363. United Nations. Yearbook on human rights . . . New York, 1946+ annual.

Records the major developments

concerning human rights in each member state during the year. Consists of extracts from national laws, constitutions, and judicial decisions in sovereign states and non-self-governing territories; the human rights clauses of international agreements and treaties and a brief statement of the work of the U.N. in the field of human rights during the year. For a detailed, documented summary of U.N. activity see "Human Rights" chapter of the U.N. *Yearbook* (H362). Subject index.

H364. The United States in world affairs. 1931+ New York, published for the Council on Foreign Relations by Harper, 1932+ annual.

Concise review of world conditions, tensions and problems as they relate to American foreign affairs. The text is documented with footnote references (usually to standard readily available sources) and is concluded with a "Chronology of World Events" for the year and a subject index. References are made to a companion volume *Documents on American foreign relations*, published annually since 1939, which contains the texts of the chief U.S. and foreign documents relating to American foreign affairs.

H365. Yearbook of the international socialist labour movement, 1956-57+ London, Lincoln-Prager International Yearbook, 1956+ annual.

Gives data and information on the parties which are affiliated with the Socialist International or the Asian Socialist Conference. Section I deals with international socialist organizations giving for each a brief historical sketch, affiliated groups, the Socialist press, voting strength and membership, as well as reproducing important documents and policy declarations. Section II treats each party, country by country, in the same manner. Volume I (1956) is largely retrospective. Volume II (1960) brings factual material up

to date, but omits the historical sketches. Index of names.

H366. Yearbook of world affairs. v. 1+ 1947+ Published under the auspices of the London Institute of World Affairs. London, Stevens. annual.

Contains 10-12 articles on topics of more or less contemporary interests and a series of bibliographic essays "Reports on world affairs." Each of the latter, nearly one half of each volume, deal with one phase of world affairs; economic aspects, geographical aspects, institutional aspects, legal aspects, psychological aspects, strategic aspects and a report of contemporary literature. A special table of books reviewed provides an alphabetical author index of all titles cited in the essays. (Between 250-600 titles per year). General index to articles and bibliographical essays.

STATISTICAL SOURCES

H367. America votes; a handbook of contemporary American election statistics. v. 1+ 1956+ New York, published for Governmental Affairs Institute by Macmillan. biennial.

A very useful compilation continuing work for earlier years done by W.D. Burnham (H368) and E.E. Robinson (H370). It goes beyond these earlier works as it includes the vote for governor, senators and congressmen. Presidential summaries precede state by state information. For each state is given: (1) a "profile" sheet indicating population, numbers of electoral votes and political subdivisions, incumbent governors, senators and representatives, composition of the state legislature (by party) and the postwar vote for governor (beginning with v. 2 postwar vote for Senator is also included); (2) a map of the state indicating counties, congressional districts and incorporated places over

25,000; (3) geographic breakdown (by county and/or assembly district) for President, Governor and Senator; (4) table of Congressional vote; and finally "notes" on the tables, including information on latest primaries.

H368. Burnham, W. Dean. Presidential ballots, 1836-1892. Baltimore, Johns Hopkins Press, 1955. 956 p.

An extension backward of the series done by Robinson (H370). This work is structured the same way as that of Robinson using the county as the smallest unit. Appendix indicates sources, (official, manuscript and secondary) notes, special cases (e.g., Soldier vote, 1864) and county organization for each state.

H369. Review of elections, 1954-1958+ London, Institute of Electoral Research, 1960+ annual.

First volume of an annual series, each number to give the election results since the previous issue. This volume contains statistics on the votes cast and seats won in the main elections in 29 non-Communist countries, plus an indication of the electoral system used in each country, the political situation, and the contesting parties. Brief notes included on elections in 10 Communist countries and a list of 27 other countries in which elections were held. A useful compilation, but information is sketchy.

H370. Robinson, Edgar E. The Presidential vote, 1896-1932. Stanford, Calif., Stanford Univ. Press, 1934. 403 p.
————. They voted for Roosevelt; the presidential vote, 1932-1944. Stanford, Calif., Stanford Univ. Press, 207 p.

In these two works will be found the first complete compilation of election returns by counties for the 13 presidential elections of the period 1896-1944. The major table, "Party vote for electors by state and by county" gives information on the

Democratic Party, the Republican Party and "Other" parties. The composition of the "other vote" is spelled out in the appendix. Other tables and maps indicate different dimensions of the election results. Excellent introductory essay. The work by Burnham (H368) carries the same tables back to 1836.

H371. U.S. *Bureau of the Census.* 1957 census of governments. Washington, Govt. Print. Off., 1957-59. 6 v. in 67 parts.

An extensive statistical analysis of state, local and municipal government in the U.S. Divided into 6 sections: (1) government organization, (2) government employment, (3) government finances, (4) topical studies, (5) taxable property values in the U.S., (6) state reports.

ORIGINAL SOURCES

H372. Code of federal regulations of the United States . . . Wash., Govt. Print. Off., 1949+

A codification of all executive and administrative rules and regulations having general applicability and legal effect issued by the administrative agencies of the federal government. The code is composed of 50 titles and a general index. These titles, similar to those of the *U.S. Code*, are divided into as many parts and chapters and published on as many volumes as required. Each volume has a pocket for supplements which are issued annually and are designed to cumulate the effective text of changes and amendments until the entire volume is revised and republished. This system of revision will keep the work going indefinitely without the need for a completed new edition. To date more than one half of the titles of the 1949 edition have been revised.

H373. Columbia University. *Legislative Drafting Research Fund.*

Constitutions of the United States; national and state. New York, Oceana, 1962. 2 v. (looseleaf)

A companion volume to *Index digest of state constitutions* (H260) this is the first compilation of state constitutions in over 20 years. Includes full texts of the present constitutions of the 50 states. An earlier work still useful historically and because it contains the organic laws of the territories and colonial dependencies of the U.S. is Charles Kettelborough's *The state constitutions.* (Indianapolis, Bowen, 1918. 1644 p.) See also F.N. Thorpe (H378).

H374. Gt. Brit. *Foreign Office.* British and foreign state papers, with which is incorporated Hertslet's "Commercial treaties." v. 1+ 1841+ London, Stationery Office.

An invaluable source of information on British and international affairs. Includes treaties (including some to which Britain was not a party), English language texts of most of the constitutions of the world, official correspondence concerning foreign affairs and many other documents of historical interest and importance. Chronological list of documents with subject and country indexes in each volume. Three general indexes cover the major portion of the series (to v. 137, 1934). Major coverage is for the 19th and 20th centuries with some material for earlier years (1373 is the earliest recorded date).

H375. Peaslee, Amos J. Constitutions of nations. 2d ed. The Hague, Nijhoff, 1956. 3 v.

The only up-to-date and reasonably complete compilation in English. Includes constitutions of 89 independent sovereign nations. The text of each constitution is preceded by a short historical introduction and summary of constitutional principles. The texts themselves are well annotated and are followed by bibliographies of sources and commenta-

ries. V. 3 contains 60 pages of comparative tables for such items as international status of nations, form of government, rights of the people, judicial departments, etc. Indexed.

H376. Peaslee, Amos J. International governmental organizations; constitutional documents. 2d ed. rev. The Hague, Nijhoff, 1961. 2 v.

A companion volume to (H375) this work compiles, in English, the basic constitutional documents of over 100 international organizations created by governments and themselves of a governmental nature. Does not include unofficial private international organizations or those created by bi-lateral agreements. A summary of the history, functions, powers, membership and other relevant data is given for each organization. Select bibliographies are appended in most cases. Index.

H377. Porter, Kirk H. and Donald B. Johnson. National party platforms, 1840-1960. Urbana, Univ. of Illinois Press, 1961. 640 p.

Brings together the party platforms of American political parties from 1840 to 1960. Includes as political parties those groups whose size, permanence and historical significance have made them of major consequence in American politics. Also includes the platforms of splinter groups where these have been important, e.g., States' Rights Party ("Dixiecrats") in 1948. The most authoritative sources available were used. Lack of an index is a handicap.

H378. Thorpe, Francis N. Federal and state constitutions, colonial charters, and other organic laws of the states, territories, and colonies, now or heretofore forming the United States of America. Washington, Govt. Print. Off., 1909. 7 v.

A compilation presenting for each state the documents of its constitutional history. Includes treaties and conventions with foreign countries relating to the areas of consideration (e.g., the treaty of 1819 with Spain ceding Florida to the U.S.). Numerous errors necessitate caution in use. Index. See also (H373).

H379. United Nations. United Nations treaty series. New York, 1946+
A compilation of treaties and international agreements registered or filed and recorded with the Secretariat of the U.N. since Dec. 14, 1946. The texts are reproduced in their original language with English and French translations. Each volume contains in an annex, where appropriate, ratifications, accessions, etc., to treaties and agreements filed, registered or recorded with the U.N. or previously with the League of Nations. Each general index covers several volumes. Supersedes the *League of Nations treaty series* (Geneva, 1920-44. 204 v.).

H380. U.S. *Dept. of State.* Foreign relations of the United States; diplomatic papers. v. 1+ 1861+ Wash., Govt. Print. Off., 1862+ one or more vols. a year.
Contains the texts of diplomatic communications, exchanges of notes, reports, Presidents' annual messages to Congress, and other official papers relating to the foreign relations and diplomacy of the U.S. Occasionally texts of treaties and agreements are included. Current time lag is 15 years. Special supplements, appendices and series appear irregularly, e.g., *The Paris Peace Conference, 1919* (13 v.). Each volume is indexed and two general indexes cover the period 1861-1918. An index to material published from 1828-1861 is Hasse (H292). Materials for the period 1789-1828 will be found in Class 1 of the *American state papers* (H382).

H381. United States. Federal register, March 14, 1936+ Wash., Govt. Print. Off. daily (except Sun. & Mon).
Contains: all Presidential procla-

mations; all Executive orders, except such as have no general applicability or legal effect; agency organization procedures; documents or classes of documents which the president determines to have general applicability and legal effect, and rules and regulations of administrative agencies. Indexes issued monthly, quarterly and annually. Superseded by the supplements to the *Code of federal regulations* (H372).

H382. U.S. *Congress.* American state papers . . . Wash., Gales and Seaton, 1832-61. 38 v.
Made up of legislative and executive documents and constitutes the only readily accessible text of documents of the first 14 congresses. Arranged in 10 classes and chronologically within each class: (1) foreign relations, (2) indian affairs, (3) finance, (4) commerce and navigation, (5) military affairs, (6) naval affairs, (7) post office, (8) public lands, (9) claims and (10) miscellaneous. The final volume in each class contains an index.

H383. U.S. *Laws, statutes, etc.* Revised statutes of the United States passed at the 1st session of the 43d Congress, 1873-74, embracing statutes, general and permanent in nature, in force December 1, 1873. 2d ed. Wash., Govt. Print. Off., 1878. 1394 p.
A codification of the laws, excluding private and obsolete enactments and including the whole body of permanent general law of the U.S. Classified arrangement under large subjects with subject index. Supplements were made and published in 1891 and 1901, but these are largely superseded by the *U.S. Code* (H385).

H384. U.S. *Laws, statutes, etc.* The statutes at large of the United States, concurrent resolutions, recent treaties, conventions and executive proclamations, 1789+ Boston, Little, 1845-1873; Wash., Govt. Print. Off., 1873+

A chronological arrangement of all laws passed since the time of the first Congress. One volume covers the laws passed during each session and is divided into 2 parts. Part 1 consists of public laws and Part 2 contains private laws, treaties, resolutions, executive proclamations, etc. Chronological arrangement necessitates the use of preliminary numerical lists, subject indexes and marginal notes in each volume.

H385. U.S. *Laws, statutes, etc.* United States code. 1958 ed. Wash., Govt. Print. Office, 1959, 13 v.

A codification of laws, first published in 1926, embracing laws general and permanent in nature, in force January 6, 1959. The laws in the code are classified and arranged under 50 titles, e.g., defense, education, public lands, etc., further subdivided by chapters and sections. Vols. 11-13 are a general index. Treaties are not included except as editorial matter where needed. Cumulative supplements are issued annually.

H386. U.S. *Treaties.* Treaties and other international acts of the United States of America, ed. by Hunter Miller. Wash., Govt. Print. Off., 1931+ (In progress)

Eight volumes of this definitive compilation have been issued to 1948. When complete it will replace the collection by W.M. Malloy (H387). V. 1 includes the plan of the work, lists, tables, etc. V. 2-8 contain documents for the years 1776-1863. Complete and literal copies of the texts of all treaties and acts of an international character in force at any time are included in chronological order by date of signature. Following the texts are extensive notes of information on the circumstances relating to the negotiations, citations to judicial decisions, historical development of the treaty and other data of value. Indian

treaties and postal conventions are excluded.

H387. U.S. *Treaties.* Treaties, conventions, international acts, protocols, and agreements between the United States of America and other powers, 1776-1937. Wash., Govt. Print. Off., 1919-1938. 4 v.

A fairly complete compilation except for postal conventions and Indian treaties. The original 2 vols. were completed by William M. Malloy and the whole set is often referred to as Malloy's treaties. V. 1-2 cover 1776-1909; vol. 3, 1910-1923; vol. 4, 1924-1937. Vol. 4 includes: (1) a chronological list of the treaties in v. 1-4; (2) a list, by country, of treaties in v. 3-4; (3) list of treaties submitted to the Senate, 1789-1957, with indication of action taken and relations to the "Treaty series" with citations to the *Statutes at large* and (5) an alphabetical index for v. 1-4.

H388. U.S. *Dept. of State.* United States treaties and other international agreements. v. 1+ 1950+ Washington, Govt. Print. Off., 1952+ annual.

From the calendar year 1950 this becomes the official place of publication and legal evidence for treaties. Prior to this they were published in the *Statutes at large* (H384). Includes all treaties to which the U.S. is a party that have been proclaimed during the calendar year, and all international agreements other than treaties to which the U.S. is a party, arranged in numerical order as originally published in pamphlet form in *Treaties and other international acts series* (see below). The treaties are printed in the language or languages appearing in the original treaties with foreign and English texts in parallel columns. Country and subject index.

Treaties have been published in separate pamphlet form for years but not until 1908 was the designation "treaty series" applied. *United States treaty series* began publication in 1908 with each treaty numbered chronologically from no. 489. Until 1929 both treaties and executive agreements were included. Starting 1929 the *Executive Agreement series* was issued (and numbered) separately. In 1946 the *Treaties and other international acts series* superseded and combined the two former series. The combined number of these two series having reached 1500, the new series begins with 1501. Each text is published separately in pamphlet form, in the original languages giving dates of signature, ratification, proclamation and effectuation.

See also: H364.

Legislative Debates and Journals

H389. Gt. Brit. *Parliament.* Parliamentary debates, v. 1-41 (1803-20), n.s. v. 1-25 (1820-30), 3d series v. 1-356 (1830-90/91), 4th series v. 1-199 (1892-1908), 5th series Commons v. 1+ (1909+); Lords v. 1+ (1909+) London, 1804+

The first 3 series were published by T. C. Hansard and the series are still referred to as *Hansard's debates.* Did not become official until 1909. Series 1-4 are neither complete nor verbatim and not all division lists are given in full. Since 1909 the official record has been substantially verbatim. Issued daily during session; cumulated in bound volumes, with a general detailed index to each session. General index to the 66 volumes of series 1 and 2. The period before 1803 is covered by William Cobbett's *Parliamentary history of England from the earliest period to the year* 1803 (London, Hansard, 1806-20, 36 v.), a retrospective compilation based on various records and sources.

H390. U.S. *Congress.* Congressional record: Containing the proceedings and debates of the 43rd

Congress+ March 4, 1873+ Wash., Govt. Print. Off., 1873+

Issued daily while Congress is in session, revised and issued in permanent form at the end of each session. Contains presidential messages, congressional speeches and debates in full and a record of voting. The text of bills are excluded. Bi-weekly indexes plus a final index to the permanent edition. Index in 2 parts: (1) Alphabetical index of names and subjects; and (2) History of bills and resolutions arranged by bill number. Section two of the index is the best source for tracing the history of a bill. For material before 1873 see: *Annals of Congress,* 1789-1824 (42 v. 1834-56); *Register of debates,* 1824-37 (14 v. in 29, 1825-37); *Congressional globe,* 1833-73 (46 v. in 108, 1834-73).

H391. U.S. *Congress. House of Representatives.* Journal. v. 1+ 1789+ Wash., Govt. Print. Off., daily.

U.S. *Congress. Senate.* Journal. v. 1+ 1789+ Wash., Govt. Print. Off. daily.

The *Journals* contain a day-by-day account of the bills, resolutions and amendments introduced each day. Text of debates and text of bills are *not* included. The section "History of bills and resolutions" contains a complete numerical list of all Senate and House bills and resolutions. If the bill was passed, the law number is given.

SOURCES OF SCHOLARLY CONTRIBUTIONS

H392. *Journals*

American journal of international law. v. 1+ 1907+ Washington, American Society of International Law. quarterly.

Bibl Fremd Zeit; Bull Anal; Bull Sig; Int Ind; Legal Per; PAIS; UN Lib.

American political science review. v. 1+ 1906+ Washington, American Political Science Association. quarterly.
Bibl Fremd Zeit; Bull Anal; Bull Sig; Hist Abst; Int Ind; Int Pol Sci Abst; PAIS; Soc Abst; UN Lib.

Foreign affairs; an American quarterly review. v. 1+ 1922+ New York, Council on Foreign Relations. quarterly.
Bibl Fremd Zeit; Bull Anal; Bull Sig; Doc Econ; Hist Abst; PAIS; RG; Soc Abst; UN Lib.

International affairs. v. 1+ 1927+ London, Royal Institute of International Affairs. quarterly.
Bibl Fremd Zeit; BR Subj Ind; Bull Anal; Hist Abst; Int Ind; PAIS; Soc Abst; UN Lib.

International conciliation. no. 1+ 1907+ New York, Carnegie Endowment for International Peace. 5 times a year.
Bibl Fremd Zeit; Bull Anal; Bull Sig; PAIS; RG; UN Lib.

International organization. v. 1+ 1947+ Boston, World Peace Foundation. quarterly.
Bibl Fremd Zeit; Bull Anal; Int Ind; PAIS; UN Lib.

International review of administrative sciences. v. 1+ 1934+ Brussels, International Institute of Administrative Sciences. quarterly. (Editions in French and English).
Bibl Fremd Zeit; Bull Anal; UN Lib.

Journal of politics. v. 1+ 1939+ Gainesville, Fla., Southern Political Science Association. quarterly.
Bull Anal; Hist Abst; Int Ind; Int Pol Sci Abst; PAIS; Soc Abst; UN Lib.

Parliamentary affairs; devoted to all aspects of parliamentary democracy. v. 1+ 1947+ London, Hansard Society for Parliamentary Government. quarterly.

Bibl Fremd Zeit; BR Subj Ind; Bull Anal; PAIS; UN Lib.

Political quarterly. v. 1+ 1930+ London, Stevens. quarterly.
Bibl Fremd Zeit; BR Subj Ind; Bull Anal; Bull Sig; Doc Econ; Hist Abst; Int Ind; Int Pol Sci Abst; PAIS; Soc Abst; UN Lib.

Political science quarterly. v. 1+ 1886+ New York, Academy of Political Science. quarterly.
Bibl Fremd Zeit; Bull Anal; Bull Sig; Doc Econ; Hist Abst; Int Ind; Int Pol Sci Abst; PAIS; Soc Abst; UN Lib.

Political studies. v. 1+ 1953 London, Political Studies Association of the United Kingdom. 3 a year.
Bibl Fremd Zeit; BR Subj Ind; Bull Anal; Hist Abst; Int Ind; Int Pol Sci Abst; PAIS; Soc Abst.

Public administration review. v. 1+ 1940+ Chicago, American Society for Public Administration. quarterly.
Bibl Fremd Zeit; Bull Anal; Int Ind; Legal Per; PAIS; Soc Abst; UN Lib.

Review of politics. v. 1+ 1939+ Notre Dame, Ind., Univ. of Notre Dame. quarterly.
Bibl Fremd Zeit; Bull Anal; Bull Sig; Cath Ind; Hist Abst; Int Ind; Int Pol Sci Abst; PAIS; Soc Abst; UN Lib.

Revue du droit public et des sciences politiques en France et à l'étranger. v. 1+ 1894+ Paris, Libraire Générale de Droit et de Jurisprudence. bi-monthly.
Bibl Fremd Zeit; Bull Anal; Bull Sig; UN Lib.

Revue française de science politique. v. 1+ 1951+ Paris, Foundation Nationales des Sciences Politiques. quarterly.
Bibl Fremd Zeit; Bull Anal; Bull Sig; Doc Econ; Int Pol Sci Abst; UN Lib.

State government; the magazine of state affairs. v. 1+ 1926+ Chicago, Council of State Government. monthly.
Int Index; PAIS; UN Lib.

Western political quarterly. v. 1+ 1948+ Salt Lake City, Utah, Western Political Science Association. quarterly.
Bibl Fremd Zeit; Bull Anal; Hist Abst; Int Ind; Int Pol Sci Abst; PAIS; Soc Abst; UN Lib.

Zeitschrift für die gesamte Staatswissenschaft. Bd. 1+ 1844+ Tübingen, J.C.B. Mohr. quarterly.
Bibl Deut Zeit; Bull Anal; PAIS; UN Lib.

Zeitschrift für politik n.s. v. 1+ 1954+ Berlin, Heymanns Verlag. quarterly.
Bibl Deut Zeit; Hist Abst; Int Pol Sci Abst; Soc Abst.

H393. *Organizations*

Académie Internationale de Science Politique et d'Histoire Constitutionelle. Paris. Founded 1936.

American Political Science Association. Washington. Founded 1903.

American Society for Public Administration. Chicago. Founded 1939.

Carnegie Endowment for International Peace. New York. Founded 1910.

Council of State Governments. Chicago. Founded 1935.

Council on Foreign Relations. New York. Founded 1921.

Deutsche Vereinigungen für Politische Wissenschaft. Berlin.

Fondation Nationale des Sciences Politiques. Paris. Founded 1945.

Foreign Policy Association. New York. Founded 1921.

International City Managers Association. Chicago. Founded 1914.

International Institute of Administrative Sciences. Brusels. Founded 1930.

International Political Science Association. Geneva. Founded 1949.

Istituto per gli Studi di Politica Internazionale. Milan. Founded 1934.

Public Administration Service. Chicago. Founded 1933.

Royal Institute of International Affairs. London. Founded 1920.

H394. *Monograph Series*

Academy of Political Science, New York. Proceedings. v. 1+ 1910+ New York.

Berlin. Institut für politische Wissenschaft. Schriften. v. 1+ 1952+ Berlin, Druncker & Humblot.

Fondation Nationale des Sciences Politiques. Cahiers. v. 1+ 1947+ Paris, Colin.

Harvard University. Harvard political studies. v. 1+ 1930+ Cambridge, Harvard Univ. Press.

International yearbook of political behavior research. v. 1+ 1961+ Glencoe, Ill., Free Press.

Princeton University. *Center of International Studies.* Research monographs. v. 1+ 1959+ Princeton, N.J.

Public Administration Service. Publications, no. 1+ 1926+ Chicago.

Rivista di studi politici internazionali. v. 1-13; 1936-1944; n.s. v. 1+ 1948+ Firenza, Sansoni.

Stanford University. *Hoover Institution on War, Revolution and*

Peace. Publications. v. 1+ 1932+ Standard, Calif.

Tulane University. Tulane studies in political science. v. 1+ 1952+ New Orleans.

University of California. Publications in political science. v. 1+ 1943+ Berkeley.

Yale University. Yale studies in political science. v. 1+ 1954+ New Haven.

SOURCES OF CURRENT INFORMATION

H395. Aussenpolitik; Zeitschrift für internationale Fragen. v. 1+ 1950+ Stuttgart, Deutsche Verlags-Anstalt. monthly.
Devoted to international questions. Carries long articles on texts of speeches by prominent authors. Regular features include reports on various countries, a chronology of events and a short section of book reviews. *Indexed in:* Bibl Deut Zeit; Bull Anal; Hist Abst; Soc Abst; UN Lib.

H396. CQ weekly report. v. 1+ 1943+ Washington, Congressional Quarterly. weekly.
Gives facts, figures and unbiased commentary on all aspects of Congressional activity, including: major issues, committee activities; floor action, etc. The annual *Almanac* contains most (but not all) of the factual information in the weekly reports. *Indexed in:* PAIS.

H397. Congressional digest. v. 1+ 1921+ Washington, Congressional Digest. monthly.
Monthly news summary. Each iuse devoted to a major controversial topic of national importance with factual background and a pro-and-con section consisting of selections from speeches, editorials, articles, Congressional testimony, etc. *Indexed in:* PAIS; RG; UN Lib.

H398. Department of state bulletin. v. 1+ 1939+ Washington, Govt. Print. Off. weekly.
Provides information on developments in the field of American foreign relations. Includes press releases on foreign policy, statements and addresses of the President and officers of the Department, special articles, information regarding treaties and international agreements. *Indexed in:* Bibl Fremd Zeit; PAIS; RG; UN Lib.

H399. Europa-Archiv. Bd. 1+ 1946+ Frankfurt am Main. semi-monthly.
A journal of political documentation whose articles, by experts, are usually followed by notes on sources and texts of pertinent documents. Includes a section of brief news notes and a chronology. Special attention given to the Council of Europe. *Indexed in:* Bibl Deut Zeit; Bull Anal; UN Lib.

H400. Foreign policy bulletin; an analysis of current international events. v. 1+ 1921+ New York, Foreign Policy Association. semi-monthly.
A small, readable, timely bulletin each issue of which contains several concise articles interpreting current international events or developments in national affairs. Frequently presents articles by two writers on opposing sides of a controversial issue. *Indexed in:* PAIS; RG; UN Lib.

H401. U.S. News and world report. v. 1+ 1933+ Dayton, Ohio. weekly.
A journal of comment and interpretation of developments in national and world political and economic affairs. *Indexed in:* Bull Anal; PAIS; RG; UN Lib.

H402. World today; Chatham House review. v. 1+ 1945+ London, Royal Institute of International Affairs. monthly.
Carries objective reports on all aspects of the international scene.

"Notes of the month" are short factual statements on recent developments. This is followed by interpretive articles on current conditions in individual countries. *Indexed in:* Bibl Fremd Zeit; Bull Anal; Int Ind; PAIS; UN Lib.

SOURCES OF UNPUBLISHED
INFORMATION

H403. "Doctoral dissertations in political science in the universities of the United States and Canada," *American political science review.* v. 6+ 1911+

Each annual listing is in two parts, 1) dissertations in progress and 2) dissertations completed. The entries are classified under 8 subject areas. Each annual list represents only additions, changes or deletions. Canadian theses were included for the

first time in the 1960 list (with listings retrospective to 1951).

H404. Royal Institute of Public Administration. Register of research in political science, 1958/59. London, 1960. 16 p. (mimeo)

A classified listing of work for higher degrees completed and in progress during the 1958/59 session in the universities of the United Kingdom and the Republic of Ireland. Covers politics and public administration, political theory, political and social history, and constitutional and administrative theory. International relations is omitted. A supplement published in 1961 includes titles approved since the 1958/59 Register. A further supplement will appear in 1962. In 1963, a comprehensive register covering the three year period will be issued.

Thompson M. Little
Carl M. White

Index

Prepared by Thompson M. Little

Cochran, R.C. The American business system, C155.

Cochran, T.C. The age of enterprise, B262; Concise dictionary of American history, B428n.

Cochran, W.G. Experimental designs, F16; Sampling techniques, F21.

Code of federal regulations, H372.

Cohen, A.K. Delinquent boys, D188.

Cohen, B.C. Political process and foreign policy, H200.

Cohen, M. Langues du monde, E196.

Cohen, Y. Social structure and personality, E42.

Coker, F. Organismic theories of the state, H38.

Cole, A.H. Business enterprise in its social setting, C156; Historical development of economic and business literature, C240; Measures of business change, C367.

Coleman, J.R. Goals and strategy in collective bargaining, C132.

Coleman, J.S. The adolescent society, D154; Politics of developing areas, A38, H23, H70; Union democracy, C134.

Collected works of Carl Menger, C. Menger, C26.

Collection des économistes et des réformateurs sociaux de la France, A. Dubois, C32.

Collectivist economic planning, F.A. Hayek, C188.

College blue book, G272.

College handbook, G273.

College placement directory, O.T. Zimmerman and I. Lavine, G288.

College teaching, J. Justman and W.H. Mais, G114.

Collingwood, R.G. The idea of history, B5.

Collison, R.L. Bibliographical services throughout the world, A163.

Colonial America, O.T. Barck, Jr. and H.T. Lefler, B205.

Colonial period of American history, C.M. Andrews, B206.

Color in business, science and industry, D.B. Judd, F157.

Coluccio, F. Diccionario del folklore americano, E189.

Columbia Lippincott gazetteer of the world, L.E. Seltzer, B427.

Columbia University. Legislative Drafting Research Fund. Constitutions of the U.S.; national and state, H373.

————. Libraries. Psychology Library. Author index to Psychological Index and Psychological Abstracts, F264.

————. Oral History Research Office. The oral history collection of Columbia University, B469.

Coman, E.T., Jr. Sources of business information, C236.

Comas, J. Bibliografía selectiva de las culturas indígenas de América, E155;

Historia y bibliografía de los congresos internacionales de ciencias antropológicas, 1865-1954, E141; Los Congresos Internacionales de Americanistas, E141n.

Coming of age in Samoa, M. Mead, E52.

Coming of the Civil War, A.O. Craven, B251.

Coming of the French Revolution, G. Lefebvre, B44.

Coming of the revolution, L.H. Gipson, B136.

Commager, H.S. Documents of American history, B450; New American nation series, B371n.

Commercial and financial chronicle, C415.

Commission on Educational Reconstruction. Organizing the teaching profession, G178.

Commodity yearbook, C374.

Common frontiers of the social sciences, M. Komarovsky, A5.

Commons, J.R. Institutional economics, C226.

Commonwealth universities yearbook, G274.

Communication and social order, H.D. Duncan, D38.

Communism, conformity and civil liberties, S.A. Stouffer, H230.

Community political systems, M. Janowitz, H129.

Community power structure, F. Hunter, D134.

Community press in an urban setting, M. Janowitz, D143.

Companion to Greek studies, L.E. Whibley, B447.

Companion to Latin studies, J.E. Sandys, B441.

Comparative analysis of complex organizations, A. Etzioni, D59.

Comparative education, N. Hans, G89; I.L. Kandel, G91.

Comparative politics, R.C. Macridis and B.E. Brown, H74.

Comparative psychology, C.P. Stone, F197.

Comparative public administration, F. Heady and S.L. Stokes, H301.

Comparative study of elites, H.D. Lasswell, *et al.*, H27.

Compendium of American genealogy, F.A. Virkus, B445.

Compendium of social statistics, U.N. Statistical Office, A178.

Competition for empire, W.L. Dorn, B135.

Competitive pressure and democratic consent, M. Janowitz and D. Marvick, H138.

Complete handbook on educational systems, L.S. Botts and J. Solomon, G297a.

Cottrell, L.S. Identity and an interpersonal competence, D97.

Cougny, G. Dictionnaire des parlementaires français, H326n.

Coulter, E.M. Historical bibliographies, B328.

Coulton, G.G. Inquisition and liberty, B101; Life in the Middle Ages, B91; Medieval village, manor and monastery, B92.

Council of Europe. Secretariat. Données statistiques, A174.

Council of State Governments. State government; an annotated bibliography, H304.

Council on Foreign Relations. American agencies interested in international affairs, H325.

Counseling and psychotherapy, C.R. Rogers, F247.

Counts, G.S. Principles of education, G5.

County and city data book, U.S. Bureau of the Census, A179, C393.

County business patterns, U.S. Bureau of Old Age and Survivors Insurance, C394.

Course of German history, A.J.P. Taylor, B167.

Courts, judges and politics, W.F. Murphy and C.H. Pritchett, H84.

Cox, G.M. Experimental designs, F16.

Cramer, J.F. Contemporary education, G87.

Craven, A.O. The coming of the Civil War, B251.

Cremin, L.A. The transformation of the school, G208.

Crestwood Heights, J.R. Seeley, D178.

Crick, B.R. American science of politics, H7; A guide to manuscripts relating to America in Great Britain and Ireland, B468n.

Criteria for the life history, J. Dollard, D205.

Critique of welfare economics, I.M.D. Little, C115.

Croce, B. History as the story of liberty, B29.

Cronbach, L.J. Educational psychology, F237; Essentials of psychological testing, F219.

Croner's world register of trade, C332n.

Cronkhite, B.B. A handbook for college teachers, G110.

Crouzet, M. Histoire générale des civilisations, B378.

Crozier, M. Mouvements ouvrier et socialiste, H276.

Crucial decade, E.F. Goldman, B284.

Crucial issues in education, H. Ehlers and G.C. Lee, G210.

Cubberley, E.P. The history of education, G34; Readings in the history of education, G35.

Cueto Fernandini, C. La Universidad en el siglo xx, G162.

Cultural anthropology, F.M. Keesing, E3.

Cultural areas of native North America, A.L. Kroeber, E182n.

Cultural background of personality, R. Linton, E50.

Cultural history of western education, R.F. Butts, G33.

Cultural patterns and technical change, World Federation for Mental Health, E97.

Culture, A.L. Kroeber and C. Kluckhohn, E72.

Culture and experience, A.I. Hallowell, E45.

Culture and mental health, M.K. Opler, E93.

Culture and personality, J.J. Honigman, E46.

Culture change, F.M. Keesing, E82, E119.

Culture historical method of ethnology, W. Schmidt, E31.

Culver, D.C. Bibliography of crime and criminal justice, D232; Methodology of social science research, A95.

Cummings, J.G. A contribution towards a bibliography dealing with crime and cognate subjects, D234.

Cumulative index to current literature on anthropology and allied subjects, India. Dept. of Anthropology, E135.

Cunliffe, M. George Washington, man and monument, B229.

Cunningham, N.E. The Jeffersonian Republicans, B225.

Currency and credit, R.G. Hawtrey, C167.

Current anthropology, E211.

Current anthropology; a supplement to Anthropology Today, W.L. Thomas, E7, E204n.

Current biography, A145.

Current Caribbean bibliography, A75n.

Current digest of the Soviet press, A59.

Current geographical publications, American Geographical Society of New York, B319.

Current history review, B449.

Current industrial reports, U.S. Bureau of the Census, C375.

Current research on Central and Eastern Europe, D. Horna, A63n.

Current researches in education and educational psychology, G245n.

Current sociological research, American Sociological Association, D296.

Current sociology, D215.

Current thought on peace and war, H258.

Curriculum planning for the gifted, L.A. Fliegler, G200.

Curti, M. The social ideas of American educators, G36.

Curtis, E.S. The North American indian, E186n.

Fundamentals of Adlerian psychology, R. Dreikurs, F66.
Fundamentals of educational leadership, C.A. Weber and M.E. Weber, G142.
Fundamentals of learning, E.L. Thorndike, F114.
Fundamentals of public school administration, W. Reeder, G137.
Funk and Wagnalls standard dictionary of folklore, mythology and legend, E190.
Fustel de Coulanges, N.D. The ancient city, B77.
Future of public education, M. Lieberman, G212.

Gabriel, R.H. Pageant of America, B423.
Gaebler, W. Politisches Wörterbuch, H313.
Gale Research Company. Acronyms dictionary, A132.
Gallois, L. Géographie universelle, B387.
Galloway, G.B. Legislative process in Congress, H102.
Gambling in Sweden, N. Tec, D196.
Ganzheit psychologie und strukturtheorie, A. Wellek, F73.
Garceau, O. Political life of the American Medical Association, H109.
Garciá Hoz, V. Principos de pedagogiá sistemática, G9.
Garfield, S.L. Introductory clinical psychology, F242.
Garner, J.W. Introduction to political science, H14.
Gaus, J.M. The frontiers of public administration, H147.
Gazetteer . . . official standard names, U.S. Board of Geographic Names, B444.
Gebhardt, B. Handbuch der deutschen Geschichte, B376.
Geiger, T. Die Klassengesellschaft im Schmelztiegel, D63.
Geldard, F.A. The human senses, F149.
Gemeinschaft und Gesellschaft, F. Tönnies, D30.
Das Gemüt, S. Strasser, F124.
Gendell, M. A sociological almanac for the United States, D76, D290.
Genealogical and heraldic history of the landed gentry, J.B. Burke, B425n.
Genealogical and heraldic history of the peerage, baronetage and knightage, J.B. Burke, B425.
General and social psychology, R.H. Thouless, F6.
General catalogue of UNESCO publications and UNESCO sponsored publications, A105.
General censuses and vital statistics in the Americas, U.S. Library of Congress. Census Library Project, D255.
General economic history, M. Weber, C223.

General education in a free society, G166.
General index to bills, reports, estimates, accounts and papers, Gt. Brit. Parliament. House of Commons, H290.
General introduction to psychoanalysis, S. Freud, F56.
General theory of employment, interest and money, J.M. Keynes, C70.
Gentz, F. von. The French and American Revolutions compared, B151.
Geoffrey of Monmouth. History of the kings of Britain, B16.
Geographical bibliography for all the major nations of the world, M. Logan, B354.
Geographical journal, B306.
Géographie universelle, P.M.J. Vidal de la Blache and L. Gallois, B387.
Geographisches Jahrbuch, B322.
Geographisches Taschenbuch, B429.
Geographisches Wörterbuch, O. Kende, B369.
George, A.L. Woodrow Wilson and Colonel House, H212.
George III and the historians, H. Butterfield, B217.
George Peabody College for Teachers. Free and inexpensive learning materials, G250.
George Washington, man and monument, M. Cunliffe, B229.
George Washington University. Report on world population migrations as related to the United States of America, D236, D241.
German and English glossary of geographical terms. E. Fischer and F.E. Elliott, B368.
Germán Parra, M. see Parra Germán, M.
Germany and the French Revolution, G.P. Gooch, B145.
Germany rejoins the powers, K.W. Deutsch and L.J. Edinger, H196.
Gershoy, L. From despotism to revolution, B141.
Gerstenfeld, M. Historical bibliographies, B328.
Gerth, H. Character and social structure, D68.
Gesammelte Aufsätze zur Religionssoziologie, M. Weber, D105.
Geschichte der Pädagogik, O.F. Bollnow, G31; W. Moog, G46.
Geschichte der soziale Bewegung in Frankreich von 1789 bis auf unsere Tage, L. von Stein, D21.
Gesell, A.L. Child development, F202.
Gesetze des Sehens, W. Metzger, F147.
Gestalt psychology, W. Köhler, F52.
Geyl, P. Debates with historians, B66; Encounters in history, B67; Napoleon, for and against, B43; The Netherlands divided, B126; The revolt of the Netherlands, B125; Use and abuse of history, B6.

Handbook of experimental psychology, S.S. Stevens, F9, F296.
Handbook of federal war agencies and their records, U.S. National Archives, H352n.
Handbook of general experimental psychology, C. Murchison, F8, F296n.
Handbook of industrial engineering and management, W.G. Ireson and E.L. Grant, C304.
Handbook of labor statistics, C383n.
Handbook of Latin American studies, A75.
Handbook of Middle American indians, R. Wauchope, E178.
Handbook of national organizations with plans, programs and services in the field of aging, White House Conference on Aging, Washington, 1961, D281.
Handbook of private schools, G277.
Handbook of psychological literature. C.M. Louttit, F251.
Handbook of psychological research on the rat, N.L. Munn, F196.
Handbook of public relations, H. Stephenson, C305.
Handbook of research methods in child development, P.H. Mussen, F209.
Handbook of Slavic studies, L.I. Strakhovsky, B443.
Handbook of small group research, A.P. Hare, F274n.
Handbook of social gerontology, C. Tibbitts, D268.
Handbook of social psychology, G. Lindzey, D51, F171, F294; C. Murchison, F295.
Handbook of sociology, W.F. Ogburn and M.F. Nimkoff, D285.
Handbook of South American indians, J.H. Steward, E177.
Handbook of the foreign press, J.C. Merrill, A164.
Handbook of the indians of California, A.L. Kroeber, E194.
Handbook on international study, Institute of International Education, G301.
Handbook on the program of the U.S. Department of Health, Education and Welfare, D286.
Handbook-directory, Association of American Geographers, B390.
Handbuch der Adels, B448n.
Handbuch der Altertumswissenschaft, B377.
Handbuch der bibliographischen Nachschlagewerke, W. Totok and R. Weitzel, A44.
Handbuch der deutschen Geschichte, B. Gebhardt, B376.
Handbuch der empirischen Sozialforschung, R. König, D35.
Handbuch der klassischen Altertumswissenschaft, B377n.

Handbuch der klinichen Psychologie, E. Stern, F223.
Handbuch der Psychologie, D. Katz and R. Katz, F7; P. Lersch, F283.
Handbuch der Soziologie, W. Ziengenfuss, D270.
Handbuch zur Geschichte der Volkswirtschaftslehre, W. Braeuer, C276.
Handlin, O. Harvard guide to American history, B289; The uprooted, B264.
Handschrift und Charakter, L. Klages, F87.
Handwörterbuch der Politik, K.H. Pfeffer, H348.
Handwörterbuch der Sozialwissenschaften, A141.
Handwörterbuch der Soziologie, A. Vierkandt, D269.
Handwörterbuch der Staatswissenschaften, H318.
Hanna, L.A. Unit teaching in the elementary school, G111.
Hans, N. Comparative education, G89.
Hansard, T.C. Parliamentary debates, H389.
Hansard's catalogue and breviate of Parliamentary Papers, Gt. Brit. Parliament. House of Commons, H291.
Hansen, A.H. Fiscal policy and business cycles, C87.
Harbison, F.H. Goals and strategy in collective bargaining, C132.
Hare, A.P. Bibliography of small group research, F274; Handbook of small group research, F274n; Small groups, D53, F274n.
Harman, H.H. Modern factor analysis, F25.
Harnack, A. von. Outlines of the history of dogma, B97.
Harriman, P.L. Encyclopedia of psychology, F284.
Harris, C.D. International list of geographical serials, B353.
Harrod, R.F. Towards a dynamic economics, C102.
Hart, A.B. American nation; a history, B371; Cyclopedia of American government, H345.
Hartmann, H. Ego psychology and the problem of adaption, F58.
Harvard business review, C247.
Harvard educational review, G225.
Harvard guide to American history, B289.
Harvard list of books in psychology, F269.
Harvard University. The behavioral sciences at Harvard, A30.
———. Graduate School of Business Administration. Baker Library. Business forecasting for the 1960's, C280; Business literature, C281; Executive compensation, C282; A guide to selected reference sources in Baker Library, C283; Kress Library of Business

Higher education in transition, J.S. Brubacher and W. Rudy, G159.

Highet, G. The art of teaching, G102.

Hildreth, R. History of the United States of America, B61.

Hilgard, E.R. Conditioning and learning, F104; Introduction to psychology, F1; Theories of learning, F103.

Hillway, T. Education in American society, G10.

Hilsman, R. Strategic intelligence and national decisions, H202.

Hinsie, L.E. Psychiatric dictionary, F280.

Hirsch, D. The sociology of science, D146.

Hirschman, A.O. National power and the structure of foreign trade, C211; The strategy of economic development, C94.

Hirshberg, H.S. Subject guide to United States government publications, H245n.

Hispanic American historical review, B473n.

Histoire de l'enseignement en France, M. Glatigny, G40.

Histoire des relations internationales, P. Renouvin, H319.

Histoire des universités, R. Aigrain, G155.

Histoire générale des civilisations, M. Crouzet, B378.

Historia y bibliografía de los congresos internacionales de ciencias antroplogicas; 1865-1954, J. Comas, E141.

Historian's craft, M.L.B. Bloch, B3.

Historical abstracts, B308.

Historical Association, London. Annual bulletin of historical literature, B300.

Historical atlas, W.R. Shepherd, B421.

Historical atlas of modern Europe, R.L. Poole, B418.

Historical atlas of the Muslim peoples, R. Roolvink, B420.

Historical atlas of the United States, C.L. Lord and E.H. Lord, B415.

Historical bibliographies, E.M. Coulter and M. Gerstenfeld, B328.

Historical development of economic and business literature, A.H. Cole, C240.

Historical evaluation of modern nationalism, C.J.H. Hayes, B173.

Historical inevitability, I. Berlin, B2.

Historical introduction to modern psychology, G. Murphy, F42.

Historical periodicals, E.H. Boehm and L. Adolphus, B325.

Historical research for university degrees in the United Kingdom, Institute of Historical Research, London University, B474.

Historical societies of the U.S. and Canada, American Association for State and Local History, B389.

Historical statistics of the United States, U.S. Bureau of the Census, A181.

Historical view of the French Revolution, J. Michelet, B47.

Histories of Herodotus, B10.

Histories of Polybius, B13.

Historische Zeitschrift, B301.

Historisch-kritische gesamtausgabe, K. Marx and F. Engels, C25.

Historisk statistik för Sverige, Sweden. Statistiska Centralbyrån, A181n.

History and historians in the nineteenth century, G.P. Gooch, B30.

History and philosophy of education, F. Eby and C.F. Arrowood, G38.

History as the story of liberty, B. Croce, B29.

History in a changing world, G. Barraclough, B1.

History of American life, D.R. Fox and A.M. Schlesinger, B379.

History of anthropology, A.C. Haddon, E8.

History of banking theory in Great Britain and the United States, L.W. Mints, C168.

History of civilization in England, H.T. Buckle, E15.

History of economic analysis, J.A. Schumpeter, C10.

History of education, E.P. Cubberley, G34; P.J. McCormick and F.P. Cassidy, G44; J. Mulhern, G47.

History of education in antiquity, H.I. Marrou, G43.

History of educational thought, R. Ulich, G50.

History of England, D. Hume, B22.

History of England from the accession of James II, T.B. Macaulay, B55.

History of England from the fall of Wolsey to the death of Elizabeth, J.A. Froude, B50.

History of England in the eighteenth century, W.E.H. Lecky, B54.

History of ethnological theory, R.H. Lowie, E10.

History of Europe, H. Pirenne, B84.

History of European liberalism, G. de Ruggiero, B170, H51.

History of experimental psychology, E.G. Boring, F38.

History of Florence, F. Schevill, B110.

History of Florence and the affairs of Italy, N. Machiavelli, B20.

History of Germany in the nineteenth century, H.G. von Treitschke, B41.

History of Greece to the death of Alexander the Great, J.B. Bury, B70.

History of libraries in Great Britain and North America, A. Predeek, G196.

History of political theories, W.A. Dunning, H39.

History of political theory, G.H. Sabine, H52.

History of political thought in the sixteenth century, J.W. Allen, H37.

History of psychology, G.S. Brett, F40.

History of Rome, T. Livy, B12; T. Mommsen, B38; B.G. Niebuhr, B39.

Tibbitts, C. Handbook of social gerontology, D268.
Tighe, L.W. A classified bibliography for the field of social work, D249.
Timasheff, N.S. Sociological theory, D14.
Time in economics, G.L.S. Shackle, C108.
Time perspective in aboriginal American culture, E. Sapir, E27.
Tinbergen, N. Study of instinct, F126.
Tingsten, H. Demokratiens Problem, D126; Political behavior, D141.
Tischener, H. Völkerkunde, E203.
Titchener, E.B. Experimental psychology, F10.
To the Finland station, E. Wilson, B171.
Tocqueville, A. de. Democracy in America, B243; Oeuvres, D22; The old regime and the French Revolution, B48.
Todd, V.E. Kindergarten teacher, G112.
Tönnies, F. Gemeinschaft und Gesellschaft, D30.
Tolman, E.C. Purposive behavior in animals and men, F115.
Tompkins, D.C. Administration of criminal justice, D232n; Drug addiction, D250; Materials for the study of federal government, H250; Sources for the study of the administration of criminal justice, D232n; State government and administration, H306; SEE ALSO Culver, D.C.
Top management handbook, H.B. Maynard, C315.
Topical bibliography of current technical literature, *International review of criminal policy*, D225.
Torgerson, W.S. Theory and methods of scaling, F31.
Torrance, E.P. Talent and education, G205.
Tostlebe, A.S. Capital in agriculture, C125.
Totok, W. Handbuch der bibliographischen Nachschlagewerke, A44.
Touraine, A. L'evolution du travail ouvrier aux usines Renault, D117.
Touring Club Italiano. Atlante internazionale, B398.
Toward a common ground, J.S. Bruner, A9.
Toward a reconstructed philosophy of education, T. Brameld, G54.
Towards a dynamic economics, R.F. Harrod, C102.
Town labourer, J.L. Hammond and B. Hammond, B160.
Toynbee, A.J. The world and the West, B118.
Trade and securities statistics, Standard and Poor's Corporation, C407.
Trade and welfare, J.E. Meade, C193.
Trade directories of the world, C332.
Trade union library, Industrial Relations Section, Princeton University, C291, C266n.

Trade unionism in the United States, R.F. Hoxie, C133.
Traité de pédagogie générale, R. Hubert, G11.
Traité de sociologie, G. Gurvitch, D266.
Traité pratique d'analyse du charactère, G. Berger, F95.
Transformation of the school, L.A. Cremin, G208.
Transportation revolution, G.R. Taylor, B245.
Trattato di sociologia generale, V. Pareto, D27.
Treaties and other international acts, H. Miller, H386; U.S. Treaties, H388n.
Treaties, conventions, international acts, protocols and agreements, W.M. Malloy, H387.
Treatise on money, J.M. Keynes, C79.
Treatise on physiological optics, H.L.F. von Helmholtz, F156.
Treatise on the law, privilege, proceedings and usage of Parliament, T.E. May, H307n.
Tree of culture, R. Linton, E85.
Treitschke, H.G. von History of Germany in the nineteenth century, B41.
Trend of government activity in the United States since 1900, S. Fabricant, C180.
Trends and cycles in economic activity, W. Fellner, C85.
Trevelyan, G.M. England under the Stuarts, B133; English revolution, B134.
Triebkräfte der Pädagogik der Völker, F. Schneider, G97.
Triffin, R. Monopolistic competition and general equilibrium theory, C57.
Troeltsch, E.D. The social teaching of the Christian churches, B113.
Tropical abstracts, A56.
Trotsky, L. The history of the Russian Revolution, B184.
Trow, M.A. Union democracy, C134.
Truman, D.B. The Congressional party, H106; Governmental process, H32, H114.
Trustees, presidents and deans of American colleges and universities, G267n.
Trusts and foundations, G.A. Keeling, A153.
Tuchman, B. The guns of August, B195.
Tudors, C. Read, B121.
Tumin, M.M. Caste in a peasant society, D177; Segregation and desegregation, D222.
Turabian, K.L. Manual for writers of term papers, theses and dissertations, G303.
Turgot, A.F.J. Oeuvres de Turgot et documents la concernant, C30.
Turner, F.J. The frontier in American history, B244; The United States, B237.
Turner, J. Party and constituency, H107.
Tuttle, E.M. School board leadership in America, G141.

Tveterås, H.L. Humaniora Norvegica, A76.
Twelve who ruled, R.R. Palmer, B144.
Twentieth century education, P.F. Valentine, G29.
Twenty years' crisis, E.H. Carr, B197.
Two cities, Otto, Bishop of Freising, B18.
Two sides of the log, R.M. Cooper, G109.
Tyler, A.F. Freedom's ferment, B242.
Tyler, L.E. Developmental psychology, F203.
Tylor, E.B. Primitive culture, E19.
Types of formalization in small-group research, J. Berger, D200.

UNESCO bulletin for libraries, A190.
UNESCO dictionary of the social sciences, W.L. Kolb and S.J. Gould, A136.
L'U.R.S.S. et les pays de l'est, A55n.
U.S.S.R. and eastern Europe, C359n.
Udy, S.G. The organization of work, C235.
Über den Schmerz, F.J.J. Buytendijk, F142.
Ulich, R. History of educational thought, G50; Three thousand years of educational wisdom, G51.
Ulman, L. The rise of the national trade union, C138.
Ulmer, S.S. Introductory readings in political behavior, H222.
Ulrich's periodical directory, A103.
Unbalanced budgets, H. Dalton, C175.
Undeclared war, W.L. Langer, B282.
Underwood, B.J. Elementary statistics, F32; Experimental psychology, F14; Psychological research, F19.
Uneasy case for progressive taxation, W.J. Blum and H. Kalven, C173.
Uniform crime reports for the United States, U.S. Federal Bureau of investigation, D292.
Union democracy, S.M. Lipset, C134, D114, H229.
Union of International Associations. Les congres internationaux de 1681 à 1899, H334; Directory of periodicals published by international organizations, A104; International congress calendar, A166n; The 1978 organizations founded since the Congress of Vienna, H335.
Unit teaching in the elementary school, L.A. Hanna et al., G111.
———. Dag Hammarskjold Library see United Nations. Library, New York.
United Nations. Dept. of Economic and Social Affairs. Analytical bibliography of international migration statistics, D251; Social welfare information series, D226; World economic survey, C366.
———. Dept. of Public Instruction. Ten years of United Nations publications, 1945-1955, H294.
———. Dept. of Social Affairs. The de-

terminants and consequences of population trends, D75; International directory of nation-wide organizations concerned with family, youth and child welfare, D280; Multilingual demographic dictionary, D262.
United Nations document index, United Nations, Library, New York. Documents Index Unit, H269.
United Nations. Economic and Social Council. Catalogue of economic and social projects, A203.
United Nations Educational, Scientific and Cultural Organization. Basic facts and figures, A172, G328; Catalogue of economic and social projects, A203; Contemporary political science, H4; Educational periodicals, G234n. General catalogue of UNESCO publications and UNESCO sponsored publications, A105; International register of current team research in the social sciences, A204; International yearbook of education, G306, G329; Liste mondiale des périodiques spécialisés dans les sciences sociales, A106; Selected inventory of periodical publications, A107; Study abroad, G295; The teaching of the social sciences in the United Kingdom, A31; The teaching of the social sciences in the United States, A32; Thèses de sciences sociales, A206; Theses in the social sciences, A206; UNESCO bulletin for libraries, A190; World list of social science periodicals, A106; World survey of education, G305, G330.
———. Education Clearing House, Education abstracts, G232.
———. Social Science Clearing House. Foundations with social science activities, A159; International organizations in the social sciences, A160; Research councils in the social sciences, A161.
———. Research Centre on the Implications if Industrialization in Southern Asia. Research information bulletin, A205; Southern Asia social science bibliography, A83.
United Nations. Library, Geneva. Monthly list of books catalogued in the library of the United Nations, A85; Monthly list of selected articles, A84.
———. ———, New York. List of selected articles, A84n.
———. ———, ———. Documents Index Unit. United Nations document index, H269.
———. Office of Legal Affairs. List of treaty collections, H287.
———. Secretariat. Dept. of Public Information. Library Services. Checklist of United Nations documents, H269n.
———. Statistical Office. Compendium of social statistics, A177; Demographic yearbook, D77, D291; Monthly bulletin of statistics, A178n; Statistical yearbook, A178; Statistics of national in-